Feminist Issues

RACE, CLASS, AND SEXUALITY

FOURTH EDITION

EDITED BY

Nancy Mandell
York University

PEARSON
Prentice
Hall

Toronto

National Library of Canada Cataloguing in Publication

Feminist issues : race, class and sexuality / edited by Nancy Mandell. — 4th ed.

Includes bibliographical references and index.
ISBN 0-13-123384-X

1. Feminism. 2. Women—Social conditions. I. Mandell, Nancy

HQ1206.F445 2004   305.4   C2004-902213-X

ISBN 0-13-123384-X

Vice-President, Editorial Director: Michael J. Young
Executive Acquisitions Editor: Jessica Mosher
Sponsoring Editor: Carolin Sweig
Executive Marketing Manager: Judith Allen
Associate Editor: Jon Maxfield
Production Editor: Charlotte Morrison-Reed
Copy Editor: Josh Thorpe
Proofreader: Dawn Hunter
Production Coordinator: Susan Johnson
Page Layout: Heidi Palfrey
Art Director: Mary Opper
Cover Design: Lisa Lapointe

1 2 3 4 5   09 08 07 06 05

Printed and bound in Canada.

Contents

Preface

This fourth edition provides an update on trends and recent developments in women's studies. Building on the strengths of their chapters written for the third edition, contributors have revised their original pieces, providing theoretical and substantive overviews of the most up-to-date material in their fields. Authors explore the range and diversity of contemporary feminist perspectives as seen through the lens of race, class, sexuality, disability, and poverty. Each chapter addresses questions and social problems that have received little attention in Canadian writing. The lives of previously forgotten and silenced women are brought to the forefront as their experiences of work, family, violence, sexuality, aging, health, religion, and education are examined. The result is an innovative, challenging, and comprehensive survey of Canadian feminist issues today.

Undergraduate students should find this book particularly accessible because authors have been asked to present their arguments in as clear and compelling a fashion as possible. Our purpose is to answer a number of central questions: How is a particular topic a feminist issue? What has feminist research in health care and religion, for instance, discovered as systemic and persistent biases against women? How has feminism addressed the inequities revealed through feminist analyses? What sorts of personal and institutional responses have been taken to redress the mislabelling and misdirection of women, such as gender tracking in high schools? And, finally, what are the immediate and long-term consequences of feminist intervention and analysis? Has the discovery of the "double day" of wage and domestic labour, for which women are responsible, in fact lessened or redistributed women's load? Students, as members of groups usually ignored and as members of institutional settings in which they are often muffled, may find, for the first time, their lives, their experiences, their feelings, and their histories explored. Students may find in this text revelations that are unsettling, contentious, validating, and liberating—it is unlikely they will emerge untouched.

Putting this book together has been a profound privilege and pleasure. An excellent group of contributors has broadened previous feminist critiques by incorporating debates about race, class, sexuality, disability, poverty, and violence into everyday explanations of women's omission and oppression. Struggling with mainstream definitions and attempting to expand the boundaries of feminist understanding is challenging.

Acknowledgments

Numerous people have read and edited versions of these chapters, suggesting significant improvements. Special notes of appreciation to Johanna Stuckey, my favourite women's studies teaching partner and the inspiration for this book; to Ann Duffy for her suggestions and support; and to my oldest son, Jeremy Mandell, for his internet skills and research assistance. At Pearson we would like to thank Jessica Mosher, Carolin Sweig, Jon Maxfield, Charlotte Morrison-Reed, and Josh Thorpe. Editorial assistance provided by Jon Maxfield and Cara Yarzab has been invaluable and very much appreciated. They have nurtured this book and intervened at important moments to ensure its successful completion. We are grateful to the following reviewers for their thoughtful comments and suggestions: Lori Chambers, Lakehead University; Pamela Downe, University of Saskatchewan; Virginia Caputo, Carleton University; Sikata Banerjee, University of Victoria; and Christabelle Sethna, University of Ottawa. And thank you to the feminist men in my life—Lionel, Jeremy, Ben, and Adam—whose love and humour I cherish.

Introduction

Most young Canadian women and men have grown up in a world in which feminism as a social and ideological movement is firmly established. Contemporary youth have lived with feminist mothers struggling to juggle work and family lives, had high school and university teachers who integrated feminist perspectives in their courses, been exposed to countless songs and images on television and in magazines that gesture toward feminism, and been exposed to an ample selection of non-traditional role models in all walks of life. Feminism has infiltrated our understanding of everyday life to such an extent that, as Mary Evans said, you would have had to have been living on Mars not to have been touched by feminism (1997).

Yet, how do young women feel about feminism, and how do they experience it in their everyday lives? Although Canadian evidence is scant, studies from abroad reveal interesting patterns. In her interviews with 33 young women aged 16–20, Budgeon (2001) shows that young women feel alienated from the second-wave feminist movement even though their identities have been informed by its feminist ideals. Bulbeck (2001) tells us that in Australia, liberal or equality feminism has significant purchase as a structural way to identify women's subordination, including explanations of patriarchy and class, but that feminism has had less of an impact at the level of consciousness and policy. Letherby and Marchbank (2001) review feminist discourses female students hear from other women's studies students revealing a legacy of ambivalence, contradiction, backlash, and marketing. Volman and ten Dam (1998) in their study of high school students in the Netherlands, reveal that even though young women and men consider gender equity the norm, traditional and often contradictory discourses on masculinity and femininity remain intact.

All of these studies show that discourses of gender difference clash with emancipation or equality discourses. Although many young adults consider equity to have been achieved, they are unaware of the ways in which traditional discourses shape their expectations and experiences. Somehow it seems old fashioned now to talk as though gender inequity existed. Liberal notions of individuals freely choosing their fates clash with feminist notions of structured inequality. As Volman and ten Dam's (1998) students put it, it's okay to explain history using discourses of feminism or inequality because "everyone knows" it was bad back then. But now that equality has been achieved, if men and women "choose" different fields, it is because they want to be in these areas or because their innate talents have led them down different family and career paths. However, when these same students come face to face with inexplicable conditions of inequality, contradiction, confusion, and ambivalence abound.

In this collection, we position women's issues at the forefront of Canadian concerns. In areas as diverse as romance, intimacy, law, education, work, beauty, spirituality, and violence, the role of women as equal participants is still uncertain. This is not to say that distinct achievements have not occurred. Women now outpace men in all areas of educational achievement. They get better grades and are more likely to achieve post-secondary education than are men. Paid work offers another glimpse into shifting gender patterns. Men, especially young men, are more likely to be unemployed and to work fewer hours than are their female counterparts (Statistics Canada, 2004). Structural changes in global economic patterns have precipitated a shift in Canadian workplace trends, but how do we account for the dramatic alteration in gendered patterns of education? And, why, given these spectacular shifts, have our ideological notions of women and men's roles in society not shifted as dramatically?

This fourth edition of *Feminist Issues* attempts to address contemporary changes in our ideas about equity. Although certainly not comprehensive, the twelve chapters in this book represent a wide range of concerns facing young Canadian women. The first section contains four entirely new chapters by a range of authors theorizing feminism through the lens of modernism and postmodernism. The second section contains four thoroughly revised chapters that focus on women's experiences of exclusion and marginalization in areas of beauty and aging, romance and intimacy, and violence and violent masculinities, capturing a range of women's experiences as they move through life's course. The final section contains three completely revised chapters and one new chapter. This section concentrates on the structural context within which women live, work, learn, worship, and receive health care.

It is important to understand the roots and diversity of women's concerns. Three York University Graduate Women's Studies' students, Shana L. Calixte, Jennifer L. Johnson, and J. Maki Motapanyane begin the book by tracing the historical and social implications of the second-wave feminist thinking of liberal feminists, socialist feminists, and radical feminists. Chapter 1, "Liberal, Socialist, and Radical Feminism: An Introduction to Three Theories about Women's Oppression and Social Change," provides an accessible review of mainstream first- and second-wave feminist theories. Canadian feminism is now about 150 years old. First-wave feminism covers the time period from the mid-nineteenth century to the end of the Second World War. It grew out of the enfranchisement movement as women began to recognize the limitations they faced without the vote. Second-wave feminism, covering the early 1950s to the early 1990s, grew out of the civil rights and antiwar movements. By showing the historical and social contexts within which feminist theories emerge, the authors show how social, economic, and cultural arrangements shape our views of what causes women's subordination. Feminist theories are roadmaps through the complexity of structural and personal features contouring women's experiences. Theories provide ways to understand and criticize these understandings, thus ensuring that feminists continually sharpen and clarify their vision. Different political positions offer distinct ways of thinking about the causes of and solutions for women's oppression. Although "waves" overlap and distort, specific political issues arising in particular historical periods have mobilized women around a common set of concerns.

Theoretical approaches to feminist studies constantly shift. As Sharon Rosenberg tells us in Chapter 2, "An Introduction to Feminist Poststructural Theorizing," postmodernism has profoundly disrupted our thinking about gender and sexuality, moving us away from dichotomous depictions of gender as binary—two genders of male and female—and opened up possibilities of multiple and fluid genders. Transgendering now captures our thinking about the ways many individuals cross gender boundaries as they live their lives, enter relationships, and create intimate relationships. Gender is both more complex and more global than it appeared ten years ago. Multiple discourses, contradictions, and active production of meaning on both an individual and social level together define possibilities for resistance and change. Gender is seen as a layered concept of symbolic constructions, social relations, and social organization. Rosenberg leads us slowly and carefully through postmodernism, showing us how to use recent theorizing about women in our everyday relationships.

Third-wave feminism began in the early 1990s and continues today. But what does it mean to claim third-wave identification? In Chapter 3, "Third-Wave Feminisms," Lara Karaian and Allyson Mitchell show how postmodern, third-wavers embrace multiplicity and diversity in their enactment of feminism in their personal, political, and work lives. Just as there is not one feminism, there is not one feminist politics, social agenda, or economic objective. Rather, young women live, display, challenge, annoy, resist, disrupt, and support multiple feminisms and ways of being feminist. With their emphasis on pop feminism, Karaian and Mitchell detail multiple resistance tactics being undertaken by young feminists through alternative media representations in art, film, and zines. Personal narratives authored by young women explore the transformative ways women interrupt traditional stories of women's motives, means, and methods for living their lives. *Turbo Chicks*, *Action Grrrls*, and *Pretty, Porky, and Pissed Off* represent contemporary sites of cultural resistance. This chapter reveals the energy with which young women have revitalized and reshaped the women's movement, a process bound to enliven classroom discussions.

All nations and their practices have been affected by processes of economic, political, and cultural globalization. How has women's equality been advanced or retarded by these forces? In Chapter 4, "Unessential Women: Race, Class, and Gender and the Implications in Education," Goli Rezai-Rashti looks at how Third-World, postcolonial, and black feminists have challenged the exclusionary discourses of Western feminism and the implications of this challenge for minority women in the classroom. Critiquing scholarship on whiteness by contesting notions of representation and authenticity, Rezai-Rashti shows how the broadening of physical borders corresponded with an opening up of ideological thinking within women's studies. Specifically, she unravels the complex intersection of feminism and antiracism as implicated in educational policy and practices, thus concretizing for young women the interplay between the international and the local.

Women's studies classrooms now comprise young women and men who assume gender equity is complete. Contemporary students represent a generation who have been raised by working mothers for whom the feminist movement has been a central force. As feminist activists or as more passive consumers of popular media, all Canadian women have experienced the challenges of achieving equity in their personal and work lives. There is no going back to the post-war traditional thinking of "men's jobs" and "women's jobs." Indeed, current generations wouldn't even consider stepping backward. Those days are firmly in the past, but old ideologies die hard. Dating, sexuality, and intimacy are shaped by notions of romance, which, whether same or opposite sex, too often turn abusive. Sharon McIrvin Abu-Laban and Susan McDaniel show in Chapter 5, "Aging, Beauty, and Status," how women are still held captive by notions of female beauty. Women learn early in life that beauty brings power and material rewards in the form of easier access to jobs and male wages. Accordingly, women starve, vomit, purge, and carve themselves up in order to become desirable sex objects. Aging women, with their wrinkles and lines and sagging bodies, are, by normative definitions of femininity, not shiny enough, not new enough, and certainly not slick enough to be considered beautiful. Beauty and aging remain gendered and raced experiences.

As Ann Duffy reminds us in Chapter 6, "Violence against Women," fear of and exposure to violence binds all women together. Regardless of their class, race, sexual orientation, or education, all women are united in their vulnerability to victimization. On December 6, 1989, Canada experienced its first mass gendercide in the Montreal Massacre when 14 women were shot at the École Polytechnique, at the University of Montreal's School of Engineering. Defined as the deliberate extermination of persons of a particular sex (or gender), gendercide is a sex-neutral term in that the victims may be either male or female. In contrast, feminists tend to use terms such as "gynocide" and "femicide" to refer to the killing of girls and women. Duffy documents the extent to which large numbers of Canadian girls and women experience or are exposed to violence in their lives.

Sexual violence, even against little girls, is not related to sexual needs. Victims are usually chosen because they are available and powerless—easy targets for male coercion and abuse. The greater women's social and individual powerlessness, the more likely they are to find themselves victimized. Native women face eight times the risk of family violence as do non-Native women. Every day the newspapers report incidents of assault directed against women with disabilities, older women, and visible minority women. Globally, women experience violence on a daily basis, underlining the patriarchal construction of social life in countries other than Canada. Despite advertising campaigns, shelters, violence hotlines, and police intervention, violence against women remains a horrendous social problem around which the entire community must unite to eliminate at home and abroad.

Chapter 7, "Men, Masculinities, War, and Sport" by Greg Malszecki and Tomislava Cavar tackles the thorny issue of men's role in the women's movement. What is a profeminist man and how does he behave? What are traditional conceptions of masculinity telling men to think and do and how can these ideas be reconciled with postmodern notions of femininity? Subjugated, complicit, and dominant masculinities form the framework within which men evaluate and adjust their behaviour to resist or conform to traditional stereotypes. Cultures of sport and war overlap, each reinforcing the other. The cultural icon of the aggressive soccer or hockey player is supported in sports bars and phone-in radio shows every day. Male adolescence marks the beginning of boys' hazardous quest for manliness, a tenuous, anxiety-ridden journey that often disappoints and discourages even the most hardy of seekers. Feminism has propelled profound alterations in our thinking and in the ways women construct their lives. Women have raced ahead of men in altering the meanings of gender roles, attitudes, and images. As Malszecki and Cavar reveal, the project of revisioning masculinity is in its infancy.

Families remain sites of intense feminist struggle. As places that offer warmth, security, and happiness, families also initiate women into their most intense experiences of pain, oppression, and suffering. Gaining, sustaining, and working at intimacy has become for many women the central project of their lives. For some women the search brings personal and emotional gratification while for others it brings economic and social costs. In Chapter 8, "Making Families: Gender, Economics, Sexuality, and Race," Nancy Mandell traces some of the ways families have been thought about and constructed in the past. Modern discourses of romance and intimacy channel their desires and contour their dreams. Recent Canadian statistics show that overall marriage is less popular while commitment remains strong. Cohabitation emerges as the new prelude to the marriage pattern taken up by most young people in their late twenties and early thirties. Canadians spend a lot of their lives trying to establish and maintain families. But what happens to those for whom building families is denied? Around the globe, many groups are denied opportunities to live with their lovers, assemble households, and parent children. Same-sex, poor, visible minority, immigrant groups, and people with disabilities struggle to build families, fighting against homophobic, racist, and sexist policies and practices.

Chapter 9, "Paid Work, Jobs, and the Illusion of Economic Security" by Susannah Wilson, details the work lives of Canadian women. Working to keep a roof over their heads and food on the table pushes many women into employment and keeps them working long hours throughout their lifetimes (Heisz and LaRochelle-Coté, 2003). Rather than being an option, employment is a basic necessity for women, especially those who are responsible for children and relatives. Falling wages, increasing taxes, and economic restructuring have decreased the number of paid jobs available for men and increased those available for women, mostly in part-time, poorly paid service positions. Racialized and immigrant women and those with disabilities face particular obstacles in finding employment. They do not have equitable access to training and education programs, and this restricts their access to the labour force. Wilson tells us how for women the gender gap in wages is maintained through occupational segregation. Moreover, sexual harassment and institutional racism keep groups of women marginalized, vulnerable, and literally shut out of certain workplaces and schools. Visible minority women occupy some of the better jobs in Canadian society as well as many of the poorly paid jobs (Boyd, 1992). Dionne Brand (1999: 90) says that today, "black women's work looks like this: cleaning white people's houses, bathrooms, and hotel rooms; serving white people breakfast, lunch, and dinner in private homes, office cafeterias, and hospitals; lifting, feeding, minding, sweeping, boxing, scouring, washing, cooking." Feminists have been central in deconstructing work as a site of emancipation for women. By examining the gendered, raced, and sexualized nature of women's labour, Wilson reveals the complex ways in which work affects women's status.

Feminist analysis of schooling has raised questions about the ways in which traditional beliefs about women and men have been used as inappropriate and inequitable sorting and streaming mechanisms. In a sweeping and comprehensive overview, Cecilia Reynolds in Chapter 10, "The Educational System," assesses the cumulative effect of the structure and practices of schooling on the life chances of females. Her conclusions are daunting. In the past, rather than promoting women's achievement, schools reproduced sexism. Rather than diminishing gender differences, schools facilitated gendered occupational outcomes. Clearly, as Reynolds suggests, some kind of "gender tracking" (Mandell and Crysdale, 1993) appears to be at work, in which extensive gender segregation of domestic labour, schooling, and workplaces means that women and men live, work, and study in different areas. Exclusion from organized forms of knowledge remains a political battle. Its effects are revealed in the intersection of school and work, or, to paraphrase Reynolds: the social reproduction processes by which gendered and raced subjects are prepared by schools to take up workplace positions.

In Chapter 11, "Understanding Women and Health," Diana Gustafson demonstrates that women's bodies remain contested terrain. Contrasting two approaches to women's health—the biomedical model and the population health model, Gustafson shows how both approaches to health and health care are socially constructed frameworks that reflect shifting understandings of what contributes to differences in health status between women and men and across groups of women. Eichler and Gustafson (1999) describe three main types of gender bias that exist in health research: androcentricity, gender insensitivity, and double standard. Gustafson uses these categories to illustrate how biomedical research constructs women as objects of health research.

While the biomedical model locates disease causality in the individual, the population health approach, especially feminist versions thereof, is concerned with a wide range of factors—including gender, culture, income, social status, employment, education, social and physical environments, childhood development, personal health practices, coping skills, health services, and social support networks—that have an impact on the health of an entire population. As mediators of care, women translate broader cultural ideas and practices of health into the everyday personal performance of health in the home and the community. Gustafson provides a comprehensive, accessible, and thorough overview of women's health issues.

In Chapter 12, "Women and Religion: Female Spirituality, Feminist Theology, and Feminist Goddess Worship," Johanna Stuckey provides a detailed overview of women's insertion into traditional religions and their creation of female-centred worship. As Clark and Whitcomb (1996: 251) comment, at its most basic, spirituality refers to the varied and differing responses people have to the universal experiences of birth, life, and death. Stuckey provides readers with a range of expressions of female spirituality and of the ways women make sense of their experiences and give meaning to their lives. Focusing here on Christianity, Judaism, and Islam, Stuckey carefully outlines the principles and traditions of each religion. Using four categories of analysis—revisionist, reformist, revolutionary, and rejectionist—Stuckey evaluates women's attempts to feminize practice within each of these religions. Revisionist Christian theologians, for example, in recovering church history, have demonstrated that women were instrumental in the establishing and spreading of Christianity.

Revisionist Jewish feminists have worked to effect change in *halakhah* Jewish law and *agunot* (women whose husbands refuse to give them a religious divorce or *get*). Muslim revisionist feminists examine *hadiths* (Muslim law) and sometimes question their authenticity. Others who work within traditional religions push the traditions to their limits, altering language and symbols of deity to include female imagery, sometimes importing language, imagery, and ritual from other traditions in their attempts to make their religion more inclusive. Still others reject the traditions, judging them to be irredeemably sexist, and set about creating new spiritual traditions. Stuckey ends her chapter with a review of the burgeoning interest in feminist goddess worship. Beginning in the 1970s, goddess worship circles ritualized sharing of experience, communal validation, and creation of safe and comfortable spaces for women. Myths, rituals, language, and practices began to emerge from this new religion or spiritual entity created by women to empower and nurture women. Humans have always sought the spiritual to nourish their souls. Stuckey's overview reminds us that women continue to search for nonsexist ways to fulfill their spiritual needs.

CONCLUDING REMARKS

The fourth edition brings together a lively and energetic series of debates about the nature of women's lives in a variety of contexts. Each chapter challenges traditional stereotypes as discursive constructions underscoring prevailing beliefs that often stray far from empirical reality. Socialization into gender is no longer seen as a linear process with fixed and well-defined outcomes, but a process full of contradictions and ambivalence. Although readers may find it unsettling to have their ideas challenged, approaching this process with an open mind can lead to fresh perspectives. This book shows that it no longer makes sense to talk about certain behaviours or beliefs as solely the domain of either men or women. The dynamic quality of social life, responding as it does to material, historical, and cultural forces, presses against static concepts, urging us to engage in the creative remaking of old ideas. The journey to new thinking can be difficult. I hope that these chapters provide readers with sustenance, encouragement, and enjoyment as they make their way along the feminist path.

Bibliography

Bulbeck, Chilla. "Articulating Structure and Agency: How Women's Studies Students Express Their Relationships with Feminism." *Women's Studies International Forum,* 24/2 (2001): 141–156.

Boyd, Monica. "Gender, Visible Minority and Immigrant Earning Inequality: Reassessing an Employment Equity Premise." In *Deconstructing a Nation: Immigration, Multiculturalism and Racism in '90's Canada*, edited by Vic Satzewich. Saskatoon: University of Saskatchewan Press, 1992.

Brand, Dionne. "Black Women and Work: The Impact of Racially Constructed Gender Roles on the Sexual Division of Labour." In *Scratching the Surface: Canadian Anti-Racist Feminist Thought*, edited by Enakshi Dua and Angela Robertson. Toronto: Women's Press, 1999.

Budgeon, Shelly. "Emergent Feminist (?) Identities: Young Women and the Practice of Micropolitics," *European Journal of Women's Studies*, 8/1 (2001): 7–28.

Carty, Linda. "The Discourse of Empire and the Social Construction of Gender." In *Scratching the Surface: Canadian Anti-Racist Feminist Thought*, edited by Enakshi Dua and Angela Robertson. Toronto: Women's Press, 1999.

Clark, Beverley and **Jo-Anne Whitcomb**. "Women's Spirituality." In *An Introduction to Women's Studies*, edited by Beryl Madoc-Jones and Jennifer Coates, 250–70. Oxford: Blackwell, 1996.

Collins, Patricia Hill. *Black Feminist Thought: Knowledge, Consciousness, and the Politics of Empowerment*. New York: Routledge, 2000.

Eichler, Margrit and **Diana L. Gustafson**. "Between Hope and Despair: Feminists Working With/For the State." Paper presented at the BAITWorM Conference, Toronto, 2000.

Evans, Mary. *Introducing Contemporary Feminist Thought*. New York: Polity Press, 1997.

Heisz, Andrew and **Sébastien LaRochelle-Coté**. *Working Hours in Canada and the United States*. Ottawa: Statistics Canada, 2003.

Letherby, Gail and **Jen Marchbank**. "Why Do Women's Studies? A Cross England Profile." *Women's Studies International Forum*, 24/5 (2001): 587–603.

Mandell, Nancy and **Stewart Crysdale**. "Gender Tracks: Male-Female Perceptions of Home-School-Work Transitions." In *Transitions: Schooling and Employment in Canada*, edited by Paul Anisef and Paul Axelrod, 21–24. Toronto: Thompson Educational Publishers, 1993.

Statistics Canada. *The Time of Our Lives: Juggling Work and Leisure over the Life Cycle*. Catalogue No. 89-584-MIE, Ottawa: Ministry of Industry, 2004.

Volman, Monique and **Geert ten Dam**. "Equal but Different: Contradictions in the Development of Gender Identity in the 1990s." *British Journal of Sociology of Education*, 19/4 (1998): 529–545.

Liberal, Socialist, and Radical Feminism: An Introduction to Three Theories about Women's Oppression and Social Change

Shana L. Calixte

Jennifer L. Johnson

J. Maki Motapanyane[1]

Simply put, feminism is a movement to end sexism, sexist exploitation, and oppression.

—hooks, 2000: 1

WHAT IS FEMINISM?

Although hooks's (2000) definition is very straightforward, feminism has come to mean many things to different people. There are a wide range of feminist ideas and practices that vary according to one's understanding of the source of women's oppression. But at its core, "[f]eminism begins with the premise that women's and men's positions in society are the result of social, not natural or biological, factors" (Andersen, 1997: 8). Feminism is a political way of being, thinking, and living in the world, the aim of which is to achieve gender equality in all spheres of life (social, political, economic, religious, and cultural). Feminism is also about seeing the connection between our day-to-day activities and experiences as women and larger social processes. These include institutions such as the political and legal systems, socio-cultural institutions such as the

---

1   The authors thank Nancy Mandell and Jon Maxfield and send a special thank-you to Johanna Stuckey and the anonymous reviewer who generously commented and offered advice on drafts of this chapter.

"family," the popular media (newspapers, television, radio, and internet), and even contemporary economic processes such as globalization.

Feminism: Theory and Practice

Feminist theory is a road map for understanding feminism. There are many different kinds of feminist theory, each with its own historical basis, theoretical predecessors, and methods of achieving social change. Theory provides a framework for explaining the complex connections between people's everyday lives and larger social, political, and economic forces. Feminist theories typically offer an analysis of systems of power in society and indicate how the unequal distribution of this power shapes the lives of men and women. An understanding of this unequal distribution can also expose other equally insidious oppressions based on factors such as race, sexuality, and class (Code, 1993: 20).

One of the main tensions between feminist theorists and activists is the idea that theorists sit back while the "woman in the street" does the work of social change. hooks (1994) argues that theory and practice are in fact inseparable and that it is pointless to engage in one without the other. She says that "by reinforcing the idea that there is a split between theory and practice, or by creating such a split, both groups deny the power of liberatory education for critical consciousness, thereby perpetuating conditions that reinforce our collective exploitation and repression" (1999: 32). We would add that even activists doing front-line work in demonstrations, women's shelters, and courtrooms have a theory behind their actions, although it may not be articulated in an academic text. hooks's idea that theory and practice are meaningless without each other is therefore a really important one to keep in mind as you read about the theories behind the actions of liberal, socialist, and radical feminists.

This chapter addresses liberal, socialist and radical feminist perspectives as they have developed in a "Western" (European, American, and Canadian) context, outlining the core concepts and critical debates in each theory. The authors therefore urge readers to consider this presentation of the theories as culturally specific to Western society. We ask readers to take feminists' achievements as important and significant in their own right but also to recognize that different women have come to understand gender inequality and women's oppression differently.

Liberal, socialist, and radical feminist theory have in common a commitment to redefining the relationship of sex to gender and to making visible relations of power between women and men. Western society has embraced the idea of a dichotomous and hierarchical relationship between "male" and "female" or "masculinity" and "femininity." These dichotomies and hierarchies in turn shape the positions, opportunities, and levels of access of individuals to political, economic, and social spaces. And yet the questionable relationship between sex and gender is often invisible to us. A central understanding in each theory is that one's biological sex (male/female) should not necessarily determine one's gender identity (masculine/feminine) and the social statuses, behaviours, and opportunities ascribed to each gender. Part of feminist theorizing is seeing the world as gendered and challenging the ways in which different characteristics, roles, and behaviours are attributed to men and women. Therefore, feminist theory seeks to identify the source of women's oppression and develop effective methods for social change and, in some cases, for revolution. Although there is a diversity of feminist theoretical approaches, and ongoing debates within and between these, what remains fundamental to each of the theories presented here is a commitment to social change through the eradication of women's oppression.

LIBERAL FEMINISM

Defining Liberal Feminism: Principles and Goals

Liberal feminist theory is founded on a core set of principles originating in liberal philosophy. Liberal philosophy developed during a period of European social change called the "Enlightenment" or the "Age of Reason" in the seventeenth and eighteenth centuries. Major shifts in European understandings of the world came about in the fields of physics, biology, and geography. Scientists such as Newton and Gallileo determined that, instead of relying on the traditions of folk wisdom or the decree of kings, the natural world can be known through careful scientific experiment. Such ways of thinking were translated by philosophers and politicians and applied to human society.

First, liberals believe that all human beings are inherently rational and, as such, people should be considered equal to one another in their shared humanity. Second, liberals believe in meritocracy. People should be able to earn their status in society, such as by earning rewards for doing well at a job or in school. To "merit" something implies that a status cannot be passed on hereditarily or through personal favours. Third, liberals believe in the principle of equal opportunity. Everyone should have the chance to merit a status or reward. If people in a society do not have equal opportunity, as in a monarchy for example, where only the heirs of the royal family can become king or queen, liberals would strive to ensure that the head of state be elected in such a way that any person might ascend to this position. Last, all rational beings should have freedom of choice unless for some reason they are incapacitated (Bryson, 1992; MacIvor, 1996). Liberalism is however, a Western philosophy that has in great part been applied to relationships between men—and specifically, white, propertied men. Women, slaves, minors, and various other groups have often been deliberately excluded or have existed outside the purview of legal and political systems that espouse a liberal point of view.

Liberal feminists take the core principles of liberalism and apply them to inequalities between men and women; they espouse the idea that women should be equally integrated into existing social, political, religious and economic institutions and that they should enjoy the same benefits that accrue to men. First, liberal feminists, past and present, are concerned first of all with establishing women's capacity for rational thought and thus their shared humanity with men. Second, liberal feminists endorse the concept of meritocracy. These first two principles have been particularly important in shaping the goal of achieving access to formal education for women, largely achieved in Western societies in the early twentieth century. Third, liberal feminists are concerned with establishing equality of opportunity for women in all areas of social, economic, legal, and political life. This principle was critical in shaping liberal feminists' goal of woman suffrage, achieved in Canada at varying points throughout the twentieth century. Fourth, freedom of choice is a principle of liberal feminism.

Liberal Feminism: A Historical Context

In a period when democracy threatened monarchy as form of government, liberal ideas upset European ways of thinking about social relations between the nobility and the peasant class. Liberalism especially questioned the hereditary rule of monarchies over the masses. Why should one man rule over another simply because he was born to it? The

French in particular did not think so and undertook a bloody revolution in 1789 to over-throw the French monarchy. They fought on the principles of liberty, equality, and frater-nity to establish a meritocracy in which, theoretically, any man could ascend to power and government. Liberalism was therefore a primary ideological goal of the French Revolution (1789) and its success gave credence to other major social reforms taking place in England, Europe, and parts of the Americas.

The "Enlightenment" was also the age of colonialism and the beginnings of industrial capitalism in the Western world. Colonialism was mainly the project of European states seeking to develop industrial capitalist economic practices through free trade. While European men fought and acquired more legal rights, the countries in whose name they fought were in effect squelching the rights of First Peoples on several continents. From 1492 onward, European nations actively undertook the conquest of many parts of the world for the riches these lands offered, including the Americas and the Caribbean. Once indige-nous populations had been subdued, eliminated, or enslaved, the Europeans found that not enough labour could be extracted from them and so began the indentureship of poor and working-class whites from Europe and then the capture, transport, and enslavement of Africans in the Americas and the Caribbean. Given that European society was a class-based society of nobility, citizens, servants, and slaves, it is hard to understand liberal feminist thought without examining the hierarchical relationships between differently racialized and classed groups of women and men that emerged during this period of colonialism.

In Canada, a complex history of trade, resistance and turf warfare between the French, English, First Nations peoples, and other European interests developed most intensely from the seventeenth century on. The Europeans may have determined that rational men shared a common humanity but applied this liberal rhetoric oppressively in the case of women, First Nations people, and enslaved Africans, arguing that these groups were not capable of rational thought.

The ideas of several liberal feminist thinkers are discussed here in order to explore the principles of liberal feminism: rationality, meritocracy, equality of opportunity, and freedom of choice.

Rational Thought and Human Worth

The ideas of Christine de Pizan (1365–1430) a widowed Frenchwoman who lived in the Middle Ages, and Mary Astell (1666–1731) an Englishwoman who lived during the Renaissance period, should be noted as early critical feminist works in Western thought. They challenged the dominant idea of the time that women are essentially weak-minded, frail, and irrational by nature, unlike men who are naturally strong of body and mind, steadfast in opinion, and inherently rational beings. In contrast, de Pizan and Astell both proposed that women have a natural capacity for rational thought, just as men do. De Pizan argued that women's status in relation to men would be improved if society acknowledged women's capacity for rational thought. Much later, Astell argued specifically for the equal-ity of the sexes based on men and women's shared humanity. These women's ideas were viciously rejected by their societies and all but erased through the repression of women's historical significance in Western history.

Mary Wollstonecraft (1759–1797) is one of the first figures in Western history to artic-ulate a basic framework for women's equality with men. In *A Vindication of the Rights of*

Woman (1792) she challenges liberal thinkers to apply the concept of liberalism to relationships between men and women and not just men. Wollstonecraft takes issue with Jean-Jacques Rousseau's depiction of children's ability to learn in his tract on education, *Émile,* in which he demonstrates the propensity of boys from any social background to be educated. Girls on the other hand, are seen to be fickle and feeble versions of their male counterparts (Bryson, 1992: 22). Instead of seeing women as inherently simple, irrational, and emotional, Wollstonecraft argues that these gender characteristics are not innate in the female sex but are the result of an environment that requires them to be so (Kramnick, 1982: 12). She argues that through formal education, women can develop their innate capabilities for intellectual thought and thus become better wives and mothers. Wollstonecraft's ideas scandalized her contemporaries for their appropriation of liberal ideology. And yet she was extremely forward thinking in her anticipation of the arguments put forward by women in later centuries.

Equality of Opportunity, Meritocracy, and Freedom of Choice

The principles of equality of opportunity and meritocracy emerge clearly in the works of Harriet Taylor Mill (1807–1858) and her long-time companion, the political philosopher John Stuart Mill (1806–1873). Harriet Taylor Mill argued radically for the desirability of women to earn and have control of their own property and money. In addition to shared humanity on the basis of their mutual capacity for rational thought, she proposed that the sexes might achieve equality through women's control over their own property. Only then would women have a chance at equality of opportunity with men in other spheres. John Stuart Mill's work also reflects a deeply held belief that women should have control of their person. In *The Subjection of Women* (1869) Mill argues that the legal subordination of women to men is in itself wrong and is actually a hindrance to human progress. Nothing less than legal equality, he believed, ought to replace this relationship of subordination (Hall, 1992).

Another way to think about what equality of opportunity, meritocracy, and freedom of choice means for women is to consider a diversity of women's experiences with these concepts. White women in Europe and the Americas might have seen hope in liberal ideas, but the status of Aboriginal and Inuit women within their own communities was particularly compromised by those acting on liberal democratic—but patriarchal and racist—ideas (Maracle, 2003: 74). First Peoples in Canada have suffered a diminished economic, political, and social status under the purview of the *Indian Act* 1867. A major intention of the act was for First Nations women and children to become subject to their husbands and fathers just as European women were. The Europeans viewed this as a path to "civilizing" First Nations people, while First Nations people found this to be an aggressive and nonsensical destruction of the diverse and strong family structures already in place throughout Aboriginal societies (Stevenson, 1999). Women who enjoyed meaningful political participation and high status in their society before the arrival of Europeans, actually had their status reversed by the presence of European liberal democratic rule. The *Indian Act* initially determined who is and is not an Indian through patrilineage and marriage. If a woman was born a registered Indian but married a non-Status Indian, the law said that she was no longer an Indian. She would be removed from the register and denied the range of protections and rights set out by the Act. An Indian man on the other hand, could marry whomever he wished and that person could gain Indian status through marriage even if she was not of Aboriginal parentage (Stevenson, 1999).

In 1951 the Act became more exclusionary, removing Indian status from any woman who married out of her band. Simultaneously, women were accorded the right to vote in band council elections, providing a formal opportunity for women's open political participation. In the 1950s, Mary Two Axe Early (1911–1996) of Kahnawake was one of the first to speak publicly about the sexism of the *Indian Act.* Jeanette Lavall and Yvonne Bedard legally challenged the legislation in 1973, but the Supreme Court of Canada declared that the Canadian Bill of Rights did not apply to the *Indian Act.* Sandra Lovelace of the Tobique Reserve, New Brunswick, took this complaint to the United Nations Human Rights Committee in 1977. The Committee found Canada to be in violation of international human rights laws on the basis of its sexual discrimination in 1981. In the meantime, frustrated with a lack of support from the National Indian Brotherhood (now the Assembly of First Nations) the Tobique Women's Group of New Brunswick marched from Oka, Quebec, to Parliament Hill in Ottawa to raise awareness of these issues (Gehl, 2000). In 1985 the federal government amended the *Indian Act* to reinstate Aboriginal peoples who had lost their Indian status either through marriage or enfranchisement (Dickason, 2002).[2] Women's experience of equality of opportunity, meritocracy, and freedom of choice are therefore heavily mediated by the ways in which their legal and political history are gendered and racialized.

Examples of liberal feminist theory in practice are given below, demonstrating the variety of methods feminists have taken up in order to achieve their primary goal of equality with men.

Women and Access to Formal Education

Early liberal feminists realized very quickly that without a formal education, women could not advance in social status or political participation. They also realized that it would be difficult to acquire other rights without an education on par with that available to men. Through women's physical presence on campuses, and informal but highly effective networks of women graduates, education for women came to be thought of as an enhancement of the young middle-class woman's "natural" qualities (Garvie and Johnson, 1999). She would, after all, one day be a wife and mother in charge of the moral instruction of her children. As women entered the labour force in greater numbers after the Second World War the number of women seeking higher education again increased dramatically.

The suggestion that women have a formal education beyond elementary or high school was preposterous to most people. Women who wanted further education found themselves up against the view that educated women were strangely divorced from their natural roles as child bearers (Garvie and Johnson, 1999; Kromnick, 1982). White women who wanted an education, or a life beyond motherhood, were accused of "racial suicide" because the racial ideas of the time presumed the moral superiority of white people and women's obligation to reproduce that "race" (Valverde, 1992). Women of colour on the other hand, such

---

2   First Nations people could be "enfranchised" after 1851 but were required to give up their Indian status and pass a battery of tests in order to receive the right to vote. Understandably, very few people deliberately took this opportunity (Dickason, 2002).

as in the large black communities in eastern Canada and southern Ontario, may have found more support for their education. Slavery in Canada was abolished in 1834 and as early as 1830 black Canadians ran separate schools, which were an important form of resistance to the racism black people experienced from white Canadians (Kelly, 1998; Sadlier, 1994).

In Canada West (what is now south-western Ontario) and Upper and Lower Canada, female teachers proliferated throughout the 1850s, providing what little education was considered necessary for girls, such as writing, reading, and needlepoint (Prentice et al., 1996). Canada's first female university students in 1858 studied at Mount Allison University, Nova Scotia. They studied a limited range of topics that typically included literature, languages, rhetoric, history, and home economics (developed specifically for female students' entry to post-secondary education). Typically, women students were segregated in all-female classrooms and required to sit apart from male students in adjoining rooms where they could hear the lecture but not be seen by the men (Garvie and Johnson, 1999). Medicine, the sciences, and engineering were off-limits to women in most Canadian universities until the 1940s, when Canada's participation in the Second World War necessitated more doctors. After the Second World War the number of female students began to parallel male students in the arts, and only at the end of the twentieth century did women's numbers creep up in the sciences. Women have worked their way slowly into universities and colleges and into traditionally male-dominated areas of study such as the sciences and engineering such that their numbers have begun to approach those of men. Access to education is one of the major accomplishments of liberal feminism.

The Vote, 1918[3]

Liberal feminist thought was both informed and developed through women's agitation for suffrage between 1850 and 1920.[4] National controversies such as the genocide and colonization of Aboriginal peoples were put aside by the state and the media to focus on the tremendous challenges to existing social and political institutions posed by immigration (Falardeau-Ramsay, 1999: 99). Social reformers and religious organizations such as the Women's Christian Temperance Union (WCTU) were concerned about the state of urban dwellers, reacting to the poverty and malnutrition of the masses that came with urbanization and industrialization. At a time when in Western Canada, for example, milk was more costly than alcohol, women began to make the connections between poverty, the availability of alcohol, and the violence of men toward women and children (Strong-Boag, 1972). The fight for the vote was premised on women's capacity for reason as well as the suffragists' understanding of women's feminine morality. Maternal feminists in particular embraced and applied the principles of equal opportunity and meritocracy but felt that women had a superior moral and racial integrity, indicating white female suitability for political participation (Roome, 2001; Valverde, 1992). Maternal feminists and liberal feminists worked together along with socialist and conservative women toward the goals of social reform and ultimately, the vote (Roome, 2001).

---

3   Some white, propertied women were occasionally allowed to vote before 1849 but all women were banned from voting after that time (Status of Women Canada, 2003).

4   It should be noted that most suffragists did not actually call themselves feminists until the early twentieth century (Roome, 2001).

Feminists lobbied the state, held demonstrations and staged mock parliamentary debates to ridicule the men who upheld women's political and legal inequality. Led by Dr. Emily Howard Stowe (1831–1903) the Toronto Women's Literary Club (est. 1876) revealed itself as the Canadian Women's Suffrage Association in 1882 when some minor rights for women to vote in municipal elections were won (Prentice et al., 1996). In Quebec, women's organizing around suffrage and social problems such as poverty and health took place largely through women's Catholic organizations, reflecting the appeal of Christian-based public service organizations such as the Women's Christian Temperance Union (WCTU) and the Young Women's Christian Association (YWCA). Their work centred on providing shelter and educational programs for young, single, and poor women. With the slight increase in women's access to formal education and legislation such as the 1884 *Married Women's Property Act* (allowing married women to hold property exclusive of their husbands' ownership), feminists built the capacity for their movement (Prentice et al., 1996). Other organizations such as the National Council of Women of Canada (NCWC) (est. 1890s), a predominantly Protestant umbrella group, had strong links to both the American and British women's and social reform movements demonstrating that Canadian women's capacity for the development of a suffrage movement had an international network of alliances (Valverde, 1992).

Suffragists used a variety of tactics to challenge the familiar dichotomy of "passive" femininity versus the "active" and political masculinity thought appropriate for political decision-making (Roome, 2001). Some felt that petitioning, letter-writing, and public speaking were the best tactics to achieve their goals. The work of maternal feminist and journalist Nellie McClung (1875–1951) in Manitoba is a good example of effective public speaking; she used wit to ridicule male politicians in the press. Maternal feminists' attachment to feminine virtues, however, limited the scope of their actions in contrast to the "militant" British feminists such as Emmeline Pankhurst (1858–1929) and her daughters Christabel (1880–1958) and Sylvia (1882–1960). Beginning in 1903, these suffragettes heckled politicians, chained themselves to the British Parliament's fences, broke shop windows, set fires, and even persisted in hunger strikes, enduring forced feedings for their cause (Bryson, 1992; Prentice et al., 1996).

Unfortunately, the efforts of liberal and maternal feminists were applied unevenly to the goal of integrating women into social and political institutions. The issues of moral and racial degeneration and woman suffrage were very much linked in the late nineteenth and early twentieth centuries. Social Darwinism dictated the meanings given to the racial and class organization of Canadian society at this time, which influenced ideas about various groups' fitness for political participation. At the extreme end of the political spectrum, Aboriginal peoples, women, people of Chinese origin, and new immigrants from Eastern and Southern Europe were viewed as biologically inferior to white men of British origin and were denied the vote on that basis (Dickason, 2002; Valverde, 1992). Social reformers who considered themselves more moderate felt that these groups had to be properly assimilated into Britishness before they should be able to vote. Neither Canada's first prime minister, Sir John A. Macdonald, or Robert Borden, the prime minister who granted some women the federal vote in 1918, were ever personally in favour of extending universal suffrage (Roome, 2001; Valverde, 1992). The suffragists were aware of these views and distanced themselves from categories of "degeneracy" by asserting white women's moral superiority. Flora MacDonald Denison, a Canadian suffragist, was particularly critical of the morals of recent male immigrants (Prentice et al., 1996), while Emily Murphy wrote extensively on the threat of Chinese and black men's corruptive tendencies to the moral purity of white women (Valverde, 1992). The white ribbons worn by WCTU activists signified white racial purity as much as it did the purity of milk over alcohol (Valverde, 1992). Despite the activities of black women such as Harriet Tubman (1820–1913) in the suffrage movement and of other women of colour in organizations such as the WCTU, the white suffragists and social reformers persisted in the belief that the "mother of the race" would be free if she could only vote (Sadlier, 1994; Valverde, 1992). Most women were granted a federal vote in 1918 but this still excluded Aboriginal people and people of Chinese origin (Cleverdon, 1974: 108). After 1918 the federal government divested itself of responsibility for granting the provincial franchise. Some Manitoban women could vote provincially in 1916, but, for example, their Québécoise counterparts had to mobilize to bring 14 separate bills in 13 years to the Quebec legislature—they enjoyed success in 1940. Status Indian women achieved the vote in 1963 when the *Universal Right to Vote* was introduced.

The Persons' Case, 1929

The Persons' Case (1929) is another early example of the ways in which feminists have used the legal system to achieve their goals of overcoming women's oppression, by ensuring that women were fully integrated as citizens in the democratic state. The "Famous Five"—Emily Murphy (1868–1933), Nellie McClung (1875–1951), Mary Irene Parlby (1868–1965), Henrietta Muir Edwards (1849–1931), and Louise McKinney (1868–1933)—challenged a provision in the *British North America Act* (1867) that excluded women from being considered "persons" in the matter of privileges and rights (Falardeau-Ramsay, 1999: 52). The success of the Persons' Case did not mean that women were entirely equal to men under the law, particularly in terms of family law and property rights, but these "rights and privileges" did include eligibility to take up public offices such as in the Senate of Canada (Cleverdon, 1974: 149).

The Royal Commission on the Status of Women, 1970 and Beyond

A new generation of liberal feminists in North America emerged in the 1960s and 1970s whose actions must be contextualized through a number of different social movements (Brown, 1989). During the Second World War the federal government empowered women working in the home to a certain extent by investing in subsidized daycare and encouraging women to join the war effort in traditionally male forms of employment (Timpson, 2001). After the Second World War women were encouraged in the media, religious institutions, and school systems to go back to the role of homemaking. The post-war welfare state did not include a national daycare programme, so many women stayed at home to fulfil their roles as mothers and wives. Women who had previously worked outside the home, and even those who had not, became increasingly frustrated with their lot as financial dependants of husbands and fathers.

During the same period, the Canadian federal government was again actively recruiting new waves of immigrants to take up jobs in Canada. Non-white immigrants created new activist networks when they encountered racism in employment and housing and were occupationally segregated in low-paying jobs (Brown, 1989; Calliste, 2001). Additionally, new challenges to the federal *Indian Act* 1867 raised by First Nations, Métis, and Inuit peoples accompanied the revitalization of Aboriginal women's leadership in their communities (Maracle, 2003: 71). These movements provided a new base of women dissatisfied with their relationship to the state and ready to do something about it.

The Royal Commission on the Status of Women, 1970 (RCSW), is a benchmark moment of Canadian women's rights. With great struggle a select group of women were making inroads to the commanding structures of the federal government. Spearheaded by Laura Sabia, then president of the Canadian Federation of University Women (CFUW), and with the help of several non-governmental organizations, they convinced the government of the need for a royal commission. They correctly recognized that a human-rights framework that had equal opportunity as its goal would be most palatable to the federal government (Timpson, 2001: 29). Headed by Florence Bird (d. 1998), the RCSW spent over a year touring the country receiving briefs and hearing presentations from individuals and groups that had something to say about the status of women in Canadian society. The entire process was televised so that the nation watched; feminists were hopeful that the public nature of the RCSW would help them hold the federal government to carrying out the recommendations.

Based on the input of more than 300 women's organizations across the country and many more individuals, the RCSW identified four major areas of importance for Canadian women: the right to choose homemaking or paid employment; the shared responsibility for child care among mothers, fathers, and society at large; the special treatment of women relating to their maternity; and the special treatment of women to help them overcome the adverse effects of discriminatory practices in Canadian society (Paltiel, 1997: 29). These recommendations supported the central liberal feminist principle of equality of opportunity for women. Liberal feminists understand women's concentration in the private sphere (the home) to be a contributor to women's oppression if women lack the choice to move between the home and the public sphere (paid work). Women are at a disadvantage if they cannot choose between paid or unpaid work because they may not be able to care financially for themselves or dependants. Being defined through their work in the home as caregivers, mothers, and housekeepers also circumscribes women's influence in society at large. Homemaking as such is not necessarily at issue, rather the lack of choice to pursue other careers is the problem. As such, contemporary liberal feminism focuses on expanding the range of choices available to women and ensuring that the doors that have already been opened (i.e., access to education and political participation) remain open. The RCSW made 167 specific recommendations to the federal government as to how women's social, political, and economic status could be improved. Some were implemented but many more were not. For example, Canada still lacks a national daycare program that would allow more women equal participation in the labour force. Many liberal-feminist organizations, while recognizing that many more issues have been added to the agenda, still use the RCSW recommendations as a measuring stick for women's equality with men in Canada.

Contemporary Liberal Feminist Thought: Breaking the Glass Ceiling?

Since the RCSW submitted its findings, liberal feminist principles have become somewhat institutionalized. In particular, the legal integration of gender into the Canadian Charter of Human Rights in 1985 was a major accomplishment. To some degree liberal feminist principles have been assimilated into institutions such as through the successful struggle to establish the federal Status of Women secretariat, led by Doris Anderson. The establishment of the National Action Committee on the Status of Women in 1973 created a non-governmental popular organization through which diverse groups of women have lobbied for women's rights. The initial goals of liberal feminists, to have access to education and political participation, would seem like fairly staid and reasonable objectives if we did not know the difficulty with which they were achieved. For example, few of Canada's elected female members of Parliament would deny that they owe something to the achievements of liberal feminists, but only a minority would call themselves "feminists." This in itself is both a fortunate and unfortunate accomplishment in the legacy of liberal feminism.

Critiques of Liberal Feminism

A primary criticism of liberal feminist theory is its selectivity and privileging of the objectives of white middle- or upper-class women. In the past, women's equality with men has not always been the primary consideration of women whose social class statuses were far removed from the average middle- or upper-class "wife." If one is subject to legislation like the *Indian Act* 1876, arguing for gender equality with men makes little difference without racial and class equality (Arneil, 2001: 54). Yet much of liberal feminist theory has not historically been written using an integrated approach to gender, race, or class. This short-sightedness played out in the way that some early Canadian feminists argued that only white women of Canadian birth should be allowed the vote (Prentice et al., 1996).

Liberal feminist understanding of women's oppression and methods of social change incorporate women's presence into existing political and economic institutions without necessarily transforming the relations of power between men and women within those organizations or even in society at large. This is so, some argue, because having meritocracy as a central principle takes for granted a level playing field between different groups of women. The following statistic is alarming at a time when the goals of liberal feminism, such as access to education and political participation, are taken as a given by many Canadian women. In 1997, university-educated women working full-time year-round made only 74 percent of their male counterparts' income (Status of Women Canada, 2003b). Women earn less not because male and female co-workers can be paid different wages, but because women are occupationally segregated into lower-paying jobs across the country (Nelson and Robinson, 2002). Unfortunately, the common reasoning presented in the media or by governments suggests that since women now have "equal opportunity" as far as the law goes, they must simply work harder to "merit" higher paying jobs. Explaining away such inequities misappropriates liberal discourse and masks structural and systemic inequalities within and between different groups of men and women. Liberal feminists continue to argue that a remedy to this inequity is possible through women's promotion into better-paying jobs and the safeguarding of their work environments from sexual harassment and discrimination.

SOCIALIST FEMINISM

Defining Socialist Feminism

Socialist feminism originates in Marxist theory and uses class and gender as central categories of analysis in its explanation of women's oppression. Socialist feminism holds several key goals in its analyses and activism. First, socialist feminism relates the oppression experienced by women to their economic dependence on men. One of the goals of socialist feminism is therefore to advocate for social conditions that allow women's economic independence. In addition, socialist feminism provides a materialist analysis of gender inequality by identifying the relationship between systems of patriarchal oppression in which women are subordinated to men, and class relations in capitalist economic systems, where working classes are subordinated to the upper classes. The gendered division of labour in the home and wage labour market (unpaid and paid work), and women's economically subordinate position in the paid labour force account for the unequal position of women in capitalist patriarchal societies. Therefore, a second goal of socialist feminism is to expose and challenge the devaluation of women's unpaid labour in the home. In doing so, socialist feminists advocate for acknowledgement of the value of women's domestic work, a sharing of domestic responsibilities between men and women, and state involvement (financial and legislative) in creating a society that is equitable and just for everyone. A third, related goal of socialist feminism is to highlight and do away with the continuing pay inequities between men and women (which lead to female financial dependency on men and/or over-representation of women among the total number of poor), and the gendered division of labour within the wage labour market (responsible for the over-representation of women in service industries).

Socialist feminism seeks to redress gender and class inequalities through changes in the state and its policies, changes that would allow for adequate incomes, pay and employment equity, state-sponsored childcare, and maternity and paternity leave for all (among other desired outcomes). Socialist feminism uses analyses of class to explain the ways in which social, economic, and political power is distributed in varying amounts to members of society, usually in relation to factors such as gender, race, and sexuality.

HISTORICAL BACKGROUND

Marxism

Karl Marx (1818–1883) and Friederich Engels (1820–1895) were influential in the development of socialist feminist thought. Marx and Engels' *Communist Manifesto* (1848) laid the foundations of Marxist theory, outlining the relationship of human beings to the ways in which we produce and reproduce for survival, as a central factor in understanding the socio-political characteristics of any particular historical period. Therefore, as Rosemarie Tong points out, "we are what we do"; unlike bees or ants, which have biologically predetermined methods of sustaining themselves (set patterns of collecting food and creating shelter), as humans, we consciously and socially manipulate our environments in particular ways in order to feed, clothe, and house ourselves (1998).

Marxists place the characteristics of the production and reproduction for the conditions of life at the centre of their understanding of history, in an analytical method called "historical materialism." A materialist analysis (an analysis that focuses on class) has been used by Marxists to explain inequality in society, particularly as it is experienced within the capitalist context. Capitalism is an economic system of production that relies on the exchange of one's labour for wages, which in turn produces profit for someone else. Thus, capitalist modes of production (as understood within Marxist theory), are characterized by a class of owners (bourgeoisie) and a class of workers (proletariat). The wealth of the bourgeoisie can only be extracted through the exploitation of the proletariat. Workers produce at a disproportionate rate to the wages they receive, resulting in market profits for owners. Capitalism is characterized by a form of mass production that alienates the proletariat from the products of their labour. In accordance with Marxist theory then, the components needed for the production and reproduction of social life (raw materials, tools, and workers) and the ways in which this production and reproduction is organized (a capitalist versus a communist economy, for example) are extremely influential to the dominant political, social, and legal ideas of any historic period (Tong, 1998).

In *The German Ideology* (1846), Marx and Engels advance an analysis of capitalist oppression that features the family as the original site of an inequitable division of labour, later to be reflected in the capitalist labour market. Marx and Engels argued that wives and children constituted a "first property" for men, whom they provided with labour, and men exerted control over the context, conditions, and environment in which this labour took place. Although gender and the oppression of women was not a point of focus for much of early Marxist thought, in *The Origin of the Family, Private Property and the State* (1884), Engels did venture an examination of the sources of women's inequality (Somerville, 2000). Engels linked the economic conditions of people to the ways in which the family is organized as a productive and reproductive unit. The change in modes of production, which saw men in charge of the domestication and breeding of animals was, according to Engels, a major factor in the unequal shifting of power between men and women. With men predominantly in charge of this new symbol of wealth and power came a devaluation of the work and material contributions of women to the community. Communal work and property came to be replaced by individual households and private property, which in turn made inheritance an important issue for men (who constituted the majority of property owners).

It is the concern over inheritance, suggests Engels, which led to the patriarchal formalization of the nuclear family unit as a method of ensuring the passing down of private property and wealth from father to children of his own blood (Somerville, 2000). Economic wealth allowed the husband to assume control of the household, subjugating his wife and children within the home. Engels advanced this as simply a reflection of the inequalities perpetuated by the capitalist labour market, with the husband representing the "bourgeoisie" and the wife taking the role of the "proletariat." Therefore, the source of women's oppression, according to Engels, lay in the fact that they did not own or have control over private property. As such, the liberation of women could be ensured only by the eradication of capitalism and the reintroduction of women on an equal footing in the production process (Brenner, 2000).

Marxist Feminism

Marxist feminism theorizes women's oppression as rooted in capitalism. It is women's economic dependence on men within the capitalist system that leads to their exploitation and inequality. This exploitation is based on a capitalist system that equates the value of an individual to paid work and the amount of money one earns in the labour market. Moreover, this capitalist economic system works simultaneously with a patriarchal socio-political system to divide and relegate certain types of work, and, subsequently, certain levels of pay to individuals based on their gender. The result is a society in which men are over-represented in the highest-paying professional jobs, women's (unpaid) domestic contributions are not regarded as work, and women are over-represented in service-oriented jobs at a lower pay. These factors listed above have implications for women's economic standing, healthcare, pension plans, childcare options, and maternity leave options (among other factors).

Women's relationship to work, both in the home and within the labour market, is a key point of analysis for Marxist feminists. Theorists such as Margaret Benston (1969) point to the division of labour according to sex, a key feature of capitalism, as central to women's oppression. One of the central functions of capitalism is to take advantage of the labour of workers for profit. Marxist feminists view this as an indication of capitalism's need to create a division of labour between home and economy. This process suggests a false notion of a supposedly clear division between private (home) and public (economy) spheres, with women and men being relegated particular responsibilities within those spheres, based on the perceived gender attributes of each (Hewitt, 2000).

Marx's discussion of the process of industrialization and the concentration of the production of goods outside the home is used by Marxist feminists to expose a shift in the popular understanding of what constitutes productivity. Working in a factory, producing goods, is viewed by capitalist states as productive, but cooking, cleaning, doing laundry, and taking care of children are not (Waring, 1999). The determinant of productivity and the value of work within a capitalist society is the wage. Marxist feminists emphasize that the ineligibility of woman's work in the home to be turned into a product that can be sold does not make it a less valuable contribution to society (Tong, 1998). Furthermore, as Mariarosa Dalla Costa and Selma James (1975) have suggested, to argue for the equal inclusion of women within the labour force (as liberal feminists have done), without socializing or making a public responsibility of childcare and housework, will only increase the oppressive conditions under which women live. The result is, as Juliet Mitchell (1971) has to some extent argued, that waking up in the morning to prepare breakfast and lunch for the kids and husband, going to the office, and returning home in the evening only to cook dinner, finish the laundry, and clean, means a double day of work for women. Women's equal numerical representation and pay in the labour market does not constitute liberation.

Marxist feminist analyses argue for the socialization of childcare and housework, and the dissolution of the nuclear family as an economic unit. They emphasize the need for women's economic independence and well being (which they see the state as having some responsibility for ensuring). Marxist feminists also link women's unequal conditions in the workforce to their exploitative positions within the nuclear family unit, calling for an end to capitalism and the oppressive policies and social, economic and political conditions it creates and perpetuates through the state. However, if women's oppression is rooted in capitalism and its exploitative characteristics (private property, gendered division of labour in the home and economy, accumulation of profit, etc.), how do we explain the existence of women's oppression prior to the existence of the capitalist system and their subordination within past and present socialist/communist states?[5]

Socialist Feminism

Socialist feminists, like Marxist feminists, consider capitalism a significant factor in the oppression experienced by women. Additionally, however, they seek to explain the oppression of women beyond their role as workers, at the hands of patriarchy. Patriarchy is an analytic category and system of distributing power in society that hierarchically ascribes importance to all things male or masculine over all things female or feminine. Socialist feminists find Marxist feminism problematic in that it locates most aspects of women's oppression within the bourgeoisie/proletariat paradigm, neglecting the more complex aspects of relationships between women and men. Although Marxist feminism has been able to explain the gendered division of labour within the home and workplace and the role of capitalism in this process, it has not been able to explain why these gendered roles, responsibilities, and attributes were assigned to women and men in the first place (Tong, 1998).

Alison Jaggar (1983) focuses on the Marxist notion of workers' alienation in a way that exposes the particular alienation experienced by women within patriarchal capitalist systems. While Marx's notion of alienation is primarily concerned with the angst experienced by workers because of their ultimate separation from the products of their labour (as can be seen in the context of mass production and factory work), Jaggar engages with the alienation experienced by women in the processes of maneuvering their bodies (shaving/tweezing body hair, dieting) for the pleasure and capitalist consumption of men. Thus, the alienation of women from their own bodies, as reflected in the efforts invested to change the body before the critical gaze of men, as well as the alienation of women from their bodies during childbirth in hospitals (with much of the process under the authority of doctors and nurses), are examples of the ways in which socialist feminism expands traditional Marxist and Marxist feminist analyses of capitalist exploitation and its relationship to gender inequality.

Socialist feminism is concerned with how capitalism interacts with patriarchy to oppress women workers more than and differently from men. In addition to the gendered division of labour in the home and economy, and women's relationship to the wage labour market, socialist feminism examines the pay inequality between men and women (contributing to female economic dependency on men and the over-representation of women among the

---

5   For example, in 1934, Russian Communist revolutionary Vladimir Lenin accused colleague Clara Zetkin of weakening the Communist Party platform by encouraging discussions of gender oppression among female party members (Tong, 1998). Discussion of women's realities were viewed as divisive to the aims of a party fighting for economic justice "for all." Additionally, Socialist feminists active in the Canadian Socialist Party and the Socialist Democratic Party of Canada during the early decades of the twentieth century frequently had to find ways of negotiating their positions within and between socialist politics (under the mandate of male-dominated parties) and socialist politics that also incorporated and supported the leading concerns of women's activism. These concerns included women's suffrage (the right of white women to vote), prohibition (the problem of alcohol), and women's positions within and in relation to the labour force (Newton, 1992).

poor) as a way of understanding the barriers and disadvantages experienced by women. Socialist feminism seeks to redress these inequalities through changes in the state and its policies, which should allow for adequate income provisions, pay and employment equity, state-sponsored childcare, and maternity and paternity leave for all (Morris, 2002).

The Household: Paid and Unpaid Labour

Socialist feminist analysis has provided important insights into the fundamental contribution of housework done predominantly by women, in the unfolding of the daily activities of individuals. As housewives and workers in the home, women contribute to the profits of the capitalist economy by ensuring that present-day and future workers in the paid labour force, be they teenagers or adults, are cared for in the home in ways that prepare and support them in their positions within the paid labour force (Morris, 2000). Whether by doing family laundry, preparing meals, cleaning and maintaining organization in the home, or transporting household members to and from school, work, and play, etc., women provide an important service—not only to their families, but also to the capitalist patriarchy that benefits from the present and future labour of these family members.

With this exposition of the intricate relationship between the home and labour market, socialist feminist theory illustrates that the oppressive power of dominant capitalist, patriarchal discourse lies not only in its perpetuation of the notion of men and women as dichotomous categories, but also in its depiction of the home and the economy as separate and relatively unrelated to each other in any significant social, political, or economic sense. The suggestion that the "private" workings of the home are isolated from the larger "public" workings of the capitalist patriarchal economic, social, and political system facilitates the acceptance of housework on the part of women as a "natural" result of their love for their family. This in turn works to legitimize the view of wage labour as "real" labour while devaluing the significant contributions of women in the home and masking the benefits and profit that capitalist and state institutions enjoy from these contributions (the reproduction of future workforce labourers, the maintenance of their physical, emotion, and mental health allowing them to continue to be productive). According to a 1997 Statistics Canada survey, 68 percent of unpaid labour in Canada is done by women, many of whom are also employed in the wage labour market (Hanson, Hanson, and Adams, 2001). Moreover, the 1996 Canadian census (the first to include questions on housework), indicated that the value of unpaid work in Canada in 1992 amounted to more than $235 billion, one-third of the GDP[6] for the total value of goods and services produced (Morris, 2000). Out of 29 of the world's most developed countries, Canada currently has the fifth-largest wage gap between male and female full-time workers (Morris, 2002). These statistics are not unrelated to the current over-representation of women among Canada's total number of poor.

The Feminization of Poverty

The "feminization of poverty" is a term used by socialist feminists to identify the disproportionate majority of women who are poor, linking their poverty to patriarchal and capi-

---

6   GDP stands for gross domestic product, a calculation of the total economic value of a country's
     yearly output of goods and services.

talist sexist and profit-based initiatives that segregate the labour market. This segregation is carried out based on constructed notions of gender ("women's work vs. men's work"); by devaluing labour in the home; by not factoring home work into official national labour-based calculations such as the GDP; and by reinforcing notions of household labour as a "natural" consequence of a woman's love for her family. As Morris (2000) points out, 2.8 million women in Canada are living in poverty. The presence of children is a factor that continues to disproportionately and negatively affect the incomes of women in comparison to those of men (Hanson, Hanson, and Adams, 2001).

Since women's responsibilities for and within the home are not recognized as "real" work, women are not compensated by the state for reducing their wage labour to part-time in order to take care of children, or for losing job training and seniority upon taking maternity leave from waged work. The relegation of women to lower-paying employment sectors long accepted as more suited to women's "feminine" characteristics (teaching, nursing, cleaning, cooking, typing), has also contributed to women's disproportionate poverty. Cindy Hanson et al. (2001) indicate that Canadian women make up 67 percent of total minimum-wage earners in the country. Childcare would be one way of supporting women's greater and more equitable participation in the paid labour force (Harman, 2000). As reflected in data collected by the National Council of Welfare in 1999, "only 1 in 4 Canadian children under 6 whose mother is employed has space in a regulated childcare" (Hanson, Hanson, and Adams, 2001). The positive impact of childcare has already been demonstrated in Quebec, which provides provincially financed childcare at five dollars a day. The Quebec Ministry of Social Welfare estimates that this policy has removed 37 percent of young mothers in Quebec from welfare (Walker, 2000). For socialist feminists, eradicating poverty and the oppression of women involves not only the equal sharing of domestic responsibilities between men and women, but additionally state policies that "increase women's choice about when and how they go back to work" (Harman, 2000).

Although these statistics are valuable in painting a picture of poverty and the economic realities of Canadian women, it is important to remember that poverty does not affect all women in the same way. Aboriginal women, non-white women, and women with disabilities are particularly vulnerable to poverty. According to Statistics Canada (2000) Aboriginal women earn an average annual income of $13,000, while their non-Aboriginal counterparts average $19,350 per year (Morris, 2002). As the National Anti-Poverty Organization (April 1999) indicates, 44 percent of Aboriginals living off reserves live in poverty, while 47 percent of Aboriginals still living on reserves average an annual income of $10,000. The successful challenge made by Jeanette Lavell, Yvonne Bedard, and Sandra Lovelace in 1985 to the sexism of the *Indian Act* 1867 alleviated one way in which systemic racism and sexism work within a patriarchal capitalist economic system to disadvantage women of Aboriginal heritage. Unfortunately, the success of their challenge is only a fraction of the economic disadvantages upheld through legislation such as the *Indian Act* (Dickason, 2002). The history of the Live-In Caregiver Program in Canada is also reflective of the ways in which women's experiences of oppression differ within the capitalist system. The interconnectedness of "race" and racism (the meanings given to one's ethnicity), gender (the ways in which one is read as a woman or man), class (the economic standing of an individual), and sexuality (how and in what ways one identifies or is identified according to sexual orientation(s) and how)—all in relation to labour—is visible in the disproportionately large number of immigrant and non-white women occupying low-wage, non-unionized jobs with no benefits.

With limited childcare spaces and a general increase in the working hours and responsibilities of employees—a consequence of contemporary economic restructuring—resorting to domestic service becomes one way Canadian women manage the responsibilities of a household and employment in the labour market (Morris, July 2002a).

The exploitation of and discrimination against foreign domestic workers primarily from the Caribbean and Philippines in Canada, has a history spanning a number of decades. Foreign domestic workers in the early 1970s were under a number of oppressive legislative restrictions and policies. Although the status of foreign domestics as temporary visa holders prevented them from accessing benefits such as paid medicare, their pay was docked for the Canada Pension Plan (CPP), Employment Insurance, and income tax. Today employees under this program must live in their employers' homes (meaning they are always on call), they can work only for the employer listed on their Employment Authorization (EA) form, and cannot stay in the country past the date listed on this form (Morris, July 2002c). These conditions are relevant to feminist theorizing and activism in Canada in that, as Himani Bannerji points out, "organization by race (or racism) is a fundamental way of forming class in Canada and this formation of class is a fully gendered one" (Bannerji, 1995).

Contemporary Socialist Feminist Analyses

Contemporary socialist feminist analyses, produced by women of colour particularly, have expanded the boundaries of materialist deconstructions of gender-based oppression, by revealing the ways in which "race," racism, colonialism/neo-colonialism, class, gender, and sexuality work simultaneously to differentiate the experiences of women with oppression. Globalization and the role of gender in transnationalism[7] have also found a place within the work of some contemporary socialist feminist theorists (Dua, 1999; Ault and Sandberg, 2001; Sparr, 1994; Carillo, 2001). This stretching of the boundaries of early socialist feminist theory to more adequately reflect the complexities and shifts of gender relations in a global economy is extremely valuable. It illustrates an understanding of the connection between, for example, an unemployed inner-city youth of colour with $200 Nike sneakers and the employed but overworked and under-paid Indonesian woman who sews these sneakers, yet barely affords to feed herself (Appelbaum, 2002). Global economic re-structuring has led many Canadian and American companies to downsize their operations and make use of the inexpensive labour available in non-Western countries. This downsizing has resulted in increased lay-offs, increased workload for those still employed, and increased part-time, temporary, low-security, low-wage, no-benefits, non-unionized jobs, largely worked by immigrants, particularly women of colour (Morris, 2000). The process of economic globalization illustrates the ways in which capitalism adapts and expands to protect its interest in profit.

In a global economic order, where one country's legislative policies can directly and indirectly influence the lives of people continents away, it is important to have analyses of gender and class that point to the interconnectedness of these processes of racialization and neo-colonialism. Socialist feminism has made important gains in the past few decades, a

---

7 The idea of economic and socio-political policies whose influences reach beyond the borders of the nation in which they originate.

number of which are reflected in Canadian government policies. The inclusion of questions on work in the household within the 1996 Canadian census for example, is an important step toward making the gendered division of labour and the economic realities of women part of a socio-political dialogue within Canadian politics and culture. The continuation of feminist agitation for state-sponsored childcare (as illustrated by the efforts of women associated with the Canadian Auto Workers Union [CAW]) is another example of socialist feminist practice that is making the contemporary economic realities of women difficult for the state to ignore.

Critiques of Socialist Feminism

Socialist feminism's use of a materialist analysis as the basis of its deconstruction of oppression leaves some questions unanswered. For example, should the equitable redistribution of power and wealth in society actually occur, and economic systems find themselves operating outside of capitalism, would, as Dooley asks, "men simply no longer harass, abuse, rape, belittle, insult and hate women?" (Dooley, 2001). The theoretical engagement of radical feminism with other social realities, such as family forms outside of the heterosexual, nuclear family model (queer-identified, non-white, immigrant, Aboriginal, and single-parent family models), has also provided legitimate critiques of socialist feminist texts and forms of activism that have used the "ideology of separate spheres for men and women" (Mandell and Elliot, 2001) as a key component of materialist analyses of oppression.

RADICAL FEMINISM

Defining Radical Feminism

Have you ever wondered when women started to "Take Back the Night," rallying for safer streets and demanding that violence against women be stopped? These demonstrations (along with demonstrations for abortion rights as well as anti-violence protests) spring from a section of the women's movement called radical feminism. Radical feminists have contributed much to feminist theory by concentrating on sexuality, control, violence, and clear-cut analyses of how men's power over women can be seen in all areas of women's lives, such as violence against women, rape, and prostitution.

The development of radical feminism in the 1960s and 1970s coincided with other movements such as the civil rights, anti-war, and broader women's liberation movements. These movements challenged the status quo as they attempted to shake up traditional societal institutions. In Canada, the Royal Commission on the Status of Women (Bird et al., 1970) suggested many ways in which equality for women could be attained. There was a sense of hope, energy, and urgency during this time.

Many scholars attribute the rise of radical feminism to a New York setting, naming groups such as the Red Stockings, the Furies, and the Radicalesbians, yet Canadian-based radical feminist groups such as the New Feminists of Toronto are important to the development of radical feminist action in Canada (Echols, 1989). Groups like these organized around many issues through consciousness-raising (CR) sessions where women came together to share stories of sexist oppression and gendered exploitation to discover that "the personal is political" (Crow, 2000: 6). The CR group or "rap session" appealed to many women. In these sessions women could hear and share accounts of oppression across class and race lines, link those accounts to a larger theoretical framework in order to build critical organizing skills, and publicly air their goals. Radical feminists active in the 1960s and 70s also used manifestos as a revolutionary method to "speak bitterness" (Freeman, 1975 in Crow, 2000: 6). Collectively, radical feminist activities formed the basis for a global sisterhood, spreading feminism internationally and building alliances around concrete concerns such as violence and pornography (Morgan, 1970).

Sites of Oppression: Patriarchy, the State, and the Family

Radical feminists argue that finding the grand theory of women's oppression is key to deconstructing it. They insist that, in order to locate the root of women's oppression, one must look past laws or economic and political critiques forwarded by liberal and socialist feminists. In the early stages of the development of radical feminist thought, sex oppression was the first and most fundamental oppression, and all other areas of repression sprang from it and were shaped by it (Crow, 2000: 2). By sex oppression, radical feminists mean that women's oppression is based on the relations of domination and subordination between the sexes, where women are seen as a sex class, whose sexuality is directly controlled by men. Radical feminists insist that, in order for women to understand their inferior roles in patriarchal society, they must look at how men have come to hold and wield power over women in all social relationships.

Radical feminists identify three main areas where women are most affected: the state, the family, and motherhood. Unlike liberal feminists, who focused on women's status in terms of individual rights and laws, radical feminists theorize from women's everyday lives. They believe that patriarchy, a "sexual system of power in which the male possesses superior power and economic privilege," is what shapes everyday life and what specifically affects women, for the benefit of men (Eisenstein, 1979: 17). Patriarchy, they argued, is constituted in and through various social structures and is reproduced and activated in everyday relations, having impacts on a global scale. It can be found in all aspects of society, including the state, the family, and other institutions, such as schools, the media, and religious institutions. In order to free themselves from the "Father Land" of patriarchy, an autonomous social, historical, and political force created by men for their own benefit, women must resist and undermine this system (Daly, 1978: 28; Donovan, 2000: 156).

As the state (which includes political institutions, laws, elected representatives, etc.) has been and continues to be founded on and emblematic of male interests, radical feminists believe that entrusting women's liberation to the state will result in them being once again taken for granted by the patriarchal order, and, in essence, "raped." State authority is male authority as it "is coercive and ensures men's control over women's sexuality; thus although the state assumes objectivity as its norm, in practice, women are raped by the state just as they are raped by men" (Andersen, 1997: 359). For radical feminists, engaging with the state is futile, as it is considered a site of male power and control.

Another area of male power and control is the family. Radical feminists voice the need to look critically at this institution and point to the family as yet another site of oppression for women. Socialist-feminists centre their analyses on the unpaid work done by women within traditional families and the negative implications of women's economic dependence on men. Building on these analyses, radical feminists identify the harms of social reproduction, describing the sexual energies women give to men in order to reproduce the family biologically and sustain it culturally. For radical feminists, ideologies of romance and love support traditional family structures. Hegemonic state apparatuses, such as marriage, as well as "opiates" such as romantic love, keep women drugged and under male control. Romantic love, beauty, dating, dieting and other cultural practices are seen as tools used by patriarchy to uphold and support heteronormativity, keeping women reliant on men's sexual attention and affection and by making women promote and service the desires of men (Firestone, 1970: 131, 146). Ti-Grace Atkinson (1970), an early radical feminist, stated that love, as an institution of male power and control, "promotes vulnerability, dependence, possessiveness, susceptibility to pain, and prevents the full development of a woman's potential" (117).

Traditional mothering ideology and practice also comes under radical feminist scrutiny. As Rich has argued, mothering under patriarchy is an exploitative responsibility (Rich, 1976). The seeming naturalness of motherhood and its institutionalization has become a duty for women in patriarchal society. Mothering is a role women need to play that restricts women's caring and nurturing energies to the family unit. In the 1960s and 1970s in particular, radical feminists pointed to the idea that women were supposed to be on the mothering job 24 hours a day, every day, with no outside contacts (Tong, 1998: 83). The patriarchal order dictates that women's ability to mother becomes conflated with their worthiness as women. Therefore, women's identity as women becomes linked to their ability to mother (i.e., if you are not a good mother, you are not a good woman) (Kreps, 1973: 236). In the past few years, radical feminist analyses of motherhood have been critiqued, especially by feminist theorists who have formulated mothering as an empowering feminist enterprise. Many feminists have reclaimed motherhood as an important step in the formation of their feminism. As Andrea O'Reilly states, "[t]hough I had identified myself as a feminist for a number of years; motherhood made feminism real for me and radically redefined it" (O'Reilly, 2000: 182–183).

Women's Bodies: Reproduction, Pornography, and Violence

Many early radical feminist theorists looked to women's reproductive roles to discover the root problem of women's oppression (Firestone, 1970): Biology separates the sexes, and that division relegates an enormous amount of reproductive labour to women. As women nurture and care for children, men are freed to participate in public life and social institutions, where they can acquire power, privilege, and property, all of which emboldens their superior social status (Hamilton, 1996: 20). This seemingly "natural" sexual division of labour (men in the public, women in the private) means that women are at the mercy of their biology; radical feminists declared a need for this to be addressed (Firestone, 1970). Within this sexual division of labour, women's bodies become an object, passed down from father to husband, placing the ownership of their sexuality squarely in the hands of men (Hamilton, 1996: 65). According to radical feminists, women clearly needed to divest themselves of these relationships.

In order to destroy patriarchy, radical feminists called for a re-evaluation of women's reproductive roles and an elimination of the traditional family. Women had little control over their reproductive functions, as abortion was illegal in Canada until 1988[8] and birth control was hard to acquire in the early phases of the women's movement in the 60s and 70s. Many, therefore, suggested that freeing women from the "tyranny of reproduction" and relying on technological advances would diminish clearly marked and oppressive gendered differences (Firestone, 1970). As a remedy, some radical feminists believed that in-vitro fertilization, artificial insemination, and eventually cloning would separate women from their wombs, therefore breaking the oppressive tie of women to biology. Others countered that although women would be liberated from reproduction through new reproductive technologies, it would only lead to male control; those who held ownership of these technologies were doctors and scientists who were usually men. Margaret Atwood's famous novel *The Handmaid's Tale* (1985) exemplifies the concerns of some radical feminists, as it recounts a dystopian future where women become uniquely defined and controlled by their reproductive roles.

Radical feminist theorists question the meaning of masculinity and femininity, arguing that masculinity is linked to dominance and that femininity is linked to subordination. Furthermore, these unequal relations of power are eroticized and in traditional heterosexual relations where women are positioned as objects of male pleasure, constantly available, constantly ready, and constantly scrutinized. In the popular media and pornography, the male gaze constructs women's sexuality and structures male and female sexual relations. Annette Koedt, in her well-known 1970 article "The Myth of the Vaginal Orgasm," discussed how medical literature about women's bodies had created the false belief that women who could not achieve orgasm solely through penetration of the vagina, and who instead achieved orgasm through clitoral stimulation, were described as "frigid" by their male partners and the medical establishment. Koedt and others challenged this notion and revealed how men owned and defined women's sexuality. In such an unequal model, women's needs and desires are ignored (MacKinnon, 1989).

Male power is still evident in much pornography and in prostitution, a sensitive area of female exploitation and domination critiqued by radical feminists. "Female sexual slavery," radical feminists argue, and the graphic depictions of women as sexual objects, are manifestations of the patriarchal domination of women by men and have the effect of shaping an acceptance of violent and coercive hatred against women (Dworkin, 1981; Barry, 1984). Some radical feminists think that male violence against women stems from an intake of violent pornography, making it acceptable to see women as purely objects of sexual gratification rather than as mutual players of love and intimacy (Tong, 1998: 66). Radical feminism still sees teenage males and females as growing up in a misogynist culture in which double standards persist. Women find themselves dieting at an early age, and the number of young women suffering from bulimia and anorexia grows daily. In a society that delivers such violent cultural messages about women and women's bodies, it is not surprising that young women starve themselves to fit their bodies into a sexist cultural ideal of beauty.

Radical-feminist theorists have also spoken strongly against rape, seeing it as a crime resulting from, and maintaining, male power. If domination and subordination are the basis for unequal sexual relations between men and women, and if these unequal sexual relations

---

8   Abortion was first decriminalized in 1969, yet access to it had to be granted by committees composed usually of men, and only if it was to preserve women's "health," a term that was often interpreted differently depending on the committee. Full access to abortion was granted in 1988.

are a maintained and constitutive of force, they ask, what is the difference between sex and rape (Dworkin, 1974; Brownmiller, 1976; MacKinnon, 1989)? If women and men are not equals in society, and if men wield power over women, then loving and sexual relationships between the two are always mediated by unequal power exchanges, where one person (man) controls the other (woman). Radical feminists conclude that women cannot experience their sexuality as pleasurable, because sexuality is male-coded and controlled. How then, they ask, do women construct their own sexuality? What would woman-defined sexuality look like?

Female Separation: Lesbian Feminism and Cultural Feminism

Radical feminists see our societies as violent and male-dominated, a world in which cultural representations of women include those of prostitution, pornography, and rape. Radical feminists argue that eliminating patriarchal society is the only viable solution to ending inequality. Patriarchy is sustained by men maintaining relationships with one another and thus ensuring that their power and privilege is maintained through interlocking systems of oppression such as racism, classism, and women's sexual oppression. Radical feminists, especially lesbian and cultural feminists, suggest that women divest themselves of patriarchy by strengthening bonds among women and by removing themselves from patriarchy's grip.

Lesbian feminism sprang from radical feminists' desire to discover and value women's contributions to society. Lesbian feminists shifted the debate from analyzing and reacting to male structures of power to focusing on how passionate bonds between women can foster a politics of emancipation. Lesbianism connotes sexual relations between women. But is also represents a political stance, a support system that allows women to turn to other women to escape from an oppressive male-dominated world. Lesbian feminists argued that every culture is infused with phallocentric social and cultural values forcing women to live lives geared toward men and heterosexual and monogamous pairings (Rich, 1980). In part, women are taught that self-worth comes from heterosexual marriage and mothering, they said. The idea of compulsory heterosexuality—where women are seen to be naturally sexually oriented toward men—restricts women socially and economically. Alternatives to this model, such as lesbian sexuality, were not well received by mainstream society and cast aside as deviant (Rich, 1980: 4).

Lesbian feminism suggests that the main way women can resist male domination and power is to refrain from having sexual relations with men. Arising from this idea came the famous slogan, "feminism is the theory and lesbianism is the practice." Or, as Catherine MacKinnon said, "feminism is the epistemology of which lesbianism is ontology" (quoted in Heller, 1997: 22). Adrienne Rich, a well-known American lesbian feminist advanced the idea of the lesbian continuum in order to operationalize that slogan. In order to separate lesbianism from being solely a sexual relation between women, Rich described a continuum, a position of compromise where all relations between women (friendships and caring relationships such as elder care) can be placed within the definition of lesbian and lesbian feminist politics (Rich, 1980). Not all feminists were comfortable with Rich's suggestion that lesbian be adopted as a political slogan. In Canada particularly, homophobic responses led to the ejection of many lesbians from feminist organizing groups, as some believed that the prominent presence of lesbians would undermine the movement (Grant, 1998; Ross, 1995).

Radical cultural feminists, successors of radical feminists, banded together and mobilized around what they saw as women's uniqueness: their femaleness. Cultural feminists espouse a "politics of disengagement," a breaking out of a male-dominated society by providing women-only cultural spaces (Adamson, Briskin, and McPhail, 1988: 192, Dononvan, 2000; 255–56). By concentrating on the positive features of women-only cultural spaces—care, sympathy, and nurturance—women would be able to promote and celebrate them and make them the basis for relationships between women. Often seen as the "separatists" in the feminist movement, cultural feminists believe that valuing women demands a woman-centered culture, where goddesses are worshipped, and bookstores, co-ops, and centres—run by women for women—can counter the negative effects of a male-dominated society.

Contemporary Theoretical Ideas

Radical feminist theorizing has been influential in shaping contemporary understandings of sex and sexuality, power and dominance. Radical feminist critiques continue to investigate patriarchy as problematic for women. Many important vehicles of feminist political action exist today because of the ideas of radical feminism.

How we understand violence against women in contemporary society has been shaped by radical feminist theories and ideas. As reported by the Canadian Research Institute for the Advancement of Women (CRIAW), half of Canadian women are survivors of at least one incident of physical or sexual violence (Morris, 2002). Women continue to "Take Back the Night" and demand safer streets and harsher rape laws for offenders. A network of government-funded shelters for women escaping abusive partners located across Canada exist because of the important theoretical insights that radical feminism has provided on violence against women. Radical feminist ideas have provided a theoretical framework for understanding women's everyday lives and continue to be relevant to contemporary theorizing.

Organizations such as Women Against Pornography and Always Causing Legal Unrest (ACLU) and journals such as *Off Our Backs* continue to uphold radical-feminist theoretical tenets and to thrive within mainstream feminist discourse. Taking up similar topics to those of 30 years ago, contemporary radical feminist theorists remain committed to providing an analytical framework around women's oppression as a result of patriarchal domination. Pornography and prostitution are still on the agenda, as is the interrogation and abolition of male privilege. Groups like the ACLU continue to demonstrate in front of sex stores, doing "zaps" as seen in the tactics of feminists working in the '60s, where small groups of people carry out symbolic protests and demonstrations. Their motto speaks to this, as they state, "we tear into sexism" (see website for ACLU in the Weblinks section).

Canadian Obscenity Laws: The Butler Case and Radical Feminist Theory

Radical feminist theories have been successful in providing a framework for understanding what is and is not considered criminally obscene in Canada. In 1992, a landmark Supreme Court decision in *Butler v. the Queen* brought into debate the definition of what constitutes criminal obscenity (Donald Butler was arrested for selling "hard-core" pornographic videos in his Manitoba store). According to the 1992 decision, the goal of outlawing certain types of material and defining them as obscene was to protect people, most notably women, from harm. What is considered pornographic and what is considered obscene is decided through one simple test: whether or not images are degrading to women. Obscenity laws were no longer seen as a matter of public morality or decency, but were evaluated according to questions of harm, especially harm of women (Cossman et al., 1997).

Catherine MacKinnon and Andrea Dworkin, two very famous radical feminists from the United States, along with the Canadian organization, Women's Legal Education and Action Fund (LEAF), were instrumental in shaping the Canadian obscenity law. These anti-pornography proponents used earlier-discussed radical feminist ideas that see pornography as essentially violent and degrading to women as a facet of the patriarchal order. LEAF submitted a legal brief with sections written with the assistance of MacKinnon, which influenced the courts' decision. It found that any images that portrayed "degrading" sex, especially of women, could be criminalized (Cossman et al., 1997: 18). This was seen as a victory for many anti-pornography feminists, who insisted that these images were detrimental to women.

This 1992 judgment affected gay and lesbian materials in unforeseen ways. What is considered "obscene" in a homophobic society, critics argue, often means demonizing images, ideas, and texts that transgress the normative bounds of heterosexual sex. Many gay and lesbian bookstores across Canada (for example, Little Sister's Book and Art Emporium in Vancouver and Glad Day Books in Toronto) maintained that Canadian customs officials were more heavily scrutinizing, seizing, and destroying shipments intended for their stores, searching for contraventions to the 1992 ruling. In 1994, Little Sister's Book and Art Emporium went to court to challenge the Butler ruling, stating that freedom of expression as well as equality (for gays and lesbians) were being violated as per the Canadian Charter of Rights and Freedoms (Cossman et al., 1997: 36). The court disagreed, ruling that "homosexual obscenity is proscribed because it is obscene, not because it is homosexual" (Cossman et al., 1997: 47). Although this ruling is clearly still a concern for many gay and lesbian businesses, a small victory occurred in 2001 when the courts agreed that customs officials were overwhelmingly heavy-handed in their appraisal of lesbian and gay materials.

Critiques of Radical Feminism

Radical feminism has strengths and weaknesses. Charges of essentialism haunt radical feminists as they are brought to task for generalizing about the fundamental nature of each sex. Theoretical writings by radical feminists often make the assumption that men are inherently violent and aggressive, while women are nurturing and caring. This of course presents concerns for many theorists, as it limits a further engagement with sex and gender, naturalizing these concepts to biological ideologies of women and men and not necessarily interrogating them further. If one's biology is the sole defining feature of a person, how does one break free from the stranglehold of biology as destiny?

Discourses of victimization also pervade radical feminist theory. Women are seen as trapped in essential roles with little hope or ability to resist. What do women do if all relations between women and men are exploitative and if there are no spaces for resistance?

Many postmodern feminists claim that radical feminist theory suffers not only from essentialism but also from romanticism, ethnocentrism, and historicism (Mandell and

Elliot, 2001). They argue that definitions given by radical feminists of patriarchy and women are homogenizing and limiting and do not account for the diversities offered by class, race, sexuality, age, history, and other aspects of women's lives that make them unique and multiple. In contrast, other radical feminists insist that we need to have a category of "woman" to rally around, for if we do not, how do we then establish a basis for feminist action and organizing (Thompson, 2001: 69)?

Many theorists of colour openly criticize radical feminists for their inattention to race, forwarding a vision of "global sisterhood" that is often racist and exclusionary. Many women of colour challenge white radical feminists on their imperialist and universalizing notions of women, where women of colour and Third-World women are often cast as "backwards" and in need of "saving." Other scholars, such as Black American feminist Angela Davis, have taken white radical feminists to task for writing about non-white communities as deviant, writing about black men and rape, naturalizing the myth of the black rapist, so prevalent during and after slavery (Tong, 1998: 223). Others also argue that the radical feminist attacks on the family are Euro- and ethnocentric, and helped to undermine the importance of family for many non-white people. As Linda Carty states, "[f]or Black people and people of colour, the family served as protection against, and a central source of resistance to, racist oppression" (Carty, 1999: 42).

Another issue of concern and contention relates to radical and cultural feminist questions about the "dangers" of transgendered people in general, and transsexual women in particular, invading women's spaces and bodies. Rather than broaden their ideas about gender, many radical feminists consider transsexual women to be committing violence: Janice Raymond says, "Rape... is a masculinist violation of bodily integrity. All transsexuals rape women's bodies by reducing the female form to an artifact, appropriating this body for themselves... Rape, although it is usually done by force, can also be accomplished by deception" (1979). Many of these ideas persist, where transsexual women are seen as a medicalized creation, out to deceive and conceal their "true" identities. Recently, the Vancouver Rape Crisis centre refused to let Kimberly Nixon, a transsexual woman, become a rape crisis counsellor out of the conviction that being born a woman is the basic and primary definition of being a woman (Wente, 2000).

Transgender feminists assert that biology should not be the sole defining characteristic of gendered identity. In fact, they argue that gender becomes politically problematic when it is so defined (Stone, 1991). As radical feminists seek to unhook women from their biology, they question the rigid mapping of sex onto gender and vice versa. Transgender feminists demand a serious re-evaluation of ahistorical and essentialist theories in their attempts to destabilize the fixity of sex/gender categories. Instead, they analyze the "social structures which enforce sex/gender identity congruity and stability at every level" (MacDonald, 2000: 289).

CONCLUSION

This chapter provides an introduction to liberal, socialist, and radical feminist theoretical approaches to understanding women's oppression. The theories are examined in terms of their central principles, their methods of challenging women's oppression, their practical goals, and their achievements.

Liberal feminism is based on the principles of women's capacity for rationality, meritocracy, equal opportunity, and freedom of choice. From the application of liberal philosophy to inequalities between men and women, we learn that at the source of women's oppression is an inequitable integration of women into society's institutions such as schools and universities, government, professions, and economic organizations. Furthermore, the avenues of opportunity that exist for women to make in-roads to full participation in society with men are insufficient. Liberal feminists have thus concentrated on achieving equal opportunity for women by ensuring that all the rights, benefits, and responsibilities that accrue to men also accrue to women.

Socialist feminists explain and advocate for women's liberation through a theoretical framework that places the interconnectedness of capitalism, patriarchy, and more recently, race, sexuality, and globalization, at the centre of its analyses of women's oppression. Socialist feminists challenge women's oppression through unions, advocating for equal pay for work of equal value, increased state investment in social services, and the eradication of poverty. The theoretical and activist contributions of socialist feminists have been instrumental in influencing the Canadian state to include, for the first time in 1996 census, questions on unpaid labour. In addition, many workplaces have passed paternity-leave provisions (although women continue to make up the majority of leaves).

Radical feminists investigate what they believe to be the root cause of women's oppression; that is, sex oppression of women by men. They argue that sex oppression in a patriarchal society can be found in social structures such as the state and the family. Radical feminists identify how women's sexuality is directly controlled by men, through an analysis of reproduction, pornography, and rape, but also through other institutions of social control in every day relations such as heterosexual love, marriage, and motherhood. Women's places within these systems are all shaped by male domination, where men wield and hold power over women, for the men's sole benefit. Radical feminist theorists posit many avenues of resistance against this system of control. Lesbian and cultural feminists argue that women need to break free from patriarchal culture, through an endorsement of lesbian relationships and women-only cultural spaces. Although radical feminist theorizing has been influential, bringing to light issues such as rape, pornography, and violence against women in a misogynist society, they have been subject to criticisms from transgendered scholars and scholars of colour who ask that they re-evaluate their essentialist ideas of the category "woman."

SUGGESTED READINGS

Bannerji, Himani. 1995. *Thinking Through: Essays on Feminism, Marxism, and Anti-Racism*. Toronto: Women's Press. *Thinking Through* provides a feminist theoretical framework for understanding the key issues related to the oppression of women and class. Bannerji addresses the relationship of feminism to Marxist thought, always within an antiracist analytical context. This book is very useful in helping think through some of the gaps left by mainstream class-oriented social justice movements.

Crow, Barbara A., ed. 2000. *Radical Feminism: A Documentary Reader*. New York: New York University Press. This compilation of key texts details the contributions of radical feminist theorizing and activism to the second-wave women's movement. Containing primary sources, such as manifestos, meeting minutes, and other published and unpublished records from the time, it provides a wealth of information on pressing issues in radical feminism, such as sexuality, lesbian separatism, race, and class.

Dua, Enakshi and **Angela Robertson**, eds. 1999. *Scratching the Surface: Canadian Anti-Racist Feminist Thought*. Toronto: Women's Press. This book is an insightful and informative reflection on antiracist feminist thought and activism in Canada. Included are discussions on the central role of racialization in the colonial settler process and the creation of the Canadian nation. The articles within provide crucial context for debates concerning class and gender.

Newton, Janice. 1992. "The Alchemy of Politicisation: Socialist Women and the Early Canadian Left." In *Gender Conflicts: New Essays in Women's History*, edited by Franca Iacovetta and Mariana Valverde. Toronto: University of Toronto Press: 118–148. Newton recovers the significant contributions of early socialist feminists to the Canadian prohibition and suffrage movements as well as to socialist and communist politics at the turn of the twentieth century. The article also includes a discussion of socialist women's activism about women's position in the labour force.

Prentice, Alison, et al. 1996. *Canadian Women: A History*. Toronto: Harcourt Brace and Company. Prentice et al. provide a substantial integrative text on Canadian women's history. Chapters are organized both thematically and chronologically, providing the reader with a helpful contextual analysis of women's history in Canada.

Rich, Adrienne. 1980. "Compulsory Heterosexuality and Lesbian Existence." *Signs: Journal of Women in Culture and Society* 5/4: 3–32. Adrienne Rich's classic discussion on the destabilizing of heterosexuality as a "natural" biological fact provides critical insight into the importance of lesbian existence and visibility in the feminist movement.

Roome, Patricia. 2001. "Women's suffrage movement in Canada." Chinook Multimedia Inc. Retrieved February 12, 2004, from the World Wide Web www.chinookmultimedia.com/poccd/registered. Roome's discussion of Canadian women's suffrage is an account of a pivotal political moment in the history of first-wave feminism. The article offers a detailed consideration of the role of women's religious organizations in achieving the vote.

Stone, Sandy. 1991. "The 'Empire' Strikes Back: A Posttranssexual Manifesto." In *Body Guards: The Cultural Politics of Gender Ambiguity*, edited by Kristina Straub and Julia Epstein. New York: Routledge. This piece, written by Associate Professor Allucquére Rosanne "Sandy" Stone (available online at http://sandystone.com/empire-strikes-back), provides a frank and important discussion on the marginalizing aspects of feminist theorizing and critically responds to Janice Raymond's 1972 work, *The Transsexual Empire*.

Valverde, Mariana. 1992. "'When the Mother of the Race Is Free': Race, Reproduction and Sexuality in First-wave Feminism." In *Gender Conflicts: New Essays in Women's History,* edited by Franca Iacovetta and Mariana Valverde. Toronto: University of Toronto Press: 3–28. Valverde provides an in-depth examination of the ways in which discourses of race, racism, sexuality, and gender were key in shaping first-wave feminists' approach to achieving suffrage. The intersection of the Canadian eugenics and temperance movements are examined and linked to the persons and organizations that also fed the early suffrage movement.

DISCUSSION QUESTIONS

1. Define each of the three theories in your own words. Which one do you most identify with?

2. Discuss how each theory defines the source of women's oppression and their approaches to social change.

3. Identify an accomplishment or goal of each group of feminists. How did theory inform their actions?

4. What are the main criticisms of each theory? Are they valid critiques? Why or why not?

5. Do you see evidence of these theories at work today? Give examples.

BIBLIOGRAPHY

Adamson, Nancy, Linda Briskin, and **Margaret McPhail.** *Feminist Organizing for Change: The Contemporary Women's Movement in Canada.* London: Oxford University Press, 1988.

Andersen, Margaret L. *Thinking About Women: Sociological Perspectives on Sex and Gender*, 4th ed. Boston: Allyn and Bacon, 1997.

Appelbaum, Richard P. "The World According to Nike: Figure IV.7." In *An Introduction to Women's Studies: Gender in a Transnational World*, edited by Inderpal Grewal and Caren Kaplan. New York: McGraw-Hill, 2002.

Arneil, Barbara. "Women as wives, servants and slaves: rethinking the public/private divide." *Canadian Journal of Political Science* 34/1 (2001): 29–54.

Astell, Mary (1694 and 1697). *A Serious Proposal to the Ladies* Parts I & II Introduction by Patricia Springborg, London, England: Pickering & Chatto, 1997.

Atkinson, Ti-Grace. "The Institution of Sexual Intercourse." In *Notes From the Third Year*, edited by Shulamith Firestone. New York: Random House, 1970.

Atwood, Margaret. *The Handmaid's Tale.* Toronto: McClelland & Stewart, 1985.

Ault, Amber and **Eve Sandberg.** "Our Policies, Their Consequences: Zambian Women's Lives under Structural Adjustment." In *An Introduction to Women's Studies: Gender in a Transnational World,* edited by Inderpal Grewal & Caren Kaplan. New York: McGraw-Hill, 2001.

Bannerji, Himani. *Thinking Through: Essays on Feminism, Marxism, and Anti-Racism.* Toronto: Women's Press, 1995.

Barry, Kathleen. *Female Sexual Slavery.* New York: New York University Press, 1984.

Benston, Margaret. "The Political Economy of Women's Liberation." *Monthly Review* 21 (1969).

Bird, Florence, et al., Commissioners. *List of Recommendations: Report on the Royal Commission on the Status of Women in Canada.* Ottawa: Government of Canada, 1970.

Brenner, Johanna. *Women and Politics of Class.* New York: Monthly Review Press, 2000.

Brown, Rosemary. *Being Brown: A Very Public Life.* Toronto: Random House,1989.

Brownmiller, Susan. *Against Our Will: Men, Women and Rape.* Toronto, ON: Bantam Books, 1976.

Bryson, Valerie. *Feminist Political Theory: An Introduction.* London: MacMillan, 1992.

Calliste, Agnes (2001). "Immigration of Caribbean nurses and domestic workers to Canada, 1955–1967" Chinook Multimedia Inc. Retrieved February 12, 2004, from the World Wide Web **www.chinookmultimedia.com/poccd/registered**.

Carillo, Teresa. "Cross-Border Talk: Transnational Perspectives on Labor, Race, and Sexuality." In *An Introduction to Women's Studies: Gender in a Transnational World*, edited by Inderpal Grewal and Caren Kaplan. New York: McGraw-Hill, 2001.

Carty, Linda. "The Discourse of Empire and the Social Construction of Gender." In *Scratching the Surface: Canadian, Anti-Racist, Feminist Thought,* edited by Enakshi Dua and Angela Robertson. Toronto: Women's Press, 1999.

Cho, Lily. "Rereading Chinese Head Tax racism: redress, stereotype and antiracist critical practice." *Essays on Canadian Writing* 75 (2002): 62–84.

Cleverdon, Catherine. *The Women Suffrage Movement in Canada.* Toronto: University of Toronto Press, 1974.

Code, Lorraine. "Feminist Theory." In *Changing Patterns: Women in Canada,* 2nd ed, edited by Sandra Burt. Toronto: McClelland & Stewart, 1993.

Cossman, Brenda, et al. *Bad Attitude/s on Trial: Pornography, Feminism, and the Butler Decision.* Toronto, ON: University of Toronto Press, 1997.

Crow, Barbara A., ed. *Radical Feminism: A Documentary Reader.* New York: New York University Press, 2000.

Dalla Costa, Mariarosa, and **Selma James.** *The Power of Women and the Subversion of the Community.* Bristol: Falling Wall, 1975.

Daly, Mary. *Gyn/Ecology, the Metaethics of Radical Feminism.* Boston: Beacon Press, 1978.

de Pizan, Christine (ca.1363–1431). *The Book of the City of Ladies.* Foreword by Marina Warner. New York, NY: Persea Books, 1982.

Dickason, Olive Patricia. *Canada's First Nations: A History of Founding Peoples from Earliest Times.* Oxford: Oxford University Press, 2002.

Donovan, Josephine. *Feminist Theory: The Intellectual Traditions,* 3rd ed. New York: Continuum Publishing, 2000.

Dooley, Chantelle. (2001). "Socialist Feminism: Is It Really Just a Class Issue?" *Suite 101.Com, Society & Culture Page.* Retrieved December 5, 2003, from the World Wide Web **www.suite101.com/article.cfm/13914/75231**

Dua, Enakshi, and **Angela Robertson,** eds. *Scratching the Surface: Canadian Anti-Racist Feminist Thought.* Toronto: Women's Press, 1999.

Dworkin, Andrea. *Woman Hating.* New York: E.P. Dutton, 1974.

———. *Pornography: Men Possessing Women.* New York, NY: Perigee Books, 1981.

Echols, Alice. *Daring to be bad: Radical feminism in America 1967–1975.* Minneapolis: University of Minnesota Press, 1989.

Eisenstein, Zillah R. *Capitalist Patriarchy and the Case for Socialist Feminism.* New York: Monthly Review Press, 1979

Engels, Friederich. *The Origin of the Family, Private Property and the State.* New York: Pathfinder, 1884/1972.

Falardeau-Ramsay, Michelle. "Gender Equality and the Law: From the 'Famous Five' to the New Millennium." *Canadian Woman Studies* 19/1-2 (1999): 52–56.

Fiamengo, Janice. "Rediscovering our foremothers again: The racial ideas of Canada's early feminists, 1885–1945." *Essays on Canadian Writing* 75 (2002): 85–117.

Firestone, Shulamith. *The Dialectic of Sex: the Case for Feminist Revolution.* New York, NY: William Morrow and Company, 1970.

Friedan, Betty. *The Feminine Mystique.* New York: Dell Publishing, 1963.

Garvie, Maureen McCallum, and **Jennifer L. Johnson.** *Their Leaven of Influence: Deans of Women at Queen's University 1916–1996.* Kingston: Queen's Alumni Association Committee on Women's Affairs, 1999.

Gehl, Lynn. "The Queen and I: Discrimination Against Women in the Indian Act Continues." *Canadian Woman Studies* 20/2 (2000): 64–69.

Grant, Ali. "UnWomanly acts: Struggling over sites of resistance." *New Frontiers of Space, Bodies and Gender.* Rosa Ainley, ed. New York: Routledge, 1998.

Hall, Catherine. *White, Male and Middle Class: Explorations in Feminism and History.* New York: Routledge, 1992.

Hamilton, Roberta. *Gendering the Vertical Mosaic: Feminist Perspectives on Canadian Society.* Toronto: Copp Clark Ltd, 1996.

Hanson, Cindy, Lori Hanson and **Barbara Adams.** *Who Benefits: Women, Unpaid Work and Social Policy.* Ottawa: Canadian Research Institute for the Advancement of Women (CRIAW), 2001.

Harman, Harriet. An Urgent Case for Modernization: public policy on women's work. In Anna Coote (ed.). *New Gender Agenda: why women still want more.* London: Biddles Ltd., 2000.

Heller, Dana A. *Cross-purposes: Lesbians, Feminists, and the Limits of Alliance.* Bloomington, IN: Indiana University Press, 1997.

Hewitt, Patricia. Gender and the Knowledge Economy: work, family and e-business. In Anna Coote (ed.). *New Gender Agenda: why women still want more.* London: Biddles Ltd., 2000.

hooks, bell. "Theory as Liberatory Practice." In *Teaching to Transgress: Education as the Practice of Freedom.* New York: Routledge, 1994.

———. *Feminism is for Everybody: Passionate Politics.* Cambridge, MA: South End Press, 2000.

Jaggar, Alison M. *Feminist Politics and Human Nature.* Totowa, N.J.: Rowman & Allanheld, 1983.

Jaggar, Alison M. and **Paula S. Rothenberg,** eds. *Feminist Frameworks: Alternative Theoretical Accounts of the Relations Between Women and Men,* 3rd ed. New York: McGraw-Hill, 1993.

Kelly, Jennifer. *Under the Gaze: Learning to be Black in White Society.* Halifax: Fernwood Publishing, 1998.

Koedt, Annette. "The Myth of the Vaginal Orgasm." *Notes from the First Year.* New York: New York Radical Women, 1970.

Kramnick, Miriam Brody, Introduction. *A Vindication of the Rights of Woman.* By Mary Wollstonecraft. Harmondsworth, England: Penguin Books, 1982.

Kreps, Bonnie. "Radical Feminism 1." In *Radical Feminism*, edited by Anne Koedt, Ellen Levine, and Anita Rapone. New York: Quadrangle Books, 1973.

MacDonald, Eleanor. "Critical Identities: Rethinking Feminism through Transgender Politics." In *Open Boundaries: A Canadian Women's Studies Reader*, edited by Barbara A. Crow and Lise Gotell. Toronto: Prentice Hall, 2000.

MacIvor, Heather. *Women and Politics in Canada.* Peterborough, Canada: Broadview Press, 1996.

MacKinnon, Catherine. "Sexuality." In *Towards a Feminist Theory of the State.* Cambridge, Mass: Harvard University Press, 1989.

Mandell, Nancy and **Patricia Elliot.** "Feminist Theories." In *Feminist Issues: Race, Class, and Sexuality,* 3rd ed. Nancy Mandell, ed. Toronto: Prentice Hall, 2001.

Maracle, Sylvia. "The eagle has landed: Native women, leadership and community development." In *Strong Women Stories: Native Vision and Community Survival*, edited by Kim Anderson and Bonita Lawrence. Toronto: Sumach Press, 2003.

Marx, Karl and **Friederich Engels.** *The Communist Manifesto*, translated by Samuel Moore. Halifax: Fernwood Press, 1998

Marx, Karl and **Friederich Engels.** *The German Ideology.* Edited by S. Ryazanskaya. Moscow: Progress Publishers, 1968.

McClung, Nellie (1915). *In Times Like These.* Introduction by Veronica Strong-Boag. Toronto: University of Toronto Press, 1972.

McKeen, Wendy. "The shaping of political agency: feminism and the national social policy debate, the 1970s and early 1980s." *Studies in Political Economy,* 66 (2001): 37–58.

Mill, Harriet Taylor (ca. 1807–1858). *The Complete Works of Harriet Taylor Mill.* Introduction by Jo Ellen Jacobs. Indiana: Indiana University Press, 1998.

Mill, John Stuart (1869). *The Subjection of Women.* Introduction by Wendell Robert Carr. Cambridge, United States: The MIT Press, 1974.

Mitchell, Juliet. *Woman's Estate.* New York, NY: Pantheon Books, 1971.

Morgan, Robin. *Sisterhood Is Powerful: An Anthology of Writings from the Women's Liberation Movement.* New York: Random House, 1970.

Morris, Marika. *Women, Poverty and Canadian Public Policy in an Era of Globalization.* Ottawa: Canadian Research Institute for the Advancement of Women (CRIAW), 2000.

Morris, Marika. *Factsheet: Women and Poverty.* Ottawa: Canadian Research Institute for the Advancement of Women (CRIAW), 2002a.

Morris, Marika. *Factsheet: Violence Against Women and Girls.* Ottawa: Canadian Research Institute for the Advancement of Women (CRIAW), 2002b.

Morris, Marika. *Factsheet: Women's Experience of Racism: How Race and Gender Interact.* Ottawa: Canadian Research Institute for the Advancement of Women (CRIAW), 2002c.

National Anti-Poverty Association. 1999 Statistics. Retrieved from http://www.napoonap.ca/en/index.html.

Nelson, Adie and **Barrie W. Robinson.** *Gender in Canada.* Toronto: Pearson Education Canada, 2002.

Newton, Janice. "The alchemy of politicisation: Socialist women and the early Canadian left." In *Gender Conflicts: New Essays in Women's History*, edited by Franca Iacovetta and Mariana Valverde. Toronto: University of Toronto Press, 1992: 118–148.

O'Reilly, Andrea. "A mom and her son: thoughts on feminist mothering." *Journal of the Association for Research on Mothering* 2/1 (2000): 179–193.

Painter, Nell Irvin. Introduction. *Narrative of Sojourner Truth.* By Sojourner Truth. Harmondsworth, England: Penguin Books, 1982.

Paltiel, Frieda L. "State initiatives: Impetus and effects." In *Women and the Canadian State/Les Femmes et L'État Canadien*, edited by Caroline Andrew and Sanda Rodgers. Montreal and Kingston: McGill-Queen's University Press, 1997.

Prentice, Alison, et al. *Canadian Women: A History.* Toronto: Harcourt Brace and Company, 1996.

Raymond, Janice. *The Transsexual Empire: the Making of the She-Male.* Boston: Beacon Press, 1979.

Rich, Adrienne. "Compulsory Heterosexuality and Lesbian Existence." *Signs: Journal of Women in Culture and Society* 5/4 (1980): 3–32.

Rich, Adrienne. *Of Woman Born: Motherhood as Experience and Institution.* New York, NY: W.W. Norton & Company, 1976.

Roome, Patricia (2001). "Women's suffrage movement in Canada." Chinook Multimedia Inc. Retrieved February 12, 2004, from the World Wide Web **www.chinookmultimedia.com/poccd/registered**.

Ross, Becki. *The House That Jill Built: A Lesbian Nation in Formation.* Toronto: University of Toronto Press, 1995.

Sadlier, Rosemary. *Leading the Way: Black Women in Canada.* Toronto: Umbrella Press, 1994.

Sethna, Christabelle (2001). "A bitter pill: Second wave feminist critiques of oral contraception." Chinook Multimedia Inc. Retrieved February 12, 2004, from the World Wide Web **www.chinook multimedia.com/poccd/registered**.

Sommerville, Jennifer. *Feminism and the Family: Politics and Society in the UK and USA.* London: MacMillan Press Ltd., 2000.

Sparr, Pamela, ed. *Mortgaging Women's Lives: Feminist Critiques of Structural Adjustment.* London: Zed Books, 1994.

Statistics Canada. *Women in Canada 2000: A Gender-based Statistical Report.* Ottawa: Ministry of Industry, 2000.

Status of Women Canada. *What Do You Mean Women Couldn't Vote? Women's History Month in Canada.* Ottawa: Government of Canada, 2003a.

————. *Women and Education and Training—Canada and the United Nations Assembly: Beijing+5 Factsheets.* Ottawa: Government of Canada, 2003b.

Stevenson, Winona. "Colonialism and First Nations Women in Canada." In *Scratching the Surface: Canadian Anti-Racist Feminist Thought*, edited by Enakshi Dua and Angela Robertson. Toronto: Women's Press, 1999: 49–80.

Stone, Sandy. "The 'Empire' Strikes Back: A Posttranssexual Manifesto." In *Body Guards: The Cultural Politics of Gender Ambiguity*, edited by Kristina Straub and Julia Epstein. New York: Routledge, 1991.

Thompson, Denise. *Radical Feminism Today.* London: Sage, 2001.

Timpson, Annis May. *Driven Apart: Women's Employment Equality and Child Care in Canadian Public Policy.* Vancouver: UBC Press, 2001.

Tong, Rosemarie Putnam. *Feminist Thought: A More Comprehensive Introduction.* Boulder, Colorado: Westview Press, 1998.

Truth, Sojourner (1850). *Narrative of Sojourner Truth.* Introduction by Nell Irvin Painter. Harmondsworth, England: Penguin Books, 1998.

Valverde, Mariana. "'When the mother of the race is free': race, reproduction and sexuality in first-wave feminism." In *Gender Conflicts: New Essays in Women's History,* edited by Franca Iacovetta and Mariana Valverde. Toronto: University of Toronto Press, 1992: 3–28.

Walker, R. "Quebec's Bargain Day Care a Hit With Parents, Educators." *Christian Science Monitor* (May 2000).

Waring, Marilyn. *Counting for Nothing: What Men Value and What Women Are Worth*, 2nd ed. Toronto: University of Toronto Press, 1999.

Wente, Margaret. "Who gets to be a woman?" *Globe and Mail,* 14 Dec. 2000.

Wollstonecraft, Mary (1792). *A Vindication of the Rights of Woman* Hardmondsworth, England: Penguin Books.

 # WEBLINKS

Status of Women Canada (SWC)

www.swc-cfc.gc.ca

Status of Women Canada is the federal government department that promotes gender equality and the full participation of women in the economic, social, cultural, and political life of the country.

National Action Committee on the Status of Women (NAC)

www.nac-cca.ca

The National Action Committee on the Status of Women is a non-governmental popular organization through which diverse groups of women can lobby the Canadian government for women's rights.

Canadian Research Institute for the Advancement of Women (CRIAW)

www.criaw-icref.ca

CRIAW is dedicated to the study of gender in Canada. It is an excellent resource for the study of gender in Canada, with many statistical resources and fact sheets.

National Library of Canada

nlc-bnc.ca

The National Library of Canada holds archives relating to Canadian history, politics, culture, and society. It is an excellent resource for the study of women's history.

Solidarity: *Against the Current Journal*

solidarity.igc.org

Against the Current promotes socialist activism and politics in North America that are rooted in democratic, feminist, and antiracist principles. Their activities are a means of changing conditions in the West and ultimately making connections to and supporting worldwide struggles for freedom.

Native Women's Association of Canada (NWAC)

www.nwac-hq.org

NWAC provides employment, training, youth, health, and human rights programs (among others) in order to advocate for the social, political, economic, and cultural well being of First Nations and Métis women within First Nations communities and Canadian society as a whole.

Always Causing Legal Unrest (ACLU)

www.nostatusquo.com/ACLU/Porn/index.html

ACLU is an American based group devoted to challenging *Penthouse* and "the porn machine" through demonstrations, letter writing campaigns, and "zaps."

Off Our Backs

www.offourbacks.org

Off Our Backs is a collectively run, radical feminist magazine, published since the 1970s.

HotHead Paisan

www.hotheadpaisan.com

HotHead Paisan is a well-known comic created by Diane DiMassa, which features the character "Hot Head Paisan, Homicidal Lesbian Terrorist."

chapter two

An Introduction to Feminist Poststructural Theorizing

Sharon Rosenberg

"Theory" is a highly contested term within feminist discourse. The number of questions raised about it indicates the importance of the debate: what qualifies as "theory"? Who is the author of "theory"? Is it singular? Is it defined in opposition to something which is atheoretical, pretheoretical or post-theoretical?... Is "theory" distinct from politics?

—Judith Butler and Joan Scott, *Feminists Theorize the Political*, 1992

INTRODUCTION

As the opening citation to this chapter suggests, "theory" is not a settled term within feminism. As you will have seen from the previous chapter, there is no singular version of feminism, nor is there one way in which feminisms define their relation to something called theory. While some argue that such non-singularity is a problem for feminism, others engage this as a vibrant and productive difference. This chapter begins from the latter position and with the proposition that attending to theoretical interrogations in and of themselves is vital to feminism's aliveness. What such a proposition suggests is that it can be important to provisionally suspend the idea that theory is only relevant to the extent that it can forecast change "now." This is not to imply that change is not important, nor that theory is of no use to making changes. Instead, it is to argue that theory can help us to think about the world differently and that the work of this thinking can be invaluable to putting into place and sustaining broader changes. Moreover, it is the argument underpinning the kind of theorizing being presented in this chapter that the categories and concepts that most usually organize our world are worth a careful look—not only as categories and concepts per se, but also for how they both produce and confine critical engagements and, hence, possibilities for change.

> Poststructuralism is not, strictly speaking, *a position* [or a theory], but rather a critical interrogation of the exclusionary operations by which "positions" are established. In this sense, a feminist poststructuralism does not designate a position from which one operates, a point of view or standpoint which might be usefully compared with other "positions" within the theoretical field. (Butler and Scott, 1992: xiv, emphasis in original)

The particular form of theorizing that this chapter will introduce is broadly categorized under the title of "postmodern" and will focus on "poststructuralism." We will look in particular at how key concepts and ideas generated by poststructural feminist thinking not only challenge central assumptions underlying "modernist" feminisms (e.g. liberal, radical, socialist), but also, in doing so, create different openings for contemporary thought and politics. A particular challenge for this chapter is negotiating, on the one hand, expectations of summary chapters (i.e. that they follow a linear, orderly, and forward-oriented narrative structure), and, on the other, that the chapter be attentive to the arguments of poststructural theorizing, which encourage a deep suspicion of universal claims, singular readings as "Truth," and coherent narratives. Thus, this chapter is formed on a paradox: It is caught in the demands of style expectations that run counter to the insights of the theorizing that is its substantive concern. That said, poststructural feminisms encourage us, as writers and readers, to live with paradoxes, to endeavour to hold contradictions, and to learn from what we might not otherwise have thought. So, in that spirit, what follows is one introduction to some key ideas and authors that I hope you might find interesting, a reading of which might invite your curiosity to further exploration.

Interruption #1: Notes from the "Author"[1]

I am writing the first draft of this chapter in Edmonton, Alberta, in the fall of 2003. It's a bright and cool autumn day and although I am sitting alone in my office, with only the companionship of books, I keep looking over the top of my computer screen, in anticipation of the faces of students who might be reading this new edition of *Feminist Issues*. Having taught various versions of introductory courses in feminist thinking and in women's studies as an arena of inquiry for more than a decade, the classes that materialize in my head range from small rooms of 15–25 students to large lecture halls of close to 300. In some ways, writing is quite different from teaching— it's likely that I won't know who is reading this chapter at all; I only have my imagined

(continued on next page)

sense of who might be reading and why. The difficulty is that I can't check to see what sense you are making; whether a particular phrasing is helpful; where one example over another would have been better. In other ways, writing this chapter is like preparing a lecture—I know that I am writing with an imagined "audience" in mind, that I must focus on a specific topic or issue, and that I have to put certain limits on the writing in order to make it through in the time we have together (whether this is measured by minutes and hours or by word and page counts). I have some sense of what chapters you will have encountered before this one and what will come after, and I can anticipate that this is one chapter in many others you may be reading in any particular week on topics as far ranging as micro-economic theory and the history of painting. The problem is that we can't really "see" each other, what we have in common is this text—the question is: What terms of commonality might that create?

POSTMODERNISM AND POSTSTRUCTURALISM

According to the *Penguin Dictionary of Sociology* (fourth edition), "postmodern" refers to "[a] movement in painting, literature, television, film and the arts generally" (Abercrombie et al., 2000: 272). The key characteristics of this movement are summarized by the dictionary compilers as irony and play, a questioning of objective standards of truth, a crossing of boundaries between genres and forms, and an emphasis on the text rather than on the author's intent for establishing meaning (272). This dictionary entry is followed by another, "postmodernity," which is defined as follows: "[a] term, usually contrasted with MODERNITY, which designates a new condition which contemporary advanced industrial societies are alleged to have reached. A large number of features are said to characterize postmodernity and they may be placed in four groups—social, cultural, economic and political" (272). The entry for "poststructuralism" is separate and it reads, in part, "[t]he fundamental idea is that we cannot apprehend reality without the intervention of language. This prioritizes the study of language—or texts. Texts can be understood only in relation to other texts, not in relation to an external reality against which they can be tested and measured" (273).

In the *Encyclopedia of Feminist Theories* (2000), "poststructuralism/ postmodernism" is given as one entry, written by Chris Weedon, whose major work, *Feminist Practice and Poststructuralist Theory* (first published in 1987), has been influential in bringing poststructural thinking to feminism. Weedon's entry is substantially longer than those in the *Penguin Dictionary*. I will summarize here some of her key points. First, she notes that "[p]oststructuralism and postmodernism are two distinct but related terms." She goes on to explain that poststructural thinking has critiqued foundational ideas of structural theories of language (hence the "post") and, in so doing, has "challenged some of the fundamental assumptions about knowledge, subjectivity and power in western philosophy" (397). In regards to postmodern, she states: "[m]ost often, 'postmodernism' and the related term 'postmodernity' are used to describe either the style and form taken by particular cultural phenomena or the present period of global late capitalism.... Like poststructuralism, postmodernism questions some of the fundamental assumptions of the Enlightenment tradition in the west. These include the belief in rational human progress, universal standards and values, and singular truth" (397).

Writing and working with definitions is tricky. On the one hand, it's helpful to have definitions of terms, particularly for an area of inquiry that is unfamiliar. Without some shared meanings, we would find it difficult to communicate with each other at all—and you would likely come away from this chapter completely frustrated that you weren't even offered a basic explanation of terms. On the other hand, definitions, by virtue of the work that they do, which is to summarize and condense a complex body of thought into a short paragraph or even a few pages, are necessarily limiting and partial. In addition, we need to consider that I have chosen two particular dictionaries to draw from (and hence not others) and have further condensed the definitions into what I think (a) are a manageable size and (b) highlight what I'm particularly interested in drawing your attention to at this point in the chapter. Thus, I suggest that we take definitions such as those outlined above as useful starting points, an orientation toward a way of thinking, *and* as matters to regard with some distrust in the recognition that no definition can be fully explanatory. With these remarks in mind, it might be a good time to pause and take note of what you understand from the definitions and the discussion to this point and what you are finding confusing. As you read each section that follows, come back to the definitions and see if they make a bit more sense.

Interruption #2: More Notes from "Me"

At this point, I need to make some decisions as the writer of this chapter. As Weedon explains, postmodernism and poststructuralism are related but distinct terms and, therefore, refer to related but distinct ways of thinking. In a 25-or-so-page chapter (and, of course, there are fewer than that number of pages left now), I could choose to try to summarize for you some key aspects of both kinds of work—how they are similar and how they may be different from each other. Or, I could work from the position that the similarities of critique are most helpful for re-engaging feminisms and write from there. In discussion with Nancy, the editor of this book, I have decided on the latter and to focus on what is generally referred to as "feminist poststructuralism," in part because this is the form of theorizing that I find most exciting the kind that I do myself, and I am eager to introduce some of that to you. More than my own desires are at issue here, however. I also think there is a strong argument to make that poststructuralism has offered particularly profound critiques of—and rich concepts to—feminism. There is a wealth of work now from scholars in disciplines ranging from education to philosophy to women's studies, who have been <u>informed</u> by, are engaging with, and are developing a form of theorizing in which feminism is in relation to poststructuralism. Because poststructuralism and postmodernism can be so closely connected, others may see this approach as best understood as "postmodern feminism." I would like to suggest that we live with this ambiguity in naming for two reasons: (a) however we name it, these modes of inquiry (as the definitions above suggest) push for a certain suspicion in regard to categorizations that attempt to mark one approach as entirely distinct and different from another (e.g. "this versus that"); and (b) getting caught up in struggles over which approach "owns" what kinds of inquiry and critique is a squabble that drains energy, resources, insights, and so on, away from how these inquiries and

(continued on next page)

critiques may help open up and change the world in which we live. Thus, what I want to propose to you by way of this "Interruption #2" is that there is more than one way this chapter could proceed, that a different way of proceeding would illuminate ideas differently and in ways I will not, and that there is no inherently better way to proceed with this chapter. In explaining to you some of my process as I write, I am trying to bring to the foreground the decisions I am making and why, rather than leaving them unstated. I am doing so so that we (myself as writer and you as reader) are both prompted to remember that this text is itself a construct, an offering of certain explanations, concepts, and insights, but not a claim to a universal truth about feminist poststructuralism or the only story that could be told.

KEY CRITIQUES AND CONCEPTS

Critiques of Modernist Knowledge Practices

By this point in the chapter, I expect it will not come as a surprise when I tell you that one of the key contributions of poststructural theorizing is a particular interrogation and critique of the practices of producing and representing knowledge that are more usually taken for granted and taught as "the right way," for example, to conduct research, write an essay, or interpret a poem. I anticipate that you are familiar with many of these practices; you were probably taught early in your school years, for instance, that it is proper to write papers and essays without use of "I," and so you learned constructs such as "one believes" and "this evidence shows that." This avoidance of the first person is one feature, among many others, of what is now known as a "modernist" approach or "enlightenment thinking." Because most of us have been so immersed in this way of thinking, not only in schools and universities but also more broadly in "Western" societies, it can be difficult to actually see this as *a* way of thinking—rather than as just "normal" or "the way we do things."[2]

One way to begin this process of beginning to see differently, if you like, is to look over the chapter to this point, to perhaps begin by identifying how it is *not* written, or cannot be easily read, on the terms that you would anticipate. If you do that, you might identify practices that stand out because they are unexpected, because they do not follow a modernist approach to representing knowledge—an approach in which the author is expected to take on an authoritative voice that is clear and distinct in his or her statements, does not draw attention to ambiguity or the limits of his or her own knowledge, and is written without engaging much with readers. (To return to an earlier point I was making, you might notice similarities here between this style of writing and a common style of lecturing.) So, if you knew there was something odd about the style of this chapter, this is an indicator that you already know something about modernist practices and enlightenment thinking.

Although one of the contributions of modernist feminisms was a critique of enlightenment notions—such as objectivity, for how it implicitly privileged and assumed a masculine point of view *as* objective—these feminisms, poststructural critics would argue, have also been caught up in other modernist forms of knowledge. For example, whereas liberal, radical, and socialist feminisms all differ in their explanation of why women's lives are limited and hindered (see previous chapter), all implicitly accept the necessity for *the* explanation that will illuminate *the* conditions that need to be addressed in *specified* ways for *all* women to be free. Such framings of explanation are known as "metanarratives" (Lyotard, 1984), theories that endeavour to provide explanations of the social world that are universal (that is, they tell "the big story").

This is an approach to practices of producing and representing knowledge that was taken on by modernist feminists, particularly as they encountered and endeavoured to establish legitimation in universities. In such contexts, not only was a focus on gender and asking questions about how a theory may and may not be applicable to women's experiences regarded as shocking enough, but also it was difficult to have feminism taken seriously without a reliance on the categories and argument structures that were already familiar and accepted (see Koldony, 2000). Moreover, as Marysia Zalewski writes, "[f]or modernist feminists often dismayed and disgusted by the centuries of false and nasty stories about women, the ideas that good and true knowledge about women was possible seemed like a dream come true.... One way to make that dream come true and ensure that innocent knowledge was collected was to have clear foundations for knowledge-building" (2000: 45–6). Such foundations came from the modernist approach that has its roots in industrialization, imperialism, and scientific thinking (see Hamilton, 1992, for example). As Zalewski goes on to note, these beliefs have carried over to much modernist feminist work that depends on the belief that there is an objective reality governed by laws independent of human perspectives; that this reality is in principle accessible to human understanding and knowledge; and that the central means for developing and establishing the truth of this knowledge is reason, a capacity that is available to all human beings (2000: 46). One further and vitally important aspect of this approach is the belief that "knowledge [is] a *progressive* force. The more we know about something, the more we understand the truth of it and can do something about it" (Zalewski, 2000: 47, emphasis in original).

Feminists attached to varying politics and modes of theorizing have challenged such modernist claims to knowledge on different fronts. As you will see in Chapter 4, antiracist feminists have been critical of the way in which the category of "women" has been deployed in modernist formulations, noting that the category is used as if it includes all women but in actuality references women with particular "race" and "class" experiences and expectations of privilege (see also Bannerji, 2000; Dua and Robertson, 1999; Hill Collins, 1990; hooks, 1984; Rothenberg, 2001). This has led, antiracist feminist critics argue, not only to partial but also to distorted explanations that cannot account for how women may be caught in and perpetuate relations of racism and colonialism in their very attempts to address sexism "for all women."

> While many types of theory appeal to *truth value* as the guarantee of their adequacy, this is not the case with poststructuralist theories. Feminist appropriations of poststructuralism tend to focus on the basic assumptions, the degree of explanatory power, and the political implications which a particular type of analysis yields. It is with these criteria in mind that I would argue the appropriateness of poststructuralism to feminist concerns, not as the answer to *all* feminist questions but as a way of conceptualizing the relationship between language, social institutions and individual consciousness which focuses on how power is exercised and the possibilities of change. (Chris Weedon, 1997: 19, emphases in original)

Feminists influenced by poststructural critiques approach difference differently (an issue to which I will return), but also offer deep critiques of the kinds of ideas that Zalewski outlines, questioning the notion of Theory as a universal explanation, questioning ideas of knowledge as "innocent" or outside of the workings of power, questioning rationality as a neutral and defining force of democracy, and questioning the assumed linear relation among knowledge, progress, and change (see, for example, Butler and Scott, 1992; Flax, 1992; Raby, 2000). Feminist poststructural critics would pose the following kinds of questions to each of these claims: Which women have to be forgotten or obscured for a single theory of women's lives to be articulated as The Theory? Whose interests does this theory serve and whose lives does it obfuscate or worsen for those interests to be served? If reason is the defining arbiter, how are we to understand the prevalence of hatred, fear, anxiety, indifference, and other such "non-rational" expressions that seem immune to, or defend against, (more) information and (more) facts? If knowledge equals progress equals change, how are we to reconcile the profusion of knowledge available, for example, on the extent and degree of violences women seem to be subject to in contemporary societies with the limited, circumscribed and ever-struggled-over efforts for change?

From an interest in feminist poststructural inquiries, the point is not to endeavour to answer such questions definitively, but to work with them as openings onto prevailing feminist explanations and political strategies, and to deliberate on how assumptions and concepts previously taken as foundational (meaning no longer open to inquiry) may be supporting not only productive but also limiting analyses and possibilities for change. I turn now to how some of this kind of critical engagement works through introducing particular concepts of feminist poststructural inquiry.

Language/Discourse

The *Penguin Dictionary* definition of poststructuralism noted earlier includes the statement that "we cannot apprehend reality without the intervention of language." And, in the previous boxed quote, Weedon suggests that poststructuralism has an interest in how power might be exercised through language. What both of these notations orient us toward is a key concern of feminist poststructural inquiry: namely, how language (and more precisely, discourses, a concept to which I will turn shortly) constitutes the world in which we live. To say that language *constitutes* the world is to say something quite distinct from, and, indeed, challenging to, prevailing ways of thinking about language. What is more familiar to many of us is the idea that language is a neutral medium through which reality passes; it has no shaping effect on that reality, but simply presents it in linguistic form. And, so, for example, from this perspective, I am sitting at a chair typing on my laptop (this is the reality) and we have the words available to describe this in English (sitting, chair, typing, laptop) that, when strung together in the grammatically correct sequence, allow me to communicate a reality to you that you, assumed to be a competent reader of English, can readily discern. To return to an earlier idea: it is a belief in the inherent neutrality of language that provides one of the supports for the notion of objective representations of reality.

Some modernist feminists, however, have been quite critical of this idea of language as neutral; in line with the critique that "objectivity" has really meant "from the perspective of privileged men taken to be no perspective at all," feminist critics of English have argued that we have inherited what Dale Spender, nearly 25 years ago, called he/man language

(1980). This is not a neutral medium, but one that is socially constructed such that "he" and "man" *appear* to stand for "everyone," but, in fact, are not generic and inscribe masculinity as (if it were) neutral, requiring that women be constantly marked in language to be recognized as not-men.[3] On the basis of this kind of critique, there have been various feminist approaches to re-working the English language, ranging from arguments for a more neutral terminology that will properly represent reality (i.e. replacing chairman with chairperson), to arguments that women cannot be represented in patriarchal languages and need to develop their own form of writing "from the body" (see, for example, Brossard, 1998; Gould, 1990; Warland, 1990).

Those informed and engaged by poststructuralism introduce another layer of critique—arguing that there is no "reality," there are no "bodies," that pre-exist how these are constituted in and through language. Rather, it is in and through language itself that the sign(s) for reality are produced, contested, and struggled over. There are no inherent meanings; there is no necessary relationship, for example, between the unit c-a-t (known as the signified) and the meaning (known as the signifier) that the word "cat" conjures (e.g. of soft, furry, four-legged, meowing creatures that have been domesticated in "the West"). If even words like "cat" and "dog," words that we are taught in the very first books that are given to us as children, are not stable and do not have inherent meaning, then you can imagine that this argument that language is constitutive of reality (rather than a neutral medium through which reality passes) is highly charged and has far reaching effects.

Interruption #3: Still Here, Shouldering the Weight of Words Not My Own

As you might expect, if you've been following this line of argument, I'm in quite a quandary here! Every sentence that I type is constituting "a reality" of feminist poststructuralism for you. But it is not as if there is a clearly demarcated and agreed upon body of work designated as "feminist poststructuralism" that I could be said to simply be re-presenting in condensed form. Moreover, the argument goes much further than this: In writing feminist poststructuralism in this chapter, I am partly constituting what counts as feminist poststructuralism (such constitutive effects will vary to the extent that this chapter is read and may be cited elsewhere with authority and/or derision). "My version" is not innocent, this chapter is not a neutral medium... meanings are made in the spaces between words as well as through the words themselves in relation to other words from which they are articulated as similar and different... all these double-quote marks all over the place: signals that no word can be taken for granted, no meaning is stable, deploying a term does not necessarily imply agreement with its prevailing meaning... versionisnotinnocentthischapterisnotaneutralmedium.

   ... b r E A k i N g d O w n... co

                     l

                  l

                         apsing

While my "breakdown" at the end of Interruption #3 is one possible response to the swirl of notions tied to the argument that language is constitutive, it does not take into account an idea I slipped in above: Language is a site of social and political struggle. From this perspective, it is not a matter of either accepting this language as it is or having a breakdown in attempting to refuse it (thankfully!). Instead, what is brought to our attention is how the notion of language-as-constitutive is productive for constituting other "realities." This is where the notion of discourse comes in. As it is used in the context of this chapter, "discourse" is a notion developed through the work of Michel Foucault and others who have worked with his ideas. Foucault did not develop a metanarrative or general theory, but rather was interested in how power, knowledge, truth were constituted through and in a variety of historically specific social practices and endeavours to produce and discipline subjects. He did not provide one singular definition of the term, but it is regarded by those who are informed by what became poststructuralism to be a pivotal idea.

Sara Mills offers some helpful orienting points for grasping some aspects of this idea. "One of the most productive ways of thinking about discourse is not as a group of signs..., but as 'practices that systemically form the objects of which they speak' (Foucault, 1972). In this sense, a discourse is something which produces something else (an utterance, a concept, an effect), rather than something which exists in and of itself and which can be analysed in isolation" (1997: 17). What Mills helpfully points us to here is the idea that we cannot actually see or grasp discourses per se (in the way that we can see a person walking into a room, for example). Rather, we can read (for) discourses through their traces, through what they produce as "the real." Follow the example of someone walking into a room: By reading how they gender themselves through hair, body language, clothing, the presence or absence of make-up, shoes, and so on, we are likely to read them as either a woman or a man (contextually). We might refer to these genderings as *effects of discourses* of femininity and masculinity, discourses that are not universal but are historically and culturally specific. From this perspective, people are not authors of their gender (gender is not inherent nor necessarily attached to a particular body), but gender regimes are produced through people's embodiment. Such gender regimes are discursive because they are bounded and repetitive.

As Mills goes on to observe: "[a] discursive structure can be detected because of the *systematicity* of the ideas, opinions, concepts, ways of thinking and behaving which are formed within a particular context, and because of the effects of those ways of thinking and behaving" (1997: 17, emphasis mine). Because discourses are not singular and do not exist in isolation, there is no such thing as one discourse of femininity and one discourse of masculinity. We might speak of femininity and masculinity as sites of discursive constitution, negotiation, struggle, and resistance, as different discourses of femininities and masculinities play out on, and are played out by, people who gender themselves and are gendered by others in ways that are intelligible. Discourses of femininity and masculinity do not have equal weight in such play, however; some are institutionalized and others are produced as "alternative," but the boundaries between these are not fixed and static. How they play out and are played out is a matter of constant negotiation though which "the truth" of femininity and masculinity is produced and struggled over.

> Why, do you suppose, some cultural phenomena are permitted to be dynamic and mutable, and so transformative, while other cultural phenomena, including gender, are considered to be static? Do you think there exists the possibility of a transformative nature in gender? And if so, how can we tap into that? (Bornstein, 1998: 20)

Although one of the key ways to trace discourses is through language (e.g. through the kinds of linguistic practices noted earlier), as the above discussion indicates, discourses do not only take form in this manner. Discourses of femininities and masculinities in particular produce and are produced through a wide variety of effects of embodiment, constituting specifically gendered subjects into "woman" and "man." It is to these ideas that I turn next.

(Gendering) The Subject

It is likely that you rarely spend anytime at all consciously trying to determine whether you or someone else is a boy or a girl. (If that's not true, my apologies; you are already ahead of me in this section of the chapter and I will try to catch up to you as quickly as possible.) This is because the prevailing ideas about gender in contemporary Western social formations, such as Canada, direct us to understanding sex/gender as a given: It is what we are. Hence, once the question "is it a girl or a boy?" has been answered correctly by caregivers (by that, I mean, by a positive response to one category *or* the other), sex/gender is no longer considered a question by most. This does not mean that what it means to be a girl or a boy, or grow up into a woman or a man, is static and uniform (as noted in the previous section), but it does mean that the distinction between girl and boy is assumed to be obvious. Indeed, such obviousness is assumed to be based on physiological and chromosomal distinctions, such that we are assumed to be born either as male or female and our gender identities of masculine or feminine develop from those bases.[4] Thus, most of us understand ourselves and each other to have a coherent and stable gender identity, such that if we have a penis and testicles and develop facial hair, we are masculine, and if we have breasts and a vagina and begin to menstruate in puberty, we are feminine.

Although these are all common-sense ideas, so much so that they are almost beyond question and rarely even considered a matter of curiosity past a young age, there are a few things going on in this previous paragraph that feminist poststructural interrogations would encourage us take a second look at. There are three key ideas that I would like to focus on: that our gender describes who we are (it is an essence of us with biological roots), that sex/gender is a stable dichotomy (boy *or* girl, no ambiguity assumed or permitted without risk), and that gender is, can, and should be always and simply mapped onto sex in a straightforward manner (and if it is not, the problem is with the individual, not the mapping).

In contrast to these ideas, feminist poststructural theorists would argue for a very different understanding of the gendering of subjects. First, the argument is that gender is not what we are, but what we do (Butler, 1999). That is, rather than an essence of being, based on sex as an underpinning of gender, be(com)ing a woman or a man is a matter of performative reiteration (Butler, 1999). This is a concept that suggests that in order to be an intelligible subject—in this case to recognize one's self and be recognized by others as a woman or a man—one must undertake a constant and consistent practice of *doing* the gender that is expected of them/us. To recall Mills' reference above: it is because of the expectation of a systematicity of gendering that we know how to do intelligible gender to ourselves and what to look for in the doing of others. The question is not, then, Are you a girl or a boy? Rather, Are you doing femininity or masculinity?[5]

If gendering is something we do to ourselves and to others and that others do to us, and is not a fixed category of being, then we might wonder, How is it that gendering looks *pretty similar* in specific times and places? If gendering is "up to us" in a sense, then doesn't that mean gendering is a choice? It may be possible that gendering could be open-ended, but the actuality of gendered life as most of us live it is not. There may be many reasons for this; I think most depend on the production of a foundational dichotomy of gender. This is the second key point of argument. Dichotomies work on a set of principles: The world is divided into two (in this case, two genders, women and men); these two are understood to be clearly demarcated, and one side of the dichotomy is assigned more value than the other (in the case of gender, this tends to be masculinity over femininity, think for example of the words associated with each side, e.g. strong, independent, and virile versus weak, dependent, and nurturing); and, by virtue of the construct of a dichotomy, if people associated with one side "appear" like those associated with the other side, they are seen to be transgressing their "natural" role and may be at varying degrees of risk (from, for example, women being called "bitch" for being "too much like a man," or men being threatened for "appearing" feminine). One other thing about dichotomies: Because they assume to divide the world into two, there are no other (legitimated) options; there is nothing else possible.[6]

Given all of this, it is hardly surprising that gendering isn't open-ended, isn't actually a choice. That is, in order to move through the world in ways that allow us to be recognized (i.e. to be loved, to be thought desirable, to be hired for particular jobs, to imagine our futures, etc.), we need to gender ourselves in ways that are intelligible within the regime of a gender dichotomy. Moreover, for gendering to work really well, gendered subjects must occupy a particularly intense paradox: On the one hand, we are told that gender is just who we are, and on the other hand, we are told that gender is an (almost impossible) achievement that takes enormous effort, resources, and labour (our own as well as others').[7]

Interruption #4: "The Author" Writing Back to Herself

But what about the ways in which legibly gendering ourselves and each other is fun? Or, how transgressing the presumed linearity and stability among sex, gender, and sexuality can be exciting? What these kinds of questions point us to is an aspect of gendering that you have not brought up in the previous critique, but one that some modes of feminist poststructural inquiry would instruct us to attend to. Such modes might also point to playing with gendering as one way to negotiate and contest regimes of reiteration—for gendering-as-doing is no mere imposition from the outside, but is a practice in which we participate and therefore can be understood as an expression of agency (a concept that I know you will be introducing in the next section). What if we were to teach students about gender as a site of discipline and play, as a regime but also a series of associated pleasures? Would that make them/you/us more interested in thinking about and playing with gender? Or less?

Power

The prevalence of dichotomous thinking that I spoke to in the previous section also under-pins how we tend to think about "power." It is typical to hear, for example, that someone has power or does not have power, a phrasing that understands power as a possession that is wielded over those who do not have it. Thus, for example, radical feminists would speak of men having patriarchal power and women not, and Marxists might speak of the bour-geoisie having power associated with the ownership of and access to resources that the pro-letariat do not. In other situations, we may speak of a "perpetrator versus victim" dichotomy, in which the position of perpetrator is understood to be a position with power and the position of victim is understood to be a passive position without capacity for action. What is further commonly held across these understandings is the notion of power as a force that oppresses, that literally and symbolically holds down people who are sub-ject to it. In this sense, power has negative connotations, is not regarded as desirable and instead as something to be cut out of visions for an equitable society.

> A story (it could be true): A man breaks into a woman's bedroom and attempts to rape her. She, realizing she cannot stop this but fearing for pregnancy or disease, insists he wear a condom. He does and proceeds to rape her. At a later point, the man is caught and charged. In his defence, it is argued that the woman cannot be considered to be a victim, nor the man a perpetrator; instead, it is argued that they participated in a consensual act. The jury agrees and the man is freed. This is a good example of how limited the notion of power as a possession of have or have not actually is. For, within the terms of this framing, it is not possible to conceive of the man as a perpetrator of an act of rape *and* a woman as having expressed limited agency in that moment. She can only be regarded as a (true) victim if she had "allowed" the rape to happen without "interference" (see Marcus, 1992 to follow up on this idea).

Feminist poststructural theorizing, drawing on the work of Foucault, offers a different reckoning with notions of power, one that can help us grasp and work with the more com-plicated expressions noted in the story in the box. Chris Weedon provides a very helpful summary of Foucault's articulation of power (recall, he did not develop a theory of Power, but offered instead theorizings, analyses of how power works contextually and specifi-cally). In my comments here, I draw heavily on Weedon's summary (1999: 119; I am work-ing from this page unless noted otherwise; the examples are mine). She notes, first, that Foucault argued against the notion that power is only repressive (or what I spoke to above as a negative force). Instead, he argued for "an analytics of power" and proposed guiding principles to consider in efforts to identify what Weedon calls "the nature and workings of power in any area of social and cultural analysis." She identifies eight such principles, which I will summarize and condense here into five points.

First, contrary to the dominant understanding of power that I described in the earlier paragraph, power is not a thing (owned or seized), but a relationship. We can't actually see relationships of power per se; instead, they exist in and take the form of specific social relations (for example, gender relations, class relations, colonial relations). Such relations both pre-exist us (that is, we enter them through subject formation) and are produced by us (that is, we are not only entered but also enter, we are not only produced, but also produce ourselves as particular subjects). Thus, relations of power can be said to be expressed intentionally and unintentionally. For example, in the story noted in the box, there are at least three social relations being expressed: first, a gendered relation between the man who entered the woman's bedroom and the woman who negotiated with him to reduce the amount of harm his rape produces; second, a policing relation between the police personnel who apprehended the man accused of raping the woman, and the man as he was apprehended and entered into the social practices and forms of policing as the criminal subject of accused rapist; and, third, a judicial relation between the man as accused rapist, the woman as accused rape victim, the lawyers, witnesses, and evidence produced for each side, and the judge and jury assigned to assess the case. Relations of gender, policing, and law are all operative in this example; they pre-exist the individuals involved in the specific circumstance, yet are given particular expression when the individuals convey intent (depending on the subject: to rape, to reduce the harms of rape, to apprehend, to judge). Note that one expression of an intent provokes and puts into play the others, but this isn't necessarily guaranteed. The man may not have attempted to rape the woman, the woman may have responded differently, the man may never have been apprehended, the event of the rape may not have become a court case. Hence, we might argue that the workings of relations power are complicated, uneven, and contextual.

Interruption # 5: A Problem that Haunts Me and One I Can't Resolve

As I work through and with the story of a rape, I know that I am on difficult and highly contested ground. Many modes of modernist feminisms, especially those attached to radical feminist conceptualizations of patriarchy, have made compelling and striking arguments about the character, extent, and effects of men's violences against women (see relevant chapters in this volume). Feminists working from these perspectives and on these social issues are often highly suspect and deeply critical of the kinds of questions and problematics I am putting forward here, arguing that they deflect attention from the real practice of men's rape of women, of what it means to be a woman and live in a "rape culture" (Buchenwald et al., 1993). For those who encounter on a regular basis the actual stories of the violences and horrors women are subject to as women, the conceptualization of power that I am articulating here may be read as abhorrent, an anti-feminist betrayal in the face of already so much struggle to have women's stories believed and taken seriously. As Ann Brooks puts it, "from the perspective of second wave feminism, postmodern and poststructuralism's effective denial of the status of all epistemologies [for example, of women's experience as authentic and true] renders feminism politically and epistemologically powerless" (1997: 46). In some ways, I am sympathetic to these critiques; in other ways, concerned by the assumptions and delimiters they keep in place. It would be an entirely other paper to grapple with these more directly.[8] What I have come to, in brief, is a

(continued on next page)

sense that—however risky and challenging feminist poststructural interrogations may feel for those (of us)[9] who are concerned with trauma, violence, loss, and suffering—I continue to think these are risks and challenges worth encountering and working through. For all of the research, activism, scholarship, panels, and support programs that feminist work on violence has produced and supported, deep changes are barely apparent. To me, that must mean that there are hard(er) questions that haven't been faced and that demand our attention. You may be wondering, What am I supposed to do with this as an undergraduate student, taking (perhaps) my first women's studies course? I don't have a single answer to that, but I do wonder, What does it mean to pass on feminist theorizing from one generation to another if these large questions aren't at the centre of what we are teaching?[10]

Second, as a series of statements in the chapter so far have suggested, power is not only restrictive, but also productive. This is an extremely important insight, I would argue. That is, if power works through relationships, then relationships are not only delimiting, but also generative of subjects and possibilities. Following the concerns I noted in Interruption #5, let me turn toward a different kind of example here that might make the potential of this conceptualization easier to grasp, separate from critique. We might say that students and professors are produced through relations of knowledge/power (a well-known Foucault couplet; see Foucault, 1980), and that the creation of these subjects ("student" and "professor") means that certain ways of living are closed down or restricted (for example, both students and professors need to abide by particular timetables for courses that take them away from other things they may like to do), *and* certain ways of living are opened up and made possible (that same timetable of courses at university may mean no early mornings, for example, so it makes sleeping in feasible). This is a rather trite example, and things certainly get much more complicated (as the rape story example and discussion illustrates), but hopefully this idea of restriction and possibility starts to make some sense.

Third, because power takes form through relationships (and forms relationships), power is not uniform, is not discharged from one central source, but comes from diverse sources and directions and takes different shapes. If we follow the example in the previous paragraph: Although professors and students are expected to abide by a schedule of courses, there are limited means to regulate this. Students can use their positioning in the relationship of power "from below" by skipping classes and will not likely receive direct punishment "from above" for doing so. Yet, in small classes, professors generally know who attends regularly and may use attendance and participation marks to both "reward" and "discipline" students. Thus, although power is not uniform in its expression, it must be exercised, through aims and objectives, in order to have effects.

This example points me in the direction of the fourth key principle: Relationships of power establish the terms of resistance specifically and agency more generally. Thus, as power is not a thing, neither are resistance or agency. Nor are agency and resistance understood on Foucauldian terms as a priori (existing outside of the workings of power somewhere). Rather, what resistance and agency look like (how they are both produced and delimited) will depend, to varying degrees, upon the specific relationship of power being negotiated.[11] If you, for example, as a student-subject, have questions about a grade on an assignment, you can speak to the TA or professor, then the department head, then the faculty office, and so on. This institutionalized set of procedures demarcates for you as a student the legitimated terms on which you can "resist" a grade. (You might fantasize about other terms, but these are not legitimated within the relations of knowledge/power at the university and thus resistance in such forms would itself be subject to further discipline through the evocation of other relations of power.) Thus, resistance is circumscribed by the workings of relationships of power that make possible a limited and provisional practice of resistance. It is within and across these that the terms of (y)our agency are made possible and delimited.

The last principle that Weedon points us to is a slight refashioning of the previous focus on the localization of the workings of power. That is, although power takes shape and shapes locally, relationships of power are not isolated and discrete but are part of broader patterns that are made manifest in institutions and social apparatuses, such as laws and policies. To follow the example of relations of knowledge/power: Individual expressions of power and resistance "locally" between a particular professor and a specific student do not exist in isolation, but are constituted by and constitutive of a broader web of university regulations and modes of appropriate practice. This web may have many dimensions, being put into play through the operation of departments and faculties, through university-wide policies, and in provincial and/or national regulations and laws.

Theorizing Difference Differently: Que(e)rying Sex/Gender/Sexuality

Throughout the chapter, I've been endeavouring not only to introduce a series of (re)conceptualizations, but also to show how they may be productive and helpful for thinking about and engaging in the social world differently. In this last section, I want to try to bring together the main points of critique, and the different modes of thinking offered by feminist poststructural inquiry, to consider their contribution to theorizing difference differently—particularly in regards to sex/gender/sexuality. Earlier in the chapter, I introduced the argument that dichotomization is a central organizing practice of late modern social formations. I spoke about this practice particularly in regard to gender, for how it constitutes gender on either/or terms (i.e. masculinity *or* femininity). Here I want to turn my attention particularly to the ways in which this practice works in regard to constituting (un)intelligible categories of sexualities. The categories that are probably most familiar to you are the ones that circulate and prevail in a variety of modes, through education, media, religion, and so on: "heterosexuality" and "homosexuality." You might also think of these as straight versus gay, or normal versus abnormal, or ordinary folk versus "I'm ok with it, so long as they don't flaunt it."

Here is where feminist poststructural critiques of knowledge-making practices can be helpful. Notice first the construct of X *versus* Y, a construct that constitutes X as meaningful by virtue of its opposition to Y, which is marked through this construct as the "other" (different, not desired, aberrant, etc.). This is a construct that has two main effects. First, it constitutes X and Y as singular and coherent categories, in which all Xs are presumed to be alike because they are Xs, all Ys are presumed to be alike because they are Ys, and, therefore, Xs and Ys are, at minimum, inherently dissimilar from each other, and, further, in opposition to each other (to be an X means one must categorically not be a Y). Secondly, Xs and Ys are not constituted as equal in this dichotomous construct; rather, the Xs are considered to be the norm/al and the Ys are considered to be the abnormal. Hence, a hierarchy is established between the two terms and one way in which the Xs are continually imagined as coherent is through the production of the Ys as some*thing* to be anxious about, feared, hated, or, at minimum, kept at a distance. Critics refer to this as a heteronormative construct; as Lauren Berlant and Michael Warner explain, "heternormativity is more than ideology, or prejudice, or phobia against gays and lesbians; it is produced in almost every aspect of the forms and arrangements of social life...as well as in the conventions and affects of narrativity, romance, and other protected spaces in culture" (1993: 359).

One response, on the part of gays and lesbians committed to social justice and recognition, has been to challenge such normative thinking by arguing that Ys are not inherently different from Xs and thus should not be considered deviant or abnormal. Rather than align with Y as a category of shame, folks have claimed Y as a category of pride and self-definition, attempting to change its meaning from derisive to affirmative. These are the characteristics of gay and lesbian liberation movements and writings, beginning in North America in the late 1960s, which have emphasized what Tom Warner identifies as the "imperatives of fostering positive identities, building community and asserting visibility" (2002: 305). Such efforts are oriented to legal and social equality for gays and lesbians; the latest manifestations of which, in Canada, as you are probably aware, have been struggles for the full and equal recognition of gay couples under marriage laws. In Michelle Owen's phrasing, this is a desire to "normalize the queer" (2001: 87); that is, to constitute gays and lesbians as *just as* committed to one another, family oriented, monogamous, etc., as heterosexual folk. (These characteristics are, of course, argued in opposition to heteronormative ideas that have designated homosexuals as promiscuous destroyers of "The Family.") Efforts to have the rights and obligations of marriage extended to gay and lesbian couples, then, depends upon being able to stretch the category of normal to include those who have been excluded. Such inclusion is made possible when gays and lesbians can be read as "normal"—not fundamentally different from straight folk—when sexual orientation is marked as a fairly neutral (meaning minimal and insignificant) difference.

If we follow the arguments outlined in earlier sections of this chapter, in regard to discourse, power, and the production of subjects, however, we begin to see traces of an inquiry that pushes for a deeper layer of questioning. For, what is clear is that the arguments for gay marriage in Canada are far from secured and settled; indeed, at stake in the debates is the question of what difference the difference of sexuality makes. Is it a neutral difference, as those arguing for gay marriage suggest? Is it an inherent difference of abnormality of being, as conservative, homophobic discourses articulate? Is it a marker of inquiry, an opening into deconstructing heteronormative systems of classification, the articulation of non- or anti-normative sexual identities or que(e)rying of sexual practices, as a way out of the "regimes of normal" (Warner in Hall, 2003: 15) that discipline us all? As you might have guessed, feminist poststructural interrogations lend themselves most readily to the latter line of questioning and hence have an affiliation with what is known as "queer theorizing."

This is a practice of critical inquiry that would propose a re-reading of the paragraph above on gay affirmative strategies for inclusion in heteronormative forms of legitimation (such as marriage). The structure of the argument would be that it will always be a failed strategy to claim Y as possible to affirm on the terms of X; Y is always and already second-class in relation to X, it can only ever be "like" X, "resemble" X, it is not valued on its own terms, and, moreover, has no grounds on which to question X. Thus, such strategies of inclusion may confront heteronormativity but do so in a very circumscribed way; to stretch the norm is not to deeply challenge, trouble, or undermine it. To queer heteronormativity is a different difference altogether; as Donald Hall, puts it, queering "may not destroy such systems [of dichotomous classification] but it certainly presses upon them, torturing their lines of demarcation, pressuring their easy designations" (2003: 14).

You might wonder why all this torturing and pressuring of categories is necessary, shouldn't gays and lesbians simply be happy to be included? The problem is with the terms of inclusion. For, folks who are demarcated as Ys and may do Y identities themselves, contrary to the premises and efforts at boundary maintenance of the X/Y dichotomy, are *not* a coherent and singular "group." Indeed, they are no more coherent and singular than Xs (but Xs aren't required to defend themselves as Xs, that is part of how normative privilege works—the burden of intelligible identification is carried by the others). What this means is that some argue for inclusion and equity, but others are more hesitant. As the brief critique above delineates, the strategy of inclusion and acceptance can only be provisional and is always at risk of being taken away. Moreover, if the boundaries between inside/outside, inclusion/exclusion, are stretched and not questioned per se as inherent in structures that both produce and delimit all of our lives (to recall a Foucauldian understanding of power as productive and limiting), then gay and lesbian inclusion can only be achieved at the cost of excluding "other queers" (e.g. gays and lesbians who don't do their identity on legitimated terms and those who queer (transgress, trouble, play with…) rather than define themselves within the normative notions of sex/gender/sexuality).

Feminist poststructural arguments can be used to support a third position here, to help us resist putting in place yet another dichotomy—in this case, inclusion versus queering—that would carry with it all the same problems of hierarchy, boundary policing, and the production of absolute rightness that inheres in such structures. This is an argument that might proceed by contending that neither position in and of itself is fully explanatory or inherently better politically (that is, neither should be made a metanarrative, nor should be regarded as outside of the complex and contextual workings of power). Instead, both need to be examined for their assumptions, conceptualizations, and strategies. Both need to be considered as theorizings of sex/gender/sexuality per se *and* for their implications for intervening politically. Similar to the questions I posed earlier in the chapter regarding modernist feminist theories, questions need to be asked of gay affirmative theories, such as Whose queer lives and what queering of identities, desires, and practices need to be forgotten or obscured for gay affirmative theories to be upheld? Whose interests does this serve? But also, questions need to be posed of queer theories, i.e., In the current political climate in Canada, is it strategic to argue for gay marriage rather than to argue against it on queer terms? Are there ways to work with the insights of queer and poststructural forms of inquiry to support multiple and diverse strategies of intervention, so that gay marriage isn't made the arbiter of what it means to be queer in Canada, but nor is not made possible for those who desire and long for such recognition? I don't propose to answer such questions here, nor do definitive answers most interest me. I offer such questions to you, however, for further discussion.

NOT AN ENDING

It's January 2004, some three months after I began to develop this chapter. Edmonton is bitterly cold and the second semester of classes is underway. There have been some changes in my life over these past few months; some wonderful, some difficult. Larger social struggles continue in a post-9/11 era in which anxiety, terror, threat, warfare, and harm are spilling over and across all of our lives, albeit very differently. As a reader, you won't be able to trace these changes and struggles as I haven't marked them explicitly, but they simmer under the surface of the writing for me. Not because I think feminist post-structural theorizing has "the answers," but because it offers a mode of inquiry and questioning of the workings of knowledge/power/subjects/difference that I think is useful in attending to what passes as normal—and may be made otherwise.

In—among—against—beside all of this, different versions of feminist theorizing are being played out in universities, as scholars struggle to instill, negotiate, and/or refuse various feminist theories and their implications for, among other things, what will be made to count as appropriate knowledge to be passed on to the next generation of students. For some, this is not really a question—they are clear about what the key texts are, how the debates are best framed, and what it is you need to know. From this perspective, the world as I signalled it above, and as it receives texture in this edited collection, presses heavily on those of us in universities, to do something with what we've learned, with what our models of making sense tell us. Thus, on these terms, there is a limit to theorizing, a point at which it stops becoming useful and slips into something else (Play? Narcissism? Theory for theory's sake?). I take this concern seriously, as I think the work of others that I have endeavoured to translate and represent to you here does also. But to take seriously does not necessarily mean to agree. And, that is where a difference is marked.

For there are those of us for whom the questioning of knowledge, learning, teaching, discipline, politics, truth, theory, representation, the making and unmaking of subjects...is not secondary, does not stop, but is crucial to why and how we find ourselves here—in these places of education. This is not to suggest that politics does not matter or is of secondary concern. Rather, to return to where I began this chapter, it is to put forward the position that it is absolutely vital to have, maintain, and struggle for spaces and places where the immediacy of the now can be suspended (provisionally, momentarily), so that we, individually and in collectivities of classrooms, reading groups, etc., can push beyond what is readily thinkable in terms of how the world *is*. This is not, I would argue, a turning away from the world, but a turning toward it differently, as we too may be different because of our encounter with ideas that shatter, unsettle, question, and press against ways of thinking that are taken as a given, in which, to varying degrees, we have all been, and continue to be, immersed. This is not a morally righteous stance. I am not proffering here a better politic that is innocent of its own investments and struggles. Rather, this is about being here, now, fully mired in the workings of power, reaching for the edges of possibility. Over to you...

ACKNOWLEDGMENTS

My deep thanks to Tanya Lewis, Tara Goldstein, and Susan Heald with whom the conversations that underpin this chapter are kept alive. My thanks to Diane Naugler for years of supporting my work, including reading an earlier version of this chapter. I am appreciative of the dialogues with students that I have had over the years in courses at York University and at the University of Alberta. I extend my gratitude also to Nancy Mandell, Jon Maxfield, and the anonymous reviewers, who understood and supported the mode of theorizing that I have endeavoured to undertake here—as an issue not only of "content" but also "form."

ENDNOTES

1. One of the oft-cited claims of postmodernism is that "the author is dead." This short-hand phrasing refers to a critique of the modernist notion that the author's intentions circumscribe and define the meaning of "their" text. Thus, titling sections such as this one as "from the author" may be read as rather contradictory in a chapter that is working with and from poststructural and postmodern ideas. Rather than read this contradiction as a problem, I offer that it may be read as a productive indicator of how relations among author, authority, and meaning might be reconfigured in and by feminist poststructuralism. For, while I am not *The Author* of this text in the modernist sense, "I" am nonetheless its writer, situated in a particular time and place; this chapter did not simply drop from the sky and land on the right desk at Pearson Education Canada, but was brought into being and negotiated through a complexity of social relations and cultural practices of which "I," with others, am a part. My interruption notes are not offered as expressions of my intentions but are initiated as an endeavour to mark the text with some particular traces of my-self-as-its-writer: breakages into expectations of this as an objective rendering.

2. You'll notice a rather heavy use of double quotation marks in this paragraph. Informed by an attention to the workings of knowledge/power/language that is being profiled in this chapter, I use such quotation marks as a signal that the term or phrase being marked in this way should be read as problematic. That is, the term or phrase needs to be used because it speaks to ideas that commonly circulate, but its prevailing meanings are open to inquiry. You might ask why every word would not then be signalled in such a way. This is a reasonable question and certainly does follow from a strict interpretation of the issues being raised here. The difficulty is that such a practice would make a text so unwieldy as to be unapproachable. Already, you may find, as did some reviewers before you, the use of such signalling a little heavy-handed at times. I have endeavoured here to strike some kind of "balance" (there I go again!) between explicitly problematizing terms and creating an approachable text. See the section on language/discourse for more on the issues at stake here.

3. One of my favourite "tests" of this position is to consider the English-language practices whereby we designate people according to the schema of Mr., Mrs., Miss, and Ms. Note that where there is one designation for men, there are three for women—all of which generate their meaning through a relation to men. Although "Ms." was introduced as a "neutral" companion to "Mr.," in practice it has come to designate divorced women and/or feminists—in and of itself a matter for curiosity.

4. Recent work on intersexuality has shown that the assumed biological basis of a sex dichotomy is actually a social construct and not a given. Critics and advocates working in this area express deep concern with how medicalization imposes this dichotomy on bodies that are deemed not to "fit" correctly. See, for example, Fausto-Sterling, 2000, and Preves, 2003.

5. This question too is up for further consideration. Note the use of the "or" and its implications (you might want to skip ahead to "Theorizing Difference Differently" or bring this issue forward when you are at that point in the chapter). One of the reviewers of this chapter suggested that bringing in some literature and contemporary theorizing in regard to transgendering would be helpful and pertinent in regard to this point and for the last substantive section of the chapter. I haven't been able to take as much space on this as I would like, but I concur with the reviewer—the recent work on playing (messing, grappling, …) with gender regimes by troubling the assumed (and reiterated) linear relation among sex, gender, and sexuality is exciting and relevant. Some of these critiques dovetail with the critiques of medicalization of intersexuality noted above; others move in different directions. Key for both, however, is the argument that there is *no necessary* relationship among one's embodiment,

one's sense of gendered self, and one's sexual desires, practices, or interests. Rather, these are highly complex configurations that are not fixed. I would argue that what is central about this theorizing is that it "queers" the dominant story of gender—not only bringing forth different stories of how people live their gendered lives, but also troubling the presumed neutrality and universality of that story for us all (on que[e]rying, see the last section; for relevant introductory reading on transgendering, see especially Bornstein, 1998, and Nestle, Howell, and Wilchins, 2002).

6. There are numerous dichotomies that are foundational to modernity, gender is but one of them. And dichotomies intersect, so gender dichotomies, for example, may intersect in particular historical moments and geo-political locations with race dichotomies, class dichotomies, and so on. This complicates what an "intelligible" gender means on whose body.

7. Feminists have generally been particularly concerned with the expenditure of energy, resources, and labour that is required for legitimated femininity (see, for example, Bordo, 1993; Brumberg, 1997; Connell, 2002). However, poststructural feminisms in particular may push for a more nuanced consideration of how such expenditures are also required by legitimated modes of masculinity, but on quite different terms.

8. Some theorists have begun to do this important work. For a formative text in this area, see Sharon Marcus (1992); for a book-length grappling, see Mayrisia Zalewski (2000). Wendy Brown's work on injurious identities is also hugely important to these debates (see her 1996 essay). I have attempted to come at these issues from a different angle in other work; see for example, my chapter in *Between Hope and Despair* (Rosenberg, 2000). I regard sustained and complex conversation between radical and poststructuralist modes of inquiry and conceptualization as an emerging area of urgently needed feminist attention.

9. In putting the "of us" in parenthesis here, I am endeavouring to, on the one hand, acknowledge that some may object to including my work in this category, and, on the other, to maintain a position that this is a category that needs to be opened to interrogation itself, to let in the difficulties that it is often bordered against.

10. These are larger questions that are currently being grappled with by a number of scholars located in (relation to) Women's Studies. See, for example, the current debate in *Feminist Theory* 4/3, 2003, and an upcoming book in which I am involved, with Ann Braithwaite, Susanne Luhmann, and Susan Heald, tentatively titled: *Troubling Women's Studies: Pasts, Presents and Possibilities* (Sumach Press).

11. I say to varying degrees, because relationships of power, inhering as they do in other social relations, do not exist in isolation, but criss-cross each other in complicated and unending ways. Thus, resistance in the context of one relationship of power may be informed and shaped in part by other relations. The more institutionalized a relation of power is, the less likely this is the case.

SUGGESTED READINGS

In addition to the texts cited in the bibliography, I recommend the following:

Davies, Bronwyn. *Shards of Glass: Children Reading and Writing Beyond Gendered Identities* (rev. ed.). Cresskill, NJ: Hampton Press, 2003.

Her writing is some of the most "accessible" and "applied" work in feminist poststructural theorizing and its implications for educative practices.

Heald, Susan. "Pianos to Pedagogy: Pursuing the Educational Subject." In H. Bannerji, L. Carty, K. Dehli, S. Heald, and K. McKenna, eds. *Unsettling Relations: The University as a Site of Feminist Struggles.* Toronto: Women's Press, 1991.

Kelly, Ursula. *Schooling Desire: Literacy, Cultural Politics and Pedagogy*. New York and London: Routledge, 1997.

Lewis, Tanya. *Living Beside: Performing Normal After Incest Memories Return*. Toronto: McGilligan Books, 1999.

Heald, Kelly, and Lewis all write and work in feminist poststructural theorizing in Canada. Although much of the "field," given the politics of knowledge transnationally, is being defined by scholars in the United States and Britain, it is important to complicate those politics and recognize "local" theorists. There are others, of course; these are some of the ones I know the best.

Richardson, Laurel. "Writing: A Method of Inquiry." In N.K. Denizen and Y.S. Lincoln, eds. *Handbook of Qualitative Research*. Thousand Oaks, California: Sage, 2000, 516–529.

Richardson's work is an excellent example of working with feminist poststructural theorizing for methodology and scholarly representation. I have been particularly inspired in this essay by the kinds of questions and suggestions she puts forth.

DISCUSSION QUESTIONS

You'll notice that I raise larger discussion questions throughout the chapter; here are a few others for your consideration:

1. Did this chapter get you thinking about how knowledge is represented? How? What difference did that make to your understanding of the ideas presented?

2. In what ways do you experience gendering yourself and others? What happens when you cannot readily read someone else's gender? How is gender produced differently across social spaces?

3. How do you read heteronormativity being kept in place and/or countered through the "gay marriage" issue in Canada? What is not being included in mainstream media discussions that might make a difference to what is considered to be at issue and for whom?

4. How do you understand the relationship between modernist and poststructural or postmodern modes of feminist theorizing?

BIBLIOGRAPHY

Abercrombie, Nicholas, Stephen Hill, and **Bryan S. Turner.** *The Penguin Dictionary of Sociology*. 4th ed. England: Penguin Books. 2000.

Bannerji, Himani. *The Dark Side of the Nation*. Toronto: Canadian Scholars Press, 2000.

Berlant, Lauren, and **Michael Warner.** "Sex in Public." *The Cultural Studies Reader*, 2nd ed. Edited by Simon During. London and New York: Routledge, 1993: 354–367.

Bordo, Susan. *Unbearable Weight: Feminism, Western Culture and The Body*. Berkeley: University of California Press, 1993.

Bornstein, Kate. *My Gender Workbook*. New York and London: Routledge, 1998.

Brooks, Ann. *Postfeminisms: Feminism, Cultural Theory and Cultural Forms*. London and NY: Routledge, 1997.

Brossard, Nicole. *She Would Be the First Sentence of My Next Novel.* Susanne de Lotbiniere-Harwood, trans. Toronto: The Mercury Press, 1998.

Brown, Wendy. "Injury, Identities, Politics." In *Mapping Multiculturalism*, edited by Avery F. Gordon and Christopher Newfield. Minneapolis: University of Minnesota Press, 1996: 149–166.

Brumberg, Joan Jacobs. *The Body Project: An Intimate History of American Girls.* New York: Random House, 1997.

Buchenwald, Emilie, Pamela Fletcher, and **Martha Roth.** *Transforming a Rape Culture.* Minneapolis: Milkweed Editions, 1993.

Butler, Judith. *Gender Trouble*, 10th anniversary ed. New York: Routledge, 1999.

Butler, Judith, and **Joan W. Scott,** eds. *Feminists Theorize the Political.* NY: Routledge, 1992.

Connell, R.W. *Gender.* Massachusetts: Polity Press, 2002.

Dua, Enakshi, and **Angela Robertson,** eds. *Scratching the Surface: Canadian Anti-Racist Feminist Thought.* Toronto: Women's Press, 1999.

Fausto-Sterling, Anne. "The Five Sexes, Revisited," *The Sciences* 40/4 (July/Aug 2000): 18–23.

Flax, Jane. "The End of Innocence." In *Feminists Theorize the Political*, edited by Butler and Scott. 445–463. New York: Routledge, 1992

Foucault, Michel. *Power/Knowledge: Selected Interviews and Other Writings 1972–1977.* Colin Gordon, ed. New York: Pantheon Books, 1980.

Gould, Karen. *Writing in the Feminine: Feminism and Experimental Writing in Quebec.* Carbondale and Edwardsville: Southern Illinois Press, 1990.

Hall, Donald E. *Queer Theories.* New York: Palgrave MacMillan, 2003.

Hamilton, Peter. "The Enlightenment and the Birth of Social Science." In *Formations of Modernity*, edited by Stuart Hall and Bram Gieben. Cambridge: Polity Press & Open University, 1992: 18–58.

Hill Collins, Patricia. *Black Feminist Thought.* Boston: Unwin Hyman, 1990.

hooks, bell. *Feminist Theory: from Margin to Center.* Boston: South End Press, 1984.

Kolodny, Annette. "'A Sense of Discovery, Mixed with a Sense of Justice': Creating the First Women's Studies Program in Canada." *NWSA Journal* 12/1 (Spring 2000): 143–164.

Lyotard, Francois. *The Postmodern Condition.* G. Bennington and B. Massumi, trans. Minneapolis: University of Minnesota Press, 1984.

Marcus, Sharon. "Fighting Bodies, Fighting Words: A Theory and Politics of Rape Prevention." In *Feminists Theorize the Political*, edited by Butler and Scott. 385–403. New York: Routledge, 1992.

Mills, Sara. *Discourse.* NY and London: Routledge, 1997.

Nestle, Joan, Claire Howell, and **Riki Wilchins,** eds. *GENDERqUEER: Voices From Beyond the Sexual Binary.* Los Angeles: Alyson Books, 2002.

Owen, Michelle K. "'Family' As a Site of Contestation: Queering the Normal or Normalizing the Queer?" In *A Queer Country: Gay and Lesbian Studies in the Canadian Context*, edited by Terry Goldie. Vancouver: Arsenal Pulp Press, 2001: 86–102.

Preves, Sharon E. *Intersex and Identity: The Contested Self.* New Jersey and London: Rutgers University Press, 2003.

Raby, Rebecca. "Reconfiguring Agnes: The Telling of a Transsexual's Story," *Torquere* 2 (2000): 18–35.

Rosenberg, Sharon. "Standing in a Circle of Stone: Rupturing the Binds of Emblematic Memory." In *Between Hope and Despair: Pedagogy and the Remembrance of Historical Trauma,* edited by Roger I. Simon, Sharon Rosenberg, and Claudia Eppert. Lanham, Maryland: Rowman and Littlefield, 2000: 75–89.

Rothenberg, Paula S., ed. *Race, Class and Gender in the United States,* 5th ed. New York: Worth Publishers, 2001.

Spender, Dale. *Man Made Language.* London: Routledge and Kegan Paul, 1980.

St. Pierre, Elizabeth, and **Wanda S. Pillow,** eds. *Working the Ruins: Feminist Poststructural Theory and Methods in Education.* New York and London: Routledge, 2000.

Warland, Betsy. *Proper Deafinitions.* Vancouver: Press Gang, 1990.

Warner, Tom. *Never Going Back: A History of Queer Activism in Canada.* Toronto: University of Toronto Press, 2002

Weedon, Chris. "poststructuralism/postmodernism." In *Encyclopaedia of Feminist Theories,* edited by Lorraine Code. New York and London: Routledge, 2000.

———. *Feminism, Theory and the Politics of Difference.* Oxford: Blackwell Publishers, 1999.

———. *Feminist Practice and Poststructuralist Theory.* Oxford and Mass: Blackwell Publishers, 1987.

Zalewksi, Marysia. *Feminism After Postmodernism: Theorizing Through Practice.* London and New York: Routledge, 2000.

WEBLINKS

Judith Butler

http://www.theory.org.uk/ctr-butl.htm

I recommend checking out the whole site. This URL will get you specifically to the page on Judith Butler's work. Lots of great, accessible information and links.

Third Space: The Site for Emerging Feminist Scholars

http://www.thirdspace.ca/

Not a site that speaks to feminist poststructural ideas explicitly but a great resource to check for those interested in exploring the many facets and energies of contemporary feminism.

Challenging Psychiatric Stereotypes of Gender Diversity

http://www.transgender.org/tg/gidr/

An information resource and activist site, informed by queer and transgender theorizing, that challenges the medicalization of gender "disorders." Useful as a practical follow-up to the critiques by and concerns of transgendered folks noted briefly in this chapter.

chapter three

Third-Wave Feminisms

Allyson Mitchell

Lara Karaian

"For me, feminism is two parts definition and one part struggle—a constant processing of defining, redefining and struggling against existing definitions."

—Mariko Tamaki (2001: 29).

INTRODUCTION

The Third Wave(s)

What does a third-wave feminist look like? Is she *Legally Blonde's* lesbian law student with a PhD in women's studies? The one that introduces herself and explains how she studied the history of conflict while she punches the guy next to her. Or is she the film's fashion-savvy, pink-clad, brainy, sexually in-charge main character? Does she sing about skater boys and wear ties like Avril Lavigne or describe herself as "trouble" like Pink? Does she look like Hailey Wickenheiser, the butchy, sporty gal who played for the Canadian Women's Hockey team?

Many of these images of third-wavers are provided to us by mainstream media, but third-wavers also comprise many young women who the media doesn't show us, such as radical cheerleaders, spoken-word artists D'bi Young or Kim Trusty, and many others who volunteer at rape crisis shelters and march (or squat) against poverty. Third-wavers are the sexy media version as well as the grass-roots activists—whom some people would call even sexier, but for different reasons.

So, our efforts to describe and problematize the diversity that exists among third-wave feminists today makes this chapter a bit of a juggling act. The complexities can be overwhelming but the end result is a more integrative feminism, one that is applicable and accessible to the lived lives of a greater spectrum of people. Third-wavers, we hope to show, are simultaneously shattering and opening up definitions of feminism. This has been heralded as the third wave's greatest strength—as well as its potential weakness.

The third wave refers to a dynamic feminist movement with no definitive shape or form. One of the main characteristics of the third wave is an active resistance to the imposition of labels, closures, boundaries, and categories. The third wave attempts to synthesize, build on, and extend what has been accomplished by the first and second waves of feminism, while attending to the particulars of our present moment in historical and feminist contexts. Another main characteristic of the third wave is its tendency to push the boundaries of the second-wave mantra "the personal is political." Young feminists have learned through their experience as activists and their education in women's studies classes to ask: Whose politics? They have learned to assert that the personal is also theoretical. Our experiences can be used to educate, trouble, disrupt, challenge, and reinforce feminism. Third wave is here and now—*doing* feminism in a society that has been transformed by the feminisms that came before us.

The word "wave" is used as a metaphor to describe the ebbs and flows of feminism occurring over time and place. Although this descriptor has been useful, we must also critique or problematize it. Some feel that breaking up feminism into waves presents an inevitable oversimplification of feminist scholarship and activism, erasing histories and sweeping over complexity and nuance. For example, the written history of the second wave in North America has largely been the record of a white women's movement. Although the second wave was organized around exclusionary notions of the category "woman," there was also a healthy anti-racist movement and women of colour were active feminists at the time (Dua and Robertson, 1999: 3). This reality demonstrates the limits and possible drawbacks of using the wave metaphor. However, there are aspects of the term "wave" that are useful in describing contemporary feminism. There are no clear boundaries between the various and multiple feminist movements just as there are no clear disconnects between waves in an ocean. Taking this into account, it may be a particularly apt description for this generation of feminists given their fluidity and their inability to be held or pinned down.

We are third-wave feminists. We defy labels, embrace contradictions, and call for complexity. From the outside we appear eclectic, fragmented, and even trite. We prefer to see ourselves as inclusive, open to change, creative, painfully conscious, funny, and really, really smart.

We distance ourselves from earlier feminisms while at the same time acknowledging that we are a generation that has grown up in a world changed by feminism and other social movements. Leslie Haywood and Jennifer Drake, authors of *Third Wave Agenda*, credit these movements with helping us develop "modes of thinking that can come to terms with the multiple, constantly shifting bases of oppression in relation to the multiple interpenetrating axes of identity" (1997: 3). They write, "We know that what oppresses me may not oppress you, that what oppresses you may be something I participate in, and that what oppresses me may be something you participate in" (1997: 3). This chapter is all about the third wave and our relationships with one another as we continue to struggle with feminism's impact on, and understanding of, oppression and privilege. In order to do this we will consider how the third wave came to be, tactics and strategies that are utilized by young feminists, and how the third wave is the same as and different from feminisms that came before it.

ORIGIN STORIES

The exact origins of the third wave are still being debated. Many argue that the third wave has come about as a result of black women's critiques of white Western feminism. Certainly, anti-racist critiques of the women's movement have altered feminism forever. The third wave comprises and takes up women of colour's argument that being critical of our positions in relation to power structures does not undermine the many struggles within feminism, meaning that it is not necessary to have what is considered to be a "common front" in order to affect social change. Others argue that the third wave is a response to dissatisfaction with what is perceived to be second-wave moralizing, especially in the area of sexuality. And still others see the third wave as a reaction to the 1990s anti-feminist or post-feminist movement that proclaimed equality to be achieved and therefore feminism to be dead. Some regard the third wave as simply "different" from the second wave; they set up a false, and not particularly useful, distinction. Regardless of the third wave's origins, it is fair to say that the dialogue between second- and third-wave feminism is complicated and often fraught with tensions.

Feminists of the third wave are uneasy claiming that identity and writing about young feminism. It is our fear that in trying to explain or define young feminisms we will leave things out or create a false history. Is it possible to talk about young feminists without, to some degree, constructing them? Are we constructing these waves out of convenience? In the introduction to *The Sub Cultures Reader*, Ken Gelder and Sarah Thorton (1997) discuss how "in the process of portraying social groups, scholars inevitably construct them" (5). The mere labelling "of a social formation is in part to frame, shape and delineate it" (5). We come to terms with this framing by recognizing how and where we are doing it. In fact, we do not lament but embrace it to the fullest, so that when we talk about "young feminism" or "the third wave" we are conscious that we are marking and defining the community and the history. We recognize that this chapter defines the subjects of the third wave through the kinds of young feminism we document and how we are positioned in the text. We struggle with the ethics of making such a map of the third wave. But at the same time, we don't see ourselves as gatekeepers; we simply wish to increase the visibility of young feminism, particularly in an academic text book that will, we hope, get more young women excited about the project of feminism.

BEING A THIRD-WAVER

How is the third wave the same as or different from the first and second waves?

Third-wavers deconstruct (take apart or problematize) the category of "women." Along with this they critique seemingly clear-cut notions of identity such as the belief that being a woman means the same thing for all women, or that being a lesbian means the same thing for all lesbians, or that all people experience their classed positions in the same way. A continuation of this is to question notions of authenticity such as those beliefs that there is a "real" way of being "black" or a "real" way of being "feminist." Some second-wavers fear this kind of exploration will prevent women from uniting in a common fight, that feminism is threatened if it can't present a united front. The argument is that if we complicate feminism too much, it may no longer look like the feminism that has provided the grounds for rallying "women" together against patriarchy. Third-wavers respond by arguing that this need for commonality is too simplistic an idea to base a resistance movement upon. They call for a greater acceptance of, and emphasis on, complexities, ambiguities, hybridity, intersectionality, and fluidity, as well as a rejection of dichotomous thinking that posits all women as good and all men as bad. Third-wavers believe fragmentation to be feminism's greatest strength, not its biggest downfall.

This generation of young feminists must still consider many of the issues that came out of the second wave such as violence against women, job equity, poverty, militarism, and the rights of children. But third-wavers' cultural context is quite different: Postmodern, post-structural, post-colonial, queer, and anti-racist theories, along with post-feminism, global capitalism, corporate media, and technological advances, make this generation's context—and thus its methods of resistance—its very own. Issues such as job equity, therefore, are now complicated by the intersections of ability, class, sexuality, and race, rather than by gender alone. When we look at the ways young women are "doing" feminism we can see that they offer new frameworks for understanding social movements and social change appropriate to our times. The following section will look more specifically at what some young women are "doing" with feminism by considering examples of activism and theory such as personal narrative, cultural production, body and sexual politics, and redefining gender. These examples will show, simultaneously, the key aspects of third-wave feminism and its methods of resistance.

What the Third Wave(s) Is/Are

Third-wave feminist scholarship is dedicated to the project of locating ourselves as feminists, academics, teachers, students, and activists. This means being as clear as possible about where we are coming from. For the authors of this chapter, a bit of self-identification is in order. Allyson Mitchell is a teacher, academic, lesbian, middle-class, white, able-bodied artist and size/body image activist. Lara Karaian is an anti-globalization and poverty activist, and a queer perpetual student doing her PhD in women's studies. She identifies as a woman of colour who experiences white-skin privilege. She is an able-bodied, struggling student with a middle-class background. We both experience a great deal of cultural capital (recognizing that we possess a knowledge of available middle-class resources—how to move through the world in a way that allows us access to privileges—even though we may not have its economic status). These positionings via race, class, sexuality, ability, and so on, have influenced and shaped this chapter and how it is constructed. The emphasis of this chapter is also dictated by the constraints of space and subject matter. We would have liked to have done a more in-depth analysis of the third wave's relationship to the second wave, an outline of young feminists' involvement in the anti-globalization and anti-war movements, and a discussion of young feminism outside of the North American context. Both of us are dedicated to various young feminist activist projects and we teach women's studies to undergraduate students. Along with our gal pal Lisa Bryn Rundle, we edited *Turbo Chicks: Talking Young Feminism*, one of the first collections of writings on feminism by young women from across Canada.

We think it's also important to outline what we mean by "youth" with regards to third-wave feminism. In this chapter we refuse to define "young" feminism by age. Does it start at 14? Does it end at 35? We try to maintain an ambiguous relationship to the membership of "young" or "third wave" so that it includes politics and aesthetics as much as it does generational positioning. We take our cue from Riot Grrrl, an anti-masculinist punk rock (some call it the original) girl-power movement that was active in North America in the 1990s. Riot Grrrl made it clear in their zines and publications that their revolution was open to all girls regardless of age and other identities. We find this approach to who belongs in the category "young feminism" or the "third wave" to be more useful than an attempt to create boundaries.

As we understand it, a simple transition from youth to adulthood does not exist in terms of movements from irrationality to rationality or from simplicity to complexity (Valentine et al., 1998: 4). Youth is a culturally, historically, and personally relative identity. The experiences, socio-economic status, personality, and age of the physical body and/or the "social body" all contribute to whether an individual is considered to be a "youth" by society, and by him or herself (James, 1986: 157). While feminism is old news, it is also "forever young." That is, young women have always been active in the practices of feminism. They have been at the centre of feminist organization in all of feminism's supposed waves and have been involved in fighting against slavery, in fighting for women's right to vote, and in insisting on access to birth control. For young women, being a part of feminism is not a new phenomenon. But there have been some changes in feminist theory, organization, and cultural expression. The ambiguity of the term "youth" or "young" is illustrated in our own use (and avoidance) of it in this chapter. Simplifying contemporary feminism to youth makes it easier to talk about … but then again the third wave is all about complicating feminism.

Third-Wave Resistance: What Does Fighting the Good Fight Look Like?

Third-wave feminists ask, What constitutes resistance and activism? How effective are these kinds of resistances? Who does this resistance benefit? All of the examples that we will outline in the following sections discuss how young women are doing feminism, enacting theories of resistance, and engaging with the above questions. Resistances in the form of personal narrative, cultural production, body politics, and trans (ex)inclusion are some of the areas that will be developed more fully.

Young feminists recognize that activism can range from the very personal to the institutional, taking up and expanding upon the second-wave mantra, "the personal is political." Civil disobedience, letter writing, street protests, culture jamming, direct action, public speaking, and education are some of the more recognizable or traditional forms of resistance. The third-wave participates in these forms of action in ways similar to those feminists who have come before us. It also questions many of these forms of action/resistance and adds to the list of possible tactics.

Third-wave feminists argue for a diversity of tactics, taking up Audre Lorde's inspirational sentiment that "the master's tools will never dismantle the master's house" (1984: 112). This means that they question some previous efforts that rely on "legitimate" strategies of resistance such as political lobbying or legal strategy. Third-wavers do not reject these strategies outright. Rather, they argue that second-wave feminists have tended to overestimate the efficacy of these methods.

Law No one can deny that the law is an important tool for change. Nevertheless, reliance upon it is problematized by young feminists who argue that particular equality-seeking movements are being forced to restructure their demands to fit within a legal framework rather than having the law change to accommodate the particular needs of their struggle. In the case of gay marriage for instance, it is argued that the use of the courts as a means of recognizing and legitimizing the union of two same-sex individuals has forced gays and lesbians to reproduce normative heterosexual relationships and to thus lose some of the transgressive and radical potential that gay identity has had when it comes to challenging notions of the family and ideas of monogamy and the nuclear family form. A great deal of time and energy on behalf of the gay and lesbian community and many third-wave feminists (queer identified or not) has gone into this issue recently. Many feminist activists reject marriage as the key issue around which to rally for change. Some also criticize the resources being spent in the courts on this issue at the expense of others. A diversity-of-tactics approach to resistance de-centres the law, not only questioning the effectiveness of the law but also rejecting it as one of the most legitimate means with which to resist. Instead, the third wave may place a greater emphasis on activism that works outside of state apparatus and gets to the heart of the communities within which the women themselves live. Institutional forms of resistance are not abandoned, rather these forms of resistance may seek to more actively subvert from within. For example, Teens Educating and Challenging Homophobia (TEACH) is a group of youth educators that resists homophobia and heterosexual privilege, both in the school system and beyond. The third wave also takes up and argues for actions such as the squats that have taken place in Toronto, Vancouver, Montreal, and Sudbury by anti-poverty activists. These actions, usually cracked down on by police, involve the reclaiming of abandoned housing by third-wave, anti-poverty activists and the homeless in an effort to publicize and meet the needs of those most impoverished in our cities. Given the fact that single mothers and elderly women make up the greatest number of poor in Canada, these actions are one way third-wavers actively address the issue of the feminization of poverty as identified by the second wave. They also move beyond gender and complicate the roots of this poverty by considering factors such as the inherent racism in changing immigration laws and cuts to social spending on mental health and disability.

Sexual orientation human rights issues and struggles against poverty do not necessarily originate within feminism, but many feminists have joined these struggles, sometimes because of direct connections to gender, such as lesbians' and trans-women's rights and the feminization of poverty. At the same time, these social movements have incorporated some feminist strategies and values. It is not productive to define the ways in which these examples of resistance are feminist. It is more useful to see these struggles as examples of the complex identification embraced by third-wavers.

Pornography   What is important to recognize when it comes to third-wave resistance is that some of its interventions are equally threatening not only to the state but also to other feminists. For example, the creation of alternative pornography is a form of activism taken up by third-wave feminists in response to dominant notions of femininity and sexuality imposed upon them by patriarchy … and by some second-wave radical feminists. Sites such as www.SSSpread.com and thatstrangegirl.com offer a different kind of porn to combat mainstream representations meant solely for the male gaze. In doing so, these third-wavers meet with the resistance of some second-wave feminists who argue that any porn is harmful to women, ignoring third-wavers' belief that alternative porn and other means of resisting mainstream representations of women's raced, classed, and sized bodies can be more liberating than destructive. Additional means of resistance to normative representations of femininity may include graffiti on public advertising that idealizes and sells, along with their products, white, emaciated women's bodies; alternative media representations in art, film, or zines; and performance art/activism such as that of Pretty Porky and Pissed Off (see the discussion of PPPO'd in the "Rethinking Bodies" section later in the chapter.)

Personal Choices   Third-wave resistance can be as personal and as private as coming out to your parents, challenging friends when they make sexist or racist jokes, or taking Wen Do self-defence classes. Third-wave resistance may even include the refusal to shop! When Western leaders urge us to save our faltering economy by hitting the malls, claiming that consumption is good, third-wavers respond by endorsing and participating in "Buy Nothing Day." Celebrated in more than 50 countries, individuals opt not to spend any money for 23 hours, enjoying instead "pranks, parades, street parties, credit-card cutups." Young feminists, a key target market in our global economy, also actively resist the reality that there are more malls than high schools in the United States by recycling clothing, arranging clothing swaps, shopping at thrift stores, and refusing to support the slave-labour practices of chains like the Gap.

Theorizing Experience: Resisting through Personal Narrative

A great deal of third-wave resistance takes place in the writings, particularly the personal narratives, of young feminists. A personal narrative can be told through autobiographical writing, manifesto, confession, ethnography, oral tradition, and testimonial. Third-wave feminist theory and activism are made up of a variety of these forms of writing and are found in edited collections, zines, and websites. The processes of self-exploration and sharing are transformative and proactive for both the writer and the audience, whose perceptions are likely to be expanded. If activism is about education, interruption, and ideological change, then these forms of writing constitute activism. Feminists of the third wave believe in the importance of their life experiences, and it has been argued that their individual stories collectively tell the tale of larger social phenomena (Siegel, 1997).

Some have argued that the third wave is actually birthed by a textual community (Siegel, 1997). For almost a decade, collections of writings by young women have contributed largely to shaping a new generation of feminists. Some of these edited collections include Barbara Findlen's *Listen Up: Voices from the Next Feminist Generation* (1995), Rebecca Walker's *To Be Real: Telling the Truth and Changing the Face of Feminism* (1995), Jennifer Baumgardner and Amy Richard's *Manifesta: Young Women, Feminism and the Future* (2000), Ophira Edut's *Body Outlaws: Young Women Write About Body Image and Identity* (2000), Lynn Crosbie's *Click!: Becoming Feminists* (1997), *Fireweed's Revolution Grrrl Style* issue (1997), and more recently *Turbo Chicks: Talking Young Feminisms* (2001), *Canadian Woman Studies'* issue on young women and activists (2001), *Colonize This: Young Women of Color on Today's Feminism* (2002), and *Yentl's Revenge: Young Jewish Women Write About Today's Feminism* (2002). These are formally bound and legitimized accounts of young women talking about, theorizing, documenting, and archiving their experiences and struggles with feminism. In most every essay, poem, and illustration within these books, young women are insisting on positioning themselves within the texts, writing in the first person and not even pretending to be objective. This is a significant and influential body of work, where young women look for connections and context to their feminism. These anthologies helped create the third wave at the same time as young women themselves were developing it. Through these accounts, young women have made connections between geographical locations, levels of academic experience, and positions of privilege and oppression. By actively seeking connections with the works of other feminists and social justice activists, third-wavers make links between their experiences and the social and institutional processes and trends that shape their lives. For example, the stories about family dynamics, hip hop culture, and hybrid identity negotiations in *Colonize This!*, although rooted in the personal, extend to the public and the political. Stories bring these elements together to create a dialogue about the continuing effects of colonization, racism, and imperialism.

It could be argued that the third wave's use of personal narratives comes out of challenges posed by black feminists such as bell hooks and Patricia Hill Collins in the 1980s and 1990s that critiqued the second wave for its inaccessible academic writing and style. The third wave's proliferation of autobiographical writing can be seen as a form of resistance to inaccessible writing. To some third-wavers it is a political tactic to write in a way that everyone can understand and be inspired or excited by. Black feminist thought, then, set the tone for new feminist theory, politics, and history (Dua and Robertson, 1999). Feminist subjectivity, as it informs personal and situated forms of writing, can be a very powerful tool to make feminism a movement that new generations and larger groups of people can relate to.

Although some may see the inclusion of personal narrative as a strength of young feminism, others see it as a weakness, regarding it as self-indulgent, unchallengeable, and theoretically weak. This is an unfair accusation if we consider how feminist academic theory has influenced young feminism. Ideas about standpoint theory, identity politics, and postmodernism have positively informed how third-wave feminists practise, process, and write their feminism. For example, many of the accounts in these collections are by women who talk about their experiences in women's studies classes in which feminist theory has been a major influence on them as feminists. Others reveal how postmodern feminism has encouraged them to be subjective and speak from experience to avoid universalizing and appropriating. They understand the significance of sharing and validating their experiences in order to comprehend the differences between women, rather than attempting to come to some false common ground. Postmodern feminist methodology insists on a reflexive theoretical practice. Young feminists use personal narratives to understand not only how the personal is political but also how the *personal* is *theoretical*. The result of this theorizing is what Gina Dent (1995) refers to in her essay "Missionary Position" in *To Be Real* as a "collective benefit." Deborah Siegel (1997), in her essay about third-wave theory, understands the anthologies listed above as "disclosures not of personal lives but the political violences inflicted on whole communities."

Zines and Zine Culture   Another prominent place where we can find examples of young feminists writing personal narratives as a means to theorize their experiences is in zines. Zines began as photocopied pamphlets that were often diaristic accounts of daily lives. Zine culture is an important vehicle for feminists in the third wave to express themselves, disseminate their ideas, and create community. This accessible form of publishing uses fast and cheap photocopying—authors avoid jumping through hoops to get their ideas published. As well, many young women are posting their zines on the web. You can read more about zines and their significance to young feminists in the section on cultural production below. It is sufficient to say here that zines, in their form and content, represent an important part of how young feminists use their lives in a kind of emergency storytelling to understand their politics, feminist or otherwise.

This returns us to one of the basic strengths of the third wave, which is to expand the idea that the personal is political. An excellent example of this type of theorizing experience can be found in the writing of Emmanuelle Pantin. Pantin tells how she used ideas in introductory political theory texts to better understand the traumas of her childhood. She talks about how silenced she felt, how angry she was, and how she applies her new understandings of her own experience to larger social corruptions such as homophobia, racism, nationalism, and classism. Pantin claims that understanding how these theories work in terms of lived lives represents how she came to understand the source of her pain—systemic power relations. Her experience changed from that of an isolated individual, as it was articulated within the form of her zine writing, to an understanding of her context and connections placed in hierarchical power relations. This is an example of how the third wave has learned from earlier feminist critiques of impersonal or falsely objective theories and made them more real and applicable by inserting, recognizing, and using their subjectivities and subsequently making the personal a part of feminist theory and action.

This part of young women's feminist theorizing and activism can be called synthesis. This defining characteristic of the third wave involves examining what works or doesn't work from pre-existing feminist thought and combining these elements with new theories and tactics. The use of narrative is a key tool for resisting, reclaiming, and engaging in dialogue with others, be they third-wavers and other generations of feminists.

Third-Wave Resistance through Cultural Production

Third-wave feminist cultural production goes beyond the written word, linking art and activism together in an effort to resist economic, cultural, racial, and gender-related inequalities. It is important to look at cultural "production" rather than cultural "consumption" when examining young feminisms. Carly Stasko discusses the importance of girls creating their own brand of feminist culture in "Action Grrrls in the Dream Machine" in the anthology *Turbo Chicks* (2001). Stasko uses pop culture material such as television and glossy magazines to make collages that illustrate the necessity for a re-evaluation of mass media. Her discussion of play as a necessary component of feminist cultural production is significant. Stasko stresses the importance of engaging with one's surroundings through cultural production rather than simply consuming it or reacting to it. With the co-optation of feminist ideologies by corporations via the Spice Girls or *Sex and the City*, Do It Yourself (DIY) anti-capitalist third-wave production is crucial.

Performing/Enacting Feminism   Young women of the third wave enact their feminism through a variety of methods of cultural production. Zine-making, songwriting, painting, sculpture, graffiti, radio, music, sticker-making, guerilla theatre, film, video, dance, and comedy are some of the types of cultural participation in which young feminists engage.

DIY Feminism   These kinds of resistance through cultural production often employ a DIY strategy. DIY politics, born out of a Riot Grrrl response to sexism in punk rock scenes, was used by girls to carve out a culture for themselves. Riot Grrrls' "learn-by-doing" approach used the media as a tool to strategically grow their movement but also reinforced a politic that commands and conveys an urgency for people to create their own culture and not to rely on the mainstream to do it for them. One riot grrrl claims that "at the heart of Riot Grrrl is the empowerment that you can do it yourself—in fact, you have to." Another describes the movement thus: "The gist of it is the strength of standing on your own and taking action" (Pedersen, 1996: 182). DIY is about people creating their own culture, partly out of economic necessity and partly out of political positioning; we should tell our own stories by any means necessary—and before someone else does it for us. Making a zine that talks about how to report a rape, how to organize a women's self-defence collective, how to address white privilege, or how to use a sound board, are all direct actions that challenge the ideological environment we live in. All are done within a third-wave DIY politic.

Young feminists use DIY cultural production tactics as a way to open up spaces where we can learn and challenge the hegemonic ideologies within our society. The efforts of artists like Miranda July increase the accessibility of women to film and video. Her networking project called "The Big Miss Moviola Project" is an excellent example. For this, July created a type of zine chain letter of women and girl-made movies. She sent out a call and asked people to submit their short works. In return, she compiled them on tapes containing 10 "lady-made" films and sent it back to the original contributor. July initiated this project in order to address what she saw as a lack of access to women-made films in the film department at her art school. The purpose was to disseminate the films to a larger audience—in this case beyond the circle of friends that the films would have been shown to without formal distribution. The result was a space to share the ideas of liberatory cultural expressions for young women. The politics of Riot Grrrl and DIY informed July's practice as a cultural producer.

After almost a decade of action and resistance, Riot Grrrl has a herstory and elders whose cultural artifacts, such as zines and films, have been archived, legitimized, and even commodified. What exists is a transformed feminist community that has been shaken up by the women who were at the forefront of this movement. Riot Grrrl has since gone underground and evolved into other forms in order to slip from the hands of mainstream media. The cultural productions of the third wave have strong affiliations with the Riot Grrrl movement, a movement that encouraged girls to tell their stories, claim their space, and crack their jokes—even if this meant writing directly on their bodies. DIY cultural artifacts are one example of how individuals communicate and proliferate shared ideologies and thus influence others. Third-wave politics creates community; it is about relationships, never only about individuals. An individual's political act or cultural production invariably links groups of people in political affiliation.

Lesbian graffiti is one type of cultural expression from which a young feminist community emerges. Understanding graffiti in a manner that gives it the power to create community and record history shows us how individual women and communities of women resist their invisibility. This sort of understanding validates a form of cultural production that usually exists under the radar of everyday perception. That is, someone who doesn't affiliate with or claim membership to any of these communities may not notice or understand the significance of its markers or presence. The lesbian (and other feminist) graffiti we see in our neighbourhoods, on bus ads, and in bathroom stalls, are acts of resistance against poverty, unemployment, the processes of gentrification, racism, and sexual conformity. Its origins lie in a number of subcultures such as lesbian, feminist, punk rock, Riot Grrrl, and youth.

However, we can't attribute all of the cultural production of the third wave to Riot Grrrl. As Kearney suggests, we must look to "other politicized ideologies and forms of cultural practice which also influence ... radical female culture" (1997: 217). Because of what the mainstream and the media define as "cultural production" and what sells in stories of "cultural producers" or even "radical subcultures," queer, trans folk, women of colour, and dis(en)abled women are often erased. We hear about the "radical" subcultures of the indie filmmaking scene or largely white zine shows, but whole other groups of people exist outside of what media deems newsworthy or what art councils deem fundable or what academics deem definable. Despite these barriers, young feminist continue to grow their own cultural productions with or without these legitimizations.

The Turtle Gals, for example, is a performance ensemble of three native woman, Michelle St. John, Monique Mojica, and Jani Lauzon. The trio blends song, dance, text, video, and comedy in order to address genocide and racism, both historical and internalized. True to third-wave tactics, the Turtle Gals employ a sharp comedic style to uncover and highlight social injustices. The three actors reclaim vaudeville as an offshoot of Indian medicine shows. They use Marx Brothers shtick, cartoon characters, and media clichés from mainstream culture to illuminate their politics. Their combination of anger, guilt, comedy, pop culture references, and memory is striking and effective. Their work is an example of political synthesis: It integrates critiques of racism, sexism, homophobia, colonialism, and anti-Semitism. The result is empowering for them as performers as well as their audiences.

> Several years ago, we gathered to talk about race, colour and sexuality. We told stories and talked about what could lie beyond the popular culture's imagery of Native women, i.e. Disney's *Pocahontas*. Out of the conversation emerged a recurring theme: scrubbing. Either we, or someone we knew had at some point tried to scrub off or bleach out their colour. This realization, whet our appetite to explore the manifestations of the internalized racism we carry. Coupled with our common theatre vocabulary in creating original and ensemble work, we felt a shared urge to form our own performance collective. (**www.turtlegals.com**)

Another example is the Toronto-based break dance troupe She Bang! This group of young women dances to address sexism in hip hop and other youth cultures. They also have a mandate to teach and empower other young women how to break dance their way out of the margins.

We can look to cultural production as a way of seeing, hearing, and tangibly touching how young feminists are "doing" feminism that is exciting and vibrant and often confrontational. Third-wave cultural production is an active political undertaking because it first identifies a lack of feminist cultural production and then functions to create alternatives for and by young feminists. Young feminists then are resisting mainstream cultural production through a diversity of artistic tactics.

Rethinking Bodies

Our body and our embodiments[1] are one of our most personal experiences. At the same time, our bodies, women's bodies in particular, are held up to hyper-scrutiny both at a micro or private level and at a macro or a public level. On the micro level, we survey ourselves through processes such as careful weigh-ins, calorie counting, plucking, shaving, and hair straightening and dying. We worry about skin tone and shading and have insecurities about toe and nose lengths and sizes. We scowl self-critically into the mirror while simultaneously spewing feminist thought and theory. We "diet talk" and dream about a carb-free, temptationless world while discussing union activism with our friends. While we competitively compare the size and tone of our butts, we critique second-wave feminists for their lack of inclusivity. How we experience ourselves and how we experience the contradictions within our feminisms is through our complex bodies.

Women's bodies are also scrutinized at the macro or public level. One way that this happens is through media. The bodies that appear to us through the media are white, thin, able-bodied, and heterosexualized. At the same time, women's bodies have been culturally constructed as a site of sin, corruption, and uncleanliness. There is an absence of the bodies of women of colour, poor bodies, bodies with disabilities, and fat bodies. When we do see these "other" bodies it is often through stereotypes that reflect racism, sizism, and profound misunderstandings about ability. Through the media, women's bodies become homogenized. That is, there seems only one (or very few) ways to be "beautiful," "normal," and "sexy," thus "acceptable," "loved," and "worthy." Women are expected (and expect themselves) to meet these criteria. As the media and social values dictate our bodies, women are preoccupied with trying to live up to impossible standards.

The body is not merely personal, it is a place where broader social phenomena are addressed in relation to power, autonomy, racism, misogyny, homophobia, and ableism. The body is always political. For many third-wave feminists, the body has been an entry point to feminist consciousness and action. Experiences of "freedoms and gains" made by the women's movement, and the lived realities that may contradict these supposed freedoms, politicize our bodies and our fluid and opposing experiences of them. The body is a place where young women connect feminist theory with practice. This is not a new phenomenon for feminism. However, it has been noted by Amelia Richards in her essay "Body Image: Third Wave Feminism's Issue?" (2000) that there is a change in the politics around

---

1   Embodiments: If you define subjectivity as who we "are," then embodiments are how we "be." That is, how we define, explore, and present our various identities and subjectivities. An identity can be embodied through clothing, body language, gestures, actions, expressions, and even the objects we possess. In her book *Volatile Bodies*, feminist theorist Elizabeth Grosz (1994) argues that, contrary to the assumptions in many theorists' work on the body as a surface to be inscribed upon, there is no prediscursive body. She claims that the body is constructed through race, sex, size, ability, and so on.

the body from second-wave feminism to third-wave feminism. The focus has moved from an external to a more internal spotlight on issues around the body.

The second wave concerns itself with violence and abuses, access to jobs, and reproductive choices. Though these issues are still concerns in the third wave, there have been institutional gains in these specific areas through law, legislation, and policy. Although there have been achievements in the public sphere, women struggle continuously with their relationships to their bodies. Feminists such as Joan Jacobs Brumberg, in her study of young women and body image (2000), have noted that the more social and economic freedoms people experience—the greater the restrictions on their bodies. In addition, the more global economic and social forces make their mark, the more all cultures are expected to measure up to white North American standards of beauty and acceptance. Our standards of body size do not exist cross-culturally or even cross-racially. For example, in the Caribbean, larger bodies—butts and breasts in particular—are seen as desirable, valuable, and attractive. However, with the proliferation of North American culture there is evidence that the body standards in other places are conforming to North American "proportions." Brumberg exemplifies this by discussing how women's experiences of "gains" in the public sphere are reflected in fashion restrictions: We see how tighter jeans, plunging necklines, and higher heels have permeated all corners of the globe.

Although fashion can be a place to reclaim feminist power and play with sexuality, it can also be a call to arms against the "standards" that dictate desirable and acceptable femininity. This is particularly true when feminists working against globalization have shown us how the dieting, fashion, and beauty industries work to oppress people not only in North America but in the so-called Third World, linking the struggles of Western women's right to shop for clothing that doesn't only fit a size six to those of the exploitation and policing of the bodies that make clothing and diet foods. In numerous different ways, then, bodies have become sites of political struggle and the redefinition of meanings about what is normal and what is not.

Body Outlaws   In her book, *Body Outlaws: Young Women Write About Body Image and Identity*, Ophira Edut (2000) argues that there is a great need to provide women with safe spaces to explore their own experiences and struggles with their bodies as a way of healing and empowerment. In her outline of body activism, she describes women who reject and disrupt discourses of beauty as "body outlaws." By "breaking the laws" of what is ascribed to our bodies, women contradict and challenge societal values and work against the interests of industries that capitalize on women's uncomfortable relationships with their bodies. Edut explains that women who resist do a kind of "shock therapy" when they openly reject the norm. By showing, through their bodies, how they exist in many shapes, sizes, colours, and abilities, young feminists articulate their politics. They are doing what Nomy Lamm (2001) describes in her essay "It's a Big Fat Revolution" in the anthology *Listen Up: Voices From the Next Feminist Generation*, as the process of using what is available (fashion for example) in a way that subverts and challenges dominant values. Lamm's politics are informed by her subjectivity as a Jewish, queer, dis(en)abled, fat woman.

Pretty Porky and Pissed Off   The fat body is a specific site where women are punished for exceeding the boundaries of femininity. The fat body disrupts these values and norms, while at the same time the individual remains influenced, prescribed, and implicated by these norms. Pretty Porky and Pissed Off (PPPO'd) is an example of how young women have used their bodies as a way to resist oppressive power structures. PPPO'd is a fat activist group that uses cultural production in the form of performance art to educate and serve up their own brand of advocacy for size acceptance. This group of "tubbies with 'tude" publicly defies stereotypes of fat women as incapable of being fashionable, sexy, smart, or active. They choose performance-based activism and humour as a way to challenge notions about the body. Sometimes this means embodying the very stereotypes they are resisting as a way of addressing and undressing them as the falsehoods they are. Rather than shrinking or hiding behind loosely fitting clothing, they perform their bodies as BIG. They dress in pink fun fur and feather boas. They teach workshops, publish zines and stickers, stage street interventions at trendy shops that don't carry their sizes, and they dance (a lot). The politics behind their work is well thought out and quite sophisticated. Pretty Porky and Pissed Off is all about alleviating and re-assigning shame. It is a *shame* that the media doesn't represent a variety of body sizes and shapes. It is a *shame* that fat women are encouraged to take up less public space. Instead they should be bursting at the seams and being applauded on stage. It is a *shame* that eating sweet and delicious foods is such a fetishized process that women feel they have to hide it, subsequently developing unhealthy relationships with food. Pretty Porky and Pissed Off says let's take that cake out of the closet and put it on the dance floor where it belongs!

Pretty Porky and Pissed Off is an excellent example of third-wave activists using the body. They look at the intersections of oppression and privilege in terms of sized bodies. They make the connections between obesity and poverty, a sizist medical establishment, globalization and junk food, and low self-esteem and the capitalist placement of guilt on the fat body in a sort of millennial moral tale. Women concerned with issues pertaining to their bodies and their experiences as sexualized, raced, classed, gendered, (dis)enabled, and fat are central to third-wave theorizing as well as organizing.

Rethinking Gender

Third-wave feminism actively resists the idea that there "good" feminists and "bad" feminists.

Referring back to our discussion about authenticity, there is no "correct" way to be a third-wave feminist. And, as young feminists have played with—there is no correct way to be female, feminine, or a "woman."

Sandra Lee Bartky describes femininity as "an artifice, an achievement" and agrees with Judith Butler's claim that femininity is performative, that it is "a mode of enacting and reenacting received gender norms which surface as so many styles of the flesh" (1990: 95). But, for Bartky, normative femininity can only ever be seen as gender conformity. The disciplinary project of femininity, as she sees it, is a process by which the ideal body of femininity is constructed and one that nearly every women fails to reproduce to some degree or another (100). Many third-wave feminists, including women with disabilities, women of colour, and fat women trouble the ideal and narrowly defined feminine body while at the same time recognizing the need to complicate the conclusion that femininity is solely imposed upon women by disciplinary structures. They argue that Bartky's analysis is lacking in any conception of female self-determination and agency since, according to Bartky, there is no way, for female femininity to be rendered a political or disruptive performance.

Third-wave feminism wrestles with the very dilemma of simultaneously destroying and reclaiming traditional notions of femininity, arguing that that we can reinsert agency and self-determination by recoding, reclaiming, misappropriating, and re-appropriating femininity for ourselves. Young feminists reject the idea that if you wear makeup, shave your legs/pits/'stache, wear heels/minis/tight-tittie-Ts, then you're a dupe of patriarchy, and definitely not a good feminist. Leah Rumack, in her article "Lipstick" in *Turbo Chicks*, recalls how in certain feminist communities she had to defend herself for simultaneously owning an eyelash comb and calling herself a feminist. Like her, third-wavers argue that any standard of beauty that is defined by others is oppressive and that includes judgments made by other feminists about what a good feminist looks like. Now she writes "with the growing cross-breeding of feminist thought into a wider arena of gender studies, with all its trannies and drag queens, the new message seems to be that its okay to be fabulous, as long as you're ironic about it (at least a little), and that beauty is okay as long as there's a wider, more active definition of what it is" (Rumack in Mitchell et al., 2001: 97).

This idea of being ironic and widening the notion of femininity has been taken up by third-wavers drawing on Judith Butler's theory of gender as performative, particularly Butler's now-famous notion that "gender parody reveals that the original identity after which gender fashions itself is an imitation without an origin" (Butler, 1990: 120). Butler uses drag queens as an example of gender performance that subverts any notion of a "true" gender identity, given that "In imitating gender, drag implicitly reveals the imitative structure of gender itself—as well as its contingency" (120). Butler goes on to claim that, "[j]ust as bodily surfaces are enacted *as* the natural, so these surfaces can become the site of dissonant and denaturalized performance that reveals the performative status of the natural itself" (1997: 126). In addition to this, there is also the movement within the third wave to articulate "femme" as a gender experience that is not tied to biological sex. Chloe Brushwood Rose and Anna Camilleri, the editors of *Brazen Femme: Queering Femininity* explore this issue and ask, What makes femme different from femininity? What would it mean to be a femme and not a woman? What would it mean to be a femme outside of a lesbian framework? What is it that femmes have in common? Although they offer the following inroad to what femme might be, they do so without claiming this as a closed definition of what a femme is or locating femme in one place, in one time, or in one tidy package (2002: 12). They write, "femme might be described as 'femininity gone wrong'— bitch, slut, nag, whore, cougar, dyke, or brazen hussy. Femme is the trappings of femininity gone awry, gone to town, gone to the dogs. Femininity is a demand placed on female bodies and femme is the danger of a body read female or inappropriately feminine. We are not good girls—perhaps we are not girls at all" (13). Femme is complicated by maleness, by racist queers and racism, by transsexuality, by politics of fat, by class, by age, and by institutionalization. It transcends the binaries of male/female and gay/straight (13).

Femininity as complicated by race is taken up by Joan Morgan, the author of *When Chickenheads Come Home to Roost: A Hip Hop Feminist Breaks It Down*. She writes about imposed prejudices experienced through stereotyped roles for women such as the "SOUTHERNBELL" and the "STRONGBLACKWOMAN." Both of these identities are based on what she calls the prejudices of the oppressor and the complex amalgamation of myths that surround white and black female identity. These are myths that she rejects for their historically racist underpinnings. She takes up and celebrates those ideas of femininity that she feels she has been denied. She resists those aspects of femininity that have been forced upon her, the myth of the black woman as superhuman, for example. She considers this myth to be both empowering and harmful in that it leads black women to wrongly believe that they can carry the weight of the world (2000: 103-104). Her turn to vulnerability is an argument for the transgressive power of femininity. She claims that it's time black women grant themselves humanity and not impose upon themselves superpower status.

Masculine Femininities   In the end, the third wave strives for less restrictive gender roles that allow for the recognition of the transgressive potential of female femininity but also alternative masculinities such as female masculinities and masculine femininities. It is with this understanding that third-wave feminism posits the question, Where does masculinity fit into the feminist movement? Third-wave feminism recognizes that masculinity extends beyond the male body and is constructed by female as well as male bodies. Judith Halberstam (1998) argues that masculinity is multiple: "Far from just being about men, the idea of masculinity engages, inflects and shapes everyone" (14). Like Halberstam, third-wave feminism takes up the belief that masculinity is produced by, for, and within women (15). This gender variance then can be used to question the dominance/submission power relations between men and women as presumed by patriarchy. Taking up the project of alternative masculinities helps the third wave "think through the messy identifications that make up contemporary power relations around gender, race and class" (18). Alternative masculinity re-presents masculinity as not always signifying power. In fact, it may undermine masculine authority by drawing attention to its performative nature and its ability to exist separately from misogyny.

Ana Marie Cox, Freya Johnson, Analee Newitz, and Jillian Sandell write in "Masculinity Without Men: Women Reconciling Feminism and Male Identification" that, "our relationship to gender—both our masculinity and our femininity—is … inflected by our understanding that such identities are socially constructed and, by implication, subject to change" (1997: 199). They argue that "Whereas second wave feminism taught us to dissociate femininity from disempowerment, perhaps third wave feminism can promote the idea of masculinity without oppression."

The performativity of gender, either of femininity or masculinity, is seen in drag queen and drag king performances. A drag king, according to Halberstam, is "a female (usually) who dresses up in recognizably male costume and performs theatrically in that costume" (232). This practice helps break up the mainstream definition of masculinity as nonperformative—that it is in fact as artificial and as open to interrogation as femininity is. Sarah Smith (2002) in, "A Cock of One's Own: Getting a Firm Grip of Feminist Sexual Power" in *Jane Sexes it Up*, shows how Judith Butler in *Gender Trouble* explains that masculinity and femininity only *appear* to be coherent sets of sex-bounded characteristics but that in actuality, stable gender roles are created and reproduced through heteropatriarchal institutions such as the family, the media, science, and government (304–305).

Transgender Politics and/Is Third-Wave Feminism

Can feminism see more than two genders? Can I? If I already know that there are boys with cunts and chicks with dicks...and people with both.... If I already know that man and woman are impossible to define...then how can I draw strength in a movement that relies on the existence of, and difference between, boys and girls?

(Cat Pyne in *Turbo Chicks*, 112)

First- and second-wave feminist thought has very much relied on a unified category of "woman"—one whose boundaries are not fluid and whose identity is therefore stable. Postmodernism and deconstruction have therefore been perceived by some as posing a threat to women by leaving them defenceless—that they are no longer able to use this identity as a solid base from which to have their voices heard. And, as Riki Anne Wilchins

(2002) says, "some feminists want to know what's in your pants and how long it has been there. Everyone's gender is subject to change in their lifetime... just like everything else about them. This scares patriarchs and feminists alike."

Third-wave feminism complicates "women" by recognizing that it isn't a unified or "victimized" category and that power relations exist between women born women and women identified women. Transgendered and transsexual persons who come before the law may have a disruptive potential with regards to the categorical imperatives of sex and the binary male/female revealing not simply the privilege of some men over some women, but some women over other women. This is not a "fictionalized hierarchy" as some anti–trans women would contend (Croson, 2001). Rather, it is a necessary confrontation of the understanding of power that says patriarchy and sexual norms are constitutive of women's oppression.

Eleanor MacDonald argues that "Feminists ... struggle over changing the meaning of what it is to be a woman, expanding the boundaries of possibilities to allow for greater freedom in women's (and men's) lives. Transgender politics, on the other hand, is often about how the categories of, and the boundary between, male and female, or masculine and feminine, are set at all" (1998: 8). The boundaries between boys and girls, men and women, have to this point acted as the basis of identity-based movements, so one can see how troubling it can be when third-wave and queer feminists question these boundaries by asking, Who is a woman? Who is a feminist? With these questions, the concerns and projects of third-wave feminism and the transgendered movement overlap. What MacDonald challenges feminism to do and what third-wave feminism is actively taking up, is the need "to move beyond identity as the basis of social movement politics and into new exploration of the ethical bases of alliances and formation of communities" (10).

Within both the third wave and the transgendered movement, there is a diverse group of people striving for self-definition. Moving away from defining feminism as solely an identity-based political movement means that the third wave is making connections and working though the lived complexities of a variety of women's lives, including those of transgendered folk. MacDonald claims that "Transgender identity is about identity experienced as problematic; the experience of being transgender problematizes the relationship of the self to the body, and the self to others. In doing so, it also problematizes issues of identity boundaries, stability and coherence" (5). It is the use of these boundaries as bases of a theory of gender oppression that the third wave questions. The third wave also recognizes that, as MacDonald argues, many transgendered experiences are paradoxical in their disruption of identity and simultaneously emphasize an internal sense of authenticity that they experience and struggle to embody. Third-wave feminism has to grapple with the relationship between transgendered individuals' integrated and authentic selves at a time when identity, particularly gender identity, is being deconstructed by postmodernism and feminism. This entails a recognition that power dynamics are complex across and within gender categories and relations. Third-wave feminism takes up the theory and activism of transgendered folk within the feminist community as a means to continue to work through and organize around this lived complexity.

The relationship between feminism and the transgendered movement has been fraught with tensions. "Feminists have denounced transgendered people as dangerous to feminism, depoliticized the experiences of transgendered people, or celebrated the transgendered identity as emblematic of the subversive character of feminist postmodern theory" (MacDonald, 1998: 3). Transgendered women have often been portrayed as threats to women-only "safe spaces" such as music festivals and rape crisis centres while transgendered men are treated as dupes of patriarchy and as traitors to their sex (3). Even within third-wave feminism, debates ensue around how to think about identities and politics. Third-wavers and transgendered folk contribute to a more complex understanding of oppressions, particularly "women's" oppression and gender relations and experiences. Third wave celebrates the diversity that transgendered individuals force feminism to acknowledge as well as second-wave feminism's dismissiveness of the transgendered as gendered and oppressed individuals.

Emi Koyama, 27, self-describes as a "multi issue, social-justice, slut" who synthesizes "feminist, Asian, survivor, dyke, queer, sex-worker, slut intersex, genderqueer, and crip politics." Emi takes on the arguments of those who defend women-only spaces and not women-born-women-only spaces:

> I take some knowledge and wisdom from Latina feminism and theories about the politics of borders. Any time we try to draw a clear boundary around gender we end up cutting somebody's flesh. It's not that they are in the borderlands, it's that the borders are arbitrarily drawn on top of their bodies. I am not one of those people who want to get rid of women-only space, but I think any attempt to draw a clear boundary and legitimize that boundary as the official one would be problematic. I may not feel comfortable with somebody who has a penis; I may not feel comfortable with somebody who has white skin, but I don't have the entitlement to eliminate whatever makes me feel uncomfortable.

> (*Bitch* Magazine, 2002)

Third-wave feminism, then, is grappling with the exclusions within it with regard to the transgendered community in the same way that second-wave feminism actively excluded women of colour or lesbians from its movement.

The issue of safety that comes up in debates about the exclusion or inclusion of transgendered folk into feminism is problematized by third-wavers like Emi who argue that the emphasis on safety can become threatening to a third-waver who embraces her multiple identities. The third wave struggles with this need to move beyond "essentialists and polemical definitions of gender" (Fireweed, 2000: 7). This is not to say that there is consensus within the third wave about trans folk and the feminist community, but as the third wave is a product of the feminism that came before it, it is also a generation of feminists who have grown up with debates surrounding the role of transgendered men and women within the movement. In some ways the debate has not really changed in 30-odd years, but the voice of the transgendered community is growing and feminism can no longer ignore it.

Grasping Sexual Power

Third-wave feminism is in part a response to the anti-sex or sex-negative feminism that has come before it. Hanne Blank (2002) in her article "Faster, Harder, Smarter, More: Finding a Political Future for Sex-Positive Smut" argues that third-wave feminists started "using explicit words and images to create a feminist, pro-sex response to the heteropatriarchal norm that discourages women's active sexuality, as well as to the anti-sex feminism that hoped to distance women from sexual oppression by distancing them from much of sex" (55). She thanks some second-wave feminists for asserting that women are allowed to experience sexual desire and sexual pleasure, but says that the third wave takes it further. "No longer asking whether consensual, beneficial, pleasurable sexuality is possible, sex positive ideologies work to improve people's access to an empowering and inclusive culture of sexuality" (57). But, she warns, the third wave must address that the production of smut and activism in this area is unbearably white and "caters … to the fantasies of people who want to believe that people of different racial or ethnic backgrounds have primary differences in their sexuality" (57).

Understandings of racism within this struggle for sexual empowerment are also complicated by the third wave's relationship with queer theory, hence its struggle not only with homophobia but also with heterophobia as it is experienced by bisexual or queer folk. Ruby Rowan writes in "Sleeping with the Enemy and Liking It" in *Turbo Chicks* that we're also still trying to reconcile those heterosexual parts of our relationships with our feminist frameworks (242). The third wave needs to make sure that women are not rejected by the feminist and queer community for heterosexuality any more than our heterosexual community rejects us for our love of women (243). Third-wave feminism runs with the critique of compulsory heterosexuality as identified by Adrienne Rich in her 1980 essay "Compulsory Heterosexuality and Lesbian Existence." She argues that heterosexuality is just that, compulsory, and that by breaking from the norm we may experience physical, economic, and emotional sanctions. Third-wavers actively queer heterosexuality; they recognize that a linear relationship among sex, gender, and sexuality is a construct that has been imposed upon us. It may not sound very revolutionary anymore, but sex can be for pleasure alone no matter what the right-wing tells us. So you can be born a girl but identify as a femmie boy who loves butchy girls. You can be a lesbian who screws men and still be a lesbian not bisexual or a "hasbian" (a lesbian that has gone straight). The combinations are endless!

The third wave also struggles with *how* it is that we love the women we love. Sarah Smith (2002) in her article, "A Cock of One's Own: Getting a Firm Grip of Feminist Sexual Power" in *Jane Sexes it Up*, explains how to have feminist sex with a dildo, penetration, objectification, and domination (300). She argues that when she penetrates her consenting lesbian partner with a dildo she's not an agent of heteropatriarchy or a "double-agent dyke." She also writes that when she's being penetrated and enjoying it she's not actually suffering from false consciousness about her own sexual desires and responses. She recognizes that a completely power-free society does not exist and neither does power-free sex *and* that this is not necessarily a bad thing (301)! She says the second-wave binary of dominance/submission as a model of power does not take into account all the complexities involved in sexual relations (303). She argues that sex-positive feminism speaks to more women as opposed to the anti-dildo feminism that seemed to thrive in the mainstream. She and other young feminists are making their sexual desires primary to a third-wave agenda in order to create models of female sexual agency and make feminism more relevant to women's lives (302).

In *Jane Sexes It Up,* third-waver Caitlin Fisher (2002) takes on second-wave assumptions and erasures about young girls' sexuality. Fisher writes, "As I enter my thirties, I find it difficult to claim a theoretical space for the girlhood I remember as sexually empowered and erotically complicated in ways that the feminism I grew up with didn't help explain" (54). She argues that few public narratives have been generated by feminism about sexually desiring girls. She asks, "Why do they play such a small part in the stories we tell ourselves as feminists? And what might be the consequences of the feminist theories we are building?" (54). These are two key questions for the third wave, a wave that reclaims female/feminine sexuality and questions some second-wave assumptions that female sexuality is all about disempowerment and vulnerability. This is not to say that the third wave doesn't recognize the systemic, public, and very private dangers that we may experience because of our female sexuality. Rather, it points to how some young feminists are strategizing by refusing to let the fear come first, to have their sexual role predefined before they can set out to experience it themselves. With a vibrator in hand, the third wave seeks out the sex workshops at Good For Her in Toronto or Venus Envy in Halifax, and then picks up its feminist porn at Little Sister's Book Store in Vancouver. Hell, we make our own porn and put it on our websites!

The pro-sex-work position of most third-wave feminists disrupts the notion that we don't own our own bodies. Through this lens, sex can be seen as a choice women make for themselves rather than something that is forced upon them. Third-wave feminists takes charge of their own sexual lives and put agency and desire back where it belongs: in the hearts, minds, and cunts of women. And the third wave is doing this well. Kristina Sheryl Wong is a third-waver that topples expectations about Asian women's sexuality. On Wong's webpage "Big Fat Chinese Mama," a porn/mail-order-bride spoof site, she lures her "oppressors" with promises of "demure lotus blossoms, geishas, and oriental sluts" and then presents them with text and images that are brash and meant to "subvert the expectations of a nasty guy in search of petite naked Asian bodies" (2002). In her FUQ section (Frequently Unasked Questions) she responds with subversive answers. For example:

> **Question**: Will my bride make an easy adjustment from her Asian Culture to the liberal American lifestyle?

> **Answer**: You may be able to buy yourself a nice little Asian porno, a Buddhist bracelet, or some other object that your capitalistic lifestyle Orientalize[s]—but you cannot buy these women. They are not for sale.

This is an example of our earlier discussion about the ways in which third-wave feminists create their own representations rather than solely responding or critiquing those that already exist. But what may be the most third-wave element about Wong's intervention is that she addresses her anger about the objectification and consumption of Asian bodies without arguing that all porn or sex is bad!

Apart from reclaiming porn, many third-wavers reclaim language. Terms such as "slut" and "whore" are emptied of their value judgments and their policing of women's bodies. Judith Butler argues in *Excitable Speech* (1997) that censoring certain words, keeping them unsaid and unsayable, works to preserve their power to injure. This, she says, may hinder "the possibility of a reworking that might shift their context and purpose" (38). Third-wave feminists have asked then whether her theory regarding the decontextualizing and recontextualizing of hate speech through "radical acts of public misappropriation" can hold for ideas of normative femininity. There's a great deal of debate about how successful we can be when it comes to reclaiming and re-appropriating images and words that have been traditionally used against women—but that isn't stopping the third wave from trying! The problem with reclaiming sex and sexuality is what Leah Rumack warns us about it her article "Lipstick." She writes that making feminism sexy may be used by mass media to take the edge off of this feminist politic. A sexually charged feminism is easily consumable; other feminist struggles that may not be as sexy aren't so readily taken up and are even ignored altogether. Rumack writes "the problem with sexual empowerment of what I call 'vibrator feminism' is this. While it's important for a young woman to feel entitled to a full, hot and self-directed sexuality, it also paradoxically makes it easier for the mainstream culture and media to eat her out, if you'll excuse the pun" (99). This brings us to our next summary that engages with pop-feminism and asks the question What happens when feminism goes mainstream?

IMPLICATIONS/CONCLUSIONS

When feminism reaches the general populous, it is called pop feminism. This returns us to our introduction and our questions about what a young feminist looks like. Is Avril Lavigne a feminist just because she wears ties, rocks out, and hangs with the boys? The irony, some would argue, is that once feminism becomes popular, it can no longer be called feminism because the politics have been removed or co-opted and commodified. That is, feminism is depoliticized and divorced from its political origins by mainstream culture and then made into a product that can be sold back to us. In the process of commodification, feminist ideas are turned into consumable objects like "pussy power" underwear or "Man Hater" baby-size tight T-shirts. Combat boots once worn by punk rockers and Riot Grrrls now adorn mannequin feet at Le Chateau. The accoutrements are no longer accessible to those who created the style, which now has a completely different politic around it. The co-optation, the ideological absorption of the ideas of a movement, means that the Gap can use revolutionary slogans such as "freedom to the people" on its store windows to sell clothing produced by slave labour. Similarly, youth culture is relabelled and redefined by dominant culture in a way that demonizes or exoticizes it. A contemporary example of this can be found in rave culture. A movement that espoused dance, community, and alternative expressions of sexuality was morphed into a dangerous drug, sex, and weapons culture that threatened to corrupt young, innocent children. The original meaning has been changed or lost. Feminism is popular as long as it's cute and non-threatening like Buffy the Vampire Slayer or magazines like *Jane*.

Any woman who is outspoken and powerful is labelled a feminist by the mainstream. This can be frustrating if the ideals and values expressed by some of these women represent classism, racism, or capitalism. Someone with a big mouth, holding a big microphone, is not necessarily a feminist. Therefore, one of the critiques of pop feminism is that it is ambiguous—that the politics are too vague and vulnerable to interpretation and may be taken the wrong way. This is the catch with pop feminism. On one hand there is the amazing opportunity to expose larger groups of people to a feminist discourse, and on the other the only things that seem to become popular are those that are easily digestible and can turn a profit. Does making feminism saleable to, or consumable by, mass culture necessarily mean dumbing or watering down its politics? Isn't the pay-off that feminism's message (even if it is diluted) reaches farther and to more remote places than was ever believed possible by a small group of women meeting weekly to discuss how to overthrow patriarchy? Feminists who work in underground ways are troubled and frustrated by these questions.

It is difficult to measure whether pop feminism actively challenges stereotypes and normative assumptions about women. What may be more effective is attaining a balance between making culture and consuming it or between owning it and sharing it. Is being co-opted by the mainstream a privilege? Most certainly, and many within feminist circles, such as women of colour and trans folk, may never experience this kind of visibility. After all, the mainstream does have its limits. Kristina Gray (2002), in her article "I Sold My Soul for Rock and Roll" in *Colonize This!*, talks about how her love for mainstream music seemed a betrayal to her race because she wasn't listening to the "right" black music and her feminist beliefs were a contradiction to her working-class background. Third-wave feminism, because of it's potential co-optation and commodification by mainstream culture, must ask some crucial questions: What is the cost popularizing feminism? Where does the third wave go from here?

SUGGESTED READINGS

Canadian Woman Studies/Les cahiers de la femme. "Young Women: Feminists, Activists, Grrrls," Volume 20–21/1 (Spring 2001).

Edut, Opheria. *Body Outlaws: Young Women Write About Body Image and Identity.* New York: Seal Press, 2000.

Findlen, Barbara, ed. *Listen Up: Voices From the Next Feminist Generation.* Seattle: Seal Press, 1995.

Fireweed. Especially these issues: Fat Issue 67 (Fall 1999); Revolution Girl Style Issue 59/60 (Fall/Winter 1997); Sex Work Issue 65 (Spring 1999); trans/scribes Issue 69 (Summer 2000).

Hernandez, Daisy, ed. *Colonize This! Young Women of Color on Today's Feminism.* New York: Seal Press, 2002.

Heywood, Leslie, and **Jennifer Drake,** eds. *Third Wave Agenda: Being Feminist, Doing Feminism.* Minneapolis: University of Minnesota Press, 1997.

Johnson, Lisa Merri, ed. *Jane Sexes It Up: True Confessions of Feminist Desire.* New York: Four Walls Eight Windows, 2002.

Mitchell, Allyson, Lisa Bryn Rundle, and **Lara Karaian.** *Turbo Chicks: Talking Young Feminisms.* Toronto: Sumach Press, 2001.

DISCUSSION QUESTIONS

1. What does a third-wave feminist look like?

2. Third-wavers argue that personal narratives can help us navigate the world and understand oppressions and our relationships with feminism and activism. Discuss.

3. What are some of the ways third-wave feminists organize and resist? Do you think that all these methods constitute activism? Why or why not?

4. How have third-wavers troubled ideas about the body? Make sure to keep in mind not only their resistance to patriarchy but also to some of the feminist thought of the second wave.

5. How does the third wave interrupt "feminist" ideas about how a feminist is supposed to behave as well as interrupt the definitions of femininity and masculinity that have been put forward and enforced by patriarchy?

6. What are the sexual politics of the third wave? What are the benefits and downfalls of feminism being brought into the mainstream?

BIBLIOGRAPHY

Baines, A., and **Avi Lewis.** *Spice Girls: Girl Power or Diet Pepsi?* On *Too Much for Much.* City TV. Much Music, Toronto. April 9, 1998.

Bartky, Sandra Lee. "Foucault, Femininity, and the Modernization of Patriarchal Power" (1990). In *Feminist Social Thought: A Reader.* D. Meyers, ed. New York: Routledge, 1997. 95.

Baumgardner, Jennifer, and **Amy Richards.** *Manifesta: Young Women, Feminism, and the Future.* New York: Farrar Straus & Giroux, 2000.

Blank, Hanna. "Faster, Harder, Smarter, More: Finding a Political Future for Sex-Positive Smut." In *Bitch* Magazine 18 (2002): 55.

Brown, Wendy. "Feminist Hesitations, Postmodern Exposures." *Differences* 3, Spring 1991.

Brumberg, Joan Jacobs. *Fasting Girls: The History of Anorexia Nervosa.* New York: Vintage, 2000.

Butler, Judith. *Excitable Speech: A Politics of the Performative.* New York: Routledge. 1997.

———. *Gender Trouble: Feminism and the Subversion of Identity.* New York: Routledge, 1990.

Brushwood Rose, Chloe, and **Anna Camilleri,** eds. *Brazen Femme: Queering Femininity.* Vancouver: Arsenal Pulp Press, 2002.

Canadian Woman Studies/Les cahiers de la femme. "Young Women: Feminists, Activists, Grrrls." Volume 20–21/1, Spring 2001.

Cox, Anna Marie, et al. "Masculinity without Men: Women Reconciling Feminism and Male-identification" In *Third Wave Agenda*, Leslie Heywood and Jennifer Drake, eds. Minneapolis: University of Minnesota Press, 1997. 178–199.

Crosbie, Lynn, ed. *Click!: Becoming Feminists.* Toronto: McFarland Walter & Ross, 1997.

Croson, Charlotte. "Sex, Lies and Feminism." *Off Our Backs,* June 2001.

Culture Jammers Network. "Fighting the Good Fight." <jammers@lists.adbusters.org> October 18, 2001.

Dent, Gina. "Missionary Position." In *To Be Real: Telling the Truth and Changing the Face of Feminis,* ed. Rebecca Walker.. New York: Anchor Books, 1995.

Detloff, Madelyn. "Mean Spirits: The Politics of Contempt Between Feminist Generations." *Hypatia* 12/3, Summer 1997.

Dua, Enakshi, and **Angela Robertson,** eds. *Canadian Anti-Racist Feminist Thought: Scratching the Surface of Racism.* Toronto: Women's Press, 1999.

Edut, Ophira, ed. *Body Outlaws: Young Women Write about Body Image and Identity.* Seattle: Seal Press, 2000.

Fireweed Collective. "Are You a Boy or a Girl? An Introduction." In *Fireweed trans/scribes* 69, Summer 2000: 7.

Fisher, Caitlin. "The Sexual Girl Within: Breaking the Feminist Silence on Desiring Girlhoods." In *Jane Sexes It Up: True Confessions of Feminist Desire,* ed. Lisa Merri Johnson. New York: Four Walls Eight Windows, 2002.

Gelder, Ken, and **Sarah Thornton,** eds., Introduction. *The Subcultures Reader*. New York: Routledge, 1997.

Giese, R. "13-Year-Old Girls Rule the World." *Toronto Star,* 14 Feb., 1998, p. N1.

Gray, Kristina. "I Sold My Soul for Rock and Roll." In *Colonize This!: Young Women of Colour on Today's Feminism,* eds. Daisy Hernandez and Bushra Rehman. Seattle: Seal Press, 2002.

Grosz, Elizabeth. *Volatile Bodies: Toward a Corporeal Feminism.* Bloomington, IM: Indiana University Press, 1994.

Halberstam, Judith. *Female Masculinity.* London: Duke University Press, 1998.

Hernandez, Daisy, and Bushra Rehman, eds. *Colonize This!: Young Women of Colour on Today's Feminism.* Seattle: Seal Press, 2002.

Heywood, Leslie, and Jennifer Drake, eds. *Third Wave Agenda: Being Feminist, Doing Feminism.* Minneapolis: University of Minnesota Press, 1997.

James, A. "Learning to Belong: The Boundaries of Adolescence." In *Symbolizing Boundaries: Identity and Diversity in British Cultures.* A.P. Cohen, ed. Manchester: Manchester University Press, 1986.

Karaian, Lara, Allyson Mitchell, and Lisa Bryn Rundle, eds. *Turbo Chicks: Talking Young Feminists.* Freemont, MI: Sumac Press, 2001.

Koyama, Emi. "MI Way or the Highway." In *Bitch* Magazine 17 (Summer 2002).

Lamm, Nomy. "It's a Big Fat Revolution." In *Listen Up: Voices from the Next Feminist Generation,* Barbara Findlen. Seattle: Seal Press, 2001.

Leonard, M. "Paper Planes: Traveling the New Grrrl Geographies." In *Cool Places: Geographies of Youth Cultures.* Tracey Skelton and Gill Valentine, eds. London: Routledge, 1988. 101–120.

Lorde, Audre. "The Master's Tools Will Never Dismantle the Master's House." In *Sister Outsider: Essays and Speeches by Audre Lorde.* Freedom, CA: Crossing Press, 1984.

MacDonald, Eleanor. "Critical Identities: Rethinking Feminism Through Transgendered Politics." *Atlantis,* 23/1, Fall/Winter 1998: 3.

Morgan, Joan. *When Chickenheads Come Home to Roost: A Hip Hop Feminist Breaks It Down.* New York: Simon and Schuster, 2000.

Nestle, Joan, Clare Howell, and Riki Wilchins, eds. *GenderQueer: Voices from Beyond the Sexual Binary.* Los Angeles: Alyson Books, 2002.

Panel Discussion. "A Fest in Distress." *Bitch* Magazine 17, Summer 2002: 71.

Pyne, Cat. "A Question for Feminism." In *Turbo Chicks: Talking Young Feminists,* eds. Lara Karaian, Allyson Mitchell, and Lisa Bryn Rundle. Freemont, MI: Sumac Press, 2001.

Rich, Adrienne. "Compulsory Heterosexuality and Lesbian Existence." *Signs: Journal of Women in Culture and Society* 5 (Summer 1980): 630–60.

Richards, Amelia. "Body Image: Third Wave Feminism's Issue?" In *Body Outlaws: Young Women Write about Body Image and Identity,* ed. Ophira Edut. Seattle: Seal Press, 2000.

Rowan, Ruby. "Sleeping with the Enemy and Liking It." In *Turbo Chicks: Talking Young Feminists,* eds. Lara Karaian, Allyson Mitchell, and Lisa Bryn Rundle. Freemont, MI: Sumac Press, 2001.

Rumack, Leah. "Lipstick." In *Turbo Chicks: Talking Young Feminists,* eds. Lara Karaian, Allyson Mitchell, and Lisa Bryn Rundle. Freemont, MI: Sumac Press, 2001.

Ruttenberg, Danya, and Susannah Heschel, eds. *Yentl's Revenge: The Next Wave of Jewish Feminism.* Seattle: Seal Press, 2001.

Smith, Sarah. "A Cock Of One's Own." In *Jane Sexes It Up: True Confessions of Feminist Desire.* Lisa Merri Johnson, ed. New York: Four Walls Eight Windows, 2002.

Tamaki, Mariko. "Robin and Me." In *Turbo Chicks: Talking Young Feminisms,* eds. Allyson Mitchell, Lisa Bryn Rundle, & Lara Karaian. Toronto: Sumach Press, 2001.

Valentine, G., T. Skelton, and **D. Chambers.** *Cool Places: Geographies of Youth Cultures.* London: Routledge, 1998.

Walker, Rebecca. *To Be Real: Telling the Truth and Changing the Face of Feminism.* New York: Anchor Books, 1995.

Wong, Kristina Sheryl. "Dis-Orient Express." *Bitch* Magazine 18, Fall 2002.

SUGGESTED WEBLINKS

Third Wave Foundation

www.thirdwavefoundation.org

Third Wave Foundation acknowledges the work of young women activists that has often been ignored by society. They help support the leadership of young women 15 to 30 by providing resources, public education, and relationship-building opportunities.

Eminism

eminism.org

Eminism.org is the website for Emi Koyama, the activist/author/academic working on intersex, sex-workers' rights, (queer) domestic violence, genderqueer, anti-racism, and other issues.

Feminista!

www.feminista.com

Feminista! is an online journal of art, literature, social commentary, philosophy, wit, humour, and respect that is currently published on a semi-regular basis.

She Made This

www.shemadethis.com

Describes itself as a live journal community and resource for grrrls who create.

Third Space

www.thirdspace.ca

Aims to raise the profile of feminist scholars and scholarship, offer emerging feminist scholars more opportunities for professional development, share information related to the politics of graduate school and careers in academia, and contribute to building a more collegial—and more productive—academic community.

About-Face

www.about-face.org

About-Face promotes positive self-esteem in girls and women of all ages, sizes, races and backgrounds through a spirited approach to media education, outreach, and activism.

chapter four

Unessential Women: A Discussion of Race, Class, and Gender and Their Implications in Education

Goli Rezai-Rashti

Our unique experiences as women of colour are frequently overlooked in discussions about women's oppression. At best, we are tokenized; at worst, we are told that our concerns seem to be less advanced, have to go with a patriarchy characteristic of our indigenous cultures. There is something missing in the women's movement that gives us an increasing sense of discomfort as we continue to participate in struggles in which only a part of our experiences as women of colour is or can be taken up.

—(Ng, 1993: 182–183)

INTRODUCTION

This chapter examines the multiplicity and diversity of feminist theories since the 1980s. It discusses the main criticisms that women of colour have directed to Western feminism. It also argues that these challenges have shifted the unitary notion of womanhood that was constructed by Western, white, middle-class women. The second part of the paper focuses on the implications of these criticisms in the education of racial and ethnic minority students in Canada.

Beginning in the 1980s, an increasing number of women of colour and women from the Third World challenged the essential notion of women that has been theorized by the mainstream feminist movement. The main focus of these criticisms was the very notion of feminism, as articulated by white liberal feminists (i.e. Amos and Parmar, 1984; Anthias and Yuval-Davis, 1993; Bannerji, 1993; Hill-Collins, 1990, 1998; hooks, 1981, 1989, 1995; Lorde, 1984; Mohanty, 1991; Ng, 1993, 1995). It was argued that white feminists had been mostly concerned about their own white, middle-class, heterosexual experiences. bell hooks, specifically, talked about the historical development of racism in the feminist movement throughout the nineteenth and twentieth centuries; she claimed that racial apartheid, as it existed in the American society, manifested itself also in the feminist movement:

> Every women's movement in America, from its earliest origin to the present day, has been built on a racist foundation—a fact which in no way invalidates feminism as a political ideology. The racial apartheid social structure that characterized 19th and early 20th century American life was mirrored in the women's rights movement. The first white women's rights advocates were never seeking social equality for all women; they were seeking social equality for white women. (1981: 124)

Focusing on Third-World women and the complexities of colonialism, nationalism, racism and sexism and the struggle for women's equal rights, Mohanty (1991: 6) argues that there is a need to go beyond the common conception of Third-World women built within the context of underdevelopment, oppressive traditions, illiteracy, poverty, and religious fanaticism. These analyses, she correctly states, "freeze Third World women in time, space, and history." Mohanty (1991: 11) describes the differences in the politics of white feminists and feminists of colour thus:

> The major analytic difference in the writings on the emergence of white, Western, middle-class liberal feminism and the feminist politics of women of colour in the U.S. is the contrast between a singular focus on gender as the basis for equal rights, and a focus on gender in relation to race and/or class as a part of a broader liberation struggle.

The contributions of feminist scholars of colour created a distinct body of knowledge that became known as race, class, and gender theories. It is important to acknowledge, however, that although this new perspective concerns itself theoretically and conceptually with race, class, gender, and their complex interaction and articulation, there are also significant differences and disagreements among these scholars in the way in which they articulate their views, both at the theoretical and political levels, within this renewed approach in feminist studies.

Historical Development

Black women were the first among women of colour to systematically challenge white feminist movements (Anthias and Yuval-Davis, 1993). The premises of their criticisms centred on three things:

a) White feminists have neglected to pay attention to race and racism as central components to the feminist struggle. The fact that black women are not only oppressed by gender relations but also by the institutional racism that is entrenched in Western societies has not been assumed as an important aspect of the feminist agenda. This includes institutional racism and sexism within the labour market or those entrenched in immigration policy, which encourage and sustain discrimination based on gender, race, and social class.

b) White feminists are ethnocentric when establishing priorities for the feminist movement, such as abortion rights and the notion of "family." In a Eurocentric framework, the complexities of race engendered in the lives of black and Third-World women in relation to such priorities were not taken into account. For example, abortion rights were a priority in the white feminist movement; however, for Third-World women abortion was not a crucial issue, as they were more concerned with the struggle for both decolonization and national independence.

c) White feminists' criticism of gender relations in other cultures, such as relations within the family (with African-Caribbean men seen as abandoning their women and children) and views that wrongly positioned Asian women as "eminently passive" individuals (because of arranged marriage and the dowry), often carry racist connotations. They are racist because white women try to impose on other women the need to abandon their cultural practices and adopt lifestyles and practices that are similar to Western feminism.

Although these early criticisms are important as a starting point of discussion, since they were among the first to identify different forms of women's oppression, they have themselves been challenged by other feminists, who point to their essentialist notion of black people as the exclusive victims of racism. These early theories tended to prioritize race or gender and failed to connect them conceptually or concretely. Hill-Collins (1990: 225) rejects the additive notion of racism and sexism and proposes instead to look at the "interlocking systems of oppression because it fosters a pragmatic shift of thinking inclusively about other oppressions, such as age, sexual orientation, religion, and ethnicity." She tells us:

> Placing African-American women and other excluded groups in the centre of analysis opens up possibilities for a both/and conceptual stance, one in which all groups possess varying amounts of penalty and privilege in one historically created system. In this system, for example, white women are penalized by their gender but privileged by their race. Depending on the context, an individual may be an oppressor, a member of an oppressed group, or simultaneously oppressor and oppressed.

Theories of race, class, and gender have been thoroughly debated in recent years. There has been a visible shift from the isolated study of a single category (race or class) toward an understanding of these categories as dynamic, relational, unstable, and complex systems. The work of feminists from the Third World, and of women of colour in Western societies, has thus helped develop a better understanding of the diversity of women's experiences.

Third-World Women's Feminism

The analysis of feminism in Third-World societies has been remarkable. The work of Kumari Jayawardena (1986) on the connection of feminism and nationalism and the anti-colonial movement has contributed to creating a framework for the analysis of the situation of women in these societies. Her work is significant because it clarifies that feminism is not necessarily a Western phenomenon and that Third-World women's struggle for national liberation and decolonization does not mean that they do not struggle also for women's overall improved conditions.

Western feminists' construction of Third-World women's subjugation and backward culture has come under considerable criticism (Amos and Parmar, 1984; Mohanty, 1991). This construction "ignores some of the trade-offs that the continued existence of certain practices might have had on the lives of women in these societies" (Yuval-Davis, 1997: 118). For example, Mohanty (1991: 53), in her systematic criticism of Western feminist analysis of Third-World women, argues that "the assumptions of privilege and ethnocentric universality on the one hand, and inadequate self-consciousness about the effects of

Western scholarship on the Third World in the context of a world system dominated by the West, on the other, characterize a sizable extent of Western feminist work on women in the Third World." She further states (72–73), that these assumptions likely lead to the production of a singular and homogeneous "Third-World difference," which includes a paternalistic attitude toward Third-World women:

> When the category of "sexually oppressed women" is located within particular systems in the Third World which are defined on a scale which is normed through Eurocentric assumptions, not only are Third World women defined in a particular way prior to their entry into social relations, but since no connections are made between first and Third World power shifts, the assumption is reinforced that the Third World just has not evolved to the extent that the West has. This mode of feminist analysis, by homogenizing and systematizing the experiences of different groups of women in these countries, erases all marginal and resistant modes and experiences.

The Western notion of women's oppression in the Third World has also been challenged by a large group of women from Muslim societies. The construction of Muslim women as oppressed, passive, and in need of adopting Western women's path to emancipation and development was criticized by, among others, Ahmed (1992) and Kandiyoti (1991). Ahmed (1992: 244), challenged the notion of universality of Western feminism, and convincingly exposed some of the limitations and ethnocentrism of the Western feminist approaches:

> As the history of Western women makes it clear, there is no validity to the notion that the progress of women can be achieved only by abandoning the ways of androcentric culture in favour of those of another culture. It was never argued, for instance, even by the most ardent nineteenth century feminists, that the European women could liberate themselves from the oppressiveness of Victorian dress only by adopting the dress of another culture. Nor has it ever been argued, whether in Mary Wollstonecraft's day, when European women had no rights, or in our own day and even by the most radical feminists, that because male domination and injustice to women have existed throughout the West's recorded history, the only resource to Western women is to abandon Western culture and find themselves some other culture. The idea seems absurd, and yet this is routinely how the matter of improving the status of women is posed with respect to women in Arab and other non-Western societies.

Although it is important to engage in a critical encounter with the white feminist theorization of Third-World women, women of colour, and Muslim women, it is also significant to look at the internal power dynamics within these communities and challenge certain cultural and religious gender-based practices that are prevalent within these groups. As Anthias and Yuval-Davis (1992: 102) argue, there has been often a tendency to fragment issues of sexism as if only those women who are the target of sexist cultural and religious practices would be able to evaluate these practices and respond to them. This, they claim, is problematic:

> We have some sympathy with the argument that struggles against culturally specific forms of sexism need to be undertaken in the full context of a racist society. None the less we do not believe that dominant cultural forms that subordinate women, from whichever context, should be immune from critique.

This is an important development that challenges and disrupts the taken-for-granted notion of gender issues in other cultures. Such challenges directed attention to the complexities of interrelations between the historical dynamics of colonization, religion, and gender relations in Muslim societies.

Feminism and Whiteness Scholarship

Another important new development in feminist theorizing has been the engagement of white feminists with antiracist feminism.[1] These feminists have tried to theorize and conceptualize the notion of "whiteness," and how white women might engage in antiracist and feminist struggles. Leslie Roman (1993) argues that rather than exclusively focusing attention on racial minorities, feminists have to engage with the enactment of power in a relational way. Roman works toward this argument with ideas raised by Gayatri Spivak's book, *Can the Subaltern Speak?* (1990). Spivak contends that the question is not whether oppressed people can speak. Rather, it is "whether privileged (European and North American) white groups are willing to listen when the subaltern speaks and how whites can know the difference between occasion for responsive listening as an excuse for silent collusion with the status quo of racial and neocolonial inequalities" (1990: 79). Taking up Spivak's work, Roman (1993) advances an alternative approach: "Speaking with rather than for, the interests of oppressed groups who are engaged in critically evaluating and transforming existing social relations" (82). She explains this provisional alternative in the following way:

> In contrast to the dominant meaning of *speaking for*, which implies that one group's voice can replace and stand for another's, I introduce the concept of *speaking with* to convey the possibility for tendential and shifting alliances between speakers from different, unequally located groups.... It also means that we can specify the conditions under which effective coalitions for social transformation may or may not be possible. (82)

Brah (1992), in discussing the recurrent issue of white and black feminist dialogue and interchange, argues against the notion of essentialism and reductionism while at the same time problematizing the issue of essentialism. She suggests that "black and white feminism should not be seen as essentially fixed oppositional categories" but rather seen in a historical context and in relation to the material and discursive practices.

Multicultural Feminism1 and Globalization

The multicultural approach is a more systematic and comprehensive perspective in feminist theorization. Multicultural feminism moves beyond the earlier critique of Western feminism and refuses to establish the hierarchy of oppression based on racial, gendered, national, sexual, and class-based struggles; rather, it stresses the relationality and intersectionality of all these axes of stratification. Ella Shohat's (1998) extensive and detailed account of this approach to feminism appears in an edited collection entitled *Talking Vision: Multicultural Feminism in the Transnational Age*, in which she situates multicultural feminism in relation to various debates—about identity, the canon, political correctness, affirmative action, the commodification of difference by transnational corporations, and the "new world order" of globalization. This approach attempts to combine the projects of multiculturalism and feminism and argues for a multifaceted feminist movement in which a large group of people can engage in dialogue and resistance as part of a community of activists. This includes "First-World" white feminist, socialism, anarchism, "Third-World" nationalism, "Fourth-World" indigenism, antiracist diasporic activism, and gay/lesbian/bi/transsexual movements. She also states, that "multicultural feminism takes as its starting point the cultural consequences of worldwide movements and dislocations of people associated with the development of 'global' or 'transnational' capitalism" (1998: 1). Another important distinction is that although multiculturalist feminists position themselves as anti-essentialist in terms of race, gender, and sexual identity—as political agents—at the same time they have supported "affirmative action" policy, which is "implicitly premised on the very categories elsewhere rejected as essentialist, leading to a paradoxical situation in which theory deconstructs totalizing myths while activism nourishes them" (1998: 6).

In terms of organization and activism around various communities, multicultural feminism acknowledges the challenges faced by such coalitions. Furthermore, multicultural feminism engages in a multifaceted dialogue that not only discusses the common aspects of women's oppression but also the diversity of women's experiences. However, it is admitted that it has been a serious challenge to creatively engage with contradictions of race, gender, social class, sexuality, religion, and globalization.

Globalization poses serious challenges to all feminists, because it necessitates that we think about our localized experiences of gender, race, and class in relation to a global context. Globalization is broadly defined as a process of social, economic, and political change on a global scale. In recent years, "globalization" has been embraced in popular discourse to explain social, economic, and political processes and events that seem beyond the influence of local communities to challenge them and indeed beyond the reach and influence of individual nation states. The actions of multi-national corporations, the exploitation of children and female workers in the "Third World" who produce commodities for "First-World" consumption, and widespread poverty seem beyond the capacity of everyday people to challenge. Globalization, in this popular context, is often used as a legitimizing discourse to make economic, political, and social changes self-evident, necessary, while leaving society with almost no alternatives to these processes (Bourdieu, 1999).

One of the significant characteristics of globalization has been precisely the shift in communication and information technology that has resulted in the compression of time/space (Cohen, 1995) or, as Giddens suggests, globalization is about transformation in time and space (1994: 4). Sassen (1998: xxxiv) argues that "globalization is a process that generates contradictory spaces, characterized by contestation, internal differentiation, continuous border crossing." Globalization affects nation-states economically, politically, and culturally.

It is in this context of globalization that multicultural feminists find ways to articulate their position. They argue that as notions of "home," "belonging," "nation," and "community" take on new complex meanings in the context of globalization, multicultural feminists should challenge the hegemonic capitalist regime across national and regional borders. As Mohanty argues:

> One concrete task feminist educators, artists, scholars, and activists face is that of historicizing and denaturalizing the ideas, beliefs, and values of global capital such that underlying exploitative social relations and structures are made visible. This means being attentive not only to the grand narrative or "myth" of capitalism or "democracy," but also to the mythologies feminists of various races, nations, classes, and sexualities have inherited about each other. (1998: 485–486)

Yuval-Davis (1997) discusses processes of globalization and their impact on local communities. She argues that the technological development in transportation and communication is shifting the notion of global and local, and of particular significance is the existence of diasporic communities. It has become easier with immigrant communities to stay in touch with their countries of origin. Also, the internet and international travel are making it easier for the "production of language and popular culture, as well as, 'keeping up' with what is happening in the 'motherland' and the diasporic communities in other countries" (65).

Sassen's (1998) focus is on the effects of globalization in the policy-making processes for immigration. She argues that the massive increase in Third-World immigration and the growth of export production caused the incorporation of Third-World women into wage labour. She sees this as a global process that assumes various forms depending on the local situation; she then argues that the employment of women in Third-World countries and immigrant women in developed countries are necessarily connected: "Immigration and offshore production are ways of securing a low-wage labour force and fighting the demands of organized workers in developed countries" (111). In addition, productive facilities that have to remain in developed countries because of demand (such as work in hospitals and restaurants) are able to use immigrant labour while production facilities that can be shifted to Third-World countries can use low-wage labour in those societies.[2]

Shohat (1998) poses a number of relevant questions in relation to the process of globalization and its impact on women. She asks that if, as it has been argued by some, this new era of globalization has resulted in the old imperial hegemonies becoming "dispersed" and "scattered," how are we to negotiate these dispersed hegemonies? As well, what are the links between such hegemonies and the national and transnational regulations of the gendered and sexualized body (48)?

It is important, however, to understand globalization not in a deterministic way in which there is no space for resistance, contestation, and difference. On the contrary, we must look at globalization both as an impetus for homogeneity and at the same time a stimulus for the production of differences. This conceptualization of globalization is significant in that it allows the local to resist, alter, and reinterpret global policies based on the histories of local conditions.

This seems to be a challenge of critical multicultural feminists. They look for possibilities of negotiation between the forces of globalization and resistance by using the development of mass communication and technologies. They avoid the binary of "bad" global and "good" local and ask for a transnational imaginary, which offers possibilities for critical affiliation. Shohat (1998) sums up this view well:

> It practices multicultural feminism, not in the simple additive sense of many histories and geographies, but as a political and cultural project which mobilizes the polycentric relationality of a constantly moving world. (52)

Implications of Antiracism and Feminism in Education

In order to provide a more empirical application of this conceptual framework, this section of the paper deals with the implications and intersectionality of race, class, and gender in the lives of racial and ethnic minority female students.

Concepts of race, gender, and social class have seldom been subjects dealt with systematically in academic curricula in the Canadian education system. The common practice has been to engage in isolated and disconnected discussion about gender equity or multicultural education (Rezai-Rashti, 1999). By and large, the study of the systematic and complex issues of antiracism and feminism has been left unaddressed. The introduction of the policy of multiculturalism in 1971, at the national level, did not bring a substantial and systematic change to the educational system. It mainly fostered a token appreciation and celebration of cultural diversity in schools, but serious issues of racism, sexism, and social class inequality remained silent in classroom discussions.

Since the 1970s, steady criticism has been directed to education systems in the Western world for their lack of attention to cultural diversity and gender equity issues (Cummins, 1986; McLeod, 1990; Gaskell and McLaren, 1992; Sadker and Sadker, 1995). These criticisms were often compartmentalized, either exclusively focusing on multiculturalism or gender equity. They were at best fragmented and did not take into account the complex articulation of race, culture, ethnicity, religion, and gender in the lives of students. The discussion of gender equity rarely touched upon race or racialization of gender issues in the school system (Sadker and Sadker, 1995). The argument about gender equity issues in the school system was mostly influenced by the theorization produced by white, Western, middle-class women, as discussed in the previous section. These gender equity issues basically focused on the access of young women to technology and sciences and their career choice.

The same could be said for the policy of multiculturalism in Canadian educational policy, which did not take into account gender and class diversity among students. In the 1980s and 1990s, the liberal approach to multiculturalism was itself the subject of considerable scrutiny. Educators called attention to the fact that multicultural education appeared to be more concerned with sustaining the status quo rather than promoting progressive changes in the education system. This view is exemplified in the following statement by Olneck (1990):

> Dominant versions of multicultural education delimit a sanitized cultural sphere divorced from sociopolitical interests, in which culture is reified, fragmented and homogenized, and they depict ethnic conflict as predominantly the consequences of negative attitudes and ignorance about manifestations of difference, which they seek to remedy by cultivating empathy, appreciation, and understanding. (166)

The criticism of multicultural education in Canada, England, and the United States, along with the introduction of antiracist education (or for Americans, critical or emancipatory multiculturalism), created a dynamic dialogue between educators, social scientists, and policy-makers in education. Antiracist advocates rightly criticized multicultural education for its additive and supplementary character, and, more importantly, for its lack of analysis of power relations. They stressed the point that multicultural education failed to integrate itself into school curriculum and everyday educational activities. For them, such activities as Black History Month and Heritage Week simply were attached to, but not part of, educational experiences. In Canada, these kinds of criticisms had a relatively positive impact at the level of policy-making in education. The Ontario Ministry of Education in July 1993 Policy Memorandum No. 119, acknowledged that the policies and programs in education have been historically Eurocentric and ignored and silenced the experiences of Aboriginal people and racial and ethnic minorities:

> There is growing recognition that the educational structure, policies and programs have been mainly European in perspective and have failed to take into account the viewpoints, experiences, and needs of Aboriginal people, and many racial and ethnocultural minorities. As a result, systemic inequalities exist in the school system that limit the opportunities for Aboriginal and other students and staff members of racial and ethnocultural minorities to fulfill their potentials. Educators, therefore, need to identify and change institutional policies that are racist in their impact, if not intent. In this regard, anti-racist and ethnocultural equity education goes beyond multicultural education, which focuses on teaching about the cultures and traditions of diverse groups. (45)

Accordingly, the Ontario Ministry of Education, under the New Democratic Party, mandated all boards of education in the province to develop an "Antiracism and Ethnocultural Equity" policy. In addition, the ministry established a unit devoted to creating a system that would support school boards and make them accountable for the implementation of the policy. It is important to mention that this mandated policy did not acknowledge gender issues, since the almost exclusive focus on antiracism kept it detached from gender issues. The policy, however, was short-lived. After the New Democratic Party was replaced by the Progressive Conservative government in 1995, the mandated policy was not enforced.

Recently, scholars concerned with race, gender, sexuality, and social class and their complex articulation have been critical of mainstream feminism (Bannerji, 1993, 2000; Ng, 1993; Yuval-Davis, 1997). Some of them have also taken issue with the analysis of both multiculturalism and antiracism (Hall, 1996; McCarthy, 1998; Rattansi, 1992). Although they agree with some of the criticisms put forward by antiracist proponents about systemic and institutional inequalities, they nevertheless remain critical of the essentialist conceptualization of both antiracism and multiculturalism.

Rattansi (1992: 34), rightly points out the inadequacies of their reductive notions of culture and ethnic essentialism. Missing in these views are a wide range of representations, as well as encouragement of a critical dialogue and interrogation of all intellectual and political frameworks. Much academic discussion and debate in recent years has evolved around the interconnection of race, class, and gender. The fashionable and rhetorical use of the terms "race, class, and gender" cannot hide the fact they are still used as separate analytical categories and not in a relational sense (Ng, 1993: 133). Ng correctly argues that gender, race, and class are social relations and not just fixed entities.

McCarthy (1998: 61–62) criticizes both mainstream and radical approaches to racial inequality and offers a more relational and contextual approach to the operation of racial inequality in schooling. Such an approach, he argues, allows us "to better understand the complex operation of racial logics in education and helps us to explore more adequately the vital links that exist between racial inequality and other dynamics—such as class and gender—operating in the school setting." As well, Cohen (1992: 77) criticizes existing theories of racism for their reductionist approach, "that is, trying to explain a complex and multifaceted phenomenon by resorting to a single, simple cause. These explanations are therefore limited since they tell only part of the story, leaving out those elements which do not fit into their chosen line of argument."

In her analysis of selected Jewish women's writing, Britzman (1998: 105) challenges the simplistic notion of race and racism and the limitations of antiracist pedagogy by arguing that:

> The modern history of European Jewry challenges commonly taught notions of white privilege as an instant, transparent, and unitary accessory to the body. Such ahistoric conceptualizations are an effect of essentialist discourses of race and perhaps of the educational desire to simplify the complex histories of racism in the name of certainty and correction.

Race, Gender, and School Practices

Since 1994, my own work (Rezai-Rashti, 1994, 1999) has attempted to engage educators with new developments in the understanding of the complexities and articulations of racism, sexism, religion, social class, and colonialism. My research has been based on some of my working experience in the school system, especially with female student minorities in Ontario. In dealing with a large number of female students from mainly the Middle East, South East Asia, and Africa, I have found that the attitudes of some school principals, teachers, and guidance counsellors continue to be influenced by colonial discourse. The belief in Western superiority is still strong among educators at all school levels, as their image of Third-World countries remains stereotypical and ethnocentric: poor, underdeveloped, and uncivilized. Likewise, women from such countries are constructed as individuals who are oppressed, powerless, and submissive. They are seen as victims who must be rescued from the oppressive influences of their families and culture. Often, that implies that they adapt to Western ways of life. This perspective creates several inter-related problems.

Sometimes, problems that are perceived by school personnel as being related to a student's "home culture" in fact have little to do with specific cultural practices. They may well be the types of problems encountered by any typical adolescent. I was once called to go to a school and talk to a Muslim student who, according to her counsellor, was experiencing "cultural conflicts." Upon my arrival at the school, the principal introduced me to the student in question. Before leaving the room, the principal looked at me and said that the girl's parents wanted to follow the "old country's rules." Then he added that the parents needed to learn that there are rules and regulations in Canada that work against sexism. After talking to the student for an hour, I found that her problems had nothing to do with her country of origin or her culture. Her school failure was the result of jealousy among siblings due to the preferential treatment that her parents gave to an older sister—nothing different from a situation that could also be found in any Anglo-Saxon family.

Educators who work with youth and adolescents are aware that intergenerational conflict between teenagers and their families is common. A normal occurrence such as this is seen and interpreted in dramatically different ways when the youth involved happens to be a young Muslim woman; more often than not, educators view the problem as a cultural one. It is immediately communicated to the student that her culture is backward. In this colonial logic, the best way to "solve" what is a common generational conflict is to break with the "old" cultural tradition and adopt the cultural way of the "new country." Culture is thus a problem and solution, a dynamic that of course sustains colonial representation of one culture as superior and as one that must be adopted if problems are to be overcome.

Students are also well aware of the stereotypical attitudes held by some educators and sometimes take advantage of a situation. For example, one day I was consulted by a school to find out if it were true that in Muslim culture girls cannot study mathematics. Surprised by the question, and after some discussion with the grade-seven student, I realized that she was using Islam as an excuse for not attending the math class and had readily convinced the principal of the school about this "cultural" rule. The student was certainly aware of the educator's attitudes toward Muslim and Islam; she also knew that any remark about the culture, however ridiculous, would be seen as acceptable provided that the remark would reinforce the stereotypical views of Muslim culture as illogical and superstitious.

On the one hand, one finds that the racialization of gender issues is practised in educational institutions by school administrators, counsellors, and teachers. In many respects, the ways in which the education systems looks at Third-World female students are truly permeated by the remnants of colonial discourse. Some teachers do hold an essentialist view of women and see their oppression as stable, homogeneous, and undifferentiated. On the other hand, there is a manipulation of multiculturalism policy by some of the families of racial and ethnic minority female students. There are instances that under the rubric of "culture," parents demand special provisions for their daughters from the school system. Not surprisingly, some educators who still cling to the colonial past appear too willing to comply with those parents' demands.

Racism and Sexism in the Education System

In Ontario, both multiculturalism and antiracism have failed to respond to the complex issues and articulation of race and gender both at the level of policy and practice. Within the multiculturalism perspective, there have been implicit and explicit assumptions of cultural homogeneity in which gender relations were perceived as the essence of the culture. Under the policy of multiculturalism, schools, at best, engaged themselves with fragmented workshops and celebrations of various cultures with little or no attention to the significance of power relations. As McCarthy (1990) argues, multiculturalism should not be limited to presenting understanding as a side topic, such as Black History Month or International Women's Day, since this suggests that all that is needed is to *add* some content about racial, ethnic, and linguistic minorities and women to the school curriculum.

In 1991, political changes resulted in school boards being mandated to develop and adopt, by 1993, a policy on Antiracism and Ethnocultural Equity. It was clear that this policy would go beyond the simple appreciation of cultures and engage administrators, teachers, and students with the problems of systemic and institutional racism. The progressive nature of the policy did not make it immune to criticism. Like multiculturalism, antiracism policy holds an essentialist and unproblematic concept of culture and identity in which ethnic and racial collectivities are mostly seen as stable, homogeneous, and undifferentiated. Such constructions do not allow space for internal power conflicts within racial and ethnic minority communities, for example, conflict along the lines of class, gender, and culture. However, before the implementation of antiracism policy had begun, the government changed; the new Conservative administration did not follow the mandated policy of the previous New Democratic Party government. Furthermore, the mechanism that was established to oversee the equity work of school boards in Ontario (the Unit on Race and Ethnocultural Equity) was dismantled by the new government.

It is clear that the theorization of antiracist feminism has not had, as yet, a strong impact on the education system. Teachers, administrators, and guidance counsellors, in their treatment of and relations with racial and ethnic minority female students, continue to use some of the essentialized way of thinking about students' culture. In doing so, they continue to see racial and ethnic minority students' complex problems and difficulties in a reductionist fashion, while simultaneously adopting too simple a solution, that these students should abandon their "backward traditions" and move to adopt Western culture. This is the same conception that dominated the white, Western, middle-class movement in the 1960s and 1970s, which, as stated earlier, has been criticized by feminist theorists of colour since the 1980s.

What needs to be understood is that in order to deal with issues concerning racial and ethnic minority female students, it is crucial to begin to interrogate and challenge those misconceptions that have so long been part of colonial discourse in the education system. Misconceptions about the essentialized notion of women and feminism should be taken up seriously. In sum, the education system should engage in an interdisciplinary and relational understanding of racism, feminism, social class, and heterosexism and their complex articulation. Only in this way will education perform one of its main tasks: making progressive changes possible.

SUMMARY

This chapter brought together the work of some of the major theorists who have put forward a valid criticism of white middle-class Western feminism. The most important point of criticism was the Eurocentric and essentialist conception of womanhood that was part of the earlier versions of the feminist movement. The second part of the paper dealt with the education system and its engagement with issues of race, class, and gender. It was argued that neither multiculturalism nor antiracism has been able to respond to the complexities that racial and ethnic minority female students face in Canadian schools. The contribution of those who advocate for a complex understanding of race, class, and gender (and their intersectionality) is a starting point of such analysis.

The theorization of women of colour, and Third World and multicultural feminism can be summarized in the following points:

a.   Women are not homogenous groups of people; they are differentiated on the basis of their race, gender, sexuality, and social class status.

b.   Any study of gender should be done in connection with a greater understanding of the articulation and intersectionality of race, ethnicity, culture, social class, and sexuality.

c.   Oppression is not quantifiable. Some of the more recent writings of feminists of colour reject the notion of double and triple oppression and instead talk about a more complex system of domination and subordination.

d.   Third-World women have to deal with the complex situation of national struggle (anti-colonial movements) and the need to articulate gender oppression alongside other forms of oppression in their societies.

e.   Multicultural feminists put forward a more systematic and comprehensive analysis of gender oppression that is more inclusive of all feminism but aware of tension and contradictions embedded in this kind of coalition.

f.   The education system has been unable to deal with the complexities of race, class, gender, and sexuality. It has been argued that neither multiculturalism nor antiracism was able to deal with race and gender issues in Canadian schools.

CONCLUSION

The significance of feminist research that engages with post-colonial, Third-World, and women-of-colour issues was the main issue addressed in this chapter. The chapter proceeded then to discuss the implications of these theories in the lives of racial and ethnic minority female students.

The contributions of feminist scholars concerned with race, class, gender, and sexuality have had a significant impact on feminist theorizing. This impact can be seen as both theoretical and political. Feminist scholars can now claim that their analysis of gender oppression includes its intersection with race and social class. At the political level, feminist organizations are striving to make themselves more inclusive of women of colour (National Action Committee on the Status of Women [NAC], for example, has deliberately chosen women of colour as leaders). Still, one needs to be aware of the fact that some feminist scholars have transformed the phrase "race, class, and gender" into a popular slogan that is used to gain scholarly and ideological legitimacy within certain circles. What is needed, however, is to take the phrase "race, class, and gender" as a matter for serious empirical investigation and analysis (Ng, 1993: 50), as well as a tool for meaningful political activism.

We are already certain that the critical mass of knowledge that has been created in the last two decades by women of colour and Third-World women can no longer be ignored. As Hill Collins asserts in the following statement about the influence of black feminist theorizing:

> African American women are no longer silenced in the same way, and the Black women public voice has gained much legitimacy. The 1980s and 1990s witnessed an explosion of works by and about Black women, designed to reclaim and highlight Black women's humanity. This highlighted visibility bears no resemblance to the past. Then Black women were virtually invisible, whereas now, Black women's visibility constitutes a "traffic jam." (1998: 50–51)

The second part of this chapter dealt with racial and ethnic minority female students and their daily encounters and experiences in Canadian schools. It was argued that neither gender equity nor multiculturalism and antiracism approaches have been able to deal with the complexities of racial and ethnic minority students' experiences. Gender equity analyses in education have often lacked connections to students' race and culture, as women are seen as a homogeneous category experiencing gender oppression in almost identical ways. In a similar way research and policies in multiculturalism and antiracism have paid little attention to the analysis of gender. The essentialism and over-generalization found in these analyses of racial and ethnic minority students' experiences misses the opportunity to give due consideration to gender as an important component of their identity.

The education system's task ahead is for it to rid itself of the simplification of race, gender, and culture and move on to engage with new perspectives that deal with the complex articulation of race, gender, and social class in education. This perspective, I believe, can help educators move toward a pedagogy that is truly empowering of all students. The contributions of antiracist feminism work can be realized only if faculties of education, which are responsible for training new teachers, take this task seriously.

In conclusion, the work of multicultural feminism is the culmination of the most comprehensive analysis of women of colour, post-colonial, transnational, and Third-World feminists. The body of knowledge produced within this framework asks feminism to challenge the disciplinary boundaries and unified feminist narrative and to imagine a feminism that is relational in its affiliation to diverse communities and constituencies.

ENDNOTES

1. In the United States, "antiracist" is not used. It is only in England and Canada that we use "antiracism" to acknowledge the existence of systemic and institutional racism. However, in the United States "multiculturalism" is used with various meanings depending on different theoretical formulations. For example, the work of multicultural feminism is very much in line with most of the literature in critical antiracism and post-colonialism.

2. I in no way am suggesting that the work of those in antiracism or gender equity education has no relevance to the lives of students. What I am arguing is that they do not engage with the complex notion of race, gender, and social class and their articulation. Their analysis of gender and race is essentialized and does not give a total picture of students' everyday experiences. For example, the research that was conducted by Sadker and Sadker (1995) does not engage with issues of race or culture. The classroom dynamic is more complicated when research considers gender, race, culture, and social class issues as an interlocking system. For instance, racial and ethnic minority male students may not be as vocal as white males.

SUGGESTED READINGS

Shohat, Ella. (ed). 1998. *Talking Visions: Multicultural Feminism in a Transnational Age*. Cambridge: Massachusetts Institute of Technology. This book consists of a collection of essays and images produced by artists, activists, and scholars from a broad range of constituencies. It is also a more systematic and comprehensive work of multicultural feminists who have introduced a relational approach in understanding feminism, multiculturalism, transnationalism, and globalization.

Bannerji, Himani. (ed). 1993. *Returning the Gaze: Essays on Racism, Feminism and Politics*. Toronto: Sister Vision Press. This anthology contains essays that make visible previously absent experiences of women of colour in Canada. Authors share a common perspective of an antiracist feminism, though they adopt different narrative and analytical strategies for exploration.

Yuval-Davis, Nira. 1997. *Gender and Nation*. London: Sage publication. This book provides an overview and critique of scholarship on gender, nationhood, and citizenship. It also deals with contesting relations between nationalism and feminism.

Hill-Collins, Patricia. 1998. *Fighting Words: Black Women and the Search for Justice*. Minneapolis, University of Minnesota Press. Focusing on black feminist thought, the book challenges the readers to think about the contemporary knowledge produced by black women. She investigates how black feminist thought confronts the injustices African-American women face today.

Ng, Roxana, et al. (eds). 1995. *Antiracism, Feminism and Critical Approaches to Education*. Westport, Connecticut: Bergin and Harvey. Contributors to this collection address relevant educational issues to women and people of colour in light of feminism and multicultural/antiracist education.

DISCUSSION QUESTIONS

1. What are the main criticisms that women of colour have addressed to white, middle-class, Western feminism?

2. How have women of colour's early criticisms of mainstream feminism changed over time?

3. What are the contributions made by multicultural feminists?

4. Do you think that the contributions made by women of colour have shifted the nature and scope of feminism and the women's movement?

5. Why is it that policies of antiracism and multiculturalism cannot deal with the complexities of gender and race issues in the school system?

6. What are your suggestions for dealing with racial and ethnic minority students' issues in the education system?

BIBLIOGRAPHY

Ahmed, L. *Women and Gender in Islam: Historical Roots of Modern Debate.* New Haven: Yale University Press, 1992.

Amos, V., and **P. Parmar.** "Challenging Imperial Feminism." *Feminist Review* 17 (1984): 3–20.

Anthias, F., and **N. Yuval-Davis.** *Racialized Boundaries: Race, Religion, Gender, Colour and Class and the Antiracist Struggle.* London: Routledge, 1993.

Bannerji, H. "The Paradox of Diversity: The Construction of a Multicultural Canada and 'Women of Colour.'" In *The Dark Side of the Nation: Essays on Multiculturalism, Nationalism and Gender.* Toronto: Canadian Scholars' Press, 2000.

Bannerji, H., ed. *Returning the Gaze: Essays on Racism, Feminism and Politics.* Toronto: Sister Vision Press. 1993.

Bourdieu, P. *Acts of Resistance: Against the Tyranny of the Market.* Trans. Richard Nice, New York: New Press, 1999.

Brah, A. "Difference, Diversity and Differentiation." In *Race, Culture and Difference*, edited by J. Donald and A. Rattansi. London: Sage, 1992.

Britzman, D. *Lost Subjects, Contested Objects: Toward a Psychoanalytic Inquiry of Learning.* Albany, NY: State University of New York Press, 1998.

Cohen, P. "It's Racism What Dunnit: Hidden Narratives in Theories of Racism." In *Race, Culture and Difference*, edited by J. Donald and A. Rattansi. London, UK: The Open University, 1992.

Cohen, P. "Out of the Melting Pot and into the Fire Next Time: Local/Global Cities, Bodies, Texts." Paper presented at the BSA conference *Contest Cities*, Essex University, 11–13 April, 1995.

Cummins, J. "Empowering Minority Students: A Framework for Intervention." *Harvard Educational Review* 56/1 (1986): 50–68.

Gaskell, J., and **A. McLaren.** *Women and Education,* 2nd ed. Calgary: Detselig Enterprises Ltd., 1992.

Giddens, A. *Beyond Left and Right: The Future of Radical Politics.* Cambridge: Polity Press, 1994.

Hall, S. "New Ethnicities." In *Stuart Hall: Critical Dialogue in Cultural Studies*, edited by D. Morleyand and K. Chen. London, UK: Routledge, 1996.

Hill-Collins, P. *Black Feminist Thought: Knowledge, Consciousness, and the Politics of Empowerment.* New York: Routledge, 1990.

———. *Fighting Words: Black Women and the Search for Justice.* Minneapolis: University of Minnesota Press, 1998.

hooks, bell. *Ain't I a Woman: Black Women and Feminism.* Boston: South End Press,1981.

———. *Talking Back: Thinking Feminist, Thinking Black.* Boston: South End Press, 1989.

———. *Killing Rage: Ending Racism.* New York: Henry Holt and Company, 1995.

———. *Black Looks: Race and Representation.* Toronto: Between the Lines, 1992.

Jayawardenna, K. *Feminism and Nationalism in the Third World.* London: Zed Press, 1986.

Kandiyoti, D., ed. *Women, Islam and the state.* London: Macmillan, 1991.

Lorde, A. *Sister Outsider.* Trumansburg: Crossing Press, 1984.

McCarthy, C. "Multicultural Education, Minority Identities, Textbook, and the Challenge of Curriculum Reform." *Journal of Education* 172/2 (1990): 118–129.

————. *The Uses of Culture: Education and the Limits of Ethnic Affiliation.* New York: Routledge, 1998.

McLeod, K. "Multiculturalism and Multicultural Education in Canada: Human Rights and Human Rights Education." Paper presented in Multiculturalism, Teaching and Learning: A Colloquium, May 27 to June 2, Vancouver, 1990.

Mohanty, C. T., et al., eds. *Third World Women and the Politics of Feminism.* Bloomington: Indiana University Press, 1991.

————. "Crafting Feminist Genealogies: On the Geography and Politics of Home, Nation, and Community." In *Talking vision: Multicultural Feminism in a Transnational Age*, edited by E. Shohat, 485–500. Cambridge: Massachusetts Institute of Technology, 1998.

Ng, R. "Racism, Sexism and Nation Building in Canada." In *Race, Identity, and Representation in Education,* edited by C. McCarthy and W. Crichlow, 50–59. New York: Routledge, 1993.

Ng, R. et al., eds. *Antiracism, Feminism, and Critical Approaches in Education.* Westport: Bergin and Garvey, 1995.

Olneck, M. "The Recurring Dream: Symbolism and Ideology in Intercultural and Multicultural Education. *American Journal of Education* 98/2 (1990): 147–174.

Ontario Ministry of Education and Training. *Antiracism and Ethnocultural Equity in School Boards: Guidelines for Policy Development and Implementation.* Toronto, ON: Author.

Rattansi, A. "Changing the Subject? Racism, Culture and Education." In *Race, Culture and Difference*, edited by J. Donald and A. Rattansi. New York: Sage Publication, 1992.

Rezai-Rashti, G, M. "The Persistence of Colonial Discourse: Race, Gender, and Muslim Students in Canadian Schools." *Journal of Curriculum Theorizing* 15/4 (1999): 47–60.

————. The dilemma of working with minority female students. *Canadian Women Studies* 14/2 (1994).

Roman, L. "White is a colour! White defensiveness, postmodernism, and antiracist pedagogy." In *Race, Identity and Representation in Education*, edited by C. McCarthy and W. Crichlow, 71–88. New York: Routledge, 1993.

Sadker, D., and **M. Sadker.** *Failing at Fairness: How America's Schools Cheat Girls.* New York: Touchstone Press, 1995.

Sassen, S. *Globalization and Its Discontents: Essays on the New Mobility of People and Money.* New York: The New York Press, 1998.

Shohat, E., ed. *Talking Visions: Multicultural Feminism in a Transnational Age.* Cambridge: Massachusetts Institute of Technology, 1998.

Spivak, G. C. "Can the Subaltern Speak?" In *The Post-Colonial Critic: Issues, Strategies, Dialogue,* edited by S. Harrasymm, 271–313. New York: Routledge, 1990.

Yuval-Davis, N. *Gender and Nation.* London, Sage Publications, 1997.

WEBLINKS

The Canadian Research Institute for the Advancement of Women (CRIAW)

www.criaw-icref.ca

CRIAW is a national, non-profit organization committed to advancing the equality of women through research about the diversity of women's experience.

The Centre for Integrative Antiracism Studies (CIARS), OISE/University of Toronto

www.oise.utoronto.ca/ciars

The Centre is housed in the Department of Sociology and Equity Studies in Education. CIARS is the first and only Centre at the University of Toronto to be devoted to Anti-racism Studies in Education. CIARS' mandate is to enhance research and teaching in the areas of equity, antiracism praxis, and alternative knowledge(s) in education.

chapter five

Aging, Beauty, and Status

Sharon McIrvin Abu-Laban

Susan A. McDaniel

It is our want of passion, our inertia, that creates emptiness in old age.

—Simone de Beauvoir (1970)

INTRODUCTION

In many ways, elders are devalued in our society, and older women are particularly disadvantaged.[1] Aging has long been seen as a women's issue (Sommers, 1976; Abu-Laban and Abu-Laban, 1977; McDaniel, 1988) and from the beginning, the issue of aging has attracted an unusual proportion of women researchers (Abu-Laban, 1981; McDaniel, 2000) compared to other research areas. Several factors, including discrimination against aging women in contemporary Western societies and the caregiving responsibilities that fall to women with aged relatives (Kaden and McDaniel, 1990; McDaniel, 1992a, 1993b; McDaniel and McKinnon, 1993), suggest ample reason for the centrality of women in age-related issues. Given this, researchers have pointed out that aging is a profoundly feminist issue (Russell, 1987; McDaniel, 1988). Women live longer than men do, they live longer in disability and poverty, and they have to live out their last years marked by the demeaning labels so often given to older women in our society. Gender and gender inequalities matter to aging, both societally and individually. How aging is interpreted and analyzed is also a feminist issue. It makes a difference whether gender inequities among the aged are seen in terms of accumulated injustices or as social problems resulting from women's greater longevity. Policies and public perceptions of what is socially problematic are filtered through the lenses of social analysts. Hence, the subordination of women that is aggravated in older age in Western societies, the institutionalization of women's inequality, and the dominant patriarchal ideologies that support this, need to be examined, questioned, and challenged.

Women are said to be older sooner than men. Although aging is seen as empowering for many men, it is not seen to be so for women. *His* facial lines are seen as signs of character; *her* lines are signs of decrepitude and decreasing sexual attractiveness. In men, power, which tends to increase with age and in itself is thought to be sexually appealing, while in women, appearance, particularly youthful appearance, is considered the *sine qua non*. Power can enhance women's appeal, but it is seldom sufficient in itself to establish that appeal, whereas appearance in women often is. For this reason some male actors nudging or exceeding the age of 70, for example, Clint Eastwood, Robert Redford, Paul Newman, or Jack Nicholson, may be characterized as attractive and sexy, and featured in films where they captivate nubile maidens sometimes young enough to be their granddaughters, yet female actors such as Elizabeth Taylor or Goldie Hawn may be seen as too old for major roles in movies or television, no matter how well-preserved they may be. Oscar Wilde suggested in a less than flattering statement both about women and society's expectations of them that "A man's face is his autobiography; a woman's, her greatest work of fiction." For aging women, a lifetime of living under patriarchal structures is reflected in their everyday lives in older age, as well as in their relationship with their own bodies. This chapter examines the social and demographic characteristics of Canadian women in older age, gender-linked age inequities, and, given the stark reality of biological aging, the incremental effect of our cultural emphasis on female appearance.

AGING AND WOMEN'S DIFFERENTIAL LIFE EXPERIENCES

It is often thought that Western society's devaluation of aging women is a relatively recent phenomenon that developed as a result of the increase in women's life expectancy and the prejudice of a youth-oriented culture. Although longevity has indeed increased and there has been more attention paid to youth over the past 30 years, a number of myths about aging women and their families have led to a sentimental view of past family life. Most important among these is the myth of large, caring families who lived together in large households, and had respect for their elders. Nett (1981) points out that "... contrary to belief, past households, although notably different in some respects from present ones, appear to have been for the most part two-generational, not much larger than current ones, with members sharing small and somewhat crowded dwellings for all but the wealthy, not entirely economically self-sufficient, and experiencing frequent changes of members and locale." This was also found in a study of pre-Confederation Newfoundland, often described as the most familial of all regions in North America (McDaniel and Lewis, 1997).

What then happened to the older generation if most families lived in two-generation households? Shorter life expectancy meant, of course, that fewer lived to see their grandchildren. Women's greater longevity, even then, often meant that women "outlived their usefulness," and the aging woman was treated with less than the mythical respect for elders.

There is no clear relation between modernization (the so-called progress of time) and a degeneration in the status of older women. It is a myth that the past was the pinnacle of good treatment of older women and that we have slid downwards ever since. At the same time, it is clear that there is cultural variation in the treatment and respect given to older women. In many First Nations societies, older women are the elders who command enormous respect. It is possible that in the past in Western societies, older people were consistently regarded with respect only among the upper classes. If this is so, then older women today may not be treated as differently from their grandmothers and great-grandmothers as we tend to think. One parallel between older women in the past and those of today is that they continue to be valued more for their utility as mothers, wives, or potential sexual partners than for what they were, or are, as individuals (de Beauvoir, 1970).

Aging is a profoundly different experience for women than for men, with much of the difference having more to do with the structural realities of women's lives than with individual differences or preferences. To understand why this is so, two factors should be explored.

The first factor is the cause of population or demographic aging, which is the unintended result not of increased life expectancy, as is often thought, but of declining birth rates. As fewer and fewer young people enter a population, the average or mean age of that population tends to increase, even with no changes in life expectancy. But if life expectancy also increases, then the mean age of the population will increase at an even faster rate. In Canada over the past two decades, there has been a precipitous decline in the birth rate, so precipitous that it has been termed a "baby bust," compared to the baby boom of the late 1940s to the early 1960s. It is the decline in the birth rate that is the most important factor in the aging of Canada's population. For a more detailed explanation of population aging, see McDaniel (1986). Birth rates have declined largely as a result of changes in women's lives, particularly their dramatically increased labour force participation. This is another factor that makes population aging particularly a women's issue.

The second factor is that women's experiences with the process of aging are different simply because women tend to outlive men. Any older population, such as that of North America, Europe, or Japan, will have many more women than men. This is particularly true at the oldest ages, where women outlive men by a considerable number of years. Currently in Canada, there are more than twice as many women as men in the 85+ age group (Statistics Canada, 2003). The ratio of women to men in the oldest age groups is increasing as greater gains are made in life expectancy at age 85 and above. Projections lead us to anticipate that by 2031, there will be only 41 men (85+) for every 100 women of the same age (*Gerontological Studies,* 1996: 15). Old men are truly hard to find! The consequence is that from time to time the gerontological literature has floated the idea of polygyny in old age (in other words, many old women sharing, in presumably "grateful" fashion, one old man). It has been noted (Abu-Laban, 1981: 5) that "while the supportive advantages of communal living can [be] and have been argued, the idea that ... one older man could meet the sexual needs of several older women is shortsighted, at best." Alternatively, it has been suggested that the problem of "partner scarcity" in old age could also be addressed by lesbian relationships (Abu-Laban, 1984), a possibility insufficiently addressed in the gerontological literature.

The life experiences of aging women are shaped by their greater longevity. Women tend to marry men about two years older than they are and can expect to be widowed, given the differential life expectancies of men and women. Even in early old age, at ages 65–74 for example, less than 8 percent of men are widowers, while more than one-third of women are (*Gerontological Studies,* 1996: 18). By age 85+, 80 percent of women are widowed, while about 39 percent of men are (McDaniel, 2001; Statistics Canada, 2003). This large and significant difference has numerous ramifications for the lives of older women.

Women, as they become middle-aged and older, have much greater likelihood of experiencing the most traumatic of life's losses: the death of a spouse. In today's world, this often means that the spouse has died of a chronic illness after being sick over some extended period of time, perhaps with the woman acting as central caregiver (Fast et al., 1997; McDaniel, 1992b, 1993a, 2000). Marriage is more than an emotional bond; it is an economic union. The death of the spouse thus also often entails loss of one's recent role in life and whatever prestige that involved. After the death of her husband, a widow sometimes finds her standard of living reduced (Townson, 1995: 48–49). This is true largely because, until recently, many private pensions in Canada did not have any survivor's provisions. And even now, survivor's pensions are often the first to go when times get tough and benefits are cut (McDaniel, 2002). Any increase in survivor's benefits in private pensions has been countered, however, by a current tendency for working people with benefits packages, still differentially men, to bargain away survivor's benefits for job security or better wage settlements. Providing survivors' benefits also means pension plan holders, still more often men, must opt for lower retirement benefits, something that many may not want to do. Women who live common-law, single, or divorced, are often ineligible for any survivor's pensions at all. Women's greater longevity has other consequences. Women who outlive their spouses and suffer grief at their death tend to be more prone to physical and mental illnesses. These illnesses, together with widows' changed living arrangements, often cause family members to intervene. Older widows lose autonomy and independence much more often than do married women or women who live on their own. The longer women live, the greater the likelihood that they will be institutionalized, either for health reasons (the longer one lives, the stronger the probability of failing health) or for social reasons (no one at home to help them out with activities of daily living). It has been estimated that more older women in Canada may be institutionalized for social reasons than for health reasons (McDaniel, 2000).

Pensions also structure women's experiences with aging differently than men's. Those women who are entitled to anything more than Canada/Quebec Pensions or Old Age Security (Gee and McDaniel, 1992; McDaniel and Gee, 1993; McDaniel, 1995a)—not a large proportion in any case because of the kinds of discontinuous work experiences that many women have—find that on retirement their pensions are often prorated for their greater longevity: the same sum in pension funds means less per month or year for a woman than for a man, so that the pension might last to the estimated end of the woman's life (Townson, 1995). And now CPP has changed, with particular implications for women, who are more dependent on public pensions than are men. Pensions for women are not user-friendly. And far fewer women than men participate in RRSP programs (Statistics Canada *Daily,* 18 February 1997). The presumption in many private pension schemes is that women are not sole supporters of themselves and others, but rather that they are spouses of someone with access to pension benefits, a presumption that for many women simply is not borne out. It is not surprising, then, that poverty among women in their older years, as for women of any age, is more common than among men (Cohen and Petten, 1997). Single mothers under 65 experienced a poverty rate of 56.8 percent in 1995, and unattached women over 65, a rate of 50.6 percent (Cohen and Petten, 1997: 12). The ratio of poor older women to poor older men is 7.3 to 1 (Cohen and Petten, 1997: 12). For aged women, poverty is a common experience indeed, with 27 percent of women over age 80 having less than $10 000 a year in income (*Gerontological Studies,* 1996: 116). With increasing numbers of Canadians being encouraged or coerced into early "retirement" before they are eligible for any pension (Schellenberg and Ross, 1997), a sharp increase in poverty among future elders may be anticipated.

Mainstream literature on women and aging often relies on the assumption that women's lives involve marriage, children, and men as well as happy family situations in both family of origin and family of choice. The many references to widowhood, caregiving by adult children, and family supports in the literature on aging suggest that women's lives are perhaps more homogeneous than they, in fact, are (McDaniel, 1997b; 1999). Unmarried women and women who have lived in untraditional families have received very little research attention (Abu-Laban, 1980, 1981, 1992; Fast et al., 1997). Ironically, the burden of caring can be denied to some women in contemporary society. In 1997 the Province of Alberta ruled against "Ms. T.," a foster mother who had successfully cared for 17 children over many years, when it became known that she had moved from a heterosexual to a lesbian relationship. Suddenly, the state felt compelled to raise questions concerning the intimate life of a foster parent caregiver and to arbitrarily deny needy children access to an apparently excellent home. Such questions were seen as irrelevant when Ms. T.'s partner was a man.

Assumptions and Presumptions about Aging Women

The research literature on social support still promulgates an image of the aged as "gray-haired Anglo-Celtic, heterosexual, life long marrieds, who have produced children and grand-children" (Abu-Laban, 1980: 196; also see Connidis, 2001). The underlying presumptions are that families of older women exist in sufficiently close proximity to assist and that this assistance is both beneficial and desired. McDaniel and Gee (1993) as well as Connidis (2001) and others make the point that current initiatives for changes in social policy in Canada often start with these presumptions. For example, much of the reasoning in regard to recent reductions in hospital stays and in funds for chronic care and recuperation facilities is based on the presumption that discharged hospital patients will have someone at home to care for them (Fast et al., 1997; McDaniel, 1997a). Often this is not true, for any number of reasons. Family mobility and immigration is one factor. Others, often overlooked, include the fact that not all families are happy families, willing and able to care for aging parents. Much is known about family violence and other negative aspects of family interactions, yet when aging is discussed, too often these realities are forgotten as questions are asked about contact with adult children, the assumption being that this contact is good, welcome, and helpful. It may well not be for many older women. More older women are divorced or separated. These women may rely on non-relatives, ex-relatives, or extended families for help and support, or they may have few resources on which to call for help. Much more needs to be known and understood about the heterogeneity of women's experience with aging.

Another factor to consider is that in the mainstream aging literature, heterosexuality is the prevailing assumption. The experiences of aging lesbian women have been largely ignored until a few recent studies (Connidis, 2001; Slater, 1995; Quam, 1996). More attention has been devoted to visible minorities, such as ethnic groups and their experiences with aging, but even that attention has been scant indeed (Chappell et al., 2003; Driedger and Chappell, 1987; Abu-Laban, 1991).

The invisibility of lesbian women generally, and aging lesbian women in particular, works in contradictory ways: both to conceal lesbians' experiences with aging and to reinforce prevalent stereotypes about lesbians. Concealment means that almost nothing is known about whether and how lesbian aging experiences differ from those of heterosexuals. (Slater [1995] provides an excellent brief summary of the issues for lesbian women, as does Connidis [2001].) Stereotypical beliefs about lesbians and aging can prevail in the absence of evidence to the contrary. Heterosexist bias and homophobia work together to instill in aging lesbians a fear of discovery and subsequent persecution. The silence that is a result of their fear helps to reinforce the stereotypes about lesbians and seals the double standard.

In sociological literature, it often happens that lesbian experience is subsumed under public gay male subcultures (Lee, 1987). The argument (see O'Brien and Goldberg, 2000) that lesbians are absent from public institutions of the gay culture—such as bars, nightclubs, and bathhouses—and therefore unavailable for sociological analysis, excludes lesbians of all ages, but older lesbians even more so. This is rather like arguing that heterosexual women cannot be studied because they are not found in strip joints, sports bars, and locker rooms. Older lesbians are overlooked not only because they do not participate in the kind of "gay subculture" that attracts sociologists, but also because they are subsumed by gerontologists under the category of aging women in general, where lesbian experiences tend to be reduced to the level of simple friendship or confidante relationships (Connidis, 2001). Even the concept of a "lesbian community" tends to ghettoize lesbian experience and isolate it further from that of other women. Ethnocultural differences among lesbians are even more invisible.

The notion that lesbians might have better experiences with aging than heterosexual women, although not without possibilities, poses further questions. This idea rests on the premise that lesbians in their younger years have learned to cope with being society's outsiders and, in essence, have learned crisis management that could serve them well as they age. Adaptive strategies involved in "coming out" could, in other words, be relied upon in coping with aging. Lee (1987), however, finds no support in his study of older gays and lesbians that crisis management skills are cumulative. He suggests instead that this view is rather like "a new version of the puritanical notion that suffering is good for you in the long run" (Lee, 1987: 53). His conclusion, based on life satisfaction scores of 47 gay men, is that "Sailing into a happy homosexual old age may be more a matter of steering clear of storms than of weathering them" (Lee, 1987: 57).

Generational conflict may be sharp and divisive among lesbians and gays because many contemporary elders who are gay or lesbian are part of the "pre-Stonewall" era,[2] when one's sexual orientation was strictly private and cautiously concealed. By contrast, for many in the post-Stonewall era, being gay or lesbian is of political and public moment. This has several important implications. One is that there are few role models—gay or lesbian elders or grandparents who can guide younger people on how to age well and gracefully. Another is the creation of a generation gap as older gays and lesbians react in fear and apprehension about the more public activities of younger gays and lesbians. Some insights into the contrasting social-historical experiences of older and younger lesbians can be gained from a recent National Film Board, Studio "D" video *Forbidden Love: The Unashamed Stories of Lesbian Lives*. The film features interviews with older lesbian women who recount their experiences some 40 years previously in the early "lesbian-friendly" beer parlours and bars in Toronto, Vancouver, and Montreal. It documents life in butch/femme subcultures and general experiences of harassment and intolerance. It is a film that challenges the erasure of lesbian history and helps to bring Canadian lesbian narratives out of the closet.

The post-Stonewall generation of lesbians may face another challenge. In "coming out," there is a need for the sort of crisis management discussed above that can prepare one for other crises, including the crisis of old age. On the other hand, coming out can have considerable costs too, including the loss of family contact and support. In later years, this can result in smaller networks on which to draw for support and aid, as well as in cumulative stress. Little is known or understood about the effects that these losses of family contact can have on elderly women—losses that do occur in the lives of many women.

Emotional Supports

Women are socially central in a demographically aging society like Canada's, as well as structurally central. Their social roles and the expectations placed on them mean that women of all ages are more often placed in situations of looking after others (Connidis, 2001; Gee and Kimball, 1987; McDaniel, 1999, 2000, 2001). In Canada, a disproportionate share of caring for the young, old, and poverty-stricken falls to women. Caring by women extends across the boundaries of race, ethnicity, class, sexual orientation, and (dis)ability—all but the rare woman become involved in caring for others in some way and to some degree at some point in their lives (Chappell et al., 2003).

Caring is, of course, not something on which women have a monopoly, yet it seems that it is a defining requirement of femininity in our society (McDaniel, 1999, 2002). A caring woman is a feminine woman, embodying the Madonna image of nurturing along with the self-sacrificing image of the woman who puts the needs of others, including the sexual needs of men, above her own interests and needs. Girls, as they become adult women, are socialized to care for others. Girls who do not care sufficiently are often labelled unfeminine, selfish, aggressive, or deviant, not to mention adjectives even less flattering. Learning to care, to be self-sacrificing and self-deprecating, is often the same as learning to be a good woman.

The socially sanctioned imperative to care extends well beyond adolescence. Kaden and McDaniel (1990) found in a study in Ontario that it is women (wives, daughters and daughters-in-law, sisters, aunts, women friends) who are called upon most often to do the caring for older relatives and friends. The same was found in a national study, although men were found to provide care too (Fast et al., 1997; Keating et al., 1999). It is also women in the paid labour force who do the caring work: day-care workers, nursing home staff, nurses generally, and others who care for the sick and those with disabilities, often in low-paying jobs. Older people prefer to call on daughters and daughters-in-law rather than on sons or sons-in-law for needs, except financial ones.

In a national study of Canadians, McDaniel (1993a, 1994) finds that it is usually women who are asked by both men and women for emotional support in times of stress or crisis. So reliant are older men on their spouses for emotional support that in situations in which they are upset with their wives, almost one-quarter of older men report that they have no one to call on for help. This compares with 16 percent of older women. Women tend to diversify their choice of whom they might rely on for emotional support, drawing on siblings, adult children, friends, and professionals more than men do. Women of all ages who are being asked for emotional support may come to see themselves and to be seen by others as more nurturing and caring than may men. The pressures on women to continue in their caring roles, often considerable in these times of economic difficulty, can have negative consequences on their well-being. Cutbacks to government programs have further negative consequences for women—as single parents, as health care and social service providers, and as family care providers—although these consequences are only beginning to be measurable (Keating et al., 1999). Women can burn out as a result of persistent and increasing expectations to be caring, to take on responsibility for the problems of others, and to put themselves and their own needs last. In such situations, women can develop a variety of stress-related problems that can eventually severely damage their health and self-esteem, as well as their families'. Caring for others can also undermine women's labour force and pension prospects.

Aging Women and Well-Being

Much about well-being among mid-life and older women is not known, largely as a result of the inadequacy of traditional social science measures to tap into the concept. Well-being includes physical, mental, and social health and often involves more than the absence of disease or disability. Asking how satisfied people are with their lives or with specific aspects of their lives typically leads to the majority reporting few dissatisfactions. It is probably not true, however, that everyone surveyed is happy and satisfied. It could be, in fact, that they are merely saying that compared to the wasted lives they see nightly on TV news programs—lives torn apart by war, disease, or famine—things could be worse. Such responses can be misleading at best.

Well-being is known to be as closely related to independence and autonomy as it is to physical health. Lack of control over one's life is well known to have adverse effects on emotional states, performance of tasks, subjective well-being, and on actual physiological indicators. Lack of control is precisely what many women experience at various stages of their lives as demands are placed on them by others, and as they are seen more as mothers, wives, and daughters than as individuals with control and autonomy. No one has been assigned the role of enhancing the development and well-being of women beyond the stage of childhood. This, combined with the popularly held stereotype of women as dependent and passive social agents, means that women are often seen as lacking in control and in the benefits to well-being that control offers.

The structural circumstances of many older women's lives make them more vulnerable to loss of control and autonomy (McDaniel, 1999, 2002). Among women who marry, those who outlive their husbands are more likely to find their lives influenced by other family members, by professionals, and by others. The privacy and judgment of a couple tends to be more respected. A long-time married couple share collective memories and can assist each other with their daily tasks. When one spouse dies, the collective memory may too. The remaining spouse, most often the woman, may be perceived as having lost her memory, if only because she can no longer rely on her spouse for the details of the shared memories. Similarly, her physical well-being can be imperiled by the need to do tasks, possibly for the first time, that previously were done by her husband. Family members also tend to observe an aging widow more closely for signs of problems with memory or well-being, signs that all of us might show but that may not be taken with the same degree of seriousness when they appear among younger family members. One of the authors (McDaniel) conducted an experiment in a large sociology of aging class: She asked the students to keep track over a week's time of how often they forgot things. The results revealed that, according to the self-reports of the students, most could be potential candidates for a diagnosis of Alzheimer's! Had the students been older and emotionally vulnerable after the death of a spouse, it can easily be imagined that doubts might have been raised about their mental competency.

The cumulative weight of women's various social obligations means that women often blame themselves for "not coping," for not being well enough organized, or for not being sufficiently capable, when in fact it would be more realistic to simply acknowledge the social forces that impinge on them and constrain their lives. Self-censure can translate quickly into self-neglect (because we are not deserving of nurturing after all) or self-abuse (substance abuse perhaps—most often nicotine and caffeine, but sometimes prescription drugs, alcohol, and/or street drugs). Donaldson (1997: 38) argues that spiritual deficits result: The traditional Western perspective of older women is so negative that most women try to make themselves invisible, externally as well as internally. In religion and mythology, the older woman has been associated with death as much as with life. Certainly, stress-related illnesses, depression, and anxiety are predictable problems for women. At the societal level, there is a potential growth not only in the feminization of social problems (inadequate mothering as the cause of crime) but in women-blaming. After all, the argument goes, women with their "selfish" demands got us into all these problems: too low a birth rate (which leads to population aging), work outside the home, demands for help in caring for children and older relatives, and altogether too many demands on the public purse (McDaniel, 1997b).

In addition to the subjective aspects outlined above, several ascriptive aspects of well-being have also been identified. Women seen by gatekeepers (medical doctors, social workers, psychologists, etc.) as healthy are those who most closely fit the culturally preferred definitions of a good woman (McDaniel, 1997b). Women who are married with children would fit the definition. White middle-class women even more so, and heterosexual women without doubt. Well-being for women, perhaps especially for aging women, is most surely obtained through this narrow definition of womanhood. Women of colour, women outside stable heterosexual relationships, lesbian women, women with disabilities, and women without children are simply not often considered in prototypical definitions of well-being for women. Any definition of well-being that includes the concept of autonomy cannot be applied to all those women whose daily lives have degenerated into survival struggles with violent partners/husbands, or to women who are so busy with their children and careers that physical (or mental) fitness is nothing but a dream, or to women who find themselves in any kind of role of subservience to others.

Social policy also has an impact on women's well-being, just as it does on their physical appearance. Compelling examples of this are provided by Gorlick and Pomfret (1993). They suggest that women on social assistance have very limited access to non-essential health services. After years of raising children, women on social assistance often find themselves with teeth that have not been treated properly by routine dental care and with cheap eyeglasses that are far from flattering. Also, they often have weight problems (either obesity or emaciation) from years of trying to feed families with an inadequate income that leaves little for mum to eat but pasta. Literally shaped in these circumstances by social policy, women have limited possibilities for putting an end to their dependence on social assistance. The prospects for women of colour, Aboriginal women, women with disabilities, or lesbian women are even worse. Aged women with out-of-date eyewear, bad teeth, unfashionably sized bodies, limited education, and whose only (or main) work experience is raising children on social assistance (no matter how much credit they might deserve for creative budgeting) are not seen as good prospects for employment in a tightly competitive job market (McDaniel, 1995). Interestingly, it is many if not all of these same attributes that limit aging poor women's marriage prospects as well. These women are not seen to be developing character or physical attractiveness as they age.

STANDARDS OF BEAUTY

Women's aging differs from that of men because of the ways in which gender is constructed and inequities are defined, reinforced, and legitimated. Although bodily changes are an expected part of human aging, they have different consequences for females than for males. Physical appearance is a key indicator of aging and old age. Over time, one's appearance undergoes significant change and, for older women particularly, these changes are subject to social judgments in some cases and social sanctions in others.

For the female child, to be assessed as "pretty" or "beautiful" is the highest accolade, one that usually makes her parents proud. They bask in the reflected praise, and their daughter learns the lesson well. To be pretty is to be approved of, liked, and rewarded. Notably, these evaluative terms that focus on the girl's facade are rarely applied to boys. Beauty is held out as an intrinsic goal for both girls and women. In infancy, females are judged by standards of "cuteness," and "prettiness," and this shifts with age into standards of "beauty" and "glamour." These beauty standards are societal creations, enshrined as ideals toward which all females should strive. But, ironically, these standards of beauty are also narrow and restrictive, and set impossible expectations for most females all of the time; by virtue of human aging, they are impossible for all women at least some of the time. There are major social consequences that stem from these unachievable standards. Beauty norms are both prescriptive and proscriptive. They tell women what ought to be, serve as mechanisms of social control, and are related to women's access to economic security, social influence, health, and intimacy. When women are reluctant to swim or engage in sports because they fear their bodies will be judged, when women prefer to stay home because of having a "bad hair day," or "nothing to wear," or because they've gained "too much weight," they succumb to powerful social constraints, constraints that define them and restrict their opportunities. Appearance becomes their measure of personal value. Socially created appearance standards are far from harmless decorative diversions. These standards have age, race-ethnic, economic, and sexual-preference biases, and, as such, they are anything but optional. Although they present an illusion of choice ("grey eye shadow or brown?"), the "options" are both constrictive and controlling.

Beauty as Constant

Beauty is often portrayed as some essential attribute that is readily apparent to everybody. However, there can be little doubt that standards of beauty are social and historical constructs that are linked to time and place, economics, ethnicity, and power. This means that standards of beauty are neither constant nor absolute. Not only do standards change, but taste and judgment are also contingent upon the observer. The opulent, full-bodied figures by the Flemish painter Peter Paul Rubens (1577–1640) stand in contrast to the slim representations of women in the work of contemporary painters such as Canadian Alex Colville or American Andrew Wyeth. Currently, as in the past, what is defined as feminine beauty may dramatically alter a woman's natural appearance. The whalebone corset of earlier times was an "unnatural" attempt to rearrange women's bodies into an idealized hourglass figure. Some enthusiasts even removed one of their ribs to better effect a wasp waist. These are only two examples of countless attempts to rework nature. Women's breasts, for example, have been subjected to various management strategies over the years—brassieres are only one example. Devices to reshape women, in whatever image happens to be currently acceptable to those with the power to define it, have resulted in sometimes painful and harmful contrivances. In some historical eras, breasts were exaggerated; in others, they were minimized. In classical Greece and Rome, female curvaceousness was "unattractive," and women wore restrictive bands to de-emphasize their breasts. Yesterday's "falsies" and today's "padded bras" were first advertised in the nineteenth century during an era when the ideal woman was pictured as inordinately slender through the waist but ample and curvaceous in breasts and hips. By the 1920s, flat chests were again fashionable and again women used bands to restrict and flatten their breasts, with the goal of achieving the "boyish" figure considered appropriate to the "flapper" look. "Push-up" padded bras were fashionable in the 1950s, and today we have the yearly spectre of thousands of North American women seeking elective breast surgery in order to increase their bra size. Beauty ideals obviously change over time, but there can be little doubt of their influence. Current efforts to surgically remove or add fat in strategic parts of the body are but a technologically upgraded version of the nineteenth-century procedure to remove an "offensive" rib. Historical fluctuations in ideal size and weight are also reflected in the average weights of *Playboy* centrefolds and Miss America contestants. Evidence indicates they too have become thinner over time (Smith, 1990). In 1951, Miss Sweden was five feet seven inches tall and weighed 151 pounds (Garner et al., 1980). In 1983, the woman selected as Miss Sweden was five foot nine (two inches taller), but she weighed a rather scant 109 pounds. Naomi Wolf (1991: 192) argues that contemporary models are some 22 percent to 23 percent slimmer than the average woman. The manifold historical variations in definitions of beauty suggest that beauty is far from a constant.

Beauty as Youth and Flawless Body

Young girls learn to worry about their appearance from an early age. Parents of newborns treat daughters differently from sons, emphasizing appearance and femininity. Beauty is emphasized for young girls both in their play and in their toys. An exercise kit (including an exercise mat, skipping rope, and exercise clothes) for girls ages five and up seeking early access to the body beautiful was advertised nationally "… not as a means of developing coordination, fitness, or athletic skill but as a way to 'work off that extra chocolate chip cookie'" (Unger and Crawford, 1992: 331).

The insidious nature of the emphasis on child-woman beauty was brutally apparent on the day after Christmas 1996. A Colorado child, six-year-old JonBenet Ramsey, was found strangled and, reportedly, sexually molested in the basement of her wealthy parents' home. The international media attention surrounding the death of this child, a former "Little Miss Colorado" and "National Tiny Miss Beauty," flooded the tabloids, television news, and talk shows. Photographs and video replays of the young girl's contest appearances showed haunting images of a heavily made-up child, not playing dress-up in her mother's clothes, but, in shadowy replay with a pirouetting walk, mimicking coquettish adult mannerisms. The sexual overtones of child beauty competitions were brought home to many. These contests are common. It is reported that "more than 100 000 children under the age of 12 compete in about 3000 beauty pageants" in the United States alone (Clark, 1997). Little girls worrying about the effects on their "figures" of too many cookies, exposed to numerous "perfect" female images, grow to be adolescents struggling to conquer their physical imperfections and media images set a demanding standard.

And demanding photographers have moved beyond the simple airbrushing of pores to digital techniques that redesign female images and obliterate presumed "imperfections" (i.e. natural human variations). Even celebrities acclaimed for their beauty may fail to make the grade. Singer-songwriter Nelly Furtado and *Titanic* star Kate Winslet both objected recently when magazines digitally manipulated photographs in order to make them more "attractive." A British magazine gave Furtado a flatter stomach while GQ magazine altered Winslet's legs to make them slimmer and more chiseled (Cott, 2003). Beauty ideals can now exceed all previous expectations; at the extreme, the commercial representations of women are neither human nor obtainable.

This beauty ideal is contingent on age; the discrepancy between "younger" and "older" women may come quite early and perhaps shockingly:

> The young girl of 18 or 25 may well believe that her position in society is equal to, or even higher than that of men. As she approaches middle age, however, she begins to notice a change in the way people treat her. Reflected in growing indifference of others toward her looks and toward her sexuality (read 'toward her as a sex object'), she can see and measure the decline of her worth, her status in the world. (Bell, 1970: 75)

Susan Sontag (1972) puts it more bluntly, arguing that, socially, women are "girls as long as possible, who then age humiliatingly into middle-aged women and then obscenely into old women."

In the 1980s, Louise Arcand, the first woman in Canada to hold a telecast anchor position with a major French-language television station, filed an age discrimination suit against the CBC. She had successfully anchored the increasingly popular dinner-hour newscast of Montreal's Radio-Canada affiliate for three years, but the position was taken away from the then 40-year-old Arcand and given to a 28-year-old woman. Louise Arcand was moved to radio and given a reduction in pay because the network wanted a more "youthful" look. Both the Canadian Human Rights Commission and the Quebec Labour Department criticized the unjust, discriminatory nature of the decision to move Arcand to radio with a reduction in pay, but neither agency had the power to restore her job or award her significant damages (*The Globe and Mail,* 1992: C4).

The physical limitations that can beset humans become increasingly prevalent with age, and aging increases the incidence of chronic conditions and disabilities. Ingeborg Boyens, (2003: 194–195) a former CBC documentary producer, describes how multiple sclerosis slowly changed her expectations of her body.

I know there are thousands of victims of chronic disease … I wish there were comfort in the sisterhood of the sick. But … I still would yearn to fit into a society that doesn't really have a place for me. It's a society that celebrates youth, beauty and sexiness. The ugly walking shoes and the unsightly industrial canes that are the backdrop of my life are a reminder that someone whose body is flawed by chronic illness has no business thinking of herself in those terms.

Yet, supposedly blemished bodies, whether "flawed" by disability or aging, may serve as exemplars of human ingenuity and resilience. Mary Lowenthal Felstiner (2000), who has arthritis, discusses the power of making her hidden disability known to her students:

> Every handicap made visible becomes an example to (others) who have covert worries about themselves. They want to know an honest job can be done with a disability. (Even if it) can't be done the same way everyone else does it. They now think that if disability strikes them, they won't wash up….
>
> So whatever disclosures we make (and this depends on our condition) we ought to be able to make without risk, without shame. That's more likely to happen if I confess and then you confess and then someone else, until it's clear we're no cowering minority in the family of humankind.

Felstiner's observations can be extended to openness in revealing or even enjoying one's true chronological age. As Chris Hewitt (2004) says, in discussing the ability of some older people to be appreciative of their own well lived-in and aging bodies, "We're here. We're not Britney Spears. Get used to it."

Beauty as the Result of Disciplined Effort

Given the numerous pressures on women to "look good," there is an implicit message that those who don't measure up to some standard of attractiveness have "let themselves go." They haven't tried hard enough to become beautiful, and this is a uniquely feminine moral failing for which women may be condemned. It is as if, in some way, they have contaminated the landscape of patriarchy. (Lest this sound extreme, it might be asked how many women have rejected their female friends because they don't look good enough?) Brownmiller (1984: 13–19) says that unattractive women can be seen as "not caring about themselves—or not taking care of themselves." The pressures on older women to "keep up" are numerous. Women "… are exhorted to stay young and beautiful, to do things to their bodies to achieve this, and to wear make-up, hair products, and clothes to conceal their real age" (Itzen, 1986: 126).

Young girls learn early that beauty rituals and preparations take time, planning, and money. Even so, plastic surgeons admit that, recently, their clientele of teenagers doubled in just five years (Alexander, 1990). With parental support, young teens are turning to elective surgery to correct their "defects."

But it is especially for older women that cosmetic surgery is held out as a way to remedy physical imperfections that, in their case, are usually the result of the natural aging process. The range of bodily alteration possibilities increases yearly. These include breast augmentations, lifts, and reductions, liposuction of any of a number of ample areas of the body, face lifts, brow lifts, eye lifts, nose alterations, lip reduction as well as lip enlargement, botulinum toxin and other injections, facial resurfacing, derriere lifts, and so on. Women now have the opportunity to shorten a "too long" second toe, to better display their foot in open-toed sandals, even though an elongated second toe was once deemed "aristocratic." Belly button surgery is an option for those hoping to wear midriff-baring fashions. An estimated 56 000 "tummy tucks" are performed each year and the incidence has tripled in the past decade. Be forewarned, however, that medical journals are in disagreement on the "ideal" shape for a woman's navel and the options are many: oval, round, elliptical, hooded, or T-shaped (Chase, 2002).

The whimsicality of surgical aesthetics is reflected in the history of cosmetic procedures on the aging eye. In the 1960s, the preferred template for surgeons doing blepheroplasties (eye lifts) was a wide-eyed Audrey Hepburn look. By the 1980s, surgeons favoured a different look, a narrower Christie Brinkley "sporty eye." Similarly, rhinoplasties (nose "corrections") have changed since the 1950s from a turned up "cute" nose to a purportedly less "operated on" more "serious" nose. Ironically, cosmetic corrections to reduce the appearance of age, may, like fads, become dated themselves.

Beauty makeover themes saturate popular culture and they too imply that disciplined effort gets results. Voyeuristic television programs such as *Extreme Makeover* or *Nip/Tuck* offer the opportunity to look into the lives of the bodily unhappy. The "before" and "after" format appeals to self-improvement themes common to our culture, and these programs offer strategies and tools for re-modelling just as surely as TV home improvement programs instruct us in the mysteries of interior design or carpentry. Even with daunting footage of actual surgeries, the transformation is made to appear seamless suggesting that beauty for all is just around the corner, if you endure the pain (and expense). Such programs assume and reinforce a cultural understanding that some body characteristics are so unacceptable, so thoroughly disgusting, there can be no question that a mass audience will agree "after" is an improvement on "before."

The expense of elective cosmetic surgery makes it inaccessible for most older women, and, as well, its risks increase with age. Without the benefits of surgical intervention, the aging woman has been characterized by one best-selling physician-author as metamorphasizing into a pitiable figure characterized by obesity and a coarse appearance, "not really a man but no longer a functional woman. These individuals live in the world of intersex" (Reuben, 1969: 92). And what if an aged woman doesn't get her act together and assemble some semblance of youth? Not meeting the expectations of society regarding physical appearance could make a difference between life and death (Abu-Laban, 1984). Sudnow's classic study of a hospital emergency room noted a sharp difference in response to a child patient and an aged female patient when both presented virtually the same symptoms at admission. An intern gave mouth-to-mouth resuscitation to the child, but he did not do the same procedure on the aged woman. When questioned, the intern explained the difference in emergency room treatment by saying "he could never bring himself to put his mouth to 'an old lady's like that'" (Sudnow, 1967: 101).

The media models available for women generally, and aging women specifically, are often economically advantaged women who have tapped into the surgeon's skill. Several years ago, *Chatelaine,* Canada's leading women's magazine, lauded actor Elizabeth Taylor, purportedly the veteran of a number of cosmetic procedures, as "the most beautiful 61-year-old on the planet" (Gooden, 1993). Unaltered 61-year-olds are not held out as models very often; instead, the surgeon's creation is set up as the physical apex of womanly aging.

Beauty as the Right Size

Ideal body sizes and shapes are part of the standards of beauty set by society, as is well known among university and college women. There is a general preoccupation about what is too much or what is too little, but very rarely an acceptance of the female body in its natural state, free of surgical or cosmetic intervention. For those who have "too much" there are diets, liposuction, guilt, and recrimination. For those with "too little" there is breast augmentation and, more recently, a reversal of liposuction that involves injection of fat or the placement of what one hopes are "harmless" substances into the body to change the contours in one manner or another. Failure to maintain a certain body size and weight carries an inherent stigma and can plague girls from an early age. Women take many health risks in pursuit of what Western, and sometimes non-Western, culture defines as an optimal figure. Smoking is often seen as a dietary aid promising weight control, albeit with cancer and other health risks. Cigarette merchants play on the obsession with slimness by targeting female consumers with slender "feminine" brands, such as Virginia Slims or Capri, that link thinness, smoking, and glamour. Indeed, Lucky Strike cigarettes launched one of the first successful tobacco ads in 1929 by urging women to "Reach for a Lucky instead of a sweet." North American women are taught to "fear" fat. They are urged to gain control, exert discipline over their wayward bodies, and establish order through slimness (Bordo, 1993). The slender woman, a homogenized body type, becomes a ubiquitous, media-enhanced cultural icon. A Canadian survey of Saskatoon high-school students found 76 percent of girls indicating that they "diet," while 17 percent vomit, and 12 percent use diet aids (Currie, 1990: 7). Recent research suggests that concern about weight is a continuing theme among older Canadian women (Clarke, 2002). In the United States alone there is a $33-billion-a-year industry concerned with diets (Wolf, 1991: 17).

Deprivatory dieting commonly has horrendous implications, including anorexia and bulimia. The US National Institute of Mental Health estimates that approximately 5 percent of adolescent and adult women, and 1 percent of men have anorexia nervosa, bulimia, or binge eating disorders (Women's Health Matters Network, 2003). Hesse-Biber (1991) estimates that some 20 percent to 25 percent of college/university women control their weight by vomiting and using diuretics and laxatives. Teens and young adult women, perhaps particularly university women, are under strong pressure to achieve, to fit in, as well as to succeed socially. Many may see super-slim models shown in fashion magazines or on television sitcoms as their role models (Thompson, C., 1996). Deep concerns about weight may start at puberty when girls see their bodies becoming womanly and they may be teased or become ashamed. This may stem from the sense that women's bodies are seen in Western societies as first and foremost sexual, so young women may feel or believe that their identities and individualities are subsumed by the stereotyped female body. Adding to the misery of eating disorders is that they are often treated as psychological or even psychiatric problems of individual women. This can convey to women that they really are mentally ill or psychologically disturbed. Rather than helping, the stigma can work to aggravate a bad situation.

A very different approach is now being embraced by third-wave feminist women, spirited in part by the path-breaking book by Becky Thompson (1994) *A Hunger So Wide and So Deep*, which revealed that many eating disorders for women were related to emotional issues, sometimes even sexual abuse. Her work began to break down the theory that eating disorders were psychological problems of largely white, middle- or upper-middle-class girls and women. Some third-wave activist movements (Reindl, 2001) have taken root around the social and cultural conditions that produce eating disorders among women. This changes the nature of the problem of eating disorders from being an individual psychological adjustment matter to one of social cause, with a social solution. It has given third-wave women a forum for social activism and for engaging social change as agents.

When dieting doesn't produce the desired effect, women may again turn to surgery. In the United States, liposuction is now the most common form of cosmetic surgery. In 2002, 372 831 lipoplasty procedures were performed, an increase of 111 percent since 1997 (American Society for Aesthetic Plastic Surgery, 2003).

A whittled-down body is not enough. The contemporary preoccupation with larger breasts and narrower hips (atypical of the human female although typical of Barbie dolls) has contributed to the rising popularity of breast alteration surgery. In 2002, there were 249 641 breast augmentation surgeries (an increase of 147 percent since 1997) and 125 614 breast reduction surgeries (an increase of 162 percent since 1997) (American Society for Aesthetic Plastic Surgery 2003). The great majority of breast implantations (80 percent) are done for elective purposes, not for post-cancer reconstruction. This has raised a host of questions regarding safety. The silicon gel Meme implant, now banned in Canada, was once hailed as boosting confidence along with cleavage. The first official acknowledgment of potential problems came in January 1991, when both Canada and the United States put a moratorium on its use because of concerns regarding surgical complications, including autoimmune problems, rupture of the implant, allergies, tumours, and repeated surgeries to correct the "problems" induced by earlier surgery. Nonetheless, in the summer of 2003, to the horror of many physicians and ethicists, a bar in Manitoba, mimicking similar events in bars in B.C. and Saskatchewan, sponsored a "Get on Track for a New Rack" contest offering free breast implants. In the words of one enthusiastic contestant, "The bigger the better. Because, like, bigger boobs: You get more attention, you get more money. You win the contests. Plus for job interviews or whatever. Seriously. In today's world, you have to look hot" (Smith, 2003). The immense popularity and acceptability of implants, is reinforced by some celebrities, whose newly enlarged and sometimes unusually spherical breasts placed inordinately close to the collar bone (if high is good, higher is better) have been described as surgeons' attempts to "better" nature by enabling their patients to resemble the elusive Barbie. Surgically created breasts have in themselves the potential to create a physical ideal.

Women can be damned if they do follow beauty standards and damned if they don't. Looking "hot" can backfire. A 1992 sexual harassment case against the giant Seattle aerospace company Boeing Corporation illustrates this problem. Part of Boeing's "defence" against the sexual harassment charge was to attack the credibility of the plaintiff by asking what *she* had done to encourage the crime. Boeing's lawyers argued that the fact that the plaintiff had cosmetic breast surgery denied the validity of the sexual harassment charge because it suggested that the plaintiff (who, it might be noted, was married) had breast augmentation surgery "to encourage overtures from male workers at Boeing" (Guteck, 1993: 209).

Ironically, size also defines power in patriarchal societies—hence the emphasis on the "little woman" who looks up to "her man." As women age, they tend to gain some weight, become larger. In fact, there is evidence to suggest that it may be to a woman's advantage to gain some weight post-menopause; among other benefits, increased body fat can contribute to the retention of natural estrogen. But the advantages of weight gain are seldom spelled out, much less the potential that larger size may carry an aura of influence. What does it mean to be "a woman of substance" or a "weighty presence"? Is there power in taking up more space in older age than is often allowed to women of any age?

Beauty as Monolith

The image of beauty that society presents to women is embodied in a female who is not only young and slim but also white (or "whitish"), heterosexual, and class advantaged. This is a monolithic image of appearance that reflects the prejudices of those who are in dominant positions in our society. For example, there is an ethnic/racial bias in the authoritative beauty ideal. Since Caucasians are a privileged racial group, the beauty messages, which are aimed at females from childhood on, reflect white privilege. Advertising imagery, therefore, reflects the status of the dominant group by using models who are tall and slim, with fair skin and light hair and eyes. This sets an ethnocultural racial standard that is northern-European and thereby excludes most of the world's women (Abu-Laban, 1991). The result is that just as we find women in general dieting, grooming, and purchasing commodities to imitate the consumer icon, we also find visible-minority women specifically using hair straighteners, skin lighteners, or cosmetic surgery to "Westernize" the eyes (that is, to alter the epicanthic folds), rhinoplasty to alter noses, liposuction to change body shape, torturous high heels to look taller. Sometimes (not always), these procedures are done in order to erase signs of racial or ethnic origin implicitly discredited by the media. Ella Shohat (1997: 204) argues that "from a multicultural feminist perspective, these cross-cultural transformations (cosmetic surgery, dyeing the hair) on one level are examples of 'internal exile' or 'appropriation,'" and for racialized women they can be a form of cultural erasure. There are ethnocultural variations in typical average height, weight, and patterns of fat distribution. Yet the standard of beauty to which all women in Canada are subjected is culturally specific. It fits a northern-European standard that is narrow even for women of northern-European descent. Even when ads portray models other than Caucasians, their features often send mixed messages—an Asian woman with "corrected" eyes; or an African woman of mixed background or with straightened hair or wearing a wig. The animated movie *Pocahantas* was described on CBC radio by a Canadian Aboriginal woman as having a body unlike any Aboriginal woman she had ever known. Interestingly, and still to be studied, some physical traits associated with aging are more common among specific ethnocultural groups, and these do not necessarily favour northern-European women (Abu-Laban, 1993). Sun damage is a major cause of skin aging; it causes wrinkling and loose skin. Darker, thicker-skinned women are less susceptible to sun damage, while women with a so-called Scottish-Irish complexion (i.e. pale, thin skin) are more susceptible to damage from ultraviolet light and, hence, their skin is more susceptible to loss of tone and elasticity over time.

Cultural notions of beauty are related to class advantage. The presence or absence of money means differential access to the facade of "beauty." Ehrenreich and English (1978: 108) describe the ideal beauty of the nineteenth century as sickly, "a beautiful invalid sensuously drooping on her cushions, eyes fixed tremulously at her husband or physician or already gazing into the Beyond." It is a description of beauty that is class-dependent. Economic advantage allows time for beauty rituals and pays for the associated expenses.

Those with marginal economic status cannot afford the luxury of leisurely draping over pillows, nor the discretionary time needed for cosmetic artifice; they cannot afford the clothes, whether haute couture or ready-to-wear, that signal style and status; they cannot afford "corrective" cosmetic surgery (even though some cosmetic surgeons are offering loan plans for future-oriented women); and they certainly cannot afford the elite surgeons who reconstruct the rich and powerful. In other words, for most aged women, access to the techniques that preserve what is defined as beauty is severely limited.

The biases of heterosexism and heterosexual privilege also interact with societal beauty standards to castigate women who are, or who are presumed to be, lesbian. Thus, the woman who openly chooses another woman as an intimate partner may be considered by the larger society as unattractive or "unfeminine." Lesbian relationships may be considered by some as second choice for women who are assumed to be "unable to attract a man." Conversely, women judged as "highly attractive" are more likely to be seen as "feminine" and less likely to be seen as lesbian (Unger, Hilderbrand, and Madar, 1982).

Jeanette Auger (1990: 33) suggests that "lesbians and heterosexual women alike are vulnerable to the myth that after menopause they are no longer sexual or attractive." Supporting this, Barbara MacDonald, a lesbian feminist, observes about her own aging:

> Sometimes lately … I see my arm with the skin hanging loosely from my forearm and cannot believe that it is really my own. It seems disconnected from me; it is someone else's. It is the arm of an old woman. It is the arm of such old women as I myself have seen, sitting on benches in the sun with their hands folded in their laps; *old women I have turned away from.* I wonder how and when these arms I see came to be my own—arms I cannot turn away from. (MacDonald and Rich, 1983: 14, italics added)

Beauty and Power

Frequently, women defined as beautiful are seen as holders of power, albeit female "power" as defined by patriarchal structures. The mistress of the ruler; the "beautiful" woman who marries upward, purportedly exchanging the rarity of her appearance for economic security; the "beautiful" woman who achieves career success that is then attributed (fairly or unfairly) to her appearance—all these women are seen as, in essence, "cashing in" on their looks.

In fact, women are often instructed in the art of appearance, with the implication that beauty pays off with material and emotional rewards. Given that patriarchy allows women few avenues to power, to the extent that it exists, beauty power is uniquely female. Advocates of this view present beauty as a facilitator, however painful the process. A book on beauty at the office advises women to wear "classic expensive-looking pumps … *as high as you can tolerate.* Keep them at your *desk if they're too uncomfortable* to wear to and from work. Remember: To look feminine is in your favor" (Schrader, 1981: 28, italics added).

The federal Liberals issued a guide for female candidates in the 1997 election (*The Globe and Mail*, 4 April 1997) that offered this advice:

> Your wardrobe is a reflection of you; therefore it should be planned with the same care that you define your policy, develop your strategy, and plan the organization of your campaign team. Remember that during the campaign, there will be no time to do things like laundry, cleaning the house, cooking, picking up the children or the dry cleaning. Complete as much as you can before the writ is dropped. Campaigns are a series of ups and downs—be prepared for mood swings.

The power of beauty is seen to open opportunities. "Being beautiful, intelligent, and in a career situation [has its] responsibilities—you can leap-frog into positions of prestige, but real power comes from ability and confidence; selection for your merit, not for your favours is what you want" (Schrader, 1981: 158, italics added). "Reverence" for youthful beauty has its bizarre aspects. In 1993, a 63-year-old Pennsylvania judge dismissed charges against a 30-year-old female model accused of driving 122 mph in a 55-mph zone because, in his view, the story she told was more likely to be true because of her appearance. In the judge's words, she was not "fat and ugly" or "an ugly broad" (*The New York Times,* 1993).

Although appearance may seem like a power advantage, still another court case suggests women can be damaged, regardless. Consider the decision made by a Canadian judge a few years ago. A 23-year-old man, armed with a knife and furious because his "girl-friend" had ended their relationship, kicked in the door of her home, pushed her into her bedroom, locked the door, and then ripped out the telephone cord when her friend tried to phone for help. The man had a lengthy criminal record, including previous convictions for forcible seizure armed with a knife, theft, break and entry, possession of drugs, assault, etc. The assailant was given a six-month sentence. The judge's comments are reflective of the bind in which women with youthful "beauty" find themselves.

> I could give him five years but I don't think under the circumstances of this case I'd be entitled to … he got mixed up with a silly little bunch of girls … a bunch of clucking females running around and they're all so scared they have to call the police … they're a free-floating type of female young for their age, very nubile, very attractive surely, but still impressionable, still stupid. You know women don't get much brains before they're 30…. (*Chatelaine*, March 1978: 58 and 118)

However our society describes beauty and femininity, these are not seen as improving with age. The woman who, figuratively or in reality, has men at her feet in awe of her beauty, enjoys an illusionary sense of power, one vulnerable to the passage of time. Where such belief circumscribes her life choices, it can come at great cost in older age. Susan Brownmiller (1986: 236) notes: "Women who rely on a feminine strategy as their chief means of survival can do little to stop the roaring tide of maturity as they watch their advantage slip by."

The conception of beauty as power implies elements of trickery and deception. It is open to question how advantageous beauty may be, but it is clear that in our society the attribution of beauty is contingent on age and that as a form of "power" it is limited by time. Beauty is assumed to be a dwindling asset. Conceiving beauty as power means that aging women must do all they can to conserve, preserve, and hide the ravages of time.

On the other hand, the aging woman who eschews some of the traditional trappings of old age runs the risk of being castigated as "mutton dressed as lamb" (Lurie, 1981: 56). It is the nature of the competitive beauty "system" that there is not much room for cooperative effort. Women may find themselves divided, in competition for the singular title of "fairest of them all." Wolf (1991: 240) argues that "since the links between generations of women must always be newly broken: Older women fear young ones, young women fear old," and the beauty myth is divisive. An ad for an anti-aging vitamin C transdermal skin patch (*Ms.*, 1997) urges, "See your mother on holidays. Not every time you look in the mirror," and the mother's image is projected as a threat, a frightening image of a future purportedly without "beauty." There is fear of being mistaken for being older than one's age, or even of accurate estimations of age. For women continually urged to "look good," to be told they look their age is not complimentary. Even more problematic, Cooper (1988) notes, "In our thirties we do not want to be mistaken for forty. In our forties we do not want anyone to assume we are fifty...." Yet the cultural displacement of aging women can be countered. Other attributes that endure and perhaps are enhanced with the advancing years of life can empower. As observed by noted feminist academic Carolyn Heilbrun (1984: 3):

> As an aging (i.e., 58) woman.... People ignore me until they know who I am. To watch their faces turn from profound indifference to pleased recognition is to become aware that the aged, until labelled unusually valuable, are assumed worthless. Through longevity I have acquired power, and I can use it in aid of younger academic women.

Ray (1997) notes that aging women compose a large part of a new avant-garde movement the "cultural creatives" who, increasingly, are espousing global concerns, environmental sensitivity, and a new spirituality. A member of the "Raging Grannies" a Canadian singing protest group that parodies old age by wearing bonnets and lace while demonstrating against war and political injustice, suggests that "Underneath the humour in the songs and costumes there is a nod to the wisdom of older women. Walt Whitman calls it "divine maternity"" (*The Globe and Mail,* 10 April 1997). Germaine Greer (1991: 378) argues: "Only when a woman ceases the fretful struggle to be beautiful can she... at last transcend the body that was what other people principally valued her for, and be set free from both their expectations and her own capitulation...." Greer argues that this can be emancipatory. What energy, authority, and power may be released in women of any age, who are less shackled by psychological, temporal, financial, and physical costs of capitulation to the beauty system?

CONCLUSION

The tendency of the dominant culture to devalue the aged is particularly harsh on women. Structural factors contribute to sharp gender inequities in older age and these play out socially and economically. Women tend to live longer than men and their experiences with aging differ, affecting their well-being, sense of control and personal autonomy, caregiving burden, income, pensions, chances of survivorship and emotional support, risk of institutionalization, and their own and others' assessment of their appearance and worth in society.

The biological realities and challenges of aging are confounded by society's idealized norms regarding women's appearance and a beauty ideal that sets oppressive standards that are the antitheses of most older women's bodies. Aged women become invisible or sometimes solely visible because of appearance alone. And they are judged. Beauty is portrayed as a monolithic constant, yet historical and cross-cultural evidence shows this to be a fallacy. The message within the larger culture is on youth and the flawless body devoid of handicap; that beauty is within reach if only women will work at it; that there is an ideal type and size of body; and that beauty achieved represents enduring female power.

Too often the research literature presents a homogenized image that fails to reflect the range of diversity among aged women. Yet, the fear of aging is a reality in the lives of many. It is hoped that this chapter will generate discussion and actions that prepare younger women and empower those who are older. Increasingly traditional beauty norms are being challenged. As women explore avenues of development beyond body alteration and adornment, they may move farther away from some of the gender-linked disadvantages that afflict today's aged women. As women of all ages question and critique current beauty norms, all of us may be freer to explore and celebrate our basic humanity.

ENDNOTES

1. Our chapter reflects research on dominant North American and Western European patterns and examines how these play out in the Canadian setting. Recognizing that Canada is a settler society with an indigenous population and immigrant diversity, nonetheless there are practices within the dominant culture that, to varying degrees, affect us all. Within this context there are variations and some ethnocultural groups may better shield their elders from the potential vicissitudes of status decline and restrictive beauty norms than others.

2. The Gay Liberation movement is usually said to have begun with the 1969 Stonewall Riot in New York City, in which gay men being rounded up by police at gay bars and bathhouses fought back. In 1981 in Canada, a similar pivotal change occurred when 3000 people protested the arrest in Toronto of 300 men as a result of police raids on gay baths.

SUGGESTED READINGS

Baldus, Bernd, and **Helga Krueger.** (1999). "Work, Gender and the Life Course," *Canadian Journal of Sociology* 24(3). This article combines survey research with interviews with both women and their husbands in Germany to examine the multiple ways in which women's life courses are contingent on husbands' life-course choices, which then makes women's life courses profoundly different from men's.

Bordo, Susan. (1993). *Unbearable Weight: Feminism, Western Culture, and the Body.* Berkeley: University of California Press. This book examines myths and ideologies concerning the contemporary female body and how these preoccupations relate to women's relationships to food, hunger, desire, and power.

McDaniel, Susan A. (2000). "A Sociological Perspective on Women and Aging as the Millennium Turns," in Dianne Garner and Susan Mercer (eds.), *Women as They Age* (2nd edition). New York: Haworth. This overview of developments in social research and theory on women and aging over the 1990s shows how far we have come and what remains to be done. New developments include new "takes" on the life course that extends from childhood to later life, new longitudinal data on women's lives as they age, and new theories that see older women as increasingly powerful. New research and theory, however, have revealed to a greater extent the constraints on women in later life.

Weitz, Rose (ed). (2003). *The Politics of Women's Bodies: Sexuality, Appearance and Behavior* (2nd edition). New York: Oxford University Press. This anthology covers a range of topics and outlines ways women's bodies are socially constructed and socially controlled, and the effects and methods of resistance.

Wolf, Naomi. (1990/1991). *The Beauty Myth.* Toronto: Vintage Books. This acclaimed bestseller critically examines the beauty industry, advertising, and general cultural expectations that can propel women and girls into a compulsive, sometimes life-endangering pursuit of "beauty."

DISCUSSION QUESTIONS

1. What are the implications of child beauty pageants for little girls, their mothers, and their fathers?

2. Humans modify their bodies in many different ways. Is the cultural pressure on women to look pleasing to others any different from the cultural pressures on men? Are the sanctions different?

3. The Baby Boomers have been associated with many dramatic societal changes. How might our attitudes toward women's aging and appearance be influenced as this group moves into old age? How might issues of dependency and vulnerability in older age change?

4. In what ways are "eating disorders" such as bulimia and anorexia feminist issues? How can we best address these problems?

BIBLIOGRAPHY

Abu-Laban, Sharon McIrvin, and **Baha Abu-Laban.** "Women and the Aged as Minority Groups: A Critique," *Canadian Review of Sociology and Anthropology* 14, no. 1 (1977): 103–16.

Abu-Laban, Sharon McIrvin. "Social Supports in Older Age: The Need for New Research Directions." *Essence* 4, no. 3 (1980): 195–210.

———. "Women and Aging: A Futurist Perspective," *Psychology of Women Quarterly* 6, no. 1 (1981): 85–98.

———. "Les femmes agées: problèmes et perspectives," *Sociologie et sociétés* 16, no. 2 (October 1984): 69–78.

———. "Family and Religion among Muslim Immigrants and Their Descendants." In *Muslim Families in North America*, edited by Earle Waugh, Sharon McIrvin Abu-Laban, and Regula Quereshi, 6–31. Edmonton: University of Alberta Press, 1991.

———. "Aging Women and Gender Disequity in Canada." In *The Elderly Population in the Developed and Developing World: Politics, Problems and Perspectives*, edited by P. Krishnan and K. Mahadevan, 444–70. Delhi: B.R. Publishing, 1992.

———. "Traversing Boundaries." Unpublished manuscript. Department of Sociology, University of Alberta, 1993.

Alexander, Suzanne. "Teens' Cosmetic Surgery Fad Causes Dismay Among Experts," *The Globe and Mail*, 25 Sept. 1990. (original in The *Wall Street Journal*).

American Society for Aesthetic Plastic Surgery. "Quick Facts" Highlights of the ASAPAS 2002 Statistics on Cosmetic Surgery" **www.surgery.org/press/quick-facts.pdf** downloaded October 04, 2003.

Auger, Jeanette A. "Lesbians and Aging: Triple Trouble or Tremendous Thrill." In *Lesbians in Canada*, edited by Sharon Dale Stone. Toronto: Between the Lines, 1990.

Bell, I.P. "The Double Standard," *Transaction* 8 (1970): 75–80.

Berger, Raymond. "The Unseen Minority: Older Gays and Lesbians," *Social Work* 27 (1982): 236–42.

Bordo, Susan. *Unbearable Weight: Feminism, Western Culture and the Body*. Berkeley: University of California Press, 1990.

Boyens, Ingeborg. "On the Water's Edge" pp. 193–200 in *Dropped Threads 2*: More of what we aren't told, edited by Carol Shields and Marjorie Anderson.Toronto: Random House, 2003.

Brownmiller, Susan. *Femininity*. New York: Linden Press/Simon and Schuster, 1984.

Chappell, Neena, et al. *Aging in Contemporary Canada*. Toronto: Prentice Hall, 2003.

Chase, Marilyn. "As fashions bare the midriff, some try navel surgery." *The Wall Street Journal*, August 06, 2002.

Chatelaine. "Ten Lousy Legal Judgements," March 1978: 58, 118.

Clark, Tony. "Child Pageants Come in for Criticism," January 22, 1997, web posted at 5:30 am EST. CNN Interactive. US News [**http: //cnn.com/us/9701 /22/child.pageant/index.html**], 1997.

Cohen, Erminie Joy, and **Angela Petten.** *Sounding the Alarm: Poverty in Canada.* Ottawa: Senate of Canada, 1997.

Connidis, Ingrid Arnet. *Family Ties and Aging.* Thousand Oaks, California: Sage, 2001

Cott, Chris. "Midas (re) touch." *Edmonton Journal*, February 2, 2003, p. D13.

Cooper, B. *Over the Hill: Reflections on Ageism between Women.* Freedom, CA: The Crossing Press, 1988.

The Crossing Press. As cited Marian and Becky Chassey, "Across Differences of Age: Young Women Speaking of and with Old Women." In *Representing the Other*, edited by Sue Wilkinson and Cecila Kitzinger, 147–51. Thousand Oaks: Sage, 1996.

Currie, Dawn. "Women's Liberation and Women's Mental Health: Towards a Political Economy of Eating Disorders." In *Women and Well-Being*, edited by Vanaja Dhruvarajan, 25–39. Montreal: The Canadian Research Institute for the Advancement of Women, 1990.

de Beauvoir, Simone. *Old Age.* Harmondsworth, England: Penguin, 1970.

Donaldson, E.L. (Betty). "Images of the Goddess: Spiritual Aspects of the Women's Life Cycle," *Canadian Woman Studies* 17, no. 1 (1997): 36–39.

Doress, Paula Brown and **Diana Laskin Siegaland.** *Growing Older. Midlife and Older Women's Book Project.* Boston: Houghton Mifflin, 1987.

Driedger, Leo, and **Neena Chappell.** *Aging and Ethnicity: Toward an Interface.* Toronto: Butterworths, 1987.

Ehrenreich, Barbara, and **Deirdre English.** *For Her Own Good: 150 Years of the Experts' Advice to Women.* New York: Doubleday, 1978.

Fast, Janet E., et al. *Conceptualizing and Operationalizing the Costs of Informal Elder Care.* NHRDP project No. 6609-1963-55. Ottawa: National Health Research and Development Program, Health Canada, 1997.

Felstiner, Mary Lowenthal. "Casing my Joints: A Private and Public Story of Arthritis," in Feminist Studies 26, no. 2 (Summer 2000): 273-285, also reprinted in Rose Weitz (ed). *The Politics of Women's Bodies: Sexuality, Appearance and Behavior* (2nd edition). New York: Oxford University Press, 2003.

Garner, David, Paul Garfinkle, Donald Schwartz, and **Michael Thompson.** "Cultural Expectations of Thinness in Women." *Psychological Reports* 47 (1980): 483–91.

Gee, Ellen M., and **Meredith Kimball.** *Women and Aging.* Toronto: Butterworths, 1987.

Gee, Ellen, and **Susan A. McDaniel.** "Social Policy for an Aging Canada," *Journal of Canadian Studies* 27, no. 3 (1992): 139–52.

Gerontological Studies, McMaster University. *Facts on Aging in Canada.* Hamilton, Ontario: Gerontological Studies, McMaster University, 1996.

Globe and Mail, The. "TV Anchor Filed Complaint Against CBC Over Age Discrimination," 15 August 1992: C4.

Globe and Mail, The. "Wardrobe as Important as Policy, Women Told," 4 April 1997: A1, A4.

Globe and Mail, The. "Goofy-Hatted Reconcilers in the Land," 10 April 1997: A24.

Gooden, Charmaine. "Knife Styles of the Rich and Famous." *Chatelaine*, April 1993.

Gorlick, Carolyne A., and **D. Pomfret.** "Hope and Circumstances: Single Mothers Exiting Social Assistance." In *Single Parent Families: Perspectives on Research and Policy*, edited by Joe Hudson and Burt Galaway, 253–70. Toronto: Thompson, 1993.

Greer, Germaine. *The Change: Women, Aging and the Menopause.* New York: Fawcett Columbine, 1991.

Gutek, Barbara A. "Responses to Sexual Harassment." In *Gender Issues on Contemporary Society*, edited by Stuart Oskamp and Mark Costanzo, 197–216. Newbury Park: Sage, 1993.

Heilbrun, Carolyn. "Aging and Raging," *Women's Review of Books* 2, no. 3 (1984): 3. As quoted in Shulamit Reinharz, "Friends or Foes: Gerontological and Feminist Theory." In *Radical Voices*, edited by Renate D. Klein and Deborah Lynn Steinberg, 222–41. New York: Pergamon Press, 1989.

Hesse-Biber, Sharlene. "Women, Weight and Eating Disorders," *Women's Studies International Forum*, 14, no. 3 (1991): 173–91.

Hewitt, Chris. "Middle-aged actors date to bare lived-in bodies." *Edmonton Journal,* 02 January 2004: D3.

Itzen, C. "Media Images of Women," In *Feminist Social Psychology*, edited by S. Wilkinson, 119–35. London: Open University Press, 1986.

Kaden, Joan and **Susan A. McDaniel.** "Caregiving and Care-Receiving: A Double Bind for Women in Canada's Aging Society," *Journal of Women and Aging* 2 no. 3 (1990): 3–26.

Keating, Norah, et al. *Eldercare in Canada: Context, Content and Consequences.* Ottawa: Statistics Canada, Catalogue no. 89-570-XPE, 1999.

Lee, John Alan. "What Can Homosexual Aging Studies Contribute to Theories of Aging?" *Journal of Homosexuality* 13, no. 4 (1987): 43–69.

Lurie, A. *The Language of Clothes.* London: Heinemann, 1981.

MacDonald, Barbara, and **Cynthia Rich.** *Look Me in the Eye.* San Francisco: Spinsters, Ink., 14, 1983.

McDaniel, Susan A. *Canada's Aging Population.* Toronto: Butterworths, 1986.

———. "Getting Older and Better: Women and Gender Assumptions in Canada's Aging Society." Feminist Perspectives, #11, *Canadian Research Institute for the Advancement of Women*, 1988.

———. "Women and Family in the Later Years: Findings from the 1990 General Social Survey." *Canadian Woman Studies*, 12, no. 2 (1992a): 62–64.

———. *Life Rhythms and Caring: Aging, Family and the State.* 23rd Annual Sorokin Lecture. Sorokin Series, University of Saskatchewan, 1992b.

———. "Emotional Support and Family Contacts of Older Canadians." *Canadian Social Trends*, Spring, 28 (1993a): 30–33.

———. "Challenges to Mental Health Promotion Among Working Women in Canada." *Canadian Journal of Community Mental Health* 12, no. 1 (1993b).

———. *Family and Friends 1990: General Social Survey Analysis Series.* Ottawa: Statistics Canada, 1994.

————. "Women, Retirement and Work in Later Life." In *Rethinking Retirement: Social Policy Challenges for the '90s,* edited by Ellen Gee and Gloria Gutman. Vancouver: Simon Fraser University Gerontology Research Centre, 1995: 75–92.

————. "Health Care Policy in an Aging Canada: The Alberta 'Experiment.'" *Journal of Aging Studies* 11, no. 3 (1997a): 211–27.

————. Towards Healthy Families: Policy Implications, Paper No. 19, *National Forum on Health.* Ottawa: National Forum on Health, 1997b.

————. "Untangling Love and Domination: Challenges of Home Care For the Elderly in a Reconstructing Canada." *Journal of Canadian Studies,* 34(3):191–213, 1999.

————. "Sociological Perspectives on Women and Aging." In Dianne Garner and Susan Mercer (Eds.), *Women as They Age* (2nd edition). New York: Haworth, 2000.

————. "The Family Lives of the Middle-Aged and Elderly." In *Families: Changing Trends in Canada* (4th Edition), edited by Maureen Baker. Toronto: McGraw Hill Ryerson, 2001: 187–204.

————. "Women's Changing Relations to the State and Citizenship: Caring and Intergenerational Relations in Globalizing Western Democracies." *Canadian Review of Sociology and Anthropology* 39(2): 1–26, 2002.

McDaniel, Susan A., and **Ellen M. Gee.** "Social Policies Regarding Caregiving to Elders: Canadian Contradictions." *Journal of Aging and Social Policy* 5, nos. 1 & 2 (1993): 57–72.

McDaniel, Susan A., and **Robert Lewis.** "Did They or Didn't They: Intergenerational Supports in Canada's Past and a Case Study of Brigus, Newfoundland, 1920–1949." in Lori Chambers & Edgar-Andre Montigny (Eds.), *Family Matters: Papers in Post-Confederation Canadian Family History.* Toronto: Canadian Scholars Press, pp. 475–497, 1997.

McDaniel, Susan A., and **Allison McKinnon.** "Gender Differences in Informal Support and Coping Among Elders: Findings from Canada's 1985 and 1990 General Social Surveys." *Journal of Women and Aging* 5, no. 2 (1993): 79–98.

Morgan, Kathryn Pauly. "Women and the Knife: Cosmetic Surgery and the Colonization of Women's Bodies." *Hypatia* 6, no. 3 (1991): 25–50.

Ms. "No Comment." March/April 1997, inside back page.

Nett, Emily. "Canadian Families in Socio-Historical Perspective." *Canadian Journal of Sociology* 6, no. 6 (1981): 239–60.

New York Times, The. "In This Courtroom, Beauty Is Truth." March 1993, sec. 1: 20.

O'Brien, Carol-Anne, and **Aviva Goldberg.** "Lesbians and Gay Men Inside and Outside Families." in *Canadian Families: Diversity, Conflict and Change,* edited by Nancy Mandell and Ann Duffy. Toronto: Harcourt Brace, 2000: 115–145.

Quam, Jean K. "Old Lesbians Research and Resources." In *The New Lesbian Studies: Into the Twenty-First Century,* edited by Bonnie Zimmerman and Toni A. H. McNaron. New York: The Feminist Press, 1996: 86–90.

Ray, Paul H. "The Emerging Culture." *American Demographics* (February 1997): 29–56.

Reindl, Sheila M. *Sensing the Self: Women's Recovery from Bulimia.* Cambridge, Mass.: Harvard University Press, 2001.

Reuben, David. *Everything You Always Wanted to Know About Sex (But Were Afraid to Ask).* New York: McKay, 1969.

Russell, Cherry. "Aging as a Feminist Issue*." Women's Studies International Forum* 10, no. 2 (1987): 125–132.

Schellenberg, Grant, and **David P. Ross.** *Left Poor by the Market: A Look at Family Poverty and Earnings.* Ottawa: Canadian Council on Social Development, 1997.

Schrader, Constance. *Nine to Five: A Complete Looks, Clothes and Personality Handbook for the Working Woman.* Englewood Cliffs, New Jersey: Prentice-Hall, Inc., 1981.

Shohat, Ella. "Post-Third-Worldist Culture: Gender, Nation, and the Cinema." In *Feminist Genealocies, Colonial Legacies, Democratic Futures*, edited by M. Jacqui Alexander and Chandra Talpade Mohanty, 183–209. New York: Routledge, 1997.

Slater, Suzanne. *The Lesbian Family Life Cycle.* New York: The Free Press, 1995.

Smith, Graeme. "Contest offers free 'boob job.'" *The Globe and Mail*, July 19, 2003: A8.

Smith, Jane E., V. Waldorf, and **D. Trembath.** "Single White Male Looking for Thin, Very Attractive ...." *Sex Roles* 23 nos. 11 & 12 (1990): 675–83.

Sommers, Tish. "Aging Is a Woman's Issue." *Response* (March 1976): 12–15.

Sontag, Susan. "The Double Standard of Aging*." Saturday Review* 55, no. 39 (1972): 29–38.

Statistics Canada. "Retirement Savings Through RPPs and RRSPs: 1991–1995." *Statistics Canada Daily*, 18 February 1997.

Statistics Canada. *Annual Demographic Statistics 2002.* Ottawa; Statistics Canada. Catalogue No. 91-213-XPB, 2003.

Sudnow, David. *Passing On: The Social Organization of Dying.* Englewood Cliffs, New Jersey: Prentice-Hall, 1967.

Thompson, Becky W. *A Hunger So Wide and So Deep: American Women Speak Out on Eating Disorders.* Minneapolis: University of Minnesota Press, 1994.

Thompson, Colleen. 1996. "Teenagers and Eating Disorders." **www.mirror-mirror.org/teens.htm** accessed 1 January 2004.

Townson, Monica. *Women's Financial Futures: Mid-Life Prospects for a Secure Retirement.* Ottawa: Canadian Advisory Council on the Status of Women, 1995.

Unger, Rhoda and **Mary Crawford.** *Women and Gender: A Feminist Psychology.* Philadelphia: Temple University Press, 1992.

Unger, Rhoda, M. Hilderbrand, and **T. Madar.** "Physical Attractiveness and Assumptions About Social Deviance: Some Sex by Sex Comparisons*." Personality and Social Psychology Bulletin* 8 (1982): 293–301.

Wolf, Naomi. *The Beauty Myth.* Toronto: Vintage Books, 1991.

Women's Health Matters Network. 2003. "Eating Disorders: Myths and Harsh Realities." Sunnybrook and Women's College Health Sciences Centre, Toronto. **www.womenshealthmatters.ca** accessed 1 January 2004.

 # WEBLINKS

feminist.com/ourbodies.htm

The book *Our Bodies, Ourselves* is a definitive women's health resource that candidly discusses a variety of issues including body image.

Status of Women Canada

www.swc-cfc.gc.ca/direct.html

Status of Women Canada (SWC) is the federal government agency that promotes gender equality and the full participation of women in the economic, social, cultural, and political life of the country. SWC focuses its work in three areas: improving women's economic autonomy and well-being, eliminating systemic violence against women and children, and advancing women's human rights.

Social Gerontology and the Aging Revolution

www.trinity.edu/~mkear1/geron.html#in

This website provides a comprehensive index to issues relating to aging.

chapter six

Violence against Women

Ann Duffy

INTRODUCTION

One of the experiential cements that binds the experiences of women is the fear and fact of male violence. All women, regardless of class, colour, race/ethnicity, ability, age, or sexual orientation, are subject to violence. Not only waitresses but also female medical students are subject to attack and abuse (Priest, 1994: A3). The wives of prime ministers, sports celebrities, doctors, lawyers, and corporate chieftains have been subject to wife battery. Daughters of executives, religious ministers, and university professors have been victims of incest and rape. A former prime minister of Japan was publicly accused by his wife of being physically abusive; in 1996, trial documents revealed that the chairman of the board of Canadian Tire and Gulf Canada Resources Limited had emotionally and physically abused his wife (Andrews, 1999); in the 1980s, an ex-Miss America claimed that for years she had been the victim of incest by her corporate-executive father. Women surgeons, senior government officials, corporate executives, and Crown attorneys have come forward to lay complaints of sexual harassment and assault. No amount of economic, racial, sexual, or class-based privilege can absolutely protect women from violence in a patriarchal[1] society. Most women recognize their vulnerability to victimization. At home, in the workplace, in the throes of giving birth, or in the last gasps of life, women have been abused and violated. The 25-year-old female college student in

Mississauga, the 90-year-old housewife in Somalia, and the 45-year-old woman religious worker in Guatemala have in common their vulnerability and their wariness. Violence and the fear of violence frame many women's lives and sculpt their identities.

The second wave of feminism was instrumental in exposing the dimensions and complexities of violence against women, especially in the more affluent and industrialized countries of the world. From sexual harassment, date rape, and incest to woman abuse in the home and in war crimes, feminists pulled away the hegemonic blinders and revealed the devastation. Third-wave feminisms have developed a more complex and nuanced understanding of violence and honed an expanded critique of the universalizing tendencies of Western feminists who tended to overlook the cultural particularities of women's victimization. Today, feminists are drawing more attention to the global and historical parameters of the violence: interconnections with colonialism (globalization), imperialism, and racism. As a result, there is growing documentation of the global toll on women's lives. However, as feminist scrutiny has expanded from a more Western preoccupation, it has become clear that violence against women must be understood in terms of localities of history, culture, and power. In short, the violence is being revealed as much more complexly interwoven with local, national, and international axes of power, privilege, and oppression.

STICKS AND STONES: THE TOLL OF VIOLENCE AGAINST WOMEN

Violence against women encompasses an enormous range of actions, actors, and social locations. Many researchers today define the concept to include psychological and emotional violence as well as economic/financial and spiritual coercion (Canadian Panel on Violence Against Women, 1993). Non-physical forms of violence, such as psychological and emotional abuse in wife battering, should not be trivialized or ignored, since they are extremely significant and prevalent. Indeed, survivors of wife assault frequently report that the emotional violence is much harder to endure and transcend than the physical blows and injuries (Schmidt, 1995: 21). Further, it is often, of course, impossible to fully separate emotional and physical violence. Physical and sexual attacks on women are frequently accompanied by vicious verbal tirades and persistent efforts to humiliate and dominate the victim. Here the preliminary focus is on feminist research (particularly in Canada), which documents the nature and extent of the violence perpetrated against women. Although it is not possible to do justice to the global literature, it is clear from this overview that violence against women in multiple forms is a common and persistent reality in most women's lives.

GROWING UP FEMALE: VIOLENCE IN THE FAMILY

Historically and cross-culturally, there is considerable evidence that, particularly in the family, women have been targeted for victimization (Mooney, 2000).[2] Indeed, many commentators have made the point that, for women and girls, the family is the most dangerous and violent institution in society. Historically, of course, many girls did not even experience the family because they were the victims of infanticide. As unwanted or insupportable burdens on family resources they were smothered or abandoned. This practice persists in some countries to this day. Indeed, analysts are expressing alarm at the increasingly skewed ratio of boys to girls in India. In North America, women compose approximately

51 percent of the population; in India between 1991 and 2001 the number of girls (six and under) dropped from 945 to 927 per 1000 boys. In some states of India it is a mere 770. Female infanticide along with ultrasound-aided selective abortion of female fetuses has meant fewer girls growing up in families (Sharma, 2003).

Sexual Abuse

Infanticide and selective abortion are not likely for girls in Canadian families, but there are other concerns. Given the pervasive patriarchal tradition of controlling and directing the sexuality of young girls, it is not surprising that much of the violence against girls and young women has been in the form of sexual abuse within the family.

The extent of the abuse was first revealed in the 1980s. Robin Bagley's groundbreaking national survey of child sexual abuse in Canada found that one in two females and one in three males had been victims of sexual offences (1984: 193). Diana Russell's breakthrough research using a probability sample of 930 San Francisco women (1986) focused more specifically on the issue of incest. She found 16 percent of the sample reported being incestuously abused. Based on a review of this and other research data, Bagley and King conclude that serious sexual abuse in childhood (much of it unreported) occurs in at least 15 percent of the female Canadian population and 5 percent of the male population (1990: 70).

The most recent Statistics Canada "Family Violence Profile 2003" corroborates the gendered pattern (see Patterson, 2003; Au Coin, 2003). Overwhelmingly it is girls who are victimized in reported family-related sexual assaults. In almost 80 percent of the police-reported cases, girls were the victims and male relatives (fathers 44 percent, brothers 9 percent, and male extended family members 12 percent) were the clear majority of accused assailants. Reflecting intersecting patterns of gender and age status, boys are at highest risk of sexual assault until age 6, while the victimization of girls continues, reaching its highest rate at 13 years of age. Even as girls mature, they remain the primary targets for both the enactment of power and the frustration of powerlessness (Au Coin, 2003: 34, 35). Among girls, certain groups are particularly at risk. Considerable research shows, for example, that Aboriginal girls are subject to high rates of victimization (Ursel and Gorkoff, 2001).

The global patterns similarly bear testimony to the extent of abuse. Where we have research on the percentage of adults who report having been sexually abused as children, statistics suggest that victimization is relatively common. In Barbados, Costa Rica, Nicaragua, Switzerland, Spain, the United States, and Australia from one in five to more than one in four women indicate they were abused. Further, where data exist, it is clearly gendered, with girls consistently more likely to be victimized than boys (Seager 2003: 58–59; Kendall-Tackett, 2001).

In addition, there are global patterns of sexual violence toward girls that are specific to certain locales. In particular, feminist activists have identified female genital mutilation as an important issue in a number of African and South American countries, notably Somalia and Kenya. Although practices vary among cultural groups, typically in this ritual all or part of the girl's clitoris is removed between 6 and 12 years of age. The practice is justified in terms of religious obligation and tradition, as a means to ensure virginity until marriage, to enhance male sexual pleasure, to bring honour to the family and to control women's and girls' sexual activities. Although the practice is banned in many countries (for example, in Kenya under the 2002 Children's Act), activists estimate that millions of girls have been subject to this practice and many have suffered serious infections along with difficulties in childbirth as a result (Munala, 2003).

Historically, girls were a form of property within the traditional patriarchal family. As evident from the Talmud and Bible, the sexual misuse of children is embedded in Western traditions—traditions later exported with colonialism. For example, according to Florence Rush, Talmudic law allows for the betrothal of a female child of "three years and one day ... by sexual intercourse" (1980: 18). From biblical times and until the late Middle Ages, child marriage[3] (when the girl was about age 12) was the norm and was generally seen as a property transaction between the father and the husband. Similarly, in biblical terms, child rape was a property crime against the father; the rapist, if unmarried, was required to marry his victim and pay a fine to her father. Within this historical tradition, with its implicit sexualization of female children and normalization of adult-child sexuality, it is not surprising that violence against many female children often takes the form of sexual abuse.

Although a law specifically prohibiting incest was introduced into the Canadian criminal law in 1890, child sexual abuse has only been acknowledged as a pervasive social problem in most Western countries since the 1970s, and, as a result, the research base has been relatively limited until recently (Sangster, 2001). There is some evidence that incest, predominantly the sexual assault of girls by older male relatives, has been a documented social problem since before the turn of the twentieth century (Gordon, 1986). However, the interesting findings presented by Freud, Kinsey, and others were dismissed by a society intent on blaming the victim, ignoring the issue, and upholding patriarchal rights. Only with the advent of the second wave of the women's movement and its explorations of violence against women were incest survivors empowered to come forward. In the late 1970s and 1980s, landmark memoirs such as Katherine Brady's *Father's Days: A True Story of Incest* (1979), Charlotte Vale Allen's *Daddy's Girl: A Very Personal Memoir* (1980), and Elly Danica *Don't Is a Woman's Word* (1988) established incest as a central feminist issue.

The horrifying magnitude of sexual abuse experiences, as well as the poor institutional response, continues to be frequently reported in the media. In a recent incest case, the judge harshly criticized Ontario's child-protection system for failing to protect five Ottawa-area sisters who were sexually abused by their father for years. As children, the five sisters slept in the same room. Each night their father would come to their bedroom and pick one of them to join him in his bedroom for sexual intercourse. Two of the daughters became pregnant by their father. Another one was kidnapped by gunpoint out of Canada to another country, where she was isolated and served as a sex slave for more than a year. One daughter managed to run away but was returned home by the police who did not take her complaints seriously. Once back home, her father beat her and threatened, with a gun to her head, that he would kill her if she ran away again. All five sisters, two brothers, and the wife were viciously beaten, terrorized, and threatened with a gun to their heads on a regular basis. It took more than 25 years to charge this father with different criminal offences. Eventually he was found too ill to stand a criminal trial and died during a civil suit (Vincent, 1999).

Rape

As girls mature, they also move out of the family to explore intimate relationships with non-family members. In the process of dating and forming cross-gender friendships, many girls all too often replicate early experiences of violence and abuse. As feminist analysts have repeatedly pointed out, this pattern of sexual violence and abuse cannot be dismissed as a natural or evolutionary feature of the human race. Rather, anthropological analysis reveals that non- or low-rape cultures are extensively documented. Cultures in which sexual equality is the norm, the sexes are seen as complementary, and women are understood to make a significant contribution to social continuity typically display socialization practices and gender dynamics that are not premised on gendered control and authority (Watson-Franke, 2002; Sanday, 1981).

In contrast, more patriarchal societies tend to endorse beliefs and attitudes that are "rape-prone."

Researchers have repeatedly reported that young men embrace notions of coercive sexuality; for example, in one study, more than half of male high school students said they believed it was acceptable for a boy to hold a girl down and force her into intercourse when, for example, she had made him sexually excited (Malamuth, 1981: 152). Similarly, Neil Malamuth, Scott Haber, and Seymour Feschbach found that 51 percent of a sample of college males said there was "some likelihood" they would rape a woman in a dating situation if they were assured they would not be punished (1980: 130).

These coercive and rape-prone attitudes appear to be more than theoretical. Mary Koss and Cheryl Oros (1982: 456) found that one in five men in a representative survey of 3862 US university students recalled "being in a situation in which they became so aroused that they could not stop themselves from having sexual intercourse even though the woman didn't want to." Approximately one in three of the women in this sample reported "being in a situation where a man because [*sic*] so sexually aroused that they felt it was useless to stop him even though the woman did not want to have intercourse." Similarly, over the past two decades "rape prevalence" research with US college students has consistently reported that one in seven female respondents was the victims of completed rape (Rozee and Koss, 2001: 296). Other research indicates that many men do not subscribe to the "no means no" script and will continue to press sexual advances after a woman has explicitly refused (Muehlenhard et al., 1996) or will interpret relatively innocuous behaviour as an invitation to sexual contact (Anderson et al., 2004). Mark Totten's interviews with male youth in Ottawa supports the view that many young men are socialized to engage in the sexual objectification and abuse of their girlfriends while embracing attitudes that define their behaviour as morally right (2000: 132, 139).

Research indicates that these beliefs and attitudes frequently result in actual rapes. In particular, the landmark[4] Canadian Violence Against Women survey (CVAW), conducted by Statistics Canada in 1993, found that dating violence is an alarmingly common phenomenon. Based on survey results, researchers estimate that 1.7 million Canadian women (or 16 percent of all women) have experienced at least one incident of physical or sexual assault by a boyfriend or date since turning age 16. If the focus is narrowed to women attending school at the time of the interview in 1993, a full 25 percent had been the victims of sexual or physical assault by a boyfriend or male date (Johnson, 1996: 112, 115).[5] The most recent Canadian statistical data rely on police-reported cases of sexual assault (problematic since only an estimated 10 percent or fewer women report their assaults to police) indicates that patterns of sexual assault have been unchanged since the early 1990s (Federal-Provincial-Territorial Ministers Responsible for the Status of Women, 2002: 19).

As with incest, rape is a global phenomenon. In the late 1990s, approximately 40 000 Chinese, 90 000 US, 7000 German, 2000 Polish, 3000 Pakistani, and 15 000 Indian women each year reported that they had been raped. Once again the reported rates vastly under-represent the actual incidence, which is estimated to be (very conservatively) ten times the numbers reported. South Africa, beset by a bitter history of colonialism and apartheid, reported the highest rape rate in the world with an estimated 4100 women a day raped (52 000 a year reported rapes) (Seager, 2003: 58–59).

Of course the direct victimization of rape victims is only one element in the issue. Although the majority of women are not themselves direct casualties of dating violence or date rape, violence is a significant feature in the sexual and social socialization of most Canadian young women as well as girls and young women around the globe (Gorkoff et al., 1999).[6] If not personally involved, they are likely to know someone who has been subjected to physical or sexual violence. Concerns about victimization, often reinforced by parents, colour the experience of forming cross-gender relationships. Young women grow up in the shadow of interpersonal violence, a shadow that crosses their most intimate relationships. The violence supports a more generalized dating culture of coercion in which young women and men in Canada act out traditional gender roles. According to this script, men are to demand, pressure, harass, and joke while women are to avoid, give in, blame themselves, and feel guilty (Littleton and Axsom, 2003).

OUT OF THE FRYING PAN AND INTO A RELATIONSHIP

Woman Abuse

For the overwhelming majority of Canadian young women, dating leads to a more or less permanent relationship and common-law or legal marriage. Unfortunately, for a surprisingly large minority of Canadian women, love and marriage lead to abuse and violence. The CVAW survey (Statistics Canada, 1993) revealed that more than one-quarter (29 percent) of ever-married women experienced violence "at the hands of a current or past marital partner" since age 16 (including common-law relationships). More than one-third of the victims of wife abuse were subjected to such serious abuse that they "feared for their lives."[7] Almost half (45 percent) of the violent episodes of wife assault resulted in physical injury to the woman and almost half (45 percent) of these injuries required medical attention (Statistics Canada, 1993: 4–6). The most recent General Social Survey (1999) indicates that spousal violence remains commonplace with 8 percent of women and 7 percent of men reporting that they had experienced violence by a spousal partner in the preceding five years (Patterson, 2003). Despite the almost equivalent reporting rates for men and women[8], research indicates that the more severe forms of violence are directed toward women. Twice as many women as men are beaten, five times as many are choked, and nearly twice as many have a gun or knife used against them. Further, twice as many women as men are subject to chronic, ongoing assaults (ten or more) (Federal-Provincial-Territorial Ministers Responsible for the Status of Women, 2002: 12).

Predictably, only an estimated 27 percent of spousal abuse incidents were reported to the police. Even within these restricted statistics, it is clear that women are particularly at risk. Of the 2549 cases reported to police in 2001, 85 percent involved female victims (Patterson, 2003). These rates of reported spousal violence have increased in recent years and presumably reflect a growing willingness to report these crimes to the police (Patterson, 2003). However, pro-charging policies that require police to lay charges in spousal violence cases independent of the victim's wishes and that require charges where the assailants counter-charge their victims ("she hit me too") may be also responsible for these increased rates of reported incidents. Victimization surveys (which sample the general population about their experience with domestic violence) suggest there has been a decline in the past five years in the rates of spousal abuse (Federal-Provincial-Territorial Ministers Responsible for the Status of Women 2002: 21). It remains to be seen whether this indicates a long-term trend.

Within these overall patterns of woman abuse, the victimization cuts across social class, immigrant status, age, sexual orientation, disability, and racial/ethnic divisions (Johnson, 1996). There appear to be no safe zones for women. However, clearly some women are more vulnerable than others. Low occupational status and low family income are commonly cited as correlates of abuse. Women who are living in low-income homes, and women whose spouses are unemployed, were twice as likely to be assaulted in comparison to those in more affluent families and with employed spouses. Also, women living in common-law relationships experience higher rates of violence (Brownridge and Halli, 2001). Moreover, men with low rates of education (less than high school diploma) had violence rates twice as high as men with university degrees, and when the effects of other variables are controlled, chronic unemployment becomes a significant predictor of wife assault (Statistics Canada, 1998: 13).

Aboriginal women have notably higher rates of woman abuse. Although, as noted previously, 8 percent of Canadian women and 7 percent of men indicate they have been the victims of spousal violence in the past five years, three times as many Aboriginal women (25 percent) and almost twice as many men (13 percent) report victimization. Similarly spousal homicide rates are 8 times higher for Aboriginal women than non-Aboriginal women (and 18 times higher for Aboriginal men than non-Aboriginal men). In contrast, the rate of spousal abuse among the immigrant population (women 6 percent, men 4 percent) and among the visible minority population (women 7 percent, men 4 percent) is slightly lower than the Canadian average. Analysts argue that factors such as systemic discrimination against Aboriginal people, economic and social deprivation, alcohol and substance abuse, intergenerational violence and the colonial legacy (as reflected in outcomes of residential schooling) result in generalized increases in violence (Baskin, 2003; Anderson, 1987, Federal-Provincial-Territorial Ministers Responsible for the Status of Women, 2002: 14, 15, 18).

Globally, evidence of woman abuse in intimate relationships is found almost everywhere. In the United States, Britain, New Zealand, Nigeria, Pakistan, India, Australia, Zimbabwe, South Korea, Egypt, and Barbados research indicates that upwards of one-third of women indicate they have experienced physical abuse at the hands of a male intimate. In some countries the figures are even higher: Pakistan (80 percent), Ethiopia (45 percent), Poland (50 percent), Portugal (53 percent), Japan (59 percent), Bolivia (62 percent), and Guatemala (49 percent) (Seager, 2003: 26–27; Shallat, 2000; Saeed, 2000). Not surprisingly, there are also important differences and distinctive issues in women's global experiences of battering. For example, in a recent study of battered women in Italy and the United States, researchers noted that women in Italy were likely to have endured more years of violence than their American counterparts and less likely to report sexual abuse (McCloskey et al., 2002). Similarly, in Uganda the problem of domestic violence interweaves with high rates of HIV infection. In this strictly male-dominated society wives report that they and their children are exposed to HIV infection by abusive HIV-positive husbands who refuse to use condoms and routinely rape and abuse them (Karanja, 2003).

This pattern of woman abuse is the enactment of a centuries-old tradition of patriarchal violence against women in intimate relations. In many countries, women's subordination in marriage was often enshrined in law. In Britain and North America, the common-law tradition ensured women's familial vulnerability. According to Sir William Blackstone's influential treatise, "The common law gave a husband almost unlimited power to control his wife's property; he was, in fact, the titled owner of all her property. He also controlled her person, and had the right to discipline her.... the husband... might give his wife moderate correction just as he is allowed to correct his apprentices or children" (as cited in Dranoff, 1977). Historical research suggests that these rights were far from theoretical. For example, Nancy Tomes's examination of trial accounts in the *London Times* between 1841 and 1875 found that working-class women were subject to a "torrent of abuse" and that violent wife-beating was so common that middle-class reformers introduced the *Wife Beaters Act* (1882), which gave magistrates the power to flog and publicly pillory men who battered their wives (1978: 340).

In Canada (and elsewhere), European colonialists transported patriarchal traditions and imposed them on indigenous peoples. For example, under English common-law tradition upon marriage, women's legal identity was submerged into that of her husband. This meant that any notion of husbands injuring wives (through slander, rape, or violence) was unthinkable. One cannot assault "oneself." When wives were given some property rights in the 1870s, they became able to sue their husbands for damage to their property but were still unable to take legal action against damage to themselves. If a husband broke his wife's nose and in the process shattered her glasses, she could sue only to recover the cost of the glasses. In 1975, Ontario became the first province to permit a wife to sue for personal injury compensation. The Napoleonic Code that influenced Quebec customs and laws also assumed the complete legal and social subordination of women to their husbands (Dranoff, 1977: 23, 12).

Within this social context, woman abuse was for generations simply experienced as part of everyday life. Just as many contemporary Canadians endorse spanking children, people saw violence between husbands and wives as, at worst, an unfortunate, shameful, and very private aspect of married life.[9] As Carolyn Strange points out, "the civil and the criminal law upheld the deeply patriarchal character of marriage, both by granting husbands enormous latitude in exercising their power, and by severely limiting married women's ability to extricate themselves from violent partners" (1995: 296). It was not until the 1960s, with the second wave of feminism, that wife battering was "named" and conceptualized as a serious social problem. In 1974, the publication of British feminist Erin Pizzey's *Scream Quietly or the Neighbours Will Hear* firmly established wife (woman) battering as a central feminist issue (Walker, 1990). The 1980 publication of Linda MacLeod's *Wife Battering in Canada: The Vicious Circle* signalled to Canadian policymakers and the public at large that violence against wives was a social issue that was not going to go away. However, as the above statistics attest, progress toward eliminating this victimization of women has been slow and uneven.

Sexual Assault in Intimate Relationships

The discussion and examination of woman abuse in turn generated new areas of concern. In particular, marital rape was identified as an important dimension of the violence against women in intimate relationships. Given the common-law tradition that women belonged "lock, stock, and barrel" to their husbands, it is not surprising that the notion of raping one's own wife was initially considered an oxymoron. Women and men assumed that a wife owed her husband sexual access. Throughout Canada and the United States, the law defined rape as an act committed by a man on a female who is "not his wife." Just as a man could not rob from himself, he could not take by force that which already belonged to him[10] (Finkelhor and Yllo, 1985; Dranoff, 1977).

By the mid-1970s, as feminists explored the nature of violence against women, marital rape was identified as an important part of the mosaic (Brownmiller, 1975). Diana Russell's survey of a random representative sample of 930 women in San Francisco revealed that 14 percent of women who had ever been married had been raped by a husband or ex-husband (1982: 2). By the late 1970s, feminists in Canada and the United States were demanding the removal of the marital rape exemption from the law.[11] In 1983, under Bill C-127, Canadian law was reformed, and it became possible for wives to lay charges of sexual assault against their husbands (Cote, 1984). Although few legal cases[12] have been pursued following this change in the legislation, the research continues to suggest that sexual assault is a significant element in woman abuse in relationships. The CVAW survey found that 8 percent of ever-married women 18 years and over had been sexually assaulted by a current or previous partner (Statistics Canada, 1993).

Once again, the victimization of women is a global phenomenon. In the late 1990s research documented that internationally large numbers of women reported that they had been subjected to sexual assault or attempted sexual assault by an intimate male partner. The rates range from slightly more than one in ten in Switzerland, to one in seven in Canada, Germany, and the United States, to roughly one in four in the United Kingdom, Zimbabwe, and India (Seager, 2003: 59). Recent research in rural Uganda reports that one in four women report having experienced coercive sex with their current male partner (Koenig et al., 2004).

Criminal Harassment

Violence by intimate partners does not necessarily end when the relationship ends. Indeed, considerable research suggests that women are particularly at risk for violence and even intimate femicide if they leave their abusive partners. According to a recent statistical report, domestic violence that increases in frequency and severity over a long period of time risks becoming lethal. And wife killings are usually preceded by a history of violence. Between 1993 and 2000, 74 percent of spousal homicides committed by ex-husbands, 57 percent of spousal homicides committed by common-law husbands, and 41 percent of spousal homicides committed by husbands in legal marriages were preceded by a history of domestic violence (Federal-Provincial-Territorial Ministers Responsible for the Status of Women, 2002: 17).

Through the 1980s and 1990s more and more media accounts appeared documenting the stalking and, sometimes, murder of women seeking to escape their abusive partners. In 1993, the Canadian federal government responded to public concerns by passing a law that afforded stalked women some protection by creating the new offence of criminal harassment (Canadian Panel on Violence Against Women, 1993). Although the legislation was not gender specific, it provided women with better legal recourse when they were followed, watched, and/or threatened by their ex-spouses and boyfriends. In order to lay charges of criminal harassment, victims must reasonably fear for their safety or the safety of someone close to them and harassers must know of, or be reckless toward, the victims' fear (Beattie, 2003).

Not surprisingly, most victims of criminal harassment are women. Indeed, women are three times more likely than men to be identified as victims in these cases. Further, most victims of criminal harassment are acquainted with their stalker. More than half of female victims (53 percent) and more than a quarter of male victims (26 percent) were criminally harassed by partners. Predictably, more than half of these partners were ex-spouses. In 2001 there were 2899 victims of "partner" criminal harassment—a 53 percent increase from 1995. The overwhelming majority (88 percent) of these victims are female.[13] Considerable evidence documents that when women are stalked by intimate partners they are at considerable risk for violence, including homicide and attempted homicide (Beattie, 2003: 8–10).

It remains to be seen whether this legislative initiative will assist women in responding to violence. The increased rates of charges since 1995 may indicate that victims are increasingly willing to involve the police and lay charges. However, incidents of women being stalked and killed by their estranged partners continue to appear in the popular media. On March 1996, Arlene May, a 39-year-old mother of five, was shot through the head in her Collingwood, Ontario, home by her estranged boyfriend, Randy Iles. One of the most tragic aspects of this murder was the fact that Iles had a long history of assaulting May and was out on bail with instructions to stay away from her. He did not follow the instructions but was granted bail again. He took this opportunity to track down May and kill her.

Intimate Femicide

Without a doubt, the killing of women by their ex-husbands and boyfriends has been instrumental in highlighting the importance and implications of violence against women. Between 1974 and 2001, 2069 women (and 612 men) were victims of spousal homicide (Patterson, 2003; Federal-Provincial-Territorial Ministers Responsible for the Status of Women, 2002). However, despite this terrible toll, in the past 27 years there has been a marked decline in the number of women (and men) killed by their spouses. Analysts speculate that this decline reflects improvements in women's economic status, delayed marriage and child-rearing, and higher educational attainment for women along with improved societal responses to woman abuse (Patterson, 2003: 7).

Intimate femicide is not, of course, peculiar to Canada. Other countries, particularly those with very strong patriarchal traditions, reveal patterns of wife murder. In India, in the past three decades "dowry murder" has emerged as a significant expression of violence against women, so much so that death by domestic violence rates are comparable to Western countries such as the United States (Rudd 2001: 514). In these instances, when the groom's family believes it has been short-changed in terms of the bride's dowry by the bride's family, it may resort to the practice of bride burning: The unacceptable bride may be eliminated by being doused with kerosene (a fuel commonly used in cooking in India) and set afire by her in-laws. The groom is, as a result, freed to marry again and obtain a new dowry.

Attention from the Western media and the growth of women's liberation organizations in India and Pakistan have not stemmed the tide of killings. Although the dowry system was banned in 1961, the practice persists. Analysts fear that as many as 11 000 young brides were killed or forced to commit suicide between 1988 and 1991 (Gargan, 1994: A1, A7). The official number of dowry deaths increased from 6758 in 1996 to 7543 in 1997 and it is estimated that in actuality 25 000 women are killed annually in this manner (Samuel, 2002; Seager, 2003: 29). Dowry-related killings have also increased in other countries. In Bangladesh, for example, 25 out of 48 femicide cases in 1993 were related to disputes over dowry (Zaman, 1999).

Honour killings also put women at risk. The term refers to "legally or socially sanctioned revenge exercised within a family against a woman" who is seen to have damaged the family's honour, typically through sexual behaviour that is defined as inappropriate (Seager, 2003). In a number of patriarchal countries (for example, Ecuador, Brazil, Morocco, Turkey, Italy, Albania, Yugoslavia, Bangladesh, Egypt, Jordan, Iraq, Afghanistan) men and women subscribe to the view that the women of the family embody the family's honour (Pervizat, 2003). If women are seen to misbehave, by disobeying their husbands or fathers, by engaging in pre-marital or extra-marital sexual relations, by wearing Western-style clothing, by putting on make-up, by venturing in public without a male family member and so on, they may be subject to stabbing, shooting, or stoning for dishonouring the family and shaming the male members of the family. This practice has extended to various Western countries in the context of migration. In several incidents, immigrant parents have resorted to honour killing to punish their Westernized daughters who were seen to be acting in inappropriate ways (Akpinar, 2003).

Similarly, intimate femicide has been embedded in patriarchal cultural traditions in some South American societies. Eva Blay, a Sao Paulo sociologist, argues, for example, that Brazilian men continue to consider women their personal property, and when their women leave, the men feel they have a right to kill them. For centuries, Brazilian magistrates have condoned this behaviour by accepting that husbands, as a legitimate defence of honour, have the right to murder wives who are unfaithful. In several high-profile trials, men who have killed wives who have separated, or threatened to separate, from them have been exonerated or have received very light sentences by appealing to this principle. Since 1979, a variety of feminist organizations have protested this pattern of intimate femicide, but to relatively little effect. (*Toronto Star,* 3 November 1990: H6). By the late 1990s, 72 percent of murdered women in Brazil were killed by a relative (husband) or friend (Seager, 2003: 28).

In sum, for women around the world, love and marriage do not provide protection from violence. Indeed, the research evidence repeatedly indicates that women are in greater peril in their home and in their close personal relationships than they are in the public domain. However, despite the perils of their private lives, most women are acutely aware that they must also confront violence in the public domain.

Public Perils and Stranger Attacks

Despite women's and girls' vulnerability in their homes, it is in public areas that Canadian women most frequently worry about their personal safety—and, often, with good reason. According to the CVAW survey 23 percent of women surveyed indicated they had been subject to a violent attack by a stranger at some point in their lives (Statistics Canada, 1993: 2, 8, 9).

Sexual Harassment and Gender Harassment

One of the important accomplishments of the second wave of the women's movement was to name sexual and gender harassment. Previous to feminist activism in the 1960s, sexual and other forms of public harassment of women were persistently trivialized as harmless, even flattering, and an inevitable feature of "office politics" or "guys being guys." Even today, situation comedies on television continue to use gender harassment, though not sexual harassment, as material for humour (Montemurro, 2003). Despite the ongoing struggle, feminists have make great strides toward "naming" public harassment of women as a serious offence and identifying the costs to women.

According to the Supreme Court of Canada, sexual harassment ranges from coerced intercourse to persistent propositions to insults and taunting. The net result is a "negative psychological and emotional work environment." Of course, the harassment is not restricted to the work context. As researchers point out, sexual harassment may also occur in streets, transit systems, and malls (Lenton et al., 1999). Gender harassment is closely related to (and in some instances considered a sub-category of) sexual harassment. It involves generalized sexist comments or behaviour that insults, degrades, or embarrasses women. For example, gender harassment might involve co-workers routinely mocking a female worker who wears pants, rather than more feminine attire, to work. The resultant "chilly" climate may have damaging consequences in terms of women's education, employment, and other public activities, and may have long-standing effects in terms of anger, frustration, depression, shame, fearfulness, and guilt (Sev'er, 1999; LeMoncheck and Sterba, 2001).

Through the last several decades, harassment has been revealed as a pervasive feature of women's public lives. Agencies and institutions ranging from the military to the ministry are all contexts for this form of violence against women. The CVAW survey found that 87 percent of Canadian women have experienced some form of sexual harassment (Statistics Canada, 1993). Although many of these incidents were perpetrated by strangers in the public domain, for example, obscene phone calls and street harassment, research indicates that workplace harassment is also commonplace. Ten percent of respondents indicated they had been subject to some form of stranger assault (including unwanted sexual touching and sexual attack) in their workplace (Johnson, 1996: 97–106). More recently, the Survey on Sexual Harassment in Public Places and at Work (1999) reported that 56 percent of Canadian working women had experienced sexual harassment in the year prior to the survey and 77 percent had experienced it at some point in their lives. Although the most common incidents were staring, jokes, and remarks about women, as well as jokes about the respondents themselves (physical force, threats, and bribery were much less common), the women did report that they were upset by the incidents (Crocker and Kalemba, 1999).

Globally, the stories sound familiar. A US study indicates that at least 40 percent, and as many as 85 percent, of American women have experienced sexual harassment on the job (Lichtman, 1993: 13A). A Madrid survey found that 80 percent of employed women reported sexual harassment, and 4 percent indicated they were subject to violent sexual harassment. In Holland, 58 percent of employed women indicated that they had been physically or verbally harassed in the workplace. In a Tokyo survey of 6500 women, 70 percent of employed women said they had been harassed while working, and 90 percent said they had been molested during commuting; about 3 percent reported they were forced to have sexual relations at work (*Toronto Star,* 7 Feb. 1992: F1). Similarly, researchers report that 85 percent of women in Hong Kong and 73 percent of women in Britain report experiencing sexual harassment in the workplace. The International Labour Organization (ILO) survey of industrialized countries found that 15 percent to 30 percent of employed women reported frequent, serious sexual harassment such as unwanted touching, pinching, offensive remarks, and requests for sexual favours (Burn, 2000). A recent examination of sexual harassment in Kenyan schools and educational institutions also documents the seriousness of violence directed against girls and women (Omale, 2000).

Predictably, certain kinds of workplaces are especially hazardous for women. Cultural norms surrounding service occupations may, for example, serve to set women up for sexual harassment (Folgero and Fjelstad, 1995). Often, a certain level of attractiveness and sexuality are implicitly expected in women holding occupations such as waitress, flight attendant, and sales "girl." Finally, although poorly documented in the research literature, women who work in explicitly sexual occupations (prostitution, pornography, and so forth) have long been subject to the most overtly physical and violent forms of harassment by both customers and managers/pimps (Miles, 2003; Canadian Panel on Violence Against Women, 1993).

In short, an extensive and growing body of research literature demonstrates that for many women there are real dangers in the public domain, including their workplace. In a significant minority of cases, the violence involves a physical attack. Research indicates that regardless of the form the violence takes, it has a dramatic impact on its targets and may lead to severe anxiety, loss of employment, intense depression, and even attempted suicide.

Stranger Rape and Murder

Ironically, the message projected in the Western mass media is that women are particularly vulnerable to stranger rape and even murder in the public domain. Women are encouraged to take numerous personal precautions so that they are not the victims of stranger attacks and research indicates that women are, as a result, fearful of travelling alone, at night, and in certain areas of their cities. Research reveals, however, that stranger attack is relatively uncommon. Although serial rapists and murders do victimize women, their role in violence against women is somewhat marginal. Women and girls are most at risk with people they know and in their homes (Mooney, 2000).

Rape, legally defined in Canada since 1983 as "sexual assault," is another form of violence against women that was saved from obscurity and trivialization by the second wave of the women's movement. Prior to feminist activism on the issue and the publication of groundbreaking analyses, such as Susan Brownmiller's *Against Our Will: Men, Women and Rape* (1975) and Lorene Clark and Debra Lewis's *Rape: The Price of Coercive Sexuality* (1977), rape was minimized and often humorously dismissed as just another example of "boys will be boys." Victims learned to blame themselves and keep quiet.

As with domestic violence and other forms of violence against women, when modern feminism focused attention on rape, the offence was re-conceptualized. Rape was no longer restricted to stranger attacks on young, sexually inexperienced women. Rape happened on dates, with family members, when women had been drinking, were dressed provocatively, or worked in the sex industry. Feminists insisted that women, regardless of occupation, situation, appearance, and all the other factors that had been used to blame the victim, always had a right to say No.

The success of this feminist initiative, particularly through the rape crisis centres that sprang up across Canada, transformed women's perception of and response to rape. The official statistical picture speaks volumes. Between 1962 and 1982 the number of rape charges laid in Canada more than tripled from 3 per 100 000 population to 10. Between 1982 and 1988, the rates almost doubled again. In 1988, there were 91 sexual assaults per

100 000 persons, 4 sexual assaults with a weapon, and one aggravated sexual assault reported in Canada (DeKeseredy and Hinch, 1991: 65B67). In 2002, there were 27 094 sexual offences reported to police. The overwhelming majority of victims were female and in 80 percent of the cases the victims knew their assailant (10 percent were friends, 41 percent were acquaintances, 28 percent were family members). Twenty percent of sexual assault cases involved stranger assailants (Statistics Canada, July 2003).

Once again, the numbers of reported rates of rape underplay sexual violence against women. The CVAW survey found that since turning 16, 19 percent of all Canadian women 18 years of age or older have been sexually assaulted by a stranger (Statistics Canada, 1993). These sexual assaults ranged from unwanted sexual touching to violent, forced intercourse. If attacks are restricted to the most violent, the figures remain alarming. Seven percent of adult Canadian women have been subject to violent sexual attack by a stranger (Johnson, 1996: 92). However, it must be reiterated that stranger violence makes up the clear minority of violence against women

Finally, a small number of women are the victims of stranger homicide. In 2002, 44 percent of all reported homicides were committed by an acquaintance, 40 percent by a family members, and only 15 percent by a stranger. Men are much more likely to be killed by a stranger, with 1 in 5 male victims being killed by strangers and only 1 in 14 female victims. In contrast, of the 84 spousal homicides in 2002, 67 involved female victims, 16 male victims, and 1 involved a same-sex couple (Statistics Canada, October 2003). Clearly, violence against women in Canada continues to be primarily, though not exclusively, situated in family and personal relationships.

UNDERSTANDING THE VIOLENCE: FEMINIST THEORIZING

> Without an understanding of male supremacy and female oppression, it is impossible to explain why the vast majority of incest perpetrators … are male and why the majority of victims … are female. (Herman and Hirschman, 1993: 47)

> The question of why men batter women can on one level be answered quite simply. Men batter women because they can. (Freedman, 1985: 41)

> Gender violence, in all of its varied manifestations, is not random and it is not about sex. (UNICEF Report as cited in Handelman, 1997: A16)

Power, Control, and Patriarchy

Second-wave feminists made an immense contribution through simply starting to identify and document the extent of violence against women. Prior to the 1970s, domestic violence, incest, sexual harassment, dowry burning, female genital mutilation, and other forms of violence against women were not on the public agenda. Rape was considered extremely uncommon and defined almost exclusively in terms of stranger violence (Chasteen, 2001). Incest was virtually ignored in most studies of the family, as was domestic violence, while sexual harassment had only recently been named (Nelson and Robinson, 2002: 316). To unearth the violence and demand that it be addressed as a societal rather than private issue was an enormous accomplishment. That the third wave also provided important theoretical perspectives from which to address the violence, speaks to the vitality of the emergent movement.

In particular, second-wave feminists located the violence in terms of patriarchal relations of power and control. Rape and incest, for example, were not about sexuality. The men involved often had access to sexual partners. Rather, the violence was about power. Men commit violence against women because their power in society allows them to do so. Their historical property rights over women and children along with their contemporary position in the social order—as heads of households, as fathers, as husbands, as brothers, as employers, as professors, and so on—provides them with the power to oppress and violate women. In this sense, violence is a reflection of male power and privilege in society. Men, regardless of their class, race, disability, and other defining characteristics, will be able to identify women whom they are superior to and whom they are able to control and abuse if they want. Rejecting more psychoanalytic explanations of the rapist or wife-beater, radical feminists pointed out that violence against women was endemic in Western societies—"rape—the all-American crime—and societal institutions such as the criminal justice system, religion, and the military both tacitly accepted and openly endorsed the control and abuse of women" (Griffin, 1971; Brownmiller, 1975).

Not surprisingly, this identification of violence against women with patriarchal societies led to a close examination into prevailing beliefs, values, and attitudes. As a result, considerable attention focused on, for example, rape-prone beliefs and attitudes. Patriarchy was understood to be embodied in the beliefs that some women were responsible for their own victimization—they were out late at night, they'd been drinking, they were wearing "provocative" clothing, and so on. As a result, radical feminists targeted these beliefs with "no means no" campaigns.

For Marxist and socialist feminists, it was not so much prevailing beliefs and values but the material conditions of women's lives—that is, their role in the family and their marginalized role in paid employment—that resulted in their relative dependence and powerlessness in the social order (Luxton, 1980). Women and their children were likely to be trapped in violence if they lacked alternative ways to survive economically. Rather than leave an abusive relationship and risk impoverishment for their children, women would stay in the family and, possibly, poorly paid and marginal female employment. Of course women's work in the home—the daily and generational reproduction of the labour force—as well as their resultant role as marginal or reserve labour force, were both vital to the interests of the capitalist economy. In this manner, capitalism and patriarchy could be understood to be complexly intertwined.

Patterns of male violence also were understood to sustain the existing patterns of male dominance and female subordination. In the past and present, violence served, not only as a male privilege, but to sustain male power and control in the family and in society in general. For centuries, in groups and as individuals, as soldiers and civilians, ordinary men have used rape to humiliate and subordinate women and to proclaim their masculine superiority to and dominance over women and other men. Similarly, the control and abuse of girls in the family could be seen as part of a socialization into male control. Witnessing the abuse of mothers similarly confirmed that men were in every sense the head of the household. Public violence completed the domination by encouraging a "protection racket" in which women would embrace personal relationships with individual men in the interests of gaining protection. Women would accept any private oppression rather than risk becoming "open territory" women—prostitutes, sluts—who were denied male (gentlemanly) protection from exploitation and abuse (Griffin, 1971). On a daily and life-long basis, gender and sexual harassment served to remind women that there were places, at work, in school, and in public domains, where they must tread carefully, and others where they were "inviting" male abuse and violence. They were safer from violence if they stayed in the home or restricted themselves to women's jobs and women's areas. In short, these various forms of violence and, perhaps more importantly, the fear of violence, perform an invaluable social control function for men and patriarchal traditions by encouraging women to tread lightly in the public domain, to restrict their activities, to accept whatever sanctuary marriage may offer, and to avoid challenging male preserves, such as male-dominated jobs and social situations (Kader, 1982).

Of course, the articulation of a power and control model necessitated questioning and dismantling opposing theoretical explanations. Considerable attention, for example, was directed against evolutionary and "human nature" explanations of male violence. Numerous analysts had argued (and continue to) that "male behaviour"—competitive, aggressive, unemotional, and so on—is the result of behaviours that bestowed evolutionary advantages on their owners and, as a result, contemporary men are genetically wired to act in this manner. Feminist efforts in biological, anthropological, and historical research challenged this perspective by pointing out the variability both in male behaviour and in societal structures (Sanday, 1981; Watson-Franke, 2002). For example, Kersti Yllo found that the rate of wife abuse reported in a random US survey varied from one state to another. Specifically, in states where women enjoy relatively high social status in terms of participation in professional and technical occupations, enrolment in post-secondary education, and representation in political office, Yllo found that women are particularly at risk for severe physical violence from their husbands when they live in a husband-dominated family. Also, wife beating is more common in states where women are accorded a low social status and the wife dominates in the family. In other words, Yllo's research suggests that when women's power in society at large is high, men have to resort to greater use of force in the family to remain dominant. Also, when women's power in society at large is low, men respond violently to what is regarded as women's illegitimate use of power in the family (1984). As explored in greater detail below, this body of research clearly suggests that the construction of masculinity varies according to cultural and historical context; human social structure is not inevitably or uniformly patriarchal.

As second-wave feminists mobilized their ideas in terms of shelters, rape crisis centres, and other anti-violence activism, they also made important advances in the theoretical conceptualization of patriarchal power and control. Domestic violence, for example, was not simply a matter of men hitting their wives. The violence could take many forms, including threats, intimidation, economic control, using children and other loved ones, and isolation. This increasingly complex understanding of violence is evident, for example, in the power and control model developed in the domestic violence movement—a model that identified not only physical, but also sexual, economic, and psychological dimensions of woman abuse (Sev'er, 2002: 57). Over the years, the model has become increasing multifaceted as analysts have incorporated an ever-greater array of violent behaviours and strategies.

This more sophisticated model of power and control was, in turn, reflected in a more nuanced understanding of the processes of violence. Concepts such as "learned helplessness" and "the battered woman syndrome" emphasized that the violence was not simply an external threat but rather could be internalized into women's sense of self. Similarly, explorations of the popular attitudes and beliefs surrounding violence against women such as rape-supportive beliefs lead to explanations that focused on the ideological structures of society. The prevailing beliefs and attitudes under patriarchy encouraged women to blame themselves and other women for their victimization. Issues of power and control were understood to permeate the individual as well as the societal levels of analysis.

As feminist theorizing progressed, analysts emphasized that the issue was not individual men (rapists, abusers), nor was it men in general, but rather a social order (patriarchy) in which men, in general, enjoyed more power and privilege than women and in which the institutional structures (family, religion, military, media, economy, education, the state) were structured to support male privilege. Rape, for example, was in part sustained by media that endorsed the sexual objectification of women in pornography as well as the popular media, by a criminal justice system that ignored or replicated the abuse of women, by religious institutions that enshrined female subordination, and so on. In short, theorizing violence was integral to a deconstruction of the patriarchal order.

Intersectionalities/Inclusiveness

It is, of course, impossible to draw a clear line between second- and third-wave feminisms (Howry and Wood, 2001). Certainly, the popularization of postmodernism and its application to feminist issues was a key milestone, but there is as much continuity as discontinuity in much feminist writings. Postmodernist feminism, however, encouraged a re-examination of the most fundamental and taken-for-granted concepts in feminist analysis. Even the conception of the woman who was the victim of violence was recast (Meintjes, Pillay, and Turshen, 2001). As Ann Cahill comments, "Where modernism emphasized the subject predicated on the autonomy and superiority of the mind, postmodern theories drew a portrait of a being who was radically divided from itself, whose identity, rather than being a static *thing*, was an ongoing process, affected by historical and cultural forces and undergoing constant change" (2002: 65). Not surprisingly, the resultant approach to violence against women was cast in profoundly different terms, "By understanding rape as an embodied experience, as an attack on an embodied subject that directly involves and invokes the sexuality of both the assailant and the victim, we can perceive the phenomenon as a threat to the possibility of embodied subjectivity, a threat to the victim's (sexually specific) personhood and intersubjectivity" (Cahill, 2002: 138).

This desire for a much more nuanced and complex understanding of subjectivity and victimization is also highlighted in two central themes of third-wave feminism: inclusivity and anti-essentialism (Diaz, 2004). Hewing out a new theoretical position, these analysts argued that second-wave feminists had theorized in ways that focused exclusively on middle-class, white Western women and tended to posit some unitary female sex-class or feminine "essence" (Hautzinger, 2002). This is, of course, not entirely true since lesbians, Aboriginal women, visible minority women, and poor and working-class women had long been active in the women's movement, and feminist analysts had long been cognizant of classism, heterosexism, ethnocentrism, and so on (see, for example, Clarke and Lewis, 1977).

There is no doubt, however, that positivist feminist accounts (such as those reviewed earlier) that present "women" as simple and undifferentiated obscure the diversity of women's experiences. In recent years analysts have devoted considerable effort to unpacking the obscured patterns of privilege and oppression that intersect in this category including, genderism (butch/femme), racism, Eurocentrism (European orientation), heterosexism, ableism (able-bodied/other-abled), educationalism (educated/illiterate), ageism (young/old), the politics of appearance, class bias, language bias (English/ESL), colourism (light/dark), anti-Semitism, rural/urban, and pro-natalism (fertile/infertile, mother/non-mother). In addition, these differences intersect with one another—elderly lesbians, upper-class Europeans—resulting in a myriad of distinctive experiences and issues. Indeed, considerable research has focused on excavating the particularities of women's experiences (e.g. black mothering) (Collins, 2000) and challenging any analyses that tend to universalize white, middle-class, Western women's lives.

This "difference feminism" perspective is reflected in a variety of recent research. Family violence, for example, was complexly interwoven with issues of class and poverty. The CVAW survey reported, for example, that unemployed men and men living in families with incomes of less than $15 000 had rates of violence twice as high as employed men and men in affluent families (Johnson, 1996: 154). It would seem that when men cannot assert their dominance over the family through economic clout, or when the foundation of their familial authority is challenged by the breakup of the marriage, they are much more likely to resort to the most direct and blunt expression of power, physical force and violence (Smith, 1990). Women trapped in violent relationships are often (although not always) unemployed or low-wage earners—women who lack the economic power to fend for themselves and their children (MacLeod, 1986: 20–21). Homeless women and other women who have been pushed to the economic perimeters of society are completely vulnerable to sexual and physical violence. Reports from shelter workers suggest that violence is an everyday occurrence for women living on the streets (Canadian Panel on Violence Against Women, 1993).

As noted above, Aboriginal women in Canada are not only at heightened risk of violence and abuse but also confront a criminal justice and social welfare system that often compounds their victimization. A recent study of northern communities reported that 75 percent to 90 percent of Aboriginal women are battered (Gurr et al., 1996: 34; Curry, 1997: D1, D7). Research into intimate femicide indicates that Aboriginal women are at least six times more likely to be victims than are non-Aboriginals (Fine, 1990: A13; Crawford and Gartner, 1992: 68, 73). Finally, the sexual abuse of Aboriginal children has been extensively documented and, although boys and girls were both violated, it appears girls once again bore the brunt of the violence (McEvoy and Daniluk, 1995). Similar patterns among black women in the United States also suggest a complex interplay among racism (especially in the criminal justice system), economic marginalization, and violence against women (Collins, 1993).

Similarly, the powerlessness and vulnerability of women with disabilities have long been ignored and obscured. Women with disabilities have been rendered invisible by the use of gender-neutral terms, such as "people with disabilities" or "the disabled." The relatively scant research does suggest that women with disabilities are particularly vulnerable to violence (Howe, 2000). A survey of 30 women who attended the 1988 Action femmes handicapées conference found that 37 percent said they had been abused by their parents, 17 percent by medical personnel, 17 percent by their spouses, and 17 percent by caregivers. Similarly, 40 percent of the women who responded to the 1989 Disabled Women's Network survey reported they had been abused or assaulted (Barile, 1992/93: 40–41; see also McPherson 1991). In recent years, feminist activists have sought to replace the old invisibility of women with disabilities with a new principle of inclusion (Stevens, 1995).

Lesbians also are subject to heightened rates of institutional and interpersonal violence. Though little has been documented in Canada in terms of "lesbian bashing," recent research suggests this is a common occurrence (Faulkner, 2001). A study of 1000 lesbians in Quebec found that 10 percent indicated they were victims of socioeconomic, psychological, and professional abuse because of their sexual orientation. Further, popular ideology has long legitimated the sexual assault of lesbians ("all she needs is a good lay") (Canadian Panel on Violence Against Women, 1993). Alarmingly, data suggest that the violence is increasing (Berrill, 1992). Further, as in other "marginalized" groups, living in a pervasively hierarchical and homophobic society may translate into violence and abuse within lesbian relationships (Ristock, 2002; Renzetti, 1992).

Age similarly affects women's experiences of violence. Older women, for example, are acknowledged to be at greater risk. For example, research into elder abuse, a relatively new field in family violence literature, tends to suggest that, in terms of abuse in domestic settings and by informal caregivers, elderly women are more likely to be physically abused than are elderly men, and that the abuse is more severe when directed against women (Vinton, 2001; McDonald et al., 1991: 11; see also the Canadian Panel on Violence Against Women 1993). This intensified vulnerability likely reflects a complex interplay among their economic plight, increased physical frailty, "ageist" attitudes in society, and the institutionalization and/or social isolation of many elderly women. Similarly, younger women are more likely to be targeted for victimization. Not only are they more available as victims, since they are more likely to be single and dating, but their age generally translates into greater social and economic powerlessness. Since the early 1970s, the sexual assault literature has consistently documented the predominance of young women as rape victims. According to official rape statistics, the "typical" sexual assault victim is a young woman, aged 15 to 25 (Duffy, 1983; Johnson, 1996: 112–113). The pattern persists today with 59.3 percent of all sexual assaults targeting women under the age of 19 and an additional 12.4 percent targeting women between the ages of 20 and 24 (Statistics Canada, 1999).

Pursuing this theoretical thread has led to greater attention being paid to the diversities of women's lives and the complex interconnections between axes of oppression and subordination. For example, attention has focused on the victimization of immigrant women who confront not only issues of domestic abuse but also economic, social, linguistic, and cultural marginalization (MacLeod and Shin, 1990; MacLeod et al., 1993). Other research has focused on the particular issues faced by abused women living in isolated rural communities and those who live in Canadian military communities (Hornosty, 1995; Harrison, 2002). Outside the Canadian context, a wealth of research has documented the diversity and complexity of women's experiences of violence.

Even the attitudes, beliefs, and values that were identified as underlying and supporting the victimization of women were found to be much more complex and differentiated. For example, attributions of blame to rape victims varied in terms of whether the victim was potentially attracted to the perpetrator (as a result, lesbians received less blame if victimized by heterosexual males) and in terms of homophobic attitudes (gay men, regardless of the orientation of their attacker were more likely to be blamed) (Wakelin and Long, 2003). A growing body of international research underscores the complexities. For example, in a study of Turkish university students, males and females were fairly similar in their attitudes toward stranger rape but women were less likely than men to blame the victim in date rape and more likely to view the assault as a crime (Golge, 2003). A recent cross-national study of attitudes toward violence against women reported that in the four countries—India, Japan, Kuwait, and the United States—important national differences (within the general pattern of men being more likely to blame the victim of spousal and sexual assault) were, predictably, identified and, more surprisingly, it appears that socio-cultural factors may in some instances be more influential than gender factors. Specifically, in Kuwait, there were negligible differences between men and women in terms of their tendency to blame the victims of woman abuse (Nayak et al. 2003).

These explorations are not only the outgrowth of a theoretical sensitivity to the ways axes of power and subordination intersect in women's lives, the research in turn has contributed to a more nuanced and open-ended understanding of central concepts including women and violence. Violence, for example, is increasingly understood as a much more encompassing process made up of relationships rather than a series of acts. For example, in a recent examination of women in a variety of national contexts who are living in post-conflict societies, the authors use the third-wave concern with diversity and anti-essentialism to point out not only the diversity of subjects included in the construct "woman" but also the important differences in the ways violence—rape in war and peace—is constructed and experienced (Sideris, 2001).

In the North American context, third-wave feminists have also pushed for a much more broadly framed understanding of violence against women. This perspective includes, for example, corporate and medical violence against women—the Dalkon Shield, DES, breast implants the feminization of poverty—as elements integral to "ordinary violence" against women (Stewart, 2002). For example, the feminization of poverty and the inadequacies of the social welfare system can be understood as an expression of "everyday assaults" on women. The outcomes of domestic violence—women fleeing their homes and becoming single parents dependent on inadequate social welfare support—cannot be theoretically amputated from the physical violence that may have triggered these results. The violence, they argue, must be understood as extending into the impoverishment and vulnerability of the single mother. Similarly, the torture of women in countries around the world—as victims of agents of the state, such as soldiers, prison guards, and police officers—cannot be hived off from the global struggle against violence and for women's equal rights (Youngs, 2003). Of course, this broadening perspective inevitably has lead to a more global framework.

Global/Localities and Postcolonial Feminism

Postmodern feminist theorizing has not been uniformly embraced by feminist theorists. Indeed, in recent years the criticisms have become increasingly heated. In a recent essay, Carine Mardorossian (2002) takes postmodernist feminists to task for failing to advance theorizing on violence against women and for engaging in psychologizing and victim-blaming. In short, she argues, they have endorsed a conservative approach while also leaving the theoretical field open to conservatives such as Katie Roiphe, Camille Paglia, and Christina Sommers—conservatives who downplay the severity of anti-woman violence and accuse feminists of encouraging a victim mentality in women (2002: 748–9). Similarly, Angela Diaz argues that in its desire to capture the differences and specificities within women's experiences postmodernist (third-wave) feminists have tended to "focus on unique personal experiences, circumstances and contexts ... deliberately turn[ing] their gaze inward to the Self and focus[ing] on ways by which the Self is produced and reproduced via lived experiences within a particular milieu" (2004: 15). In the process, Mardorossian suggests, the political has been reduced to the personal and the important issues such as the relations between gender and patriarchal capitalism and "between rape and 'the systematic working of wage labor and capital and the way that such a system needs the superexploitation of women'" (2002: 772) have been relentlessly obscured. As a result, she argues much postmodernist feminist activism and theorizing is increasingly irrelevant to the victims of rape and the struggle for change (2002: 772).

Other analysts have taken issue with postmodern feminists' preoccupation with anti-essentialism and diversity. The feminist project, as articulated in second-wave analyses, appears to rest on some acknowledgment of commonalities among women, despite differences of class, race, ability, and so on. An emphasis on diversity tends to promote a segmentation of women's experience that does not lend itself to social action or social change. For example, Sarah Hautzinger (2002) explores the notion of anti-essentialism in her study of Brazil's creation of all-female police stations as a response to violent crimes against women. As she points out, as important as it has been to acknowledge "difference" among women, anti-essentialism remains a tension in feminist theorizing. It is not clear where to draw the line between essentialism and, as bell hooks (2003) describes it, "the authority of experience" that women share with one another. As Hautzinger points out it is precisely some belief in essentialism—in our shared experience as women across boundaries of class, ethnicity, nationality and so on—which often animates the "imagined communities" which enable women's collective struggle (249).

Perhaps feminisms informed by globalization and postcolonialism may provide the much needed antidote to the extremes of postmodernism. As feminist analysis has been established around the globe and has focused on an increasing diversity of women's experiences, much feminist theorizing has moved toward an examination of local-global intersections in specific national contexts. Working from a feminist postcolonialist perspective, these theorists often focus on the lives of women in the aftermath of colonialism. They specifically reject Eurocentric approaches to reality, for example, the principles of binary oppositions such as civilization/barbarism and us/them that have created a "monolithic" image of Third-World women as passive, powerless, backward, uneducated, and so on. Here, the emphasis is on locating women's experiences in a specific set of historical and material conditions. The localities of women's experience in a specific time and place is understood as an intersection between local and global realities—realities in which the local must be understood as shaped by, for instance, historical and contemporary imperialism (Diaz, 2004).

Diaz (2004) provides a provocative example of this approach in her examination of Filipino women's identities and experiences. She explores the historical construction of social institutions—notably, economic, religious, and educational—that establish the boundaries of Filipino women's day-to-day and overall lives. She also explicitly rejects traditional third-wave approaches to feminism on the grounds that they tend to be oblivious to the implications of the intersections of local and global realities for Third-World women. For instance, she points out, she lives a daily life in which she cannot help but be complexly aware of the Philippine-American neocolonial connection as it is embodied in the valuation of local currency, the price of gasoline, the presence of US military in the Philippines, the presence of American media on Philippine radio, television, and film, and so on. Diaz argues that it is precisely this exploration of the interconnections between the global and the local and an understanding of the personal and cultural implications of these connections that is not reflected in third-wave feminism.

It is very much this perspective that seems also to animate several recent feminist analyses of domestic violence and dowry murder in India. Here, the analysis locates the violence against individual women in the context not simply of marriage, tradition, and culture but also in terms of social class, the response of the state, and the global division of labour. Dowry murder, it is argued, must be seen as a recent phenomenon that owes much to shifts in the economy, increased middle-class consumerism, and changes in the status of women. In this way, researchers make connections among the individual victimization of women and the suspension of US aid to India, the arrival of millions of refugees in India as a result of the India/Pakistan conflict, the decrease in agricultural production, and OPEC's oil pricing. The economic stagnation that resulted from these events has meant that many families were in increased need of cash and in this particular time and place the result was an escalation in dowry deaths. In short, the theoretical approach not only acknowledges the "differences" of Indian women's lives but also their interconnectedness with global as well as local events. Importantly, in light of criticism of postmodern feminism, it is also pointedly concerned with social change and is unwilling to be drawn in to collaborations with the state (Rudd, 2001; Samuel, 2002). Similarly, Pande's (2002) examination of domestic violence in India is located in the context of development policies, patterns of literacy, and popular campaigns for social change. The personal and political are understood as woven together and the analysis seeks to explore the complex connection between structure and personal issues. Most important, in terms of critiques of postmodernist feminist perspectives, the analysis is embedded in issues of social change and women's empowerment.

Gender Studies and Hegemonic Masculinities

Although, increasingly complex and global understandings are emerging in feminist literature, so too is a provocative examination of the ways in which masculinities are socially constructed, deployed, and supported. Drawing from the anti-essentialist positions of postmodern feminism, analysts working from this perspective consider the ways in which certain scripts for "being a man" are valued, especially in Western countries, while others are stigmatized (Connell, 1995; Messerschmidt, 1993; Kimmel, 1987; Kaufman, 1993). Although this line of analysis has deep roots in elements of the contemporary men's movement and second-wave "power and patriarchy" feminism, it has expanded into a dynamic resource for contemporary feminist theorizing with important applications to violence against women.

The research and analysis coming out of gender studies has revealed the diverse ways—historically and cross-culturally—in which growing up male is experienced and understood and in which specific conceptions of masculinity are socially valued and legitimated over others. As with much feminist discussion, this has entailed in-depth examinations of the ways in which diverse men—those with disabilities, racial minorities, gay men, immigrants, working-class men, young men—both confront and construct masculinities (hooks, 2003; Murtadha-Watts, 2003; Gerschick and Miller, 2000; Connell, 2000; Sampath, 2001). Further, these diversities are conceptualized as embedded in specific institutional arrangements and considerable work has been done on the roles played by education, the military, the media, the economic order, sports, and so on, in reinforcing particular understandings and enactments of masculinities (Messner, 2003; Thorne, 2003; Connell, 2002; Gardiner, 2003; Williams, 2003; Jensen, 2003).

Most recently, this literature has increasingly focused on the global positioning of masculinities and the interweaving of gender with material interests and practices (production/reproduction; wage work/housework) (Connell, 2000). Viewed from this perspective, economic and cultural globalization can be seen as gendered; for example, colonialism and imperialism (past and present) are gendered processes in which indigenous gender orders are disrupted and new gender divisions of labour and gender ideologies are imposed (Connell, 2000; see, for example, Diaz 2004). This approach provides support for a vital feminist approach to the "new world order."

Not surprisingly, this attention to gender and to masculinities, in particular, has been a powerful stimulus in the analysis of violence against women. Some of the core issues—what would cause a man to abuse a woman he loves or to harass and attack women who are strangers to him—can be approached in terms of the ways in which "being a (real) man" and in which men and women relate in historically, culturally, socially, and economically constructed ways, and in terms of the ways in which specific dominant institutions—the economy, military, media, sports—construct and reinforce certain expressions of masculinity. Further, this vantage point addresses not only interpersonal violence but also the organized violence that often targets women and girls as victims (Connell, 2000; Totten, 2000). Finally and importantly, the critical exploration of masculinities has lent itself to fresh initiatives in opposing violence against women. For example, the White Ribbon campaign launched in Canada in response to the 1989 massacre of women at the University of Montreal has become an important instrument nationally and internationally for mobilizing men who want to actively oppose the victimization of women.

CONCLUDING REMARKS

This discussion does not invite conclusions. Clearly, the work on violence against women is very much "in progress." Year after year, the documentary evidence of violence against women—nationally and internationally—is being compiled and expanded. In the course of these investigations there is a growing appreciation of the complexity and diversity of women's experiences of violence. Understanding and theorizing the violence has similarly evolved, somewhat unevenly. Admittedly, these developments have been matched by continuing opposition and backlash as even the statistical documentation of violence is challenged (Doob, 2002), as feminists are castigated for propagating a victim mentality in women, and as analysts argue for a mutuality of violence (men as victims of female violence and women as violent aggressors) (Straton, 2000).

However, despite the continuing struggle over the most basic aspects, there is a place for cautious optimism. In less than a lifetime, violence against women has been dragged into the light and extensively documented and theorized. Recent developments in theorizing anti-woman violence are promising, particularly in light of the growing wealth of transglobal perspectives and increased attention to both the material relations and the international and the institutional arrangements that frame violence against women. Finally, and most importantly, the dream of a world in which women and girls could "walk free" remains very much alive.

ENDNOTES

1. Patriarchy is here used to loosely define societies that are male-dominated; that is, societies in which men tend to occupy the positions of power and authority and rewards and privileges tend to accrue to men. It is acknowledged that this understanding of patriarchy suggests a lengthy continuum, ranging from societies that overtly and harshly repress women to societies in which male dominance is less obvious and more contested. The concept of patriarchy is central to feminist analyses of violence. Although patriarchal societies do not necessarily render women powerless or lacking in "rights, influence, and resources," women tend always to have "less" than men. Within this social context, men's violence against women is explicitly or tacitly legitimated and/or tolerated. Even though in Canada the family patriarch has been steadily replaced by the patriarchal state, the gender inequality between men and women has persisted (The Canadian Panel on Violence Against Women, 1993: 14).

2. Both boys and girls are abused in families. However, it appears that boys are consistently abused at a younger age while the victimization persists for girls. One explanation is that in a patriarchal society, as boys become more adult they are seen as increasingly unacceptable subjects for victimization while girls continue to be seen as suitable. Or, given the contradiction between male adult status and being a victim, boys may be increasingly unwilling to identify themselves as a victim.

3. Child marriage was banned in 1950 in India (Rush, 1980). However, there is some evidence that girls continue to be "married off" while very young. For example, in Kebbi state in Nigeria the average age of first marriage for girls was 11 (Seager, 2003: 22).

4. Based on a random representative sample of women in Canada, this telephone survey using an in-depth interview format provided a wealth of data pertaining to violence against women.

5. The significance of these patterns of violence is also borne out by research into resulting injuries. Though both young women and young men report engaging in dating violence, young women are four times more likely to report sustaining moderate to severe injury as a result (Sugarman and Hotaling, 1989: 10).

6. Predictably, women who have been victimized as children, for example, as the victims of childhood or adolescent sexual abuse, are at increased risk for date rape (Lundberg-Love and Geffner, 1989: 175).

7. Women's fear for their lives is understandable when taking into consideration that violent attacks often occur during pregnancy. One Canadian study found that 30 percent of assaulted wives were pregnant when beaten, and 40 percent of the women indicated that the abuse became more severe when they were pregnant. The CVAW survey found that 50 percent of assault victims were pregnant during the abuse (1993: 34). As a result of this and other studies, doctors and prenatal care workers are being asked to routinely inquire about domestic violence. Predictably, many women miscarry as a result of the abuse. In this sense, they already know the abuse is lethal.

8. Considerable research indicates that women are not necessarily passive victims in wife-abuse situations. For example, a national US survey found that wives and husbands were equally likely to report that they hit, shoved, and threw things in relationship disputes. In other words, both partners acted violently. Research, however, consistently indicates that women are much more likely than men to report that they had been injured in these conflicts (Brush, 1993). Even when both husband and wife are injured, the wife's injuries are usually three times as severe as her husband's (Kurz, 1993: 258; Duffy and Momirov, 1997). Considerable media attention has focused on the issue of men as victims of domestic violence.

9. Traditionally, wife abuse has been the subject of humour. An example is the ditty: "A woman, a horse, and a hickory tree/The more you beat them the better they be." As many will recall, the serious introduction of the issue of wife abuse into the Canadian House of Commons was met with peals of laughter. There have been persistent efforts in the academic and scientific literature to muddy the issue by referring to the "battered-husband syndrome" and "spousal abuse," with the implication that the violence is mutual and the consequences shared.

10. It is interesting to note that the first wave of feminism (the so-called suffrage movement) had identified coerced sex in marriage (and, as a consequence, coerced childbearing) as an important feminist concern in the late nineteenth century (Finkelhor and Yllo, 1985: 3–4).

11. Change came somewhat more slowly in the United States. As late as January 1985, 27 American states still allowed marital exemption for husbands accused of raping a wife with whom they were currently living (Finkelhor and Yllo, 1985: 140).

12. In 1991, British courts imprisoned a man for raping his wife. This was the first conviction in which the assailant was living with his wife at the time of the offence (*Toronto Star,* 20 Apr. 1991: A13).

13. Between 1995 and 2001 there has also been an increase in the proportion of male victims (from 8 percent to 12 percent) (Beattie 2003: 11).

SUGGESTED READINGS

Sev'er, Aysan. 2002. *Fleeing the House of Horrors: Women Who Have Left Abusive Partners.* Toronto: University of Toronto Press. The book provides an excellent overview of woman abuse while also providing insights into the personal lives of abused women. It is particularly helpful in exploring women's efforts to transcend their victimization.

Harrison, Deborah. 2002. *The First Casualty: Violence Against Women in Canadian Military Communities.* Toronto: Lorimer. This book is an in-depth examination of violence against women in Canadian military communities. The authors' interviews with 100 abuse survivors clarify the complex relationships among culture, institutional structures, and personal lives.

Johnson, Holly. 1996. *Dangerous Domains: Violence Against Women in Canada.* Scarborough: Nelson Canada. The book provides an overview of the main issues regarding violence against women, especially spousal abuse. It analyzes data from the first-ever Violence Against Women Survey conducted by Statistics Canada.

Totten, Mark D. 2000. *Guys, Gangs and Girlfriend Abuse.* Peterborough: Broadview Press. The author's research serves as the foundation for an examination of the roots of male violence and the linkages among the abuse of girls, gays, and racial minorities. This book is particularly helpful in sorting out the ways in which gender ideologies are embedded in young men's lives.

DISCUSSION QUESTIONS

1. Discussions of violence against women tend to discuss "women" as a category. What important differences among women are obscured by these discussions and what are the implications of ignoring these differences?

2. In what ways do specific social institutions—the military, media, religion—contribute to patterns of violence? How would these patterns vary in other parts of the world?

3. The prevailing beliefs and values in a society serve to support (or challenge) patterns of violence against women. What beliefs and values in Canada and elsewhere have been instrumental in perpetuating the abuse of women?

4. How would second- and third-wave feminists differ in their approach to domestic violence in Canada? What contributions would be provided by paying attention to the interplay between global and local contexts?

BIBLIOGRAPHY

Akpinar, Aylin. "The Honour/Shame Complex Revisited: Violence Against Women in the Migration Context." *Women's Studies International Forum* 26 (September/October 2003): 425–442.

Allen, Charlotte Vale. *Daddy's Girl: A Very Personal Memoir.* New York: Wyndham Books, 1980.

Anderson, Karen. "A Gendered World: Women, Men, and the Political Economy of the Seventeenth-Century Huron." In *Feminism and Political Economy: Women's Work, Women's Struggles,* edited by Heath Jon Maroney and Meg Luxton. Toronto: Methuen, 1987.

Anderson, Veanne N. et al. "Gender, Age, and Rape-Supportive Rules." *Sex Roles* 50 (January 2004): 77–90.

Andrews, Audrey. *Be Good, Sweet Maid: The Trials of Dorothy Joudrie.* Waterloo: Wilfrid Laurier University Press, 1999.

Au Coin, Kathy. "Violence and Abuse Against Children and Youth by Family Members." In *Family Violence in Canada: A Statistical Profile 2003,* edited by H. Johnson and K. Au Coin. Ottawa: Ministry of Industry, 2003: 33–45.

Bagley, Christopher, and **Kathleen King.** *Child Sexual Abuse: The Search for Healing.* London: Tavistock/Routledge 1990.

Bagley, Robin. *Sexual Offences Against Canadian Children.* Vol. 1. Ottawa: Minister of Supply and Services, 1984.

Barile, Maria. "Validation as Prevention of Women with Disabilities." *Women's education des femmes* 10 (Winter 1992/93): 40–41.

Baskin, Cyndy. "From Victims to Leaders: Activism Against Violence Towards Women." In *Strong Stories: Native Vision and Community Survival,* edited by K. Anderson and B. Lawrence. Vancouver: Sumach Press, 2003: 213–227.

Beattie, S. "Criminal Harassment." In *Family Violence in Canada: A Statistical Profile 2003,* edited by H. Johnson and K. Au Coin. Ottawa: Ministry of Industry, 2003: 8–11.

Berrill, Kevin T. "Anti-Gay Violence and Victimization in the United States: An Overview." In *Hate Crimes: Confronting Violence Against Lesbians and Gay Men,* edited by G. Herek and K. Berrill. Newbury Park: Sage, 1992.

Brady, Katherine. *Father's Days: A True Story of Incest.* New York: Seaview Press, 1979.

Brownmiller, Susan. *Against Our Will: Men, Women and Rape.* New York: Bantam Books, 1975.

Brownridge, Douglas A., and **Shiva S. Halli.** *Explaining Violence against Women in Canada.* Lanham: Lexington Books, 2001.

Burn, Shawn M. *Women Across Cultures: A Global Perspective.* London: Mayfield Publishing Company, 2000.

Brush, Lisa D. "Violent Acts and Injurious Outcomes in Married Couples: Methodological Issues in the National Survey of Families and Households." In *Violence Against Women: The Bloody Footprints,* edited by Pauline B. Bart and Eileen Geil Moran, 240–51. Newbury Park: Sage, 1993.

Cahill, Ann J. *Rethinking Rape.* Ithaca: Cornell University Press, 2002.

Canadian Panel on Violence Against Women. *Changing the Landscape: Ending Violence— Achieving Equality—Executive Summary.* Ottawa: Minister of Supply and Services Canada, 1993.

Chasteen, Amy L. "Constructing Rape: Feminism, Change and Women's Everyday Understandings of Sexual Assault." *Sociological Spectrum* 21 (April 2001): 101–140.

Clark, Loreene, and **Debra Lewis.** *Rape: The Price of Coercive Sexuality.* Toronto: The Women's Press, 1977.

Collins, Patricia Hill. "The Sexual Politics of Black Womanhood." In *Violence Against Women: The Bloody Footprints,* edited by Pauline B. Bart and Eileen Geil Moran, 85–104. Newbury Park: Sage Publications, 1993.

Collins, Patricia Hill. *Black Feminist Thought: Knowledge, Consciousness and the Politics of Empowerment.* New York: Routledge, 2000.

Connell, R.W. *Masculinities.* Cambridge: Polity, 1995.

———. *The Men and the Boys.* Cambridge: Polity, 2000.

———. *Gender.* Cambridge: Polity, 2002.

Crocker, Diane, and **Valery Kalemba.** 1999. "The Incidence and Impact of Women's Experiences of Sexual Harassment in Canadian Workplaces." *Canadian Review of Sociology and Anthropology* 36:4 (November): 541–558.

Cote, Andree. "The New Rape Legislation: An Overview." *Status of Women News.* November, 1984: 8–12.

Crawford, Maria, and **Rosemary Gartner.** *Woman Killing: Intimate Femicide in Ontario, 1974–1990.* Women We Honour Committee, 1992.

Curry, Don. "Indian Women Face Battle against Violence." *Toronto Star,* 3 April 1997: D1, D7.

Danica, Elly. *Don't Is a Woman's Word.* Charlottetown, P.E.I.: Cynergy, 1988.

DeKeseredy, Walter S., and **Ronald Hinch.** *Woman Abuse: Sociological Perspectives.* Toronto: Thompson Educational Publishing Inc., 1991.

Diaz, Angeli R. "Postcolonial Theory and the Third Wave Agenda." *Women and Language* 26 (January 2004): 10–17.

Doob, A. "Understanding the Attacks on Statistics Canada's Violence Against Women Survey." In *Violence Against Women: New Canadian Perspectives,* edited by K. McKenna and J. Larkin, 55–62. Toronto: Inanna Publications and Education Inc., 2002.

Dranoff, Linda Silver. *Women in Canadian Life: Law.* Toronto: Fitzhenry and Whiteside, 1977.

———. *Everyone's Guide to the Law.* Toronto: Harper Collins, 1997.

Duffy, Ann, and **Julianne Momirov.** *Family Violence: A Canadian Introduction.* Toronto: Lorimer, 1997.

Duffy, Ann. "Women, Youth Culture and Coercive Sexuality." Paper presented at the Family Life Conference, York University, Toronto, April 1983.

Faulkner, M. Ellen. "Empowering Victim Advocates: Organizing Against Anti-Gay/Lesbian Violence in Canada." *Critical Criminology* 1 (2001): 1–16.

Federal-Provincial-Territorial Ministers Responsible for the Status of Women. *Assessing Violence Against Women: A Statistical Profile.* Ottawa: Status of Women Canada, 2002.

Fine, Sean. "Study of Native Women Says 80 Percent Have Suffered Abuse." *The Globe and Mail,* 19 Jan. 1990: A13.

Finkelhor, David, and **Kersti Yllo.** *License to Rape: Sexual Abuse of Wives.* New York: The Free Press, 1985.

Folgero, I.S., and **I.H. Fjelstad.** "On Duty-Offguard: Cultural Norms and Sexual Harassment in Service Organizations." *Organization Studies* 16(2) (1995): 299–314.

Freedman, Lisa. "Wife Assault." In *No Safe Place: Violence Against Women and Children*, edited by Connie Guberman and Margie Wolfe, 41–60. Toronto: The Women's Press, 1985.

Gardiner, J.K. "*South Park*, Blue Men, Anality and Market Masculinity." In *Masculinities: Interdisciplinary Readings,* edited by M. Hussey, 100–115. Upper Saddle River: Prentice Hall, 2003.

Gargan, Edward. "Dowry Disputes Bring Murder To Middle-Class Homes." *The Globe and Mail*, 1 Jan. 1994: A1, A7.

Gerschick, T.J., and **A.S. Miller.** "Gender identities at the crossroads of masculinity and physical disability." *Masculinities* 2 (2000): 34–55.

Golge, Z. Belma, et al. "Turkish University Students' Attitudes Toward Rape." *Sex Roles* (December 2003): 653–661.

Gordon, Linda. "Incest and Resistance: Patterns of Father-Daughter Incest, 1880–1930." *Social Problems* 33 (1986): 253–67.

Gorkoff, Kelly, et al. "Violence Prevention and the Girl Child: Final Report." *The Alliance of Five Centres on Violence*, February, 1999.

Griffin, Susan. "Rape: The All-American Crime." *Ramparts* 10 (September 1971).

Gurr, Jane, et al. *Breaking the Links between Poverty and Violence against Women*. Ottawa: Ministry of Supply and Services Canada, 1996.

Handelman, Stephen. "Violence Killing Millions of Women: UNICEF." *Toronto Star,* 22 July 1997: A1, A16.

Harrison, Deborah. *The First Casualty: Violence Against Women in Canadian Military Communities*. Toronto: James Lorimer, 2002.

Hautzinger, Sarah. "Criminalising Male Violence in Brazil's Women's Police Stations: from flawed essentialism to imagined communities." *Journal of Gender Studies* 11 (2002): 243–251.

Herman, Judith with **Hirschman, Lisa.** "Father-Daughter Incest." In *Violence against Women: The Bloody Footprints*, edited by Pauline B. Bart and Eileen Geil Moran, 47–56. Newbury Park: Sage Publications, 1993.

hooks, bell. "Reconstructing Black Masculinity." In *Masculinities: Interdisciplinary Readings*, edited by M. Hussey, 298–316. Upper Saddle River: Prentice Hall, 2003.

Hornosty, Jennie. "Wife Abuse in Rural Regions: Structural Problems in Leaving Abusive Relationships (A Case Study in Canada)." In *With a Rural Focus*, edited by F. Vanclay, 21–34. Australia: Charles Sturt University, 1995.

Howe, Keran. "Violence Against Women With Disabilities: An Overview of the Literature." **www.wwda.org.au/keran.htm,** 2000.

Howry, A.L., and **J.T. Wood.** "Something old, something new, something borrowed: Themes in the voices of a new generation of feminists." *Southern Communication Journal* 66 (2001): 323–336.

Jensen, R. "Using Pornography." In *Masculinities: Interdisciplinary Readings*, edited by M. Hussey, 262–270. Upper Saddle River: Prentice Hall, 2003.

Johnson, Holly. *Dangerous Domains: Violence against Women in Canada*. Toronto: Nelson, 1996.

Kadar, Marlene. 1982. "Sexual Harassment as a Form of Social Control." In Maureen Fitzgerald et al. (eds.) *Still ain't satisfied: Canadian Feminism Today*. Toronto: The Women's Press, pp. 169–180.

Karanja, Lisa W. "Domestic Violence and HIV Infection in Uganda." *Human Rights Dialogue* 10 (Fall 2003): 10–11.

Kaufman, M. *Cracking the Armour: Power, Pain and the Lives of Men.* Toronto: Viking, 1993.

Kendall-Tackett, Kathleen A. "Victimization of Female Children." In *Sourcebook on Violence Against Women*, edited by C.M. Renzetti, J.L. Edleson, and R.K. Bergen, 101–116. Thousand Oaks: Sage Publications, 2001.

Kimmel, M.S. "Rethinking 'masculinity': New directions in research." In *Changing Men: New Directions in Research on Men and Masculinity*, edited by M. Kimmel, 1–22. Newbury Park: Sage, 1987.

Koenig, Michael, et al. "Coercive sex in rural Uganda: Prevalence and associated risk factors". *Social Science and Medicine* Vol. 58, Issue 4, February 2004.

Koss, Mary P., and **Cheryl J. Oros.** "Sexual Experiences Survey: A Research Instrument for Investigating Sexual Aggression and Victimization." In *Journal of Consulting and Clinical Psychology* 50 (June 1982): 455–457.

Kurz, Demie. "Social Science Perspectives on Wife Abuse: Current Debates and Future Directions." In *Violence against Women: The Bloody Footprints*, edited by Pauline B. Bart and Eileen Geil Mora, 252–69. Newbury Park: Sage, 1993.

Lenton, Rhonda, et al. "Sexual Harassment in Public Places: Experiences of Canadian Women." *Canadian Review of Sociology and Anthropology* 36 (November 1999): 517–555.

LeMoncheck, Linda and **James P**. **Sterba** (eds.). *Sexual Harassment: Issues and Answers.* New York: Oxford University Press, 2001.

Lichtman, Judith L. "How Can We Fight Harassment." *USA Today*, 14 October 1993: 13A.

Littleton, Heather L., and **Danny Axsom.** "Rape and Seduction Scripts of University Students: Implications for Rape Attributions and Unacknowledged Rape." *Sex Roles* 49 (November 2003): 465–475.

Lundberg-Love, Paula, and **Robert Geffner.** "Date Rape: Prevalence, Risk Factors, and a Proposed Model." In Maureen A. Pirog-Good and Jan E. Stets, eds, *Violence in Dating Relationships: Emerging Social Issues.* New York: Praeger, 1989, pp. 169–184.

Luxton, Meg. *More than a labour of love.* Toronto: Women's Press, 1980.

MacLeod, Linda. *Battered But Not Beaten: Preventing Wife Battering in Canada.* Ottawa: Canadian Advisory Council on the Status of Women, 1986.

MacLeod, Linda. *Wife Battering in Canada: The Vicious Circle.* Ottawa: Supply and Services Canada, 1980.

MacLeod, L., et al. *Like a Wingless Bird: A Tribute To the Survival and Courage of Women Who Are Abused and Who Speak Neither English Nor French.* Ottawa: National Clearinghouse on Family Violence, 1993.

MacLeod L. and **M. Shin.** *Isolated, afraid and forgotten: The Service Delivery Needs and Realities of Immigrant and Refugee Women who are Battered* Ottawa: National Clearing House on Family Violence, 1990.

Malamuth, Neil M., Scott Haber, and **Seymour Feschbach.** "Testing Hypotheses Regarding Rape: Exposure to Sexual Violence, Sex Differences and the 'Normality' of Rapists.'" *Journal of Research in Personality* 14 (March 1980): 121–137.

————. "Rape Proclivity Among Males." *Journal of Social Issues* (Fall 1981): 138–157.

Mardorossian, Carine M. "Towards a New Feminist Theory of Rape." *Signs* 27 (2002): 743–775.

McCloskey, Laura Ann, et al. "A Comparative Study of Battered Women and Their Children in Italy and the United States." *Journal of Family Violence* 17 (March 2002): 53–74.

McDonald, P. Lynn, Joseph P Hornick, Gerald B. Robertson, and **Jean Wallace.** *Elder Abuse and Neglect in Canada.* Toronto: Butterworths, 1991.

McEvoy, Maureen, and **Judith Daniluk.** "Wounds to the Soul: The Experiences of Aboriginal Women Survivors of Sexual Abuse." *Canadian Psychology* 36 (3) (August 1995): 221–235.

McPherson, Cathy. "Tackling Violence against Women with Disabilities." *Canadian Woman Studies* 12 (Fall 1991): 63–65.

Meintjes, S., A. Pillay, and **M. Turshen.** "There is No Aftermath for Women." In *The Aftermath: Women in Post-Conflict Transformation* edited by S. Meintjes, A. Pillay, and M. Turshen, 1–18. London: Zed Books, 2001.

Messerschmidt, J.W. *Masculinities and Crime: Critique and Reconceptualization of Theory.* Lanham: Rowman & Littlefield, 1993.

Messner, M. "Boyhood, Organized Sports, and the Construction of Masculinities" In *Masculinities: Interdisciplinary Readings,* edited by M. Hussey, 140–152. Upper Saddle River: Prentice Hall, 2003.

Miles, Angela. 2003. "Prostitution, Trafficking and the Global Sex Industry: A Conversation with Janice Raymond." *Canadian Women Studies* 22:3, 4 (Spring/Summer): 26–37.

Montemurro, Beth. "Not a Laughing Matter: Sexual Harassment as 'Material' on Workplace-Based Situation Comedies." *Sex Roles* 48 (May 2003): 433–445.

Mooney, Jayne. *Gender, Violence and the Social Order.* New York: Palgrave, 2000.

Muehlenhard, C.L., et al. "Beyond 'Just saying no': Dealing with men's unwanted sexual advances in heterosexual dating contexts." In *Sexual coercion in dating relationships,* edited by E.S. Byers and L.F. O'Sullivan, 141–168. New York: Haworth Press, 1996.

Munala, June. "Combating FGM in Kenya's Refugee Camps." *Human Rights Dialogue* 10 (Fall 2003): 17–18.

Murtadha-Watts, K. "Theorists on Constructions of Black Masculinities: Identity, Consumerism, and Agency." In *Masculinities: Interdisciplinary Readings,* edited by M. Hussey, 323–330. Upper Saddle River: Prentice Hall, 2003.

Nayak, Madhabika B., et al. "Attitudes Toward Violence Against Women: A Cross-Nation Study." *Sex Roles* 49 (October 2003): 333–342

Nelson, Adie, and **Barrie W. Robinson.** *Gender in Canada.* Toronto: Prentice-Hall, 2002.

Omale, Juliana. "Tested to their Limit: Sexual harassment in schools and educational institutions in Kenya." In *No Paradise Yet: The World's Women Face the New Century,* edited by J. Mirsky and M. Radlett, 38. London: Panos, 2000.

Pande, Rekha. "The Public Face of a Private Domestic Violence." *International Feminist Journal of Politics* 4 (December 2002): 342–367.

Patterson, J. "Spousal Violence." In *Family Violence in Canada: A Statistical Profile 2003,* edited by H. Johnson and K. Au Coin, 4–20.Ottawa: Ministry of Industry, 2003.

Pervizat, Leyla. "In the Name of Honor." *Human Rights Dialogue* 10 (Fall 2003): 30–31.

Pizzey, Erin. *Scream Quietly or the Neighbours Will Hear.* London: Penguin Books, 1974.

Priest, Lisa. "Medical Students at U of T Report Harassment." *Toronto Star,* 1 February 1994: A3.

Renzetti, C.M. *Violent Betrayal: Partner Abuse in Lesbian Relationships.* Newbury Park, CA: Sage, 1992.

Ristock, Janice L. "Responding to Lesbian Relationship Violence: An Ethical Challenge." In *reclaiming self: issues and resources for women abused by intimate partners*, edited by L. Tutty and C. Goard, 98–116. Halifax: Ferwood and RESOLVE, 2002.

Rozee, Patricia D., and **Mary P. Koss.** "Rape: A Century of Resistance." *Psychology of Women Quarterly* 25 (2001): 295–311.

Rudd, Jane. 2001. "Dowry-Murder: An Example of Violence Against Women." *Women's Studies International Forum* 24 (2001): 513–522.

Rush, Florence. *The Best Kept Secret: Sexual Abuse of Children.* Englewood Cliffs, N.J.: Prentice Hall, 1980.

Russell, Diana E.H. *Rape in Marriage.* New York: MacMillan Publishing Inc., 1982.

Russell, Diana E. H. *The Secret Trauma: Incest in the Lives of Girls and Women.* New York: Basic Books, 1986.

Saeed, Rahal. "File under 'Hurt': Domestic violence in Sri Lanka." In *No Paradise Yet: The World's Women Face the New Century*, edited by J. Mirsky and M. Radlett, 157–174. London: Panos, 2000.

Sampath, Niels. "'Crabs in a Bucket': Reforming Male Identities in Trinidad." In *The Masculinities Reader*, edited by S. Whitehead and F. Barrett, 330–340. Cambridge: Polity, 2001.

Samuel, Edith. "Dowry and Dowry Harassment in India: An Assessment Based on Modified Capitalist Patriarchy." *African and Asian Studies* 1 (2002): 187–229.

Sanday, Peggy. "The Socio-Cultural Context of Rape: A Cross-Cultural Study." *Journal of Social Issues* 37 (1981): 5–27.

Sangster, Joan. *Regulating Girls and Women: Sexuality, Family, and the Law in Ontario, 1920–1960.* Toronto: Oxford University Press, 2001.

Schmidt, K. Louise. *Transforming Abuse: Nonviolent Resistance and Recovery.* Gabriola Island, British Columbia: New Society Publishers, 1995.

Seager, Joni. *The Penguin Atlas of Women in the World.* New York: Penguin Books, 2003.

Sev'er, Aysan. "Sexual Harassment: Where We Were, Where We Are and Prospects for the New Millenium." *Canadian Review of Sociology and Anthropology* 36 (November 1999): 469–497.

———. *Fleeing the House of Horrors: Women Who Have Left their AbusivePartners.* Toronto: University of Toronto Press, 2002.

Shallat, Lezak. "Democracy in the Nation but not in the Home: Domestic violence and women's reproductive health in Chile." In *No Paradise Yet: The World's* Women *Face the New Century*, edited by J. Mirsky and M. Radlett, 137–156. London: Panos, 2000.

Sharma, Dinesh C. "Widespread concern over India's missing girls." *Lancet* 362 (2003): 1553.

Sideris, Tina. "Rape in War and Peace: Social Context, Gender, Power and Identity." In *The Aftermath: Women in Post-conflict Transformation*, edited by S. Meintjes, A. Pillay and M. Turshen, 142–158. London: Zed Books, 2001.

Smith, Michael D. "Sociodemographic Risk Factors in Wife Abuse: Results From a Survey of Toronto Women." *Canadian Journal of Sociology* 15 (1990): 39–58.

Statistics Canada. *Women in Canada: A Statistical Report.* Ottawa: Minister of Supply and Services, 1990.

———. "Homicide" *The Daily*. October 1, 2003.

———. "Sexual Assaults" *The Daily*. July 25, 2003.

————. *Canadian Violence Against Women Survey.* Ottawa: Ministry of Industry, 1993.

————. *Canadian Crime Statistics*, 1998. Ottawa: Ministry of Industry, 1999.

Stevens, Kathy. "Stopping Violence Against Women with Disabilities." In *Listening to the Thunder: Advocates Talk About the Battered Women's Movement*, edited by L. Timmins, 223–34. Vancouver: Women's Research Centre, 1995.

Stewart, Mary White. *Ordinary Violence: Everyday Assaults Against Women.* Westport, Connecticut: Bergin & Garvey: 2002.

Strange, Carolyn. "Historical Perspectives on Wife Assault." In *Wife Assault and the Canadian Criminal Justice System*, edited by M. Valverde, L. MacLeod, and K. Johnson, 293–304. Toronto: Centre of Criminology, University of Toronto, 1995.

Straton, J.C. "The Myth of the 'Battered Husband Syndrome.'" In *Gender Through the Prism of Difference*, 2nd ed., edited by M. Zinn et al., 126–128. Boston: Allyn and Bacon, 2000.

Thorne, Barrie. "Girls and Boys Together … But Mostly Apart: Gender Arrangements in Elementary School." In *Masculinities: Interdisciplinary Readings*, edited by M. Hussey, 79–91. Upper Saddle River: Prentice Hall, 2003.

Tomes, Nancy. "A 'Torrent of Abuse': Crimes of Violence Between Working-Class Men and Women in London, 1840–1875." *Journal of Social History* 11 (Spring 1978): 328–345.

"Sexual Harassment: Issue in Japan." *Toronto Star* 7 February 1992: F1.

Totten, Mark D. *Guys, Gangs and Girlfriend abuse.* Peterborough: Broadview Press, 2000.

Ursel, Jane and Kelly Gorkoff. "Court Proceedings of Child Sexual Abuse Cases." In *Pieces of a Puzzle: Perspectives on Child Sexual Abuse*, edited by D. Hiebert-Murphy and L. Burnside, 79–94. Halifax: Fernwood and RESOLVE, 2001.

Vincent, Donovan. "System Failed Abused Sisters." *Toronto Star*, 23 September 1999: A5.

Vinton, Linda. "Violence Against Older Women." In *Sourcebook on Violence Against Women*, edited by C.M. Renzetti, J.L. Edleson, and R.K. Bergen, 179–192. Thousand Oaks: Sage Publications, 2001.

Wakelin, Anna, and **Karen M**. **Long.** "Effects of Victim Gender and Sexuality on Attributions of Blame to Rape Victims." *Sex Roles* 49 (November 2003): 477–487.

Walker, Gillian. "The Conceptual Politics of Struggle: Wife Battering, the Women's Movement, and the State." *Studies in Political Economy* 33 (Autumn 1990): 63–90.

Watson-Franke, Maria-Barbara. "A World in which women move freely without fear of men." *Women's Studies International Forum* 25 (November/December 2002): 599–606.

Williams, C.L. "The Glass Escalator: Hidden Advantages for Men in the 'Female' Professions." In *Masculinities: Interdisciplinary Readings*, edited by M. Hussey, 231–247. Upper Saddle River: Prentice Hall, 2003.

Yllo, Kersti. "The Status of Women, Marital Equality, and Violence against Wives." *Journal of Family Issues* 5 (September 1984): 307–320.

Youngs, Gillian. "Private Pain/Public Pease: Women's Rights as Human Rights and Amnesty International's Report on Violence against Women." *Signs* 28 (2003): 1209–1229.

Zaman, Habiba. "Violence against Women in Bangladesh: Issue and Responses." *Women's Studies International Forum*, 22 (1), 1999: 37–48.

 ## WEBLINKS

National Clearinghouse on Family Violence

www.hc-sc.gc.ca/hppb/familyviolence/

The National Clearinghouse on Family Violence is a national resource centre for all Canadians seeking information about violence within the family and looking for new resources being used to address it. Professionals, front-line workers, researchers, and community groups need to know what their colleagues and counterparts are doing across the country. By sharing the latest research findings and information on all aspects of prevention, protection, and treatment, the Clearinghouse helps Canadian communities work toward the eventual elimination of all forms of family violence.

Status of Women Canada

http: //www.swc-cfc.gc.ca/about/about_e.html

Government of Canada website with links to useful publications on violence against women and on special events such as the Day of Remembrance.

Statistics Canada

http: //www.statscan.ca

Government website with links to useful publications, notably, the Family Violence in Canada Profile, which is published yearly.

White Ribbon Campaign

http: //www.whiteribbon.ca/

The White Ribbon Campaign organizes men who want to oppose violence against women. The campaign originated in Canada and now exists worldwide.

chapter seven

Men, Masculinities, War, and Sport

Greg Malszecki

Tomislava Cavar

THE HERO: CULTURAL ICON OF MALE SUPREMACY

Since the late 18th century, the women's movement has encouraged women and men to rethink the oppressive gender order based on belief in male supremacy. Feminists erode patriarchy by analyzing sexist gender identities as socially constructed. Genetics is not gender. Literary, historical, linguistic, cultural, and philosophical conventions tend to universalize essentialist manhood. Yet, feminists point out that, like women, men vary according to class, ethnicity, racialism, abilities, region, and sexual orientation. Nevertheless, as an overarching social category, men enjoy the privileges and unearned advantages of sexism. Why so little change so far?

Feminists deconstruct masculinity as critical to their goal of dismantling misogyny. Men have been encouraged to join this project for human equality. So far, not many have taken up the challenge. Most men seem united in opposition to feminism, even if their attitudes have no consensus. Why have few men joined the feminist struggle? Let us examine basic ideas about masculinities and consequences of rethinking social roles, attitudes, and ideas held onto by men. In particular, let us critique the Western ideal of the hero expressing forceful virility in violent action; the worlds of sport and the military are traditional arenas of struggle where heroic manhood is created, celebrated, and reproduced. Studying how boys become men is a feminist issue.

Achieving "real" manliness is a perpetually anxious, hazardous quest for males. Along the way, most boys find contradictions: the promise of rare manliness recedes and yet sexism seems to assure its accessibility. Still, most struggle to adhere to the ancient norms, scripts, and rules of patriarchal masculinity, linking fathers and sons. The icon of hero represents the Western epitome of force personified. This archetype saturates males in images of man as protector (using violence to maintain law and order), as triumphing over evil by protecting the weak, and as a symbol of virility in daily contests. Men wanting to command respect in men's eyes strive to achieve this image in different locations: a working-class Afro-Canadian pro football player; an upper-class British-Canadian national rowing team athlete; a straight middle-class Asian-Canadian store manager; a gay Euro-Canadian university professor; a Francophone primary schoolteacher; an Indo-Canadian millionaire; a Maritime miner with a disability; a Cree constitutional lawyer; or a Ukrainian-Canadian police officer in Montreal. Despite obvious class/ethnic differences and cruel vertical ranking of social power, what unites these men is their accelerating heritage of tough virility expressing male supremacy. Hero-images from the deep past and anxious present appeal to almost all men. That patriarchal ideal dramatizes the success of strength, something that men embody and women cannot. Although there are different avenues to achieve this ideal (conquest through money, power, sex, fame, etc.) and although apparent accomplishment is obviously rare, all men are urged to try and all boys overexposed to its attractions. Growing into a man often means struggling to achieve this impossible ideal, a lifelong project of competitive camaraderie. The most visible arenas to be a hero are institutions of sports and war. Fighting or play-fighting, sexists believe, bring out the *real man* in action. If a hero emerges from struggle, he is measured by his ability to use force against punishing opponents. "The only real test of a man … is when the firing starts" (Keegan and Holmes, 1999).

Sport and war receive vast attention and human energy. These global institutions require feminist study in order to reveal the distorted formation of manhood as oppressive. War and sport decisively nurture gender hostility, male violence, homophobia, and inferiorization of females. Exclusive domains of physical contests lock females into sexual apartheid. Boys understudy how to transform themselves into "men." Paradoxically, the last few decades have seen more women entering sport and the military, causing writers to wonder what it is that women seek from institutions that historically teach men to act superior? Perhaps it is seeking the same benefits that attract males, but it is a revolt against caste of some kind. After all, more women play soccer worldwide than there are people in Canada. And how are men reacting? Tradition-bound heroic masculinity is a chief obstacle to gender equality. How can pro-feminist men and feminist women engage with sport and the military to eradicate icons of courage making only men heroes?

THE SOCIAL CONSTRUCTION OF MASCULINITIES AND MANHOOD

At birth we are socially defined by our gender. Boy or girl? One's life is forever-after a response to that question. Gender identity from infancy triggers reflexes from our society and continuously regulates our behaviour. We become entangled progressively in "doing gender." How caregivers touch newborns, hold them, handle, clothe, talk to, and attend one shapes gender construction. Motivating both male and female caregivers are idealized notions of appropriate responses to infants. Stereotypes define babies' lives. Everyone usually corrects traits that do not fit with the assigned gender. Social practices are sculpting tools sexism requires to carve children into expected identity. No way out.

Key to the patriarchal creation of male supremacy is inculcating opposite core traits coercively stereotyped into men and women. Social agents work incessantly to turn boys into men by disciplining them to be tough, forceful, competitive, aggressive, rational, dominating, emotionally controlled and ("when necessary") violent. In contrast, women are conditioned to be obedient, submissive, nurturing, attractive, and docile. Both *must* be assumed heterosexual. The toughening up for males and beautifying for females begins at birth. Comments such as "Oh, isn't she a pretty girl!" or "What a strong boy!" express sexist gender ideals. This ubiquitous process of separation is necessary to superiorize boys over girls. Society specifically prepares boys to acquire an appropriate location among peers in the hierarchy of male ranks. Through these practices, personal growth for all is stunted. Thus, organized beliefs bind frustrated awareness to patriarchal presumptions of heterosexism as "normal" desire punishing resistance or exceptions. Systematic, coercive social patterning recently termed "heteronormativity" is promoted as universal and "natural" in human history by our dominant sexist culture (Kimmel, 2003). And so the intergenerational patriarchy replicates itself by eating the young. What now?

Robert Connell (1995) points out that there are different knowledges competing to define *gender*: biology, psychology, genetics, the social sciences, and the humanities. Differences historically simplistic are absurdly complex as categories. What of biology, one might ask? Doesn't nature produce only two sex types? No! Although we all start as females at conception as XX chromosomes, in fetal development the introduction of Y chromosomes make males the variants. Yet, life sciences acknowledge more than the dichotomy we know as "opposite sexes." Genetic combinations, morphology, and variations of the endocrine system in physiology question boundaries of our caste system. Social scientists also argue that thinking of gender as comprising only male and female is not only socially constricting, but also an inaccurate description of our lives, and definitely an invalid regime for how people feel about themselves. What if there are five or more sexes? Feminist research questions the binary standard of science and society, as do queer theorists, not to mention those lifestyle-explorers resisting heteronormativity.

The sexist duality of "male/female" could expand beyond a range of combinations not confined by body signifiers such as genitalia, muscle mass, body hair, voice production, and so on, which also bind the person to gender apartheid. Psychologists and social scientists also invoke role theory to explain gender as a product of social scripts beyond innate essence. But in trying to explain gender differences without a critique of sexist assumptions, life sciences and social sciences have failed to attend to total structures frameworking individuals that feminists in and out of the academy call "patriarchy." The systemic differential of men's controlling power over females replicates itself in countless ways daily in lives all over the world. Western global dominance reproduces it profitably wherever there is resistance, through its IMF (the International Monetary Fund) or the Olympics or the arms trade or oil business or its cultural products like running shoes or media. To be truly valid, analysis in all disciplines should include a coherent explanation of the institutionalized relationships that privilege male over female. The order of the sexes is not an automatic complementary psychological role or natural social balance; it needs sexist stereotypes and bad science to prevent questioning of misinformation. Anthropologists have recorded an astonishing range of cross-cultural variations on identities. By both nurturing and extinguishing so-called masculine or feminine traits in the preparation of properly assigned children for a male-dominated life, our society demands compliance to the enforced gender order. What most societies end up with is a dangerous hierarchical patriarchy instead of equality so that few resist to realize fully humane potential.

Nullifying gender as the prime factor of worth, identifying essentialism with oppression, and challenging the ideology of male supremacy, feminism threatens the status quo of virility above all. Patriarchal societies like ours raise boys to believe unearned entitlement is natural; but anatomy is not destiny. Patriarchy requires constant energy to separate and reinforce gender differences, insisting on a history of heroes without women. Equality threatens our reactionary status quo by allowing equal inherent human worth for all without reference to markers of identity. Rearranging society on this basis, we would raise "for the first time in human history, the possibility of a fully human community, a community structured by a variety of connections rather than separation and opposition" (Hartsock, 1985). The UN Declaration of Human Rights then becomes word made flesh, and gender becomes an incidental like eye-colour. The past will be past.

Heroic manhood, most precious and fragile idealized identity, requires relentless cultivation, fortified by all the institutions that men control: governments, business, religion, the military, media, and sport. "Within the context of white supremacist capitalist patriarchy one can assert manhood simply by demonstrating that one has the power to control and dominate women" says bell hooks (1995). Before feminism, men theorized very little about the construction of masculinity even though successive generations glorified manliness, obsessed with its pursuit. Past and current sexual division of labour benefits all men, though it stunts their human spirit.

Besides examining how men control women and children as subordinates, feminists study how restrictively men relate to other men according to their social locations and ranking within our ranked dominant culture. Although men may appear as equals in society-wide patriarchy, such appearances are basically deceptive. "Man" is no longer an unproblematic concept. It has been methodically considered in recent feminist studies and demythologized by female thinkers and their pro-feminist male allies. Especially important for study are settings in which men exclude women to re-affirm their manhood, the men's houses Kate Millett refers to in *Sexual Politics,* especially sport and the military (1970). In the early 1980s, pro-feminist male writers like Sabo and Runfola (1980) and Joseph Pleck (1981) made connections between masculinity and sport with books like *Jock: Sport and Male Identity* and *The Myth of Masculinity*. It was not until the late 1980s that a concentrated body of work emerged on the nature of manhood and masculinities. Robert Connell's *Gender and Power*, Michael Kaufman's edition of *Beyond Patriarchy: Essays by Men on Pleasure, Power, and Change*, Hearn's *The Gender of Oppression,* and Michael Kimmel's edition of *Changing Men: New Directions in Research on Men and Masculinity* were all published in the same year (1987). In England, Vic Seidler published *Rediscovering Masculinity* in 1989, followed in 1990 by Lynne Segal's review of men's awakening to feminism in her *Slow Motion: Changing Masculinities*. There are discernible splits in theoretical findings. Robert Bly's *Iron John* (1990) and Sam Keen's (1991) *Fire in the Belly* are arguments for a back-to-man-the-warrior mythopoetic movement. Stoltenberg examined this topic in *Refusing to Be a Man* (1990) and *The End of Manhood* (1993). Other studies are Harry Brod and Michael Kaufman's *Theorizing Masculinities* (1994), Michael Messner's *Power at Play* (1992), and Rotoundo's *American Manhood: Transformations of Masculinity from the Revolution to the Modern Era* (1993).

Although these writers differ on meanings of manliness, most agree that the chief concept is based on the warrior as man of action. Bach (1993) urges that "new forms and images of masculinity must be uncovered, created, constructed as a resource men can draw upon in reconstructing themselves." Ideals for translating boys into men are part of the past's stranglehold upon the present (Pollack, 1998). Unless patriarchy experiences resistance by men, social change is in danger of absorption and assimilation to the status quo. Yet becoming a man is the main lifetime project for most males; its model is the warrior-hero spanning narratives from the Trojan War epics to the films of Terminator cyborg battles. Super Bowls and Stanley Cups share ancient deep roots, but drop by your local arena or hoops court and the lust for heroism will prove our point.

Are sexist heroes the ultimate expression of courageous humanity? In a global population of more than six billion (with slightly more females than males) estimates for the Opening Ceremonies of the 2004 Athens Olympic Games is expected to command an audience of half the world, in a world where half its people have no phone. No collective activity for any group of women can command anything like this, nor is it likely in your lifetime. Spectacular dramas of war and sport are concrete manifestations of sexist priorities and values of privilege; in these domains, women's assumed inferiority and suffocating insignificance rarely surface. Omitting women in these arenas of manly endeavour is the norm. Warrior-heroes who never give up are replayed in photos, histories, yearbooks, films, broadcasts, and news roundups, captivating anxious boys and men by holding out exemplars of *achieved* real-manhood in action. Rather than repudiate phallocentric privilege and patriarchal control, false promises of virility appeal to boys big and small. Those promises daily drown men's love of justice and sabotage equality.

Following Simone de Beauvoir's 1953 analysis of women in *The Second Sex*, Kimmel and Messner (1992) are among critics who argue that men are not born but made. Males must be taught that they should demonstrate invincible toughness, strength, aggression, determination, and action. Insistent focus on manhood filters through the complicated lenses of culture, class, race, sexuality, and ethnicity. Each combines with the others to enhance or reduce one's social power as a male, yet the singular ideal binds most into a cult of virility. Within the context of a boy's location in family, peer group, and community, expectations urge him to embody the heroic warrior. Hargreaves (1994) discusses the process as role theory in which social behaviour is a performance in which individuals act out scripts shaped before history was written. Progressive rewards for convincingly absorbing the ideals of "acting like a man" are many for the maturing boy. Though ancient nomadic warrior societies might seem far away, similar purposes continue today in boys' lives, including rites of passage, brutal ordeals of teasing or torture, and male-only activities that are intended to build the real man. Material and psychological rewards are impressive enough that there are few incentives for abandoning the quest, even for the vast majority of males who fail to achieve it.

BECOMING A MAN: GROWING INTO OLDER, BIGGER BOYS

Harris (1995) marks six developmental stages in the construction of male identity: early childhood (ages 0–6), youth (ages 6–18), early adulthood (ages 18–30), adulthood (ages 30–40), maturity (ages 40–50), and seniority (over 50). Throughout this life-cycle, males work at absorbing, moulding, and validating their manliness by other men's approval. During the adult and mature phases, men may choose whether to relive their masculine youth, finish masculine tasks left uncompleted, resolve any past issues of masculinity, or create alternative identities resisting traditional ones. Even though later stages of life offer men opportunities to reflect and revise their ideas of masculinity, the strong cultural imperative is refreshed daily. Refuting this ideal involves risking benefits that society offers conformists. Still, sexism requires imposing men's gender order on intimate relations and inferiorizing all females, suppressing healthy equality.

Assume "opposite sexes" is the root of differential treatment for male and female children. Usually dressed in different clothing, given contrasting toys, we are channelled then disciplined into significantly different behaviours. Conditioning works! Children can distinguish between the sexes themselves by age three. According to Harris (1995) boys begin to mimic masculine role play by age six, following behaviour they witness in male relatives, neighbours, action heroes, and media images. Barrie Thorne (1993) analyzes how gendered play patterns teach proper roles by encouraging strenuous physical experiences for boys and modifying those for girls as weaker. Acquiring male identity also involves emotional distancing before puberty from close bonds with females such as mothers, aunts, grandmothers, sisters, friends, teachers, and female role models. What are the personal costs for males scarred through loss incurred in distancing themselves from female significant others and the stunting of humane feelings for women and other men? Obviously, there is elastic variation in occurrence and degree, even among people sharing the same schools and communities. But no matter how uneven the process, across the spectrum of our society there is consensus on the real man, traits assumed to be quite different from those characterized as female. Boys coming of age cannot be left to chance, choice, or nature.

Adolescence for boys requires demonstration of traditional male role-playing. Stereotypical characteristics of warriors—toughness, strength, aggression, and emotional control—are enforced by rewards and sanctions (Kilmartin, 1994). Since the codes of our culture are inscribed upon our bodies, sport obviously functions as a showcase for prowess. Misogyny patrols homophobic boundaries for any behaviours that are deemed "feminine." Homosexuality is equated with hated femininity: "weakness" to be brutalized by threatened males. Consequently, flagrant shows of appropriate masculinity become normal for boys, beginning in the pre-pubescent years to the end of the teens. Schools, sports, families, and friendships become arenas of testing oneself and others. Media re-affirms compulsory heterosexuality broadcasting only it as acceptable. No surprise armies like to recruit boys while still in their late teens, for the adolescent's need to prove himself makes him compliant and malleable for soldier-building. And after several millennia of success, techniques are reliable.

Even if a male senses a firm masculine identity in early adulthood, all his efforts win him little security since he must continue to prove himself. In fact, performance anxiety is one of the key components of sustaining manliness. Males learn that they are only as good as their current performance. Past achievements do not count. In sports (as in war) victory is what counts—results, *not* relationships; performance is measured in goals, in touchdowns or baskets or reaching military objectives, all of which translate into social and sometimes financial recognition. Adolescent boys often display enormous anxiety as they learn adult male cultural performance scripts. They see little variation on the script, little room for negotiation, few role models who offer alternative scripts. Some boys drop out of situations like organized hockey where exaggerated scripts are enacted, since they realize winning is unobtainable for them there. Yet emasculation threatens all, even champions.

Male identity acquisition within the hierarchy continues throughout adulthood in the work men assume, their educational levels, their choices of partner, residences, and so on.

Kilmartin (1994) asserts that adult masculine identity bases itself on self-esteem associated with work, wealth, achievement, and perceptions of significant others such as spouse, friends, family, and associates. Of course, class and ethnicity tailor each man into acceptable versions of masculinities in the dominant culture's hierarchy. Again, war and sport provide manly images for men's eyes. Heroic manhood binds males across and down the ranks, wherever women are excluded.

Men must try to sustain this identity for the rest of their lives despite aging bodies and competition from younger men. In the maturity phase, from 40 to 50 years of age, many men experience a mid-life crisis that coincides with physiological and psychological changes eroding the certainties of early manhood, possibly generated by andropause. Declining vitality and accumulated problems in the physical-emotional realms unleash questions of worth. Since manhood is defined by emotional control and suppression of vulnerability, many men have spent most of their lives hiding their emotions. Some may now release their empathy more consciously toward caring for others; others deny themselves this expression. This phase often requires reconciliation between idealized heroes of youth with middle-aged self-knowledge. In the last stage of life, men attempt to resolve issues from the past in a number of ways. Some refute the persona they have absorbed. Others spend considerable time in confusion about their identity, while most cling more ferociously to the original conditioning. Although it is more acceptable for a mature man to be emotive, he does so as a proven man or a failed one. A few men might try to redeem their misogynist wrongs, but most strive to imprint their standards in succeeding generations. Often men finish their lives confused about the hideous price they paid for their manly identity: emotional estrangement, a body broken by violence or overwork, suppressed or stunted emotions, and a life dedicated to securing power over others instead of encouraging equal relationships. Often spouses are the sole intimates men retain while pursuing recessive manliness, and the loss of that only connection through separation or death often signals the end of the will to live, triggering murderous rages in a few.

Males learn to disguise and suppress their true emotions under layers of masks. According to Pollack (1998) male supremacist elites promote "gendered strait jackets" to bind up the feelings of most males, thus inhibiting their capacity to empathize with others inferiorized in the social power grid, such as women and children. Just as in slave-owning societies (and women have been referred to as the world's first and last slaves), members of our sexist society are discouraged or prevented from acting and thinking freely because such activity threatens the social order (castes of the privileged and the powerless) by fostering ideas of equal personal worth. Although both genders find their self-esteem affected by the roles they play as stereotyped, males continue to align themselves with power that confers privileges on them. The use of force is primary in the world of men; force, tough discipline, and control of self or others mark the essence of the real man. Under Western patriarchy, a man's life-cycle generically reflects expected stages of life, while varying in particulars among social classes, ethnicities, and subcultures (such as the gay community); historical conditions affect actual lives, but ideally the lifelong process of making boys into men matches the template of the warrior-hero model. Joining the ranks of "true" men requires accepting layered social practices, coat upon coat, until a boy's feelings become armoured by the ideology of male supremacy. Michael Kaufman (1994) demonstrates how this process is one of tremendous anxiety, painful isolation, and emotional suffocation, mixed with misogyny and homophobia in *Cracking the Armour: Power, Pain, and the Lives of Men.* Jackson Katz explores the pressures on boys and the possibilities to become more humane masculinities in his powerful video analysis *Tough Guise: Violence, Media, and the Crisis of Masculinity* directed by Sut Jhally (1999). Released by feminist insight, more men are rejecting the insecurities of misogyny and the pretense of the sexist habit of manhood. Refusing the patriarchal agenda with enthusiastic love of justice instead of numbing conformity to gender scripts, "new men" aspire to become fully realized humans instead of needy beggars for other men's approval. But sexism still rules; denial is widely shared panic. A Toronto radio station specializing in man-talk advertises itself with billboards pleading "Save the Males." Can extinction be far away?

WAR AND SPORT AS PRIME SITES OF SOCIAL CONSTRUCTION OF MASCULINITIES

"There is no comparison to any other line of work in the world than the military for male bonding," writes ex-Armed Forces member James Davis in *The Sharp End: A Canadian Soldier's Story* (1997). Military units and sports teams remain apart in contemporary society from other public spaces, such as workplaces and schools, in which men and women increasingly mix. These two represent domains where men display "superior" prowess before vast appreciative audiences magnified by both broadcasts and print journalism. Gender segregation reinforces the worlds of war and sport as refuges from threatening sexual politics. There men form close male friendships without censure or doubt of virility. In fact, these arenas cultivate fan-fantasies of being a "man among men," as celebrity heroes. Our society puts such images beyond the reach of women, who may only exceptionally glory in fame as honorary males. Female athletes certainly exist in huge numbers and are serious about sport, increasingly honoured as champions. The military female is now among us as both rare occupation and possible combat personnel, making up around 13 percent of Canadian Forces in mostly non-combat roles. But women-soldiers are nevertheless still perceived as a cultural anomaly in contrast with their male counterparts. Power, violence, and heroic action still are categorized as male. Why?

War is not only a constant in Western history, but it is also our metaphor for defining human experience and understanding the world: life, disease, relationships, politics, and competing interests are described as fights. History, nature, and human conflicts are seen in Western culture as contests between the strong and weak. After Darwin, the survival of the fittest came to be interpreted as survival of the strongest. However, feminists have refuted our bias that war is about natural male fighting urges or emotional testosterone-induced aggression, arguing instead that war is actually a highly rational, social activity involving battle plans of mass attacks organized by politicians and generals who have long-range and political strategies for using trained forces of soldiers. As Michael Ignatieff says, "It is not that males are made for war but that war makes males into men, over the millennia transforming masculinity into machismo. War has been the decisive influence in the shaping of human instinct, institutions, and character. War militarizes the male" (1997). War requires a complex movement of troops and supplies with battle plans and tactical shifts. It is a social institution that trains boys and men as combatants and influences greater society with its needs and values. Males do not naturally make war. But rather, violent powerful men train young male minds through bodies already schooled from childhood to fight when ordered.

There are distinct advantages for males in restricting women from combat. During revolutions women function as irregular troops, substituting for men. In very recent times armies of developed nations have been forced to officially accept the first women in small numbers for combat units. But 99 percent of the thirty million armed soldiers in the world are males, even if the USA has around 15 percent of its military strength in female troops. In warlike societies men are believed to be active protectors, while women in their lesser role are either framed as either the defenceless protected or the passive victims. Women in these cultures protecting themselves as trained and armed combatants makes sense only when wars are fought out in the home country. These beliefs neglect compelling historical proofs of women as fighters equal to men in both regular warfare and revolutionary conflicts (Jones, 1997). But the status quo of armed men has prevailed in human history despite good sense and good use of human personnel. If women could fight just as well as men, what then would be the difference between them? Heightened value of male bonding without females in the "pure" world of military combat service confers both the heroic role to men alone and solidarity among males extends into both public and private life, as noted by Klein in her study of the Israel military (1999). The perceived inability of women to fight reduces claims of equal dignity whenever war threatens. Hartsock (1985) concludes in her study that "heroism is the supremely masculine role" and that heroic myths serve as seductive catechisms in the education of young men. In Homer's *Iliad,* the Trojan hero Hector pointedly informs his wife Andromache (who is holding their baby son), "War is man's business, and this war is the business of every man in Troy." From the time of Homer to the present manhood has been equated with the use of force in violence, willing to kill or to risk being killed, to conquer or die. Militarization means that every routine of men's lives is measured against the behaviour and standard of performance of the anticipated potential death struggle. Western patriarchy needs the myth of the real man, the hero, because it cannot exist without either the possibility of war or the benefits of sexism passed from father to son.

Sport is a competitive representation of hostile combat, an image of battle played for amusement, profit, practice, and glory. Men and boys are to play at fighting and they are to fight as if playing. We find this approach as much in today's *Sports Illustrated* as in the *Iliad*. Sport's language, uniforms, strategies, and tactics (extending down into youth sport to T-ball at least) mimic the world of the armed forces with both soldier and athlete intent on toughening the body and mind and training to perform hard tasks against adversaries in the pursuit of victory. In history and parallel function as a man-making institution, sport has much in common with war, though with obvious differences in objectives and results. In the heat of rivalry sometimes those differences are forgotten. And every sports banquet has celebrated the similarities. But both make heroes out of sons and inspire the feelings of comradeship for brothers-in-arms. Which came first?

Sport precedes war in human development, since verifiable instances of war and mass armed movements only date back to about 10 000 years ago and play pre-exists the first hominids as far as we can tell. Based on artifacts and the study of prehistoric sites, scholars believe that our early ancestors did not experience organized warring, but that organized games and recreation are believed to be a part of the very earliest cultures. Communal religious rituals of contests and seasonal amusements, physical activities and sporting events were already ancient before the onset of organized mass murder of humans. The discovery that the human body could be trained as a weapon, using the implements of hunting, was one of the most revolutionary moments in history. War-making extends to absorb almost all other social activities into its lethal orbit. The sharply gendered nature of warfare is present throughout recorded history, sifting apart irrevocably lived experiences of men and women. The discipline, training, brotherhood hazing, ritual ordeals, and the violence of battle divide the destinies by gender. Boys must be hardened to kill and be killed upon command, while girls must be prepared to bear and nurture children who may have to do either one. The ancient machine runs on fresh blood; and the patriarchy must ensure that there is a constant supply of boys.

Both war conflicts and sports contests are useful training grounds for warriors and warrior-athletes. Comparatively, women's sport and low-caste men's sport are seen as play worthy of no attention. In warlike societies, the supreme sports, the combat sports such as hunting or the medieval noble's jousting, are exclusively reserved for the class that specializes in that society's forms of battle. Noblewomen sometimes hunted but hardly ever jousted, a skill requiring years of expensive and exclusive training. Those peasants lowest in status in medieval Europe played an early form of football (both men and women), a game just for amusement. But when infantry and artillery became the norm in modern warfare, who served as soldiers? Every man but not women. Is this social pattern still reflected in the seriousness with which we treat men's professional basketball contrasted with the much less attention paid to women's basketball? When we observe sexual apartheid at work in modern sports, we see the oldest paradigm rooted in the Western militarism of male supremacy. This paradigm denies the idea of strong women, especially ones who might equal or learn the traits, efforts, skills, and successes of men. Sexism cannot abide the presence of women as heroes, as warriors, as equals in the fields of glory that exude the essence of manly strength and courage.

SPORT AND MANLINESS: FEMINIST ISSUES IN MEN'S LIVES

Industrialization, urbanization, and technological innovations have created the rise of today's sport. An important factor in the crisis of masculinity is male anxiety regarding the huge influx of females this past century into the labour market as rivals for wages. Growing demands of women in all classes for social equality, political participation, access to all education, and fully sufficient economic independence have attacked the heart of male privileges. Men, already feeling diminished by the lessening need for raw muscle power that the machine age had replaced, look more intensively to sport as daily reassuring proof of deserving superior status over women, especially feminists (Burstyn, 1999; Connell, 1995; Hargreaves, 1994). Sport's contests have become central to patriarchy's modern production of manliness. The best defence is a great offence.

Modern sport grew out of the nineteenth century and early twentieth century determination to counter so-called feminizing influences in the workplace, schools, homelife, and society in general. As a hostile reaction, sport became that male preserve—football fields or hockey rinks or stadiums or high-school gyms—which celebrated male victory, aggression, virility, physical strength, and grace away from the interference or demands or rivalry or performances of skilled females. Male fans, journalists, commentators, spectators, and sponsors could enjoy the high achievements of talented athletes in the inherently exciting context of sport, pretending always that this at least was something men would always best women in. As Baron de Coubertin, the founder of the modern Olympics, believed, women could only be tolerated as an admiring audience, but sport at his Olympics was to be about strengthening the virility and power of men in contests for men. From 1896 Athens onward, the Olympic Games have been a showcase for manly endeavours even if women always have pushed to be included. By the 1996 Atlanta Games, there were still two male athletes for every female. At the rate of glaciation, this is not "progress." And women's closing of the gap is not welcome nor is it sports news. Sport sells heroic masculinity to those needing it most.

VIOLENCE AND SPORT: MALE BODIES AS WEAPONS

Sport offers an antidote to our increasingly routinized, time-pressured, work-obsessed lives. Sport offers an immediate, alive, exciting, and uncertain contest in which tough players compete. Even at more orchestrated levels of pro sport and Olympic competitions, the masculinity psychodrama prevails. Sport as a business feeds the commercial demands for the consumption of masculinity images in action. We can understand what pure sport offers everyone without reference to gender, including action developing positive qualities of self-confidence, discipline, fellowship, and initiative. Males have always been attracted to sport for these benefits, so it is no surprise that females are searching for similar experiences. The positive qualities of engaging in sport, the fun and good friends, often got lost in early feminist critiques that only understood sport as an arena where men exclude women. More recently, feminist theorists have investigated sport as a site for theorizing the body where women have been excluded from its challenging and transformative experiences. Feminist writers like Helen Lenskyj, Laura Robinson, Susan Bordo, Ann Hall, Lynne Segal, Susan Birrell, and Cheryl Cole ask, What distinguishes the sexes? Should only men be strong?

Michel Foucault (1978) surveyed the social impact on the reflective characteristics of our physical selves. The disciplining of the body, together with its pleasures and its discourses, shapes the personality inhabiting that body. We appreciate from his work how elastic the body is, how malleable, how adaptable to the systemic demands of its reference group. Foucault exhibits how saturated the body is with political notions in a web of power relations. Are we our physiques? Men tend to over-identify with the heroic body, carrying scars with pride. What happens when women enter the same sports as contested terrain?

In the 1970s, neo-Marxist scholars like Jean-Marie Brohm (1978) were among the first to connect competitive sport with sophisticated forms of machine-like work in which the body is subjected to excessive demands for performance, even before the major drug problem of steroid enhancers. Today we see professional sport, a lucrative industry, as a form of work rather than play. Indeed, many athletes refer to "doing their job," even if they still claim a "love for the game" while commanding fortunes in salaries. More recently, sport sociologists like Varda Burstyn, Don Sabo, Michael Messner, Bruce Kidd, and David Whitson have written searing critiques of the physical and emotional damage men do to themselves and other men in the furiously aggressive spectacles we know as pro sport. The pride players show in their ability to "'take it like a man" cannot hide the cumulative damage of repetitive violence visited upon the bodies of players, particularly in the contact sports we call "collision sports," such as boxing, ice hockey, football, lacrosse, and even soccer and basketball, which lately have been taking on more aggressive styles of play. What makes hurting others or absorbing hurt oneself a fun or worthwhile activity to endure or watch? Winning seems the goal, but proving one is a real man at any cost is apparently also of the most intense and greatest interest: "no pain, no gain," or, more pointedly, "no guts, no glory." Comradeship in adversity fosters a fighting spirit that makes a man afraid of losing "what he holds more dear than life itself, his reputation as a man among men" (Keegan, 1985). Joseph Kuypers (1992) points to the traditional code of dominant masculinity that centres itself upon violent force, the ability to "dish it out" and the ability "to take it." Such attitudes and practices in sport (and other places such as the business world) perpetuate the warrior model. Recent studies on hazing and initiations in college team sport identify the desire and need to test, to inferiorize, to torture, and to control (Johnson, 2000). Don Sabo and Joe Panepinto (1990) compare hazing in team sports to coming-of-age rituals in tribal societies where boys were expected to "toughen up," to "sacrifice the body," to "push beyond" the pain and humiliation in graduating from boyhood to manhood. Of course, war is also a metaphor for the ultimate male experience; as one coach is quoted as saying "football is the closest thing to war you boys will ever experience. It's your chance to find out what manhood is all about." Laura Robinson (1998), in *Crossing the Line*, investigates ritualized sexual assault of females among junior hockey circles and the extreme role-playing typical of team atmosphere. Johnson (2000) reveals common but horrifying underground practices of team initiations among male athletes (and among females athletes too, though in usually less severe forms). Andrew Thornton (1998) shows how persistent sexism is even in the "new" sport of ultimate Frisbee. Boys learn to make the body a weapon.

Ironically, team owners, coaches, peers, fans, and media reward physical assault on the playing fields or in the rink even though it is outlawed elsewhere in society. Most of the physical and verbal abuse encountered by players at all ages is considered completely unacceptable in any other place in society. In work situations "trashtalk" or assault would constitute grounds for dismissal. Yet, such abuse is fostered in sport. The law of the land does not stop at a sheet of ice for hockey games, yet in the NHL only two charges have been laid for assault: Dino Ciccarelli in Toronto in 1988 and Marty McSorley in Vancouver in 2000. The current situation of abuse in organized sport—its prevalence and perpetuation—is reminiscent of the repugnant discourse that used to surround domestic abuse. Yet sport-culture advances all kinds of abuse as normal play. The "hit of the week" is a treat for television audiences eager to see vicious assaults in detail. Don Cherry can turn out a series of "Rock'em Sock'em" videos that sell in the millions. Even at the youngest levels, virility is tested by violence.

Some parents, particularly fathers, often placed boys in physically abusive sports to harden them for a competitive world and to eliminate any effeminate qualities. Although sport claims to build character, in its brutal forms sport more often reveals compliance to aggression. At all levels fine athletes have their careers ended by injury. Sport can be extremely unhealthy, sometimes even lethal. But even an increase in career-ending injuries has not blunted the rationale that legitimates violence and abusive behaviour. Despite the chronic pain and risk of permanent damage from playing hurt, most athletes see it as part of the game. They are correct. Injuring the opposition is taught as an instrumental tactic to help the team win by attacking talented rivals. Sport as a healthy activity must be seriously questioned by anyone who totals the medical costs of accumulated injuries in sports, especially given the fact that athletes are in peak physical condition. Drug-enhanced performance is also part of this dangerous world. Steroid use, for example, is symptomatic of the self-violence among athletes. The list of self-damage athletes risk is lengthy, including permanent disabilities, chronic conditions, brain damage, cumulative concussions, destroyed or surgically repaired joints, heart problems, post-retirement obesity, substance addictions, and emotional trauma. Owners and coaches too often view bodies as machines, weapons, or raw resources from which they extract maximum performances. If one human machine breaks down, a replacement will be found.

Yet sport does not teach boys and men just to sacrifice their bodies for victory or for the team; it educates athletes in techniques of actual violence to be used on opponents. There is a dark side to the effect of such training. Those who study aggression directed at intimate partners, acquaintances, or strangers outside of sport believe the attitudes and techniques useful in the pursuit of victory are carried over. Although there is no empirically conclusive evidence of a connection between sport and violence yet, evidence is accumulating. Profound misogyny in men's sport incites some athletes and their fans to acts of violence against women. Such studies investigate the increased likelihood of athletes committing criminal acts of violence, including spousal assault (Schwartz and DeKeseredy, 1997). Michael Smith's study, *Violence and Sport* (1988), has become a standard text on the factors that support violence in and out of sport; Smith identifies how thoroughly sport violence is justified in the quest for victory but more so with the motive of proving masculinity. He divides sport violence into four types: brutal body contact, borderline violence, quasi-criminal violence, and criminal violence. Within varying degrees, each type of violence is seen as excusable in a sporting context because of the "consent" of players. Smith dissects the interpersonal factors such as the direct and indirect encouragement of young athletes in violent styles of play by the leagues, coaches, teammates, parents, fans, and media. Violence varies from sport to sport and individual athletes, but fosters player-on-player fights, bench-clearing brawls, fan disturbances, hooliganism, and all-out riots. Smith quotes the rules for the successful aggression: be first, be fast, be final, and be careful. Many players refuse to fight, but readiness to do so is the expected norm. And the pressure of peers often compels non-combatants to attack.

White and Young (1999) compile a horrifying cross-section of sports injuries that are seen as acceptable as the price of playing. Playing while hurt is universally rationalized as part of the game, but it deserves classification as self-violence. The adaptation to pain and accompanying insensitivity is a highly prized trait among soldiers; its salient presence in men's sport is another bond with the cult of the hero. Pain among athletes spills out much farther than the arena or playing field. It surfaces in aggressive driving, in fighting in civilian settings, in substance abuse, in frightening loss of temper with family members, in partner abuse, and in date rape. Pro athletes who have been adored for their skilled performances since childhood (and who have been protected by platoons of stakeholder "fixers" whenever they did something wrong) have little patience for those who irritate them. If they are up because they won a game, or down on themselves because they lost a game, or got told off by the coach, or were frustrated for simply not getting their way, many star athletes have acted badly. Androcentrism produces sports heroes who embody heroic masculinity to tens of millions of men and boys. Despite the psychic, emotional, and physical damage to these heroes and their victims, such are the mainstay of an enormously lucrative industry that sells masculinity to males who are anxious about their identity and status in the changing gender order. Sport has many positive social and personal values, but these are distorted in the daily production of deep sexism. Patriarchy nullifies transformative possibilities of play.

MUSCLE = MANHOOD = MONEY: THE BUSINESS OF MALE SPORT

Varda Burstyn (1999) examines men's fascination with male sport in her book, *The Rites of Men: Manhood, Politics, and the Culture of Sport.* She finds that sport both generates and perpetuates the ideal of a warring masculinity she calls "hypermasculinity." Of prime significance is the glorification of male power through the nexus of sport and media delivered to a thirsty mass market. The public marketing of masculine ideals to a large sport market audience magnifies the visibility of heroic icons. As long as stereotypical propaganda remains vivid, more humane alternatives do not have much attraction. "Sport as spectacle" is really big business. Corporate monopolies are profiting from globalizing Western sport. FIFA World Cup Soccer opens new markets for Coca Cola and Nike. The NBA carries enormous prestige in markets far from North America. Primarily male sports audiences have more extensive disposable income than females. Men buy big-ticket items like cars, electronics, even season tickets or sport collectibles that fuel profits in the NFL, NBA, NHL, Major League Baseball, PGA Golf, and World Tennis, international soccer and cricket, the Olympics, the networks, cable television, and internet companies.

Such massive profits have incited expansion of pro teams in all sports to new markets whether in North America or worldwide. Owners, star athletes, broadcasters, and corporate businessmen have become absolutely wealthy by marketing everything in sport: merchandising team logos on everything from water bottles to jerseys; fans spend billions of dollars on sports shoes, clothes, cereals, and non-sport equipment endorsed by the most popular athletes who then open name-restaurants, sports stores, and other businesses. Certainly some elite athletes have been splendid human beings defying discrimination and championing philanthropy, yet their very accomplishments within the system extend the status quo rather than challenge it in fundamental ways. Almost none condemn homophobia or misogyny in sport settings. Why not?

According to Burstyn, the fourteen teams of the NFL who originally negotiated as a league under Pete Rozelle as Commissioner in 1964 made $15.4 million, but the expanded version of the league in the early 90s accumulated $3.6 billion from a negotiated contract 30 years later for a 233 percent increase over the same period of wage stagnation for working people. Baseball, basketball, and hockey also have increased revenues to the point where sports agents can handle deals for a hundred million dollars plus pay for contracts with bonus options, and even greater rewards for endorsement deals. Michael Jordan, for example, is reported to have made almost 150 percent of his playing salary in endorsement deals, particularly with Nike. His endorsement fee alone for one year is said to be greater than the annual wages of all the workers (mostly female) making the shoes he endorses. Moreover, athletes' celebrity status as heroes is threatened by equity concerns, since their appeal and profitability relies upon male anxiety. As in the wage competition for jobs, women are rivals. Women's sport erodes rich male-only markets.

The commercialization of men's sports stands in strong contrast to the branding of even the most popular women's sports, tennis and golf (no team sports), which produce exceptionally skilled players who will play for less prize money and accept less media coverage than men. Even the much-praised Women's NBA, with start-up funding from the NBA (and benefited by the media deals that such a powerful organization can negotiate) has not managed to put most female pros into six-digit salaries; the average salary was reputed to be around $27 000 (US) in 2000. The historical marketing of "sport as spectacle enter-tainment" cuts women out as equal or coming players since their sports, their audience, and their values are discounted by the almost entirely male decision-makers who run sport, the media, and the industries who buy advertising. Yet women are a huge untapped audience as indicated by the Olympics viewership. Whether it is television, newspaper, magazine, radio, internet, film, video, gambling, or fashion, still only male sports matter. It is a world seemingly devoid of women, except for figure-skating, gymnastics, tennis, or golf. Even though girls and women have increased their participation by nearly 1000 percent in the past two decades, they play largely unseen. Men claim sport as their own because they see no women doing sports at the highest levels, defined as supremely male in skill and power. Outstanding female athletes are considered exceptions, honorary males who can have that honour withdrawn anytime, like Hayley Wickenheiser or Annika Sorenstam.

Men's sport expresses the agony of all-out effort in the quest for victory. Male sport frames its commentary with the language of battle. Only male athletes inspire a passion-ate concern with statistical records as historical measures of skilled performance. The spo-ken or unspoken assumption is that no normal women match men's play (the few exceptional woman acknowledged as champions "must" be lesbian or a truly rare hetero-sexual athlete—they were even sex-tested for thirty years). In the caste system of male supremacy how could even highly trained and motivated females approach a man's per-formance, let alone equal or best it? Men and many women have been conditioned to see women's athletic performance at all levels relative to their male equivalents as categori-cally second-class. No one except feminists ever dreams of discussing the fact that the average man would be hopelessly outmatched in competition with any elite female cham-pions. Raising the topic would guarantee arguments at any barbecue or Thanksgiving din-ner. Images of the strong female athlete, better than the average man, more daring and more skilled, more confidently aggressive and more committed to winning, cannot be per-mitted to ruin the fantasy that men everywhere are better than women anywhere and that institutions like war and sports substantiate this belief.

Images of male muscle sell manhood in action on the playing field. Muscle is the sign of hard power, a phallic icon, for those who need to consume this image. Such vicarious feelings of power compensate for the anxiety males experience now that virility is under siege. The feminist threat of de-privileging through equality sends tremors through the market for sport. Although women and girls are challenging the power relations in other domains, men and boys continue to insist on male supremacy in sport as they watch their heroes at play without women in sight except as cheerleaders or dates. Selling manhood is a growing global industry.

TENSION BETWEEN HOMOEROTICISM AND HOMOPHOBIA

Questions dangerous to status quo heterosexuality arise when men excite feelings for other men. As Brian Pronger (1999) writes, "the reason why homosexuality is a controversial issue in our society is because it undermines the *myth of gender*, a myth upon which all human relations are based... homosexuality is a violation of masculinity in our culture." Following Foucault's (1978) analysis of the central role sexuality plays in our conformity or resistance to the regimented "norms" of the dominant culture, Pronger sees that the aggrandizement of men's power occurs at the expense of humanity's other half (1999). Both genders have their perceptions locked up within stereotypes that highlight apparently opposite traits and hide overlapping similarities. Male erotic attraction between equals is dangerous. The cult of virility must intensify yet subvert the attraction between men loving men. Male bonding expressed through sexual desire threatens the required heterosexism of patriarchy. Gay relationships invalidate the beliefs of the gender order. Therefore, denial of sexual attraction to hard men's bodies skillfully performing in agonistic sport collects into targeted hatred of homoeroticism in sport, namely homophobia. Tension is maximized by negotiating homosociality with fear.

Homophobia in sport guards the boundaries of sexism relying upon heteronormativity. Any sexual attraction between players or fans must be repressed into socially acceptable forms of behaviour, often aggression. Homoeroticism is yoked rather than exterminated. Attraction to men encourages close affiliation among teammates and buddies. Such intense mutual attractions among men are inevitable and even desirable, but must be guarded. Men in groups openly scorn gay men even more than women in presenting themselves as real men. Attraction to same-sex partners is unacceptable, unnatural, and unmanly. Tough-guy sport is for separating men (supposedly) from gays and women as inferiors. The more aggressive and violent the sport, the closer is its embodiment to the warrior-ideal of manhood. Boxing, wrestling, fighting in hockey, collisions in football, body contact in basketball, rough tackles in soccer, and discharges of anger in baseball, golf, or tennis proves manliness through aggression. Homophobia patrols the borders of the minds of male athletes. They cannot talk about how much they love another athlete and can never voice desire for a player as sexual partner. Think of how few have come out as gay over the past century. Rather, coaches, fellow players, fans, and journalists can talk about how hard they hit, how accurately they score, how smartly they play, and how massive are their biceps. They can collect pictures of their heroes, or items of clothing or equipment, visit shrines in halls of fame. Manliness here is erotically charged but not acknowledged. That would ruin everything.

There are gays in male sport of course, as there are in every field of human endeavour. The ancient Greeks were not the only gay athletes. However, just as we have very little modern commentary on the erotic dimensions of the ancient Greek sports festivals like the Olympics that ran for nearly 1100 years, we have silence about discussions of gays in men's pro or high-performance sport (with the exception of figure-skating and diving). Homosexual athletes who are out have to play in gay leagues or in sports events like the queer-positive Gay Games, held every four years (started by an American decathlete, the late Dr. Tom Waddell). These games offer competitions for all gay-positive people—gay and lesbian, bisexual, transsexual, questioning, and heterosexual—and they have actually included more athletes than the Olympics. But very few gay male athletes have come out and continued to play their sport. Dave Kopay, professional football player and journeyman quarterback, came out after ten years of pro ball, and the negative, hostile treatment he received was a clear message to others that there are vicious punishments for unmasking homoeroticism in sport. Silence rules for good reason. Sport is one of the narrow areas left where males can openly show and receive physical affection from other males without compromising their status as heterosexuals. But it is a dangerous topic.

WOMEN IN SPORT AND MEN'S REACTIONS TO FEMINISM

In spite of severe opposition, women have entered the realm of sport. Although women and girls have always played sports, there are no references in our received histories.

Ambiguous allusions to the Heraean Games among the ancient Greeks, for example, have not been sufficiently investigated, nor has the involvement of women in medieval and early modern Europe. Jennifer Hargreaves (1994) argues, "large numbers of men and boys were seen to play sports and women generally were not—the evidence confirmed that this was in the 'natural' order of things."

Mary Wollstonecraft (1792) in *Vindication of the Rights of Woman* claimed that boys and girls ought to be raised exactly the same way with the same intellectual and physical education. She believed that women's physical disabling through restrictive education resulted in diminished capacities, further supporting her argument that women's weakness was cultivated instead of natural. Until girls were raised to be strong, one could never know whether males were really stronger or not. It was a radical position in 1792 and it still is today. Feminists have often refused to accept women's second-class status as absolute. By the late nineteenth century some women disproving biological myths of social Darwinists. Clergy, medical experts, and social theorists widely agreed that females have a weak, vulnerable constitution to be conserved for birthing and raising children. "Vital energy" theorists of spermatic economy contradicted themselves on social class. Standards of polite society were repulsed by and discounted the physical labour expected of working-class women in factories, on farms, or in domestic service of the middle class.

Women had been participating in gymnastics events in Sweden, Denmark, and Germany since early in the nineteenth century as part of a patriotic rejuvenation of national populations. Domestic duties and childcare were principal responsibilities for females in all classes and nations (as they still are), but there was developing interest in Anglo-Canadian-American society in the so-called new woman who sought out higher education, paid work, and active recreation. Women's fashions at the time—corsets, long dresses, yards of heavy material, and hats—were not conducive to playing sports, although one could manage lawn sports like croquet and tennis. The 1881 invention of the safety bicycle became revolutionary for women who had to adapt style in order to ride the bicycle, choosing split-skirt "bloomers." So many first-wave feminists rode bicycles to meetings they were known as "bloomer girls." This was real liberation, as women were liberated from binding fashions, from chaperones, from lack of physical conditioning, and from dependency for transportation. The American social justice activist Frances Willard learned to ride a bicycle at age 53 in 1892 and wrote a book entitled *A Wheel within a Wheel* encouraging other feminists to learn to do so. She writes "the old fables, myths, and follies associated with the idea of woman's incompetence to handle bat and oar, bridle and rein, and at last the crossbar of a bicycle, are passing into contempt in the presence of the nimbleness, agility, and skill" (Sandoz and Winans, 1999).

Private schools for girls and women provided the first kind of regular sports programs for females. In the United States, Catherine Beecher set up female institutes in the early 1820s that required calisthenics classes. The American female-only universities of Mt. Holyoke (1837), Vassar (1861), and Smith and Wellesley College (1871) promoted exercise and games for women as a reinforcement of their energy for study. In England, Queen's College (1848), North London Collegiate School, and Cheltenham Ladies College (1850s), and residential schools like St. Leonards and Roedean in the late 1870s implemented movement education including sports as part of the curriculum. In Canada, Mount St. Vincent in Halifax, founded in 1873, followed the pattern of cultivating independent women through a full program. The large number of women entering the teaching profession by the last quarter of the nineteenth century focused on physical education as a necessary health component in a well-rounded student's development. Enthusiastic proponents like Dudley Sargent at Harvard welcomed women instructors as physical educators, even though the theory of separate realms for males and females was still in place and remains so in most places today. Nevertheless, team sports for women were a reality before the twentieth century, even extending to interschool competition. When James Naismith, a Canadian working as athletic director for the YMCA in Springfield, Massachusetts, invented the game of basketball in December of 1891, he recommended it as a good non-contact recreational sport for high-school girls and college women. He even played it with his fiancée. The 1896 Stanford-Berkeley women's game had more than 500 enthusiastic spectators and sports coverage from the San Francisco newspapers. Later, Naismith would say that the incredibly successful Edmonton Grads basketball team was the finest team he had *ever* seen play the game.

Middle-class recreation eventually generated women's tournaments in the late nineteenth century in sports such as swimming, tennis, golf, figure-skating, cycling, ice hockey, field hockey, baseball, and lacrosse, even charity games of soccer in England drawing very large crowds. The first ladies' single championship was played at Wimbledon in 1884 just seven years after the men's was established. Isobel Stanley, daughter of the donor of the Stanley Cup, took part in a hockey game in 1891 in Ottawa between two club teams. Although the Baron de Coubertin, founder of the modern Olympic Games, was strictly opposed to women's participation at the games, a Greek woman named Melopomene protested against exclusion by successfully running in the first-ever Olympic marathon race in 1896 at Athens, although she refused to enter the stadium when she finished (women's marathon would not become an official Olympic event until 1984). Female sports pioneers established impressive lists of firsts in areas of sporting feats thought impossible for women. First-wave feminism motivated and encouraged women to intrude, enter, and compete against women in the male domain of sport. Female champions defied assumed male superiority over the "weaker sex" but were almost never allowed to compete against male opponents, except among Afro-Americans.

In countering traditional notions of inferior minds in inferior bodies, pro-feminist students and faculty of the new schools for girls insisted that the body as well ought not to be subject to sex discrimination. Character-training that boys derived from sports was also seen as potentially beneficial for girls. Reformers did not directly challenge the status quo by trying to compete with boys or even play like them but instead created play for women: "a girl for every sport and a sport for every girl." Athletic girls felt empowered.

Although the International Olympic Committee initially refused to entertain the idea of women as competitors, the organizing committees in Paris (1900) and St. Louis (1904) consented to women competing in tennis and golf and eventually even in archery. By 1908, the London Games committee added figure-skating and allowed a female into an open sailing event. In 1912, 55 women competed in swimming events. Mme. Alice Milliat organized women's sports organization to challenge the IOC rules, hoping females would be included in more events in the 1920 Games. When nothing more than tennis and swimming were added, women from Europe and the United States held their own sports festival in Monte Carlo in 1921 and arranged to have an impressive one-day program of athletic events including track and field before 20,000 spectators. This resulted in the formation of the Federation Sportive Feminine Internationale (FSFI), which proceeded to lobby for inclusion in the Olympics and to create the World Games for Women—decidedly successful. Despite

ferocious hostility from lots of groups (including women's advocacy groups feeling threatened by eroding separation of the sexes), the FSFI managed to grow independent women's
games. Finally, on de Coubertin's retirement as president of the IOC, women's sporting
events were included into the 1928 Olympic program where Canada's "Matchless Six"
emerged as champions. The FSFI had to compromise on the number of competitions and
the type, a compromise that inspired a boycott by British female athletes. Yet successes for
FSFI also elicited resistance from many women, especially female physical educators in the
United States who opposed the abandonment of separate sexes in sport. Opponents worried
that the closing of the gap between sport for females and males would mean that women
would absorb masculine values of competition into pursuits previously played for ladylike
enjoyment only. Concern was voiced by medical and academic authorities that competition
would have a deleterious effect upon the female body, so that the uterus might fall out in
elite competition. However, phenomenal female athletes such as Canada's "Bobbie"
Rosenfeld and America's "Babe" Didrickson broke through many of the gender stereotypes
and won widespread approval as well as press coverage for wit.

Women have since defied perceived limitations and established new records at rates of
improvement much faster than those of men, once they got access to long-denied sporting
opportunities and training. Although females seemed limited in skilled performance at the
beginning of the century, boundaries proved to be much more elastic (and nearly useless at this
writing) when tested. The percentage of female competitors in the Olympics climbed from 12
percent in the Melbourne Games of 1956 to nearly 34 percent in the Atlanta Games in 1996.
Lori Bawden of Canada in 1998 in Hawaii's twentieth world-famous Ironman Triathlon for
men and women (the event involves a 2.5 mile swim in heavy surf, a 112 mile bike race, and
a full marathon) came in under 9.5 hours after the first female champion had completed the
course in 12 hours and 55 minutes in 1979, better than 99 percent of the male competitors.

However, the point is not that individual woman are "better" than individual men but
rather that sport is still almost entirely male-controlled and defined by male standards.
Indicators such as the dismal media coverage of women's sports and business practices that
promote male sport for profit have been confronted by worldwide revolution in participation of women and girls in every variety of sport and game: marathons, women's rugby,
women's ice hockey, women's World Cup Soccer, professional volleyball and basketball
leagues in Europe as well as in Japan, plus the Women's NBA appearance in the late 90s.
Of course, women's tennis, golf, and figure-skating represent steadily growing professional opportunities for aspiring females. Despite labelling of lesbianism, attacks upon the
feminine physique, extremely low pay for women in sport, and few jobs in management or
coaching (and none in men's sport) after active playing days are finished, women have
managed to compete in areas believed impossible for them. Their results shatter illusions
of male supremacy. National teams provide some job opportunities in sports administration, coaching, sports medicine, and sports psychology, and more women are insisting
upon remaining in professional careers outside of limited sporting opportunities designated and controlled by men. The IOC remains resistant to female participation as voting
members. As late as 1999, there were only fifteen female members of the one hundred
twenty-five. Yet, the phenomenal global participation of women in sport has unforeseen
revolutionary consequences. No one really knows what.

Several key events have produced dramatic changes in women's sport. Title IX as an
amendment to the Civil Rights Act of the United States put forth a formula for equalizing

educational opportunities in schools receiving federal funds (and aimed especially at athletic participation and access) that has helped women's college sports grow. Billy Jean King's defeat in tennis of Bobby Riggs in the "Battle of the Sexes" at the Houston Astrodome before a huge television audience in 1973 had a huge impact on the way men and women see female athletes. The impressive medal results that former Communist countries enjoyed from their teams of highly trained females to the Olympics drew both criticism (regarding alleged drug use) and emulation. Women's strength now is acknowledged; Heywood signals this new element as a thrust of feminism in her book analyzing women's bodybuilding, *Bodymakers* (1998). Finally, the politicizing of women's sport at every level from recreational and leisure activities to high-performance sport has had a generally positive visible effect on women's struggles for access, funding, public presence, and self-images. The stereotypes cannot last. Women have heroes of their own, though recognition of even the best athletes continues to be a serious problem given inconsistent, mediocre, pathetic media coverage. Class, race, and ethnic inequalities among women mean that working-class women have far fewer opportunities than middle- or upper-class women, and women of European backgrounds in North America find far more acceptance than do women of colour or those from non-European cultures. And even if some lesbians have been able to come out, there is still formidable pressure to stay in the closet. Attitudes towards lesbianism, especially from men, continue to be biased and misogynist. Women with disabilities can now compete in the Paralympics with full honour in a range of activities that would have been unimaginable a generation ago, although this area of competition needs more funding and valid appreciation.

It is clear that the huge numbers of women attracted to sport as athletes from preschoolers to master's-level competitors in their 90s find tremendous satisfaction. Leagues, teams, and clubs for females are organizing everywhere with great success, and competitions in team sports are rapidly moving to world-class level, such as women's ice hockey and women's soccer, two sports that now match in skill and depth Olympic and professional women's basketball. In the martial arts, weightlifting, bodybuilding, wrestling, boxing, billiards, auto racing, windsurfing, snowboarding, and so many other sports, women have moved beyond the traditional aesthetically judged sports such as gymnastics and figure-skating (which still retain huge popularity). Synchronized swimming and women's skiing provide excellent competition for female athletes, but now women's teams are also competing against men as master sailors in the America's Cup and they are ready for more. The bonding and team cohesion that affirmed personal strengths and peer support for men now fortify women in action on teams.

Many feminist theorists argue cogently that this is empowerment and anti-sexism. The Women's Sport Foundation set up in 1973 by Billie Jean King with money she won against Bobby Riggs has been followed by the creation in 1981 of the Canadian Association for the Advancement of Women in Sport and the British Women's Sport Foundation in 1984. In 1994 the first international conference on Women and Sport was held at Brighton, England, establishing the importance of women supporting women's sport through its Universal Declaration. Although the movement of global sport for women has its roots in patriarchal Western capitalist culture and the middle-class/heterosexual experience of women with European ancestry, it has evolved into a worldwide challenge to male supremacy and sexism. Strong, self-confident women are intent on playing, on winning, on defining their own body image, and on strengthening themselves for themselves. Women's success in sport undercuts heroic myths about women as the weaker sex.

MEN'S RESPONSES TO FEMINISM

Jennifer Hargreaves (1994) reminds us that women struggle, but not uniformly, where "they are manipulated *and* resistant, determined by circumstance *and* active agents in the transformation of culture." Males as well are not their stereotypes. Simplistic history produces images of solid agreement rather than the reality of contradictions and shifting viewpoints. Overall there is ubiquitous male privilege but neither conspiracy nor consensus. Reactions to feminism have produced some male allies in the fight for women's emancipation, even though most men remain conditioned enough by sexism to sustain male supremacy. However, first-, second-, and third-wave feminists of the past century have sharply increased the number of men willing to oppose misogyny and condemn inequality. They would aspire to become humane persons whose love of justice rejects the distortions generated by androcentrism. And many have allied themselves through support of female athletes. Most female champions had male encouragement.

Although mostly male academics and political radicals have declared themselves profeminists, within the context of sport there are many who demand the end of sexism; male athletes, coaches, administrators, media broadcasters, journalists, club managers, physical educators, and therapists are vocal about it. Male PE teachers and coaches are able to challenge gender with innovative practices, providing a more inclusive and rewarding experience for both female and male participation in school PE and sport (Cavar, 2004). Sexism is problematic for all sexes. Men who can identify with compassionate empathy and love of justice show courage and strength, not just the traditional aggression levels and muscle mass in action before male fans.

Christine de Pisan found men in the medieval courts of Europe who supported her writing on warfare, chivalry, and the *debat des femmes*. Castiglione's *The Courtier* insults the warrior-ethos as narrowing of human capacity without either moral value or civil manners. Mary Wollstonecraft found kindred spirits to share her hopes for women, and even Thomas Paine, the American revolutionary, in documents that precede the Declaration of Independence argued that women should be included in nation-building because they have equal right to virtue. Michael Kimmel (1995, 1998) charts support for women's equality in activities of certain American men since Frederick Douglass attended the Seneca Falls Convention and there played a key role in the suffrage debate in 1848. Emerson and Thoreau both supported women's right to vote. The anti-slavery movement compared the power relations of the slavery system to those of men and women within the gender system just as Mary Wollstonecraft compared the fall of the aristocracy in the French Revolution with the eventual demise of a male privileged class in the domestic aristocracy. Male educators and donors rallied around the foundation of women's colleges as well as nineteenth century public schooling for girls. During labour movements and first-wave feminism, supportive men encouraged the resolve of key feminist leaders. "Male suffragettes" at the threshold of the twentieth century stood up to abuse and ridicule shoulder to shoulder with activists in order to bear moral witness to the equal right of females to be independent and in control of their bodies and destinies. In sport there were always individual men who championed the right of females to engage in competitions, marketing, coaching, and providing equipment, opportunities, funding, and encouragement. Wherever women agitated for reforms that would emancipate them, they were sure to find a few men brave enough to support them publicly and more who were sympathetic. Many have seen that emancipation for women means men too would be freed from oppressive roles disregarding their individual well-being and personal growth. Male supremacy, after all, does not fulfill its promises to most men. Men are exploited and subjugated in brutal hierarchies that provide little comfort and few actual rewards except the dubious one of status above women and the privilege of dominating them. Class-bound, racist heterosexism lures boys into reactive masculinity with seductive promises of heroic success, while cutting men off from fulfilling intimate connections with significant others. Neither military duty nor civilian status proves either satisfying or healthy for most men. Thanks to feminism, some can repudiate patriarchy, remembering there is nothing natural about strong boys and weak girls, aggressive manhood and passive womanhood. Without sexism, we discover overlapping capacities beyond the confines of gender, sexual apartheid, and prescribed stereotyped opposite roles.

The men's rights movement predictably reacts to feminist actions; aggrieved males organize around beliefs that men are "subjected to numerous generally unrecognized injustices of a legal, social, and psychological nature" (Clatterbaugh, 1990). Essentialist groups seem intent upon reinforcing men's traditional roles while damning feminism. The mythopoetic men's movement headed by patriarchal figures like Robert Bly and Sam Keen has directed men's attention to recovering the "warrior within" as an imputed blend of Jungian archetypes and fairy tale psychology combined with New Age therapies and First Nations' initiation rituals for males reaching adulthood. Problems for them stem not from patriarchy nor misogyny but from current social conditions "softening" men to the point where they have forgotten their gifts of male bonding, having lost ways of bringing boys properly into manhood. Sweat lodges, drumming, wildman campouts, all-male encounter groups, and ritual induction into holy manhood appeal to men and boys who are anxious in the face of feminist challenges. They are determined to reclaim privileges in previously male-dominant institutions such as the bedroom, churches, politics, the workplace, the military, and sport. Dedicated men's groups coalesce around divorce laws and custody court, such as father's rights advocates in custodial arrangements. They push arguments of "reverse discrimination" concerning legislation about sexual harassment or affirmative action, citing total feminist control of society. Patriarchal religions crusade against slippage in male authority. In Christian circles especially, men proclaim biblical passages regarding marriage practices that re-inscribe males as household heads. The Promisekeepers in the United States aim to resurrect the "rightful" place of men. Basing their campaigns on doctrines of "separate but equal" natures and destinies for men and women, these retro-groups aim to relieve women of the burden of male decision-making they have been forced to accept because men have not performed their "natural" duties. In North America, family-values rhetoric has become code for restoring male familial authority. If men really valued their family, they would ensure that boys learn from girls that no one need become a stereotype.

Girls are free now to disbelieve there are any restrictions on their range of choices; it is time boys learned they too can be free from terrible pressures of our gender regime. Although females attempt to try everything human inspired by feminism, male peers are *not* being mentored to seek true equality. Instead they sense wrongly without pro-feminist mentoring that social justice means their painful de-privileging and humiliation, with young Euro-Canadian males particularly threatened by change. They move from illusion to delusion without escaping from sexism. Sport is a chief retardant, war another.

At the extreme of misogyny, sexists violently reject equality as the Montreal Massacre of 6 December 1989 illustrates. The killer cited feminists in his suicide note as his targets and ordered men out of the classrooms before executing female engineering students and staff. Men saw it as a crazed murderer while women saw it as a lethal man mad at women. In the note he refers to the Olympic Games and war as proof that there are natural differences that superiorize men. Women as engineers are unnatural as would be female athletes outside graceful events or women combat troops. The horror is usually spread out with daily reports of domestic assaults and partner murders. Women *belong* to men and are property, not equals, in this grammar of homicide. When all other serious crimes dropped in frequency after the year 2000, sexual assaults and assaults against women significantly increased. Violent patriarchy uses force to perpetuate itself, pushing those males feeling most threatened by accomplished, strong females. Amid the misogynist numbness of marginal males, revenge scenarios are spawning to hurt women whose success offends them and whose claims to equality are obscene. Sexist internet pornography betrays deeply rooted twinned hatred/fear of liberated women. Male-controlled media extends depersonalization by omitting women from news. Sports broadcasts rarely feature women as heroes with strength enough to challenge men.

When we look at the harassment of females in the military, or male athletes who have committed criminal acts of abuse against females, we see rage about distinctly unhealthy entitlement of caste. From rink-side sexism of minor hockey coaches who encourage boys to prove that they are not "hitting like girls" to the claims of innocence from repeat pro sport spousal abuse offenders, we are reminded that such men are insulated by the reverence they earn from embodying the warrior ideal. War and sport continue to nourish the deepest beliefs of patriarchal thinking, male supremacy, and its privileges. Studying men, masculinities, and sport is a necessary feminist issue and contested terrain to confront essentialism. Sexual apartheid naturalizes stereotyped differences in the gender order. But critical theory dismantles the sexist paradigm, pitting men against women in a "Battle of the Sexes." There is no such thing but rather a constructed system of privilege unable to tolerate equality or accept social justice. Women who defy stereotypes and men who support them refute the patriarchal hierarchy and its requisite violence. Questioning links among men, masculinities, sport, and war reveals essentialism as a sexist trap built in ancient times but destroying lives now as well. War does not protect life, equality does. All are heroes; let us play!

SUGGESTED READINGS

Burstyn, Varda. 1999. *The Rites of Men: Manhood, Politics, and the Culture of Sport*. This is the most comprehensive analysis of the historical role of sport and its function in sustaining the gender order, the warrior-cult, and aggressive masculinity.

Connell, R.W. 1995. *Masculinities*. This critique of sexual politics reveals the complexities in the changes of male identity, while offering fresh and sophisticated views of gender. Connell reviews theories of masculinity and offers portraits of actual men working to change notions of manhood and power dynamics within a feminist framework.

Gilligan, James. 2001. *Preventing Violence*. Presenting violence as a public health problem, Gilligan analyzes social causes of violence, devoting a chapter, in particular, "Violence as Proof of Masculinity."

Goldstein, Joshua S. 2001. *War and Gender*. Testing evidence for possible explanations for exclusion of females from combat and concluding that gender norms shape lives according to the needs of warring societies, Goldstein finds that war does not come naturally to humans.

Kuypers, Joseph A., ed. 1999. *Men and Power*. This collection of essays addresses the ways manhood is constructed to include power at someone else's expense. Ten authors examine the struggle to face this and redefine both.

White, Philip, and **Kevin Young,** eds. 1999. *Sport and Gender in Canada*. These essays demonstrate how sport is experienced differently by males and females yet always dominated by heterosexual males. The range of topics indicates the possible transformation through analysis of gender and its inequities in Canada.

DISCUSSION QUESTIONS

1. Why are the ideals of manhood, heroic models of manliness, and the concepts of virility feminist issues?

2. How does sport perpetuate the ideology of male supremacy as misogyny?

3. What attracts women to enter into sport and with what results?

4. How does sexuality conform to or resist dominant cultural norms in both sport and war?

5. What risks would men willing to oppose male sexism face? What benefits would these pro-feminist males enjoy? Why are younger males reluctant?

BIBLIOGRAPHY

Bach, Michael. "Uncovering the Institutionalized Masculine: Notes for a Sociology of Masculinity." In *Men and Masculinities: A Critical Anthology*, edited by T. Haddad, 37–55. Toronto: Canadian Scholars' Press Inc., 1993.

Bly, Robert, *Iron John: A Book about Men*. Reading, MA: Addison-Wesley, 1990.

Bordo, Susan. "My Father the Feminist." In *Men Doing Feminism*, edited by Tom Digby. New York: Routledge, 1998.

Brod, Harry, and **Kaufman, Michael,** eds. *Theorizing Masculinities*. Thousand Oaks, CA: Sage Publications, 1994.

Brohm, Jean-Marie. *Sport: A Prison of Measured Time*. Trans. Ian Fraser. London: Ink Links, 1978.

Burstyn, Varda. *The Rites of Men: Manhood, Politics, and the Culture of Sport*. Toronto: University of Toronto Press, 1999.

Cavar, T. *Breaking Down Barriers: Male Physical Education Teachers' and Coaches' Role in Female Students' Physical Education and Athletic Programs*. Unpublished master's thesis, Ontario Institute of Studies in Education-University of Toronto, 2004.

Clatterbaugh, Kenneth. *Contemporary Perspectives on Masculinity: Men, Women, and Politics in Modern Society*. San Francisco: Westview Press, 1990.

Cole, Cheryl. "Resisting the Canon: Feminist Cultural Studies, Sport, and Technologies Of the Body." In *Women, Sport, and Culture*, edited by Susan Birrell and Cheryl L. Cole. Champaign, Ill.: Human Kinetics, 1994.

Connell, Robert. *Gender and Power*. Palo Alto, CA: Stanford University Press, 1987.

Connell, R.W. *Masculinities*. Berkeley: University of California Press, 1995.

Davis, James R. *The Sharp End: A Canadian Soldier's Story*. Toronto: McIntyre, 1997.

de Beauvoir, Simone. *The Second Sex*. Trans. and ed. H. M. Parshley. New York: Vintage Books, 1953/1974.

Digby, Tom, ed. *Men Doing Feminism*. New York: Routledge, 1998.

Dyer, Gwynne. *War.* New York: Crown, 1985.

Eby, Cecil D. *The Road to Armageddon: The Martial Spirit in English Popular Literature 1870-1914*. Durham, NC: Duke University Press, 1988.

Foucault, Michel. *The History of Sexuality: Volume I: An Introduction*. Trans. Robert Hurley. New York: Pantheon, 1978.

Gilligan, James. *Preventing Violence*. Volume of the *Prospects for Tomorrow series*, edited by Yorkick Blumenfeld. New York: Thames & Hudson, 2001.

Goldstein, Joshua. *How Gender Shapes the War System and Vice Versa*. Cambridge: Cambridge University Press, 2001.

Gray, Chris Hables. *Postmodern War: The New Politics of Conflict*. New York: The Guildford Press, 1997.

Gray, J. Glenn. *The Warriors: Reflections on Men in Battle*. Lincoln, NA: University of Nebraska Press, 1998.

Grossman, David. *On Killing: The Psychological Cost of Learning to Kill in War and Society*. Boston: Little, Brown, 1996.

Guttmann, Allen. *Women's Sports: A History*. New York: Columbia University Press, 1991.

Hall, M. Ann. *Feminism and Sporting Bodies: Essays on Theory and Practice*. Champaign, Ill.: Human Kinetics, 1996.

Hargreaves, D.J. "Psychological Theories of Sex Role Stereotyping." In *Understanding Masculinities*, edited by M. Mac An Ghaill. Philadelphia: Open University Press, 1996.

Hargreaves. Jennifer. *Sporting Females: Critical Issues in the History and Sociology of Women's Sports*. London: Routledge, 1994.

Harris, Ian M. *Messages Men Hear: Constructing Masculinities*. London: Taylor & Francis, 1995.

Hartsock, Nancy. *Money, Sex, and Power: Toward a Feminist Materialism*. Boston: Northeastern University Press, 1985.

Hearn, Jeff. *Gender of Oppression: Men, Masculinity, and the Critique of Marxism*. Brighton: Wheatsheaf, 1987.

Hearn, J., and **Morgan, D.,** eds. *Men, Masculinities, and Social Theory*. London: Unwin Hyman, 1990.

Hedges, Chris. *War Is a Force that Gives Us Meaning*. New York: Anchor Books, 2003.

Hedges, Chris. *What Every Person Should Know About WAR*. New York: Free Press, 2003.

Heywood, Leslie. *Bodymakers: A Cultural Anatomy of Women's Bodybuilding*. New Brunswick, NJ: Rutgers University Press, 1998.

Homer, *The Iliad*. trans. E. V. Rieu. London: Penguin Books, 1950.

hooks, bell. *Killing Rage: Ending Racism*. New York: H. Holt and Company, 1995.

Ignatieff, Michael. *The Warrior's Honor.* New York: Henry Holt, 1997.

Johnson, Jay. "Hazed and Confused: Hazing Experiences versus Anti-Hazing Policies; A Case Study of Two Southern Ontario Universities." Unpublished thesis. 2000.

Jones, David E. *Women Warriors: A History.* Dulles, VA: Brassey's, 1997.

Katz, Jackson. *Tough Guise: Violence, Media, and the Crisis of Masculinity.* (video) Dir. by Sut Jhally. Media Education Foundation, 1999.

Kaufman, Michael. *Crack In the Armour: Power, Pain, and the Lives of Men.* Toronto: Penguin, 1994.

Kaufman, Michael, ed. *Beyond Patriarchy: Essays by Men on Pleasure, Power, and Change.* Toronto: Oxford University Press, 1987.

Keegan, John, and **Holmes, Richard.** *Soldiers: A History of Men in Battle.* New York: Prospero Books, 1999 [re-issue of 1985 version].

Keen, Sam. *Fire in the Belly: On Being a Man.* New York: Bantam Books, 1991.

Kidd, Bruce. "The Men's Cultural Centre: Sports and the Dynamic of Women's Oppression/Men's Repression." In *Sport, Men, and the Gender Order: Critical Feminist Perspectives*, edited by Michael A. Messner and Donald F. Sabo. Champaign, Ill.: Human Kinetics, 1990.

Kidd, Bruce. *The Struggle for Canadian Sport.* Toronto: University of Toronto Press, 1996.

Kilmartin, Christopher T. *The Masculine Self.* Toronto: Maxwell Macmillan Canada Inc., 1994.

Kimmel, Michael, ed. *Men and Masculinities: A Social, Cultural, and Historical Encyclopedia.* New York: ABC-CLIO, 2003.

Kimmel, Michael. "Masculinity as Homophobia: Fear, Shame and Silence in the Construction of Gender Identity." In *Men and Power*, edited by Joseph A. Kuypers. Halifax: Fernwood Publishing, 1999.

Kimmel, Michael. "From 'Conscience and Common Sense' to 'Feminism for Men': Profeminist Men's Rhetorics of Support for Women's Equality." In *Feminism and Men: Reconstructing Gender Relations*, edited by Steven B. Schacht and Doris W. Ewing. New York: New York University Press, 1998.

Kimmel, Michael. *Manhood in America: A Cultural History.* New York: Free Press, 1995.

Kimmel, Michael, *Changing Men: New Directions in Research on Men and Masculinity.* Thousand Oaks, CA: Sage Publications, 1987.

Kimmel, Michael S., and **Messner, Michael A.** *Men's Lives.* Toronto: Maxwell Macmillan Canada, Inc., 1992.

Kimmel, Michael S., and **Mosmiller, Thomas E.** *Against the Tide: Profeminist Men in the United States, 1776–1990.* Boston: Beacon Press, 1992.

Klein, Uta. "'Our Best Boys': The Gendered Nature of Civil-Military Relations in Israel." *Men and Masculinities*, 2:1 (July 1999) 47–65.

Kuypers, Joseph A. *Man's Will to Hurt: Investigating the Causes, Supports and Varieties of His Violence.* Halifax: Fernwood Publishing, 1992.

Kuypers, Joseph A. *Men and Power.* Halifax: Fernwood Publishing, 1999.

Lenskyj, Helen. *Out of Bounds: Women, Sport, and Sexuality.* Toronto: Women's Press, 1988.

Lenskyj, Helen. *Out on the Field: Gender, Sport, Sexualities.* Toronto: Women's Press, 2003.

Malszecki, Gregory. *"He Shoots! He Scores!": Metaphors of War in Sport and the Political Linguistics of Virility.* Unpublished PhD thesis, Social and Political Thought, York University, 1996.

Messner, Michael A. *Power at Play: Sports and the Problem of Masculinity.* Boston: Beacon Press, 1992.

Messner, Michael A., and **Sabo, Donald F.** *Sport, Men, and the Gender Order: Critical Feminist Perspectives.* Champaign, Ill.: Human Kinetics, 1990.

Millett, Kate. *Sexual Politics.* New York: Avon, 1971.

Moss, Mark. *Manliness and Militarism: Educating Young Boys in Ontario for War.* Don Mills, ON: Oxford University Press, 2001.

Pleck, Joseph. *The Myth of Masculinity.* Cambridge, Mass.: MIT Press, 1981.

Pollack, William. *Real Boys.* New York: Random House, 1998.

Pronger, Brian. "Fear and Trembling: Homophobia in Men's Sports." In *Sports and Gender in Canada*, edited by Philip White and Kevin Young. Toronto: Oxford University Press, 1999.

Robinson, Laura. *Black Tights: Women, Sport and Sexuality.* Toronto: HarperCollins, 2002.

Robinson, Laura. *Crossing the Line: Sexual Assault in Canada's National Sport.* Toronto: McLelland and Stewart, 1998.

Rotundo, Anthony E. *American Manhood: Transformations in Masculinity from the Revolution to the Modern Era.* New York: Basic Books, 1993.

Sabo, Donald F., and **Panepinto, Joe.** "Football Ritual and the Social Production of Masculinity." In *Sport, Men and the Gender Order: Critical Feminist Perspectives*, edited by Michael A. Messner and Donald F. Sabo. Champaign, Ill.: Human Kinetics, 1990.

Sandoz, Joli, and **Winans, Joby,** eds. *Whatever It Takes: Women on Women's Sports.* New York: Farrar, Straus and Giroux, 1999.

Schacht, Steven P., and **Ewing, Doris W.,** eds. *Feminism and Men: Reconstructing Gender Relations.* New York: New York University Press, 1998.

Schwartz, Martin, and **DeKeseredy, Walter.** *Sexual Assault on the College Campus: the Role of Male Peer Support.* Thousand Oaks, CA: Sage Publications, 1997.

Segal, Lynne. *Slow Motion: Changing Masculinities, Changing Men.* London: Virago, 1990.

Seidler, Victor. *Rediscovering Masculinity: Reason, Language, and Sexuality.* New York: Routledge, 1989.

Smith, Michael D. *Violence and Sport.* Toronto: Canadian Scholars' Press Inc., 1988.

Stoltenberg, John. *Refusing to Be a Man.* London: Fontana, 1990.

Stoltenberg, John. *The End of Manhood: A Book for Men of Conscience.* New York: Dutton, 1993.

Thorne, Barrie. *Gender Play: Girls and Boys in School.* New Brunswick, NJ: Rutgers University Press, 1993.

Thornton, Andrew. *Ultimate Masculinities: An Ethnography of Power and Social Difference in Sport.* Unpublished thesis. 1998.

Walmsley, Kevin B. "The Public Importance of Men and the Importance of Public Men: Sport and Masculinities in Nineteenth-Century Canada." In *Sport and Gender in Canada*, edited by Philip White and Kevin Young, 24–39. Toronto: Oxford University Press, 1999.

White, Philip, and **Kevin Young,** eds. *Sport and Gender in Canada.* Toronto: Oxford University Press, 1999.

Whitson, David. "Sport in the Social Construction of Masculinity." In *Sport, Men, and the Gender Order: Critical Feminist Perspectives*, edited by Michael A. Messner and Donald F. Sabo, 19–30. Champaign, Ill.: Human Kinetics, 1990.

Wollstonecraft, Mary. *A Vindication of the Rights of Woman.* ed. Carol F. Poston. 2nd ed. New York: W. W. Norton & Company, 1792/1988.

 WEBLINKS

Men for Change

www.chebucto.ns.ca/CommunitySupport/Men4Change/the_group.htm

Men for Change is a pro-feminist organization dedicated to promoting gender equality and positive masculinity, and ending sexism and violence.

The White Ribbon Campaign

www.whiteribbon.ca

The White Ribbon Campaign was started in 1991 as a response to the Montreal Masscre and is the world's largest effort by men to end men's violence against women through volunteers, events, education, and community-building.

The American Men's Studies Association

members.aol.com/amsapage

The American Men's Studies Association is a not-for-profit professional organization of scholars, therapists, and others interested in the exploration of masculinity in modern society.

The History of the Men's Movement

www.amazoncastle.com/feminism/menhist.htm

Visit this site to read an article by Tom Williamson on the history of the men's movement.

chapter eight

Making Families: Gender, Economics, Sexuality, and Race

Nancy Mandell

INTRODUCTION

Feminists suggest that making families and nurturing intimacy is for many women the central project of their lives. But accomplishing this project places women in a profound dilemma. On the one hand, the love and support women receive in families is powerful and not easily dismissed. On the other hand, nurturing and sustaining family takes tremendous time and effort, sometimes threatening women's equity. Feminists ask why the project of making family compromises women's equality and if it is possible for women to achieve both in other ways.

Feminists have been central to questioning the meaning of family and intimacy in women's lives, noting that family is often conflated with intimacy. Sixty years ago, expectations about marriage were straightforward, desire was channelled, and life projects were clearly circumscribed. Young adults had two tasks: secure a job and find a mate. Both were expected to last a lifetime. Today youth face a wide range of choices in forming families and achieving intimacy. Parenting is not necessarily linked to marriage. Intimacy no longer demands sexual exclusivity. Romance can be experienced many times in a life.[1]

New terms are beginning to crop up to capture this multiplicity: the negotiated family, the alternating family, the same-sex family, the multiple family, and the post-divorce family. All recognize that intimacy and family are now diverse, fluid, and porous arrangements. Although still searching for intimacy, women have more opportunities for achieving personal and emotional connections. But although for some women this search opens up new possibilities, for others it is achieved at great social and economic cost.

Marriage, partnerships, and family are far from dead, but how they fit into the lives of young women is an open question. A full 98 percent of Canadians in legal marriages, and 96 percent in common-law unions feel that a long-term relationship is important for their happiness, and many believe strongly in the institution of the family (Statistics Canada, 2003f). However, for economically insecure women, women with disabilities, immigrants, and racialized women, material challenges make the project of achieving family far more difficult than popular culture suggests. Demands of childcare take precedence over individual needs for emotional gratification and women's lives become completely organized around caring for and protecting their children.

In this chapter, after reviewing briefly some of the contributions feminists have made to theorizing about families and intimacy discourse, I turn to examining contemporary trends indicative of postmodern families. I then focus on groups of women for whom forming families has been a struggle: those with disabilities, poor, racialized, same-sex, and female-headed single-parent families.

FAMILIES OF THE PAST

The Emergence of the Modern Family

About four hundred years ago, the long and mostly European march toward modernity began in the period historians call the Age of Reason or Age of Enlightenment. Industrialization, urbanization, and the emergence of global capitalism ushered in the modern era, transforming the social landscape. Profound economic and social forces altered the living conditions of individuals and opened up possibilities for new ways to earn livings, create families, and craft personal relations. Rather than living on feudal estates, people moved to the cities in search of work in the new industrial factories. Wages were poor, living conditions were bleak, and slums, pollution, and crime grew in cities (Peplar, 2002).

In Canada, intense modernization began in the early nineteenth century and lasted for about 150 years until the early 1980s (Bernard, 1982). In the nineteenth century, the pattern of agricultural and household production was one in which the family functioned as a "mini-manufacturing unit." Work and family lives were intermingled as people produced much of what they consumed. Goods and services were traded directly and people had little need for cash. Workers whose primary occupation was making manufactured goods expected eventually to work for themselves as master craftsmen. Journeymen or apprentices worked in their employers' households learning skills that they could use to set up their own businesses (Coontz, 1992).

The spread of industrialization meant that over time, production moved out of the home and into the factories. Work lives and family lives increasingly became physically separated. Employers moved employees out of their households into central shops—and later factories—where they could be supervised by a boss (a new word in the 1830s) (Coontz, 1992). Most people—women and men—became employees earning wages.

Throughout this transition from subsistence to market or money economies, the daily lives of working-class, immigrant, and visible minority women were sharply different from those of economically secure women. Working-class women coped with lengthy days as subsistence labourers such as domestics, maids, seasonal farm workers, hotel cleaners, and factory workers. The meager earnings of working-class men meant that women found ways to contribute to family incomes through producing household goods, taking in washing, boarders, and home work.

Whether contributing to family incomes, parenting children on their own after husbands deserted or died, or confronting racist encounters in the workplace, most women faced daily struggles to eke out a subsistence living for themselves and their children. Children also participated in the labour force, as their wages were financially essential to household survival. Visible minority women remained a source of readily available, underpaid, exploited labour (Brand, 1999). Being a racial/ethnic woman in the past century meant having extra work both inside and outside the home (Dill, 1988). It also meant that neither visible minority women nor their female children were seen as the "weaker sex," in need of protection from the brutal conditions of manual labour (Brand, 1999).

Whether or not women worked for wages outside the home, the transformation from a co-provider to a wage-earning family structure changed the relationships between gender and work identities. Gender identities and work identities came to define each other. Women became associated with the "private" realm of the home, including domestic labour and child-rearing tasks, while men were associated with the "public" world of wage earning. Men became defined as good or bad providers depending on the size of their paycheque while women were seen as good or bad mothers depending on the way their children turned out.

Domesticity idealized middle-class white women as "angels" in the household. Rising standards of cleanliness, larger homes, sentimentalization of the home as a "haven in a heartless land," new emphasis on childhood, and the mother's role in nurturing children, all served to enlarge middle-class women's reproductive responsibilities at a time when technology had done little to reduce the physical drudgery of housework. Rather than challenging gender norms, middle-class women participated in defining and enlarging domestic discourse.

Poor, immigrant, and working-class women performed the dirty, heavy manual labour of cleaning and caring for middle-class families. A modern pattern was established in which some women left their own families to perform domestic labour in the homes of middle- and upper-class women, freeing them for volunteer work, leisure, and more recently for careers. Today, we continue this trend by importing domestic labourers from Third-World countries.

By 1945, traditional family discourse assumed "normal" families were nuclear with wage-earning fathers and stay-at-home mothers. Even when few families matched this ideal, the ideals themselves were hegemonic. Romance was firmly grafted onto marriage. Popular culture reflected the view that there is a right man or women for every person. A woman's suitable life project became finding and marrying the right individual for a lifetime (Shumway, 2003: 20–21).

The "Good Wife's Guide" is an example of 1950s traditional family discourse. "Working" at a good marriage was thought to be a wife's job:

- Have dinner ready. Most men are hungry when they come home and the prospects of a good meal is part of the warm welcome needed.
- Prepare yourself. Take 15 minutes to rest so you'll be refreshed when he arrives. Touch up your makeup, put a ribbon in your hair and be fresh looking. He has just been with a lot of work-weary people.
- Be happy to see him. Greet him with a warm smile. Show sincerity in your desire to please him.

- Listen to him. Let him talk first—remember, his topics of conversation are more important than yours.
- Don't ask him questions about his actions or question his judgment or integrity. Remember, he is the master of the house and as such will always exercise his will with frankness and truthfulness. You have no right to question him.
- A good wife always knows her place.

(The "Good Wife's Guide," from *Housekeeping Monthly*, 13 May, 1955.)

Traditional family discourse was spread through the concrete practices of local, provincial, and federal governments. Marriage laws, divorce restrictions, child welfare policies, workplace policies, birth control information, housing policies, welfare provisions, employment and pension benefits, and schooling practices were just some of the many official policies that assumed and encouraged a nuclear family.

Second-Wave Feminists Confront the Modern Family

Women's rights movements developed in the nineteenth and twentieth centuries, what we now call the "modern" era. Modernization refers not only to changes in the economic, political, and social structures of society but also to changes in the consciousness of individuals, their values, norms, and ideas (Berger, 2002). Scientific advances in biology, geography, and physics emphasized empirical knowledge, objectivity, and rationality over tradition. With the spread of reason came new ideas about the relationship of the individual to the social order, altering public opinion about who should and could participate in modern social life. Previously held beliefs about feudal and church authority, the divine right of kings and aristocrats to rule, and the lack of political participation by the masses were replaced by modernist notions of individual enfranchisement, equality, and rationality. Principles of individual liberty, freedom of choice, and equality of opportunity were seen as basic rights that ought to be extended to all citizens (Elliot and Mandell, 2001: 25).

Liberation movements, especially those led by liberal feminists, focused on extending to women those rights and privileges held by men, including the right to own property, have custody of children, gain a divorce, control their own money, obtain a university education, and vote. Women were second-class citizens in public and subservient in the home. Liberal feminists thought that equalizing woman's economic, social, political, and cultural status would automatically result in equalizing their status with men in intimate, private relationships.

Socialist feminism also emerged during the tumultuous period of industrialization. Marxist feminists thought the origin of women's subordination lay in their material or financial dependence on men. Economic status shapes people's social, political, and cultural relations. Marxists and socialists argued that economic production in pre-industrial Europe was integrated into the household with men, women, and children working in tandem. Industrial capitalism, with its corresponding system of ownership and progressive division of labour, served to undermine this balance.

Males moved out of the household and into the public as wage labourers while women, especially married women, were confined to wageless domestic work and made increasingly subservient to men (Berger, 2002: 37–40). For women, financial dependence upon men resulted in their social and political dependence as well. According to socialists, until women earned wages comparable to men and were able to satisfy their material needs for food, clothing, and shelter, they would remain domestic servants of men, subordinate to male needs and desires.

Socialist feminists (Luxton and Corman, 2001; Vosko, 2000) expanded definitions of labour to include activities not previously recognized as work, including unpaid work in the household and social reproduction. Referring to the array of activities and relationships involved in maintaining people both on a daily basis and intergenerationally, social reproduction includes such activities as purchasing household goods, preparing meals, washing and repairing clothing, maintaining furnishings and appliances, socializing children, providing emotional support for adults, maintaining community and kin ties.

The argument advanced by socialist feminists that social and reproductive labour ought to be considered work is an argument now taken for granted by Canadian policy makers and measured by the Canadian census. This extremely important argument revealed that domestic labour is work disproportionately performed by women, invisible, unpaid, and unrecognized since it lies hidden in the household. Domestic labour props up the industrial economy and directly benefits men and children who are freed up to concentrate their efforts in paid employment. Moreover, gender divisions in the home interact with and reinforce the gender divisions found in paid work.

Antiracist feminists of the second wave, especially those using materialist analyses, demonstrated that race is integral to the structuring of labour markets. Occupational segregation by gender combines with race to create a dual labour market. As antiracist feminists tell us, racial ethnic women are disproportionately employed as service workers in institutional settings to carry out lower-level "public" reproductive jobs while cleaner, white-collar supervisory or lower, professional positions are filled by white women. The less desirable or more onerous jobs have devolved on visible minority women, "freeing" white women for higher level pursuits (Glenn, 1999).

White women and men gain material and ideological advantages from the racial division of paid and unpaid labour. Throughout the twentieth century, racial ethnic women were employed as servants in white households. Visible minority women were seen as being particularly suited for service. In the past fifty years, the substantial growth of the service sector has meant that many services, such as food preparation, home health care, sewing of clothes, and personal services are now purchased. Lower-level service jobs are among the fastest growing sectors of the economy. Women, and especially visible minority women, disproportionately fill these jobs as nurses' aides in hospitals, kitchen workers in restaurants and cafeterias, maids in hotels, cleaners in office buildings, and food processors in fast-food outlets. In contrast, white women are disproportionately employed as supervisors, professionals, and administrative staff. Just as domestic work is hidden, most commodified service work takes place out of sight, at night, behind institutional walls.

Radical feminists agreed with many of the structural arguments put forth by liberal and socialist feminists. Modernity destroyed the conventional nuclear family anchored in kinship, community, and religion and turned marriage into a primarily financial arrangement in which women traded reproductive and domestic services for financial security (Berger, 2002: 33). Love and sexuality became commodities traded in the market. Men were free to dominate and exploit those who depended on them. But while socialist feminists thought male power and economic advantage derived from their superior location within capitalist economies, radical feminists thought male superiority also came from the social system they called patriarchy.

Defined as a sexual system of power in which the male possesses superior power and economic privilege, patriarchy is viewed as an autonomous force through which men dominate and control women's behaviour and sexuality. The "patriarchal family" mirrors and reproduces patriarchal relations in the wider society. The family represents a site, a description, and an explanation for the conventional nuclear-family household in which women play a subordinate and servicing role to men. The economic and cultural superiority of men carries over into intimate relationships in which male needs, desires, expectations, and demands come to dominate marital life. "His" experience of marriage is profoundly different from "hers" (Bernard, 1982). The only way to correct this imbalance lies in dismantling old structures and creating new, separate spheres of intimacy between equals.

Second-wave feminists—liberal, socialist, radical, and antiracist—launched a stinging critique of family discourse and practice. Study after study showed that patriarchal families deny women personal and material opportunities for independence; women's financial dependence on male wages makes them vulnerable to physical, sexual, and emotional abuse; domestic ideals make women responsible for family caregiving, child rearing, kin keeping, and domestic labour; and women are held responsible for "successful" family life and asked to bear responsibility for family disappointments. Antiracist feminists were particularly successful in revealing how white women are more able to meet hegemonic standards of womanhood by denying opportunities to poor and marginalized women. Staggering under what felt like constant attacks from a wide variety of women, the Canadian media declared that feminists were out to destroy the family.

Third-Wave Feminists Confront Postmodern Families

Sometime during the 1990s, feminist writing about families stagnated, just as traditional families began to disappear. Some critics questioned the economic determinism of socialist feminism, noting that the movement of women into wage labour had not brought about equality. Other critics questioned radical feminist assumptions that there is a unique and special female nature found in every culture and in every society. Still others questioned the predominately white, middle-class bias of second-wave writing, noting that women differ enormously from one another in terms of income, education, race, age, dis/ability, and so on. How is it possible to talk about universal sisterhood when so many differences exist (Brand, 1999; Das Gupta, 2000)?

Postcolonialists expanded the antiracist feminist argument (see Chapter 4, this volume). Antiracist feminists accused early feminists of "colonizing" the study of family by ignoring how First Nations, poor, immigrant, and working-class families struggled to earn a living wage and keep family units together. Antiracist feminists reveal the racism inherent in immigration policies, labour force trends, and assessments of scholastic achievement? (Brand, 1999; Carty, 1999). They showed how the policies, assessments, and procedures of governments, schools, workplaces, courts, and social welfare agencies assume a white, middle-class family norm that automatically positions any other type of family activity or configuration as deviant. Furthermore, antiracist feminists acknowledge women's subordination in traditional family structures but also recognize that family has been a haven from racist society, a source of nurturance and protection (Dua, 1999a, 1999b). Feminists did not know how to talk about the family as a site of both oppression and opportunity. It is only recently that antiracist feminists have felt ready to reveal stories of sexist mistreatment within their families while also emphasizing families as sources of strength (Collins, 2000: 88).

Queer theory animated feminist debates. In his introduction to *Fear of a Queer Planet: Queer Politics and Social Theory*, Michael Warner (1994) coined the term heteronormativity to refer to the practice of organizing patterns of thought, basic awareness, and raw beliefs around the presumption of universal heterosexual desire, behaviour, and identity. Queer theorists led the way in postmodern rethinking of family. They began by detaching marriage from family and challenging traditional ways of thinking about family. Traditional nuclear families with their rigid gender role prescriptions seemed thoroughly heterosexist and out of step with the ways many young people create family. New lifestyles and family forms open up new possibilities for creating intimate relations.

Today we are experiencing a social and economic transformation every bit as wrenching and far-reaching as that of the early nineteenth century—a total rearrangement of the links between families and the wider economy, along with a reorganization of work, gender roles, race relations, family structures, intergenerational expectations, and personal rights. Contemporary trends in family reflect not only changing material conditions but also shifting ideas about what constitutes intimacy and how best to achieve it.

Marriage, Intimacy, and Romance: Are They Related?

In Canada, marriage remains popular. Around 84 percent of women aged 20 to 29 surveyed in 2001 will marry at least once in their lives, and 94 percent of women between the ages of 30 and 69 will live as part of a couple. With the legalization of same-sex marriage, the percentage will climb even higher.

The pull of marriage remains powerful. Even if women decide to go it alone, as increasing numbers do, all women devote time to sorting out their feelings about marriage. Intimate relations have fewer fixed forms, more choices, more beginnings, and more farewells (Beck-Gernsheim, 2002: 41). Youth anticipate disruption and fluidity to characterize their intimate lives. The relationship principle of "until the next best thing" prevails meaning that stable periods in relationships alternate with others, before, alongside, or after marriage or cohabitation (Beck-Gernsheim, 2002: 40).

But although patterns of forming relations are changing, powerful discourses[2] of romance and intimacy remain. These discourses contour women's life choices as women continue to structure their hopes, desires, and lives around notions of romance and intimacy, which in turn work to prop up marriage. Romance, separate from, and often a prelude to, intimacy, offers adventure, intense emotion, and the possibility of finding the perfect mate. Intimacy promises "deep communication, friendship, and sharing that will last beyond the passion of new love" (Shumway, 2003: 17). Intimacy promises lifetime love and psychological transcendence will be achieved by obtaining a degree of personal closeness, autonomy, and comfort offered when one finds and lives, not with one's companion, but with one's "soul mate" (Shumway, 2003: 156). Both point toward marriage.

These two discourses, romance and intimacy, are told over and over again in our society (Giddens, 1992; Beck and Beck-Gernsheim, 1995). Television, self-help books, magazine articles, talk shows, and movies tell young women the same marriage story: It's okay to dream about finding the right mate and living with her/him for your whole life because it is through romance that one finds happiness and self-fulfillment. Most young women assume they will realize their dream.

In early modern times, the nuclear family was thought to be the form in which both romance and intimacy could be obtained. Romantic love led to a companionate marriage based on gender inequality and mutual dependence through clearly defined gender-segregated roles. Monogamous and usually heterosexual relationships were seen as the only forms in which intimacy could be achieved. Today, contemporary discourses have enlarged to include same-sex relationships, but for both heterosexual and same-sex couples, happy marriage remains the goal. Neither type of relationship endorses rampant individualism but rather insists that relations of responsibility, duty, and obligation be fulfilled within contractual arrangements. These contracts may be short-lived and embrace a wide range of alternatives,[3] but they nonetheless remain institutional, exerting numerous duties, obligations, and responsibilities upon members. Romance and discourse, in other words, continue to assume marriage as a paradigm.

Is Heterosexual Marriage Unequal?

Heterosexual marriage and cohabitation offer women and men different experiences (Luxton and Corman, 2001). Marriage offers more rewards to men than to women, especially among whites (Berk, 1985). Men like to be married because they benefit a great deal in terms of quality of life, mental health, and professional opportunities (Simpson, 1998). Women report lower levels of marital satisfaction than men and experience higher rates of mental illness than single women or married men (Steil, 1997).

Even though a heterosexual married or cohabiting couple may begin as equal partners, the work of marriage sets in motion a wife's duties to household and children and a husband's duties to earning money for the family (Schwartz and Rutter, 1998). Most men earn more than women do, and this financial difference is often assumed to be what tilts the division of responsibility. The norm of the man being the provider is so strong that, even if the woman has money from her family or earns more money than her husband,[4] the man will still be granted the perks of the provider status (Beaujot, 2000; Mandell, 2001).

Is Same-Sex Marriage Equal?

Same-sex marriages and cohabitations seem to be more equal. Lesbian relationships are described as more companion-oriented, more flexible in social roles, less bound by traditional gender divisions of labour, and more egalitarian. Lesbian couples value intimate relationships that are equal, emotionally close, supportive, and sustaining. As Dunne (1999: 79) reports, a lesbian's partner is usually her best friend, or at least one of them, and the operation of power is more likely to elaborate upon the rules of friendship (equality, support, balancing the differences, reciprocity) than the rules of heterosexual romance (the eroticization of difference, "intimate strangers" possessing different emotional vocabularies, institutional and sexual power imbalance). Lesbian couples report intense bonding and discovery of mutuality of sexual passion and emotional connectedness in their partnerships (Pearlman, 1989). Many describe this bonding, interdependence, and intensity as unlike any other relationship they have encountered (Baber and Allen, 1992: 46).

Domestic Labour in Same-Sex Partnerships: Movement toward Equality

Participation in finances and household decision-making are two areas in which married and cohabiting lesbians share more often equal relations. In turn, literature reports that lesbians in partnerships exhibit high levels of self-esteem, an intangible that equality confers (Dunne, 1999; Patterson, 2000). In virtually all gay and lesbian relationships, both partners are wage-earners. Many lesbian partnerships enjoy a high level of "material self-sufficiency" (Weston, 1991: 148; O'Brien and Goldberg, 2000). Domestic labour tasks are negotiated according to skill, preference, and energy (O'Brien and Goldberg, 2000: 128).

Domestic Labour: Inequality Continues for Heterosexual Couples

Do heterosexual women's gains in the labour market translate into improvements in redistributing domestic labour? Apparently not! Canadian time-use surveys show that women and men spend about equal amounts of time on paid and unpaid work.[5] Men spend more time on wage earning while women are more likely to take responsibility for domestic tasks. However, if we only examine domestic work, then we see that women perform about two-thirds of the domestic work in households (Duxbury et al., 2003; Beaujot, 2000: 183).

The 2001 census was the second to include questions on unpaid work[6] asking people how much time they spent in the week prior to the census providing care or assistance to seniors, doing unpaid housework or home maintenance, and taking care of children without pay (Statistics Canada, 2003c: 17). Women still do most of the unpaid work: about 21 percent of women devoted more than 30 hours in a week compared with 8 percent of men; 16 percent of women devoted 30 hours or more on childcare compared with 7 percent of men; about 20 percent of women, compared with 15 percent of men, reported taking care of a senior generally for fewer than 10 hours a week (Statistic Canada, 2003c: 17).

The more education and the more income women secure, the more likely they are to share domestic labour with family (Marshall, 1993). Wives who work part-time,[7] have shift jobs, or are self-employed do more domestic labour. Some of these women seek out these employment strategies as ways to manage their domestic responsibilities (Beaujot, 2000; Frederick, 1995; Statistics Canada, 2003c). The most equal relationships were found among those over age 65 and among young partners with no children.

Women do most of the physical maintenance of the household and childcare, work that is non-discretionary and needs to be done frequently. Husbands may help, but their family work is less likely to be part of their daily routine than it is for women and often it can be delayed (Marshall, 1993; Porter and Kauppi, 1996). Women do most of the interaction work of building and maintaining communication in heterosexual relationships, and women are responsible for the "stroking function" (Bernard, 1982). Women "make family" in the sense of being responsible for coordinating schedules and activities and managing a long list of family-related responsibilities. Women keep social calendars for their children and partners; plan graduations, weddings, anniversary parties; care for aging relatives; and generally do the social, emotional, and physical work associated with maintaining family (Duxbury et al., 2003; Goldscheider and Waite 1991: 9).

Even when they do not intend to, husbands and wives fall into gendered patterns of domestic, economic, and emotional labour. Everyday interactions reinforce gendered roles of women and men, reminding us that Mom should remain the primary parent with caretaking her main preoccupation. Fathers report being ignored at parent-teacher interviews. Doctors consult with mothers while sports coaches seem to prefer to confer with fathers on their sons' performance.

Women carry a greater burden of domestic labour than men do, even when they are working full-time and even when they are earning more than their partners (Steil, 1997). Obviously the pressures for single parents and for women of low incomes are even more enormous. Women, especially those who are divorced, single parents, and young, report high rates of dissatisfaction with the domestic distribution of labour (Spain and Bianchi, 1996: 171).

Why don't young men do more domestic labour? What little data we have suggest that some young men have difficulty adjusting to changing gender and family expectations, many of which conflict with the model of hegemonic masculinity reflected in the media and in society (Lees, 1999: 74). However, this model is proving to be increasingly dysfunctional and inefficient in helping partners figure out how to manage the load of paid work, domestic work, and childcare (Dubeau, 2002).

Starved for Time

Women with children are starved for time (Clark, 2002; Sauve, 2002). Fifteen percent of households headed by lesbians have children. Three percent of households headed by gay males have children. In total, about 63 percent of Canadian families (lone parent, married, and cohabiting) have children (Statistics Canada, 2003c). In her in-depth study of executives and factory workers in an American company, American sociologist Arlie Hochschild (1997) describes not two, but three shifts that working mothers experience. As the first shift (at the workplace) takes more time, the second shift (at home) becomes more hurried and rationalized. The longer the workday at the office or plant, the more we feel pressed at home to hurry, to delegate, to delay, to forgo, to segment, to hyper-organize the precious remains of family time. Both the time deficit and what seem like solutions to it (hurrying, segmenting, organizing) force parents to engage in a third shift—noticing, understanding, and coping with the emotional consequences of the compressed second shift.

Children, for example, respond to the new cult of efficiency in their own ways as they act out their feelings about the sheer scarcity of family time. Fathers, or the second mother in same-sex units, "handle" children who throw tantrums when play dates keep getting put off. Mothers buy children toys every time they travel on business. Part of modern parenthood for same- and opposite-sex partnerships now includes coping with children's resistance to the tight-fitting schedules required when home becomes work and work becomes home. What happens to mothers parenting children alone with no outside supports and no "extra" money to purchase help? When one adds the stresses of daily encounters with disability, racism, and sexism, the pressures seem overwhelming.

Women who parent in either same- or opposite-sex relationships respond in a variety of ways to evade the time bind (England, 1996; Sauve, 2002; Silver, 2000). Some try to redefine their roles by becoming "supermoms." Economically secure women purchase domestic services or cut down on the number of hours they work for pay. Others may choose to marry men who plan to share work at home. Still others, following marriage, try to change their partner's behaviour by forcing greater involvement in domestic work and some cope by trying not to impose change on their husbands thereby avoiding conflict altogether (Mandell, 1989). Still others call upon grandparents to help (Milan and Hamm, 2003; Rosenthal and Gladstone, 2000).

For those with no partners, family, or kin to call on, the lack of additional money and community resources makes it extremely difficult to find ways out of the time bind. Many resort to emotional asceticism as a common personal strategy, meaning parents downsize their emotional needs. If we don't see a need, how can we imagine we need time to meet it? Women develop ideas that minimize how much care a child, a partner, or they themselves "really need." They make do with less time, less attention, less fun, less relaxation, less understanding, and less support at home than they once imagined possible. No one expects that women will win the time lottery. Still, parents dream about evenings or weekends fishing, camping, sailing, or hiking with children or partners. They fantasize about a time-rich future, in which they are able fully to meet the needs of loved ones (Hochschild, 1997).

The growing "time industry" tempts women to buy themselves out of the time bind by purchasing goods and services such as summer camps, retirement homes, fast foods, cleaners, day-care centres, domestic help, and so on. For those women who can afford to buy services, domestic help is often the first purchase. Each year about 75 000 women leave South and South East Asia to work as domestic servants, nurses, and service industry workers in Australia, Canada, the USA, and Western Europe (Seager, 2003: 72). The "maid trade" is a distinct form of labour migration from poorer to richer countries. In 2002, up to 1.5 million women were working outside their own countries as foreign maids (Seager, 2003: 72).

Most women cannot afford these services, especially those who parent alone or are low income. With the generally low wages most women earn and with state policies still pathologizing single parents and refusing to provide any help with childcare, Canadian women face enormous stresses with few realistic avenues for help.

Delaying Commitments/Delaying Children

Is it any wonder that Canadian families are shrinking?[8] Young women feel caught in a basic dilemma. Child? Job? Or both? As Beck-Gernsheim (2002: 73) point out, while many desire children, if they act on this wish, they need to reckon with considerable costs for their own lives in terms of limited job opportunities, excessive daily workloads, reduced leisure, financial insecurity in old age, and a risk of poverty in the event of divorce. Broadening employment opportunities for women has simply doubled their workload while not substantially altering the parenting or domestic labour practices of men. Few men take parental leave. Few men share childcare tasks equally with women. The work of raising children is still mainly the work of women, especially mothers and, increasingly, grandmothers. As Beck-Gernsheim (2002: 73) tells us, for most women these choices do not seem to offer either freedom or equality. What had once appeared a matter of course—the combination of children with other goals in life, especially a job—now seems fragile and open to doubt.

The vast majority of young Canadians report that they intend to have at least one child. In 2001, only 7 percent of Canadians, aged 20–34, indicated that they did not intend to have children (Stobert and Kemeny, 2003: 7). Women carefully plan when to have children (Beck-Gernsheim, 2002: 62). Many delay marriage and parenthood until well into their 30s. And some delay indefinitely. Cognizant of the stress that lies ahead, "responsible" parenthood becomes measured by a number of factors from relationship stability through income and housing to the time in a working life chosen to have a child.

Are Relationships Happy?

The gradual extension of the life span means that a marriage today has the potential to last three times longer than a marriage a few centuries ago. That statistic ought to give young adults pause! As the population ages, there are more marriages reaching 40 years. But what is the quality of these partnerships?

Valerie Oppenheimer (1988) suggests we are experiencing a polarization between increasing numbers of very high quality, long-lasting marriages and increasing numbers of low-quality, short-lived, "starter" marriages. Those in the low-quality relationships do not want to be trapped for life while those in the high-quality ones seemed to have moved away from the traditional model of the past (Alford-Cooper, 1998). Little is known about the vast array of marriages in the middle, those of medium duration and medium quality. Nor do we know how children interpret these relationships, even though most children, 79 percent, live with both biological parents (4 percent live with one biological parent and a step-parent,[9] 16 percent live with a lone parent, and 1 percent live with adoptive parents and foster parents).

Gay couples report greater relationship satisfaction and more intimacy, autonomy, and equality than married couples as well as higher levels of problem solving (Ambert, 2003: 5). Lesbian couples with children report being happier with their relationship than those without children (Koepke et al., 1992; Ambert, 2003). Kurdek (2001) compared gay, lesbian, and heterosexual couples in terms of conflict concerning power, social issues, personal flaws, distrust, intimacy, and personal distance. The rate of violence in same-sex relationships is thought to approximate that found in heterosexual ones, between 12 percent and 33 percent depending on the sample and measures (Straus and Gelles, 1990; Ambert, 2003; Statistics Canada, 2003e: 20). Intimacy and power were most frequently mentioned sources of conflict by all couples, which makes feminists wonder about the role of gender-based explanations for relationship happiness. Lesbian women report more frequent use of constructive conflict resolution styles and report a greater effort to resolve conflict (Ambert, 2003; Kurdek, 2001).

Partnerships are no longer expected to last until "death do us part." Canadians understand why divorce[10] occurs, and almost all think that no woman should tolerate an abusive or disrespectful partner. More than one-third think that constant arguments about money or an unsatisfactory sex life are grounds for divorce. Less than one-fifth think that conflict over raising children, sharing household tasks, or disagreements over fertility issues justify leaving a marriage. Less than 50 percent would stay in an unhappy relationship because of the children (Ambert, 2002; Frederick and Hamel, 1998). Yet, the search for happiness continues to drive the serial monogamous pattern in which many Canadians engage. Even though remarriages are even more tenuous propositions than first marriages, women continue to seek intimacy through marriage, remarriage,[11] and/or cohabitation.

STRUGGLING TO BUILD FAMILIES: SEXUALITY, DISABILITY, RACE, AND ECONOMICS

Canadians spend a lot of their lives trying to establish intimacy through families. But what happens to those for whom building families is denied? Around the globe, what Porteous and Smith (2001) call "domicide," the global destruction of home, is taking place. There are many contemporary and historical Canadian narratives of groups denied opportunities to live with their lovers, assemble households and parent their own children.

SAME-SEX FAMILIES

The early years of 2000 have been exciting. After years of concerted effort, provincial and federal legislation has been introduced that extends to same-sex couples the same rights and responsibilities as heterosexual partnerships. This confirms what sociologists have long said: in every civil marriage, there are really three partners: two willing spouses and an approving state. Since 2003, when Ontario and British Columbia legalized same-sex marriages, Toronto and border towns such as Windsor have experienced a flood of weddings of Canadians and non-Canadians whose marriages may not be recognized in their own provinces or countries but who nonetheless want to be married.[12]

At the time of writing this chapter, the Supreme Court of Canada is considering whether or not the traditional definition of marriage as the union of a man and a woman[13] violates the Charter of Rights and Freedoms, as indeed lower courts have ruled. The applicants in the court challenge cite three reasons why gay and lesbian couples want to marry. First, some gay and lesbian couples want to have full and equal recognition of their relationship as is extended to other couples. Marriage is a ceremony in which the couple formally announces to their families, friends, and the state their commitment to each other and their intention to make the relationship last. Second, married couples are recognized immediately upon registering their marriage and become eligible for benefits and subject to federal law, while common-law couples must wait one year to qualify. Gay and lesbian couples do not want to wait a year. Third, access to marriage provides their families and children with full protection of the law. Without it, their children may be stigmatized (Department of Justice, 2002: 5).

In July 2003, Jen Woodill and Alex Vamos, graduates of York University's Graduate Women's Studies Masters' program, were among one of the first same-sex couples in Ontario to marry. Commenting on what marriage means to her, Jen states:

> Marriage signifies a great deal—two people coming together, loving each other and making a commitment to one another to build a life together through all the trials and tribulations, to raise a family together, to make a contribution to society together. Gay and lesbian couples have been making this kind of commitment for a long time—building family, sharing love, building community, but this commitment has not been recognized by society as anything positive. Extending marriage to include gay and lesbian couples is SO essential in recognizing the contribution that gay couples make to building family and community in Canada, and it is SO essential in defusing homophobia and normalizing gay and lesbian relationships. Calling this by another name is at least recognizing the relationship which is much better than the past silence, but to use a different name only serves to say to the Canadian public that gay and lesbian relationships are different from heterosexual relationships, and are not good enough to be called marriage. (Woodill, 2004)

Canadians support gay and lesbian marriage. A 2002 Environics poll conducted for the Centre for Research and Information on Canada found that that 53 percent of respondents were in favour of gay and lesbian couples marrying; 40 percent were opposed (Department of Justice, 2002: 6).

Within the lesbian community, disagreement exists over marriage. Some reject legal marriage, seeing the institution as symbolic of patriarchy, while others insist that marriage within one's belief or religious traditions validates the sanctity of the lesbian union (Conway-Turner and Cherrin, 1998: 53). Some hold neither position but feel that, until same-sax marriages are legal, lesbian rights remain unfulfilled. A study published by Janet Lever (1994, 1995) in the American national gay and lesbian magazine *The Advocate* indicates that 92 percent of homosexual men and women favour being in a couple. Lever found that almost 75 percent of the lesbians and 85 percent of the gay men surveyed would legally marry if allowed to do so, and some have even put the right to marry at the top of their political action and advocacy agenda (Schwartz and Rutter, 1998). As Jen Woodill says,

There is a reason why people are so up in arms about this whole marriage thing—and that is because society sees marriage as special and beautiful and a cornerstone of society. I just got married to Alex, my partner, and it was special, it was beautiful, and we got married because we believe that in our life together, our love (and our love is so huge) will continue to grow and this love will be the centre of our building family, building community, and giving to the world. I am married, and I cannot or will not use any other word to describe it. This is the most profound relationship that I have been in over my 28 years of life, and my time with Alex fills me with wonder, with love, with absolute joy. I feel that I am closer to God, closer to the spiritual essence of life, when we are together. I call this marriage, and there is no other word to use. (Woodill, 2004)

As the battle over same-sex marriage reveals, current marriage laws institutionalize heterosexual marriage and privilege this form of sexual preference as the only socially and legally valid foundation for family life. Lesbians may escape the constraints of patriarchal marriage but they are also denied its privileges[14] (Jackson, 1997).

The 2001 census estimates there are 34 200 same-sex couples in Canada, of which at least 3000 are raising children (Ambert, 2003; Statistics Canada, 2002a). Early works on lesbian mothers attempted both to fill the information gap and to demonstrate how ordinary and how similar lesbian mothers are to heterosexual mothers in comparable social and economic circumstances. Literature shows few differences between children raised by lesbian mothers and children raised by heterosexual mothers. What minor differences there are stem largely from the homophobia children experience in society, which has the effect of making them more tolerant, empathetic, and contented (Ambert, 2003). This information was used to challenge custody decisions that positioned lesbian mothers as abnormal and as unfit mothers not only because they lived with another woman but also because they constituted father-absent households (Lewin, 1993: 4–6; Weston, 1991). If lesbian mothers lose custody of their children, their partners have no legally sanctioned relationship to a child they have helped raise unless they have been formally appointed as legal guardian by the court or by the mother.

The growing literature on lesbian partnerships and mothering makes visible relationships, families, friends, leisure activities, and lives previously hidden (Arnup, 2005, 1995; Tobin and Anonymous, 1996). Emerging studies deconstruct the relation between gender and sexuality as well as broaden the concept of family to include ones we create as substitutes for families into which we are born. Lesbians raising children often create support networks comprising both gay and non-gay adults including relatives, friends, and former partners, who provide social and emotional support (Ambert, 2003; Oswald, 2002). Often gays and lesbians opt out of blood families and into families they choose (Ali, 1996; Arnup, 2004; Dunne, 1999; Nelson, 1996; Oerton, 1997; Oswald, 2002; Seyda and Herrera, 1998).

Same-sex relations have revealed heteronormative discourses underlying traditional constructions of family. As Cheshire Calhoun (1997: 133) states,

Lesbians are uniquely positioned to violate conventional gender expectations that they, as women, would be dependent on men in their personal relations, would fulfill the maternal imperative, would service a husband and children, and would accept confinement to the private sphere of domesticity.

POOR FAMILIES

Many Canadian families struggle their entire lives to maintain a roof over their heads, to put food on the table and to purchase clothes and basic necessities for their children. In

2000, the median income of Canada's 8 million or so families was $55 016 (Statistics Canada, 2003d: 7). Just over one million families (1 050 000) were below Statistics Canada's 2000 low-income cutoffs based on before-tax income. Nearly 18 percent or 1 245 700 children were living in low income in 2000. Half of these children live in what we call "working poor"[15] families, nuclear families with two parents.

Most families need more than one source of income in order to survive. In 2000, 76 percent of families with children under 18 consisted of dual earners (Statistic Canada, 2003d: 14). The number of two-parent families below the poverty line would increase by 78 percent if only one person earned an income. Two-earner families are working longer hours just to maintain a family living standard that could have been provided by one earner in the 1950s and 1960s.

Family incomes have been falling in Canada since 1989, while high taxes and high unemployment have continued to erode family incomes. Real wages (the amount a worker can actually buy with a paycheque) have been declining since 1973. What a worker has left in her or his pocket from her or his hourly wage, after taking out income taxes and adjusting for inflation, has fallen by nearly 1 percent each year since the early 1970s. Many families search for third incomes by having their children work part-time or by having husbands or wives moonlight, with one or both taking on a second job.

In 2000, almost 231 000 children with at least one immigrant parent who arrived in Canada during the 1990s were living in low income. Despite the fact that immigrants of the 1990s were more educated, they have had more difficulty matching the earnings of their Canadian-born counterparts than did immigrants of the 1970s and 1980s (Statistic Canada, 2003d: 11).

Young families are particularly hard-hit by economic decline. They cannot afford family life so "economic adolescence," the period when young adults are working full-time but not earning enough to support a family or be fully self-sufficient has lengthened (Lochhead, 1998). Americans estimate that a young man under 25 years of age working full-time in 1994 earned 31 percent less per week than his counterpart in 1973.

Lone-parent families are now a mainstream family type (Rowlingson and McKay, 2002: 3). Single-parent families have increased at four times the rate of husband-wife families over the past decade. According to the 2001 census, there are about 1.3 million lone-parent families in Canada, of which 1 065 365 are headed by women and 245 825 are headed by men. Each of these lone-parent families has an average of 1.5 children at home (Statistics Canada, 2002b).

For the majority of female-headed lone-parent families, money is a nagging problem. Without access to male wages, most female-headed lone parents are poor. Based on their before-tax income, 46 percent of lone-parent families with children were in the low-income category in 2000. This figure is very significant, as it is four times higher than the rate of 11 percent observed among two-parent families with children. In 2000, the median income of lone-parent families was around $26 008. Four percent of all children lived in lone-parent families in 2000 in which the single parent had no earnings (Statistic Canada, 2003d).

Duncan and Edwards (1999) identify four overlapping discourses around lone motherhood: lone parents as a social threat; lone parents as a social problem; lone parents as escaping patriarchy; and lone parents as a reflection of lifestyle change. The social threat discourse sees lone parents as women who have been encouraged by feminism to live alone and burden the state; as women who choose to have children to get welfare; as women who don't want to work; as women who are promiscuous; as women who produce delinquent boys and girls owing to a lack of a father; and as women who wreck society.

The social problem perspective sees lone parents as victims in need of help; as economically and socially disadvantaged; as wanting to but being unable to work because of poverty and childcare costs; as producing delinquent boys and promiscuous girls owing to the lack of a father.

The discourse of lone parents as escaping from patriarchy sees lone mothers as innovators who are escaping male control and enjoying financial and emotional advantages over women trapped by marriage.

The discourse of lone parents reflecting a lifestyle change sees this family type as a rational choice made by people who advocate their rights to divorce, have decent wages and exercise their rights to equal and independent decision-making around family forms (Rowlingson and McKay, 2002: 58–59). Clearly, discourses influence perceptions of lone parents and state policies that are enacted.

All families have to absorb economic shocks: increased social inequality, unemployment, recession and restructuring, increased welfare dependency, decreased state assistance, and declining family incomes. For poor, young, and female-headed lone-parent families, these shocks hit particularly hard. Families resist by engaging in creative income-generating strategies to accommodate changing market demands.

Women often bear the brunt of "managing" poverty. As providers for and caretakers of their families, it is often women's labour and their personal austerity that typically compensate for diminished resources of the family or household (Seager, 2003: 86). Globally, women are the "shock absorbers" of economic crises. When governments cut back on social and health services to cope with their debt burden, poor households, of which women-headed households are a disproportionate share, bear the brunt of these cuts (Seager, 2003: 88).

According to the *World Atlas on Women* (Seager, 2003), the majority of the world's population is poor. As the majority of the world's poor, women tend to be among the poorest of the poor. Women's poverty results from their status as women. Gender ideologies still encourage women to focus their energies on marriage and motherhood even while they hold down jobs. They must wrap the demands of wage labour around their domestic responsibilities. Inadequate childcare and parental leave policies, and the juggling of paid and unpaid labour, often forces women to "choose" part-time, casual, or contract employment, or to "choose" to spend time at home with the children. For these so-called personal choices, women are financially punished by having no pensions, no steady incomes, and few opportunities to accumulate transferable skills or resources. When marriage ends in divorce, when women face widowhood, or when women opt for unmarried, single parenthood, their financial state becomes even more precarious.

All over the world, women's limited access to income, property, and credit means they lack the resources to climb out of poverty. Globalization has further deepened women's property disadvantage as cash economies have replaced household-based or communal land use (Seager, 2003: 84). Most of the world's women do not own homes or land. In Canada there is no legal discrimination but some women are subject to social pressures to turn over property or financial matters to male relatives or not to exercise their full inheritance rights, and are socialized to believe that men are better at financial matters (Seager, 2003: 84).

Older women are especially vulnerable to poverty. In 2002, 17 percent of seniors were living below the low-income cutoff. Of the seniors living with low income, the vast majority,

71 percent, or almost 428 300 were women. The gap is due to living alone and the likelihood of not receiving private pension income (Statistics Canada, 2003d: 10). Their family "choices" have left them financially exposed. Close to half of all Canadian women aged 65 in 1995 did not have enough money to live on. Past responsibilities for caregiving delayed or deterred their wage earning for significant periods of their lives. Labour market inequalities, including wage discrimination and occupational segregation, means fewer than 50 percent of older women receive pension benefits and very few have sufficient savings for retirement (Khosla, 1993). Many Canadian women now between the ages of 45 and 65 are also expected to retire in poverty (Baines et al., 1998).

Poverty exacts an enormous social, economic, and physical toll on families. Inadequate housing means that poor children live with substandard heating, too little hot water, poor ventilation, often unsafe living conditions, and too little play space. There are New Brunswick children living in dwellings with mud floors, leaking roofs, and no running water (Spears, 1991: A21). Providing children with sufficient food becomes a weekly challenge for poor mothers. Too many children get by on too little food or low-quality, high-fat or high-sugar content food (Kitchen et al., 1991: 7). Infant deaths are higher for poor families. Native children have an infant death rate five times higher than the rate among non-Native children. Native children are also much more prone to committing suicide than are other 10- to 19-year-olds in Canada (Boyle, 1991: 99–100).

What psychological, emotional, and cultural damage is done to poor families? Fear, anger, isolation, frustration, and despair characterize their daily lives. Rather than experiencing efficacy, a sense that they can alter their situations, poor women feel defeated. Working poor women, those with low-paying jobs, work endless hours and still do not make enough money to support their dependants. Those without jobs battle welfare stereotypes. Women have to deny their children "treats" such as money for school teams or trips. Luxury items for themselves are non-existent (Duffy and Mandell, 2000). The following is a quote from 20 years ago. Unfortunately, it remains as relevant today as it was then:

> If I say "no" to the children, they feel very depressed when they see other children taking things to school. The children feel very disappointed. They kind of lose love for you. They think that you don't love them. (Women for Economic Survival, 1984: 23)

Poor women describe themselves as "observers of life," constantly on the outside looking in. They do not see themselves reflected in television sitcoms, in magazine stories or on billboard ads. Their experiences, fears and dreams rarely reach mainstream attention except during holiday food or toy drives.

For these women and their children, feminism seems a luxury. As one woman put it:

> The majority of poor women haven't a hope of a "career" which is personally satisfying, financially rewarding or even pleasant. Mostly, we get jobs. And our jobs give us no prestige or power, very little pay and often are bad for our health. Yet feminist theory continues to assume that all women want to work-for-pay because of the "personal satisfaction" we get from our "careers." (Pierson et al., 1993)

Poor women and their families are washed out of social consciousness.

DISABILITY AND FAMILIES

Feminists have been slow to incorporate women with disabilities[16] into women's studies courses. Many women with disabilities find their invisibility distressing and academically debilitating. As one young woman with disabilities told Karen Swartz, Coordinator of York University's Office for Persons with Disabilities, the absence of disability-related content marginalizes their experiences:

> I won't take a women's history course because it doesn't cover disabled women. You can't tell me that disabled women don't exist ... I think we need to make professors more aware and almost demand that it get put on the curriculum. I mean if they can study women's issues, gay issues, African/Canadian issues. We are part of society and we deserve to be studied. (Swartz, 1996: 22)

Removing women with disabilities from texts has the effect of rendering invisible their experiences.

The vast majority, 93 percent, of all persons aged 15 and over with disabilities live at home in private households while 7 percent live in institutions. Of those living in households, 69 percent are members of a family: 56 percent are husbands, wives, or common-law partners, 5 percent are lone parents, and 8 percent are dependent children. These figures reflect the correlation between disability and aging. Disabilities are most common among seniors. In 1991, 46 percent of all persons aged 65 and over had disabilities, compared with 8 percent of those aged 15–34 (Statistics Canada, 2001a, 2001b).

People with disabilities, especially young people, face significant discrimination. Underlying our treatment of people with disabilities is a discourse of normality, which assumes that everyone can see, walk, and hear well; that everyone is healthy; and that everyone is physically strong. Our society is physically, socially, and culturally constructed on this assumption. Feminists and critical disability activists challenge this assumption and point out that we are all in the process of becoming disabled.

> In 1985, I fell ill overnight with what turned out to be a disabling chronic disease. In the long struggle to come to terms with it, I had to learn to live with a body that felt entirely different to me—weak, tired, painful, nauseated, dirty, unpredictable. I learned at first by listening to other people with chronic illnesses or disabilities; suddenly able-bodied people seemed to me profoundly ignorant of everything that I most needed to know. Although doctors told me there was a good chance I would eventually recover completely, I realized after a year of waiting to get well, hoping to recover my healthy body, was a dangerous strategy. I began slowly to identify with my new, disabled body and to learn to work with it. As I moved back into the world, I also began to experience the world as structured for people who have no weaknesses. The process of encountering the able-bodied world led me gradually to identify myself as a disabled person, and to reflect on the nature of disability. (Wendell, 1989)

Disability takes place on a continuum ranging from mild to severe. Some disabilities are not easily recognized nor easily defined, such as women with low vision, chronic pain, and learning and psychiatric disabilities. Other disabilities fluctuate. Women may appear limited at some points in time while at other times, their experience of disability is very severe (Hulett, 2004: 25).

For the most part, disability is regarded as a family problem rather than a matter of social responsibility. People with disabilities are expected to overcome obstacles to participation by their own extraordinary efforts or the efforts of their families. Yet, social and economic barriers have made it difficult for people with disabilities to construct families. Although schools, workplaces, transportation systems, cultural activities, and leisure events may be accessible, their social organization assumes their clients are able-bodied. Completing school, finding jobs, and securing housing thus become enormous struggles that make it nearly impossible for people with disabilities to obtain the material resources on which families and households are built.

Consider these statistics. People with disabilities are underrepresented at all levels of education, in the labour market, and in income. The International Adult Literacy Survey conducted in Canada in 1994 found that Canadians with disabilities have lower average literacy scores, had less formal schooling, and were less likely to be employed.[17] Low levels of education make it difficult for people with disabilities to find employment.

Low educational attainment translates into lower lifetime earnings.[18] The average income of persons with disabilities is below that of people without disabilities in all age groups (Statistics Canada, 2001a, 2001b). People with disabilities earn lower wages for longer periods of time than non-disabled persons. Statistics Canada reports that only 28 percent of women with disabilities had full-time, full-year employment during 1998, as compared to 64 percent of women with disabilities. For employed men with disabilities, the rate is slightly higher at 47 percent. Aboriginal people with disabilities are more than twice as likely to be unemployed (12 percent) than Aboriginals without disabilities (28 percent). Many earn far below the weekly Canadian average of $752 (Statistics Canada, 2003c).

Women with disabilities usually take up typically female jobs, such as secretary or receptionist, jobs linked with stereotypical images of female beauty. Women with disabilities earn the lowest wages in the lowest-paid jobs. One-quarter of women aged 15 to 64 with disabilities that limit them at work are manual workers while the majority work in clerical jobs. If and when they get to work, they encounter further barriers such as inaccessible work sites, washrooms, and cafeterias; problems for wheelchair users; lack of adequate transportation; and biased attitudes of employers and co-workers.

Women are traditionally defined by their roles as daughters, wives, and mothers but women with disabilities are not expected to become "women" (Wendell, 1989). They are assumed to be unable to fulfill caretaking and partnership roles. Popular opinion does not expect these women to marry, have intimate relationships, bear children, or become mothers. If women want access to these roles, they are encouraged to deny their disabilities.

There are few positive images of women with disabilities in our society and even fewer marital images. Today, an attractive, marriageable woman is young, slim, medium-height, and able-bodied. Women with disabilities, particularly non-white, older, heavy, and tall ones are seen as defective, unattractive, and unmarriageable. The constant media message is that they are unlovable, undesirable, and unacceptable. For these women, their bodies become sources of embarrassment, anguish, guilt, and shame. As a young, female university student told Karen Swartz (1996: 33),

> The mass media portrays women to be beautiful. You must be a skinny model, you must be this and that ... I did not fit that model and it was very hard to take because there was that perception of "Oh, you have a disability, part of your body is broken so therefore you're not a sexual being, therefore you're not attractive you know ... I don't want to be seen around with you because my friends are going to reject me"....You know, that kind of mentality thinking and I just felt really at a loss.

Negatively positioned as sexually unattractive women, they experience ambivalence and confusion over their own sexuality. They are characterized as asexual, or, at best, as having inferior sexual desires. Overprotection by caregivers means young girls are often raised in ignorance of their own sexuality and denied access to information about sex, pregnancy, birth control, gynecological procedures, abortion, and reproductive rights.

Read the words of Frances, a 44-year-old woman with cerebral palsy:

> The wheelchair is not the confining part of my life. What is the confining part of my life is, is the myths that people have about people with disabilities. It's other people's attitudes that have impacted most on my life. The fact that they think of me, when I was younger that I wasn't smart. That I was gonna amount to nothing. I'm this sexless sort of woman... I don't even think that they think of me in terms of a woman even. I mean I'm sort of this nothing ... nothing about my life affirms me in that way. Really, I find that really, really difficult. Because that for me is the most confining part. I cannot genuinely feel that I can affirm myself as a woman in this society. It just doesn't, there's no ability for me to do that. (Rice, 2003)

Even though women with disabilities have the same dreams, hopes, fears, and desires as women without disabilities, if disabled in their youth, they are less likely to establish partnerships. Women with disabilities are more likely to never marry, to marry later, and to divorce. Women who become disabled during their lifetimes have a 99 percent divorce rate compared with men who become disabled, who face a 50 percent divorce rate. Women with disabilities who are also immigrants, visible minorities, Aboriginal, or elderly experience additional oppression.

Women with disabilities report extreme social isolation, especially Aboriginal women living in rural and northern communities. For all women with disabilities, the dual expression of both sexism and handicapism makes it extremely difficult for them to establish intimate relations and build families.

RACIALIZED FAMILIES

First Nations Families

Canadian immigration history is replete with racist policies and practices.[19] At different times, different groups have been subject to intense cultural racism. To Canada's continued discredit, Aboriginal peoples have always been targets of discrimination. Processes of colonization, reserves, residential schools, and transracial adoption are some of the state-sanctioned processes, that have attempted to abuse Aboriginal families. "Government policy, denial and suppression of information about Aboriginal heritage have operated thoroughly at public levels (schools, churches, government institutions) and with mixed result at family levels to eradicate or bury the fact of our heritage" (Leclair and Nicholson with Hartley, 2003: 57–58).

Colonialism destroyed women's authority and prestige within Native communities. Sylvia Maracle tells us why it was primarily men who occupied formal positions of leadership:

> When the treaty parties came to us, the Europeans didn't bring their women. In turn, they didn't want to deal with the women who were leaders of our families, clans, communities and Nations. Colonial government policies and laws, including the Indian Act, reinforced political practices that excluded women. This interference ensured that only men carried titles like chief, band councillor and band administrator until very recently. (2003: 73)

More recent policies attacked Native families through their children. Transracial adoption, for example, like taking children off reserves and putting them into white religious boarding schools, was an attempt to assimilate Natives into Canadian society. As a transracially adopted child sent to a white family, the effects of this cultural genocide, or what Spears calls symbolic annihilation, are devastating.

As Shandra Spears tells us:

> ... I was robbed of a political, historical, spiritual, linguistic and cultural base which could have given me a great sense of self-esteem and strength. This position acknowledges that a large proportion of Native people who ended up homeless, incarcerated, addicted or psychologically scarred were products of this "better life". Native people who remained connected to community and culture did not come over to our house for dinner. I never heard my language spoken, and I was never given accurate information about my culture. I grew up within an ideology that said I did not exist, because Native people did not exist, except as mascots or objects of desire. (2003: 83)

In 2001, there were just over 1.3 million people, or 4.4 percent of the total population of Canada, who identified as having some Aboriginal ancestry. Close to one million persons (976 305), or 3.3 percent of the population actually self-identify as Aboriginal, 30 percent of whom are Metis, 62 percent North American Indian, and 5 percent Inuit (Statistics Canada, 2003a: 6).

Language is essential for cultural survival. As Deerchild says, "Over the course of 500 years, our ancestors were told not to speak their language or to show their Aboriginality, but to adopt the European ways. This was termed as civilizing the Indian, or assimilation" (2003: 102).

About one-quarter of those who identify as Aboriginal report they have enough knowledge of an Aboriginal language to carry on a conversation in Dene, Inuktitut, Notagnasi-Naskapi, Micmac, Oju-Cree, Attikamekw, Dakota/Sioux, Blackfoot. Regular use of language is key to maintaining it. Most who know the language speak it at home (Statistics Canada, 2003a: 8). The majority of Inuit, about 70 percent, can carry on a conversation in Inuktitut and 65 percent speak it regularly in their home (Statistics Canada, 2003a: 17).

Native women make great efforts to keep families intact and secure. Almost half (49 percent) of the Aboriginal identified population live in urban areas, while 31 percent live on reserves, and about 20 percent live in rural non-reserve areas. About 65 percent of Aboriginal children on reserves live with two parents compared with only 50 percent in cities. Among the non-Aboriginal population, 83 percent of non-Aboriginal children live with two parents. About 32 percent of Aboriginal children on reserves live with a lone-parent compared with 46 percent for those in cities. Only 17 percent of non-Aboriginal children live with a lone parent. One-half of the Inuit population live in the new territory of Nunavut, where almost three-quarters of all Inuit children aged 14 and under live with two parents (Statistics Canada, 2003a).

Native families struggle against systemic racism. Native groups have shorter life expectancies, lower marriage rates, higher rates of single parenthood, less education, and greater occupational segregation by gender. Women and men in all three groups are less likely to have married than are Canadians overall. Relatively large percentages of Native women 15 years of age and older have never married. Young Indian women experience the highest unemployment rates, making them the most disadvantaged of an extremely disadvantaged group (Gerber, 1995: 474).

The extreme oppression of Aboriginal women shows the ways in which gender and race are mutually reinforcing processes. At the level of cultural representation, symbols, language, and images are deployed to express and convey the inferiority of Native life. "As targets of male domination and violence, women and children bear the brunt of the social disruption that colonization has brought" (Fernandez, 2003: 242). At the level of social structure, power and material resources are allocated along race/gender lines to subject Aboriginal families to cultural elimination. Native women resist by building healthy communities and restoring self-esteem to their children. What can feminism offer Aboriginal women? As Deerchild explains, Lita Fontaine is trying to bring women into drum ceremonies:

> ... tribal feminism does not mean defiance or rejection of values, philosophies and ceremonies that have been practiced for thousands of years prior to and after European contact. It is not a matter of trying or even wanting to change these Aboriginal traditions. For her [Fontaine], it is the same reasons that more and more women are picking up the drum. It is about bringing back the balance and restoring the matriarchy: "Women are reclaiming, taking back their rightful place within our Aboriginal societies. I think it is about time to bring back that balance." (Deerchild, 2003: 105)

Immigrant Families

Immigrants have built Canada. Blacks first arrived in Canada as servants, labourers, and slaves used to build the colony of New France. Slavery was institutionalized in 1685 and from the late seventeenth until the nineteenth century, African-Canadian slaves were held in Quebec, Nova Scotia, New Brunswick, and Ontario. The "Code Noir," a set of practices to regulate the behaviour of black slaves, was adopted from France. It was harsh and punitive: "Si le noir s'évade, on lui coupe les oreilles et on le marque au fer rouge d'une fleur de lys à l'épaule; s'il recidive, on lui coupe les jarrets. S'il ose recommencer une troisième fois, c'est la mort" (Williams, 1989:10). (Translated: If the Negro escapes, his ears will be cut off and he will be branded on the shoulder with a fleur de lys; if he tries again, he will be hamstrung. If he dares a third attempt, he will die.)

The first underground railroad was established to help slaves escape from the provinces under British rule to the slave-free northern United States (Winks, 1969). Slavery ended in Canada in the early 1820s. Significant numbers of American blacks moved to Canada between the 1820s and 1850s. Many American blacks settled in southern Ontario, especially in St.Catharines, Windsor, Amherstburg, and Collingwood. By 1837, there were at least 50 black families living in Toronto. They successfully started businesses, purchased homes, built churches, and organized benevolent and fraternal organizations (Hill, 1963).

Immigrants have been denied opportunities to sustain families. Chinese workers who first arrived in Canada from China and San Francisco in the 1860s and 1870s were men. Women were specifically excluded on the grounds that Chinese men were merely temporary workers. Cultural racism worked to keep Asians from establishing families.

> No yellow slave shall eat our children's bread Let no Chinese leper cross our threshold. (Ward, 1978: 41)

To discourage entire families from immigrating, the head tax (1885–1923) and the Chinese Exclusion Act (1923–1947) were implemented. Initially set at $100, the federal head tax was levied on any Chinese immigrant. The tax increased to $500 in 1903; by 1923, an outright ban was effected (Ponting, 2000). The tax was sufficiently high to discourage wives or other relatives. The Exclusion Act was not repealed until 1947.

The first Chinese women who came to Canada were merchants' wives who were excluded from the head tax, prostitutes bought and sold by men, and "slave girls" or female servants imported to work as domestic labourers. Slave girls performed domestic work thus freeing Chinese women to engage in piecework sewing at home, to work in tailor shops, laundries, restaurants, and small grocery stores. Women's labour, frequently unrecognized and unremunerated, enabled Chinese businesses to succeed (Adilman, 1984; Man, 2003).

South Asians were also discouraged from building families in Canada. In the mid-1890s, South Asian men began to arrive, leaving behind their families. Racist immigration laws banned Indian women from entering Canada until the 1917–1919 Imperial War Conference agreement legislated their entry (Doman, 1984). The Continuous Journey Stipulation of 1908 allowed access into Canada only to those South Asians who had "come from the country of birth or citizenship by continuous journey and on a through-ticket, purchased before leaving the country of their birth or citizenship (Simms, 1993). Sometimes this policy had fatal ramifications. In 1914, 400 would-be Indian immigrants were denied entry to Canada because their freighter, the *Komagatu Maru*, had picked up passengers from different ports on its journey. For two months the ship sat in a Vancouver port. One passenger died and several others became seriously ill because of lack of food and water. Twenty-six others were killed in on-board skirmishes before the ship eventually returned to India (Elliott and Fleras, 1992; Dhruvarajan, 2003; Das Gupta, 2000).

Although non-white immigrants were actively discouraged from relocating families to Canada, other groups were actively encouraged. *Bring Your Families to Canada*, proclaimed a poster by the Canadian Pacific Rail Company during the early twentieth century (Statistics Canada, 2003b). At the time of Confederation, in 1867, 61 percent of Canadians were of British origin, 31 percent were French, and Aboriginal peoples and other groups made up the rest. Immigration authorities assumed that the more a prospective immigrant resembled a white Anglo-Saxon Protestant in appearance and manner, the more likely he or she was to "Canadianize," that is, adjust to Canadian life and contribute to building the nation.

Since 1901, Canada has welcomed 13.4 million immigrants. Half a century ago, most immigrants came from Europe, with the United Kingdom, Italy, Germany, and the Netherlands being the primary source of immigrants. In 2001, 5.4 million people, or 18.4 percent of the total population, were born outside the country. Only in Australia is the proportion of population born outside the country higher than it is in Canada (22 percent). More than 200 ethnic groups were recorded when Canadians answered the 2001 census question on ethnic ancestry (Statistics Canada, 2003b).

The three largest visible minority[20] groups in 2001—Chinese, South Asians, and Blacks—account for two-thirds of the visible minority population. South Asians represent just under a million people, or 3.1 percent of the population, while blacks account for 2.2 percent of the country's total population or 662 200. By 2016, the visible minority population will account for one-fifth of Canada's population (Statistics Canada, 2003b).

Immigrant families are heterogeneous, diverse, and complex. Their only commonality lies in their difference, thus making any comprehensive analysis of issues they face in creating families the subject of an entire text (Anisef and Kilbride, 2003; Tykksa, 2001). Here only a few issues can be discussed.

Canada needs the skills and knowledge of immigrants in order to grow. Census data show that immigrants who landed in Canada during the 1990s, and who were in the labour force in 2001, represent almost 70 percent of the total growth of the labour force over the decade. If current immigration rates continue, it is possible that immigration could account for virtually all labour force growth by 2011 (Statistics Canada, 2003c: 5).

Yet, recent immigrants face more difficult labour market conditions than individuals born in Canada. Census 2001 shows that only 65.8 percent of recent immigrants are employed compared with 81.8 percent of Canadian born. Male recent immigrants are more likely to be employed than female recent immigrants are, perhaps because a large proportion of females enter as family members of a male economic immigrant. Canada's immigration policy favours more highly educated immigrants, meaning that about a quarter of recent immigrants have university degrees and enter as entrepreneurs and especially as skilled workers in information technology, accountancy, engineering, and natural sciences. A large proportion of recent immigrants, 43 percent, is still in low-skilled jobs (Statistics Canada, 2003c).

Black women's wages have always been essential for maintaining families. The types of jobs black women are doing have not changed significantly since slavery. Up until the 1930s, black women worked as indentured labourers. Domestic work represents the contemporary version of this form of bondage (Brand, 1993). For example, in 1941, 80 percent of black adult females in Montreal were employed as domestic servants (Walker, 1980). Until World War Two, black women were denied access to factory jobs (Pierson, 1986). Nursing, teaching, and other professions open to white women remained closed to black women. Black women recall that the only available jobs were as cleaners or domestics:

> You couldn't get any position in Toronto in 1920, regardless of who you were and how educated you were, other than housework, because even if the employer would employ you, those that you had to work with would not work with you. (Brand, 1992: 37)

A 1981 study noted that black women are concentrated in job ghettos as nursing assistants (as aides and orderlies), personal service occupations, nursing, and electronic data-processing equipment operations (Reitz et al., 1981). Not much has changed in the intervening years. Becoming a nurse is seen as an escape from domestic work (Brand, 1993). Black women, along with immigrant women and women of colour, are the lowest-paid workers. Visible minority women are overrepresented in service occupations, machining, and product fabrication. Racial-minority women are underrepresented in middle- and upper-level management positions, overrepresented in the manual fields, and heavily concentrated in clerical work (Agocs and Boyd, 1993).

The low wages paid to black women, and black men, make it extremely difficult to build families. Women learn not to depend on men's wages and thus learn to become self-sufficient, to value education, and to prepare for a lifetime of hard work. As Dionne Brand (1993: 231) says:

> Every black woman has a mother or grandmother who has told her that she had to do it, probably alone, and that she had to continue to find ways of surviving, that she must be cognizant that no man would rescue her. This vision is reflected in the proportion of women-headed households in the black community (35 percent) an in our participation in waged work.

Immigrant families face numerous cultural, material, and interpersonal barriers including the stress of finding secure employment; learning English; educating and socializing children; adjusting to marital role shifts; and balancing home life between old and new traditions. Gender interacts with race and ethnicity to create a range of family practices. As bearers of family, women take on most of the work and pressure of maintaining families. Yet, as racially inscribed women, material and cultural factors often make this accomplishment a struggle.

What unites Aboriginal, non-white, and immigrant families are their feelings of isolation and alienation from mainstream Canadian society. Immigrant families report feeling ashamed and afraid to report domestic abuse, in part because of the notion of the family as a private matter. Religious beliefs, language barriers, and cultural practices combine to point the individual inward to the ethnic community as a source of information, through the ethnic media, and to community services as a source of support (George, 1998).

The contemporary extended family in the black community is a woman-built system resting on three social building blocks: the imperative of waged work; the stress of child-bearing and raising; and an understanding of children as grace. The extended family is basically matrilineal, including sisters, grandmothers, nieces, aunts, as well as older children. Its scope may extend to women in the family of the child's father and to friends and neighbours. The rearing of children is its central feature (Brand, 1993; Calliste, 2003).

Black families reveal the household as a woman's domain and the mother-child relationship as the cornerstone of family life. Motherhood routinely involves a woman's providing financially for the family in order to compensate for the disadvantaged labour force position of black men. Working-class black families, along with immigrant and other minority families, engage in family strategies to reverse their economically and racially disadvantaged position.

Although black, Aboriginal, and immigrant families are not homogeneous, certain barriers are common to them. Language is one. In 2001, 61 percent of the immigrants who came to Canada in the 1990s used a non-official language as their primary home language. Research by the Coalition of Visible Minority Women and reported by Jacqueline Scott (2003: 109) tells us that constantly being misunderstood eventually affects a person's self-esteem. People who feel they are being watched, may become passive and quiet, and may be sensitive to negative reactions:

> In the West Indies, we have some words in our dialect, which are different from plain English. And I think that is what made the problem in school for most of these kids. That's why they said they are not speaking English. The Jamaican dialect that we have, the Canadians don't understand. It's not that we don't speak English. (Caribbean female parent)

A South Asian male talks about how he deals with questions of identity and belonging in a new culture:

> I speak Punjabi all the time ... I am proud of my culture. If I'm going to speak English and act like a White person that ain't going to make me White, right?? ... So I just say ... if you're going to be classified by culture or your colour, represent your culture all the way. (Desai and Subramanian, 2003: 137)

Officially, Canada promotes a policy of multicultural tolerance, but unofficial pressures to fit in and assimilate result in generational tension and individual confusion. Some young women desire to alter their appearance by become "whiter" (Rice, 2003). Others report not feeling that they belong, of being "othered," of being sexualized as seductive objects of desire and racialized as overly fertile, undesirable, smelly, and oily-haired (Aujla, 2000). Most young women feel as if they live in two worlds, not quite belonging in either.

Children clash with parents over schooling, employment, traditions, clothing, dating, and marriage. In South Asian tradition, women are seen as "custodians" of family values and culture, making parents more anxious about their daughters retaining traditional values and customs (Desai and Subramanian, 2003: 243).

> I think a lot of Indian families—South Asian families, for that matter—just don't understand the youth or today's culture. They just go back into their days when they were young and say, "We couldn't do this when we were your age, so why should you be able to do it? (Desai and Subramanian, 2003: 142)

For parents, excessive insistence on children maintaining traditions is less about enforcing patriarchy, as some suggest, and more about resisting cultural homogenization.

Intermarriage of visible minorities is increasing. In 2001, there were 217 500 mixed unions (marriages and common-law unions) involving a visible minority person with a non-visible minority person. The most common type was between Chinese and non-visible minorities. Intermarriage gives rise to an increase in the numbers of binational/bicultural children who are in the vanguard of erasing cultural boundaries. For these children, it is completely ludicrous to ask them to name their race or ethnicity.

Overall, children from immigrant families start school with less developed skills in reading, writing, and mathematics. With the passage of time, children with immigrant parents catch up to, and sometimes surpass, the academic performance of their classmates with Canadian-born parents (Statistics Canada, 2003b: 9). Sheer persistence, hard work, and determination mark their careers.

Studies from Britain reveal that young black women are in the vanguard of gender change. Black girls, in contrast to black boys, white girls, and white boys, are more likely to aspire to high-status occupations, be more confident that their aspirations will be realized, be more likely to choose non-gendered occupations, be employment-oriented rather than marriage-oriented, be strongly committed to economic independence rather than seeing their earnings as part of family income, and be less guilt-ridden about childcare as they believe in shared childcare. Being marginalized shifts the centre and allows new and more innovative family arrangements to emerge.

Immigrant families have always encountered a wide range of barriers to establishing and nourishing families. Community organizing has been an effective strategy to resist cultural and systemic racism. Most immigrant groups have extensive ties to the community through religious groups, political organizations, homework clubs, and sports and activity clubs for children, to mention only a few. Knowledge of and membership in these organizations provides women with strength to combat the many ways in which discrimination makes "making family" difficult.

CONCLUSION

Social, economic, and cultural transformations alter family practices and family structures. Changing employment expectations, cultural and ethnic diversity, norms of gender equity, and technological developments shifted the reasons for living with others and our expectations and responsibilities within partnerships (Carbone, 2000). New possibilities open up while more traditional forms tend to disappear. Families of choice, friendship networks, cross-household familial relationships, and serial monogamy are all patterns challenging the hegemony of heteronormative arrangements. Young people remain in parental homes for longer periods of time, non-familial households emerge in which accommodation is shared among friends, lovers, acquaintances, and strangers, and solitary living grows in popularity. Aboriginal, visible minority, and immigrant families are characterized by their resilience, flexibility, and resourcefulness in resisting racism and sexism. Cultural boundary-crossing deconstructs traditional ideas about ethnic identity, allowing more hybrids and fluid families to emerge.

Diversity in social, emotional, and domestic relationships allows feminists an opportunity to trouble taken-for-granted ideas about the family. Feminists have been key to questioning what we have assumed to be natural and normal family forms and practices. The result has been an engaging and ongoing dialogue within Canadian society about women, family, and intimate relations.

ENDNOTES

1. Although most women will enter a conjugal union, more than 53 percent of women aged 20 to 29 will choose common-law as their first conjugal experience. Most of these women will eventually marry (Statistics Canada, 2002: 3). Of all couples sharing a household (married and cohabitating) 0.5 percent are same-sex (Ambert, 2003).

2. Discourses are groups of related narratives in terms of which men and women have projected the "natural" course of their lives. They provide sets of terms in which differing thoughts might be formulated. Discourses produce many variations but at the same time they exclude others entirely.

3. Canada has about 30 million people, about 80 percent of whom live in urban areas in families with an average of 2.6 people per private household. Canadian families come in many sizes and in many forms. Few traditional families remain. In 2001, married or common-law couples with children represented only 44 percent of all families, down from 55 percent in 1981. Couples with no children living at home accounted for 44 percent of all families. Lone-parent families increased to 16 percent of all families. Same-sex common-law couples represented 0.5 percent of all couples, or 34 200 people. Step-families represented 12 percent of all Canadian couples with children (Statistics Canada, 2003f: 11). Part of the demographic shift in family types has to do with the aging population. The fastest growing population group is that aged 80 and over. About one-quarter of the country's total population comprises Canadians aged 45 to 64 years. The population ages while the number of children being born each year decreases (Statistics Canada, 2003e: 4). Even premarital patterns assume marriage. About 40 percent of men and 36 percent of women live together before age 30 or before marriage. Heterosexual cohabitation is seen as a type of courtship pattern or preliminary stage before marriage. It is seen as easier to enter and exit, thus accounting for its high rate of dissolution (Ambert, 2002). Lesbian cohabitation is also very common although precise statistics are not readily available.

4. Women's wages are essential to keep the family above the poverty line. A growing number of wives earn more than their husbands do. In 1997, the proportion of homes in which the wife earned more than her husband soared from 5 percent in 1967 to 23 percent in 1992 and has remained unchanged for six consecutive years.

5. Women's participation in the labour force continues to grow substantially. In 2002, 56 percent of all women aged 15 and over had jobs and women accounted for 46 percent of the employed workforce. In 2002, 76 percent of women between the ages of 25 and 54 were part of the paid workforce than women in other age ranges. There have been large increases in the numbers of employed women with children. In 2002, 72 percent of all women with children less than age 16 living at home were employed and 62 percent of women with children younger than 3 were employed (Statistics Canada, 2003g: 7–8).

6. A relatively large percentage of women work part-time. In 2002, almost 2 million employed women, 28 percent of all women in the paid workforce, worked fewer than 30 hours per week at their main job, compared with just 11 percent of employed men. Young women are particularly likely to work part-time. In 2002, over half, 53 percent, of employed women aged 15 to 24 worked part-time, citing reasons such as not wanting full-time employment or because part-time work is more appropriate for their personal situation. Many women work part-time because of childcare or other family responsibilities. In 2002, more than one in five female part-time employees said they worked part-time because of personal or family responsibilities (Statistics Canada, 2003g: 8). Highly skilled occupations normally requiring a university education accounted for almost one-half of total labour force growth (Statistics Canada, 2003e: 18–20). Despite their rising levels of education, in 2002, 70 percent of

all employed women were working in one of the following: teaching, nursing and related health occupations, clerical or other administrative positions, or sales and service occupations (Statistics Canada, 2003g: 8).

7. In 1996, for the first time, the Canadian census measured unpaid work, making Canada one of the few countries to gather national data. Unpaid, domestic labour is defined under the following categories: domestic work (meal preparation, cleaning, clothing care, repairs and maintenance, and other domestic work); help and care (childcare and adult care); management and shopping; transportation and travel; other unpaid work (volunteer work, other help and care, and travel related to volunteer work and other help and care) (Jackson, 1997). Data are gathered on all social classes and racial-ethnic groups but it does not distinguish between same-sex and opposite-sex partnerships. Ninety percent of Canadians report some unpaid work: 89 percent for housework or home maintenance; 38 percent for childcare; 17 percent for eldercare. In each category, women did more domestic work than men did.

8. Canada has undergone a substantial decline in its fertility rate. In 1921, the total fertility rate per woman was 3.5 children compared with 1.5 in 1999. In addition to women having fewer children, more are not having any children at all (Stobert and Kemeny, 2003g: 7). In 2001, the census counted 1.7 million children aged 4 and under, down 11 percent from 1991. The declining fertility is expected to continue (Statistics Canada, 2003e: 3). Reasons for not having children include medical conditions, having careers, not having the right partner, not interested in children, and religious and environmental reasons (Stobert and Kemeny, 2003: 8).

9. Many children adapt to the presence of a step-parent in their household and some are required to form domestic bonds with half-brothers or sisters. Half of all step-families contain only the female spouse's children, 10 percent contain only the male spouse's children and the remaining 40 percent are blended, usually with new children from the new union plus the children from the first marriages. In 2001, Canada had more than half a million step-families, representing an increase of 17 percent since 1995. Step-families accounted for 11.8 percent of all Canadian couples with children in 2001 (Statistics Canada, 2002a: 8–9).

10. Studies show us that about one-third, 31 percent–36 percent, of all marriages end in divorce. Of these, about 50 percent do not include dependent children. Ambert estimates that at least 15 percent of divorces are re-divorces for one or both spouses (Statistics Canada, 2002a, 7). The average duration of marriages ending in divorce in 1998 was 13.7 years. The average age at divorce was 42 years for men and 39.4 years for women. Even still, young people in their twenties and early thirties are the most susceptible to divorce (Ambert, 2002: 7–9). Couples who cohabit before marriage are more likely to divorce than those who are married. In the 20- to 30-year-old group surveyed by Le Bourdais et al. (2000), 63 percent of those women whose first relationship was a cohabitation had separated by 1995 compared with 33 percent of those who had married first. Poverty, low incomes and youthful marriages are other risk factors to divorce (Ambert, 2002: 17). Serial monogamy, or remarriage, is popular. Following divorce, 70 percent of divorced men and 58 percent of divorced women remarry in Canada, except Quebec where the preference tends to be cohabitation (Ambert, 2002: 10). In 2001, 12 percent of families comprising a couple with children were step-families. About 10 percent of all Canadian children under the age of 12 are living in a step-family.

11. Remarriages have a higher rate of dissolution with the projected rate of re-divorce around 41 percent (Glossup, 2002). Reasons include acceptance of divorce as a solution; less willingness to compromise; and fewer role guidelines available to navigate the complex structure of relationships that accompany remarriages and step-families (Glossup, 2002).

12. The Canadian Constitution divides the power to make laws over marriage between the federal Parliament and the provincial and territorial legislatures. The federal Parliament has authority over the legal capacity to marry (i.e. who can marry whom). The provincial and territorial legislatures have the authority over solemnization, which includes requirements for such things as licences, who can conduct the ceremony and how, and registration. When marriages break down, the Constitution gives

authority to the federal Parliament to regulate the legal consequences through divorce. The *Divorce Act* sets out a legal framework applied across Canada, which includes grounds for divorce and allows for spousal support, child support, and custody and access orders (Department of Justice, 2002: 9).

13. Who is a spouse? In June 2003, the Ontario Supreme Court legalized same-sex marriage. British Columbia followed a few months later. Fifty-three percent of Canadians favour gay and lesbian couples marrying (Department of Justice, 2002: 6). Same-sex relationships challenge notions of partnership, spouse, and marriage. Since 1999, the Supreme Courts of Ontario, Quebec, and British Columbia have declared that same-sex couples are entitled to receive the same legal and economic benefits as other couples. The definition of spouse has been changed to include any two persons who have lived together in a "marriage-like" relationship for at least two years. In 2000, the federal government extended benefits and obligations to common-law couples, be they of opposite sexes or the same sex. In many provinces, same-sex couples can now adopt children (Ambert, 2003).

14. What recent changes have occurred? In 2000, the federal government passed *The Modernization of Benefits and Obligations Act,* extending benefits and obligations under 68 federal statutes to common-law opposite-sex and same-sex couples. As a result, the majority of the legal consequences of marriage federal law now apply to all couples in committed common-law relationships (Department of Justice, 2002: 4). These changes were in accordance with the views expressed by 75 percent of Canadians polled in 1998 who agreed that human rights legislation in Canada should protect gay and lesbians from discrimination based on their sexual orientation (Department of Justice, 2002: 6).

15. A typical Canadian family needs to work close to 77 weeks a year just to support themselves, 16 weeks to pay their income taxes, and almost 10 weeks to pay for food (Lochhead, 1998). Among the 4.5 million individuals living without a spouse or children of their own (people termed "non-family persons" by the census), median income reached just over $20 213 (Statistics Canada, 2003d: 7). The median income of couples with children under 18 was just over $66 000 (Statistic Canada, 2003d: 13). About 21 percent of low-income children live in two-parent families in which only one parent has employment earning; about 17 percent in families in which both parents have earnings; and another 12 percent in families in which neither parent reported earning. Low-income children are disproportionately concentrated in lone-parent families, and in particular, in lone-parent families in which the single parent has no employment earnings (Statistics Canada, 2003d: 10).

16. Disability includes the following: 72 percent of people with disabilities report mobility issues, 70 percent pain, 67 percent agility, 30 percent hearing, 17 percent seeing, 15 percent psychological issues, 13 percent learning, 12 percent memory, 11 percent speech, 4 percent developmental, and 3 percent unknown. Among the people with disabilities, 33 percent report mild disabilities, 25 percent report moderate disabilities, 28 percent report severe, and 14 percent report very severe. Among the 3.4 million adults with disabilities, the 2001 national Participation and Activity Limitation Survey (PALS) distinguished four levels of severity: mild, moderate, severe, and very severe (Statistics Canada, 2001b: 19). Most adults with disabilities, 34.1 percent, experience a mild disability while 26.9 percent experience severe activity limitations, and 14 percent report having a very severe disability. Men are more likely to experience mild disabilities, while women are more likely to report a severe level of activity limitation. In terms of the total population aged 15 and over, more than 480 000, or 2 percent, report a very severe level of disability (Statistics Canada, 2001a). Mobility and/or agility disabilities are the most commonly reported type, that is limitation in ability to walk, move from room to room, carry an object a short distance, or stand for long periods (Statistics Canada, 2001a: 3).

17. Persons with mild disabilities are more likely than those with moderate or even severe disabilities to be employed. In 1991, 62 percent of those aged 15–64 with mild disabilities were part of the paid workforce compared with 19 percent of those with severe disabilities. About 14 percent of those aged 15–64 with disabilities are unemployed, compared with 10 percent of those without disabilities (Statistics Canada, 2001a: 4–5).

18. Many people with disabilities receive income, which is related to their condition, such as social assistance and Canada/Quebec Pension Plan disability benefits. Many others report having considerable disability-related expenses that are not reimbursed.

19. Racism refers to ideas or behaviour that delineates group boundaries by reference to race or to real or alleged biological characteristics, and that attribute groups so racialized with other negatively evaluated characteristics. Racialization refers to "those instances where social relations between people have been structured by the significance of human biological characteristics in such a way as to define and construct differentiated social collectivities" (Solomos, 1993: 23).

20. Visible minority is defined by the Employment Equity Act as "persons, other than Aboriginal peoples, who are non-Caucasian in race or non-white in colour." Under this definition, regulations specify the following groups as visible minorities: Chinese, South Asians, Blacks, Arabs, West Asians, Filipinos, Southeast Asians, Latin Americans, Japanese, Koreans and other visible minority groups, such as Pacific Islanders (Statistics Canada, 2003b).

SUGGESTED READINGS

Anderson, Kim, and **Bonita Lawrence,** eds. *Strong Women Stories: Native Vision and Community Survival.* Toronto: Sumach Press, 2003.

An excellent edited collection of women's stories exposes the tremendous resilience of Native women as they work to build strong communities and families.

Anisef, Paul, and **Kenise Murphy Kilbride,** eds. *Managing Two Worlds: The Experiences and Concerns of Immigrant Youth in Ontario.* Toronto: Canadian Scholars' Press, 2003.

An in-depth look at issues identified by immigrant youth in the areas of race, gender, employment, family, language, and adaptation.

Mandell, Nancy, and **Ann Duffy,** eds. *Canadian Families: Diversity, Challenge and Change*, 3rd ed. Toronto: Nelson Thomson, 2005.

An edited collection of articles looking at contemporary issues facing Canadian families.

Rowlingson, Karen, and **Stephen McKay.** *Lone Parent Families: Gender, Class and State.* Harlow, England: Pearson Education Ltd., 2002.

An excellent discussion of the ways postmodern and feminist discourses have affected our thinking about lone-parent families in England over the past century.

Shumway, David R. *Modern Love: Romance, Intimacy and the Marriage Crisis.* New York: New York University Press, 2003.

An engaging look at discourses of intimacy and romance that shape individuals' notions of partnering.

DISCUSSION QUESTIONS

1. Define and describe the discourses of intimacy and romance. To what extent are contemporary television shows based on these discourses?

2. Discuss the ways in which race, class, economics, and gender both shape and are shaped by family practices.

3. Consider the interaction between labour markets and family practices. What are the consequences for the organization of family life?

4. How are same-sex marriages challenging patriarchal families?

5. Demonstrate the ways gender intersects with race to affect family experiences of Aboriginal, visible minority, and immigrant families.

BIBLIOGRAPHY

Adilman, Tamara. "Preliminary Sketch of Chinese Women and Work in British Columbia, 1885–1950." In *Not Just Pin Money: Selected Essays on the History of Women's Work in British Columbia,* edited by Barbara Latham and Roberta Pazdro, 53–78. Victoria, British Columbia: Camosun College, 1984.

Adult Literacy Survey. 1994. Human Resources Development Canada, available at **www.nald.ca/nls.**

Agocs, Carol and Monica Boyd. "The Canadian Ethnic Mosaic Recast for the 1990s." In *Social Inequality in Canada,* 2nd ed., edited by James Curtis, Edward Grabb, and Neil Guppy, 330–52. Toronto: Prentice Hall, 1993.

Alford-Cooper, Finnegan. *For Keeps: Marriages that Last a Lifetime.* New York: M.E. Sharpe, 1998.

Ali, Turan. *We Are Family: Testimonies of Lesbian and Gay Parents.* London: Cassell, 1996.

Anderson, Kim, and **Bonita Lawrence.** *Strong Women Stories: Native Vision and Community Survival.* Toronto: Sumach Press, 2003.

Anisef, Paul, and **Kenise Murphy Kilbride,** eds. *Managing Two Worlds: The Experiences and Concerns of Immigrant Youth in Ontario.* Toronto: Canadian Scholars' Press Inc., 2003.

Ambert, Anne-Marie. *Same-Sex Couples and Same-Sex Parent Families: Relationships, Parenting, and Issues of Marriage.* Ottawa: The Vanier Institute of the Family, 2003.

———. *Divorce: Facts, Causes, and Consequences.* Ottawa: The Vanier Institute of the Family, 2002.

Arnup, Kathleen. "Sexuality and Power: Same-sex Families." In Nancy Mandell and Ann Duffy (eds). *Canadian Families: Diversity, Challenge and Change.* Toronto: Thomson, 2005.

———. *Lesbian Parenting: Living with Pride and Prejudice.* Toronto: Gynergy Books, 1995.

———. "Lesbian and Gay Parents." In Nancy Mandell and Ann Duffy (eds.), *Canadian Families: Diversity, Conflict, and Change,* 3rd Edition. Toronto, Thomson Nelson, 2005.

Aujla, Angela. "Others in Their Own Land: Second Generation South Asian Canadian Women, Racism, and the Persistence of Colonial Discourse." *Canadian Woman Studies* 20/2, (Summer 2000): 41–47.

Baines, Carol, Patricia Evans, Sheila Neysmith, eds. *Women's Caring: Feminist Perspectives on Social Welfare,* 2nd ed. New York: Oxford University Press, 1998.

Baber, Kristine M., and **Katherine R. Allen.** *Women and Families: Feminist Reconstructions.* New York: The Guilford Press, 1992.

Beaujot, Roderic. *Earning and Caring in Canadian Families.* Toronto: Broadview Press, 2000.

Beck, Ulrich, and **Elisabeth Beck-Gernsheim.** *The Normal Chaos of Love.* London: Polity Press, 1995.

Beck-Gernsheim, Elisabeth. *Reinventing the Family: In Search of New Lifestyles.* Cambridge: Polity, 2002.

Berger, Brigitte. *The Family in the Modern Age.* New Brunswick and London: Transaction Publishers, 2002.

Berk, Sarah Fenstermaker. *The Gender Factory: The Apportionment of Work in American Households*. New York: Plenum, 1985.

Bernard, Jessie. *The Future of Marriage*, 2nd ed. New Haven, CT: Yale University Press, 1982.

Boyle, Michael. "Child Health in Ontario." In *The State of the Child in Ontario*, edited by Richard Barnhorts and Laura C. Johnson, 92–116. Toronto: Oxford University Press, 1991.

Brand, Dionne. "Black Women and Work: The Impact of Racially Constructed Gender Roles on the Sexual Division of Labour." In *Scratching the Surface: Canadian Anti-Racist Feminist Thought,* edited by Enakshi Dua and Angela Robertson, 89–96. Toronto: Women's Press, 1999.

———. "A Working Paper on Black Women in Toronto: Gender, Race and Class." In *Returning the Gaze: Essays on Racism, Feminism and Politics,* edited by Himani Bannerji, 220–41. Toronto: Sister Vision Press, 1993.

———. *No Burden to Carry: Narratives of Black Working Women in Ontario, 1920s to 1950s.* Toronto: Women's Press, 1992.

Calhoun, Cheshire. "Family's Outlaws: Rethinking the Connections between Feminism, Lesbianism, and the Family," In *Feminism and Families*, edited by Hilde Lindemann Nelson, 131–50. London: Routledge, 1997.

Calliste, Agnes. "Black Families in Canada: Exploring the Interconnections of Race, Class and Gender." In *Voices: Essays on Canadian Families*, 2nd ed., edited by Marion Lynn. Australia: Scarborough, Ont.: Nelson Thomson, 2003.

Carbone, June. *From Partners to Parents: The Second Revolution in Family Law.* New York: Columbia University Press, 2000.

Carty, Linda. "The Discourse of Empire and the Social Construction of Gender." In *Scratching the Surface: Canadian Anti-Racist Feminist Thought*, edited by Enakshi Dua and Angela Robertson, 35–47. Toronto: Women's Press, 1999.

Clark, Warren. "Time Alone. *Canadian Social Trends* 66 (Autumn 2002): 2–6.

Collins, Patricia Hill. *Black Feminist Thought: Knowledge, Consciousness, and the Politics of Empowerment*, Second edition. New York: Routledge, 2000.

Conway-Turner, Kate, and **Suzanne Cherrin**. *Women, Families and Feminist Politics: A Global Exploration*. New York: Haworth Park Press, 1998.

Coontz, Stephanie. *The Way We Never Were: American Families and the Nostalgia Trap*. New York: Basic Books, 1992.

Deerchild, Rosanna. "Tribal Feminism Is a Drum Song." In *Strong Women Stories: Native Vision and Community Survival*, edited by Kim Anderson and Bonita Lawrence, 97–105. Toronto: Sumach Press, 2003.

Das Gupta, Tania. "Families of Native People, Immigrants and People of Colour." In *Canadian Families: Diversity, Conflict and Change*, 2nd ed., edited by Nancy Mandell and Ann Duffy, 146–87. Toronto: Harcourt Brace, 2000.

Desai, Sabra and **Sangeeta Subramanian.** "Colour, Culture and Dual Consciousness: Issues Identified by South Asian Immigrant Youth in the Greater Toronto Area." In *Managing two worlds: The experiences and concerns of immigrant youth in Ontario*, edited by Paul Anisef and Kenise Murphy Kilbride, 118–161. Toronto: Canadian Scholars' Press Inc., 2003.

Department of Justice. *Marriage and Legal Recognition of Same-sex Unions*. Ottawa: Ministry of Industry, 2002.

Dhruvarajan, Vanaaja. "Hindu Indo-Canadian Families." In *Voices: Essays on Canadian Families*, 2nd ed., edited by Marion Lynn. Australia: Scarborough, Ont.: Nelson Thomson, 2003.

Dill, Bonnie Thornton. "Our Mother's Grief: Racial Ethnic Women and the Maintenance of Families." *Journal of Family History*, 1988: 415–31.

Doman, Mahinder. "A Note on Aisan Indian Women in British Columbia, 1900–1935." In *Not Just Pin Money: Selected Essays on the History of Women's Work in British Columbia,* edited by Barbara Latham and Roberta Pazdro, 53–78. Victoria, British Columbia: Camosun College, 1984.

Dua, Enakshi. "Canadian Anti-Racist Feminist Thought: Scratching the Surface of Racism." In *Scratching the Surface: Canadian Anti-Racist Feminist Thought*, edited by Enakshi Dua and Angela Robertson, 7–31. Toronto: Women's Press, 1999a.

————. "Beyond Diversity: Exploring the Ways in Which the Discourse of Race Has Shaped the Institution of the Nuclear Family." In *Scratching the Surface: Canadian Anti-Racist Feminist Thought*, edited by Enakshi Dua and Angela Robertson, 237–59. Toronto: Women's Press, 1999b.

Dubeau, Diane. *The Involved Father*. Ottawa: The Vanier Institute of the Family, 2002.

Duffy, Ann and Nancy Mandell. "The Growth of Poverty and Social Inequality in Canada: Losing Faith in Social Justice." In *Canadian Society: Meeting the Challenges of the Twenty-First Century*, edited by Dan Glenday and Ann Duffy, 77–114. Toronto: Oxford University Press, 2001.

Dunne, Gillian A. "A Passion for Sameness: Sexuality and Gender Accountability." In *The New Family*, edited by Elizabeth Silva and Carol Smart, 67–82. Thousand Oaks, California: Sage, 1999.

Duncan, S., and **R. Edwards.** *Lone Mothers, Paid Work and Gendered Moral Rationalities*. Basingstoke: Palgrave, 1999.

Duxbury, Linda Elizabeth, Christopher Higgins, and **Donna Coghill.** *Voices of Canadians: Seeking Work-Life Balance*. Hull, Quebec: Human Resources Development Canada, Labour Program, 2003.

Elliot, Patricia and **Nancy Mandell.** "Feminist Theories." In *Feminist Issues: Race, Class and Gender*, 3rd ed., edited by Nancy Mandell, 23–48. Toronto: Prentice Hall, 2001.

Elliott, Jean Leonard and **Augie Fleras.** *Unequal Relations: An Introduction to Race and Ethnic Dynamics in Canada.* Toronto: Prentice Hall, 1992.

England, Kim. "Mothers, Wives, Workers: The Everyday Lives of Working Mothers." In *Who Will Mind the Baby? Geographies of Child Care and Working Mothers*, edited by Kim England, 109–23. London: Routledge, 1996.

Frederick, Judith. *As Time Goes By: Time Use of Canadians*. Ottawa: Statistics Canada, cat. No. 89–544, 1995.

Frederick, Judith and **Jason Hamel.** *Canadian Attitudes to Divorce*. Statistics Canada, cat. No. 11-008-XPE, 1998.

Fernandez, Carl. "Coming Full Circle: A Young Man's Perspective on Building Gender Equity in Aboriginal Communities." In *Strong Women Stories: Native Vision and Community Survival*, edited by Kim Anderson and Bonita Lawrence, 242–254. Toronto: Sumach Press, 2003.

George, Usha. "Caring and Women of Colour: Living the Intersecting Oppressions of Race, Class and Gender." In *Women's Caring: Feminist Perspectives on Social Welfare,* edited by Carol Baines, Patricia Evans and Sheila Neysmith, 69–83. Toronto: Oxford University Press, 1998.

Gerber, Linda M. "Indian, Metis, and Inuit Women and Men: Multiple Jeopardy in a Canadian Context." In *Gender in the 1990s: Images, Realities and Issued*, edited by E. D. Nelson and B. W. Robinson, 466–77. Toronto: Nelson, 1995.

Giddens, Anthony. *The Transformation of Intimacy: Sexuality, Love and Eroticism in Modern Societies*. Stanford, California: Stanford University Press, 1992.

Glenn, Evelyn Nakano. "The Social Construction and Institutionalization of Gender and Race: An Integrative Framework." In *Revisioning Gender*, edited by Myra Marx Ferree, Judith Lorber, and Beth Hess, 3–43. Thousand Oaks: Sage, 1999.

Glossup, R. Personal Communication between Ambert and Glossup, as cited in Ambert's 2002 Divorce paper for the Vanier Institute. Ottawa: The Vanier Institute of the Family, 2002.

Goldscheider, Frances and **Linda J. Waite.** *New Families, No Families?* Berkeley: University of California Press, 1991.

Hill, Daniel G. "Negroes in Toronto, 1793–1865." *Ontario History* 55, 1963.

Hochschild, Arlie Russell. *Time Bind: When Work Becomes Home and Home Becomes Work.* San Francisco: Henry Holt, 1997.

Housekeeping Monthly. 1955. *The Good Wife's Guide*, 13 May.

Hulett, Terri. *Women with Disabilities: Barriers to Achieving Postsecondary Education.* Major Research Paper submitted to the Graduate Program in Women's Studies, York University, January 2004.

Jackson, Stevi. "Women, Marriage and Family Relationships." In *Introducing Women's Studies*, 2nd edition, edited by Victoria Robinson and Diane Richardson, 323–48. Washington Square, New York: New York University Press, 1997.

Khosla, Punam. Review of the situation of women in Canada. Toronto: National Action Committee on the Status of Women, 1993.

Kitchen, Brigitte, Andrew Mitchell, Peter Cluttervuck, and **Marvyn Novick.** In *Unequal Futures: The Legacies of Child Poverty in Canada.* Toronto: Child Poverty Action Group and the Social Planning Council of Metropolitan Toronto, 1991.

Koepke, L., Hare, J., and **Moran, P. B.** Relationship Quality in a Sample of Lesbian Couples with Children and Child-Free Lesbian Couples. *Family Relations* 41 (1992): 224–229.

Kurdek, L. A. Differences between Heterosexual-nonparent Couples and Gay, Lesbian, and Heterosexual-parent couples. *Journal of Family Issues* 22 (2001): 728–755.

Le Bourdais, C., Neil, G., Turcotte, P., et al. *The Changing Face of Conjugal Relationships. Canadian Social Trends* 56 (2000): 14–17.

Leclair, Carole and **Lynn Nicholson,** with **Elize Hartley.** "From the Stories that Women Tell: The Metis Women's Circle." In *Strong Women Stories: Native Vision and Community Survival*, 55–69. Toronto: Sumach Press, 2003.

Lees, Sue. "Will Boys Be Left on the Shelf?" In *Changing Family Values*, edited by Caroline Wright and Gill Jagger, 59–76. London: Routledge, 1999.

Lever, Janet. "The 1994 Advocate Survey of Sexuality and Relationships: The Men." *The Advocate: The National Gay and Lesbian Newsmagazine*, August 23, 1994: 17–24.

———. "The 1995 Advocate Survey of Sexuality and Relationships: The Women." *The Advocate: The National Gay and Lesbian Newsmagazine*, August 22, 1995: 22–30.

Lewin, Ellen. *Lesbian Mothering: Accounts of Gender in American Culture.* Ithaca, New York: Cornell University Press, 1993.

Lochhead, Clarence. *From the Kitchen Table to the Boardroom Table: The Canadian Family and the Work Place.* Ottawa: The Vanier Institute of the Family, 1998.

Luxton, Meg and June Corman. *Getting By in Hard Times: Gendered Labour at Home and on the Job.* Toronto: University of Toronto, 2001.

Man, Guida. "The Experience of Middle-Class Women in Recent Hong Kong Chinese Immigrant Families in Canada." In *Voices: Essays on Canadian Families*, 2nd ed., edited by Marion Lynn. Australia: Scarborough, Ont.: Nelson Thomson, 2003.

Mandell, Nancy. "Women, Families and Intimate Relations," In *Feminist Issues: Race, Class and Gender*, edited by Nancy Mandell, 3rd ed., 193–218. Toronto: Pearson Educational, 2001.

———. "Juggling the Load: Employed Mothers Who Work Full-time for Pay." In *Few Choices: Women, Work and Family*, edited by Ann Duffy, Nancy Mandell, and Norene Pupo. Toronto: Garamond, 1989.

Mandell, Nancy, and **Ann Duffy** (eds.). *Canadian Families: Diversity, Conflict, and Change.* Toronto: Harcourt Brace, 2000.

Maracle, Sylvia. "The Eagle Has Landed: Native Women, Leadership and Community Development" In *Strong women stories: Native Vision and Community Survival*, edited by Kim Anderson and Bonita Lawrence, 70–80. Toronto: Sumach Press, 2003.

Marshall, Katherine. "Dual Earners: Who's Responsible for Housework?" *Canadian Social Trends*, Cat. No. 11-008E (Spring and Winter) 1993: 11–14.

Milan, Anne, and **Brian Hamm.** "Across the Generations: Grandparents and Grandchildren." *Canadian Social Trends*, 71 (Winter 2003): 2–7.

Nelson, Fiona. *Lesbian Motherhood: An Exploration of Canadian Lesbian Families.* Toronto: University of Toronto Press, 1996.

O'Brien, Carol-Anne, and **Aviva Goldberg.** "Lesbians and Gay Men Inside and Outside Families." In *Canadian Families: Diversity, Conflict and Change*, 2nd ed., edited by Nancy Mandell and Ann Duffy, 115–145. Toronto: Harcourt Brace, 2000.

Oppenheimer, Valerie. "A Theory of Marriage Timing." *American Journal of Sociology* 94 (1988): 563–91.

Oerton, Sarah. "Queer Housewives? Some Problems of Theorizing the Division of Domestic Labour in Lesbian and Gay Households." *Women's Studies International Forum* 20/3 (1997): 421–430.

Oswald, R. F. "Resilience within the Family Networks of Lesbians and Gay Men: Intentionality and Redefinition." *Journal of Marriage and the Family*, 64 (2002): 374–383.

Patterson, C. J. "Family Relationships of Lesbians and Gay Men." *Journal of Marriage and the Family,* 62 (2000): 1052–1069.

Pearlman, S. F. "Distancing and Connectedness: Impact on Couple Formation in Lesbian Relationships." In *Loving Boldly: Issues Facing Lesbians*, edited by E. D. Rothblum and E. Cole, 77–88. Binghamton, New York: Harrington Park, 1989.

Peplar, Michael. *Family Matters: A History of Ideas about Family Since 1945.* London:Pearson Education Ltd., 2002.

Pierson, Ruth. "The Mainstream Women's Movement and the Politics of Difference," In Canadian Women's Issues, Vol. 1: *Strong Voices*, edited by Marjorie Griffin Cohen, Paula Bourne and Philandra Masters, 186–263. Toronto: Lorimer, 1993.

———. *They're Still Women After All: The Second World War and Canadian Womanhood.* Toronto: McClelland Stewart, 1986.

Ponting, Rick. "Race and Resistance." In *Canadian Society: An Introduction*, edited by Dan Glenday and Ann Duffy, 84–100. Toronto: Oxford University Press, 2000.

Porteous, J. Douglas, and **Sandra E. Smith.** *Domicide: The Global Destruction of Home.* Montreal and Kingston: McGill-Queen's University Press, 2001.

Porter, Elaine, and **Carol Kauppi.** "Women's Work Is (Almost) Never Done (By Anyone Else)." In *Changing Lives: Women in Northern Ontario*, edited by Margaret Kechnie and Marge Reitsma-Street, 162–73. Toronto: Dundurn Press, 1996.

Reitz, Jeffrey G., Livianna Calzavara, and **Donna Dasko.** *"Ethnic Inequality and Segregation in Jobs."* Research Paper, Toronto: Centre for Urban and Community Studies, University of Toronto, No. 123, 1981.

Rice, Carla. *Becoming Women: Body Image, Identity, and Difference in the Passage to Womanhood.* PhD dissertation, York University, Graduate Program in Women's Studies, 2003.

Rosenthal, Carolyn J. and **James Gladstone.** *Grandparenthood in Canada*. Ottawa: The Vanier Institute of the Family, 2000.

Rowlingson, Karen and **Stephen McKay.** *Lone Parent Families: Gender, Class and State.* Harlow, England: Pearson Education Ltd., 2002.

Sauve, Roger. *Connections: Tracking the Links between Jobs and Family: Job, Family and Stress among Husbands, Wives and Lone-parents 15–64 from 1900 to 2000.* Ottawa: The Vanier Institute of the Family, 2002.

Schwartz, Pepper, and **Virginia Rutter.** *The Gender of Sexuality*. Thousand Oaks: Pine Forge Press, 1998.

Scott, Jacqueline L. "English language and Communication: Issues for African and Caribbean Immigrant Youth in Toronto." In *Managing Two Worlds: The Experiences and Concerns of Immigrant Youth in Ontario*, edited by Paul Anisef and Kenise Murphy Kilbride. Toronto: Canadian Scholars' Press Inc., 2003.

Seager, Joni. The Penguin Atlas of Women in the World, third edition. New York: Penguin Books, 2003.

Seyda, Barbara, and **Diana Herrera.** *Women in Love: Portraits of Lesbian Mothers and Their Families*. Boston: Bullfinch Press, 1998.

Shumway, David R. *Modern Love: Romance, Intimacy and The Marriage Crisis.* New York and London: New York University Press, 2003.

Silver, Cynthia. "Being There: The Time Dual-Earner Couples Spend with their Children." *Canadian Social Trends*, 57 (Summer 2000): 26–29.

Simms, Glenda P. "Racism as a Barrier to Canadian Citizenship." In *Belonging: The Meaning and Future of Canadian Citizenship.* Montreal: McGill-Queen's University Press, 1993.

Simpson, Bob. *Changing Families: An Ethnographic Approach to Divorce and Separation.* New York: Oxford, 1998.

Solomos, John. *Race and Racism in Britain*, 2nd ed. Houndmills, Basingstoke, Hampshire: Macmillan, 1993.

Spain, Daphne, and **Suzanne Bianchi.** *Balancing Act: Motherhood, Marriage and Employment among American Women.* New York: Sage Foundation, 1996.

Spears, Shandra. "Strong Spirit, Fractured Identity: An Ojibway Adoptee's Journey to Wholeness." In *Strong Women Stories: Native Vision and Community Survival*, edited by Kim Anderson and Bonita Lawrence, 81–94. Toronto: Sumach Press, 2003.

Spears, John. "N.B. Seeks Answer to Childhood Poverty." *Toronto Star,* 31 May 1991: A21.

Statistics Canada. *Aboriginal Peoples of Canada: A Demographic Profile.* 2001 Census: analysis series. Catalogue No. 96F0030XIE2001007, 2003a. **www.statcan.ca/cgi-bin/downpub/freepub.cgi.**

———. *Canada's Ethnocultural Portrait: The Changing Mosaic.* 2001 Census: analysis series. Catalogue No. 96F0030XIE2001008, Ottawa: Ministry of Industry, 2003b. **www.statcan.ca/cgi-bin/downpub/freepub.cgi.**

————. *The Changing Profile of Canada's Labour Force.* 2001 Census: analysis series. Catalogue No. 96F0030XIE2001009, Ottawa: Ministry of Industry, 2003c. **www.statcan.ca/cgi-bin/downpub/freepub.cgi.**

————. *Income of Canadian families.* 2001 Census: analysis series. Catalogue No. 96F0030XIE2001014, Ottawa: Ministry of Industry, 2003d. **www.statcan.ca/cgi-bin/downpub/freepub.cgi.**

————. *Profile of the Canadian population by age and sex: Canada ages.* 2001 Census analysis series. Catalogue No. 96F0030XIE2001002, Ottawa: Ministry of Industry, 2003e. **www.statcan.ca/cgi-bin/downpub/freepub.cgi.**

————. Update on families, *Canadian Social Trends*, Ottawa, Summer, 11–13, 2003f.

————. *Women in Canada: Work chapter updates.* Catalogue No. 89F0133XIIE, Ottawa: Ministry of Industry, 2003g.

————. *Profile of Canadian families and households: Diversification continues.* Catalogue No. 96F0030XIE2001003, Ottawa: Ministry of Industry, 2002. **www.statcan.ca/cgi-bin/downpub/freepub.cgi.**

————. *Changing Conjugal Life in Canada.* General Social Survey—Cycle 15. Catalogue No. 89-576-XIE, Ottawa: Ministry of Industry, 2002. **www.statcan.ca/cgi-bin/downpub/freepub.cgi.**

————. *Canadians with Disabilities.* Canadian Centre for Justice, Statistics Profile Series Catalogue No. 85F0033MIE, Ottawa: Ministry of Industry, 2001a. **www.statcan.ca/cgi-bin/downpub/freepub.cgi.**

————. *A Profile of Disabilty in Canada, 2001.* Catalogue no. 89-577-XIE, Ottawa: Ministry of Industry, 2001b. **www.statcan.ca/cgi-bin/downpub/freepub.cgi.**

Steil, Janice M. *Marital Equality: Its Relationship to the Well-Being of Husbands and Wives.* Thousand Oaks: Sage, 1997.

Stobert, Susan, and **Anna Kemeny.** "Childfree by Choice." *Canadian Social Trends*, Ottawa: Statistics Canada, Summer, 7–10, 2003.

Straus, M.A., and **Gelles, R. J.** *Physical Violence in American Families: Risk Factors and Adaptation to Violence in 8,145 families.* New Brunswick, NJ: Transactional Books, 1990.

Swartz, Karen. *Life Transitions of Women with Disabilities' Personal Reflections on Education: A Participatory Research Approach.* Master's Thesis, York University, Graduate Program in Education, 1996.

Tobin, Pam, and **Anonymous.** "Invisible Lives, Visible Strength: Stories of Northern Ontario Lesbians." In *Changing Lives: Women in Northern Ontario*, edited by Margaret Kechnie and Marge Reitsma-Street, 94–104. Toronto: Dundurn Press, 1996.

Turcotte, P. *Changing Conjugal Life in Canada.* The Daily, Statistics Canada, July 11, 2002. **www.statcan.ca/cgi-bin/downpub/freepub.cgi.**

Tyyska, Vappu. *Long and Winding Road: Adolescents and Youth in Canada Today.* Toronto: Canadian Scholars' Press Inc, 2001.

Vosko, Leah. *Temporary Work: The Gendered Rise of Precarious Employment Relationship.* Toronto: University of Toronto Press, 2000.

Ward, W. Peter. *White Canada Forever: Popular Attitudes and Public Policy Towards Orientals in British Columbia.* McGill-Queens University Press, Montreal, 1978.

Warner, Michael. *Fear of a Queer Planet: Queer Politics and Social Theory,* Minneapolis: University of Minnesota Press, 1994.

Walker, James W. *A History of Blacks in Canada: A Study Guide for Teachers and Students.* Supply and Services, Hull, Quebec: Minister of State Multiculturalism, 1980.

Wendell, Susan. "Towards a Feminist Theory of Disability." *Hypatia* 4/2 (Summer 1989).

Weston, Kath. *Families We Choose: Lesbians, Gays, Kinship.* New York: Columbia University Press, 1991.

Williams, Dorothy W. *Blacks in Montreal, 1628–1986: An Urban Demography.* Cowansville, Quebec:Editions Yvon Blais, 1989.

Winks, Robin. "Negroes in the Maritimes: An Introductory Survey." *Dalhousie Review* Winter 1968–69.

Women for Economic Survival. *Women and Economic Hard Times: A Record.* Victoria: Women for Economic Survival and the University of Victoria, 1984.

Woodill, Jennifer and **Alex Vamos.** *Personal Communication.* January, 2004.

WEBLINKS

http://www.vifamily.ca

The Vanier Institute of the Family website contains the most up-to-date statistics and analysis of Canadian families.

http://www.statscan.ca

Statistics Canada provides the most recent Canadian information on all aspects of marriage including marital status, common-law status, families, dwellings, and households.

Equality for Gay and Lesbian Everywhere.

http://www.egale.ca

The Centre for Families, Work and Well-Being, University of Guelph.

http://www.uguelph.ca

This site provides up-to-date information on issues affecting family policy in Canada.

http://www.parentswithoutpartners.org

This organization is devoted to providing information for single-parent families.

chapter nine

Paid Work, Jobs, and the Illusion of Economic Security

Susannah J. Wilson

Women, like men, work primarily for economic reasons, although jobs also provide a sense of individual self-worth, economic security for families, and social cohesion for communities. At the beginning of the twenty-first century women's employment has become institutionalized to the extent that women want and expect to work. It is not institutionalized in that both work and household organization complicate the reconciliation of the conflicting demands of paid and family work. Given the dramatic increase in female labour force participation since the 1960s, we might have expected to see a parallel shift in unpaid work, but this has not been the case. Women continue to do most of the housework and take responsibility for dependant care. The fact that younger and more highly educated men do more housework is a positive sign, but generally change has been very slow.

From 1950 until the 1970s, the Canadian economy was buoyant, and women were pulled into the labour force by expanding opportunities. The picture in the last quarter of the century, following a recession in the early 1980s and a second in the early 1990s was far more bleak. In this period, real incomes declined, and the labour market became less stable. Jobs for both men and women were less secure, and more jobs were part-time or temporary. More men and women have become self-employed, but few entrepreneurs are well paid. It is too early to tell what the impact of this persistent job insecurity has been on unpaid work at home. There has been an increase in the number of "stay-at-home" dads, but this seems less a decision to focus on fathering than an adjustment to unemployment.

This chapter looks at changes in women's paid employment, at increasing employment rates but high rates of part-time and self-employment. It also looks at how unemployment and job insecurity, coupled with the erosion of the safety net, have affected women and their families. Finally it considers how education, collective bargaining, and work-family policies have altered labour market inequalities. What changes have helped most? What have been the greatest barriers? As will be clear in the discussion, the problems of labour market segmentation and low pay are well entrenched. Addressing labour force inequality through legislative change was a key strategy for both first- and second-wave feminists.

First-wave feminists were concerned about a range of labour, health, and welfare issues and sought institutional changes to protect women and children. The early reformers were blocked in their efforts to institute change because they could not vote, or run for office, so obtaining the vote became a focus. What began as a means to an end became a lengthy campaign as "suffragettes" in Great Britain, the United States, and Canada worked for more than half a century to gain the right to vote. Although women continued to lobby for educational, labour, health, and welfare reforms during this period, and during the Great Depression and World War Two, it was not until the 1960s that feminists found another powerful catalyst. Although Canadian women's groups were influenced by the increasingly vocal women's liberation movement in the United States, liberal feminists in Canada were drawn together in their demand for a Royal Commission on the Status of Women (RCSW).

Liberal feminists initiated the RCSW with the intention that it "ensure for women equal opportunity with men in all aspects of Canadian society" (RCSW, 1970: viii). When published in 1970, the RCSW report provided a detailed analysis of inequalities in Canada, and its 167 recommendations set the liberal feminist agenda for the next 15 years. The focus of liberal feminism was equality of opportunity in education and work. Working within the system, liberal feminists pushed for legislative changes to remove barriers and counter discrimination. Educational barriers, inadequate childcare, discriminatory hiring and promotion, and unequal pay were all focal points for change. Indeed it was not until 1964 in Canada that the practice of wage discrimination became illegal, and not until 1972 that lower minimum wages for women were disallowed.

The focus of socialist feminists is more on the relationships between paid and unpaid work and women's attempts to reconcile the two reinforce inequities in both areas. Because women assume responsibility for housework and children, they are more likely to work part-time, not be promoted, be absent for family reasons, and so on. Because women earn less and appear less committed to the labour force, they, not fathers, stay home with sick children, work part-time, and so on. Labour force inequalities and imbalances in the distribution of housework therefore become self-fulfilling prophecies. In addition, as Marxist feminists' analysis of housework shows, domestic work in private homes serves the interests of capitalism as well as the interests of family members. So, socialist feminists want to change the organization of domestic labour *and* the organization of paid work. An important vehicle for change has been the union movement, particularly public-sector unions where inroads have been made in support of family issues. Socialist feminists also draw our attention to ways sexual oppression is confounded by race, class, sexual orientation, and ability. Women are not equally oppressed; men are not equally privileged. Social feminists are critical of the white, middle-class heterosexual, Western bias of mainstream liberal strategies that ignore these differences.

WOMEN'S INCREASED LABOUR FORCE PARTICIPATION

Canadian women have among the highest rates of labour force participation in the world. The following paragraphs describe women's increased labour force participation rates, the increased employment of married women and mothers, and the effect of children on women's paid work. Although some women worked for pay in the nineteenth century, until the 1950s, the typical working woman was young, single and childless. In 1951, fewer than 8 percent of married women were in the labour force. In 2002, 56 percent of Canadian women had jobs, and participation rates for married women, including mothers of young children, were very similar to the rates for single women.[1]Most of the growth took place in the late 1970s and 1980s. Predictably, women's participation rates increase during periods of economic expansion and slow down during recessions. Rates peaked in 1989, prior to the 1990–92 recession. During recessionary cycles, young women are affected most. They have the least experience and are most likely to remain in school.

In the 1970s participation rates were highest for young women (aged 15–24). By the 1980s participation rates were higher for women 25–54 than for younger (or older) women. Although these rates remain high, they are lower than participation rates for men in this age range. In the 1980s married women were less likely than single, separated, or divorced women to be in the labour force. Now, participation rates for single and married women 25 and over are very similar, and young (15–24 years) married women have higher participation rates than young single women.

The labour force participation rate for immigrant women 25–44 was 63.9 percent in 2001, and the employment rate was 38.4 percent. For all immigrants (men and women) over 15, participation and employment rates increase with educational qualifications. 51.8 percent of university educated immigrants are employed compared with 43.5 percent with high school graduation. Employment is also influenced by region of birth (highest for immigrants from the United States and Oceania and lowest for immigrants from Africa) and is much higher for immigrants with knowledge of English or French (Statistics Canada, *Longitudinal Survey,* 2003).

Having young children remains a deterrent to women's labour force participation, although the labour force participation of women with school-aged and preschool-aged children has dramatically increased over the last two decades, particularly for mothers with children under three. According to Gunderson (1998), women with children were 14 percent less likely to be in the labour force in 1991 than women without children. The 1995 Statistics Canada *Survey of Work Arrangements* found that mothers of preschool children were slightly less likely to work a Monday to Friday schedule (59 percent compared with 64 percent), and slightly more likely to do shift work (29 percent compared with 25 percent). Mothers of young children were also more apt to work part-time (31 percent compared with 21 percent), have flexible work schedules (28 percent compared with 25 percent), and work from home (13 percent compared with 11 percent) (Akyeampong, 1997).

Employed women typically have more work interruptions than men, but this difference too has declined over time. This is because women today marry later, have smaller families, and take shorter maternity leaves. About 60 percent of women return to work within six months of giving birth. Ninety percent return within a year. Self-employed women and women who do not receive maternity benefits are more likely to return to work within a few weeks, suggesting that these decisions are economically driven (Marshall, 1999). Not surprisingly, mothers who contribute all or much of the total family income are more likely to remain employed, exit from employment more slowly, and return to employment more quickly after childbirth.

In December 2000, parental leave benefits were increased from 10 to 35 weeks. Parental leave may be used by either parent or split between them. This is in addition to 15 weeks of maternity benefit. When Katherine Marshall (2003) looked at the impact of this increase she found that there was a significant increase in maternity leave *for those who receive benefits*. The problem of course is that 40 percent to 45 percent of mothers of newborns are not covered by maternity or parental benefits. About 10 percent of fathers participate in the parental benefits program.

Since 2000, the employment of lone parents whose youngest child is 6–15 has increased to the point that their participation rates are only slightly lower than women with partners whose children are at this age (Statistics Canada: *Women in Canada,* 2003: 16). This increased labour force participation has resulted in an increase in the average income of female lone-parent families and a decrease in the proportion of these families living with low income. Female lone parents also have higher rates of unemployment (Statistics Canada, *Women in the Labour Force,* 1994: 47). Clearly, barriers to employment are extremely high for these women. Recently Ontario sole-support mothers on social assistance were asked what they saw as the biggest problem in finding employment. The first issue was that the jobs for which they qualified would not provide enough income to support their families. They also worried about the loss of benefits associated with finding employment and leaving welfare (Lynn and Todoroff, 1999: 72).

Part-Time Employment

An important characteristic of women's labour force participation is the extent of part-time work (defined as less than 30 hours a week). Part-time work developed as a way of encouraging first married women, then youth, and, more recently, retirees, into sales and service jobs. Early on, married women were encouraged into the labour force by part-time work opportunities. In 1999 one in five Canadian workers worked part-time. Seventy-three percent of these would rather have worked full-time (Marshall, 2000: 25) Now, women dominate the ranks of part-time employees. More than 70 percent of part-time work is done by women and one-quarter of employed women work part-time, compared with about 10 percent of men. Teenagers and young people are more likely to work part-time, and the male/female differences are smaller for young workers. As we might predict, the numbers of part-timers increase during a recession and decrease during an upturn. Thus, in the late 1980s the numbers of part-time jobs declined but increased again in the recession of the early 1990s. In the last quarter of the century the proportion of women working part-time increased. The fact that men's part-time employment increased as well (although rates are much lower) suggests that part-time work is less a choice than a force of circumstances.

Part-time employment is a double-edged sword. The key advantage is flexibility, and the flexibility extends to both employees and employers. But the advantages to the employer (low labour costs) are disadvantages to employees (low pay, no benefits). Technology has meant that many part-time jobs require little skill or training. The conditions of low-skilled work are not appealing, and there are few if any opportunities for advancement. Few part-time jobs are unionized. From the employer's point of view, these conditions make it easy to manage fluctuating demand. When demand increases, new employees can be trained easily. When demand tapers off, employees can be let go.

For many women, part-time work was a good compromise, allowing the opportunity of combining paid work and family responsibilities or leisure. Fast and Frederick (1996) found that women who work part-time feel less time pressure than women who work full-time—but they do more housework than full-time employees. The fact that a higher proportion of women with children work part-time, especially mothers of young children, suggests that this is a way for some women to reconcile the competing demands of paid and unpaid work. Duffy and Pupo (1992) interviewed women working part-time in Ontario, most of whom were married mothers. Their decision to work was based on the economic pressure they felt. Part-time work was preferable because it was more manageable. The 2002 Labour Force Survey asked Canadian men and women their reasons for working part-time. The most significant reasons given by 75.1 percent of young men and 72.3 percent of young women was "going to school." The most important reason women aged 25–44 work part-time is "caring for children." More than half of the young men in this age group said they worked part-time because of business conditions or an inability to find full-time work. Approximately the same proportions of men (56.5 percent) and women (54.4 percent) over 45 indicated that they work part-time because it is their personal preference, but a significant proportion of men (30.4 percent) and women (25.4 percent) over 45 couldn't find full-time work (Statistics Canada: *Women in Canada,* 2003: 19).

Part-time jobs are more common in the sales and service sectors and rare in manufacturing. Indeed, growth in sales and service accounts for most of the growth in part-time work. Women, and more recently teenagers and retirees, have been available for this kind of work. As might be predicted, the majority of the increased number of seniors working part-time are women. As Duffy (1997: 174) suggests, part-time employment for seniors may be an increasingly important aspect of the gendering of work. Whether employed full-time or part-time, women typically work in a narrow range of jobs where they earn less than men.

Segregation and the Wage Gap

Labour force segregation and pay differentials have deep historical roots. Indeed, what made women attractive to employers was that they were inexpensive to hire. At the base of these entrenched patterns are assumptions about women's family and domestic responsibilities. The wage gap persists whether one is measuring full- or part-time work, or calculating on the basis of hourly wage or annual income. According to Statistics Canada the earnings ratio (the ratio of women's to men's earnings) has remained relatively stable for the last decade. Women earn between 62 percent and 65 percent of what men earn. The wage gap is only partially explained: the explained portion includes productivity-related factors such as education and work experience, the unexplained portion is presumed to be due to discrimination. Over time, the unexplained portion has declined. Indeed, the wage gap has narrowed to about 90 percent for young people and is also narrow for those with high education and for unionized workers. It does, however, remain large for middle-aged and older workers, reflecting the high price these women have paid for accommodating family responsibilities. The key to the recent narrowing of the wage gap is neither effective legislation nor changing attitudes. The big change in the 1990s has been the fact that men's wages have stagnated or declined.

In the 1950s, the impetus to women's increased involvement in paid work was the expansion of jobs in health, education, welfare, financial services, and retail sales. The growth of the public sector in the 1960s and 1970s provided jobs for women in schools, hospitals, and in the provincial and federal governments. As Luxton and Reiter (1997) argue, the growth of *some* public-sector jobs both provided employment to women *and* filled some unmet needs (such as childcare) for working women. In other words, women found employment in services such as childcare—and the availability of childcare services enabled women to enter the work force.

The concentration of women in service and sales jobs has been a persistent aspect of the labour force since these figures were first calculated in the 1891 census. From the early years of women's paid employment, women have worked in a limited number of jobs, and jobs in which they are the majority. The leading occupations for women in 1961 were "stenographers, typists, and clerk-typist," and 96.8 percent of people doing this work were women! By 1993, one-third of employed women were clerical workers, and 80.2 percent of clerical workers were women. Occupational segregation has implications for the instability of women's work, because of the extent of part-time work in the sales and service sector, and for economic security, because the jobs that women dominate are low paying.

The discussion of labour force segregation and pay inequity obscures a fundamental point about diversity among women. Women are not equally disadvantaged in paid employment. Nor are men equally privileged. Disadvantage is multidimensional and related to race, ethnicity, immigration status, ability, and sexual orientation as well as gender. Statistics Canada provides aggregate labour force data for immigrant and visible-minority Canadians, but it is difficult to untangle the effects of gender, race, recent immigration, and language as predictors of labour market "success." Labour force participation rates for visible-minority women and immigrant women are slightly lower than for non-visible-minority and Canadian-born women, but the differences are small. Immigrant women are also less likely to be unemployed (Statistics Canada, *Women in Canada,* 1995). However, labour force participation varies by country of origin and race, with Filipino women and Blacks having the highest rates. West Asian, Southeast Asian, Arab, and Latin-American women were less likely to be employed (Kelly, 1995).

Immigrant women earn less than Canadian-born women and far less than immigrant men. Some of this difference can be explained by recent immigration. Recent immigrants earn considerably less than immigrants who have been in Canada for a number of years. A study of immigrant earnings found that the real earnings of recent immigrant men fell in the years between 1980 and 2000, while the real earnings of recent immigrant women rose (Statistics Canada, *The Daily,* October 8, 2003). This reflected the pattern of wages for Canadian-born men and women. Thirty-eight percent of women who immigrated to Canada between 1995 and 1999 had university degrees, compared with 22 percent of employed Canadian-born women—but this was not reflected in earnings. Visible-minority immigrants have lower average employment income than other immigrants, and Canadian-born visible minorities earn less than non-visible-minority Canadian-born workers (Statistics Canada, *The Daily,* March 12, 1998). Christofides and Swidinsky (1994: 45) found a predictable additive effect: White females face the same pay disadvantage as minority males in the labour market, and minority women are more disadvantaged than either.

If racial and ethnic minority women are doubly disadvantaged compared with majority or "White" women, immigrant visible-minority women are triply disadvantaged. Asian immigrant women who speak English or French are disproportionately employed in health and welfare and earn higher incomes than Canadian-born women. Asian women who do not speak English or French are employed in service, accommodation, and food industries and earn low wages (Boyd, 1999). Visible-minority women are less likely than non-visible-minority women to work in professional occupations and are more likely to be underemployed (Gabriel, 1999: 148). Immigrant and visible-minority women are over-represented among homeworkers where they receive very low pay—typically below the legislated minimum wage (149).

ECONOMIC INSECURITY IN THE 1990S

Participation rates for women continued to rise in the 1980s, and, increasingly, work patterns of younger men and women were similar—although they continued to work in different industries and do different kinds of jobs. But the recession of the early 1990s was deep, and, when coupled with the erosion of the welfare state, created a period of deeply felt economic insecurity for Canadian families. Only 51 percent of Canadians who worked at some point in 1995 worked full-time, full-year. Another 8 percent worked part-time full-year. The rest of the labour force—more than 40 percent—of Canadians did not work a full year (Statistics Canada, *The Daily*, March 17, 1998). The period of erosion of the welfare state between 1980 and 1995 created a double jeopardy for women "as workers whose jobs were threatened and as people who use the threatened services" (Luxton and Reiter, 1997: 198).

Although fewer than half of all families in 1996 were married couples with children, most Canadian women live with someone else—a partner, a child, or a parent. Although all families feel some degree of economic insecurity, two-income families will be buffered and single-parent and poor families most disadvantaged. In the face of declining male employment rates, and a stagnation of men's real earnings over the past 20 years, women's paid work has become an increasingly important part of family economic survival. Family incomes have risen because more wives are employed—and more employed wives work full-time. In short, families increasingly rely on women's incomes. We have also seen an increase in the number of families in which wives earn more than husbands and an increase in the number of families in which wives are the *only* breadwinner.

In 1997, husbands were the only income earners in 16.5 percent of husband-wife families, and 61.3 percent of husband-wife families were dual-earner (Statistics Canada, Catalogue 13-215-X1B, 1999). Some (17.4 percent) of the remaining families had no earners, and in 5 percent of families, wives were the only earners. In addition to the wages of two parents, many families rely on children's earnings as well. Wives' earnings relative to husbands' have also increased since the 1960s. One of the consequences of this shift is an increase in the number of families in which wives earn more than their husbands. In 1997 in 14.3 percent of husband-wife families, wives earned more than husbands. The fact that these numbers accelerated during the recessionary years of 1990–92 supports the idea that some wives may have become main breadwinners. Indeed, in approximately one-third of families in which wives earned more, husbands had been unemployed at some point during the year. Almost half of those husbands had been unemployed 26 weeks or more.

In 1997 only 31 percent of husband-wife families with at least one child under 16 were single-earner compared with 59 percent in 1976. In an increasing number of these single-earner families, it is wives who are breadwinners. Although they represent a small proportion of all families, the numbers are increasing dramatically (Marshall, 1998b). (We do not know how many families choose to have a "stay-at-home dad.") Part of the increase is presumably due to job loss, limited employment opportunities, and underemployment.

"Among the stay-at-home parents who have worked in the past year, 67 percent of fathers and 43 percent of mothers said they had lost their last job" (Marshall, 1998b: 14).

The importance of a second income is clear when we consider the high risk of poverty faced by single mothers. In 1996, 61.4 percent of single mothers under 65 with children under 18 were poor. More than 90 percent of single mothers under 25 were poor (National Council of Welfare, 1998: 35). Family income and unemployment fluctuate with the economy, and poverty rates for working Canadians are normally 3–5 percentage points above the unemployment rate (National Council of Welfare, 1998: 13). Although single-parent families are at far greater risk of poverty than two-parent families, there are more poor children living with two parents than one. Is child poverty more affected by changes in the labour market or by family structure changes? An analysis of the probability that Canadian children will move in to or out of low income found that for individual children, marriage, separation, and divorce have greater impact on children's economic well-being than parental job change. However, changes in family status are infrequent compared with job changes, so in the aggregate, the effect of the two factors is almost equal (Picot, Zyblock, and Pyper, 1999).

In the last two decades world economic restructuring resulted in plant closures, extensive layoffs in the public and private sectors, and periods of high unemployment in Canada. When coupled with government cutbacks and the continued erosion of the safety net, these changes have threatened the economic security of many Canadian families. The bulk of job creation during this period was in part-time work and self-employment. Indeed, self-employment accounted for 80 percent of all job growth in Canada between 1989 and 1997. Part-time work accounted for all net gains in paid (compared with self-) employment. However, as we will argue later in this chapter, although self-employment and part-time work have some advantages for some women, they share the disadvantages of low pay and low job security. Women and young people are more likely to be employed in these marginal areas of the labour market. They are also (at different stages of economic cycles) more apt to be unemployed.

UNEMPLOYMENT

The unemployment rate typically varies with the economy, rising during recessions and falling with economic expansion. Unemployment levels were higher during the recessions of the early 1980s and 1990s than at any time since the Depression. In 1989 Canada's unemployment rate was 7.5 percent. Three years later, in November 1992, unemployment reached a high of 11.9 percent. By June 1999 the rate had dropped again to 7.6 percent (Statistics Canada, *Labour Force Update*, Summer, 1999: 8). Seasonally adjusted unemployment rates fluctuated between 6.7 percent and 8 percent between January 2000 and June 2003 (Statistics Canada, *The Labour Force Survey*, July 2003). Rates for men and women differ, and youth unemployment is typically much higher than for older, experienced workers (Gower, 1996). Immigrant women, women who speak neither English nor French, and women with low education also have high unemployment (Gunderson, 1998: 197).

The 1990s were particularly hard for *young* Canadians seeking work. During the early 1990s young women were less affected by unemployment than young men. This is a reversal of the situation in the late 1980s, when young women had higher unemployment (Statistics Canada, *Women in the Labour Force*, 1994: 24). Youth unemployment remained high for the whole of the 1990s, and teenagers were hardest hit. The unemployment rate for 15- to 19-year-olds actively seeking work was 20 percent in 1998. Forty percent of this group had no work experience. Youth participation rates declined during this period primarily because more young people were in school. Prolonged low youth employment rates have been accompanied by higher rates of school attendance (Sunter and Bowlby, 1998). Labour force participation for young people who were also students was 36 percent in 1980, 47.3 percent in 1989, 42.6 percent in 1993, and 40.3 percent in 1997 (Sunter and Bowlby, 1998: 17).

Core-aged (25–54) unemployment is considerably lower than youth unemployment. In the 1970s and 1980s women had higher unemployment than men—except during the recession of the early 1980s when men's unemployment was greater. In the early 1990s women's unemployment was again lower than men's. This can be explained by labour market segregation. Layoffs in the early 1990s were greatest in manufacturing, construction, forestry, fishing, mining, oil, and gas—all areas where male workers far outnumber females (Statistics Canada, *Labour Force Update*, Summer, 1999: 10). Women typically experience a shorter period of unemployment than men, although the duration of unemployment increases with age (Statistics Canada, *Women in the Labour Force*, 1994: 22–24).

Unemployment for older workers (55+) is low. This in part reflects the advantage of experience and seniority. It also reflects that older workers may move into retirement if permanently laid off. On the other hand, when older workers are unemployed, they tend to stay unemployed for a longer period than their younger counterparts. Labour force participation rates for men aged 55 to 64 have declined over time (from 77 percent in 1976 to 59 percent in 1995). Participation rates for women in this age group are much lower but have risen slightly from 32 percent in 1976 to 36 percent in 1997 (Sunter and Bowlby, 1998: 20). As the wave of women baby boomers enters this age group, we might expect to see even higher participation rates. We will have to wait to see whether age or gender has the greatest impact. In other words, will older women's rates continue to climb or will they, like men's rates, begin to decline?

It is hard to determine how much older men's declining participation reflects push and how much pull. The 1994 General Social Survey compared reasons for retirement in two periods: 1983–88 and 1989–94. In both periods health and personal choice were the main reasons given. The proportion retiring because of early retirement packages almost doubled in the 1990s, but the proportion retiring because of unemployment rose slightly (Sunter and Bowlby, 1998: 20). We have no way of knowing how many retirees are more appropriately called discouraged workers. Discouraged workers are those who are unemployed and have stopped looking for work because they believe no one will hire them. An increased number of men in the 55 to 64 age group are neither employed nor retired (Cheal, 1998: 15). Male unemployment has implications for women's employment and for family economic security.

POLARIZATION OF JOBS

Against this background of unemployment, the current labour market is characterized by an increased polarization of jobs, job conditions, hours worked, and income. Although there has been job growth in technically demanding and high-paying jobs, most new jobs have been in part-time, contract, and temporary employment, or self-employment. There are a relatively small number of well-compensated, skilled, stable new jobs alongside a large number of new jobs requiring little skill, where pay is low, and there is little stability. This phenomenon has been referred to as the casualization or polarization of the labour market. Because of low rates of job creation and high unemployment, the early 1990s amounted to a jobless recovery. Slight improvements in the latter half of the decade have been described as job-poor growth (Burke and Shields, 1999). Participation rates for men and women in the 1990s did not return to pre-recession levels.

Polarization is also reflected in income distribution. In the face of declining real wages, the number of people living in poverty has increased, as have numbers in the highly compensated group, while the middle is shrinking. As Yalnizyan (1998: 27) explains in her study *The Growing Gap,* there is a "remarkable symmetry" emerging in the labour market. Some workers are underemployed; others work excessively long hours. One-fifth of jobs are part-time while one-fifth of employees work overtime. More overtime is unpaid, although men are more likely to get paid for their overtime hours. Among women who work overtime, 62 percent don't get paid. "Unpaid overtime is increasingly the price one is expected to pay for maintaining a position in the full-time labour market."

PART-TIME WORK AND SELF-EMPLOYMENT: COMPROMISE OR ACCOMMODATION?

The most important source of new jobs in the 1980s was part-time employment. The most important source of new jobs in the 1990s was self-employment. Women have long dominated part-time employment, and their rates of self-employment are increasing faster than men's. Are these non-standard forms of employment good or bad for women?

In December 1999, 17.9 percent of jobs were part-time (Statistics Canada, *The Daily,* January 7, 2000). Women, teenagers, and seniors filled the part-time ranks, not always out of choice. Part-time work is both a promise and a problem for women (Duffy and Pupo, 1992: 39). For some women, part-time work is a manageable choice allowing them to combine work and family responsibilities. For other women it is insecure and poorly paid but the only type of work available. Although women are no more or less likely than men to moonlight, they are more likely to combine two part-time jobs (Kimmel and Powell, 1999). "The major policy implication here is that a combination of multiple part-time jobs may result in full-time hours of work but will not generate the employment benefits usually associated with full-time jobs" (Chaykowski and Powell, 1999: S12).

During the early 1990s, 34 percent of women working part-time said they would have preferred full-time work—up from 20 percent in 1989 (Statistics Canada, *Women in the Labour Force,* 1994: 13). This group is referred to as involuntary part-timers, or as underemployed. Usually underemployment trends parallel unemployment, rising in recessions and dropping during recovery periods. This did not happen in the 1990s. Unemployment improved, but underemployment did not—which is why this period is described as a jobless or job-poor recovery. Almost half (46 percent) of the underemployed were core-aged (25–54) women (Statistics Canada, *Labour Force Update,* 1999: 20). Increasingly, jobs in sales, service, health care, and so on, are done on a part-time or temporary basis. Regions with the highest unemployment have the highest proportions of involuntary part-time work. We do not know the extent to which women turn to self-employment because they are dissatisfied with their employment options.

The increased number of self-employed women is a widespread pattern, occurring in the United States, Britain, Belgium, Finland, Germany, Italy, and Spain (Hughes, 1999: 3). The proportion of women who are self-employed is higher in Canada than in other OECD countries, including the United States (Hughes, 2003: 4). Indeed, much of the growth in the Canadian economy has come from small business and self-employment, and the self-employment sector is growing faster than the paid employment sector. From 1990 to 1998 the labour market expanded by 775 000 jobs. Three-quarters of these were in the self-employed sector (Lin, Yates, and Picot, 1999: 3). In 2002 more than 2.3 million Canadians were self-employed (Statistics Canada, *Women in Canada*, 2003: 20). Although there are twice as many self-employed men as women, the number of women entrepreneurs is rising. In 1997, 21.1 percent of men were self-employed compared with 13.9 percent of women (Hughes, 1999: vi) and about one-third of the self-employed labour force were women (compared with 1 in 25 in 1931). Immigrants have higher rates of self-employment than the Canadian-born population, and this holds for immigrant women as well as men (Gardner, 1994: 15–16). The business immigrant program created during the 1980s added to the number of immigrant entrepreneurs. Indeed immigrants who arrived in Canada in the 1990s are more likely to be self-employed than immigrants who arrived earlier.

As with part-time work, this growth is in part a result of a shift to a service economy. Self-employment also reflects organizational strategy. Employers have been able to fill the gaps created by downsizing and restructuring with temporary and contract employees. The fact that the majority of self-employed jobs are poorly compensated suggests that self-employment is not always an attractive choice. Many people, it seems, become self-employed because they cannot find other jobs.

Are people drawn or pushed into self-employment? Lin, Yates, and Picot, (1999: 11) found that women's self-employment entry rate is more responsive to the unemployment rate than men's, suggesting that women are pushed by unemployment to consider self-employment. For some women, self-employment may be a positive alternative to paid work. There are also some clear disadvantages. The fact that the incidence of self-employment is higher for women who did not complete high school may indicate opportunities for women with low formal education. Women appear to use self-employment as a way of balancing work and family demands (Hughes, 1999: vii). In a survey of self-employed Canadians, both men and women indicated that one of the aspects they liked best about self-employment was "entrepreneurial values." Second for women was flexible hours and the ability to work from home. Both men and women disliked the insecurity, long hours, and income fluctuations (Statistics Canada, *The Daily*, January 7, 2002). Ostensibly, the self-employed have more control over their work. Yet the self-employed work many more hours per week than employees, although women work fewer hours than men.

Earnings for self-employed workers are polarized, and the wage gap between men and women is greater than among paid workers. A small percentage of the self-employed earn very high incomes; the majority earn very little. In 1995 more than half of "own account self-employed" earned less than $20 000 (Hughes, 1999: vii). Self-employed women earn less than women who are paid employees—about half of what self-employed men earn. The earnings ratio for self-employed women was 46.1 percent in 1967 and 63.8 percent in 1997 (Drolet, 1999: 15). Hughes (2003: 11) argues that there is greater polarization of earnings among self-employed women compared while women paid workers. One of the reasons for the discrepancy is the extent of part-time work among self-employed women. Another reason is that women entrepreneurs work in fields (sales and service) where earnings are typically low (Cohen, 1996). Among the self-employed, women work in a narrower range of jobs than men. As in paid employment, self-employed women are concentrated in sales and service. In 1994, 37 percent of self-employed women worked in service occupations, and an additional 21 percent worked in sales. These workers will not receive benefits available to paid workers.

Self-employed workers tend to be older, presumably because they can draw on a base of experience as employees. Age also explains the higher rates of self-employment for married persons. At least one of the partners is self-employed in one-third of dual-earning families (Marshall, 1998a: 10). In many of these families the couple works together. The most common businesses were agriculture and retail. These couples worked long hours but had relatively low combined incomes of less than $40 000 (Marshall, 1998a).

To summarize, we have argued that the early post-war years saw an unprecedented increase in women's labour force participation. The rapid changes in women's paid work can be explained by a combination of factors. The expansion of the economy, particularly in health, education, and welfare, pulled women into the labour force with the lure of jobs. The jobs women filled, and the extent of part-time work, reflected women's domestic strengths. Women taught school, nursed, and did clerical work, but they also continued to care for their families. In some ways, family responsibilities have been less demanding for women since the 1960s than for earlier generations. The age of marriage increased, and families were smaller. Rising standards of living meant that more labour-saving appliances were available to ease the burden of housework. In the 1950s and 1960s, married women's earnings provided luxuries that families could not otherwise afford. But, beginning in the 1970s, the rules changed. Real wages began to stagnate in the mid-1970s, and it became less possible to live well on the wages of a single breadwinner (Wilson, 1996: 110–11). An increasing number of women worked, not for luxuries, but because their income was necessary for their own or their family's economic security.

On the positive side, women now experience fewer overt barriers to employment. More women have attended university and became qualified for professional or managerial work. More women work in "non-traditional" fields, and the earning gap has been reduced for younger and better-educated women and for union members. But the recession of the early 1990s and the restructuring that followed have exacerbated women's economic insecurity. Labour market restructuring resulted in increasingly precarious relationships with work. More jobs are temporary, contract, part-time, and self-employed. Countless reasonably well-paid jobs held by women in the public sector and social services have simply been lost to restructuring.

One way to determine whether Canadian women have gained more than they have lost is to compare the labour market "success" of women who entered the market at different points in time. Did baby boom women who came of age in a period of economic expansion have an easier time than those who went before or than the Generation X women who followed? Louise Earl (1999) compared baby boom women to the preceding and succeeding generations using four indicators of labour market success: participation rates, full-time employment rates, unemployment, and earnings.

In 1977, baby boom women had higher labour force participation rates than women a generation older and were more likely to work full-time. They had higher unemployment rates than women 20 years older, but younger people typically have higher unemployment rates because they have less experience. But the inexperience of baby boomers was not reflected in their earnings. In 1977, young women earned *more* than women 20 years older—even though they worked fewer hours. Education was an equalizer then as now. Fifteen percent of baby boomers in the 1977 labour force held degrees compared with 6 percent of the older group, but older women with degrees earned more. In short, baby boom women had more labour market success than the preceding generation. They have also been more successful than women 20 years younger.

By 1997, employment patterns for younger and older women were very similar. In 1997, 77 percent of the baby boomers (now aged 45 to 49) were employed; 77 percent of them full-time. Generation X women, who were 25 to 29 in 1997, had a participation rate of 78 percent, and 78 percent of them were employed full-time. Twenty-seven percent of the younger group had degrees (compared with 19 percent of baby boomers), but baby boomers worked longer hours and earned more money. So, baby boom women entered an expanding labour market in 1977, out-earning women 20 years older. They maintained this advantage and out-earned younger women in 1997.

Education *has* provided an entry to better-paying, more-secure employment for women, and a buffer against unemployment. Unemployment rates for university graduates are far lower than for those with less education, particularly for younger workers. Educational differences in unemployment decline with age. Young women are better educated than young men, and women currently are a majority among undergraduate (but not graduate) students. Women make up 57 percent of full-time undergraduates in the 18- to 24-year-age group (Statistics Canada, *Perspectives*, 2002: 48). According to the 2001 census, 21 percent of men and 20 percent of women over 25 were university graduates. Eighteen percent of women and 13 percent of men were college graduates. There are, however, persistent patterns of educational segregation, and although women with university degrees earn more than women without, university-educated women still experience an earning differential compared with men.

Finnie and Wannell (1999) looked at the gender earning gap for new graduates of bachelor's level programs. They used the National Graduate Survey, a large representative sample of graduates who completed their program in 1982, 1986, and 1990. Each group of graduates was interviewed two and five years after graduation. Their findings confirm the persistence of patterns of program concentration. Women are more likely to have graduated with degrees in teaching, education, fine arts and humanities, social sciences, and other health disciplines. They were underrepresented in economics, engineering, computer science, mathematics, and the physical sciences. Employment patterns were equally consistent. Although unemployment rates were more or less equal for men and women, more women graduates worked in temporary and part-time jobs. Interestingly, men and women graduates were equally satisfied with both jobs and incomes. To no one's surprise, male graduates earned more two years after graduation, and their earnings grew at a faster rate than female graduates. Both field of study and hours of work explain part of the earning gap.

Rates of unionization for women increased in the 1960s so that now almost as many women as men belong to unions (although unionization generally has declined in Canada). The increases in unionization were due to the growth of public-sector unions. Now unionization rates stand at 30.9 percent for men and 29.3 percent for women (Statistics Canada, *The Daily*, August 24, 1999). The rate of unionization among women in the public sector was 72.5 percent, slightly higher than the men's rate. This reflects women's dominance in education and health care.

On average, unionized female workers employed full-time earn 90 percent of the hourly wages earned by their male counterparts, and both men and women members earn higher wages than non-unionized employees (Statistics Canada, *The Daily*, August 24, 1999). Unionized workers also receive better benefits including benefits specifically related to domestic and family responsibility. Public-sector unions have also led the way in protecting workers against discrimination and sexual harassment, reducing health and safety risks, and extending benefits to same-sex couples. "The major advances that women have made in achieving concrete gains in paid employment have been through the union movement" (Luxton and Reiter, 1997: 209).

WOMEN'S DOUBLE DAY

The need to manage both family care and paid employment has been necessary as long as women have been in the labour force. But it was not until the 1970s that women's labour force participation reached the point that balancing became widespread. The need to balance is an issue for parents of young children and those with both child and adult family responsibilities. An increasing number of Canadians care for dependent adults, responsibilities that also affect working life. The 1996 General Social Survey found that 15 percent of women and 10 percent of men who had a job outside the home were providing care to someone with a long-term health problem. Half said that caregiving affected their employment, for example, causing them to arrive late for or miss work. The situation for all those with dependant care is exacerbated by the aging of the population and cutbacks in social service supports.

Study after study documents the stability of the traditional division of labour. For example, the 1996 census, the first to ask about unpaid household work, found that although more than 90 percent of Canadians said they did some form of unpaid household work, the burden fell on women. More women than men did housework and childcare, and provided assistance to a senior. Women also devoted more hours to these activities than men (Statistics Canada, *The Daily*, March 17, 1998). There has been increased involvement in housework by young, highly educated men, but employed women still do most household work in most homes. The fact that men earn more money reinforces this division of labour and (in the absence of institutionalized social or workplace supports) leaves women dependent on the good will of a spouse or employer to manage.

Hessing (1993) interviewed Canadian mothers who worked in full-time clerical jobs about how they managed the demands of work and family. Her study illustrates several key coping strategies. Typically, these mothers experienced the double day not as discrete and sequential tasks or responsibilities, but as overlapping "webbed" demands. Their coping strategies emphasize the importance of supportive work-family policies. Many were able to use the daycare facilities at their place of employment. Others worked a compressed week to take every tenth working day off to run errands, pre-prepare meals, and spend time with children. These women became skilled time managers in order to squeeze more household tasks into the time available. They worked long hours, using evenings for housework, not leisure. Noon hours were used for grocery shopping and household errands, or occasionally visiting children's schools. They borrowed time by preparing bag lunches the evening before and making several meals at once. They rarely had the luxury of doing one job at a time.

A key coping strategy for women in Hessing's study was to develop a support network including partners, family, and friends. Older children were enlisted to help take responsibility for younger ones, but it is the extended family who provide most emergency help. Managing the support system is a necessary additional part of the employed mother's responsibility.

Although adept at coping, these women found the combination of full-time employment and household management stressful, physically exhausting, and emotionally draining. They were frustrated that they could not do better at both jobs and with the assumption that one should not allow home problems to interfere with paid work. They recognized that their clerical jobs held little potential for long-term satisfaction or advancement. Yet an additional coping mechanism was to portray the work as voluntary and temporary (Hessing, 1993: 57). This way of viewing work allowed women to rationalize their own lack of job success. Such a definition also created the illusion of a way out of a stressful situation.

In 1994 and 2000 the General Social Survey (GSS) asked a representative number of Canadians about workplace stress (Williams, 2003). In both years the most significant source of job stress was "too many demands or too many hours." Regardless of age, women were more likely to report feeling stressed by this. Midlife women (aged 45 to 64) experienced greatest stress in this regard. This seems to reflect women's double day. It may also reflect the way home computers have helped blur the distinction between work time and individual or family time. In 1994 when unemployment rates were high, more than one-fifth employed Canadians worried about a layoff or job loss. This was far less frequently mentioned as a source of stress in 2000.

WORK AND FAMILY POLICY

Women's long-term connection with domestic work and childcare meant that the resolution of work and family conflicts was initially defined as a woman's issue. Increasingly, women's work patterns resemble men's, and men are assuming a larger share of domestic and family work, so that men too are affected by work and family conflicts. These conflicts are costly to both men and women in terms of stress, missed employment opportunities, (Fast and Frederick, 1996) and, we may assume, missed family opportunities as well.

Surveys confirm that the problems of work-family conflict in Canada are widespread. Duxbury and Higgins (2001) used data they collected in 1991 and 2001 to see whether the work-family conflict increased during the 1990s. Their findings suggest that more workers are experiencing greater difficulty balancing work and family responsibilities. Workers experience greater stress and deteriorating health. Jobs have become less satisfying. It is not surprising, then, that women with children experience greater stress and are more likely to suffer from depression than either childless women or men.

Until recently there was little expectation that work organizations would bend to the needs of employed parents. Consequently, work structures and work cultures were largely unresponsive to family care issues. As Hochschild noted (1989: 267), "Corporations have done little to accommodate the needs of working parents and government has done little to prod them." Some employers, in some cases as a result of union demands, have begun to develop policies and practices to recognize the dependant-care responsibilities of employees. Flexible work schedules including job sharing, flex-time, telecommuting, and flexible working hours, including part-time work with benefit and family leave, are means of accommodating employees with family responsibilities.

Most employees would like to have more control over when and where they work, as well as more control over the total number of hours of work. The 1992 General Social Survey asked Canadians about work arrangements and stress. Fast and Frederick (1996) found that part-time work and flex-time were associated with reduced stress for parents, but compressed work weeks and on-call work were actually more stressful. (There was no relationship between stress levels and self-employment, shift work, or flex-place options.) The more family-friendly the workplace environment, the greater the ability of parents to cope with competing demands.

There are three general categories of workplace supports for helping employees deal with work-family conflict: policies that allow for a reduction in hours worked, policies that allow for increased flexibility of scheduling, and policies that provide workplace supports (Glass and Estes, 1997: 294).

Reduced hours of work may be taken in part-time employment or in family leave policies such as maternity leave. Flexible scheduling may be either flex-time or flex-place options. Support policies may include provision of on-site childcare, or, more typically, information and referral services for employees. In weighing the impacts of these policies, Glass and Estes (1997: 306) conclude that the ability to work a reduced number of hours benefits both the employer and the employee, although the economic penalty makes this option unattractive for many employees. Flexible scheduling is typically defined narrowly, in terms of the ability to flex around the 10:00 a.m. to 3:00 p.m. band. Ironically, employees without primary childcare responsibilities greatly appreciate the benefit of flex-time options.

In Canada, existing supports fall short of easing the burden for employed women with family responsibilities. In part this reflects the inadequacy of relevant employment policies and in part it reflects the success of frontline managers in discouraging access to available services and supports (Skrypnek and Fast, 1996: 809). Perhaps both remain issues because of the unresolved debate about work and family strategy. Should the focus be on ways of freeing employees from work responsibilities to enable them to care for children and other family members? Or should the focus be on securing care alternatives for children and dependent adults? "These divergent perspectives suggest different policy alternatives—extended parental leave for newborns versus infant day care, paid sick days for family illness versus sick-child care, reduced or part-time work hours for parents versus extension of the school day or school year" (Glass and Estes, 1997: 292).

Canada stands between Western Europe and the United States in the development of family-supportive policies. For example, in western Europe there are universally available childcare provisions for three- to six-year-olds. The anglo countries of the United States, Canada, Australia, and the United Kingdom are the exceptions in failing to provide such coverage. Creating policy support for Canadian families is more difficult because of jurisdictional differences. Access to family-related leave, child and adult dependant-care provisions, and alternative work arrangements varies tremendously from province to province (Skrypnek and Fast, 1996).

CONCLUSION

Women's employment has always responded to economic fluctuations and changing demands in the labour force. The economic expansion of the late nineteenth century provided opportunities for paid work for men and single women, attracting immigrants and rural migrants to industrial centres. The expansion of clerical and sales jobs drew more women into paid employment in the early years of the twentieth century. However, it was not until the 1960s that large numbers of Canadian women worked for significant periods of their adult lives. It is this period of rapid increases in women's paid work that has been the focus of this chapter.

Two patterns characterize the history of women's paid work: labour force segregation and low pay. Eroding these two patterns has been the focus of liberal feminist legislative reform, and there have been significant improvements in both areas. However, it is important to remember that the most important reason for a narrowing of the income gap is the decrease in men's wages, not because of attitude change or effective legislation. More women are educated in, and later find employment in, what were only a few years ago referred to as non-traditional fields. However, the greatest gains have been made by White, middle-class, Canadian-born women. Minority and immigrant women, lesbian and bisexual women, and women living with disabilities continue to face discrimination in hiring, promotion, and pay, as evidenced by pay differentials and segregation trends.

Jobs have become increasingly insecure over the last decade. What is neutrally referred to as labour market flexibility has meant the loss of thousands of jobs. Women have been particularly affected by losses in clerical and fabricating jobs, although unemployment was high in the early 1990s for both men and women. Optimistic newspaper reports of increased employment opportunities downplay the fact that a majority of new jobs have been part-time, temporary, or self-employment. The majority of part-time workers and an increased number of the self-employed are women. These jobs, which are typically low-paid and insecure, are in sharp contrast to the small number of well-paid jobs for highly skilled employees. The labour market has become increasingly polarized in terms of both jobs and income. The *growing gap* refers to the increased divide between well-paid, secure jobs and non-standard jobs with low pay. This is a serious problem for Canada as an increasing number of workers are being marginalized at a time when social supports are being eroded.

Women's employment experiences are shaped by race, class, ability, marital status, and the number and ages of children for whom they accept responsibility. But all women are engaged in the struggle to reconcile the competing demands of paid and unpaid work. Most women, but particularly mothers of young children, work a double day. Canadian women have one of the highest rates of labour force participation in the world. But there have not been parallel adjustments in unpaid work, nor have work organizations created environments that support the needs of employed women with dependant-care responsibilities. The inequity this creates has repercussions for family life and for women's economic security. At the very least, women work longer hours than men, are paid less, have less job security, and less leisure.

Labour market insecurities have serious repercussions for family life as well. Women have fewer children, but take less time from paid employment to recover from childbirth or to spend time with their newborns. More women are single earners in two-parent families or earn more than their partners—a sign of men's job insecurity, not equality of opportunity. Women who are single parents find it extremely difficult to manage paid and unpaid work, and many are excluded from the labour force. Families with no income from employment are seriously marginalized. Clearly, dual-income families have greater economic security than single-income families, and it is women's employment that creates this security. But have we addressed the social costs of this commitment to paid employment? We know that trying to balance work and family life is particularly stressful for women and contributes to their ill health. What gaps in the quality of family life are created when parents deal with a regular diet of job insecurity and intermittent employment? Is the quality of life for the majority diminishing with increased polarization? The baby boomers experienced expanding opportunities, worked long hours, and earned high salaries on average. Their daughters had higher educations but worked less and earned relatively less. Their granddaughters are children now. What factors will shape their experience in the labour force?

ENDNOTES

1   Labour force participation rates refer to the number of people in the labour force (employed and unemployed) as a percentage of the total population. The employment rate refers to the number of people employed as a percentage of the population. For example there were 7 149 800 women over 15 in Canada in 2002, and 56.4 percent of these were employed (Statistics Canada, *Women in Canada: Work Chapter Updates,* 2003: 12)

SUGGESTED READINGS

Andrew, C., P. Armstrong, H. Armstrong, W. Clement, and **L. Vosko,** eds. 2003. *Studies in Political Economy: Developments in Feminism.* Women's Press, Toronto. This book is a collection of articles from the journal *Studies in Political Economy* looking at the intersection of feminism and political economy in the Canadian context.

Chaykowski, R., and **L. Powell,** eds. 1999. *Women and Work.* Montreal and Kingston: McGill-Queen's University Press. The papers in this collection address key issues in Canadian women's labour force participation.

Duffy, A., D. Glenday, and **N. Pupo,** eds. 1997. *Good Jobs, Bad Jobs, No Jobs: The Transformation of Work in the 21st Century.* Toronto: Harcourt Brace. This collection of papers looks at labour market dislocation in manufacturing and service industries in Canada.

Statistics Canada. 2003. *Women in Canada: Work Chapter Updates.* Catalogue No. 89F0133XIE. This is an annual publication that adds the most current data to historical trends for a complete picture of women's paid work in Canada.

DISCUSSION QUESTIONS

1. Describe ways in which part-time and self-employment are both traps and opportunities for women. What are the short-term and long-term costs and benefits of non-standard work?

2. Generation X women experience less labour market success than baby boomers. What are the social costs of this discrepancy?

3. What workplace supports are most helpful for women managing the conflicting demands of paid and unpaid work?

4. Do you predict that women and men will eventually share household work? Do men become increasingly involved in housework as women gain economic power?

BIBLIOGRAPHY

Akyeampong, Ernest. "Work Arrangements: 1995 Overview." *Perspectives on Labour and Income,* Spring, 1997: 48–52. Statistics Canada Catalogue No. 75-001-XPE.

Boyd, Monica. "Immigrant Women: Language, Socioeconomic Inequalities and Policy Issues." In *Ethnic Demography: Canadian Immigrant, Racial and Cultural Variations,* edited by Shiva Halli, Frank Travato, and Leo Driedger, 275–95. Ottawa: Carleton University Press, 1999.

Burke, Mike, and **John Shields.** *The Job-Poor Recovery: Social Cohesion and the Canadian Labour Market.* Toronto: The Ryerson Social Reporting Network, 1999.

Chaykowski, Richard, and **Lisa Powell.** "Women and the Labour Market: Recent Trends and Policy Issues." *Canadian Public Policy/Analyse de Politiques* 25 (1999) Supplement: S1–S25.

Cheal, David. *Poverty and Relative Income: Family Transactions and Social Policy.* Ottawa: Renouf Publishing Company, 1998.

Christofides, L. N., and **R. Swindinsky**. "Wage Determination by Gender and Visible Minority Status: Evidence from the 1989 LMAS." *Canadian Public Policy/Analyse de Politiques,* 20(1), 1994: 34–51.

Cohen, Gary. *Women Entrepreneurs: Perspectives on Labour and Income.* Spring 1996: 23–28, Statistics Canada Catalogue No. 75-001-XPE.

Drolet, Marie. *The Persistent Gap: New Evidence on the Canadian Gender Wage Gap.* Statistics Canada, Income Statistics Division, 75F002MIE – 99008, 1999.

Duffy, Ann. "The Part-time Solution: Toward Entrapment or Empowerment?" In *Good Jobs, Bad Jobs, No Jobs: The Transformation of Work in the 21st Century*, edited by A. Duffy, D. Glenday, and N. Pupo, 166–88. Toronto: Harcourt Brace, 1997.

Duffy, Ann, and **Norene Pupo.** *Part-time Paradox*. Toronto: McClelland and Stewart, Inc., 1992.

Duxburg, Linda, and **Chris Higgins.** *Work-life Balance in the New Milennium Where Are We? Where Do We Need to Go?* Ottawa: CPRN Networks, 2001.

Earl, Louise. *Baby Boom Women—Then and Now: Perspectives on Labour and Income.* Autumn: 26-29. Statistics Canada Catalogue No. 75-001-XPE, 1999.

Fast, J. E., and **Frederick, J. A.** "Working Arrangements and Time Stress: *Canadian Social Trends*, Winter, 14–19. Statistics Canada Catalogue 11-008XPE, 1996.

Finnie, Ross, and **Ted Wannell.** "The Gender Earnings Gap amongst Canadian Bachelor's Level University Graduates: A Cross-Cohort, Longitudinal Analysis." In *Women and Work*, edited by R. Chaykowski and L. Powell, 1–50. Montreal and Kingston: McGill-Queen's University Press, 1999.

Gabriel, Christina. "Restructuring at the Margins: Women of Colour and the Changing Economy." In *Scratching the Surface*, edited by Enakshi Dua and Angela Robertson. The Women's Press: Toronto, 1999.

Gardner, Arthur. "The Self-Employed." *Focus on Canada* Series Catalogue No. 96-316E. Toronto and Ottawa: Statistics Canada and Prentice Hall Inc., 1994.

Glass, J. L., and **S. B. Estes.** "The Family Responsive Workplace." *Annual Review of Sociology* 23 (1997): 289–313.

Gower, Dave. *Canada's Unemployment Mosaic in the 1990s. Perspectives on Labour and Income.* Spring: 16–22. Statistics Canada Catalogue no. 75-001-XPE, 1996.

Gunderson, Morley. *Women and the Canadian Labour Market: Transitions Toward the Future.* Census Monograph Catalogue No. 96-321-MPE No. 2. Ottawa and Toronto Statistics Canada and ITP Nelson, 1998.

Hessing, Melanie. "Mothers' Management of Their Combined Workloads: Clerical Work and Household Needs." *Canadian Review of Sociology and Anthropology*, 301 (1993), 37–63.

Hochschild, A. *The Second Shift: Working Parents and the Revolution at Home*. New York: Viking, 1989.

Hughes, Karen D. "How are Women Faring in the Entrepreneurial Economy?" Presented to "Breakfast on the Hill." Canadian Federation for Humanities and Social Sciences (CFHSS), Ottawa, May 1, 2003.

———. *Gender and Self-Employment in Canada: Assessing Trends and Policy Implications.* Ottawa: Canadian Policy Research Networks Study No. W04 Changing Employment Relations Series, 1999.

Kimmel, J. and **L. M. Powell.** "Moonlighting Trends and Related Policy Issues in Canada and the United States." *Canadian Public Policy/Analyse de Politiques* 25/2 1999: 207–31.

Lin, Zhengxi, Janice Yates, and **Garnett Picot.** "Rising Self-Employment in the Midst of High Unemployment: An Emperical Analysis of Recent Developments in Canada." Analytical Studies Branch, Research Paper Series, Statistics Canada No. 11F0019MPE No. 133, 1999.

Luxton, Meg and **Ester Reiter.** "Double, Double, Toil and Trouble ... Women's Experience of Work and Family in Canada 1980-1995." In *Women and the Canadian Welfare State*, edited by P. Evans and G. Wekerle, 197–221. Toronto: University of Toronto Press, 1997.

Lynn, Marion and **Milana Todoroff.** "Sole Support Mothers on Social Assistance in Ontario." *Canadian Women's Studies* 18/1 (1999): 2–75.

Marshall, Katherine. "Benefiting from extended Parental Leave." *Perspectives on Labour and Income*, Summer 15–21. Statistics Canada Catalogue no. 75-001-XPE, 2003.

———. "Part-time by Choice." *Perspectives on Labour and Income*. Spring: 20–26. Statistics Canada Catalogue No. 75-001-XPE, 2000.

———. "Employment after Childbirth." *Perspectives on Labour and Income*. Autumn: 18–25. Statistics Canada Catalogue No. 75-001-XPE, 1999.

———. "Working Together—Self-employed Couples." *Perspectives on Labour and Income*. Winter: 9–13. Statistics Canada Catalogue No. 75-001-XPE, 1998a.

———. "Stay-at-home-dads." *Perspectives on Labour and Income*, Spring: 9–15. Statistics Canada Catalogue no. 75-001-XPE, 1998b.

National Council of Welfare. *Poverty Profile, 1996*. Ottawa: Supply and Services, 1998.

Picot, G., M. Zyblock, and **W. Pyper.** "Why Do Children Move into and out of Low Income: Changing Labour Market Conditions or Marriage and Divorce?" Statistics Canada, Analytic Studies Branch. No. 132, 1999.

RCSW (Royal Commission on the Status of Women in Canada), *Report*, 1970. Ottawa: Information Canada.

Skrypnek, B. J., and **J. E. Fast.** "Work and Family Policy in Canada: Family Needs, Collective Solutions." *Journal of Family Issues* 17/6 (1996): 793–812.

Statistics Canada. *The Daily*, October 8, 2003.

———. *Longitudinal Survey of Immigrants to Canada: Process, Progress and Prospects*. 2003. Catalogue 89-611-XIE. Available online at www.statscan.ca/english/freepub/89-611-XIE/index.htm.

———. *Women in Canada: Work Chapter Updates*. Ottawa. Catalogue 89F0133XIE. May, 2003.

———. *Labour Force Survey*, 2002 (and 2003).

———. *Perspectives*. Spring, 2002: 47–51. Catalogue 75-001-XPE.

———. *The Daily*, January 7, 2000**.**

———. *The Daily*, August 4, 1999.

———. *Labour Force Update*. Summer. Ottawa: Catalogue 71-0056-XPB, 1999.

———. "Key Labour and Income Facts," *Perspectives on Labour and Income*. Autumn 1999: 72–77. Statistics Canada Catalogue no. 75-001-XPE.

———. *Characteristics of Dual-Earner Families*. 1999. Catalogue 13-215-XIB.

———. *The Daily*, March 12, 1998.

———. *The Daily*, March 17, 1998.

———. *Women in Canada.* Catalogue 89-503E, 1995.

———. *Survey of Work Arrangements,* 1995.

———. *General Social Survey,* 1994.

———. *Women in the Labour Force*, 1994 edition. Statistics Canada Catalogue 75-507E, 1994.

Sunter, D., and **G. Bowlby.** "Labour Force Participation in the 1990s." *Perspectives on Labour and Income.* Autumn 1998: 15–21. Statistics Canada Catalogue 75-001-XPE.

Williams, Cara. "Stress at Work." *Canadian Social Trends.* Autumn 2003: 7–13. Statistics Canada Catalogue 11-008.

Wilson, Suzannah J. *Women, Families and Work,* 4th edition. Toronto: McGraw-Hill, 1996.

Yalnizyan, Armine. *The Growing Gap.* Toronto: The Centre for Social Justice, 1998.

 # WEBLINKS

The Canadian Council for Social Development

www.ccsd.ca/index.html

A national, self-supporting, non-profit organization, the CCSD focuses on concerns such as income security, employment, poverty, child welfare, pensions, and government social policies.

Canadian Policy Research Networks

www.cprn.com

This web site contains a myriad of sources on the work and family life and health of Canadians.

Statistics Canada—Employment

www.statscan.ca/english/Pgdb/labour.htm

Visit this site for interesting Canadian statistics on employment.

The Canadian Research Institute for the Advancement of Women

www.criaw-icref.ca/

CRIAW is committed to advancing the position of women in society, to encouraging research about the reality of women's lives, and to affirming the diversity of women's experience.

The Educational System

Cecilia Reynolds

INTRODUCTION

"When I went to school, there were separate entrances for boys and for girls. You can still see that on the outside of some of those old buildings. Nobody expected girls to get too much education. They were supposed to get married and raise a family on the farm and that was what most of them did" (grandmother) (Reynolds, 1993).

"In my day, there were three choices for girls. You could be a teacher, a nurse or a secretary. You were only supposed to do that until you got married but most of my friends ended up having to support themselves and their children. A lot of them went back to school later in life" (mother) (Reynolds, 1993).

"I don't remember any discrimination when I went to school. We were always told we could be anything we wanted to be and most of us believed it. When I look back now, however, I realize that the boys had a lot of advantages in the classroom which they just expected. My biggest worry is how I'm going to have a family and still work as hard in my career as I need to in order to be a success" (daughter) (Reynolds, 1993).

These excerpts from an interview study in Ontario (Reynolds, 1993) reveal the changing nature of schooling experiences for three generations of women. They also help us see how gender, along with race, class, and sexual orientation, among other factors, affect the access that individuals have to the educational system, the experiences they have within that system, and the outcomes they come to expect.

Much of our popular culture, as expressed in films about schools or news reports about teachers and students, fosters the view that even though we know there are many problems within our schools, they still offer each of us the most direct route to material success. A number of feminist critiques of the educational system, however, have challenged such views.

This chapter explores an important educational issue that feminists have brought to our attention: the legacy of exclusion of girls and women from education. It also examines studies that show how traditional structures across elementary, secondary, and post-secondary levels of schooling have created a "chilly climate" for females from grade school to graduate school, and how this adversely affects women as they move from school to work. Finally, the chapter examines how traditional gender relations and the distribution of power within educational systems in Canada can affect students and teachers in negative ways.

A LEGACY OF EXCLUSION AND SEPARATION

In the early history of British North America, formal schooling did not play a large part in most people's lives. Access to schools was easier for some groups than for others, and not everyone held schooling experiences in high esteem. Thus, early school traditions and structures were predicated on the needs of only a small and privileged group within the newly developing society.

Our knowledge of native cultures reveals oral traditions and skills training but little formal instruction outside of what may have occurred within Jesuit missions or the Ursuline or Notre Dame convent schools set up in New France in the seventeenth and eighteenth centuries. Since immigrants to New France came largely from urban areas, they were likely to have had some schooling (Prentice et al., 1988).

Convent and parish schools were largely sex segregated and run by nuns or priests, but some lay teachers were employed and some "petites écoles" in rural areas had both male and female students—although an ordinance issued by the Bishop of Quebec in 1727 specified that teachers should not teach those of the opposite sex. Such early traditions supported the separation of males and females within schools. Such separations were largely predicated on fears about sexuality but also encompassed beliefs about the need for different types of education for females, who were to spend most of their lives in the private sphere, and for males, who were to spend their lives in the public sphere (Prentice et al., 1988).

Schooling opportunities were not as plentiful for the New England Loyalists who came to Nova Scotia, New Brunswick, or Prince Edward Island after the transfer of Acadia to the British Crown in 1713, or those who immigrated from the British Isles in the 1830s and 1840s after the Napoleonic Wars. For black children who travelled the underground railroad in the first half of the nineteenth century or for the children of immigrants who pioneered the Canadian west, attendance at a school needed to fit in around the tasks required at home. But a wide variety of schools existed during this period and, while some catered to the well-to-do, others had a clientele of pupils fairly well mixed in terms of gender, class, race, and ethnic background. Also, although many teachers came from religious orders, such as that of the Grey Nuns, established in the Red River colony in 1846, others, such as Angélique and Marguerite Nolin, who set up a school for Metis children in Red River in 1829, were part of a growing number of lay women who looked to teaching as a form of paid labour through which they could either support themselves or supplement the income of their household.

By the middle of the nineteenth century in most of Canada, publicly funded "common schools" developed; these were supported by the taxes of property owners and of business and industry. Most of these common schools included only the elementary grades and were coeducational even though some educators, such as Egerton Ryerson in Ontario, felt that there was a "moral danger" in girls attending school along with boys. In many school buildings of this era there were separate entrances for boys and girls, with the separate designations etched in the stone walls above the doorways.

The British North America Act of 1867 declared that schooling issues would come under the control of each province. School boards developed in both rural and urban areas. Elected school trustees had decision-making powers with regard to the hiring of teachers and the building of schools. In many areas, parallel "Catholic" and "Public" boards operated, and many previously existing privately funded schools continued, most of them run by clergy of a variety of religious denominations. Thus, although the rhetoric of Canadian educators was that of equality, the realities of school life and the outcomes of schooling varied enormously for rural and urban students, for those from poor and wealthy families, for those from native Canadian or immigrant backgrounds, and for males and females within each of these categories.

Records of school attendance (Gaskell et al., 1989) reveal that female students were more likely than males to attend classes regularly and to complete their formal schooling with graduation from high school. Despite this reality, women were not allowed entrance to the universities. When Emily Howard Stowe wanted to enter medical school in Canada in the 1860s, no school would admit her and she had to go to the United States for her education. It was not until 1883 that two separate women's colleges for medical education were established in affiliation with Queen's University and the University of Toronto. In 1890, Clara Brett Martin was refused admission by the Law Society of Upper Canada and it was not until 1897 that she was allowed, by provincial decree, to become the first woman in the British Empire to practise law. Not until 1941 were women in Quebec able to become lawyers.

And what about women who wanted to become teachers? By the beginning of the twentieth century the growth of "common schools" and the development of secondary schooling, along with many provincial policies requiring compulsory school attendance between the ages of 6 and 16, created a demand for qualified and inexpensive teachers (Gidney and Millar, 1990). Despite evidence that trustees and educational experts were initially doubtful about women's abilities to teach, by 1901 (Reynolds, 1983) three-quarters of all those engaged in the educational profession were women and, indeed, apart from domestic service, teaching was the largest category of paid employment for women in Canada at that time.

However, despite the hiring of female teachers in large numbers, they were usually placed under the control of male teachers, principals, inspectors, or trustees and were seldom allowed to teach in the senior grades. In Victoria, British Columbia, in 1903 the board stated that "in the interests of tactful discipline and the cultivation of strength and character in boys" (Wilson, 1970: 317) more male teachers should be hired. Often, as in Toronto in 1870 (Graham, 1974), there were differences in salaries paid to male and female teachers despite comparable teaching credentials (the average female salary was $220–$400 per year, while the average male salary was $600–$700 per year).

Historical records also reveal different patterns of participation in teaching and administrative roles for males and females. In Canada, men have tended to teach older students and to predominate numerically as professors in universities (Rees, 1990). Men have also been far more likely than women to become school principals or hold the most powerful administrative roles such as that of the director of the school board. Women, on the other hand, have tended to teach young children and have only recently been appointed as school principals or professors in universities in percentages equivalent to those of men. Formal policies have been overcome barring women teachers in the nineteenth century and requiring women to resign from teaching upon marriage in the twentieth century, and yet, despite ostensibly equal access, most women and men still continue to follow different career patterns within the teaching profession in this country.

Both as students and as teachers, females have needed to argue for acceptance within the educational system at all levels. Formal barriers excluding female students have diminished in Canada and, in 2001, women made up 62 percent of all Canadian university students aged 20 to 24 (Statistics Canada, 2003). In that year, 62 percent of all bachelor's degrees in this country were earned by women, up from 42 percent in 1975. Women in 2001 also earned 59 percent of all master's degrees and 50 percent of all doctoral degrees, a substantial growth from having earned only 28 percent of master's and 16 percent of doctoral degrees in 1975. However, women continue to earn fewer degrees than men in mathematics, physical sciences, engineering, and applied sciences, and they earn more degrees than men in health and education. Thus, although women have had formal access to most forms of schooling for more than 100 years in Canada, their participation in such schooling has been different from that of their male peers. This raises many questions about how formal structures and informal patterns (which still exist) channelled students by gender into different positions within the educational system.

In the 1960s, many feminists began to raise questions about equal access for male and female teachers and students within Canada's educational system. Throughout the 1970s and 1980s there was much documentation of the numerical disparities by gender within our schools. Such documentation revealed the patterns just described but did little to explain them or suggest steps toward fostering equality. Indeed, a debate arose about whether equality, defined as sameness, was what women really needed or wanted from schooling. Perhaps, some feminists suggested, we do not want women and men to be the same, especially if that means that females as students or teacher/administrators have to fit into a male model. Breaking down formal and informal barriers for women in terms of access was a part of the solution to the "problem" and something that continued to need attention, but many feminists began to discuss the need to study such issues as female experiences in classrooms, the transference of female schooling experiences into activity in the paid labour force, and the whole issue of power within schools, its distribution, and its maintenance mechanisms. It is to these three areas that we will now turn.

EXPERIENCES IN SCHOOLS

To understand the part that gender plays in a person's experiences of schooling, we need to grapple with different definitions of gender. We need also to consider how gender is connected to other factors, such as race, class, age, and ableism. School experiences are only one part of a complex system of socialization in our society, but as "official" state-run or state-sanctioned institutions, they carry out a legitimization function that is important.

Much controversy exists about the beginnings of status differences between men and women and about differences across cultures regarding understandings of gender and its importance.

Biological theories emphasize differences in chromosomes, hormones, and genitals that allow us to distinguish between two sexes, male and female (Richmond-Abbott, 1992). Social and cultural theories emphasize learned behaviours and focus on gender as masculine or feminine.

Thus, we have sex roles based on biology, and gender roles based on social expectations of appropriate behaviours. What some feminists have argued is that this has resulted in a complex and often hidden sex/gender system that dictates certain gender relations based on power. Within such a system, gender stereotypes (or oversimplified descriptions of a group of people) have developed, and stratification (or a different ranking or valuing of the two groups) has formed. In almost every society, it is men who decide on the rules, control the economy, and define dominant cultural rituals and ideologies. This male control of the laws and institutions so that men have a superior status to that of women has been defined as patriarchy.

Feminists in the 1960s and 1970s became concerned that schools and their formal curricula were part of a system of early socialization that helped to sustain gender stereotypes, inform male and female students of their traditional rankings in the society, and thereby act as institutions that perpetuated patriarchy. Early efforts focused on school readers and other textbooks in an effort to counter stereotypical images of girls and women as passive social actors with limited potential beyond motherhood and other nurturing roles. Attempts were made to raise the consciousness of teachers, parents, and students to the shortcomings of a continuation of such traditional patterns in our schools. Unfortunately, much of this early work focused on a "deficit model" (Gaskell et al., 1989), which argued that the schools were the place to intervene and compensate for the deficits (a) in parental knowledge and abilities; (b) in societal shortcomings, such as those found in the media; and (c) in girls themselves, who were accused of being afraid of success, having a phobia about mathematics, and not being assertive enough for their own good. As with earlier issues of access to education, it was erroneously believed that if only people knew about the uncovered injustices in our educational system, they would be moved to act in such a way as to alleviate them.

More recent studies stress how both the "hidden curriculum" that is passed on by the structures of classroom life and the expressed beliefs of students and teachers alike need consideration as well as the formal plan of study and the choice of textbooks. Also, theories of social construction, such as those outlined by Phillip Shaver and Clyde Hendrick in *Sex and Gender* (1987), posit a biosocial-interactionist perspective that argues that both sexuality and gender are constructed within societies for specific purposes. To alter sexism in the schoolhouse, then, means attending to all forms of communication—both verbal and non-verbal—and it means recognizing the social locations of male and female teachers and students.

Studies of classroom interaction patterns in Canada, the United States, Britain, and elsewhere have uncovered sexism from grade school to graduate school. The influential work of Myra and David Sadker in the United States has documented how both male and female teachers across different grade levels give more attention (both positive and negative) to male students, and educators are generally unaware of the impact of their own bias in classroom interaction patterns (Sadker and Sadker, 1986). Studies also indicate that males in most classrooms make greater use of verbal and non-verbal communication. Largely because of this dominance of "air time," most teachers try to select topics of interest to the males in the group in order to maintain control of the situation, tend to give more praise and reprimands to the males, and assess males as having greater ability overall (Richardson and Robinson, 1993).

Michelle Stanworth in Britain (quoted in Richardson and Robinson, 1993: 339) described how teachers used the phrase "faceless bunch" to describe those perceived as the passive female students in their classroom. Much work in Canada has focused on the "chilly climate" (Briskin, 1990) for women in Canadian colleges and universities and on possible interpretations of the relative female silences in classrooms at all levels.

Carol Gilligan's *In A Different Voice* (1982) suggested that we needed to encourage girls and women to break their silences and, indeed, we needed, as researchers and theorists, to listen attentively to what was said, recognizing that perhaps existing measures and scales were normed on male and not female experiences. She urged us to consider the importance of differences and not automatically assume that difference meant deficit.

The scales and measures that are used in standardized tests in schools are particularly problematic when we consider gender. Data from the Education Quality and Accountability Office for Ontario in 2002, showing province-wide results of standardized tests in mathematics, reading, and writing for students in grades three and six, revealed that girls had more positive attitudes and achievement than boys in reading and writing. In mathematics, boys had more positive attitudes than girls but boys' higher level of confidence was not well-founded since girls actually had higher achievement levels in mathematics. The data also showed substantially different reading interests and activities, in that girls were more likely than boys to read novels and poetry.

Other Canadian studies have also shown gender differences. In 1998, a study by the Council of Ministers of Education looked at performance levels for 4600 students aged 13 and 16. They found that girls were reading and writing at higher levels than boys. A study by the Fraser Institute in 1999 looked at six years of exam and classroom marks from more than 200 secondary schools in British Columbia and found that "even though boys do better than girls on five of the eight most commonly written provincial exams, girls consistently earn higher average marks on all eight of the classroom subjects" (Council of Ministers of Education, Canada, 2000). This finding prompted a leader of the BC Teachers' Federation to come to "one very simple conclusion about why girls do better than boys in secondary school: they work harder" (Council of Ministers of Education, Canada, 2000).

Similar findings in studies in many other countries in the 1990s have once again raised questions about what some have termed the "boy's crisis." Parents and educators have once again struggled to understand patterns of male violence in light of incidents such as mass shootings in schools by boys. Michael Kimmel (1999), in his summary of much of the research on masculinity and male development, comes to the conclusion that rather than being at the root of the problem, as some have suggested, feminism is the place to look for the solution to "boys' fragility, hidden despair, and despondence" (Kimmel 1999: 88). He goes on to discuss that what needs addressing is male entitlement, in order to "confront racism, sexism, and homophobia—both in our communities and in ourselves" (Kimmell 1999: 90) if we hope to counter the real boy crisis. Christine Skelton (2001) in Britain and Bob Pease (2000) in Australia are in general agreement with Kimmel's perspective regarding masculinity.

A collection of Canadian studies edited by Jane Gaskell and John Willinsky, *Gender In/forms Curriculum* (1995), offers further evidence of the negative experiences of many Canadian females in our schools at all levels and provides several useful theories to help explain why this is the case and what we should try to do about it. Two special issues of *Orbit* (edited by P. Bourne et al., 1997; P. Bourne and C. Reynolds, 2004) also take up the theme of gender and schooling from the perspective of students, teachers, and researchers from across the country.

Gaby Weiner and Madeline Arnot in *Gender and the Politics of Schooling* (1987) suggest an equal-opportunities/girl-friendly approach that would advocate ways of enticing females into science and technology courses so they could reap the rewards of higher-paying careers in these areas. Critics of this approach such as Ursula Franklin point out that it often veils the diversity within the category "girl" by such factors as race, class, ethnicity, etc., and it can lead to what Franklin has called the "sandbox phenomenon," that is, women and girls can enter the science and technology sandbox but the powers that be will not allow them to play with any of the toys or change that sandbox in any substantial way. Such critics propose a more radical reform of curriculum, including pedagogy, so that entire discourses within disciplines, such as science, are altered to include and to value the perspectives of girls and groups of boys who have traditionally been silenced by traditions within those discourses.

Canadian materials for teachers encompass both approaches and although many are available for science, math, and computers, fewer exist for subjects such as history, the arts, or physical education, although individual teachers often work to construct their own resources. As parents and teachers strive to improve girls' schooling experiences, writers such as Janice Streitmatter, in her book *For Girls Only* (1999), make the case for the merits of single-sex schooling, even if that means girls only classes within coeducational schools. Of major importance in the endeavour to consider how to improve gender equity in all types of schools is the growth of Women's Studies in our colleges and universities.

In 1970, the Royal Commission on the Status of Women stated that Women's Studies courses indicated the necessity for change, helped show the ways this could be accomplished, and suggested that such courses could improve the conditions for women in future educational systems. In 1982, the Jean Commission in Quebec concluded that "women's studies were essential for the improvement of women's opportunities for learning" (Brodribb, 1987: 1).

Women's studies programs provide the infrastructure in Canada for the continuing study of women's experiences and the provision of material in the various disciplines for feminist teachers to use with their students. They also assist feminist teachers in understanding how they themselves are situated as social actors in their attempts to bring about school reform. In *Women Teaching for Change* (1988), Kathleen Weiler studied how difficult it is for feminist teachers to work toward antisexist approaches in their classrooms. Also, Patti Lather in *Getting Smart* (1991) has described "student resistance to liberatory curriculum" even within women's studies courses.

At the centre of much of this reported resistance is the issue of language and communication, which is central to the educational enterprise. As Dale Spender points out in *Man Made Language* (1980), until fairly recently, conventions that posited the superiority of males and the inferiority of females, such as the use of the "generic he," served to limit our abilities to think in non-gendered ways. In the *Oppositional Imagination* (1989), Joan Cocks delineates how even our non-verbal communications have traditionally been predicated on the gender of the persons involved and how our very imaginations have been limited by the gendered vocabularies available to us. Indeed, Deborah Tannen in *You Just Don't Understand* (1990), used data on men and women in same-sex and mixed-sex conversations to describe two "genderlects" and explained that in most public settings, such as classrooms, it is the male conversational style that prevails. Thus, in traditional classroom discourse, females must speak an unfamiliar genderlect: They must, as Adrienne Rich has put it, "tell it slant," an activity that robs them of energy and often serves to silence them. Rich urges us to "listen to a woman groping for language to express what is on her mind, sensing that the terms of academic discourse are not her language, trying to cut down her thought to the dimensions of a discourse not intended for her" (1979: 243–244).

This perspective on language and communication raises feminist questions not only about how students should be treated in classrooms but also about what they should be taught. Jane Roland Martin, in *Reclaiming a Conversation: The Ideal of the Educated Person* (1985), has argued that because the school has traditionally been viewed as preparation for public life, it has been based on the ideal of "the cultivated, educated gentleman," even for females. We have discarded Jean-Jacques Rousseau's ideas of overtly separate educational goals for males in the public sphere and for females in the private sphere. Although Martin does not advocate that we return to a "domestic science" approach to the education of female students, she does point out that at present the three Cs (caring, concern, and connection) seem, through informal differentiation of the curriculum by gender, to be more frequently stressed for girls than for boys. This, she argues, is particularly problematic in an era when old paradigms of enlightenment, rationality, autonomous individuality, and unlimited consumerism are being called into question by post-modernist theorists in a wide variety of disciplines, from physics to art history.

What is important for some feminist educational reformers, then, is an examination of "epistemology" or knowledge itself. No longer can we unquestioningly accept established canons or lists of great contributions to civilization when these exclude women's accomplishments and experiences. We need to question what is worth knowing and how we have come to know. Mary Belenky and a number of other researchers did just that in a book entitled *Women's Ways of Knowing* (1986). In that work they argued that not only females, but many males as well, would be better served by a teaching method that posed problems and let learners search for connections between knowledges rather than by lecture techniques that compartmentalized knowledges and asked students to be interested spectators and consumers.

Indeed, Sheila Tobias argues in *They're Not Dumb, They're Just Different* (1990), that current techniques used in the teaching of math, science, and technology, especially at the college and university level, are aimed at gatekeeping: only a few students, who resemble in thought patterns, learning styles (and, often, in such characteristics as gender and race) those in power positions within these disciplines, will be allowed the chance to study and eventually work in these areas. Although those who have invested in maintaining the status quo of any discipline may benefit by this procedure, the development of truly "new" innovations in the discipline is severely hampered.

What feminists suggest is that the experiences of all students, teachers, and school administrators be considered by those involved in the educational system in Canada. Some feminist reformers are focused on improving the participation and success of females; others have focused on countering sexism, racism, homophobia, ableism, and other forms of harmful discriminatory structures and practices; still others are working toward a transformation not only in pedagogical or teaching techniques that have favoured certain groups of males, but also in (a) the actual knowledge bases used, (b) the underlying theories about humans and ways they learn, and (c) assumptions about their roles in the world. Books such as Ruth King's *Talking Gender* (1991) describe how we can alter traditional communication patterns; Diane Richardson and Victoria Robinson's *Thinking Feminist* (1993) tells us how women's studies concepts are crucial to change. In their book, *Scratching the Surface: Canadian Anti-racist Feminist Thought* (1999), Enakshi Dua and Angela Robertson challenge us to consider how institutions such as schools continue to reproduce marginalization and how we might work to bring about change. In her edited book, *The politics of women's bodies: sexuality, appearance and behaviour* (2003), Rose Weitz counters the split between mind and body and shows implications for schools.

To be successful, such reforms need to consider the interrelationship between education itself and the larger economic and political structures of our time. Thus, we need to consider the connections between the educational system and forms of paid and unpaid work.

LINKAGES BETWEEN SCHOOL AND WORK

Since World War Two, a number of analyses of the relationship between school and work have been offered. Although it is not possible here to detail all of this work, four major theories will be discussed. The first is the functional approach of Talcott Parsons in the 1950s and 1960s. In brief, Parsons postulated that schools were institutions that served major functions for the economy: They socialized students, developed their skills, developed their capacities to be productive, and allocated them to occupational roles needed in society. To do so efficiently, schools should make rational use of economic resources. This framework was used by John Porter (1965) in Canada in his influential analysis. In many provinces we are currently seeing a return to such Parsonian views of schools justified by reference to current economic restraints in increasingly competitive global markets.

Closely related to Parsons's work was that of Howard Becker, who argued that if a single person could advance in the society through merit and hard work, then the society itself could improve its economic position through educational improvement. In *Human Capital Theory* (1964), Becker argued that investment in education would be positively related to economic growth and that educated workers would be more productive workers. These ideas are also making a strong resurgence in the popular imagination of Canadians as we increasingly ask the homeless and the unemployed to pull themselves up by their bootstraps. However, both Parsons and Becker assumed that the individual was the basic economic unit and that paid labour was all that counted in the economy, a view countered by New Zealand feminist Marilyn Waring and many others who see women's roles in unpaid labour as vital in the development and sustainability of any economy.

A contrasting view to that of Parsons and Becker was put forward by Bowles and Gintis in *Schooling in Capitalist America* (1976). They argued that schools reflect the dominance of some groups over others and serve the needs of the dominant groups rather than the collective good. The meritocracy that was the basis for differentiation between students in Parson's theory was viewed by Bowles and Gintis as a camouflage for a system that was stacked from the beginning against working-class students. Among the Canadians influenced by this approach was George Martell, who wrote *The Politics of the Canadian Public School* (1974).

The work of Paul Willis in *Learning to Labour* (1977) added an important new dimension to the theory of Bowles and Gintis. Willis argued that "social reproduction" of a class-biased system was not inevitable. Indeed, he detailed in his study of British working-class "lads" how the individual negotiated in an ongoing way the contested and contradictory processes of schooling and paid work. In Willis's view, the participants in schooling were active agents who produced a culture, a set of decisions, and some concrete behaviours out of their interpretations of the social conditions in which they found themselves. They understood part of what they were contesting, they resisted some of it, and they complied with other aspects in a way that made sense to them.

For Parsons, women's schooling was primarily related to their unpaid domestic work, and women were often left out of studies using a functional framework, or they were allocated to the category of "housewife." For Becker, women's lower rate of return on their educational investment remained a mystery he could not explain. For Bowles and Gintis, class equity was their major concern and, although they noted women's discontent, they themselves did not explore issues of sexism or indeed issues of racism or other issues outside of class-based discrimination within the educational system. For Willis, males were more interesting than females for the purpose of his theory. His work has come under severe criticism by feminists such as Angela McRobbie (1978). She found that although Willis uncovered misogyny clearly expressed by the working-class lads, he did not explore this and treated it and other gender-related aspects of his findings as only tangential. His framework, however, has been effectively used by Jane Gaskell in her Canadian study of working-class students in British Columbia in *Gender Matters From School to Work* (1992).

Along with different theories about the relationship between school and work, Jack Nelson, Stuart Palonsky, and Kenneth Carlson point out in *Critical Issues in Education* (1990) that our political beliefs affect our views about what schools are supposed to do and whose interests they should serve.

On the political "right" are those who believe that government's role is to ensure that parents can be free to choose the kind of education they want for their children and that each of us can best help the less fortunate by contributing to the national welfare rather than by giving handouts or special privileges to certain students.

Those on the political "left" demand that the government guarantee that every child have equally good schooling despite parental circumstances. They argue that to date we have had a system that has not equalized the condition of poor people or women but has instead only allowed them to remain dependent upon the well-to-do, most of whom are white males. They state that whenever improved conditions become available to disadvantaged children, those in the advantaged group find some way to provide some form of additional or improved schooling for their children that negates the gains made.

To varying degrees, feminists, like others in our society, can be found across this spectrum of theories and political locations. What they agree upon, however, is that most female students are less advantaged than most male students when it comes to cashing in on their educational investment. Some feminists believe that this is because female students make some unfortunate choices during their schooling, such as dropping math classes. These choices limit the possibilities for females in the world of paid work. Other feminists argue that there are few role models for females to follow in non-traditional occupations and that this contributes to aspirations by females to work in fields where women have always worked and to avoid trying to enter the less comfortable and somewhat risky terrain of such fields as engineering.

In 2001 about 8 percent of those who attained doctorates in engineering were women. This compares with women making up 45 percent of those gaining doctorates in education in that same period. In the health professions over those same years, women constituted

34 percent of those claiming their doctorate (Statistics Canada, 2003), but women owned only about 34 percent of businesses in the country.

These statistics indicate that despite some historical improvements, most girls and women within our educational system still seem to "track" into traditional areas, particularly the teaching area. This goes against the popular wisdom that women have been moving into non-traditional areas in rapid numbers and are actually threatening the previous privileged location reserved for white males. Reports from women, however, suggest that no matter where they find themselves working for pay, balancing home and career responsibilities remains a major challenge.

This raises questions about how schools might alleviate the difficulties experienced by females in the paid labour force. Suggestions by feminists include the following: counselling girls and women into taking courses that "keep their options open"; encouraging them to gain firsthand knowledge from female mentors in non-traditional roles for women; educating both male and female students about the realities of and need for increased employment equity policies and practices in the paid labour force; equipping students, both male and female, with the desire and skills needed to continue to work toward greater equity for a variety of groups in our economy; and transforming the schools themselves so that those who work within them can offer a model to all students of how paid labour need not be designated by gender and how existing traditions and power structures can be altered to increase equity. It is in regard to this last strategy that we now turn to the final section of this chapter: a discussion of the distribution of power within educational hierarchies.

THE DISTRIBUTION OF POWER IN EDUCATIONAL HIERARCHIES

Webster's defines a bureaucracy as "a system of administration marked by officialism, red tape and proliferation." Public resentment over the costs of maintaining such bureaucracies has recently led to a series of education cuts in many provinces and an outcry for accountability. What has this meant to women?

When we trace the historical development of elementary, secondary, and post-secondary schooling across Canada, we see that, over time and particularly following World War Two, the administrative side of schools increased dramatically. For example, in the Toronto Board of Education in 1940, 20.5 percent of the teachers were in such administrative roles as principal or vice-principal. By 1980, that percentage had risen to 47.6 percent. Clearly, the structures and processes of power had become more complicated than those used to operate one-room rural schools. Hierarchies of many varieties had developed. In terms of post-secondary schooling, again we can trace historically a proliferation of universities and colleges with increasingly complex administrative structures and processes. Provincial ministries of education also had large staffs of decision-makers.

Most women and men within these educational hierarchies did not participate equally. It was primarily white men who were appointed as deans and presidents in universities, as directors and supervisory officers in school boards, as principals and vice-principals in elementary and secondary schools, and as ministers and deputy ministers at governmental levels. By and large, it was women who taught and men who managed and set policy. This pattern in the United States is spelled out by Jackie Blount in *Destined to Rule the Schools: Women and the Superintendency 1873–1995* (1998). The similar pattern in Australia is discussed by Jill Blackmore in *Troubling Women: Feminism, Leadership and Educational Change* (1999).

Canadian patterns are documented in the collection edited by Cecilia Reynolds and Beth Young, *Women and Leadership in Canadian Education* (1995). In that book, several authors present data from different provinces suggesting that although employment equity has significantly improved the participation of women in official leadership roles in our schools at all levels, it has often not really made much difference to overall power structures, which continue to disadvantage most women and some groups of men within the unchanged bureaucracy. In *Women and School Leadership: International Perspectives* (Reynolds, 2002) the discussion is broadened to include data from several countries.

In an article in the *Canadian Journal of Education* (1995), I have argued that power differentials are partly explained by the web of rules within such bureaucracies, which are designed to absorb small changes without causing an overall disturbance in the dominant structures. Another explanation is that when women move into powerful roles, like immigrants to a new land, they may be more interested in fitting in than in working to change a system from which they now stand to gain at a personal level.

Some feminists, as well as others, have suggested that what we really need are alternative non-bureaucratic approaches to the problems of organization in education and elsewhere in our society. Kathy Ferguson, in *The Feminist Case Against Bureaucracy* (1984), is only one among many who offer a systematic analysis of the problems of bureaucratization not only for women but also for all those in minority positions within the larger society. She also points to examples of alternative structures and cites feminist egalitarian approaches to getting things done as important sources of clarification and resistance to traditional patterns of power distribution.

But there is little to suggest that such transformations would occur easily. Those interested in maintaining the status quo are unlikely to see merit in change in this direction. Even those currently being exploited by existing systems may not agree with suggested alternatives unless they are assured that these will not offer just a different form of exploitation. There are problems, too, in helping individuals come to grips with their beliefs and actions at a level beyond lip service and "politically correct" rhetoric.

Employment equity policy within current educational systems seems to offer a good example of the possibilities for new forms within educational hierarchies. It also offers us examples of the difficulties that must be overcome before any deep-seated and lasting changes can occur.

In 1984, in *Equality in Employment: A Royal Commission Report*, Judge Rosalie Abella stated:

> Employment equity is action to achieve equality in the workplace so that no person shall be denied employment opportunities or benefits unrelated to ability and to correct the conditions of disadvantage in employment experiences by women, aboriginal peoples, persons with disabilities and persons, who, because of their race, creed, colour, or religion, are in a minority. (quoted in Rees, 1990: 3)

A study conducted in 1990 by the Canadian Educational Association (Rees, 1990) revealed that progress across Canada in provincial ministries of education, school boards, and teachers' associations varied greatly according to employment equity policies and procedures and in related matters dealing with such issues as sexual harassment and inclusive language. Overall, the distribution by gender for teachers and administrators continues to show an overrepresentation of men in the highest ranks. Despite some provincial declarations, such as Memorandum 111 in Ontario, which declared that by the year 2000 women should constitute 50 percent of all administrative positions in the educational system, most policies do not set targets or goals, nor do they apply rewards or sanctions to those who comply or fail to comply with the policy. Outcries about "reverse discrimination" have been heard in many sectors, and some regions actually show a decline in the participation of female administrators as a result of recent retirements or amalgamation of school districts.

Early reactions from some sectors of the school system to efforts to increase the number of women in powerful roles in schools has often been described as a backlash. At present, it could even be called a whiplash, that is, a quick jerking stop in what was a forward movement. As I have argued with my colleague Harry Smaller in an article in the FWTAO/FAEO Newsletter (January 1996), we may be watching patterns similar to those in the 1930s when female teachers were more adversely affected than their male peers by the economic downturn and its effect on schools. Once again, as before, we are seeing jobs primarily held by women being those that school systems are choosing to cut. Power is being taken away from the most vulnerable members within the bureaucracies. For example, when school boards came under pressure, many decided to cancel junior kindergarten classes, an area with primarily female teachers. As universities cut back, female support staff lost their jobs, and junior faculty (many of whom are women who achieved their positions as a result of employment equity initiatives) were asked to increase their workload without increased wages.

Within colleges and universities, the Canadian Association of University Teachers, through its Status of Women Committee, has, over many years, made a sustained effort toward employment equity and educational equity. Mirrored in many provincial associations, such committees have kept open for debate the need for a redistribution of power and new possibilities regarding old structures. Much of that debate recently has focused on "the inclusive university" as an alternative to the traditional version of "academe." Discussing this theme, Joyce Forbes declares:

> The masculinist power structure of the university has no right to set its own limitations on others. By seeing as tangential all that is not traditional, by naming as whole that which is partial, the university has consolidated into an absolute what is partial vision and partial judgment.... To affirm another's self-respect is to ferret out the words that acclaim diversity. This is to transform education: make it relevant. (Forbes, 1993: 3)

Following these ideas, the Canadian Federation of University Women and others have identified aspects of a "woman-friendly" university that are similar to those discussed by many in colleges and in elementary and secondary schools when they address employment equity.

This includes such things as support services, for staff and faculty and for full-time and part-time students, including child care and elder care; a safe and harassment-free environment; recognition of work experience; salary equity; incentives for increased participation by women in light of their household and family commitments, including access to scholarships and all academic programs; equity in hiring and promotion procedures and outcomes; attention to the inclusion of female experience in all course content; gender-inclusive language as the norm throughout the institution; and, finally, structural recognition of women's studies as an accredited area of scholarship.

CONCLUSION

The historical origins of educational systems in Canada reveal that females were somewhat grudgingly admitted to schools primarily designed to meet the needs and learning styles of males. Only relatively recently have the material conditions and lives of female students and teachers in classrooms been deemed worthy of study or comment. Examinations of those experiences have indicated that despite their greater compliance overall with the demands of school life, females have been less valued by teachers, given less attention in classrooms, and have had their experiences and accomplishments largely left out of curriculum materials or treated in a stereotypical fashion. Women have also been less likely than men to realize the same economic gains from their educational investment. Their participation in the paid labour force, while expanding, remains largely in traditional sectors. The overall location of women within the power structures of educational systems, despite some progress related to employment equity initiatives, still remains less secure and less influential than the overall location of men within those structures. Indeed, current economic and political climates appear to threaten hard-fought gains.

Feminists, as already stated, have diverse views about the importance of the educational system in bringing about improvements in our society for girls and women. They often disagree about what strategies should be employed and what changes are necessary. Those who accept the basic traditions of schooling in this country are working largely to ensure that women and other minorities have equal chances to use schooling to help them gain economic viability. Those who are critical of traditional Canadian schooling practices and structures are working to alter them so that the status quo will be changed and possibilities for new forms of organization can develop over time.

In some ways, feminists concerned with the educational system alternate between fatalism and romanticism. They constantly search for clarity of vision regarding existing realities, whether those are the realities of the current economic or political climates within which they must work for change, or the realities of classroom life that inform them about the success or failures of their attempts. Perhaps the clearest way to think about how feminists are working within the educational system is to imagine, as Virginia Woolf did in *A Room of One's Own* (1929), that Shakespeare had a sister who, like all great poets, has never died but will come back to life when the opportunity permits. Her possible return motivates many feminists to work for educational reform. As Virginia Woolf explains:

> As for her coming without that preparation, without that effort on our part, without that determination that when she is born again she shall find it possible to live and write her poetry, that we cannot expect, for that would be impossible. But I maintain that she would come if we worked for her, and that so to work, even in poverty and obscurity, is worth while. (Woolf, 1929: 123)

CHAPTER SUMMARY

- Feminist critiques of schooling challenge commonly held beliefs (supported by popular culture), which suggest that schools can answer all of society's problems.
- Girls and women in Canada, as in several other countries, have systematically been excluded from the highest levels of education and from certain areas of study.
- Females have had to argue for access both as students and as teachers.
- Formal barriers in education for females have given way to informal barriers and these have been identified from grade school to graduate school.

- Controversy remains about whether nature and/or nurture explains observable differences between the ways that males and females learn and the ways they behave in schools.

- Gender bias can be found in overt and "hidden" curriculum and classroom practices.

- Research shows that although boys tend to get more attention in schools and to speak out more often than girls, girls tend to get higher grades and to work harder at school-work than boys.

- Worries about violence in schools have brought new attention to sexual harassment in schools and patterns of male and female development.

- Efforts by teachers and parents to create "female-friendly" classrooms and inclusive curriculum have gone a long way to improving sexist, racist and homo-phobic practices in many classrooms.

- The growth of women's studies programs in colleges and universities is important to sustaining efforts to improve gender and racial equity in schools since this is one of the major areas in which theory develops and new approaches are designed.

- There are many competing theories about the relationship between school and work and not all feminists agree about how we can move forward to improve gender equity in both realms.

- Often, school systems themselves reproduce a gendered division of labour that favours men and allows only a very few women into positions of power and influence.

- Although not all feminists agree which strategies might be best for improving society for girls and women, few feminists would deny that a closer look at our educational systems is an important step toward fostering a better future for us all.

SUGGESTED READINGS

Blackmore, J. 1999. *Troubling Women: Feminism, Leadership and Educational Change.* Buckingham: Open University Press.

This book is based on the author's study of women school leaders in Australia. It outlines the gendering of educational work and questions traditional notions about women as "trouble" within the school bureaucracy. Blackmore offers a critique of current gender equity policy initiatives and describes a feminist politics for leadership in post-modern times.

Dua, E., and **A. Roberston** (eds.). 1999. *Scratching the Surface: Canadian Anti-racist Feminist Thought.* Toronto: Women's Press.

This collection brings together the work of a number of Canadian feminists concerned with the marginalization of women and others in our institutions, including schools. Race and gender are brought together in important discussions of such issues as colonialism, the economy, labour markets, and the Canadian state.

Reynolds, C. (ed.). 2002. *Women and School Leadership: International Perspectives.* New York: State University of New York Press.

In this book, feminist researchers from Canada, Australia, New Zealand, and the United States discuss women's experiences as school leaders in elementary, secondary, and post-secondary settings. The authors provide gender-focused theories concerning leadership in today's environments and they outline important questions for future studies.

Reynolds, C., and **A. Griffith** (eds.). 2002. *Equity and Globalization in Education.* Detselig Enterprises: Temeron Press.

This collection delineates how an emphasis on school effectiveness has served in many developed and developing nations to sidetrack equity initiatives in today's schools. The current context in Canada is explored in depth in the final section of the book.

QUESTIONS

1. Many people believe, contrary to what research indicates, that there are no longer any gender-related problems in classrooms. List the reasons why it is so hard for parents, teachers, and students to recognize gender-related inequities in elementary, secondary, and post-secondary schools.

2. There continues to be considerable controversy about whether or not girls and boys should be educated together. How do single-sex school settings benefit girls? How do they benefit boys? Why do we have so many coeducational schools?

3. Women's studies programs are relatively recent additions on most campuses. How are such programs viewed on your campus? Why? What are the contributions such programs can make to our society?

4. Some people have argued that if more women had powerful roles in school systems, gender equity would improve. Do you agree? Why or why not? Do we still need employment equity policies in school systems? Why or why not?

BIBLIOGRAPHY

Becker, H. *Human Capital Theory.* New York: Columbia University Press, 1964.

Belenky, M., B. Clinchy, N. Goldberger, and **J. Tarule**. *Women's Ways of Knowing: The Development of Self, Voice and Mind.* New York: Basic Books, 1986.

Blackmore, J. *Troubling Women. Feminism, Leadership and Educational Change.* Buckingham: Open University Press, 1999.

Blount, J. *Destined to Rule the Schools: Women and the Superintendency, 1873–1995.* Albany: State University Press, 1998.

Bourne, P., L. McCoy, and **M. Novogrodsky**, eds. "Gender and Schooling." *Orbit* 28/1 (1997): 1.

Bourne, P,. and **C. Reynolds**, eds. "Girls, Boys and Learning." *Orbit* Vol. 34, No. 1, 2004.

Bowles, S., and **H. Gintis**. *Schooling in Capitalist America.* New York: Basic Books, 1976.

Briskin, L. "Gender in the Classroom." *CORE: Newsletter of the Centre for the Support of Teaching* (York) 1/1 (1990).

Brodribb, S. *Women's Studies in Canada: A Discussion.* Resources for Feminist Research/ Documentation sur la Recherche Feministe, 1987.

Cocks, J. *The Oppositional Imagination: Feminism, critique and political theory.* New York: Routledge, 1989.

Council of Ministers of Education. 1998. Available online at **http://www.cmec.ca/nafored/english/ update.pdf.**

Council of Ministers of Education. "Science Learning: The Canadian Context." In *SAIP School Achievement Indicators Program 1999*. Toronto: The Council of Ministers of Education, 2000.

Dua, E., and **A. Roberston**, eds. *Scratching the Surface: Canadian Anti-racist Feminist Thought*. Toronto: Women's Press, 1999.

Education Equality and Accountability Office (EQAO). *The Grade 3 and Grade 6 Assessments of Reading, Writing and Mathematics, 2001–2002*. Queen's Printer for Ontario, 2002.

Ferguson, K. *The Feminist Case Against Bureaucracy*. Philadelphia: Temple University Press, 1984.

Forbes, J. "The Inclusive University." *CAUT Status of Women Supplement,* 1993.

Gaskell, J. *Gender Matters from School to Work*. Toronto: OISE Press, 1992.

Gaskell, J., and **J. Willinsky**, eds. *Gender In/forms Curriculum*. Toronto: OISE Press, 1995.

Gaskell, J., A. McLaren, and **M. Novogrodsky**. *Claiming an Education. Feminism and Canadian Schools*. Toronto: Our Schools/Our Selves Education Foundation, 1989.

Gidney, R., and **W. Millar**. *Inventing Secondary Education*. Montreal: McGill-Queen's University Press, 1990.

Gilligan, C. *In a Different Voice*. Cambridge: Harvard University Press, 1982.

Graham, E. "Schoolmarms and Early Teaching in Ontario." In *Women at Work 1850–1930*, edited by L. Kealy. Canadian Women's Educational Press, 1974.

Industry, Science and Technology Canada. *Women in Science and Engineering. Volume 1: Universities*. Ottawa: University and College Affairs Branch, Science Sector, 1991.

Kimmel, M. "What Are Little Boys Made of?" *MS Magazine* Oct/Nov 1999: 88–91.

King, R. *Talking Gender: A Guide to Nonsexist Communication*. Toronto: Copp Clark, 1991.

Lather, P. *Getting Smart: Feminist Research and Pedagogy with/in the Postmodern*. New York: Routledge, 1991.

Martell, G. *The Politics of the Canadian Public School*. Toronto: James Lewis & Samuel, 1974.

Martin, J. R. *Reclaiming a Conversation: The Ideal of the Educated Woman*. New Haven: Yale University Press, 1985.

McRobbie, A. "Working Class Girls and the Culture of Femininity." In *Women Take Issue*. Centre for Contemporary Cultural Studies, Women's Studies Group. Birmingham: University of Birmingham, 1978.

Nelson, J., S. Palonsky, and **K. Carlson**. *Critical Issues in Education*. Toronto: McGraw-Hill Publishing Company, 1990.

Pease, B. *Recreating Men: Postmodern Masculinity Politics*. Thousand Oaks, CA: Sage Publications, 2000.

Porter, J. *The Vertical Mosaic*. Toronto: University of Toronto Press, 1965.

Prentice, A., P. Bourne, G. Brandt, B. Light, W. Mitchinson, and **N. Black**. *Canadian Women: A History*. Toronto: Harcourt Brace Jovanovich, 1988.

Rees, R. *Women and Men in Education: A National Survey of Gender Distribution in School Systems*. Canadian Educational Association, 1990.

Reynolds, C. "Ontario Schoolteachers 1911–1971: A Portrait of Demographic Change." Unpublished Master's thesis. University of Toronto, 1983.

———. "Looking Back Through our Mothers." Unpublished manuscript. 1993.

————. *Women and School Leadership: International Perspectives.* SUNY Series in Women in Education. State University of New York Press, 2002.

————. "In the Right Place at the Right Time: Rules of Control and Woman's Place in Ontario Schools, 1940–1980." *Canadian Journal of Education* 20/2, 1995: 129–145.

Reynolds, C., and **B. Young**. *Women and Leadership in Canadian Education.* Calgary: Detselig Enterprises, Temeron Press, 1995.

Reynolds, C., and **Smaller, H.** "Economic Downturns Affect Women and Men Differently." *FWTAO/FAEO Newsletter,* 1996: 50–57.

Rich, A. *On Lies, Secrets, and Silence: Selected Prose, 1966–1978.* New York: Norton, 1979.

Richardson, D., and **V. Robinson**. *Thinking Feminist: Key Concepts in Women's Studies.* New York: The Guilford Press, 1993.

Richmond-Abbott, M. *Masculine & Feminine. Gender Roles Over the Life Course.* Toronto: McGraw-Hill, Inc., 1992.

Sadker, M., and **D. Sadker**. *Sexism in the Classroom: From Grade School to Graduate School.* Phi Delta Kappan, 1986.

Shaver, P., and **C. Hendrick**. *Sex and Gender.* Newbury Park: Sage, 1987.

Skelton, C. *Schooling the Boys: Masculinities and Primary Education.* Philadelphia: Open University Press, 2001.

Spender, D. *Man Made Language.* London: Routledge and Kegan Paul, 1980.

Stanworth, M. *Gender and Schooling: A Study of Sexual Divisions in the Classroom.* London: Hutchinson, 1983.

Streitmatter, J. *For Girls Only. Making a Case for Single Sex Schooling.* Albany: State University Press, 1999.

Tannen, D. *You Just Don't Understand: Women and Men in Conversation.* New York: Ballantine Books, 1990.

Tobias, S. *They're Not Dumb, They're Different: Stalking the Second Tier.* Tucson: Research Corp., 1990.

Weiler, K. *Women Teaching for Change: Gender, Class & Power.* Massachusetts: Bergin & Garvey Pub., Inc., 1988.

Weiner, G., and **M. Arnot**. "Teachers and gender politics." In *Gender and the Politics of Schooling,* edited by M. Arnot and G. Weiner, eds. London: Hutchinson, 1987.

Weitz, R. *The Politics of Women's Bodies: Sexuality, Appearance, and Behaviour.* New York: Oxford University Press, 2003.

Willis, P. *Learning to Labour.* Farnborough: Saxon House, 1977.

Wilson, D., ed. *Canadian Education: A History.* Scarborough: Prentice Hall, 1970.

Woolf, V. *A Room of One's Own.* Triad Grafton Books, 1977, 1929.

 **WEBLINKS**

Organizations:

Canadian Association of University Teachers
www.caut.ca

Canadian Federation of University Women
www.cfuw.org

Canadian Research Institute for the Advancement of Women
www.criaw-icref.ca

Education Quality and Accountability Office
www.eqao.com

Resources for Feminist Research
www.oise.toronto.ca/rfr/

Federal Government:

Industry Canada
www.ic.gc.ca

Women in Small Business
http://strategis.ic.gc.ca/epic/internet/insbrp-rppe.nsf/vwGeneratedInterE/rd00649e.html

Women Business Links
http://strategis.ic.gc.ca/epic/internet/incontact-contact.nsf/vwGeneratedInterE/mi06730e.html

Statistics Canada
www.statscan.ca

Education Links
www.statscan.ca/english/Pgdb/educat.htm

Education Search
www.statscan.ca/english/search/browse-people.htm

Free Publications
www.statscan.ca/english/freepub/89F0133XIE/free.htm

Census 2001 Tables
www12.statscan.ca/english/census01/products/standard/themes/Index.cfm

Status of Women Canada
www.swc-cfc.gc.ca

chapter eleven

Understanding Women and Health[1]

Diana L. Gustafson

How do we define health? How do we understand women's health? Some describe good health as being physically and mentally fit, free of disease, and able to engage in everyday activities of living. Many say that health is a general sense of well-being that results from healthy lifestyle choices such as eating nutritious meals, getting plenty of rest, participating in regular exercise, getting an annual PAP smear and regular dental care, and learning to cope better with the stress of mother work and paid work. Others may add that being born with good genes gives some women a healthy advantage. That some of us reduce health to functioning of the body and mind that can be measured, monitored, and managed is not surprising. Nor is it surprising that many of us believe that we are personally responsible for our state of health. These understandings of health are consistent with biomedical research developed from a predominantly white masculinist perspective (Murray and Chamberlain, 2000). In turn, these understandings are institutionalized in the health practices, education, policies, and programs that shape women's health, exemplify and contribute to social disparities, and are the site of women's resistance.

This chapter invites you to think about women's health as it is defined by the dominant biomedical model and the population-health approach advanced by the World Health Organization (WHO). A critical discussion of disparities in women's health organized

---

1   My thanks go to Nancy Mandell, Sue Wilson, Natalie Beausoleil, Sharon Bueller, and Maria Mathews for their guidance during the writing of this chapter.

around population-health determinants complicates gender as a category of analysis and reveals the connections between women's health, social location, and differential access to power and resources. Doing so also shifts from descriptions and measurement of health and illness as abstract concepts in institutionalized knowledges to understanding tangible concepts "reflected through other realms or spheres of everyday life" (Radley, 1999: 27).

The discussion begins with an overview of the biomedical and the population-health approaches to women's health. Outlining key differences between the approaches is one way of getting at the kinds of gender bias that structure biomedical research, and in turn, women's relationship to the dominant health care system as recipients and providers of health care. To illustrate some of the key challenges facing women in these two realms, examples drawn from Canadian health research, education, policy, and programs are organized around health determinants. The discussion reveals how a critical feminist approach expands our understanding of women's health as an equity issue.

UNDERPINNINGS: TWO APPROACHES TO WOMEN'S HEALTH

The biomedical and population-health approaches to health and health care are socially constructed frameworks that reflect shifting understandings of women's health and factors contributing to health differences between women and men, and across groups of women.[2] The biomedical approach centres on the body, its function and malfunction, its disease, its diagnosis, and its cure. Knowledge is generated through empirical research in which researchers seek to objectively measure the pathology of the physical body, identify the constellation of clinical factors that signal disease, the internal factors (genes or germs) that cause or protect against disease, and the appropriate strategies for screening, treating, and managing *disease*.[3] Because women's bodies share some common primary and secondary sex characteristics that differ from men's, these common attributes are used to construct women's and men's health and disease causality differently. Biomedical research directs little or inappropriate attention to health priorities as women define them, to subjective experiences of health, or to the socio-structural factors that contribute to broader health disparities (Denton and Walters, 1999; Walters, 1992).

By comparison, the population-health approach, as the label suggests, is concerned with a wide range of factors that affect the health of a population. Both approaches recognize that biology and genetic endowment, gender, culture, and personal health practices and coping skills influence health status. In addition to these health determinants, population-health research also measures the impact of income and social status, employment, education, social environments, physical environments, healthy childhood development, health services, and social support networks.

The biomedical model deals with individuals—usually one at a time—who have, or are at risk of having a health problem. Access to health care professionals and services is

---

2   Feminists critique both approaches to women's health. For a more detailed discussion of the strengths and limitations of the biomedical model, see Sherwin (1998), and of the population-health approach, see Ussher (2000). Both are listed in the suggested readings.

3   Juanne Clarke (2000) distinguishes disease from illness and sickness. Disease refers to a pathological condition of the body, diagnosed by a physician and potentially curable using specific biomedical interventions. Illness refers to the subjective feelings of unwellness experienced in a social context.

considered a cornerstone of biomedicine. The physician-client relationship locates the physician as the primary health care provider and repository of health knowledge, and women as consumers of health practices, services, and products. In this relationship, women are expected to make appropriate lifestyle choices to promote health, prevent disease, and cope successfully with health problems. As women, we are expected to monitor our bodies, know the date of our last menstrual period, the lumpiness of our breasts, desired body weight, and optimal heart rate during aerobic exercise. As Rail and Beausoleil (2003: 3) argue convincingly, the focus on making healthy choices shifts responsibility from external to internal control where "the desire to achieve health has become a new form of corporeal (self) control and guilt has become intimately tied to an individual's failure to achieve it."

From the biomedical perspective, health is an important life goal and an "unproblematic good" (Rail and Beausoleil, 2003: 3). Health status is improved by curing disease through chemo-pharmaceutical, surgical, and other "heroic," high-tech treatments (Clarke, 2000: 292). The efficacy of treatment is determined using randomized clinical trials that are believed to generate the most valid, reliable, and value-free knowledge (Clarke, 2000: 354). Finding the most cost-effective way to reduce indicators such as *mortality* and *morbidity* rates,[4] for instance, drives health research, policies, and programs.

By comparison, the population-health approach views health as a valuable resource that allows human collectives to engage in productive lives. The cause of health problems is linked to social factors and access to the resources that support health. Promoting or restoring health is achieved through a more equitable distribution of social resources across a population. An ongoing challenge in an advanced industrial capitalist economy is that social goals that are more difficult to assess and give a dollar value receive less attention than goals that can be financially justified and statistically measured. As Armstrong and Armstrong (2003, 111) say, "What counts is what can be counted."

Together, these two approaches give us discrete tools for describing and measuring health and the causes of health problems, one at the body systems level and the other at the population systems level. When a woman gets sick or hurt, biomedicine offers her an organized system of health providers and services for the management of physical expressions of her illness or injury. When women as a collective get sick or hurt because of the poor working conditions in which we live and work, the population-health approach offers an organized system of determinants for describing and measuring that problem within a larger social context.

Feminists argue, however, that description and measurement contribute only one piece to the understanding of women's health. For instance, a low blood hemoglobin does not tell us about a woman's experience of being tired and poor and unable to get enough dietary iron. Neither does statistical information on high rates of obesity and substance use among Aboriginal women help us understand cultural marginalization, colonialism, poverty, and hopelessness. Measurement suggests trends without conveying the local materiality of women's health experiences. Bringing a critical feminist lens to the interpretation of the quantitative and qualitative research generated by both models contributes to a richer understanding of women's health as an abstract concept and a lived experience. The next section illustrates this point using gender-based analysis to explore how biomedical research measures and constructs women's health.

---

4   Mortality rates refer to the frequency of deaths in a given population, while morbidity rates refer to the incidence of disease within a given population.

UNDER THE MICROSCOPE: WOMEN AS OBJECTS OF BIOMEDICAL RESEARCH

Women have seldom been in a position to determine what is studied, how it is studied, and what is done with the findings. Although women's health issues have received increasing attention over the last 30 years, much of the emphasis is on women's reproductive functions. Until the early 1990s, women's perspectives and priorities were of little interest in setting medical, academic, and government agendas for women's health. Vivienne Walters (1992) was among the first to explore women's views of our health needs as a starting point for women's health research.

Increasingly, feminist scholars are partnering with grassroots organizations and feminists bureaucrats in redefining women's health as a complex relationship of biological and social processes. One initiative to come out of these partnerships is *gender-based analysis* (GBA). GBA facilitates the development and evaluation of policies and programs and the research that informs both. The goal of GBA is to eliminate gender-bias problems and contribute a better understanding of women's health. In a synthesis of 160 Canadian and international GBA documents, Eichler and Gustafson (2000) describe three main types of gender bias that exist in health research: androcentricity, gender insensitivity, and double standard. These categories are used here to illustrate how biomedical research constructs women as objects of health research.

Historically, men's bodies, minds, and natures were taken as the norm against which women's were measured, evaluated, and with astounding regularity found to be "essentially and dangerously inferior to men's" (Morgan, 1998: 102). This type of gender bias, *androcentricity*, is encountered frequently in health research and takes several forms (Eichler and Gustafson, 2000). One form that involves excluding or underrepresenting females in studies and was a common practice in drug trials. Findings drawn from all-male populations were typically generalized to both men and women, raising concerns about validity. More importantly, this bias can result in serious negative consequences for women. In 1996, guidelines regulating drug companies were amended, requiring that women be included in drug trials in the same proportion as are expected to use the drug.

Women are also underrepresented in AIDS/HIV research. We know that women are at higher risk of infection through intercourse, that increasing numbers of women are affected, and that women have a lower survival rate than men (Health Canada, 2000). Underrepresentation leaves important knowledge gaps concerning health promotion, disease prevention, treatment, and support of women. Stevens and Tighe-Doerr's (1997) in-depth narrative study of women's responses to learning about their serostatus exemplifies the importance of including women in research populations. Their study identifies the wide range of responses and varying needs for care and counselling among a racially diverse group of low-income women.

Victim blaming is another form of androcentricity and appears in literature and intervention material on violence against women (Eichler and Gustafson, 2000). Violence against women is a cause of physical and emotional injury, permanent disability, and death and is, therefore, an important area of health research. Statistics Canada (2000) data indicate that 78 percent of female victims are assaulted by someone they know and 58 percent of female homicide victims are murdered by a family member. Women with disabilities are particularly vulnerable to abuse (Morris, 2001). Literature on codependence locates the problem of so-called domestic violence in women's problematic psycho-social development, implying that women contribute to their own victimization (Morgan, 1998). Feminists argue that legal and social interventions are better directed at protecting women from the perpetrators of violence and at funding for community agencies and grassroots organizations that provide comprehensive, long-term support (Transken, 2000).

Another form of androcentricity concerns women's over-identification with issues affecting family, household, or procreation, resulting in the overrepresentation of women and underrepresentation of men in some health research (Eichler and Gustafson, 2000). This bias is premised on two notions: First, men and women are assumed to operate in separate life spheres and therefore men are inappropriately excluded from research located in the so-called private sphere. Second, the supposed uniqueness of women's biology is assumed to require "special types of care and specific kinds of research" (Statistics Canada, 2000: 47). The critical reader who asks, Unique, special and specific as compared to whom? must conclude that such research assumes a masculinist perspective that essentializes and naturalizes women's bodies.

Overrepresenting women and underrepresenting men in some health research results in several negative outcomes: The scope of women's health research is narrowed, placing disproportionate emphasis on issues such as birth control and fertility, and directing attention away from other significant issues such as heart disease and stroke, which claim more women's lives than all cancers combined (Morris, 2001).

Another outcome is the *medicalization*[5] of normal biological processes such as menstruation, pregnancy, and childbirth as well as other health problems such as mental illness and depression. Postpartum depression is a good example of the pathologizing of women's health. New motherhood is defined as a psychiatric illness grounded in women's supposed biological uniqueness rather than understandable in the context of women's lives, their relationships, social supports, and institutionalized expectations. Feminists like Natasha Mauthner (1999) call for a "relational reframing" of postpartum depression. Her qualitative study of 40 women's experiences characterizes postpartum depression as a "normal" response to the "public-world losses of identity, autonomy, independence, power, and paid employment."

Ideally, all health research should include females *and* males to avoid the narrowness of focus and androcentric perspective. When this is not possible for some reason, the underlying assumption should be that a sex/gender difference exists unless empirically shown otherwise (Eichler and Gustafson, 2000).

Gender insensitivity is the second type of gender bias and involves ignoring sex or gender as an important variable in a context in which it is, in fact, significant (Eichler and Gustafson, 2000). This problem is captured by the terms *gender neutrality* and *gender blindness*—both of which have been used erroneously to represent a movement toward gender equality. Heart disease in women is an area in which women are inappropriately treated like men. Typically, both women and men with heart disease are evaluated using a clinical profile developed through empirical studies on men. Because women do not typically present with the same clinical picture as men, they are misdiagnosed, appropriate treatment is delayed, and they have more complications (Cunnius and Kerstein, 2002).

---

5   Kathryn Morgan (1998: 173) describes *medicalization* as a problematic social process in which human experiences are intentionally and unintentionally reduced to pathological conditions that are treatable as a medical problem. Morgan's model complicates the monolithic social control model of medicalization.

Gender insensitivity occurs in everyday medical practice when physicians assume that women can and will assert themselves in ways similar to men. This is insensitive to the gendered differences in power in the typical male physician, female patient relationship (Clarke, 2000: 264). Focus group interviews with women indicate that women want to participate in making treatment choices but need to be encouraged to do so (Health Canada, 1999: 16). But dichotomizing this relationship along gender lines assumes gender homogeneity and does not reflect the growing diversity of the Canadian patient population or the increased numbers of women and minoritized groups entering medicine. Power relations between physician and patient are influenced by differences in education, income, social status, and race/ethnicity in both groups. Relative to their male counterparts, female health care practitioners tend to have less power within the health care system and the physician-patient relationship (Gross, 1997). Racialized and newcomer women tend to participate less than men or white women in making decisions about their own health (Guruge et al., 2000).

Given the pervasive importance of sex and gender in our society, the safer way to undertake health research is to assume that sex and gender *are* socially significant, unless a GBA shows that this is not the case in a particular situation or context (Eichler and Gustafson, 2000). Moreover, it is important to consider the intersecting vulnerabilities across groups of women rather than assuming gender homogeneity.

A third type of gender bias is the *double standard* and involves evaluating substantially the same or identical situations, traits, or behaviours differently on the basis of sex (Eichler and Gustafson, 2000). For instance, research on unintended pregnancies, and public education programs and media messages that emerge from it, have traditionally been directed at young women and girls. These messages reinforce the social expectation that women and girls have the power to negotiate safe sex and assume the burden of responsibility for contraception (Health Canada, 2000). In this case females and males are treated differently in a situation that disadvantages females. To counter this type of gender bias, effective and appropriate prevention programs should be directed at both sexes and evaluated for their effectiveness.

The next section looks at how gender bias in health research is reflected in and influences policies, programs, and practices about women's health. Attention is given to alternative ways of understanding these structures.

UNDER PRESSURE: GETTING AND "GIVING" CARE

Biomedical research directs our attention to a multitude of genetic, biochemical, physiological and lifestyle factors linked to women's health problems. We hear about "bad" genes that predispose some women to breast cancer and how HIV crosses the placental barrier from mother to fetus, making women a vector of disease. We hear that eating disorders are associated with certain personality types and chemical imbalances in the brain. We hear that sexually transmitted infections, endometriosis, and infertility are linked, and that more young girls are smoking, putting them at greater risk of lung cancer. Print and television advertising reminds women that we need the right products for light days, heavy nights, and mid-cycle leaks to manage the unpredictability of our bodies' menstrual flows and the purported limits placed on our normal activities. Some women place their fetal sonograms on the fridge along with other family photos, demonstrating how public and taken-for-granted the surveillance of women's reproductive function has become.

The following discussion of specific women's health issues is organized around health determinants and draws on qualitative studies of women's health and quantitative data from health information databases.[6] Two cautionary notes are included here for the critical reader. First, many health information databases that claim to measure *health* actually present indicators of *disease* (such as mortality and morbidity rates) and the quality of health care services. Currently, there is no widely accepted measure of population health that incorporates subjective and objective expressions of health with ideas and practices of health as they are given meaning in structural and historical contexts. Second, organizing this discussion based on health determinants is only one way of mapping out and offering examples drawn from the broad field of women's health. Health determinants are social and political constructs that tend to simplify and compartmentalize factors that are, in the living of them, complex and interconnected. Therefore, understanding women's health must begin from an explicit feminist theory of society that assumes the dynamic interrelationship among social vulnerabilities that result in disparities in health status and quality of life, and the biological and social processes through which these differences are expressed.

Gender

Women make up more than half the Canadian population and have one of the longest *life expectancies*[7] in the world, at an average 81.4 years for females born in 1996 (compared with 76 years for men). This is a significant increase from 1921, for example, when life expectancy for girls at birth was 61 years. Although life expectancy is not, in itself, an indicator of good health, the increase seems to suggest that Canadian females are living longer, healthier lives than men. Interestingly, however, women and men have similar overall rates of hospitalization, disability and chronic disease—all measures of morbidity (Health Canada, 2003). Although significant findings, these mortality and morbidity indicators do not help us understand theoretically the differences in life expectancy and illness experiences.

In general, both health models tend to treat sex, race, and socio-economic status (SES) as demographic variables and, with the exception of SES, individual physiological attributes. Critical feminists contextualize these categories, linking them to patterns of access to power and social and material resources that include health determinants. In this way the physiological and social attributes of sex and gender can be linked with other social locations in exploring health disparities.

Challenging the gender homogeneity suggested by gender as a demographic variable reveals another new picture of women's health. Life expectancy among Aboriginal peoples, for instance, is significantly lower than the overall Canadian averages due to higher rates of infant mortality, suicide, and fatal unintentional injuries. Similarly, illness experiences and quality of life vary among groups of women. Women living in poverty, Aboriginal women, women who are differently abled, and women who hold certain jobs, have shorter life expectancies and fare less well on quality-of-life indicators than women as a whole. Aboriginal women, especially those living in northern communities, have a higher incidence of preventable disease because of limited access to clean water, adequate sanitation, and sufficient income to provide sufficient nutritious foods that many white, middle-class women take for granted.

---

6   Unless otherwise noted, all statistics are drawn from a gender-based analysis of Statistics Canada survey data published in 2000.

7   Life expectancy is the average length of life predicted for those persons born in any given year.

Biology

Both approaches to women's health recognize that biological factors affect women's mortality and morbidity rates. Both agree there are some physiological differences between men and women, but the extent of these differences, as well as the extent to which these differences account for disparities in health status, is in dispute. Feminist criticism says that bodies, and bodily processes and experiences, cannot be isolated from the social and historical contexts that give meaning to them.

For instance, menopause is portrayed in the popular print media as a negative experience or disease that requires medical intervention. Jennifer Blake who studies hormone replacement therapy reinforces the need for medical intervention when describing menopause to family physicians as "one of the most intriguing areas for physicians to *manage*" (1998: 1205, emphasis added). However, a cross-cultural study of the meanings of menopause reveals that negative emotions and symptoms that are treated with hormone replacement therapy in Canada are rarely reported in cultures where menopause signals the beginning of a highly valued stage of life (Gannon, 1999).

From a feminist perspective, women's bodies are contested terrain (Morgan, 1998). Historically, women have been constructed as subject to the appetites, desires, and functions of the body and therefore less rational and more emotional beings than men. In contrast, men are constructed as being able to transcend the body and therefore are more rational and less sensitive beings. The mind-body-spirit split, the intellectual denigration of the body, and the valuing of mental over physical labour have philosophical roots in the writings of Plato and Aristotle and are institutionalized in biomedical practices (Morgan, 1998; Ng, 2000b).

Some feminists challenge social, cultural, and biomedical representations of the negative body and the emphasis on bodily differences between women and men. The literature on embodiment, for example, celebrates the healthy female body as a source of pleasure and satisfaction rather than the object of male desire and medical intervention. Feminists reclaim women's sexuality, reproductive lives, and health by advancing the body as site of transgression (Monaghan, 2001; Morgan, 1998) and epistemology (Gustafson, 1999; Ng, 2000b). However, another body of feminist literature challenges the celebratory approach to the body. Susan Wendell (1993: 117) says that images of the ideal female body and bodily experiences reinforce an oppressive hierarchy between able-bodied women and those living with disability, chronic illness, and pain, for whom the body can be "a source of frustration, suffering and even torment." Rather than seeking embodiment as a means of reclaiming the female body, identity and self, she argues that some women seek to transcend or disengage from the body.

Body image and body weight are significant health issues for women who are bombarded by conflicting and dangerous messages. Consider for a moment the multi-billion-dollar weight loss industry that makes money on misplaced dreams while competing with the multi-billion-dollar fast food industry pushing easy meal solutions for busy women. Add to this biomedical research linking obesity with heart disease, stroke, diabetes, and other health problems that affect life expectancy and quality of life. According to WHO standards, 24 percent of Canadian women are overweight (as cited in Morris, 2001). Although excess weight is a problem for some women, a far greater percentage of women express some level of dissatisfaction with their bodies. Disordered eating and plastic surgery are two expressions of this dissatisfaction (Wendell, 1993). The tension between promoting healthy practices and the obsession to attain a flawless, thin, youthful, white body ideal is part of the web of social contradictions that makes women's bodies a site of social control and capitalist enterprise.

Income and Social Status

Income is the most sensitive predictor of health and life expectancy (Morris, 2001). Although wealthy women live the longest, there are many more poor than rich women and more poor women than men in all age groups. Women over 65 years, women living with disabilities, Aboriginal women, and lone mothers are among Canada's poorest. The term, the *feminization of poverty*[8] names this phenomenon.

How is poverty measured in Canada? The low income cut-off or LICO is the indicator of poverty used most widely by Canadian social policy experts.[9] Individuals and families who spend, on average at least 20 percent more of their pre-tax income than the Canadian average on food, shelter, and clothing are classified as low-income. The indicator takes into account the number of family members and the size of the urban or rural area where the family lives.

An adequate income is essential to good health and determines access to the necessities of life. Barbara Ehrenreich (2001) details her efforts to provide herself with the necessities of life on the salary available to the average low-paid, unskilled worker. As a healthy, white, English-speaking woman with no child-care responsibilities, her three-month research venture is a window into the struggles faced by differently positioned women for whom poverty is a full-time, year-round experience with no escape clause to a better life.

International studies suggest that small improvements in income at the low end of the income scale translate into significant improvements in health for those living in poverty. Moreover, narrowing the gap between the rich and the poor improves health status across all income groups (Wilkinson as cited in Morris, 2001). Although poverty is a predictor of poor health among the poor, income inequality or the size of the gap between the haves and the have-nots is a predictor of poorer health for the whole population. Despite this evidence, priority is given to reorganizing the health care system and changing individual health practices rather than to social policies that would increase the minimum wage to a living wage (Morris, 2001).

Physical Environments

The physical environments where women live and work influence health. Environmental hazards in the water, air, and land have increased dramatically over the last century. Many diseases reproductive problems, and more than 60 percent of all cancers are thought to be environmentally caused and therefore potentially preventable (Clarke, 2000: 73). Feminists

---

8 Feminization of poverty recognizes how income inequality and inadequate financial and social support leave many single, widowed, and divorced women with dependent children living in poverty (Pearce, 1978).

9 There is active debate about the use of the LICO. Some policy agencies such as the conservative Fraser Institute argue that the LICO defines poverty too broadly and therefore defines too many people as poor. Others such as the Canadian Council on Social Development lobby for indicators that are even broader than the LICO. Finally, government documents consistently assert that the LICO is not an official poverty line nor should it be used for that purpose (Statistics Canada, 2000: 140).

and environmentalists are calling for more research that identifies linkages between cancers and environmental factors as a way to eliminate hazards and prevent disease (Batt, 1994; Epstein, 1998). Currently only a fraction of cancer research dollars is directed toward primary cancer prevention, with most directed toward early detection and treatment.[10]

Clean water, pollution-free air, and safe housing are prerequisites for long-term health. Having safe drinking water is a resource that many Canadian women take for granted. Data gathered by the WHO indicates that 100 percent of Canadians in urban areas and 99 percent of those in rural areas have access to clean water. However, some women living on reserves and in northern Innu and Inuit communities do not have indoor running water and must draw water from a community tap. In 1985 at the World Conference on Women in Nairobi, the Canadian federal government voiced their commitment to women's equality and guaranteed safe water for all Canadian women by pledging to introduce a safe drinking water act in 1990. Ten years passed without meeting that commitment (Stienstra and Roberts, 1995: 74). In 1995, the federal government earmarked $250 million to provide clean drinking water to 92 percent of existing reserve homes. Still, this amount falls short of meeting a basic need afforded other Canadian women (Stienstra and Roberts, 1995, 67). In May 2000, seven people died and 2000 more became ill as a result of contaminated water in Walkerton, Ontario. A public inquiry recommended that the Ontario government spend up to $280 million to implement a safe drinking water act (CBC News Online, 2002). Time will tell whether the public outrage evoked by an event in the small rural predominantly white southern Ontario community will be the catalyst that brings long overdue improvements in water safety to Native women in isolated northern communities.

Waste disposal is another environmental problem in advanced industrial capitalist economies. Hazardous toxins and solid waste from homes, hospitals, and industry are sent into the air, water, and landfill sites. Housing located near landfill sites or downwind from industrial sites tends to be less expensive than housing located in more environmentally friendly spaces. Racialized and Aboriginal women, women living with "disabilities," old and young unattached women, and lone mothers who have difficulty finding safe, stable, and affordable housing, are all more likely to be concentrated in such unhealthy living environments.

Women with low incomes face long waiting lists for co-operative and public housing units (McCracken and Watson, 2004). Band-Aid solutions such as homeless shelters, which are overcrowded, are a breeding ground for the spread of diseases such as tuberculosis. To better meet women's needs, McCracken and Watson recommend that federal, provincial, and city governments adopt GBA when developing and evaluating all new housing policies and programs. They go on to say that meeting women's basic housing needs requires public participation in decision-making, and a restructuring of social assistance and disability assistance policies.

Employment

Women in the paid workplace face a wide array of physical, chemical, biological, and psychological hazards that affect health and safety. Newcomers, racialized women, and those with little formal education tend to be concentrated in job ghettos characterized by repet-

---

10   The concept of prevention is undergoing an alarming redefinition. Powerful drugs such as tamoxifen used in breast cancer treatment are being tested as preventative agents for "high-risk" women (Epstein, 1998). Another example described as prevention is the practice of removing normal ovaries in women over 45 years who are undergoing hysterectomy even when cancer is not suspected.

itive and monotonous tasks and shift work that offers lower wages, lack of autonomy over product, and limited or no health benefits or opportunity for promotion. These factors are a recipe for workplace stress (Clarke, 2000) and ill health.

To have an income, some women work in unhealthy environments that predispose them to acute and chronic illnesses (Messing and Grosbois, 2001). Sweat shops in the Toronto garment district exploit the labour of newcomer women who work under appalling physical conditions for extended hours doing piece work that results in income below minimum wage (Ng, 2000a). Women with little formal education take jobs as domestics using organochlorines and other toxic chemicals linked to cancer. Cashiers, hairdressers, retail, and service workers who stand for long hours experience varicose veins and back and foot problems that can become chronic health concerns. Nurses and other hospital workers are exposed to radiation and toxic chemicals linked to cancer and other diseases. Health care providers, teachers, and child-care workers are exposed to contagious diseases, violence, and abuse in their daily work. Clerical workers may perform in ergonomically poor workspaces where they are subject to excessive noise and poor ventilation and lighting (Clarke, 2000).

Women's occupational health issues are obscured by an androcentric research bias that assumes that women's concerns are captured by studying male workers (Messing and Grosbois, 2001). Women and men face different hazards because of differences in the kinds of work each do. Moreover, women's working conditions can differ from men's even within the same setting. Male-dominated unions and other governing structures put emphasis on addressing more visible health and safety issues leaving these normal routes of redress less available to women (Messing and Grosbois, 2001).

Education

Although women with a university education earn on average more than women without post-secondary education, women earn less than their male counterparts at all levels of educational attainment. For example, women with university degrees earn about 74 percent as much as their male colleagues. Newcomer women with formal education in health professions are restricted in their access to the labour market because of credentialing, language requirements, and other structural barriers (Guruge et al., 2000; Lum and Williams, 2000). These barriers negatively affect the emotional well-being of women who accept a lesser-paying job to support their families, providing cheap but competent labour within a restructured health care system (Lum and Williams, 2000).

Social Environments

The social environment in which women work and live influences health and responses to disease. Women who have positive connections to family and community tend to lead happier, healthier lives. When ill or injured, having an established social network speeds recovery.

The population-health approach measures healthy practices and risk-taking behaviours. Feminists argue that women's sexual and reproductive health is better understood by looking at the influence of social environment on sexual behaviour and practices. Here are three examples: Current regulations for provincial and private health insurances mean that some lesbians and bisexual women do not have the same health coverage as heterosexual women. Add this structural bias to the homophobia lesbians face in day-to-day interaction and you have some insight into the differences between lesbians and straight women in morbidity rates and uses of health services (Morris, 2001).

Smoking is high-risk behaviour clearly linked with lung cancer. Lung cancer represents 21 percent of all female deaths from cancer. Eliminating smoking is an important health goal. The biomedical approach is visible in anti-smoking campaigns directed at changing individual health behaviours. See Lorraine Greaves (1996) for a thorough discussion of the cultural pressures that influence women's smoking habits and the benefits that accrue for a society that promotes women's smoking while simultaneously mounting prevention programs.

As the number of cancer diagnoses rises, the financial and human costs also rise. Some women face greater challenges when faced with a cancer diagnosis, for example. Cancer treatment is covered by provincial health insurance but other costs associated with a cancer diagnosis are not. There are indirect costs such as lost wages and loss of caregiver income. There are out-of-pocket expenses such as dispensing fees, transportation and parking at outpatient clinics, child-care, and prosthetics (Moore, 1999). These greater burdens help us understand why women who are living in precarious social and material circumstances tend to have limited or restricted access to health resources and are at increased risk of premature death due to cancer (Hislop et al., 2000).

Culture

In the medical and population-health documents, *culture* is so broadly inclusionary that it is rendered almost meaningless as a social category. This is a contested term among feminists as well. As a health indicator, culture appears to measure race, ethnicity, Aboriginal status, immigrant status, language spoken, and so on.

Living in a racist society affects all of us but is experienced differently by various groups of women. Racism and social marginalization can lead to feelings of powerlessness and hopelessness among Aboriginal and racialized women. For some, racism is a chronic stressor that negatively affect health, as Vines et al. (2001) describe in their study of black women. Many women who are newcomers to Canada or whose first language is not English or French have difficulty gaining access to health care, negotiating the system, developing a comfortable relationship between them and a care provider, understanding treatment regimes, and giving informed consent (Guruge et al., 2000).

Feminists propose a number of strategies for improving the health of racialized women and their families: developing culturally and linguistically sensitive health services, facilitating women's participation and representation in decision-making organizations, and forging working alliances among feminist activists, bureaucrats, and specific communities of minoritized women to implement change that begins from women's expressed needs (Guruge et al., 2000).

Healthy Childhood Development

Canada has one of world's lowest rates of infant and maternal mortality (Health Canada, 1999). These rates have fallen dramatically over the last century. The reasons for this are in dispute.

Healthy childhood development is said to begin at conception. Poorly nourished women are more likely to bear stillborn, low-birth-weight, or neurologically impaired infants. Low birth weight is an important indicator of future health (Clarke, 2000). One researcher goes so far as to say that women should eat nutritiously out of concern for their potential role as birthing agents. John Callis bases his assertion that on research done by a team of scientists from Canada, Australia, and New Zealand who are studying pre-term births in sheep. "Women need to think about proper diet and food intake before they even know they're pregnant because proper nutrition after pregnancy may not compensate for the lack of it beforehand. Even a modest restriction around the time of conception could have far-reaching consequences." (Callis as cited in Wong, 2003). The original study on sheep found that maternal nutrition at the time of conception was associated with long-term adverse health effects in offspring (Wong, 2003).

From a population-health perspective, healthy childhood development can be linked to family income and family status. Women tend to have less income than men, with lone-mother families among the poorest. Women are more often responsible for the care of children in and outside of civil unions. Less income means that some women's children have less access to adequate amounts of nutritious food. Thus, family income, family status, and the health of mother, fetus, and child are dynamically connected. Pregnant and breast-feeding women may not get sufficient amounts of dietary iron, iodine, and vitamin A to support healthy fetus and infant development. We also tend to feed our children before ourselves, lowering our resistance to illness (Clarke, 2000).

Some population-health researchers attribute falling infant and maternal mortality rates to overall improvements in sanitation and nutrition, while biomedical researchers point to better maternal care. Critical feminists argue that the surveillance and monitoring of a normal reproductive function plays on women's fears and reshapes it as a high-risk function requiring medical intervention. Arguments favouring the medicalization of women's experience of childbirth skim over the benefit that accrues to medical practitioners, third-party payers, and biotech companies (Cawthorne, 2000). In the debate where medicine and midwifery are set up as mutually exclusive models of maternal care, some describe obstetrics as institutionally sanctioned violence against women while others claim "home birth is child abuse in its earliest form" (as cited in Cawthorne, 2000: 107–26). Rhetoric aside, midwives provide safe and effective care to women with low-risk pregnancies while obstetricians provide care for women with high-risk pregnancies (Cawthorne, 2000). Midwifery has only recently returned as a viable ideological and financial option in some parts of Canada. In Ontario, midwifery services are covered by the provincial insurance plan rendering unambiguous, enthusiastic support for a safe alternative for pregnant women at all income levels.

Personal Health Practices and Coping Skills

The majority of women consider themselves to be in very good or excellent health, with 10 percent of women saying they have no health problems (Walters, 1992). Almost all women make at least one visit in a year to a health professional such as a doctor, dentist, ophthalmologist, or medical specialist. Far fewer consult other health professionals such as nurses, chiropractors, social workers, or physiotherapists.[11] Although physician and biomedical practices are the starting point for most women, a growing number of white,

11 For the first time in 1996, Statistics Canada included questions about health care providers in their survey.

well-educated, middle-class women are turning to so-called alternative healers to promote health (Shroff, 2000; Ng 2000b).

As women age, we are less likely than younger women to describe ourselves as being in good health. This may be due in part to the increased prevalence of *chronic illness*[12] and degenerative conditions that limit activity, decrease quality of life, and may lead to hospitalization and death. Statistics Canada (2000) reports the most common chronic problems among females 12 years and older are non-food allergies, chronic pain, arthritis or rheumatism, back problems, high blood pressure, migraines, and asthma. Compare this to women's view of their most immediate health concerns: Stress, anxiety, and depression top the list (two of which are not considered chronic illnesses by the Statistics Canada definition), followed by migraines, arthritis, obesity, back problems, and blood pressure problems (Walters, 1992, 1993).

Physical activity is a personal health practice that gets lots of attention. Regular exercise is linked with positive physical and mental health outcomes such as lower rates of heart disease, osteoporosis, and depression. Data from a 1996–7 national population-health survey shows that 60 percent of women are sedentary. Activity levels vary across age groups, with older women generally less active than younger women and women in all age groups generally less active than their male counterparts. The higher a woman's income the more likely she is to engage in healthy practices such as regular activity and in fewer risky behaviours such as smoking and binge drinking (Health Canada, 2003). How do we explain these differences?

Compared with men, women have less free time available for leisure activities. Married women employed full-time spend more time doing unpaid work and have less free time than their male counterparts. Having children affects the way that married women and men allocate their time. Although both experience a decrease in the amount of free time and sleep time, as well as changes in patterns of paid and unpaid work, women continue to experience more dramatic changes and assume greater responsibility for unpaid care work.

Another possible explanation for differences in physical activity relates to the configuration of living and working spaces. Few workplaces provide women with safe facilities to regularly engage in physical activities during or after work hours (Morris, 2001). With the exception of walking and cycling, there are few inexpensive options for low-income women. Urban neighbourhoods often lack community centres, public parks, cycling paths, and other safe spaces needed for such activities. Where these are available, many lone mothers do not have dedicated personal time and daycare to engage in regular physical exercise.

Social Support Networks

Social support networks are another important determinant of mental and physical health. Mental health is often measured using indicators of self-esteem or self-worth—also a person's sense of coherence, a person's perception of life as meaningful and manageable, or a person's sense of mastery and control (Forbes, 2001). These measures locate mental health within the individual and place less emphasis on the systemic factors that structure women's lives and experiences differently from men's. For example, although women tend to have the same levels of self-esteem and coherence as our male counterparts, we are less

---

12   Statistics Canada defines a chronic illness as any disorder that has been diagnosed by a health
     professional and lasts for at least six months.

likely to have a high sense of mastery. And in a society in which social locations are linked to power, women more than men, and marginalized women more than women in general, face greater structural obstacles, leaving some with good grounds for feeling less masterful.

Although most women are able to deal successfully with life's challenges, women are twice as likely as men to have a depressive episode (6 percent versus 3 percent). Young women 15–19 years old are more likely than any other age group to exhibit symptoms of depression. Although a depressive episode may last an average of 5 weeks for women aged 15–19 years old, women over 75 have symptoms lasting an average of 10 weeks. This latter group also accounts for the largest number of women hospitalized for mental illness. Although women are far less likely than men to complete suicide, suicide rates among Aboriginal women, for example, are significantly higher than in the general female population.

One cause of stress is attributable to the additional family caregiving women are expected to assume. Increased "role complexity" or the number of tasks a woman undertakes can lead to higher levels of stress (Statistics Canada, 2000: 111). Married mothers with full-time jobs are almost twice as likely to be severely time-stressed as their counterparts without children. By contrast, there is no difference in the incidence of severe time stress for employed married men with or without children. Restructured families and new family forms as well as the resurgence of the discourse of traditional family values may contribute to women's reports of higher rates of stress (Eichler, 1997).

Health Services

How health services are organized, the quality of care provided, and the impact of those services on health are measured by both health models. Women are the majority of the users of the health care system. As the numerical majority in the Canadian population, we use the system to access services for ourselves and family members. Women also constitute the majority of unpaid care providers as well as the majority of paid health care workers. Nursing is the single largest health professional group. At 97 percent female-dominated, the nursing profession holds less institutionalized power, authority, and legitimacy than the traditionally male-dominated medical profession.

Over the last two decades, more women have gained entry into medicine and dentistry, with women making up 47 percent of all doctors and dentists in 1999. Female physicians are changing the day-to-day practice of medicine, emphasizing collaboration over compliance in decision-making about women's health issues. As Kathryn Morgan (1998) points out, biomedicine is not a monolithic enterprise. Although there are common themes and patterns notable at the macro level, differences in interpretation and practice play out among individual practitioners. But physicians operate within a funding structure that ideologically and financially encourages the treatment of women's physiological processes independent of social variables. Structures such as fee for services reduce opportunities for collaborative decision-making by making a physician's income dependent on quantity rather than the quality of interactions.

Some women express their dissatisfaction by opting out of unsatisfactory relationships with their physicians. A health survey reports that two-thirds of Canadian women who changed doctors did so because they were dissatisfied with their doctor's attitude (as cited in Health Canada, 1999: 17). Not all women have that option, such as those living in rural, northern, and isolated communities who experience persistent physician shortages.

Hospital downsizing, amalgamations, and closures have a profound impact on a labour-intensive health sector largely comprising women (Armstrong and Armstrong 2003; Aronson and Neysmith, 1997). Job cuts and work redesign intensifies historical tensions between categories of nurses and between nurses and other bedside workers that play out along race and class lines (Lum and Williams, 2000). Full-time jobs are replaced with part-time and casual labour. Women who cannot get full-time positions work two or three part-time jobs. Part-time and casual work involves irregular schedules, no health benefits, and lower wages. Activities previously performed by well-educated and highly skilled workers are shifted to workers with less skill and training who are also less costly to the system.

Rationalization and regionalization of health services results in cuts in local services and longer waiting lines for emergency and specialty services. Women in northern and rural communities are hit especially hard, with longer distances to travel for abortion or cancer treatment, for instance. Higher patient turnovers, more day surgery, and shorter hospital stays means more and sicker people are discharged into the community or the home (Armstrong and Armstrong, 2003).

Traditionally, work done in the home was presented as different from work done outside the home. Recognizing that work comes in two forms—paid and unpaid—involved an important redefinition of work as an economic term. One way to think about women's caring functions in an advanced industrial capitalist economy is as providers, mediators, and negotiators of health (Graham as cited in Clarke, 2000).

As care *providers* (Graham as cited in Clarke, 2000), women provide wide range of paid and unpaid material, psychological, and emotional services. Women are the primary care providers to children, seniors, differently abled, and sick and housebound adult relatives. Wives, daughters, and daughters-in-law provide most of the support for aging parents (Aronson, 1998). Although both men and women engage in caring activities, the types of activities they engage in differ. Women are more likely to provide personal support and intimate care while men are more likely to engage in less intimate care activities such as shopping, transportation, and household maintenance. In 1996, over one million women aged 25–54 provided unpaid child care and elder care. As the guardians of family health, the gender-neutral term "sandwich generation" belies the disproportionate burden of care assumed by women in this age group.

As *mediators* of care (Graham as cited in Clarke, 2000) women translate broader cultural ideas and practices of health into the everyday personal performance of health in the home and the community. Typically, women educate family members about nutrition, healthy lifestyle choices, and how to maintain their health. Child-rearing books are directed at new mothers, reinforcing women's responsibility as "Doctor Mom" for monitoring, diagnosing, and treating childhood illnesses, maintaining immunization records, and teaching and enforcing personal health practices.

Women also serve as *negotiators* of care (Graham as cited in Clarke, 2000) among paid care providers, and between care providers and individuals. This role is most evident during health care restructuring, as women operate in all arenas, trying to negotiate the best care situation for themselves as paid and unpaid care providers on behalf of themselves or family members who are care recipients.

Health care restructuring downloads care work from paid to unpaid, from formal, institutional settings such as hospitals to community-based settings and private homes, from more skilled to less skilled paid workers, from paid workers to unpaid relatives and friends, and, in some cases, "from someone to no one" (Aronson, 1999). Some services previously covered by provincial insurance are now available through private agencies, downloading the cost of care to individuals. Some women and their families must assume this additional burden or do without. These changes affect the health and well-being of health professionals and family care providers as well as those who receive their care. Armstrong and Armstrong (2003) argue convincingly that the disproportionate burden of cost containment has resulted in significant costs in women's health and well-being.

UNDER/TAKING CHANGE: WOMEN AND HEALTH

A 1994 report of the Advisory Committee on Women's Health Research Issues estimated that only 5 percent of the Medical Research Council's funds supported research dedicated to women's health issues (Health Canada, 1999). A year later, the Canadian federal government unveiled "Setting the Stage for the Next Century: The Federal Plan for Gender Equality," which includes eight goals for promoting women's equality. Although equality is a core principle in the history of Canadian legislation and the medicare system, the federal plan acknowledges the need to invest equality with substantive meaning.

GBA is a key component in the federal plan that has the potential to broaden our understanding of what constitutes good health research, policies, and programs. GBA has the expressed support of governments at all levels. Responsibility for implementing GBA is decentralized with each federal, provincial, and territorial department and agency accountable for incorporating a gender perspective into the development and evaluation of its policies and programs. The federal government is voicing support for GBA through programs such as Centres for Excellence in Women's Health. The Canadian Institute for Health Research is a federal initiative that is funding research specifically related to women's health issues and the interconnections between biological and sociological processes. At the provincial level, one Manitoba-wide campaign launched by the Women's Health Network publicly announced that "poverty is hazardous to women's health." The message directed at policy makers and the general public pushes for health policies and programs that take down the structures that sustain poverty rather than dealing with the outcomes arising from it.

Critical feminists bring to the exploration of women and health an explicit theory of society that assumes the dynamic interrelationship among social vulnerabilities. This theoretical approach to women's health makes visible the disparities in health status and quality of life, and the biological and social processes through which these differences are expressed. This means using an inclusionary model to revise women's health. Good health policy reduces social inequalities. This can mean affordable housing policies, pay equity, and better access to education. Good health programs begin at the local level, are driven by community needs, and are implemented through public participation. This can mean any program, such as safe public spaces and affordable care for children and seniors, that fills gaps in material and social needs. Good health services are responsive to all women's health needs. This can mean developing linguistically and culturally appropriate services.

Women's health is an equity issue. Good health for women means good health for all.

SUGGESTED READINGS

Baines, Carol, Patricia Evans, and **Sheila Neysmith,** eds. 1999. *Women's Caring*, 2nd ed. Toronto: Oxford. This collection of articles explores theoretical questions about women's paid and unpaid caring work and offers empirical research on various aspects of both paid and unpaid caring.

Miedema, Baukje, Janet M. Stoppard, and Vivienne Anderson, eds. 2000. *Women's Bodies Women's Lives: Health, Well-Being and Body Image.* Toronto: Sumach Press. This collection provides a historical and contemporary overview of processes that shape our understandings of women's health, bodies, and lives.

Sherwin, Susan, ed. 1998. *The Politics of Women's Health.* Philadelphia: Temple University Press. This collection provides a largely theoretical approach to a wide range of issues related to women's health.

Ussher, Jane M, ed. 2000. *Women's Health: Contemporary International Perspectives,* Leicester: British Psychological Society. This collection offers a theoretical approach to a wide range of women's health issues in an international context.

DISCUSSION QUESTIONS

1. What do we mean by health?
2. What factors contribute to health disparities between women and men and among groups of women?
3. How will gender-based analysis contribute to our understandings of women's health?

BIBILOGRAPHY

Armstrong, Pat, and Hugh Armstrong. *Wasting Away: The Undermining of Canadian Health Care,* 2nd ed. Toronto: Oxford University Press, 2003.

Aronson, Jane. "Women's Experiences of Receiving Home Care: Responsive Community Care?" Paper presented at the Canadian Research Institute for the Advancement of Women Conference, Sudbury, 1999.

Aronson, Jane. "Dutiful Daughters and Undemanding Mothers: Constraining Images of Getting and Receiving Care in Middle and Later Life." In *Women's Caring,* 2nd ed., edited by Carol Baines, Patricia Evans, and Sheila Neysmith, 114–138. Toronto: Oxford, 1998.

Aronson, Jane, and Sheila M. Neysmith. "The Retreat of the State and Long-Term Care Provision: Implications for Frail Elderly People, Unpaid Family Carers and Paid Home Care Workers." *Studies in Political Economy* 53(Summer 1997): 37–66.

Batt, Sharon. *Patient No More: The Politics of Breast Cancer.* Charlottetown, PEI: Gynergy Books, 1994.

Blake, Jennifer. "Hormone Replacement." *Canadian Family Physician* 44, (1998): 12050–6, 1216–7.

Cawthorne, Jane. "Obscuring a Crisis: The Obstetricians' and Gynecologists' Job Action and Maternal Child Care in Alberta." In *Care and Consequences: The Impact of Health Reform,* edited by Diana L Gustafson, 107–26. Halifax, NS: Fernwood Press, 2000.

CBC News Online. *Inside Walkerton: A Water Tragedy.* Posted at: **http://www.cbc.ca/news/ indepth/walkerton/** May 2002. Accessed Feb 16, 2004.

Clarke, Juanne Nancarrow. *Health, Illness, and Medicine in Canada.* 3rd ed. Toronto: Oxford University Press, 2000.

Cunnius, Peter, and Morris Kerstein. "The Silent Worker." *Emergency Medical Services* 31/6 (June 2002): 32.

Denton, Margaret, and **Vivienne Walters.** "Gender Differences in Structural and Behavioral Determinants of Health: An Analysis of the Social Production of Health" *Social Science and Medicine* 48/9 (May 1999): 1221–1235.

Eichler, Margrit. *Family Shifts: Families, Policies, and Gender Equality.* Toronto: Oxford University Press, 1997.

Eichler, Margrit, and **Diana L. Gustafson.** *Between Hope and Despair: Feminists Working with/for the State.* Paper presented at the BAITWorM Conference, Toronto: May 2000.

Ehrenreich, Barbara. *Nickel and Dimed: On (Not) Getting By in America.* New York: Metropolitan, 2001.

Epstein, Samuel S. *The Politics of Cancer Revisited.* Fremont Centre, NY: East Ridge Press, 1998.

Forbes, Dorothy A. "Enhancing Mastery and Sense of Coherence: Important Determinants of Health in Older Adults." *Geriatric Nurse,* 22/1 (Jan–Feb 2001): 29–32

Gannon, Linda. *Women and Aging: Transcending the Myths.* London: Routledge, 1999.

Greaves, Lorraine. *Smoke Screen: Women's Smoking and Social Control.* Halifax, NS: Fernwood, 1996.

Gross, E. B. "Gender Differences in Physician Stress: Why the Discrepant Findings?" *Women and Health,* 26/3 (1997): 1–14.

Guruge, Sepali, Gail Donner, and **Lynn Morrison.** "The Impact of Canadian Health Care Reform on Recent Women Immigrants and Refugees." In *Care and Consequences: The Impact of Health Reform,* edited by Diana L Gustafson, 222–42. Halifax, NS: Fernwood Press, 2000.

Gustafson, Diana L. "Embodied Learning: The Body as an Epistemological Site." In *Meeting the Challenge: Innovative Feminist Pedagogies in Action,* edited by Maralee Mayberry and Ellen Cronan Rose, 249–73. New York: Routledge Press, 1999.

Health Canada. *Women's Health Surveillance Report: A Multi-dimensional Look at the Health of Canadian Women.* Ottawa, ON: Canadian Institute for Health Information, 2003.

Health Canada. *Health Issues Snapshots.* Ottawa, ON: Women's Health Bureau, Health Canada, 2000. Last modified: July 17, 2000. Posted at: **www.hc-sc.gc.ca/women/english/ snapshots.htm#body.**

Health Canada. *Health Canada's Women's Health Strategy,* Ottawa, ON: Minister of Public Works and Government Services Canada, 1999. Last modified: April 16, 2002. Posted at: **www.hc-sc.gc.ca/pcb/whb.**

Hislop, T. Gregory, Chong Teh, Agnes Lai, Tove Labo and **Victoria M. Taylor,** "Cervical Cancer Screening In BC Chinese Women," *BC Medical Journal* 42/10 (December 2000): 456–60.

Lum, Janet M., and **A. Paul Williams.** "Professional Fault Lines: Nursing in Ontario after the Regulated Health Professions Act." In *Care and Consequences: The Impact of Health Reform,* edited by Diana L. Gustafson, 49–71. Halifax, NS: Fernwood Press, 2000.

Mauthner, Natasha S. "Women and Depression: Qualitative Research Approaches." *Canadian Psychology,* 40/2 (May 1999): 143–61.

McCracken, Molly, and **Gail Watson.** *Women Need Safe, Stable, Affordable Housing: A Study of Social, Private and Co-op Housing in Winnipeg,* Prairie Women's Health Centre of Excellence, February 2004. Posted at: **http://www.pwhce.ca/safeHousing.htm.**

Messing, Karen and **Sylvie de Grosbois.** "Women Workers Confront One-Eyed Science: Building Alliances to Improve Women's Occupational Health." *Women and Health* 33/1–2 (2001): 125–41.

Monaghan, Lee F. "Looking Good, Feeling Good: The Embodied Pleasures of Vibrant Physicality." *Sociology of Health and Illness* 23/3 (May 2001): 330–56.

Moore, K. "Breast Cancer Patients' Out-Of-Pocket Expenses." *Oncology Nursing Forum,* 22/5 (1999): 389–96.

Morgan, Kathryn Pauly. "Contested Bodies, Contested Knowledges: Women, Health, and the Politics of Medicalization." In *The Politics of Women's Health,* edited by Susan Sherwin, 83–121. Philadelphia: Temple University Press, 1998.

Morris, Marika. *Women, Health and Action: A Fact Sheet.* Canadian Research Institute on the Advancement of Women, July, 2001. Posted at: **http://www.criaw-icref.ca.**

Murray, Michael, and **Kerry Chamberlain.** "Qualitative Methods and Women's Health Research." In *Women's Health: Contemporary International Perspectives,* edited by Jane M. Ussher, 40-49. Leicester: British Psychological Society, 2000.

Ng, Roxana. "Restructuring Gender, Race and Class Relations: The Case of Garment Workers and Labour Adjustment." In *Restructuring Caring Labour: Discourse, State Practice and Everyday Life,* edited by Sheila Neysmith, 226–45. Toronto: Oxford University Press, 2000a.

Ng, Roxana. "Re-visioning the Body/Mind from an Eastern Perspective: Comments on Experience, Embodiment and Pedagogy" In *Women's Bodies Women's Lives: Health, Well-Being and Body Image,* edited by Baukje Miedema, Janet M. Stoppard, and Vivienne Anderson, 175–93. Toronto: Sumach Press. 2000b.

Pearce, Diana. "The Feminization of Poverty: Women Work and Welfare." *The Urban and Social Change Review* 11/1-2 (1978): 28–36.

Radley, Alan. "Social Realms and the Qualities of Illness Experience." In *Qualitative Health Psychology: Theories and Methods,* edited by Michael Murray and Kerry Chamberlain, 16–30. London: Sage, 1999.

Rail, Geneviève and **Natalie Beausoleil.** "Introduction to 'Health Panic and Women's Health.'" *Atlantis* 27/2 (Spring-Summer 2003): 1–5.

Shroff, Farah M. "Forget Reform—We Need a Revolution! Better Health for Canadian Women through Holistic Care." In *Care and Consequences: The Impact of Health Care Reform,* edited by Diana L. Gustafson, 271–94. Halifax, NS: Fernwood Publ., 2000.

Statistics Canada. *Women in Canada 2000: A Gender-Based Statistical Report.* Catalogue no. 89-503-XPE, Ottawa, ON, Ministry of Industry, 2000.

Stevens, P. and **Tighe-Doerr, B.** "Trauma of Discovery: Women's Narratives of Being Informed They Are HIV-infected." *AIDS Care,* 9/5 (1997): 523–38.

Stienstra, Deborah and **Barbara Roberts.** *Strategies for the Year 2000: A Woman's Handbook.* Halifax, NS: Fernwood, 1995.

Transken, Si. "Dissolving, Dividing, Distressing: Examining Cutbacks to Programs Responding to Sexual Violation." In *Care and Consequences: The Impact of Health Care Reform,* edited by Diana L. Gustafson, 127–53. Halifax, NS: Fernwood Publ., 2000.

Vines, A.I., M.D. McNeilly, J. Stevens, I. Hertz-Picciotto, M. Baird, and **D.D. Baird.** "Development and Reliability of a Telephone-Administered Perceived Racism Scale (TPRS): A Tool for Epidemiological Use." *Ethnicity and Disease* 11/2, (Spring–Summer 2001): 251–62.

Walters, Vivienne. "Women's Views of Their Main Health Problems." *Canadian Journal of Public Health* 83/5 (Sept.–Oct. 1992): 371–75.

————. "Stress, Anxiety and Depression: Women's Accounts of Their Health Problems." *Social Science and Medicine,* 36/4 (1993): 393–402.

Wendell, Susan. "Feminism, Disability and Transcendence of the Body." *Canadian Woman Studies Journal* 13/4 (Summer 1993): 116–22.

Wong, Janet. "Premature Birth Linked To Lack of Nutrition." *News@UofT.* April 24, 2003. Posted at: **http://www.newsandevents.utoronto.ca/bin4/030424a.asp**.

WEBLINKS

Canadian Research Institute for the Advancement of Women

www.criaw-icref.ca/

The Canadian Research Institute for the Advancement of Women (CRIAW) is a national, not-for-profit organization that addresses a range of women's issues though partnerships between the academy and community, through research and action. Access numerous publications and fact sheets about racism, violence, poverty, peace and security, and other issues affecting women's health.

The Canadian Women's Health Network

www.cwhn.ca/indexeng.html

The Canadian Women's Health Network (CWHN) is a network of individuals, groups, organizations, and institutions concerned with women's health. The CWHN recognizes the importance of information sharing, education, and advocacy for women's health and equality.

Women's Health Bureau

http://www.hc-sc.gc.ca/english/women/

Learn more about the objectives and key activities of the Women's Health Strategy developed by Health Canada's Women's Health Bureau. Explore links to fact sheets about gender-based analysis, the health concerns of lesbians, seniors, and Aboriginal women as well as other hot topics like hormone replacement therapy and breast implants. Also check out links to national and international associations concerned with women's health.

World Health Organization:Women's Health

www.who.int/health_topics/womens_health/en/

This World Health Organization's page provides links to information relating to women's health around the world including such topics as reproductive health, HIV/AIDS, aging, tuberculosis, environment, and tobacco use.

chapter twelve

Women and Religion: Female Spirituality, Feminist Theology, and Feminist Goddess Worship[1]

Johanna H. Stuckey

AIMS AND SCOPE

Religion and spirituality are today areas of much feminist concern. This chapter will acquaint readers briefly with the importance of female spirituality and examine how spiritual feminists handle the main issues in three old religious traditions and one new one. I have chosen to focus on the traditions that have had the most impact on Western consciousness: Christianity, Judaism, and Islam. They are, of course, all monotheistic. However, as a scholar of goddess worship, I could not omit consideration of one of the fastest-growing new religions in the West today: Feminist Goddess Worship.[2]

THE IMPORTANCE OF SPIRITUALITY FOR FEMINISTS

Many feminists and feminist theorists condemn religion as irredeemably patriarchal and think feminist spirituality at best quirky and at worst dangerous (Magee in King, 2000: 101; Beattie in Sawyer and Collier, 1999). So why study female spirituality and women's involvement in religions?

First, feminist commitment to recognizing diversity demands that we honour the myriad forms of women's spirituality and explore in "a positive way" women's spiritual experiences (King, 1989: xii).

Second, what could be more personal than the spiritual? Spiritual orientations and choices shape views of the world and are usually integral to political and social behaviour, yet feminist analysis often ignores them (King, 2000: 219–220).

Third, study of spirituality and religions reveals a major way in which male-dominated political systems have maintained control over women and men. In some societies, religion remains *the* central control mechanism. Gendered religious symbols continue to reflect and influence cultural and political assumptions.

Fourth, Western feminists have to eschew the male habit of separating women's (or people's) lives and selves into compartments. By now we know that mind and body are not unrelated, and spirituality is related to both.

Fifth, until recently, the study of religions, in the West particularly, has meant the study of *male* religious roles, *male* understandings of spirituality, and *male* symbols. Half the human population has not existed for most religious-studies scholars.

Sixth, feminist theology examines change in women's lives. Its importance stems from the fact that it facilitates conversion of "mind, heart, and ways of living and judging" (Finson, 1995: 2).

FEMINIST THEOLOGY

Webster's Dictionary defines theology as "the field of study and analysis that treats of God and of God's attributes and relations to the universe; the study of divine things or religious truth…" (*Webster's*, 1996, 1967). All theology comes from experience. Both women and men have the transforming and revelatory experiences that give rise to theology. Feminist theologians, within or outside established religions, generally agree that Western religions have devalued and even betrayed women. They also accept that the spiritual/religious is meaningful and valid. Many women need to develop their spirituality in a feminist context and their feminism in a spiritual context.

Feminist theology refers mainly to the work of women (and men) who remain inside, and strive to change, male-dominated monotheistic traditions (Reuther in Haddad and Esposito, 2001). Feminist theology not only demonstrates that past theological thinking has almost completely ignored female experiences but also uses women's experiences to expose both traditional theology and sacred texts as focused on *male* not universal experience (Reuther, 1983: 13). Thus, feminist theologians tend to concentrate on connected issues: for instance, sexism inherent in both sacred texts and religious organizations, problems caused for women by male God-language and images in sacred books and liturgy, and the paucity of female leadership in religious institutions (Green-McCreight, 2000). Even though they may not deal with them, criticisms by feminist theologians have affected most religious traditions (Sawyer and Collier, 1999; Russell and Clarkson, 1996)

CATEGORIES OF FEMINIST THEOLOGY

Feminist theology fits into four categories that often overlap: *Revisionist* theology argues that sacred material has been incorrectly interpreted and that correct interpretation makes obvious the liberating message at the religion's core. Many whose work falls into this category insist that using sex-neutral language in, say, liturgy, while keeping the core ideas intact, provides a satisfactory solution to the problem of sexism. Going a step further, *Renovationist*[3] theology seeks to remodel religious traditions to make them hospitable to women: "Revealing a religion's liberating core" is not enough, for we must expose, and refuse to accept, sexism in the tradition. Further, the use of sex-neutral language is not an adequate response to sexism in sacred material. Renovationist theology seeks to emend the language and symbols of deity, as well as liturgical language, to include female imagery. Even more extreme is *Revolutionary* theology, which pushes a tradition to its limits. For instance, it advocates importing from other traditions language, imagery, and occasionally ritual. Those taking a Revolutionary stance often have close connections with feminists who practise goddess spirituality. Finally, *Rejectionist* theology judges monotheistic religions to be irremediably sexist. Its proponents leave them, usually to create new spiritual traditions, often by employing ancient ideas, symbols, and rituals. Many now practice Feminist Goddess Worship, which they understand as altogether different from other forms of spirituality.

CHRISTIANITY AND FEMINISM

Christianity divides into three basic groups: Eastern or Orthodox, Roman Catholic, and Protestant, the latter having two main streams, liberal and conservative (Bowker, 1997; McManners, 1990).

(1) *Eastern or Orthodox*: This Eastern European, North African, and Eastern Mediterranean tradition, a community of self-governing churches, maintains strict hierarchy, usually with females subordinate. It accepts married priests, all male, and permits divorce. It disapproves of contraception, condemns abortion and sexuality outside marriage, and opposes homosexuality (Ware, 1997).

(2) *Roman Catholic*: The largest Christian tradition worldwide, Roman Catholicism is hierarchical, its supreme head being the Pope. Its priests, all male, cannot marry. It opposes divorce and sexuality outside marriage, does not permit abortion or artificial means of birth control, and disapproves of homosexuality.

(3) *Protestant*: All Protestant churches refuse the authority of the Pope, and almost all Protestant priests can marry. Otherwise, Protestants hold a wide spectrum of views on such topics as divorce, birth control, abortion, sexuality outside marriage, and homosexuality. Protestantism divides roughly into two groups:

(a) Conservative: Pentecostal churches concentrate on possession by the Holy Spirit. They often allow women to take spiritual leadership roles, although they normally hold traditional views of women's domestic role. Evangelical churches, hierarchical in structure, focus on Jesus and his (male) nature. They see males and females as essentially different, with women subordinate.

(b) Liberal: Mainline churches and sects belong here. Structures vary from hierarchical to increasingly communal, emphasizing female-male equality. Many liberal churches ordain women as priests and even bishops. A number also ordain lesbians and gays.

The Dominant Stream in Christian Feminist Theology

According to Charlotte Caron, most Christian feminist theologians subscribe to 10 principles:

- Women's experiences are central.

- "The personal is political," meaning that individual salvation is impossible: None can be saved unless everyone is saved.
- Patriarchy is an evil, hierarchical system that oppresses women.
- There is no such thing as objectivity.
- Everyone, including gays/lesbians, people of colour, and people with disabilities, must participate freely, fully, and publicly in "the naming and shaping of the common good."
- Women have a right to control their own lives and, especially, bodies.
- The basis of everything is the community: Influential members are accountable to the least powerful.
- Exclusively male God-language and imagery are not acceptable. Now God is "Creator" and "Mother."
- Pluralism is essential—feminism has so far dealt primarily with the concerns of white, middle-class, heterosexual, able-bodied women.
- Ambiguities and contradictions are expected, and Christian feminists must live with them (Caron, 1993).

Topics in Christian Feminist Theology

Feminist theologians deal with such issues as sexism in the churches; the education, ordination, and ministry of women; pastoral care of women and by women; recovering the history of Christian women; Christian ethics; the meaning of Christ (Christology); Bible interpretation; and rewriting language, liturgy, and ritual.

Beginning in the second wave, feminist theologians undertook a radical exposure of the sexism of the texts and practices of Christianity. Christian theology at the time was androcentric, neither objective nor universal. Feminist theology demanded that churches and theologians take into account women's experience. Feminist Christians then developed a theology with women's experience at its core. The earliest and perhaps most historically significant remains Mary Daly, whose books *The Church and the Second Sex* (1968), *Beyond God the Father* (1973), and *Gyn/Ecology* (1978) reveal religious language and liturgy as androcentric and, finally, affirm the Goddess as the life-loving "be-ing" of women and nature. Also very influential is Rosemary Reuther, whose books *Religion and Sexism* (1974), *Sexism and God-Talk* (1983), *Gaia and God: An Ecofeminist Theology of Earth Healing* (1992), and *Gender, Ethnicity, and* Religion (2002) restate Christian insights in the context of women's experiences.

Today, women constitute between 50 and 80 percent of the students of many theological schools. This influx over a 20-year period has had an enormous effect on Christianity, especially Protestantism. In the 1980s, women began to enter the Protestant ministry in considerable numbers. Soon there was a flood of experiential and scholarly studies of women and ministry, to which Canadian scholars have contributed: women in Canadian churches (Muir and Whiteley, 1995; Anderson, 1990), the ordination movement in the Anglican Church (Fletcher-Marsh, 1995), Canadian women in missions to Asia and Africa (Brouwer, 2002, 1990; Rutherdale, 2002), women preachers in Upper Canada (Muir, 1991), and modern women in the ministry, including lesbians and Native and Japanese Canadians (Lebans, 1994).

The consequent discussion of pastoral care of women and by women covers topics such as violence and sexual abuse, poverty, and aging. Perhaps the most controversial work is *Christianity, Patriarchy, and Abuse*, which addresses the possibility that images of Jesus' suffering might recall painful memories to survivors of abuse (Brown and Bohn, 1989).

Since the latter half of the 1980s, an area of burgeoning publication has been Christian ethics, exploring issues such as abortion, homophobia, the function of power in pastoral counselling, power and sexuality, and suffering and evil. In 1992, Marilyn Legge examined ethically the concerns of Canadian women in their daily lives.

Christology, or examination of the meaning of Jesus, has produced heated debate (Finson, 1995). Rosemary Reuther envisions Christ as "our sister" (1983: 138). Others suggest constructing different visual images. One such attempt, the statue "Crucified Woman," which stands outside Emmanuel College, University of Toronto, provoked a storm of controversy (Dyke, 1991).

Recovery of religious and church history has also been a very productive area of research (Finson, 1995: 38–41). Historian-theologians have demonstrated that women were instrumental in the establishment and early spread of Christianity (Kraemer and D'Angelo, 1999; Kraemer, 1992; Torjesen, 1993; Pagels, 1979). They have also researched women of the past such as early martyr Perpetua, twelfth-century prophet-mystic Hildegard of Bingen, fourteenth-century mystic Julian of Norwich, Shaker Christ/Messiah Ann Lee, and Roman Catholic social activist Dorothy Day (King, 1998; Setta, Campbell in Falk and Gross, 1989). Also, a collection of four centuries of American women's religious writing appeared in 1995 (Keller and Reuther, 2000).

Examinations of Biblical texts attempt to develop interpretive methods for uncovering revelatory messages for women (Laffey in Haddad and Esposito, 2001; Fiorenza, 2001, 1992; Newsom and Ringe, 1992; Trible, 1984, 1978). In an influential book (1983), Roman Catholic feminist Elizabeth Schüssler Fiorenza discusses the widely used phrase "the hermeneutics of suspicion" (56) and calls for Christian women to form an "*ekklesia* of women," a gathering of equals to decide on spiritual and political matters (344). Today, this "Women-church" movement is a worldwide phenomenon (King, 1989: 202–204).

Language, especially that referring to God, continues to be a central focus for feminist theologians (Finson, 1995: 16–17, 42–44). Mary Daly was one of the first to call attention to the problem of the maleness of both God and Jesus, as well as androcentric God symbolism (1973, 1985: 180–183). Labelling the use of exclusively male language for God as a kind of idolatry, Rosemary Reuther proposes instead the word *God/ess* (1983: 66, 67).

Since the mid-1970s, women have been rewriting hymns, prayers, and liturgies; collecting women's poetry for use in ritual; and even composing new hymns, complete with music (Finson, 1995: 44–47). They have also been developing liturgies for girls' coming-of-age rituals and lesbians' coming-out ceremonies, as well as rites of passage for divorce and healing rituals, especially for victims of violence and sexual abuse (Reuther, 1985; Procter-Smith and Walton, 1993).

Revisionist solutions include the interpretation of God-language and symbols in ways that are not oppressive. Renovationist ones involve making language neuter or, more extreme, adding female symbols. Revolutionary solutions routinely use female language for God and female symbols. Rejectionists, of course, are already deeply involved with goddesses.

Womanist Theology

Fifteen years after Daly's 1968 pioneering work *The Church and the Second Sex*, African American writer Audre Lorde (1983) published a devastating critique of Daly's *Gyn/Ecology* (1978). Lorde faults Daly for generalizing about women's experience from white women's experience, which is not the same as African American women's experience (Kamitsuka, 2003: 46). African American feminist theorist bell hooks had been making similar criticisms since 1981 (1981, 1984). From these beginnings came "Womanist" or African American feminist theology. "Womanist" is Alice Walker's term for a feminist woman of colour (Walker, 1983: xi–xii; Williams in King, 1994).

Womanist theologians adhere to four principles. First, putting African American women's experiences at the centre of their endeavour, they aim to assist African American women to rely on their own experiences to control the "character" of Christianity in their communities (Williams, 1993: xiv). Womanist theologians argue that African American women experience Jesus differently from the way white people do. Black women see him as co-sufferer, symbol of freedom, equalizer, and liberator (Grant, 1993: 66–69). They identify with him because he identifies with them. For them, Jesus is black. Since, in their prayers, black women do not distinguish among the members of the Trinity (Grant, 1989: 211), Jesus is the one to whom they pray. Womanist theologians have also been developing rituals for Womanist worship (Powell and also Williams in Procter-Smith and Walton, 1993)

Second, Womanists understand all systems of oppression (gender, race, class, ability) as interrelated in "one overarching structure of domination" (Eugene, 1992: 140). They emphasize communal commitment to the survival and wholeness of an entire people, without the sacrifice of any woman's individuality. Effective liberation has to work for all their people and all other oppressed people (Cannon, 1988).

Third, they maintain that "Afrocentric" ideas about family and community, which are quite different from those of the dominant culture, must be a focus of inquiry (Williams in King, 1994: 79; Eugene, 1992: 140–143). Womanist theologians point out that many black women perceive white feminism, with its attack on family, as a threat to black family life and to African American survival (Grant, 1989: 201).

Fourth, with the high value they place on the African American community, Womanists see themselves as linked to the community's folk tradition and consider it important to communicate in the language of ordinary black people (Eugene, 1992: 146). Most Womanists also understand themselves as connected to the traditions of American black churches (Paris, 1993: 120; Grant, 1982).

The contributions of Womanist theologians to feminist theology in general are enormous. Through their criticisms of white feminist theology, they have offered feminism new insights. Not only have they developed a set of theological principles of their own, but they have also spurred other women of colour and women of other ethnicities to follow suit: for instance, Latinas, Mujeristas, and Chicanas (Aquino, Macado, and Rodriguez, 2002; Isasi-Díaz, 1996) and Asian American women (Southard in King, 1994).

Third-World Feminist Theology

With the proliferation of feminist theology from the "developed" countries, Asian and African feminists began theologizing from their own perspectives. Latin American women were already doing Liberation theology (King, 1996: 3, 63). For some years, *Inheriting Our*

Mothers' Gardens was the best known introduction, though the bulk of its articles discuss American women of colour (Russell, Kwok, Isasi-Díaz, and Cannon, 1988). The 1994 appearance of *Feminist Theology from the Third World* provided essays by prominent Asians, Latin Americans, and Africans. Recent studies include Kwok Pui-lan's book on Asian feminist theology (2000) and Mercy Oduyoye's on African women's theology (2001).

Lesbian Voices

Lesbian issues began to surface in feminist-theological discussion in the late 1980s: ethics of lesbian choice, friendship, suicide, lesbian priests and ministers, and eroticism. Episcopal (Anglican) priest and feminist theologian, Carter Heywood is openly lesbian; topics she addresses include a specifically lesbian view of Christianity (1989a), ethics (1984), and theology and the erotic (1989b), as well as rituals for lesbians (Cherry and Sherwood, 1995). Lesbians raised as Roman Catholics examine their relationship to that faith (Zanotti, 1986), and 50 lesbian nuns present their personal stories (Curb and Monahan, 1985). Other works examine lesbians and gays within organized religions (Comstock, 1996), the Lesbian and Gay Christian Movement (Gill, 1998), lesbian and gay clergy (Hazel, 2000), and lesbians and gays in African American congregations (Comstock, 2001). The journal *Sinister Wisdom* devoted a special issue to "Lesbians and Religion" (1994–1995).

JUDAISM AND FEMINISM

From the eighteenth century, many Jews were questioning traditional Judaism, with its numerous, strict rabbinical laws. Some developed what became Reform Judaism, which aimed to remodel Judaism for the modern world. At this time traditional Judaism acquired the name "Orthodox Judaism." The *Hasidim*, "pious" ones (Epstein, 1990: 271), fall into this category (Harris 1985). Extremely traditional, "Ultra-Orthodox" Jews are also called *haredim*, "those who tremble." In Orthodox Judaism, women have traditionally had a very strong, if separate, role in the domestic sphere, but no role in the religion's public life (El-Or, 1994; Schulman in Wessenger, 1996: 312).

Well ahead of its time, Reform Judaism's Breslau Conference of 1846 concluded with a call for equality of the sexes in religion, with little response. In the 1890s, feminist fore-mother Henrietta Szold worked for equality, attended the Jewish Theological Seminary in New York, and ended her days in Palestine, where she founded the network of health care that became modern Israel's Hadassah Medical Organization. The first woman rabbi, Regina Jones, who died in Auschwitz, was ordained in Germany in the 1930s (Nadell, 1998).

In 1875, Reform Rabbi Isaac Mayer Wise founded Hebrew Union College in Cincinnati and encouraged women to study there. Though in 1921 the college's faculty voted to allow women to study for ordination, the Board did not approve. Finally, in 1956 the Board agreed to ordain women who managed to achieve the requirements (Carmody, 1989: 152).

Other attempts to update the tradition resulted in Conservative Judaism and Reconstructionist Judaism. The goal of Conservative Judaism, the largest denomination in the United States today, is to confront the challenge of integrating tradition with modernity. In 1886 its Jewish Theological Seminary was founded. Its ordained rabbis form the Rabbinical Assembly that set up a Committee on Jewish Law and Standards to advise on interpretation of rabbinic law (*halakhah*[4]). Although Conservative Judaism understands *halakhah* as binding, member synagogues can accept or reject committee decisions (Schulman in Wessenger, 1996: 314).

Mordecai Kaplan (1881–1982), founder of Reconstructionist Judaism, was a strong advocate of equality for women (Alpert and Milgram in Wessenger, 1996: 291). A Reconstructionist conference in 1967 set up the Reconstructionist Rabbinical College in Philadelphia. The Reconstructionist Rabbinical Association and the Federation of Reconstructionist Congregations govern the movement, which opposes hierarchy in Judaism. Reconstructionist Jews consider *halakhah* a sacred but non-binding tradition that needs to take into account contemporary ethical standards (Alpert and Milgram in Wessenger, 1996: 291).

Feminism and Feminist Theology

During the past two decades, Jewish feminists, stimulated by parallel work in other religions, have been revising basic tenets and premises that have underpinned Judaism in some cases for as much as three millennia. For example, they question male dominance; are involved in forming and naming the tradition (Plaskow, 1990: vii); analyze sacred and legal texts (Levine in Haddad and Esposito, 2001); and examine the relationship of feminist theory and Judaism (Plaskow, 1994).

Not until recently have feminist theologians dealt with theological issues arising from the Holocaust of World War II (1939–1945). For all Jews the Holocaust was a major occurrence, but for Jewish women it is "the single most important historical event," because the Nazis particularly targeted Jewish women as bearers of "communal and religious continuity" (Stuckey, 1998: 34). Indeed, "Nazism placed women in 'double jeopardy' as object both of anti-semitism and misogyny" (Raphael, 2003: 1). To answer the central question, "Where was God?" Melissa Raphael wrote a Jewish feminist theology of the Holocaust (2003).

With considerable success, Jewish feminists have been taking part in public ritual and filling leadership roles (Nadell, 1998). Today, in the non-Orthodox streams, there are a number of women rabbis, including some in Conservative Judaism (Nadell, 1998; King, 1989: 43). In Conservative, Reform, and Reconstructionist Judaism, women can publicly read from the Torah, the first five books of the Hebrew Bible. Even in Conservative Judaism, they can usually form part of the *minyan*, the prayer quorum of 10 adults, traditionally all-male (Elwell in Wessenger, 1996).

Feminist theologians also ask what sort of a religion Judaism would be if it incorporated not only the participation of women, but also their points of view (Plaskow, 1994: 81).

Revisionist Views The earliest Jewish feminist work concentrated on recovering lost women and their contributions (Plaskow, 1994: 67). Today, feminist historians continue to do recovery work, for example, Ellen Umansky and Diana Ashton (1992) and Tikva Frymer-Kensky (1994, 1992). Other studies examine women's place in the synagogue (Goldman, 2000; Brooten, 1982), women and American Judaism (Nadell and Sarna, 2001), women in rabbinic literature (Baskin, 2002), and women's history, 600 BCE to 1900 CE (Taitz, Henry, and Tallan, 2003).

At the First International Conference on Orthodoxy and Feminism in New York, February 1997, most attendees described themselves as "modern or centrist Orthodox." The conference discussed such issues as effecting changes in *halakhah*; the ordination of women; and the *agunot*, women whose husbands refuse to give them religious divorces (*gets*). Participants had already heard that some Orthodox women were performing all rabbinic roles except in public ritual. They had also received a report that a group of Orthodox rabbis had formed a religious court to deal with the *agunot* problem; it had already managed to find ways inside Jewish law to annul the marriages of six women. Speaker after speaker insisted that rabbis could interpret *halakhah* so that Orthodox women could become increasingly active in their own religious lives (Cohen, 1997).

Over the past 20 years, Orthodox women have been expanding their areas of religious expression, for instance, by celebrating women's rites like *Rosh Chodesh*, a monthly new-moon gathering, and by meeting in women's prayer groups; there are now a few in Canada and a number around the world. Often these prayer groups meet to celebrate a *bat mitzvah*, a girl's coming-of-age ceremony. In some synagogues, after the men have read the Torah scroll aloud, they pass it behind the screen separating the women from the men, so that the women may touch it (Cohen, 1997). Orthodox feminists, like most at the 1997 conference, intend to stay "firmly within the bounds of generally accepted halacha [*sic*]" and, from that position, reveal the liberating core of the tradition and the power and influence of women in their families and communities (Frankiel, 1990: xiii, xi).

In the 1990s, a small but vocal feminist group demanded more drastic change in Orthodox Judaism, including Talmud[5] studies for women, the formation of all-women *minyan*s, and regular performance by women of the obligations (*mitzvot*) that traditionally only men observe. Such demands, obviously threatening, were "severely criticized from within" (Myers and Litman, 1995: 69). Despite their insistence on remaining Orthodox, we should probably class such women as Renovationist.

Most feminists working inside Conservative Judaism are also Revisionist. Judith Plaskow argues that the educational opportunities now available to women in Conservative Judaism lead only to contradictions. Her example is the *bat mitzvah*, which represents a girl's *final* participation in the congregation, not the beginning, as the *bar mitzvah* does for a boy (1990: ix).

Feminist pressure, however, has produced alterations even in this stream of Judaism. Starting in 1972, the Conservative Jewish Women's Group began requesting changes that eventually led to women's full involvement in education for the rabbinate. Women were admitted to the Jewish Theological Seminary in 1983. However, the Seminary accepted women only if they voluntarily undertook to perform all the obligations enjoined on males. Some female students had problems with this logic, for it implies that women as women are unacceptable, that they must become quasi-males. As one student pointed out, women have to conquer their femaleness to gain equality with males (Schulman in Wessenger, 1996: 315–16). From May 1985 to May 1993, the seminary ordained 52 female rabbis, and most explained that, in becoming rabbis, they were seeking not just authority and "equality of obligation," but also "authenticity" in the tradition (Schulman in Wessenger, 1996: 327–28). In the mid-1970s, the committee of the Rabbinical Assembly that interprets *halakhic* matters pronounced that women could participate in a *minyan* (Schulman in Wessenger, 1996: 314).

Renovationist Views   Although Reform Judaism had ordained at least two women before 1940 (Neudel in Falk and Gross, 1989: 180), American Sally Preisand, ordained in 1972, is usually named as the first woman to become a Reform rabbi (Preisand, 1975). A decade later, there were 61 female Reform rabbis and by 1986 a total of 131 (King, 1989: 43).

By 1991, 10 percent of all Reform rabbis were women, and 40 to 50 percent of all applicants to the rabbinic program at Hebrew Union College were female. Recent graduating classes at the College have been close to 50 percent female (Marder in Wessenger, 1996: 287).

Feminist theologians have been quick to attack the sexism in Judaism, the Torah and especially *halakhah*. Plaskow, raised in the "classical Reform" tradition (1990: viii), says that Jewish feminist aims must include restructuring the foundations of Jewish life; that entails developing a new way of interpreting the Torah, because the Torah is profoundly unjust (in Heschel, 1995: 230). *Halakhah* change has been central to feminist demands, and some hope to improve the status of women through it. However, to date, feminists have challenged only specific laws, not the law's basic assumptions (Plaskow in Heschel, 1995: 224).

Jewish feminists are committed to challenging male-centred language and God imagery (Spiegel, 1996: 126–27). Rita Gross argues for the necessity of reuniting "the masculine and feminine aspect of God" and of using female language to refer to God (in Christ and Plaskow, 1979: 167–68). She considers female imagery, however, to be more important than female language. Only a decade later, Gross discusses developing Jewish female God imagery: the use of female language, especially pronouns, and the collection of female images of God from inside and outside the Jewish tradition. She concludes by advocating the addition of "Goddess" to Judaism, a claim that surely pushes the tradition beyond its limits (Gross in Heschel, 1995).

Feminist theologians have also been examining liturgy, especially the Passover order of service (*Haggadah*) and various prayers and blessing formulae. Women have constructed feminist and women's *Haggadah* texts; they add references to Biblical foremothers, women in legends, and historical women, and they often expand the *Haggadah's* focus on oppression and liberation to include women's oppression and need for freedom (Elwell in Wessenger, 1995; Cantor in Christ and Plaskow, 1979). A particularly rich resource is Marcia Falk's collection of feminist prayers and blessings (1996), many of which are now part of ritual in liberal synagogues. In addition, some liberal-synagogue rituals incorporate liturgical/musical prayers by Debbie Friedman (2000).

Renovationists have been instrumental in the creation of women's rituals (Spiegel, 1996: 128ff; Orenstein, 1994; Orenstein and Litman, 1994). They have constructed rituals to mark the female life cycle and other important events, for instance, rites of passage for women in mid-life (Fine, 1988, Adelman, 1986) and rituals for the welcoming of daughters into the Jewish community (Plaskow in Christ and Plaskow, 1979).

For Judith Plaskow, remaining Jewish was not just a rational decision, for she felt that "sundering Judaism and feminism would mean sundering [her] being" (In Christ and Plaskow, 1979: x, xi). In the introduction to her important book *Standing Again at Sinai*, Plaskow observes that in non-Orthodox Judaism women's efforts have resulted only in their becoming participants in and teachers/preservers of a male religion. What Plaskow advocates instead seems very Revolutionary: a complete transformation of Jewish religion and society, so that the tradition incorporates women's experiences (Plaskow, 1990: xiv–xv).

For feminist Jews who already belonged to the Reconstructionist stream it should have been easy to become Revolutionaries. The movement is egalitarian and non-hierarchical and understands God as gender neutral (Alpert and Milgram in Wessenger, 1996: 292). In fact, although feminist activities inside Reconstructionist Judaism have been quite successful, most feminist theology in this stream remains Renovationist. By the early 1980s, there were 14 female Reconstructionist rabbis, almost 20 percent of all rabbis ordained since the establishment of the Reconstructionist Rabbinical College in 1968; in 1983 the College ordained 47 students, of whom 23 were women (Carmody, 1989: 152–53). Women rabbis have devised "theologies" and rituals that express the experiences of women. They have also worked on text interpretation, inclusive language, and God names (Alpert and Milgram in Wessenger, 1996: 303, 309). In 1983, however, Susannah Heschel could write that, like the Conservative stream, Reconstructionist Judaism was still emphasizing a historical consciousness of Jewish civilization (1995: xlviii).

The Jewish Renewal Movement, the "vision" of which "began over thirty years ago" (Goldberg, 2002: 13), seems Renovationist, though some of its practices are Revolutionary, and some fit "well within a Rejectionist viewpoint, albeit the authors tenuously hold to a Jewish ethos" (Goldberg, 2002: 24). The movement allows "liberal" Jewish women to articulate their "spiritual understandings" (Goldberg, 2002: iv) in a context that welcomes feminist ideas.

Revolutionary Views   Very few Jewish feminist theologians take fully Revolutionary stances in their work. In arguing that Judaism needs a goddess, Rita Gross had already moved by 1983 into the Revolutionary category and even beyond it. With the drastic changes that she envisions, Judith Plaskow too may already have one foot in the Revolutionary feminist-theological camp (1990). The brave women who carried a Torah to the holy West Wall of the Temple in Jerusalem ("Wailing Wall") did a Revolutionary act, though it is unlikely that any would label herself Revolutionary (Chesler and Haut, 2003; Zuckerman, 1992).

In *She Who Dwells Within*, Lynn Gottlieb shows herself to be firmly Revolutionary, and her spiritual history suggests that she has long held such views (1995). Gottlieb focuses on the female "Presence of God," the *Shekinah* (1995: 20). She advocates borrowing from other spiritual traditions, like Native American or ancient eastern Mediterranean. Further, she revitalizes and reinterprets elements of the Jewish tradition, and she draws on her own vision for new material from which to construct prayers, rituals, sacred stories, and meditations. What Revolutionary Gottlieb envisions would entail the complete alteration of the Judaism that Judith Plaskow has spoken of (1990: xiv–xv).

Judaism, Multiculturalism, and Difference

Most of the feminist theologians discussed above are Ashkenazi (Bowker, 1997: 98–99). Ashkenazic women have been the subjects of most research, as well as being the researchers. However, the voices and theological views of Sephardic women (Bowker, 1997: 875) and those of other origins are not absent from the record, but are not widely available in North America. Special issues of the journals *Bridges* (7/1: 1997–1998) and *Canadian Woman Studies* (16/4: 1996) have begun to improve the situation. Recently, Jewish feminists have been discussing both multiculturalism and difference "without and within" (Plaskow, 2003:91), as articles by six scholars in *Journal of Feminist Studies in Religion* demonstrate (Brettschneider and Rose, Plaskow, Falk, Cohler-Esses, and Levine, 2003).

Lesbian Voices

Jewish feminists taking a Revolutionary stance are often lesbians, who usually have difficulty finding acceptance even in liberal streams (Alpert and Milgram in Wessenger, 1996:

308). However, Rebecca Alpert mentions six openly lesbian Reconstructionist rabbis (1997). The best-known Jewish lesbian publication collects essays, poetry, and stories about women's identity (Beck, 1982). Another contains a number of articles by Jewish lesbians (Balka and Rose, 1989). Lesbians too have devised rituals and liturgy (Butler, 1990; Stein, 1984). A special issue of the journal *Sinister Wisdom* is devoted to "Lesbians and Religion" (1994–1995).

ISLAM AND FEMINISM

In most Muslim societies, women manage to express their spirituality despite their involvement in what has developed as a thoroughly male-dominated religion (Shehadeh, 2003). Feminists can be found in Muslim countries and communities worldwide, even though "Islamic feminism" might seem a contradiction to most Western feminists.

In some countries, Muslim feminists are able, more or less freely, to express their views. However, in countries that are experiencing powerful fundamentalist pressure or have fundamentalist governments, an avowed feminist can suffer considerable distress and even face real danger (Moghissi, 1999; Alam, 1998). Not surprisingly, many feminists writing about Islam work in Western societies (Webb, 2000; Yamani, 1996: ix–xii).

Monotheistic like Judaism and Christianity, Islam builds on the other two, but has "original" traits (Buturovic, 1995; Haddad and Esposito, 2001: 1). *Islam* means "surrender" or "submission" to the will of God (Ruthven, 1997: 2–3). Thus, a Muslim is anyone submitting to God and observing His Commandments. Muslims base their faith on the Qur'an (The Koran, 1994), their sacred book, which God revealed to the prophet Muhammad over a period of about 23 years. Islam is characterized by "indivisibility between the sacred and the secular" (Cleary, 1993: VII). For Muslims, their religion *is* their way of life.[6] Thus, Muslim feminists are often torn in finding that they cannot leave Islam (Khan in Saliba, Allen, and Howard, 2002: 327)

Islam and Women

Possibly "more explicitly than any other [monotheistic] sacred text," the Qur'an deals with women both separately and fully (Buturovic, 1995). It states that God made women and men from "one soul" (Qur'an, Chapter (*Sura*), 4: 1) and sets out the obligations of the sexes in matters of both social behaviour and faith, expressly understanding the female-male equality in the latter (Buturovic, 1997: 53). In principle, the Qur'an expects women to fulfill all religious obligations.

Chapter four of the Qur'an is traditionally called "Women." Since the Qur'an is, for Muslims, the revealed word of God, what it says about women has always been central to Islam's treatment of them. It proclaims that women and men are equal in faith (*Sura* 4: 124–26). As in every other sphere of life, in male-female relationships, the first duty of Muslims is to keep God in the forefront at all times, for God sees and knows everything (*Sura* 4: 1).

The Qur'an permits a man to marry up to four women, provided he can support them economically and treat them equally (*Sura* 4: 3). However, the preference of both the Qur'an and Muslim custom is monogamy, and the ideal relationship is that of Muhammad and his first wife, Khadijah (Carmody, 1989: 191).

The Qur'an states that women can inherit a woman's portion, but men inherit the equivalent of two women's portions (*Sura* 4: 11). Marriage is a contract in Islam, not a sacrament, as in Christianity. A Muslim wife has legal rights. She can insist on the terms of the contract, and she retains her dowry. She also has the right to refuse marriage. If her husband does not support her, she can seek redress from the law. She can also sue for divorce, though traditionally divorce has been easier for men than for women. The Qur'an forbids incest (*Sura* 4: 23), as it does adultery. Four witnesses have to corroborate an accusation of "lewdness" against a woman; if she is guilty, incarceration in the house until death may be her sentence. The law punishes both partners in fornication.

On the other hand, *Sura* 4: 34 states that men are in charge of women because God has given men superior qualities and because men support women. Good women are obedient and chaste. Men should banish disobedient women from their beds and whip them. The Qur'an prescribes modesty for both men and women, and it makes clear that a woman's primary role is to be a good wife and mother. If a woman is pregnant or menstruating, she is exempt from the duties of fasting and pilgrimage. Islam does not forbid women to study the Qur'an or to read prayers in mosques (Buturovic, 1995).

Later interpretation of the Qur'an, as well as a body of material relating to Prophet's life (the *Sunna*), and the development of Islamic law (*Sharia*) in the light of local custom often resulted in the subjection of women to very restrictive demands concerning obedience and family honour. Increasingly, Muslim society placed emphasis on woman's role as mother. Certain sayings of the Prophet (*hadith*s), as well as writings by prominent men, have disparaged women; for instance, Muhammad is reported to have said, "Consult [women] and do the opposite" (Carmody, 1989: 195).

Discussing women in Turkey, Julie Marcus examines women's involvement in rituals mainly to do with the life cycle, especially birth and death. She concludes that the female world view is egalitarian (1992: 121ff.). She also demonstrates that, even in extremely male-dominated religions, women make spiritual space for themselves.

Perhaps the most important point to remember about Muslim women is that, as with women of other traditions, there is enormous variation in their social, political, economic, and religious experiences. There can be vast differences between Muslim women even in basically the same religious context. Thus, context is extremely important (Buturovic, personal communication, 17 May 1997).

Feminism and Feminist Theology

A wide variety of feminisms exists in Islam (Buturovic, personal communication, 17 May 1997). Many women who wish to remain Muslims, however, have adopted "Islamist" or "Islamic" feminism. Egyptian feminist Margot Badran opts for the term "Islamist woman," rather than "Islamist feminist" (Buturovic, personal communication, January 1998). Since the adjective "Islamist" usually describes fundamentalist movements that advocate total adherence to Islamic law (Yamani, 1996: 1), the term "Islamic" seems preferable, and so I will use it here.

Islamic feminism is not "a coherent identity." Rather it is "a contingent, contextually determined strategic self-positioning" (Cook, 2001:59). It deals with issues that challenge the religious and political establishment of Islam, particularly its scholars (Cook, 2001: vii). All Islamic feminists have as their goal female empowerment from inside "a rethought

Islam." They plan to achieve their goal mainly through appeal to the rights that Islam grants women (Yamani, 1996: 1–2). An Islamic feminist engages in dialogue with tradition and tries to bring out the best in it because she thinks that women can feel empowered inside Islam without needing to reject values important to them (Buturovic, personal communication, 17 May 1997).

This kind of feminism does not go far enough for Yasmin Ali, who insists that it leads only to "a limited extension of opportunity" for a small number of women. Ali sees Islamic feminism as elitist (in Saghal and Yuval-Davis, 1992: 12). Leila Ahmed also has reservations about it (1992: 236).

Though she stays involved with Islam, long-time feminist activist and Egyptian writer Nawal el Saadawi has declared Islamic tradition sexist (Saadawi, 1980, 1997). Leila Ahmed considers el Saadawi's criticisms to proceed from assumptions and ideas stemming from Western capitalism (Ahmed, 1992: 235–36). Indeed, Islamic feminists describe women like Nawal el Saadawi as Western-style "feminists."

In elucidating the attitude of Muslim women to Western feminism, Leila Ahmed argues that, in colonial times, male colonizers appropriated the language of Western feminism—their enemy in their own countries—to attack Muslim men for abuse of women and so justify the subversion of colonized cultures. In Ahmed's opinion, Western feminists have not been much better, because, "in the name of feminism," they have attacked many practices of Muslim societies, especially the *hijab*, head scarf or veil (Ahmed, 1992: 243–44).

Today, Ahmed maintains, these manipulations are "transparently obvious." She accuses Western media and scholarship, including Western feminist scholarship, of invoking the oppression of women to validate, and "even insidiously" support, antagonism toward Muslims and Arabs (1992: 246). It is no wonder that, for many women in Muslim countries, identification as a feminist or a women's liberationist connotes giving in to "foreign influences" (Mernissi, 1987: 8).

According to Fatima Mernissi, the Prophet's message, the Qur'an, is egalitarian (1991: ix). However, Amila Buturovic has qualified such a statement by identifying the message's egalitarianism as applying to faith (1997: 53). Further, Muslim women often insist, usually to the incredulity of non-Muslims, that the tradition is non-sexist. Leila Ahmed attributes this sincere belief to the fact that Muslim women respond to "ethical, egalitarian" Islam, rather than the "technical," legalistically focused Islam of the male establishment. It is the latter that is powerful politically (Ahmed, 1992: 239). By making the distinction between what Mernissi has called "political Islam" and "spiritual Islam" (1993: 5), Muslim feminists can begin to expose sexism in their societies. Islamic feminist scholars scrutinize not only political Islam, but also the widely varied religious practices of Islamic communities, most of which get their validation, rightly or wrongly, from the sacred texts of Islam, primarily the Qur'an.

Getting involved in Qur'an interpretation is difficult for women not only because, for all Muslims, the Qur'an is the revealed word of God, but also because most Muslim women do not have access to the necessary education. However, the Qur'an is the very centre of Islam. On it rests women's role in Islamic societies. When dealing with the Qur'an, most feminist theologians explicate its message and ignore, or try to explain, its sexism, but they do not question its authority. For instance, an Islamic feminist cannot reject polygamy because the Qur'an expressly permits it (*Sura* 4: 1–10); she can, however, decide not to deal with it.

A few feminists do study the Qur'an critically. In her early work, Mernissi rejected the Qur'an's sexism. In her later work, she accepts the sacred book and attributes women's condition mainly to societal factors (1987: 165–77). For instance, in discussing *Sura* 4: 34, which states that men have charge of women and may beat them for disobedience, she resigns herself to living with contradictions. Muhammad, she notes, was opposed to violence (1991: 154–55).

Recently, following in a venerable and previously exclusively male tradition, some feminist theologians have begun in earnest the difficult process of Qur'an interpretation (Yamani, 1996: 2). Such scholars include Najla Hamideh (in Yamani, 1996) and Riffat Hassan (1997). What seems to be the first thorough examination of the sacred book from a woman's perspective appeared in 1992 (Wadud, 1999).

If the Qur'an is inviolable, the collection of sayings and deeds of the Prophet (the *Sunna*) is another matter. Of course, it is almost as sacred as the Qur'an, but Islam has had a long tradition of study and validation of these texts. Thus, some feminist scholars question the authenticity of certain of the sayings (*hadith*s). Mernissi addresses one of them: "Those who entrust their affairs to a woman will never know prosperity" (1991: 1). This *hadith* is widely quoted in Muslim societies. Thus, it is extremely important for attitudes to women. A consensus of Islamic scholars holds it authentic, despite the fact that its authenticity was a matter of fierce debate (Mernissi, 1991: 61).

Mernissi points out that Muslim society has two universes: that of men, which consists of the worldwide religion and all public power, and that of women, focused on the domestic realm, including sexuality (1987: 138). The five obligations or Pillars[7] of Islam connect the two (Marcus, 1992: 65). As to the Five Pillars, women have no problem fulfilling the first, daily witness to the Oneness of God. Though God is understood as male, He is not Father, like the God of Christianity and Judaism, nor does He have feminine characteristics. Thus, since Islam does not emphasize the sex of God, it is not an issue for women. The second, the giving of alms, causes no problem either (Marcus, 1992: 66).

The other three duties (observation of Ramadan, pilgrimage to Mecca, and daily prayers) are public and require ritual purity. Menstruation and having recently given birth render women impure. Further, no woman who is still menstruating can fast for the full 30 days of Ramadan. The same is true for the time it normally takes a pilgrim to make the journey to Mecca (*hajj*). Both of these obligations a woman must postpone until after menopause. Consequently, she has little chance, until she is middle aged or old, to garner the great respect that comes to a person who has made the *hajj*. Prayer at a mosque on Friday and at dawn on feast days demands total purification beforehand, again impossible for women much of the time. So, though Muslims value communal prayer more highly, women usually have to pray in private. There are no women's mosques (Marcus, 1992: 65–69). In practice, then, few women can, at least while young, fully observe the main obligations. Nonetheless, since God excuses them, they can still remain good Muslims.

Feminist theologians deal with other topics and issues, among them family law and its abuses (Ahmed, 1992: 64ff, 241ff; Fernea, 1985), sexuality (Mernissi, 1987), and the controversy over the veil (Alvi, Hoodfar, and McDonough, 2003; Khanum in Saghal and Yuval-Davis, 1992; Mernissi, 1987). Some scholarship recovers women's history (Mabro, 1996; Mernissi, 1993; Tucker, 1985). One researcher has produced a history of birth control in Islam (Musallam, 1989). Scholars are also making available women's stories and recording their voices (Sharawi, 1986; Fernea and Bezirgan, 1977). In addition, they have studied women and women's movements both in the Muslim world in general and in various Muslim countries (Afshar, 1993; Badran, 1995; Beck and Keddie, 1978; Lateef, 1990; Mumtaz and Shaheed, 1987; Minces, 1982; Musallam, 1989; Sansarian, 1992; Tabari and Yeganeh, 1982; Wikan, 1991).

In the concluding chapter of *Beyond the Veil*, Mernissi maintains that Muslim male writers have insisted that any change in the situation of women necessarily involves religion. Therefore, any attempt to alter the status of women and the conditions they endure would represent a frontal assault on God's ruling and ordering of the world. Mernissi argues, however, that making changes to benefit women in any society is actually primarily a matter of economics (1987: 165). So society needs to be completely reshaped, beginning with economics and finishing with language structure (176). This reshaping is a matter for political Islam, not spiritual Islam (Moghadam, 2003; Abu-Lughod, 1998). Nevertheless, Muslims in general make no such distinction.

Lesbian Voices

Commonly, today's Islamic communities regard heterosexuality as the only acceptable form of sexual expression, appealing to the Qur'an's comment on Lot and Sodom for support (*Sura* 27:54). They generally agree in condemning homosexuality as unnatural, though lesbian scholar Shahnaz Khan states that there are no *suras* in the Qur'an expressly against homosexuality (In Saliba, Allen, and Howard, 2002: 329). It's not surprising that I have found very little material on Muslims who were, may have been, or are lesbians, though some Islamic feminists discuss the topic (Imam, 1997; Ahmed, 1992: 184–87; Mernissi, 1987: 27–64). Recently, Canadian feminist lesbian writer and broadcaster Irshad Manji published a controversial book in which she describes Islam as, among other things, homophobic (2003).

FEMINIST GODDESS WORSHIP

Today's keen feminist interest in spirituality comes from women's attempts to develop, or rediscover, language, sacred stories, and myths that speak to their experiences (Christ in Christ and Plaskow, 1979: 228). Emerging alongside feminist spiritualities in the three monotheistic traditions is a new religion, Feminist Goddess Worship, also called Feminist Spirituality and Spiritual or Goddess Feminism (Raphael, 1996). Over the past decade it has become a separate entity committed to women's spiritual and political issues while seeking spiritual expression that empowers women and helps them change their lives (Eller, 1993: ix). Already it has its *thealogy* and its *thealogians* (Raphael, 2000a).

In the late 1960s, I was a member of Toronto New Feminists, a radical-feminist group firmly opposed to religion. I remember intense consciousness-raising (CR) sessions at which we exchanged significant stories, personal myths, and aspirations. In retrospect, I realize that they were a combination of therapy session, discussion group, healing circle, and prayer meeting. One of the reasons many feminists turned to spirituality and goddess-worship circles in the mid-1970s was to recapture the elation accompanying ritualized sharing of experiences and communal validation, as well as the comfort, safety, release, and support that CR groups provided.

Another reason for the growth of Feminist Goddess Worship was the power of Elizabeth Gould Davis' *The First Sex*, an early statement of its enabling myth (1971). Davis' aim was to empower women by demonstrating that women had once ruled. She dismissed received history as "two thousand years of propaganda" about female inferiority, as she searched myth, literature, findings of archaeology, and patriarchal history for the "Lost Civilization" of the female-dominated past (Davis, 1972: 18–19). Davis was a prophet for a new religion that would be 20 years in the making.

In 1976, Merlin Stone published her enormously influential *When God Was a Woman*, and Feminist Goddess Worship had one of its sacred books. Stone's pivotal work inspired women to seek out goddesses. Since then, a myriad of books have contributed heavily to the spread of Feminist Goddess Worship (for example, Eisler, *The Chalice and the Blade* (1987); Gadon, *The Once and Future Goddess* (1989); and Baring and Cashford, *The Myth of the Goddess* (1991).

The Myth or Sacred Story

Feminist Goddess Worship has a very powerful enabling myth (Raphael, 2000a: Chap. 3): For millennia, prehistoric peace and harmony prevailed in goddess-worshipping, woman-centred cultures. Then violent conquerors erupted from desert or steppe, devastated the gentle matriarchal societies, and, by force, instituted male dominance or patriarchy (Davis, 1971; Stone, 1977; Gimbutas, 1982, 1989, 1991; Eisler, 1987; and others). The sacred history follows societal development from the arrival of the patriarchal invaders through to the present day, the witch-hunts of the early modern period forming a major example of the continuing persecution of goddess worshippers. Donna Read's visually stunning and extremely popular film *Goddess Remembered* (1989) is an evocative testimony to the myth.

Though many devotees no longer insist that events in the "sacred history" actually happened, the myth comes alive in each retelling, made new by each interpretation. A number of women have written it down, but it remains, like all true myth, essentially oral, recounted at parties, celebrations, and, above all, rituals. The myth tells women about ancient goddess worship and matriarchies, patriarchal takeover, women's creativity and wonderful bodily functions, their natural power and strength, and the return of the Goddess and women's re-empowerment in a Goddess-centred religion. Given the tremendous validation women receive from worshipping the Goddess, it is no wonder that Feminist Goddess Worshippers get annoyed at scholars who argue that events may not have happened exactly as the story says (Eller, 2000; Christ, 1997: 70–88; Frymer-Kensky, 1994; Hurtado, 1990)!

The Goddess

Carol Christ, feminist the*a*logian (student of the female divine), explains why women need the Goddess: to help them acknowledge that female power is "beneficent," independent, and legitimate; to validate the female body and "the life cycle expressed in it"; to symbolize "the positive valuation of will" in Goddess rituals; and to permit women to re-assess their connections to one another and to "their heritage" (in Christ and Plaskow, 1979: 75–83).

Sometimes the Goddess is One, sometimes Many. Her Oneness answers the Oneness of the traditional God (Raphael, 2000a: Chap. 2). The Goddess chant "Isis, Astarte, Diana, Hecate, Demeter, Kali—Inanna" invokes the Goddess by some of Her myriad names. The Goddess's many aspects relate to women's experiences of their bodies, their cyclical natures, and their intertwining relationships over generations. Whether She is one or many, Feminist Goddess Worshippers often have a special relationship with a particular goddess, who is obviously Herself and not just an aspect of the Goddess.

The Triple Goddess, much-revered in Feminist Goddess Worship, is the epitome of the One and the Many. She is the Moon, whose three phases are represented by specific goddesses. She also corresponds to the phases of womanhood: maiden, mother, and crone. The Triple Goddess seems to be the Feminist Goddess Worship's Holy Trinity (Christ, 1997: 109–112).

Principles

First, the deity is a goddess or goddesses, not just the inclusion of the female in a pair or as an aspect of divinity (Christ, 2003: 227; Raphael in Sawyer and Collier, 1999). The religion puts female and feminine at the centre of "its system of symbols, beliefs, and practices" (Eller, 1993: 3). Since it also regards the Goddess as validating the female body, it refuses to accept the body/mind-spirit dualism of Western culture (Christ, 1997: 30, 100).

Second, Feminist Goddess Worshippers understand that female empowerment, which often means healing, is the primary aim of their religion. As long as they are not harmful to others, whatever means women employ to achieve that end are valid (Christ, 1997: 165ff).

Third, they are almost universally in agreement that Nature is alive and sacred, often personified as a Goddess—Mother Earth, Mother Nature, Gaia. Some see human psychological problems as the result of alienation from Nature (Low and Tremayne, 2001). Others regard the concept of progress with a jaundiced eye and consider the "ascent of man" to be the reason for today's ecological disasters. Thus, ecological activism often attracts them (Christ, 1997: 134).

Fourth, tolerance of other people's differing views and actions or non-actions is, with few exceptions, a given in Feminist Goddess Worship (Christ, 1997: 152–53), as it is generally among Neo-pagans and Wiccans (Adler, 1979: 101).

Fifth, almost all accept "the revisionist version of Western history" (Eller, 1993: 6). Further, many are serious students of ancient cultures and myths, reading widely, attending classes, and passing on their knowledge (Christ, 1997: 50ff.).

Sixth, decentralization is an absolute rule; there can be no central authority and no hierarchy in worship. Feminist Goddess Worship groups are small and independent. In addition, there are no received and inviolate scriptures and no collective liturgy, though much sharing and borrowing goes on (Christ, 1997: 29).

There is also general, if not universal, agreement about the following: Many regard their religion as forcing them into political action, while for others spirituality separates them from politics; for most devotees, the sacred is neither transcendent, nor immanent, but both (Christ, 1997: 101ff.); borrowing from Wiccans, a number of worshippers think that sexuality is sacred, whatever its expression, with, of course, the proviso that it not harm another (Christ, 1997: 147).

There are some disagreements among Feminist Goddess Worshippers. One tension concerns men in the movement and the nature of females and males. Are women and men similar or different? Are women superior to men? The nature/culture controversy also produces debate. Some disagree over the structure and organization of ancient matriarchies, the origin and definition of patriarchy, and the form of a truly woman-centred culture. Occasionally there is dispute over the nature of the Goddess. In addition, questions arise about the ethics of appropriation from other traditions and about ideas of good and evil, especially with respect to the practice of "magic."

Practices

Feminist Goddess Worship manifests itself primarily in ritual (Northup, 1997). Ritual connects participants to the Goddess. Ritual also brings worshippers back into harmony with Nature. Thus, many groups meet monthly, or more often, to celebrate the new or full moon (Christ, 1997: 25–30).

Gatherings also contain social and therapeutic elements. Goddess groups provide support for members, validation for changes they may be making in their lives, and, when necessary, group therapy and healing.

Women come together to celebrate with special rituals events in one another's life cycle or the life cycles of relatives and friends: menarche, middle age, and menopause; conception and birth, as well as abortion and miscarriage; marriage and divorce. In addition, Feminist Goddess Worshippers celebrate cosmic events like solstices and equinoxes. Sometimes these latter rituals are large, when women gather for a festival (Eller, 1993: 1ff).

Feminist Goddess Worshippers are creative in constructing rituals, borrowing freely from many cultural traditions. Addressing the four directions, the spirits of west, east, south, and north, seems now to be obligatory, as is "smudging," burning of sage or some other aromatic plant to purify participants with smoke.

In principle, Feminist Goddess Worship groups are leaderless, and all members are priestesses. However, in larger gatherings, those with an aptitude for religious leadership normally take these roles.

A typical ritual starts with the setting up of an altar, the introduction of participants, and the creation of sacred space and time, "casting of the circle." Worshippers do this by "calling in the four directions." When the circle is "closed," the ritual begins. Chanting almost always occurs. One chant, which encapsulates the essence of the religion, goes: "We all come from the Goddess, and unto Her we shall return, like a drop of rain flowing to the ocean." Meditation is another ritual technique, along with role playing and rhythmic dancing. Sometimes a participant will go into trance, sometimes become possessed by a goddess or other spirit. Worshippers bless one another and themselves and listen to the telling of myths or to short homilies.

The core of the ritual is the creation of a "cone of power." Focusing their collective energy through dance, drumming, and chant, the ecstatic participants direct the power they have "raised" to specific ends, often healing (Eller, 1993: 93). Then the group "grounds" the energy through a precise ritual technique. Worshippers conclude the ritual by releasing the spirits of the four directions and pronouncing the circle "open, but unbroken." The group then relaxes to enjoy the food and drink that always accompany such occasions. Many of these practices Feminist Goddess Worshippers have borrowed piecemeal from Wicca (Starhawk, 1979: 133).

The use of magic in ritual is a controversial topic, magic being understood as the ability to contact the power of the Goddess and focus that power through the will. Starhawk defines magic as changing "consciousness at will," an alteration that can, and does, change the world (1979: 109). Most Feminist Goddess Worshippers believe that magic exists and that it is very potent.

Feminist Goddess Worship defies categorization. Women are creating, from day to day, an empowering, fulfilling alternative to other religions. Although it is difficult to foresee its future form, most adherents believe, as a lapel button announces, "The Goddess is here, and SHE is ORGANIZING."

Lesbian Voices

According to Cynthia Eller, Feminist Goddess Worshippers in the United States are dis-proportionately lesbian, the spirituality being "the civil religion of the lesbian feminist community" (1993: 18, 20–21, 35, 41). Unquestionably, there is a "strong lesbian element" in Feminist Goddess Worship (Raphael, 1996: 13, 272). Even more, the new religion has benefited greatly from the strength and energy of lesbian women (Adler, 1993: 340). Lesbian feminist writers, Audre Lorde and Adrienne Rich, for example, have made impor-tant contributions to the literature of Feminist Goddess Worship (Lorde, 1989; Rich, 1976).

CONCLUSION

Modern religious-studies scholarship has, until very recently, ignored female spirituality, so that we are only just beginning to find out about it. Nonetheless, women have always expressed their spirituality as fully as their situations have allowed. It is, then, important to listen to what women say about their spiritual experiences and about what those experi-ences mean. Feminist theologians are correct, therefore, to point to women's experiences as the key. They are the key to our accepting a woman's satisfaction with a fundamentalist religion. Despite our feminist conviction that religion is generally sexist and demeaning to women, the individual woman's experience tells another story. Women's experiences are also the key to our understanding what it is about religions of complementarity between female and male that makes women inside them insist that they are egalitarian. And it is women's experiences to which we must turn to seek the reason why, despite the obvious appeal of Feminist Goddess Worship, Jewish, Christian, and Muslim feminists stay in their contradictory and ambivalent positions of deep emotional commitment to sexist traditions. Finally, the empowering experiences of feminists who worship the Goddess speak to the power of the new religion to nurture and heal women.

ENDNOTES

1. To Nancy Mandell goes my deep gratitude for her unstinting help and support. In addition, Aviva Goldberg's knowledge and insights, as well as research assistance, have been invaluable. Further, I owe appreciation to Amila Buturovic, Charlotte Caron, Beth Cutts, Jordan Paper, and Jane Robin for their advice on this chapter. Needless to say, any errors herein are totally my responsibility.

2. "Feminist Goddess Worship" is my term for the new religion. I settled on it after considering "Feminist Spirituality," used by many (for example Gross, 1996; Christ, 1997), and "Modern Goddess Worship." I eliminated the latter because it names the worship of goddesses in Hinduism, Chinese religion, and other modern polytheistic traditions. My conviction that many Jewish, Christian, and Muslim feminists are also practicing "Feminist Spirituality" forced me to find another term.

3. In the first version of this chapter, I called this category "Reformist," but altered it to avoid confusion with "Reform" Judaism. Carol Christ's 1983 essay on symbols of deity in feminist theology was my starting point in developing these categories. In that essay Christ distinguishes three feminist-theological positions, equivalent to Revisionist, Renovationist, and Rejectionist. Since 1983, however, a fourth position has emerged, Revolutionary. Though other scholars use different names for these positions, Christ's article has influenced almost all of them (1983: 238).

4. Over time, rabbinical interpretation of the Torah, as well as the rest of the Hebrew Bible, and the Talmud (see note 4) produced *halakhah*, "the path," rabbinic law. As Plaskow points out, behaviours,

not beliefs, are the defining characteristic of Judaism, and *halakhah* elaborates behaviours. *Halakhah* ideally enjoins the observant Jew to fulfill a number of obligations, or *mitzvot*, traditionally 613 in all. However, the rabbis judged that, although adult males who were free, not slaves, were bound by all obligations, women should be exempt from all but three which apply only to women: *challah*, breaking of the bread at Sabbath; *hadlik ner*, lighting of Sabbath candles; and *niddah*, observing laws of family purity (women are to practice sexual abstinence during menstruation and for seven days after, and, before resuming marital relations, to immerse themselves in a purifying ritual bath, *mikveh*) (Frankiel, 1990: 74–85).

5. The Talmud contains the *Mishnah*, the code of Jewish law, and commentaries on it. In 63 volumes it explains and amplifies the Torah.

6. Though, in the late 600s, Muslims divided into two groups: Sunnis and Shi'ites, all Muslims accept three basic beliefs: *Tawhid*, the Oneness of God, absolute monotheism; *Nubuwah*, Prophethood, and *Aakhirah*, Life after Death. All Muslims undertake the five duties called "Pillars" (see note 6). All Muslims revere the *Qur'an* and the *Sunna*, a collection of sayings and deeds of the Prophet. Together the *Qur'an* and the *Sunna* constitute the main source of Islamic law, the *Sharia*.

7. The "Five Pillars of Islam" are five duties or acts of worship: *shahadah*, daily witness to the Oneness of God; *salah*, prayer five times a day; *zakah*, alms-giving; *sawm*, abstinence in the month of Ramadan; and *hajj*, pilgrimage to Mecca at least once in a lifetime.

SUGGESTED READINGS

Christ, Carol P. 1997. *Rebirth of the Goddess: Finding Meaning in Feminist Spirituality*. Reading, MA: Addison-Wesley. The first systematic and theoretical thealogy of Feminist Goddess Worship.

Cooey, Paula M., William R. Eakin, and **Jay B. McDaniel,** eds. 1997 (1991). *After Patriarchy: Feminist Transformations of the World Religions*. Maryknoll, New York: Orbis. Articles by well-known feminist scholars on various traditions, including Judaism, Christianity, and Islam.

Hampson, Daphne. 1993 (1990). *Theology and Feminism*. Oxford: Blackwell. British "post-Christian" feminist theologian presents a full and controversial examination of Christianity.

Plaskow, Judith. 1990. *Standing Again at Sinai: Judaism from a Feminist Perspective*. San Francisco: Harper and Row. The foremost American Jewish feminist theologian analyzes Judaism in detail and concludes that radical change is necessary.

Stuckey, Johanna H. 1998. *Feminist Spirituality: An Introduction to Feminist Theology in Judaism, Christianity, Islam, and Feminist Goddess Worship*. Toronto: Centre for Feminist Research, York University. Presents the background, normative practices, and feminist theology of four religions, with introductory bibliographies on other traditions.

Yamani, Mai, ed. 1996. *Feminism and Islam: Legal and Literary Perspectives*. New York: New York University. Articles by Islamic feminists on the effect of Islam on women in general and in a number of Muslim countries.

DISCUSSION QUESTIONS

1. Into what feminist theological category or categories (Revisionist, Renovationist, Revolutionary) do the suggested readings by Daphne Hampson and Judith Plaskow fit? How does Hampson react to the views of Daly or Reuther, and how would Plaskow react to those of Gottlieb? How would both respond to Christ's *Rebirth of the Goddess*?

2. In what ways is Carol Christ's position in *Rebirth of the Goddess* Rejectionist? Discuss the criticisms implicit in her book of the three monotheistic traditions.

3. Using Plaskow, the articles in Yamani, and the works of Reuther or Fiorenza, discuss critically the reasons why feminists remain inside admittedly sexist religious traditions.

4. What major changes would be necessary in each of Judaism, Christianity, and Islam to satisfy feminist theologians, especially the Revolutionaries?

BIBLIOGRAPHY

Abu-Lughod, Lila. *Remaking Women: Feminism and Modernity in the Middle East.* Princeton, NJ: Princeton University, 1998.

Adelman, Penina V. *Miriam's Well: Rituals for Jewish Women Around the Year.* NY: Biblio, 1990 (1986).

Adler, Margot. *Drawing Down the Moon: Witches, Druids, Goddess-Worshippers, and Other Pagans in America Today.* Boston: Beacon, 1979.

Afshar, Haleh, ed. *Women in the Middle East.* London: Macmillan, 1993.

Ahmed, Leila. *Women and Gender in Islam: Historical Roots of a Modern Debate.* New Haven, CT: Yale University, 1992.

Alam, S. M. Shamsul. "Women in the Era of Modernity and Islamic Fundamentalism: The Case of Taslima Nasrin." *Signs* 23/1 (1998): 429–61.

Alpert, Rebecca. *Like Bread on the Seder Plate: Jewish Lesbians and the Transformation of Tradition.* New York: Columbia University, 1997.

Alvi, Sajida S., Homa Hoodfar, and **Sheila McDonough,** eds. *The Muslim Veil in North America: Issues and Debates.* Toronto: Women's Press, 2003.

Anderson, Grace M. *God Calls, Man Chooses: A Study of Women in Ministry.* Burlington, ON: Trinity, 1990.

Aquino, Maria Pilar, Daisy L. Macado, and **Jeannette Rodriguez,** eds. *A Reader in Latina Feminist Theology: Religion and Justice.* Austin, TX: University of Texas, 2002.

Badran, Margot. *Islam and Nation: Gender and the Making of Modern Egypt.* Princeton, NJ: Princeton University, 1995.

Balka, Christie, and **Andy Rose,** eds. *Twice Blessed: On Being Lesbian, Gay, and Jewish.* Boston: Beacon, 1989.

Baring, Anne, and **Jules Cashford.** *The Myth of the Goddess: Evolution of an Image.* London: Arkana, 1991.

Baskin, Judith R. *Midrashic Women: Formations of the Feminine in Rabbinic Literature.* Hanover, NH: Brandeis University, 2002.

Beck, Evelyn T., ed. *Nice Jewish Girls: A Lesbian Anthology.* Watertown, MA: Persephone, 1982.

Beck, Lois, and **Nikki Keddie,** eds. *Women in the Muslim World.* Cambridge, MA: Harvard University, 1978.

Bowker, John, ed. *The Oxford Dictionary of World Religions.* Oxford: Oxford University, 1997.

Brettschneider, Marla, and **Dawn R. Rose.** "Meeting at the Well: Multiculturalism and Jewish Feminism. Introduction." *Journal of Feminist Studies in Religion* 19/1 (2003): 85–90.

Bridges Special Issue 7/1: 1997-98.

Brooten, Bernadette. *Women Leaders in the Ancient Synagogue.* Chico, CA: Scholars, 1982.

Brouwer, Ruth C. *New Women for God: Canadian Presbyterian Women and India Missions.* Toronto: University of Toronto, 1990.

———. *Modern Women Modernizing Men: The Changing Missions of Three Professional Women in Asia and Africa, 1902–69.* Vancouver: University of British Columbia, 2002.

Brown, Joanne, and **Carol Bohn,** eds. *Christianity, Patriarchy, and Abuse: A Feminist Critique.* New York: Pilgrim, 1989.

Butler, Becky, ed. *Ceremonies of the Heart: Celebrating Lesbian Unions.* Seattle, WA: Seal, 1990.

Buturovic, Amila. "Islam," Guest Lecture, Humanities 2820.06 "Female Spirituality" course, Division of Humanities, Faculty of Arts, York University, Toronto, 17 January, 1995.

———. "Spiritual Empowerment Through Spiritual Submission: Sufi Women and Their Quest for God." *Canadian Woman Studies/les cahiers de la femme* 17/1 (1997): 53–56.

Canadian Woman Studies special issue 16/4: 1996.

Cannon, Katie G. *Black Womanist Ethics.* Atlanta, GA: Scholars, 1988.

Carmody, Denise L. *Women and World Religions.* 2nd ed. Englewood Cliffs, NJ.: Prentice Hall, 1989.

Caron, Charlotte. *To Make and Make Again: Feminist Ritual Thealogy.* New York: Crossroad, 1993.

Cherry, Kittredge, and **Zalmon Sherwood,** eds. *Equal Rites: Lesbian and Gay Worship, Ceremonies, and Celebrations.* Louisville, KY: Westminster John Knox, 1995.

Chesler, Phyllis, and **Rivka Haut,** eds. *Women of the Wall: Reclaiming Sacred Ground at Judaism's Holy Site.* Woodstock, VT: Jewish Lights, 2003.

Christ, Carol P. "Symbols of Goddess and God in Feminist Theology." In *The Book of the Goddess, Past and Present: An Introduction to Her Religion,* edited by Carl Olson, 231–251. New York: Crossroad, 1983.

———. *Rebirth of the Goddess: Finding Meaning in Feminist Spirituality.* Reading, MA: Addison-Wesley, 1997.

———. *She Who Changes: Re-Imagining the Divine in the World.* New York: Palgrave Macmillan, 2003.

Christ, Carol P. and **Judith Plaskow,** eds. *Womanspirit Rising: A Feminist Reader in Religion.* New York: Harper and Row, 1979.

Cleary, Thomas, ed. *The Essential Koran: The Heart of Islam.* San Francisco: HarperSanFrancisco, 1993.

Cohen, Debra H. "Chasm between Orthodoxy and Feminism Closing." *Canadian Jewish News* Feb. 27, 1997: 49.

Cohler-Esses, Dianne, "A Common Language Between East and West." *Journal of Feminist Studies in Religion* 19/1 (2003) 111–118.

Comstock, Gary D. *Unrepentant, Self-Affirming, Practicing: Lesbian/Bi-Sexual/Gay People Within Organized Religion.* New York: Continuum, 1996.

Comstock, Gary D. *A Whosoever Church: Welcoming Lesbians and Gay Men into African American Congregations.* Louisville, KY: Westminster John Knox, 2001.

Cook, Miriam. *Women Claim Islam: Creating Islamic Feminism Through Literature.* New York: Routledge, 2001.

Curb, Rosemary, and **Nancy Monahan,** eds. *Lesbian Nuns: Breaking Silence.* Tallahassee, FL: Naiad, 1985.

Daly, Mary. *Beyond God the Father: Toward a Philosophy of Women's Liberation.* Boston: Beacon, 1973.

———. *Gyn/Ecology: The Metaethics of Radical Feminism.* Boston: Beacon, 1978.

————. *The Church and the Second Sex. With Feminist Postchristian Introduction and New Archaic Afterwords*. Boston: Beacon, 1985 (1968).

Davis, Elizabeth G. *The First Sex*. Baltimore, MD: Penguin, 1972 (1971).

Dyke, Doris J. *Crucified Woman*. Toronto: United Church, 1991.

Eisler, Riane. *The Chalice and the Blade: Our History, Our Future*. San Francisco: Harper and Row, 1987.

Eller, Cynthia. *Living in the Lap of the Goddess: The Feminist Spirituality Movement in America*. New York: Crossroad, 1993.

————. *The Myth of Matriarchal Prehistory: Why an Invented Past Won't Give Women a Future*. Boston: Beacon, 2000.

El-Or, Tamar. *Educated and Ignorant: Ultraorthodox Jewish Women and Their World*. Boulder, CO: Lynne Rienner, 1994.

Epstein, Isadore. *Judaism: A Historical Presentation*. London: Penguin, 1990 (1959).

Eugene, Toinette M. "To Be of Use." *Journal of Feminist Studies in Religion* 8/2 (1992): 138–47.

Falk, Marcia. *The Book of Blessings: New Jewish Prayers for Daily Life, the Sabbath, and the New Moon Festival*. San Francisco: HarperSanFrancisco, 1996.

————. "My Father's Riddle, Or Conflict and Reciprocity in the Multicultural (Jewish) Self." *Journal of Feminist Studies in Religion* 19/1 (2003): 97–103.

Falk, Nancy A., and **Rita M. Gross,** eds. *Unspoken Worlds: Women's Religious Lives*. Belmont, CA: Wadsworth, 1989.

Fernea, Elizabeth W., ed. *Women and the Family in the Middle East: New Voices of Change*. Austin, TX: University of Texas, 1985.

Fernea, Elizabeth W., and **Basima Q. Bezirgan,** eds. *Middle Eastern Muslim Women Speak*. Austin, TX: University of Texas, 1977.

Fine, Irene. *Midlife—A Rite of Passage: The Wise Woman—A Celebration*. San Diego, CA: Women's Institute for Continuing Jewish Education, 1988.

Finson, Shelley D. *A Historical Review of the Development of Feminist Liberation Theology*. Ottawa: Canadian Research Institute for the Advancement of Women, 1995.

Fiorenza, Elisabeth Schüssler. *In Memory of Her: A Feminist Theological Reconstruction of Christian Origins*. New York: Crossroad, 1983.

————. *But She Said: Feminist Practices of Biblical Interpretation*. Boston: Beacon, 1992.

————. *Wisdom Ways: Introducing Feminist Biblical Interpretation*. 2001.

Fletcher-Marsh, Wendy. *Beyond the Walled Garden: Anglican Women and the Priesthood*. Dundas, ON: Artemis, 1995.

Frankiel, Tamar. *The Voice of Sarah: Feminine Spirituality and Traditional Judaism*. San Francisco: HarperSanFrancisco, 1990.

Friedman, Debbie. *Timbrels and Torahs: Celebrating Women's Wisdom*. Berkeley, CA: Jot of Wisdom, 2000. Video.

Frymer-Kensky, Tikva. *In the Wake of the Goddesses: Women, Culture, and the Biblical Transformation of Pagan Myth*. New York: Free, 1992.

————. "The Bible and Women's Studies." In *Feminist Perspectives on Jewish Studies*, edited by Lynne Davidman and Shelly Tenenbaum, 16–39. New Haven, CT: Yale University, 1994.

Gadon, Elinor W. *The Once and Future Goddess: A Symbol for Our Time*. San Francisco: Harper and Row, 1989.

Gill, Sean, ed. *The Lesbian and Gay Christian Movement: Campaigning for Justice, Truth and Love*. London: Cassell, 1998.

Gimbutas, Marija. *The Goddesses and Gods of Old Europe, 6500 to 3500 BC*. Berkeley, CA: University of California, 1982 (1974).

———. *The Language of the Goddess: Unearthing the Hidden Symbols of Western Civilization*. San Francisco: HarperSanFrancisco, 1989.

———. *The Civilization of the Goddess: The World of Old Europe*. San Francisco: HarperSanFrancisco, 1991.

Goldberg, Aviva. *Re-Awakening Deborah: Locating the Feminist in the Liturgy, Ritual, and Theology of Contemporary Jewish Renewal*. Toronto: York University Ph.D. thesis, 2002.

Goldman, Karla. *Beyond the Synagogue: Finding a Place for Women in American Judaism*. Cambridge, MA: Harvard University, 2000.

Gottlieb, Lynn. *She Who Dwells Within: A Feminist Vision of a Renewed Judaism*. San Francisco: HarperSanFrancisco, 1995.

Grant, Jacquelyn. "Black Women and the Church." In *All the Women Are White, All the Blacks Are Men, But Some of Us Are Brave: Black Women's Studies*, edited by Gloria T. Hull et al., 141–52. New York: Feminist, 1982.

———. *White Women's Christ and Black Women's Jesus: Feminist Christology and Womanist Response*. Atlanta, GA: Scholars, 1989.

———. "'Come to My Help, Lord, For I'm In Trouble': Womanist Jesus and the Mutual Struggle for Liberation." In *Reconstructing the Christ Symbol: Essays in Feminist Christology*, edited by Maryanne Stevens, 54–71. Mahwah, NJ: Paulist, 1993.

Green-McCreight, Kathryn. *Feminist Reconstructions of Christian Doctrines: Narrative Analysis and Appraisal*. New York: Oxford University, 2000.

Gross, Rita. *Feminism and Religion: An Introduction*. Boston: Beacon, 1996.

Haddad, Yvonne Y. and **John L. Esposito,** eds. *Daughters of Abraham: Feminist Thought in Judaism, Christianity, and Islam*. Gainesville, FL: University of Florida, 2001.

Harris, Lis. *Holy Days: The World of a Hasidic Family*. New York: Summit, 1985.

Hassan, Riffat. "Muslim Women and Post-Patriarchal Islam." In *After Patriarchy: Feminist Transformations of the World Religions*, edited by Paula M. Cooey, William R. Eakin, and J. B. McDaniel. Maryknoll, NY: Orbis, 1997.

Hazel, Dann. *Witness: Gay and Lesbian Clergy Report from the Front*. Louisville, KY: Westminster John Knox, 2000.

Heschel, Susannah, ed. *On Being a Jewish Feminist*. New York: Schocken, 1995 (1983).

Heywood, Isabel Carter. *Our Passion for Justice: Images of Power, Sexuality and Liberation*. New York: Pilgrim, 1984.

———. *Speaking of Christ: A Lesbian Feminist Voice*, ed. Ellen C. Davis. New York: Pilgrim, 1989a.

———. *Touching Our Strength: The Erotic as Power and the Love of God*. San Francisco: Harper and Row, 1989b.

hooks, bell. *Ain't I a Woman? Black Women and Feminism*. Boston: South End, 1981.

———. *Feminist Theory: From Margin to Center*. Boston: South End, 1984.

Hurtado, Larry, ed. *Goddesses in Religions and Modern Debate*. Atlanta, GA: Scholars, 1990.

Imam, Ayesha. "The Muslim Religious Right ('Fundamentalists') and Sexuality." Women Living Under Muslim Laws. *Dossier* 17: 7–25 (boit postale 23, 3474, Gravelle, France), 1997.

Isasi-Díaz, Ada María. *Mujerista Theology: A Theology for the Twenty-First Century*. Maryknoll, NY: Orbis, 1996.

Isherwood, Lisa and **Dorothea McEwan,** eds. *Introducing Feminist Theology: Second Edition*. Sheffield, UK: Sheffield Academic, 2001.

Kamisuka, Margaret D. "Reading the Raced and Sexed Body in *The Color Purple*: Repatterning White Feminist and Womanist Theological Hermeneutics." *Journal of Feminist Studies in Religion* 19/2 (2003): 45–66.

Keller, Rosemary S. and **Rosemary R. Reuther,** eds. *In Our Own Voices: Four Centuries of American Women's Religious Writings.* Louisville, KY: Westminster John Knox, 2000.

King, Ursula. *Women and Spirituality: Voices of Protest and Promise.* New York: New Amsterdam, 1989.

———, ed. *Feminist Theology from the Third World: A Reader.* Maryknoll, NY: Orbis, 1994.

———. *Christian Mystics: The Spiritual Heart of the Christian Tradition.* New York: Simon and Schuster, 1998.

———, ed. *Religion and Gender.* Oxford: Blackwell, 2000.

The Koran. Translated by J.M. Rodwell. London: Dent Everyman, 1994.

Kraemer, Ross S. *Her Share of the Blessings: Women's Religions Among Pagans, Jews and Christians in the Greco-Roman World.* New York: Oxford University,1992.

Kraemer, Ross S., and **Mary Rose D'Angelo,** ed. *Women & Christian Origins.* New York: Oxford University, 1999.

Kwok Pui-lan. *Introducing Asian Feminist Theology.* Cleveland, OH: Pilgrim, 2000.

Lateef, Shahida. *Muslim Women in India: Political and Private Realities.* London: Zed, 1990.

Lebans, Gertrude. *Gathered by the River: Reflections and Essays of Women Doing Ministry.* Toronto: United Church, 1994.

Legge, Marilyn J. *The Grace of Difference: A Canadian Feminist Theological Ethic.* Atlanta, GA: Scholars, 1992.

Levine, Amy-Jill. "Multiculturalism, Women's Studies, and Anti-Judaism." *Journal of Feminist Studies in Religion* 19/1 (2003): 119–128.

Lorde, Audre. "Uses of the Erotic: The Erotic as Power." In *Weaving the Visions: New Patterns in Feminist Spirituality*, edited by Judith Plaskow and Carol P. Christ, 208–13. San Francisco: Harper and Row, 1989.

Low, Alaine, and **Soraya Tremayne,** eds. *Sacred Custodians of the Earth? Women, Spirituality, and the Environment.* New York: Berghahn, 2001.

Mabro, Judy, ed. *Veiled Half-Truths: Western Travellers' Perceptions of Middle Eastern Women.* London: Taurus, 1996.

Manji, Irshad. *The Trouble with Islam: A Wake-Up Call for Honesty and Change.* New York: Random House, 2003.

Marcus, Julie. *A World of Difference: Islam and Gender Hierarchy in Turkey.* London: Zed, 1992.

McManners, John, ed. *The Oxford History of Christianity.* Oxford: Oxford University, 1990.

Mernissi, Fatima. *Beyond the Veil: Male-Female Dynamics in Modern Muslim Society.* Bloomington, IN: Indiana University, 1987 (1975).

———. *Women and Islam: An Historical and Theological Inquiry.* Oxford: Blackwell, 1991.

———. *The Forgotten Queens of Islam.* Minneapolis, MN: University of Minnesota, 1993 (1990).

Minces, Juliette. *The House of Obedience: Women in Arab Society.* London: Zed, 1982.

Moghadam, Valentine M. *Modernizing Women: Gender and Social Change in the Middle East.* Boulder, CO: Lynne Rienner, 2003.

Moghissi, Haideh. *Feminism and Islamic Fundamentalism: The Limits of Postmodern Analysis.* London: Zed, 1999.

Moraga, Cherrie and **Gloria Anzaldua,** eds. *This Bridge Called My Back: Writings by Radical Women of Color.* New York: Kitchen Table, 1983.

Muir, Elizabeth G. *Petticoats in the Pulpit: The Story of Early Nineteenth-Century Methodist Women Preachers in Upper Canada.* Toronto: United Church, 1991.

Muir, Elizabeth G. and **Marilyn F. Whiteley,** eds. *Changing Roles of Women within the Christian Church in Canada.* Toronto: University of Toronto, 1995.

Mumtaz, Khawar and **Farida Shaheed.** *Women of Pakistan: Two Steps Forward. One Step Back?* London: Zed, 1987.

Musallam, B.F. *Sex and Society in Islam: Birth Control Before the 19th Century.* Cambridge: Cambridge University, 1989.

Myers, Jody and **June R. Litman.** "The Secret of Jewish Femininity: Hiddenness, Power, and Physicality in the Theology of Orthodox Women in the Contemporary World." In *Gender and Judaism: The Transformation of Tradition,* edited by T.M.Rudavsky, 51–77. New York: New York University, 1995

Nadell, Pamela S. *Women Who Would Be Rabbis: A History of Women's Ordination, 1889–1985.* Boston: Beacon, 1998.

Nadell, Pamela S. and **Jonathan D. Sarna,** eds. *Women and American Judaism: Historical Perspectives.* Hanover, NH: Brandeis University, 2001.

Newsom, Carol and **Sharon H. Ringe,** eds. *The Women's Bible Commentary.* Louisville, KY: Westminster John Knox, 1992.

Northup, Lesley A. *Ritualizing Women: Patterns of Spirituality.* Cleveland, OH: Pilgrim, 1997.

Oduyoye, Mercy Amba. *Introducing African Women's Theology.* Cleveland, OH: Pilgrim, 2001.

Orenstein, Debra, ed. *Lifecycles: Vol. 1 Jewish Women on Life Passages and Personal Milestones.* Woodstock, VT: Jewish Lights, 1994.

Orenstein, Debra and **Jane R. Litman,** eds. *Lifecycles: Vol. 2 Jewish Women on Biblical Themes in Contemporary Life.* Woodstock, VT: Jewish Lights, 1994.

Pagels, Elaine. *The Gnostic Gospels.* New York: Random House, 1979.

Paris, Peter S. "From Womanist Thought to Womanist Action." *Journal of Feminist Studies in Religion* 9/1–2 (1993): 115–25.

Plaskow, Judith. *Standing Again at Sinai: Judaism from a Feminist Perspective.* San Francisco: Harper and Row, 1990.

———. "Jewish Theology in Feminist Perspective." In *Feminist Perspectives on Jewish Studies,* edited by Lynn Davidman and Shelly Tenenbaum, 62–84. New Haven, CT: Yale University, 1994.

———. "Dealing with Difference Without and Within." *Journal of Feminist Studies in Religion* 19/1 (2003): 91–95.

Preisand, Sally. *Judaism and the New Woman.* New York: Behrman, 1975.

Procter-Smith, Marjorie and **Janet R. Walton,** eds. *Women at Worship: Interpretations of North American Diversity.* Louisville, KY: Westminster John Knox, 1993.

Raphael, Melissa. *Thealogy and Embodiment: The Post-Patriarchal Reconstruction of Female Sacrality.* Sheffield, UK: Sheffield Academic, 1996.

———. *Introducing Thealogy.* Cleveland, OH: Pilgrim, 2000a.

———. "When God Beheld God: Notes Towards a Jewish Feminist Theology of the Holocaust." In *Challenging Women's Orthodoxies in the Context of Faith,* edited by Susan F, Parsons, 73–87. Aldershot, UK: Ashgate, 2000b.

———. *The Female Face of God in Auschwitz: A Jewish Feminist Theology of the Holocaust.* London: Routledge, 2003.

Read, Donna, director. *Goddess Remembered.* Studio D, National Film Board of Canada, 1989.

Reuther, Rosemary Radford, ed. *Religion and Sexism: Images of Women in the Jewish and Christian Traditions*. New York: Simon and Schuster, 1974.

———. *Sexism and God-Talk: Toward a Feminist Theology*. Boston: Beacon, 1983.

———. *Women-Church: The Theology and Practice of Feminist Liturgical Communities*. NY: Harper and Row, 1985.

———. *Gaia and God: An Ecofeminist Theology of Earth Healing*. San Francisco: HarperSanFrancisco, 1992.

———, ed. *Gender, Ethnicity, and Religion: Views from the Other Side*. Minneapolis, MN: Fortress, 2002.

Rich, Adrienne. *Of Woman Born: Motherhood as Experience and Institution*. New York: Norton, 1976.

Russell, Letty M., and **J. Shannon Clarkson,** eds. *Dictionary of Feminist Theologies*. Louisville, KY: Westminster John Knox, 1996.

Russell, Letty M., Kwok Pui-lan, Ada María Isasi-Díaz, and **Katie G. Cannon,** eds. *Inheriting Our Mothers' Gardens: Feminist Theology in Third World Perspective*. Philadelphia: Westminster, 1988.

Rutherford, Myra. *Women and the White Men's God: Gender and Race in the Canadian Mission Field*. Vancouver: University of British Columbia, 2002.

Ruthven, Malise. *Islam: A Short History*. Oxford: Oxford University, 1997.

Saadawi, Nawal el, ed. *The Hidden Face of Eve: Women in the Arab World*. London: Zed, 1980.

———. *The Nawal El Saadawi Reader*. London: Zed, 1997.

Saghal, Gita, and **Nira Yuval-Davis,** eds. *Refusing Holy Orders: Women and Fundamentalism in Britain*. London: Virago, 1992.

Saliba, Therese, Carolyn Allen, and **Judith A. Howard,** eds. *Gender and Politics in Islam*. Chicago: University of Chicago, 2002.

Sansarian, Eliz. *The Women's Rights Movement in Iran: Mutiny, Appeasement, and Repression from 1900 to Khomeini*. New York: Praeger, 1992.

Sawyer, Deborah F. and **Diane M. Collier,** eds. *Is There a Future for Feminist Theology?* Sheffield, UK: Sheffield Academic, 1999.

Sharawi, Huda. *Harem Years: The Memoirs of an Egyptian Feminist* (1879–1924). London: Virago, 1986.

Shehadeh, Lamia R. *The Idea of Women in Fundamentalist Islam*. Gainesville, FL: University of Florida, 2003.

Sinister Wisdom. 54 (1994–1995) Winter. "Lesbians and Religion" issue.

Spiegel, Marcia C. "Spirituality for Survival: Jewish Women Healing Themselves." *Journal of Feminist Studies in Religion* 12/2 (1996): 121–37.

Starhawk (Miriam Simos). *The Spiral Dance: A Rebirth of the Ancient Religion of the Great Goddess*. San Francisco: Harper and Row, 1979.

Stein, Judith. *A New Haggadah: A Jewish Lesbian Seder*. Cambridge, MA: Bebbeh Meiseh, 1984.

Stone, Merlin. *The Paradise Papers* (US title: *When God Was a Woman*). London: Virago, 1977 (1976).

Tabari, A. and **N. Yeganeh.** *In the Shadow of Islam: The Women's Movement in Iran*. London: Zed, 1982.

Taitz, Emily, Sondra Henry, and **Cheryl Tallan.** *The JPS Guide to Jewish Women: 600 BCE–1900 CE* Philadelphia: Jewish Publication Society, 2003.

Torjesen, Karen Jo. *When Women Were Priests: Women's Leadership in the Early Church and the Scandal of Their Subordination in the Rise of Christianity*. San Francisco: HarperSanFrancisco, 1993.

Trible, Phyllis. *God and the Rhetoric of Sexuality*. Philadelphia: Fortress, 1978.

————. *Texts of Terror: Literary-Feminist of Biblical Narratives*. Philadelphia: Fortress, 1984.

Tucker, Judith E. *Women in Nineteenth-Century Egypt*. Cambridge: Cambridge University, 1985.

Umansky, Ellen and **Diana Ashton,** eds. *Four Centuries of Jewish Women's Spirituality: A Sourcebook*. Boston: Beacon, 1992.

Wadud, Amina. *Qur'an and Woman: Rereading the Sacred Text from a Woman's Perspective*. New York: Oxford University, 1999 (1992).

Walker, Alice. *In Search of Our Mothers' Gardens: Womanist Prose*. San Diego, CA: Harcourt Brace Jovanovich, 1983.

Ware, Timothy. *The Orthodox Church: New Edition*. New York: Penguin, 1997.

Webb, Gisela, ed. *Windows of Faith: Muslim Women Scholar-Activists in North America*. Syracuse, NY: Syracuse University, 2000.

Webster's Encyclopedic Unabridged Dictionary of the English Language. New York: Gramercy, 1996.

Wessenger, Catherine, ed. *Religious Institutions and Women's Leadership: New Roles Inside the Mainstream*. Columbia, SC: University of South Carolina, 1996.

Wikan, Unni. *Behind the Veil in Arabia: Women in Oman*. Chicago: University of Chicago, 1991.

Williams, Delores S. *Sisters in the Wilderness: The Challenge of Womanist God-Talk*. Maryknoll, NY: Orbis, 1993.

Yamani, Mai, ed. *Feminism and Islam: Legal and Literary Perspectives*. London: Ithaca, 1996.

Zanotti, Barbara, ed. *A Faith of One's Own: Explorations by Catholic Lesbians*. New York: Crossing, 1986.

Zuckerman, Francine, ed. *Half the Kingdom: Seven Jewish Feminists*. New York: Crossing, 1986. Also Canadian National film Board video.

WEBLINKS

WSSLINKS

www.earlham.edu/~libr/acrlwss/wsstheo.html

This site, part of WSSLINKS, a project of the Women's Studies Section of the Association of College and Research Libraries, contains links on women and religion, feminist theology, and the feminine divine.

House of the Goddess

www.hogonline.co.uk/

Visit this site to learn more about Goddess Spirituality.

Christian Lesbians

www.christianlesbians.com

Visit the christianlesbians.com homepage for links to other related sites, a chat room, daily devotions, and current articles.

Notes on Contributors

SHANA L. CALIXTE is a PhD candidate in the School of Women's Studies at York University in Toronto. She holds an MA in Women's Studies and a Bachelor of Journalism and Women's Studies from Carleton University in her home city, Ottawa. Her current academic work focuses on young Caribbean feminist women organizing around issues of sexuality and globalization. She has also examined the use of oral histories to document stories of migration, home, and displacement for second-generation Caribbean women. She currently works as the project manager of Caribbean Tales (www.caribbeantales.org), an interactive, educational website that documents the stories of Caribbean peoples through music, literature, and oral histories.

    TOMISLAVA CAVAR is a young feminist completing her Honours degrees in Kinesiology and Health Science as well as Sociology at York University. She is pursuing her interests in media portrayals of women athletes and violent acts of male athletes. Involved in community activities such as promoting health at York, assisting at a local high school, and serving as a residence Don, she uses sport to create equal opportunities for females and healthy lifestyles for all.

    ANN DUFFY is a Professor of Sociology at Brock University, where she also teaches in the Women's Studies and Labour Studies programs. In 1995, she was awarded an Ontario Confederation of University Faculty Associations Excellence in Teaching Award. She is the co-author of several books on the sociology of work, Canadian society, and the sociology of the family. She has also co-authored (with Julianne Momirov) the first Canadian text on family violence, *Family Violence: A Canadian Introduction* (J. Lorimer, 1997).

    DIANA L. GUSTAFSON is an assistant professor with the Faculty of Medicine at Memorial University, where her teaching and research interests include health care reform, embodiment, community-based carework, and motherwork. Her interest in social justice issues emerged during her youth: "Long before I had labels for feminism and antiracism, I was concerned about equity."

    JENNIFER L. JOHNSON holds degrees from Queen's University and the University of Oxford and is currently a PhD candidate at the School of Women's Studies at Toronto's York University. Her research focuses on international trade relations between Canada and the English-speaking Caribbean, using feminist anti-imperialist critiques of globalization. She has worked at the Department of Foreign Affairs and International Trade, assisting in research on the export activities of Canadian businesswomen, and acts as management counsel on gender equity in sound management practice at the Manitoba Institute of Management. Her publications include research on the impact of globalization on local communities and the history of women's education in Canada.

    LARA KARAIAN is currently completing her PhD. in Women's Studies at York University where she is also a teaching assistant for Women and the Law. Her research interests include feminist, postmodern, and queer legal theory, and the Canadian Charter of Rights and Freedoms and its S. 15 equality jurisprudence. Lara is a co-editor of *Turbo Chicks: Talking Young Feminisms* (Sumach, 2001) and was a member of the guest editorial board for *Canadian Woman Studies'* "Young Women: Feminists, Activists, Grrrls" issue (20–21/1, 2001). Lara is also an activist and a runner who sometimes manages to combine the two!

    GREGORY MALSZECKI teaches in the Kinesiology and Health Science Department, York University. He has been teaching Women and Sport at the fourth-year level since 1991. Besides investigating issues of gender in sport, he has been associated with the Centre for Feminist Research and the LaMarsh Centre for Research on Violence and Conflict Resolution, at York University. A book, *Homo Furens: Violence and Virility in Sport and War,* is upcoming.

    NANCY MANDELL teaches in the Sociology and Women's Studies programs at York University. She has published on mid-life women's experiences of intimacy and family; gendered social capital; academic-community research partnerships; married women's juggling of wage and domestic labour; adolescent interpretations of work, family, and school life; violence against women; and the feminization of poverty in Canada.

    SUSAN A. McDANIEL is a professor at University of Alberta. As of July 2004, she will be Vice President of Research, University of Windsor as well as Professor of Sociology. She is the author of seven books and more than 160 research articles, and her work appears in prominent journals as well as several texts on family, aging, and women's issues. She is Chair of the Science and Technology Advisory Committee at Statistics Canada, Chair of a national Task Force on Enhancing Social Science Research Capacity in Canada, and is appointed to the National Statistics Council. She is also Vice President (Publications) of the International Sociological Association, and a frequent keynote speaker on family and women's issues. She is a Fellow of the Royal Society of Canada, listed in *Who's Who of the World's Women* and a recipient of numerous awards, including the Kaplan Award for Research Excellence (1999), the University Cup (2002), in acknowledgment of continuous excellence in both teaching and research, and a Distinguished Service Award from the Canadian Sociology and Anthropology Association (2003).

SHARON McIRVIN ABU-LABAN is a Professor of Sociology at the University of Alberta, specializing in comCREDtive family, gender, social gerontology, and international development. Her scholarly work has appeared in a wide range of professional journals and anthologies, and she is co-editor of *Muslim Families in North America and The Arab World: Dynamics of Development* (University of Alberta Press, 1991).

ALLYSON MITCHELL teaches Feminist Activism at York University. She is currently completing her PhD in Women's Studies. Her research interests include women who identify as fat, geographies of power, independent cultural production, body image and size activism, and queer politics. Her writing is published in *Brazen Femme: Queering Femininity* (Arsenal, 2002) and the forthcoming *PHAT!* (Penguin, 2002), as well as various independent publications. Allyson is also a visual artist and filmmaker (her films can be previewed at www.cfmdc.org).

MAKI MOTAPANYANE is a PhD student in York's Women's Studies Program. Her research centres on postcolonial feminist analysis of the political activism of township women in post-apartheid South Africa. She is specifically concerned with the ways in which the style of activism, as well as the issues and concerns of township women, have changed in the decade following apartheid.

GOLI M. REZAI-RASHTI teaches at the University of Western Ontario's Faculty of Education. She has a scholarly and activist interest in the areas of post-colonial and antiracist feminism. She is the author of several articles in scholarly journals and books. Her most recent work "Educational Policy Reform and Its Impact on Equity Work in Ontario: Global Challenges and Local Possibilities" appears in the journal *Education Policy Analysis Archives* 11/51, 2003.

CECILIA REYNOLDS is Dean of the College of Education, University of Saskatchewan. A former director of the Women's Studies program at Brock University, she continues to use interdisciplinary and collaborative approaches to develop critical perspectives on education. Her current research includes intergenerational work on mothering and teaching, a longitudinal study of gender and teachers' work, and questions about globalization and school changes.

SHARON ROSENBERG is currently assistant professor in Theory/Culture in the Department of Sociology at the University of Alberta; she was previously on faculty in the School of Women's Studies at York University. She teaches courses primarily in feminist theory, gender/sexuality, critiques of modernity, and cultural politics. Much of her published work has been concerned with questions of violence, loss, trauma, and memorialization. With Roger I. Simon and Claudia Eppert, she is an editor of *Between Hope and Despair: Pedagogy and the Remembrance of Historical Trauma* (Rowman and Littlefield, 2000). She is currently editing a special issue of *torquere*, "Memorializing Queers/Queering Remembrances."

JOHANNA H. STUCKEY is a Professor Emerita in the Humanities Division of the Faculty of Arts (Women's Studies and Religious Studies programs) at York University. She teaches courses on goddess worship and female spirituality at York University and at the School of Continuing Studies, University of Toronto. She published a book entitled *Feminist Spirituality: An Introduction to Feminist Theology in Judaism, Christianity, Islam, and Feminist Goddess Worship* (Centre for Feminist Research, York University, 1998) and is currently working on a new book on goddesses and "dying" gods.

SUSANNAH WILSON teaches research methods and family sociology in the School of Nutrition at Ryerson Polytechnic University in Toronto. Her published work includes the text *Women, Families, and Work*, which reflects her longstanding interest in women's work and family sociology. One of her current research projects is a longitudinal study of full-time undergraduate students with dependant-care responsibilities, focusing on the ways overburdened students cope with the conflicting demands of family, work, and full-time study.

Index